PHILOSOPHIAE MORALIS
INSTITUTIO COMPENDIARIA
WITH
A SHORT INTRODUCTION
TO MORAL PHILOSOPHY

NATURAL LAW AND
ENLIGHTENMENT CLASSICS

Knud Haakonssen
General Editor

Francis Hutcheson

Philosophiae Moralis
Institutio Compendiaria
with
A Short Introduction
to Moral Philosophy

Francis Hutcheson

Edited and with an Introduction by Luigi Turco

*Collected Works and Correspondence
of Francis Hutcheson*

LIBERTY FUND

Indianapolis

This book is published by Liberty Fund, Inc., a foundation established
to encourage study of the ideal of a society of free and responsible individuals.

𒂼𒄄

The cuneiform inscription that serves as our logo and as the design motif for
our endpapers is the earliest-known written appearance of the word
"freedom" (*amagi*), or "liberty." It is taken from a clay document written
about 2300 B.C. in the Sumerian city-state of Lagash.

Frontispiece: Detail of a portrait of Francis Hutcheson by Allan Ramsay (ca. 1740–45),
oil on canvas, reproduced courtesy of the Hunterian Art Gallery, University of Glasgow.

11 10 09 08 07 C 5 4 3 2 1
11 10 09 08 07 P 5 4 3 2 1

Library of Congress Cataloging-in-Publication Data

Hutcheson, Francis, 1694–1746.
[Philosophiae moralis institutio compendiaria. English]
Philosophiae moralis institutio compendiaria:
with a short introduction to moral philosophy/Francis Hutcheson;
edited and with an introduction by Luigi Turco.
p.   cm.   (Natural law and enlightenment classics)
(Collected works and correspondence of Francis Hutcheson)
Includes bibliographical references and index.
ISBN-13: 978-0-86597-452-4 (hc: alk. paper)
ISBN-13: 978-0-86597-453-1 (pbk.: alk. paper)
1. Ethics—Early works to 1800. 2. Philosophy, Modern—Scotland—Early works to 1800.
3. Philosophy, Modern—18th century. I. Turco, Luigi. II. Title.
B1501.P4513 2007
171'.2—dc22   2006024255

LIBERTY FUND, INC.
8335 Allison Pointe Trail, Suite 300
Indianapolis, Indiana 46250-1684

CONTENTS

INTRODUCTION

Francis Hutcheson is considered by many scholars to be the father of the Scottish Enlightenment. His thought variously influenced leading figures in eighteenth-century Scotland, such as David Hume, Adam Smith, and Thomas Reid, in the rest of Europe, and in America. Hutcheson, like Shaftesbury and other neo-Stoic philosophers, viewed philosophy, not as a mere theoretical exercise, but as having a practical function. His argument for a virtuous life and for an active involvement in public life was based on his belief in the benevolence of God, the harmony of the universe, and men's sociable dispositions. Hutcheson had the great merit of turning Shaftesbury's aristocratic language into clear and concrete prose that well matched the empirical turn of mind in eighteenth-century Britain and could be understood by a wide readership. Hutcheson criticized the pessimistic account of human nature inherent in the legalistic conception of morality and justice in seventeenth-century Protestant theology and jurisprudence.

Philosophiae Moralis Institutio Compendiaria was aimed at university students and had a large circulation within Scottish universities, Irish and English dissenting academies, and American colleges. The aim of the text was twofold: on one hand, to put forward an optimistic view of God, human nature, and the harmony of the universe; on the other hand, to provide students with the knowledge of natural and civil law required by the university curriculum.

This work was preceded by *An Inquiry into the Original of our Ideas of Beauty and Virtue* (1725), a work largely influenced by the thought of Lord Shaftesbury and Richard Cumberland and reacting to the skeptical moral teaching of Mandeville's *Fable of the Bees;* and by *An Essay on the Nature and Conduct of the Passions and Affections. With Illustrations on the Moral*

Sense (1728), an answer to his critics. Hutcheson considered the two *Inquiries* on beauty and virtue, the *Essay* on passions, and the *Illustrations* to be complementary and referred to them as "the four treatises" which constituted his moral teaching. From 1725 to 1742 he carefully made additions and corrections to these works, a sign that he never judged them to be surpassed. However, Hutcheson's moral thought is also presented in his *Philosophiae Moralis Institutio Compendiaria,* published in 1742 with a revised second edition in 1745—and translated into English with the title *A Short Introduction to Moral Philosophy* in 1747—as well as in *A System of Moral Philosophy,* published posthumously in 1755 by his son Francis, but already circulating among his friends in 1737.

Therefore, we have three different versions of Hutcheson's moral thought, and scholars have always found some difficulties in explaining their different aims and in finding consistency among them. In a celebrated monograph of 1900, William Robert Scott argued that there was a development in Hutcheson's moral thought and identified four phases, from the Shaftesburian *Inquiries,* through the influence of Bishop Butler in the *Essay* and *Illustrations,* to the Aristotelian *Institutio,* and finally to the Stoic *System.* However, given Hutcheson's remarks in the preface to the *Philosophiae Moralis Institutio Compendiaria,* it is more reasonable to consider this work to be an elementary book addressed to the young who study at universities, and not to a learned, adult public audience. Hutcheson was aware that "many such compends have been published by very learned men," but added that "every teacher must use his own judgment on these subjects." He thought that the "method and order which pleased" him "most" was "pretty different from what has of late prevailed," and that it would "be of use to the students to have in their hands an abridgement, containing the method and the principal heads of argument, to recall to their memories the points more largely insisted upon in their lectures." Combined with comments we have from William Leechman, James Wodrow, and William Thom on Hutcheson's teaching, these remarks clearly suggest that the *Institutio* mostly reflects Hutcheson's "private" (that is, advanced) afternoon lectures in Latin and were designed to help his students to elaborate their theses, according to the custom of the time. Also, the evidence suggests that his *System of Moral Philosophy* reflects his early morning public (that is,

more basic) lectures in English.[1] As will be evident to the modern reader, this does not mean that the *Institutio* and the *System* were not elaborate works.

Hutcheson's remarks may also help us solve some problems about the order of composition of the two works. In 1737 he stated that the *System* "has employed my leisure hours for several summers past," and it is possible that the composition of the *Institutio* dated to the same early years of his teaching in Glasgow as the *System* since the second and third books seem to be an enlargement of the *Institutio*. Some scholars have conjectured that the *Institutio*, as well as Hutcheson's *Logic* and *Metaphysics*, could even have been composed during the twenties when he was teaching in the Dublin Academy that he then ran. This could explain why he wrote Latin compends in subjects he never taught in Glasgow.[2]

While it is possible that an early manuscript version of the *Institutio* existed in the early thirties or even in the twenties, the first edition published in 1742 might differ at least as much from it as the two published editions differ from each other. In any case, a careful reading of the parallel chapters in the *Institutio* and the *System* does not allow us to establish a definite order of composition. In many cases the *System* seems to enlarge on subjects already treated in the Latin work, but there are chapters of the *Institutio* that present a more ordered and concise exposition than the corresponding chapters of the *System*.

1. See Leechman's cited Preface quoted by W. R. Scott, *Francis Hutcheson: His Life, Teaching and Position in the History of Philosophy* (Cambridge: Cambridge University Press, 1900), pp. 62–65. Cf., particularly, this sentence in Hutcheson's letter to Tom Drennan of June 15, 1741: "I . . . am adding confusedly to a confused book all valuable remarks in a farrago, *to refresh my memory in my class lectures on several subjects"* (*ibidem,* p. 114. Italics mine).

2. Cf. James Moore, "The Two Systems of Francis Hutcheson: On the Origins of The Scottish Enlightenment," *Studies in the Philosophy of Scottish Enlightenment,* ed. M. A. Stewart (Oxford: Clarendon Press, 1990), pp. 57–58. See also J. Wodrow's and W. Thom's Letters quoted by P. Wood in "'The Fittest Man in the Kingdom': Thomas Reid and the Glasgow Chair of Moral Philosophy." *Hume Studies* 23, no. 2 (1997), pp. 280–84.

The Institutio

Hutcheson found himself in the difficult position of having to instruct his students in the principles and subtleties of natural and civil law even though he was a keen critic and severe judge of one of the most important systems of such law, that of Pufendorf. In a letter to the *London Journal* of 1724, he had criticized Pufendorf for his "grand argument" that "the belief of a deity" "is true" "because it is necessary to support society."[3] In his inaugural lecture at Glasgow in November 1730, he castigated Pufendorf for his pessimistic account of the state of nature and for assuming that "men were driven in society only for the sake of external advantage, and for fear of external evils, but in opposition to their natural turn of mind and to all natural affections and appetites."[4]

Pufendorf's *De officio hominis et civis* (an abridgement of his *De jure naturae et gentium*) was a standard text in the teaching of natural law in Protestant universities, and Hutcheson keeps close to the order of Pufendorf's exposition while modifying its moral foundations. In Book III of the *Institutio* Hutcheson accurately summarizes Pufendorf's discussion in Book II of *De officio* (the duties of the citizen). The contents of Book I of Pufendorf's *De officio,* on the duties of mankind or the law of nature, are dealt with in two different books of Hutcheson's work: In Book II of the *Institutio* (*Elements of the law of nature*) Hutcheson refers to juridical notions he derives directly from Pufendorf (law of nature, classification of rights, acquisition and transferring of property, contracts, oaths, obligations, etc). In Book I he replaces Pufendorf's legalistic ethics with the ethics of his own *Inquiry.* The two first chapters are devoted respectively to the description of human nature and its basic sociability, and to the *summum bonum* or happiness and virtue, according to the Stoic perspective, especially as set out in Cicero's *De finibus* and *Tusculanae Disputationes,* Books 4 and 5.

3. The letter is reproduced in *Francis Hutcheson: On Human Nature,* ed. Thomas Mautner (Cambridge: Cambridge University Press, 1993), p. 98. Cf. Pufendorf, *De officio hominis et civis,* I.2.10.

4. I quote from Mautner's translation of Hutcheson's *Oratio Inauguralis, op. cit.,* p. 135.

The first chapter of Book I, the longest of the *Institutio,* is a careful description of the several powers of human nature. Hutcheson begins from the peculiarities of the human body as compared with the bodies of animals, and passes to the external senses and to the faculties of understanding and will, to concentrate his account on his preferred theme, the reflex or internal senses. Different sections are dedicated to the sense of beauty, sympathy, the moral sense, the sense of honor, and the sense of ridicule, as well as to the affections and the passions of the soul. It is by the sense of beauty that we receive pleasant perceptions in observing proportion, harmony or grandeur, and novelty in the objects of nature or the fine arts. Sympathy or *sensus communis,* as Hutcheson calls it following Shaftesbury, is the reflex sense by which we rejoice in the prosperity of others, or sorrow with them in their distress.

However, the most important sense is the moral sense or the "sensus decori or honesti," as Hutcheson calls it following Cicero,[5] by which we approve every action springing from benevolent affections or passions and disapprove any contrary disposition. To the moral sense is connected the sense of honor and shame which gives us pleasure or pain when others approve or condemn our conduct. Hutcheson stresses not only the innateness but also the supremacy of the moral sense over every other sense and its authority in regulating our conduct. With this thesis, absent in the first editions of the *Inquiry,* Hutcheson approaches the ethics of Butler, where conscience has a hegemonic role. However, he explicitly opposes Butler's ethics when he considers benevolence to be as ultimate and basic a principle of human conduct as self-love. Hutcheson carefully distinguishes, in accordance with Stoic and Ciceronian doctrine, between the calm and rational desires and aversions inspired by these senses, and the turbulent motions of the passions. The multitude of these instinctive senses and desires is a proof "that man was destined by nature for action." Further, the stress on human industry, another Ciceronian feature, is a novelty in the *Institutio.*[6]

5. In the English version, *A Short Introduction to Moral Philosophy* (Glasgow, 1747), "sensus decori et honesti" is translated as "conscience," a Butlerian term Hutcheson never uses in the *Institutio* with reference to the moral sense.

6. *Short Introduction,* p. 15.

In Book V of *De finibus* and in *Tusculan Disputations* Cicero discusses whether virtue is the only good (the Stoic thesis) or we need also some natural good, such as health or riches (the Aristotelian thesis). So the argument is about the relationship between virtue and happiness, and Cicero says that we need some external prosperity. In the second chapter of the first book of the *Institutio,* Hutcheson considers the relationship between virtue and happiness, or, more generally, between our senses and happiness. Happiness and misery are the sum of pleasures and pains that differ according to their dignity or quality and according to their duration. Considering in turn the external and internal senses and the pleasures we get from them, he reaches the conclusion that "happiness consists in the virtues of the soul, and in the continued exercise of them in good offices" together with "a moderate degree of external prosperity,"[7] again a conclusion close to the Stoicism of Cicero, mitigated by the teaching of the Peripatetic school.

Three chapters are devoted to the duties of man toward God, other men, and himself. In this way Hutcheson follows a common division, present also in Pufendorf's *De officio* but quite different in content from Pufendorf. For example, Pufendorf's chapter on the duty to oneself focuses on the right to self-defense, but Hutcheson's chapter is a warm invitation to the practice of virtues and to the control of the passions, a duty we owe to ourselves, if we want to be happy (cf. Chapter 2). The three chapters on duties are preceded by a chapter dedicated to the classification of virtues, according to the Platonic, Aristotelian, and Ciceronian division, into the four cardinal virtues.

How is the ethics of moral sense of the first book connected with the doctrine of rights in the second book? From the beginning, Hutcheson's ethics has an antilegalistic feature that renders problematic its connection with the natural law legacy. The conception that moral behavior depends on the law of a superior who threatens sanctions debases morality, in Hutcheson's eye. Moreover, the moral sense discovers moral excellence in those actions or characters that are inspired by benevolent intentions. Actions which

7. *Ibidem,* p. 56.

spring from self-love or personal interest, as legal actions do, are *indifferent* from a moral point of view. In each of his three works—the "four treatises," the *Institutio,* and the *System*—Hutcheson finds different ways to escape from his impasse.

In the *Institutio,* Hutcheson attaches a moral value to the common good of the system of human creatures. The moral sense makes us approve benevolent affections; in combination with natural religion it lets us discover a God provided with the same kind affections toward his creatures and, possibly, an analogous moral sense. In this way the common good of the system, as well as every action which contributes to it, acquires a moral value. Every action that is morally innocent, even if inspired by interest or self-love, and that contributes to the common good of the whole has the status of a right guaranteed by the law.[8] So Hutcheson is able to arrive, independently, at the notion of a "divine law of nature" that commands us to worship God and promote "the common good of all and of particular men and societies,"[9] as well as at the notion of right "as a faculty or claim" guaranteed by a law "to act, or possess, or obtain something from others."[10] An alternative way to arrive at the same conclusion is provided by Hutcheson's moral calculus. This computation was first proposed in the *Inquiry* in order to ascertain the degree of benevolence or virtue implied in any action, moving from the idea that, *ceteris paribus,* there is a relation between the degree of benevolence and the amount of good produced. Since the aim of morally good affections is to maximize the common good, every action that contributes to this goal has a moral value and therefore has to be guaranteed by natural and civil laws.[11] In this light, it makes sense that Hutcheson puts forward the discussion of the state of nature in the second book while Pufendorf treats it only in his book on government.

---

8. See K. Haakonssen, *Natural Law and Moral Philosophy: From Grotius to the Scottish Enlightenment* (Cambridge: Cambridge University Press, 1996), pp. 77–78.

9. *Short Introduction,* p. 117.

10. *Ibidem,* p. 120.

11. These different lines of approach are present in all three works, but with different emphasis. If the deduction of the basic concepts of natural law from the ethics of moral sense had been more straightforward, the order of chapters and sections might have been the same in Hutcheson's works.

The natural condition of man is a state of innocence and sociability. Hutcheson does not use the traditional term "state of nature," but prefers to call it a state of freedom, reacting, as Titius and Barbeyrac before him, to the pessimism of Hobbes and Pufendorf. He distinguishes between perfect rights that are necessary to the survival of society and that must be sanctioned by civil law, and imperfect rights that cannot be rendered a matter of compulsion in society without greater loss than benefit; he lists the rights of individuals, such as rights to life, reputation, and private judgment. The explanation of the origin of property and the method of acquiring and transferring it is followed by contracts, the conditions of their validity, and the obligations implied in speech and oaths. The concluding chapters of the second book explain that recourse to violence is licit when rights are violated. Hutcheson also enlarges on the rights of war and on the ways in which controversies must be decided in the state of natural liberty. In short, Book II touches upon all the subjects treated by Pufendorf in the first book of *De officio,* and when Hutcheson deviates from Pufendorf, it is in most cases under the influence of Gershom Carmichael's annotations to Pufendorf's work, as we will see.

The third book of Hutcheson deals with the subjects treated by Pufendorf in his second book. On the themes of marriage, parental power, and master-servant relationships, Hutcheson stresses the equal obligation of man and woman to fidelity in marriage and their equal partnership and authority in the education of children, and he challenges the principles on which natural jurists defend slavery. Every man is born free, and no just war can justify slavery for the population or conquest of its territory. Hutcheson also challenges the violent origin of the state and espouses Pufendorf's doctrine that the state is founded on the consent of people expressed in three acts: (1) a contract of union among citizens, (2) a decree of the people concerning the form of government and the nomination of governors, and (3) a covenant between the governors and the people "binding the rulers to a faithful administration of their trust, and the people to obedience."[12] As a state is "a society of free men united under one government for their common

12. *Short Introduction,* p. 286.

interest," Hutcheson defends the right of resistance,[13] even in the state where the prince's power has not been limited by the original contract. He denies the existence and legitimacy of monarchies founded on a pretended "divine right," the patrimonial states, and is sarcastic about the subtleties of inheritance in hereditary monarchies.[14] He follows Locke in the division of powers among the different organs of the state, Aristotle in his discussion of the forms of government, and Harrington in stressing the importance of the different forms of government and the necessity of some agrarian law to moderate the amount of lands owned by a single citizen. According to Hutcheson, the state has the duty, not only to provide for the safety and prosperity of the citizen, but also to provide for general religious instruction and to promote all the incentives to cultivating the four cardinal virtues. In the last chapters of the third book, on the laws of war, on treaties, and on ambassadors, Hutcheson follows not only Pufendorf, but also the Dutch natural jurist Cornelis van Bijnkershoek; this is a sign, perhaps, that Hutcheson thinks his compendium fit for a larger audience than the students of Glasgow or for Glaswegian students who have to complete their legal studies abroad.

Hutcheson and Carmichael

In his Preface Hutcheson declares that much of his compendium "is taken . . . from Pufendorf's smaller work, de officio hominis et civis, which that worthy and ingenious man the late Professor Gershom Carmichael of Glasgow, by far the best commentator of that book, has so supplied and corrected that the notes are of much more value than the text."[15] In addition to minor points that Hutcheson receives from Carmichael, there are basic and deep agreements between the pupil and his former teacher. First of all they agree on the two precepts in which the law of nature is summarized,[16] veneration of God and promotion of the common good, though Hutcheson does not want to start from the law of nature as a commandment of

13. *Ibidem,* p. 304.
14. *Ibidem,* pp. 303, 313, and 308–9.
15. *Short Introduction,* p. i.
16. *Ibidem,* pp. 117 and 244.

God, but rather wants to derive it from his teleological recognition of providence and the powers of human nature. Hutcheson follows Pufendorf and Carmichael's theory of the original contract, concurs with Locke and Carmichael that even in a just war the conquerors have no right to enslave a nation, and concurs with Carmichael that most of the people in a conquered nation are innocent, that a slave is not property, and that children of slaves are born free. He shares Carmichael's defense of the right of resistance and his strictures against the peculiar sanctity of the sovereign authority and against the legitimacy of patrimonial states. Hutcheson's chapter on quasi-contracts[17] is derived from Carmichael, and he clearly acknowledges the implications of this doctrine for his view of the duties of children to their parents, of orphans to their adoptive parents, and for his polemic against slavery; he uses it also to state that the original contract binds posterity without consent.[18]

Hutcheson and Hume

Hutcheson received a copy of the first and second books of David Hume's *Treatise of Human Nature* from Henry Home early in 1739, and, months later, Hume sent him the manuscript of the third book, *Of Morals.* Very likely he received a visit from David Hume in the winter of 1739–1740. Whereas Hutcheson's reaction to the first two books was positive, differences appeared between the two men concerning morality.

We know of these differences through four extant letters from Hume to Hutcheson. Whereas Hume had to defend himself against the accusation of lacking "warmth in the Cause of Virtue," he criticized Hutcheson for founding the notion of "natural" on final causes.[19] Since they agreed that morality is founded on sentiment and not on reason, they must also agree

17. Quasi-contract is a juridical fiction of Roman law through which a party acquires an obligation to another party without an actual former agreement.
18. See *Natural Rights on the Threshold of the Scottish Enlightenment: The Writings of Gershom Carmichael,* ed. James Moore and Michael Silverthorne (Indianapolis: Liberty Fund, 2002), pp. xv–xvi and 117 note 17.
19. *The Letters of David Hume,* ed. J. Y. T. Greig (Oxford: Clarendon Press, 1932), pp. 32–33.

that "it regards only human Nature and human life" and that nothing is known about the morality of superior Beings.[20] They had a number of differences also concerning the notion of virtue. According to Hume and in contrast to Hutcheson, benevolence is not the sole or chief virtue, justice is an artificial virtue, natural abilities like the accomplishments of body and mind are virtues, and utility perceived through sympathy is the foundation of merit. Hume also declared that he took his "Catalogue of Virtue from *Cicero's Offices.*"[21]

In 1742 Hutcheson presented Hume with a copy of his *Institutio Compendiaria* and received the fourth of Hume's letters. While Hume reassured Hutcheson on the purity and elegance of his Latin, he added some critical reflections on particular points of Hutcheson's book. He could not approve the distinction between calm affections and passions, Hutcheson's adoption of Butler's hegemonic moral sense, his explanation of the origin of property and justice, or his fear of deriving "any thing of Virtue from Artifice and human Conventions." Moreover he repeated, as a common opinion, that Hutcheson "limited too much" his "ideas of Virtue."

Did Hutcheson answer Hume's criticisms? The first edition of the *Institutio* is already in many ways an answer to Hume. The first chapter of the first book presents a teleological approach to ethics that we cannot find in the earlier "four Treatises," and the first chapter of the second book culminates in two general laws of nature, where the first states, "God is to be worshipped with all love and veneration." In the second chapter on the *summum bonum,* Hutcheson presents a general catalogue of virtues in which the four cardinal virtues appear after the kind affections. Moreover, he begins to talk about "some natural sense, different from the moral one, but not unlike it, by which we relish and value some powers of the mind and the body," that is, Hume's "natural abilities." In his *System of Moral Philosophy,* he will enlarge on this sense, calling it "a sense of *decency* or *dignity*" and stressing its independence "from any indications of advantage by the spectators."[22] Moreover, Hutcheson, in his third chapter, adds a large

20. *Ibidem,* p. 40.
21. *Ibidem,* pp. 33–34.
22. *A System of Moral Philosophy* (Glasgow, 1755), vol. I, pp. 27–28.

list of virtues as specifications of the four cardinal virtues, a catalogue no-
where else so detailed, not even in the works of Cicero, Aristotle, or Henry
More, to whom Hutcheson refers his readers.

In his second edition of 1745, Hutcheson does not change any word in
the passages criticized by Hume, but his answer to Hume becomes more
evident. In his Preface he declares: "The design of Cicero's books de officiis,
which are so very justly admired by all, has been mistaken inconsiderately
by some very ingenious men, who speak of these books as intended for a
compleat system of morals or ethicks." But "The doctrine concerning virtue, and the supreme good, which is the principal <and most necessary>
[three words omitted from the 1747 translation] part of ethics, is to be
found elsewhere. Nay in his own books *de finibus,* and *Tusculan questions.*"
According to the Stoics, "the officia, or external duties of life" are "things
indifferent, neither morally good nor evil." Therefore, Cicero's *de officiis*
show "how persons in higher stations, already well instructed in the fundamentals of moral philosophy, should so conduct themselves in life, that
in perfect consistence with virtue they may obtain great interest, power,
popularity, high offices and glory." Hume is certainly a likely target of this
criticism.[23]

Hutcheson adds also two sections to the second chapter of the first book,
presenting a detailed account of the passions according to the common
Aristotelian and Ciceronian distinction—also adopted by Hume—of three
classes of goods and evils: of the body, of the soul, and external goods.[24]
In this way Hutcheson can complete his account of human nature without
renouncing his distinction between calm affections and turbulent passions.
Finally, Hutcheson adds a seventh and last chapter to his first book. This
chapter does not present new matter: the first section stresses the teleological
and religious perspective of his ethics, the second section returns again to
the four cardinal virtues, while the third is a warm encouragement to the
practice of virtue and to confidence in God, with long quotations from
Cicero. We can say that Hutcheson, fearful of the secularization of morals

23. See also below p. 4, note 2.
24. Hutcheson had touched on the subject of turbulent motions of the soul or passions in the first edition, drawing, as usual, from Cicero's *Tusculan Disputations,* IV.16
ff., in a short paragraph, which was canceled in the second edition.

that Hume derives from human sentiments, tries to enforce the religious foundation, expands on his original idea that virtue is based on benevolence by tying it to the classical tradition of the four cardinal virtues, and presents his system as authorized by the most approved and cherished of the classical authors, Marcus Tullius Cicero, who used Aristotelian ideas to mitigate the rigorous teaching of the Stoics.

Editorial Principles

This edition is based on the second edition published in 1745, *Philosophiae Moralis Institutio Compendiaria, Libris III. Ethices et Jurisprudentiae Naturalis Elementa Continens,* Glasguae, Typis Roberti Foulis, M DCC XLV, and compared with the 1742 first edition, published with the same title and by the same publisher. The revisions that may have a substantial relevance have been included in the text by internal citations. While almost all additions and deletions are pointed out, more than 50 percent of the substitutions of mere stylistic relevance are not indicated: these include changes in capitalization, differences in spelling, minute changes of punctuation, changes in the order of words, and changes of verbal tenses and modes, of synonymic conjunctions, prepositions, and adverbs. Other relevant changes, such as a different order of paragraphs, are noted. In sum, the changes included in the text are indicated in the following way:

1. Strings of text (sentences or words) *added* to the 1745 edition are enclosed in {braces}.

2. Strings of text (sentences or words) *deleted* from the 1745 edition are enclosed in <angle brackets>.

3. Strings of text *changed* in the 1745 edition are indicated as follows: both the new and the old strings are enclosed in [square brackets] with the 1745 text first. To ease reading, the square brackets around 1745 text have been left out in cases where the change concerned no more than three words and the same number of words as in the 1742 text. So, for example, at page 3, line 4, "cognitu facilier [cognitione prior]" means that "cognitu facilier" of the 1745 edition is a substitution for "cognitione prior" of the first edition. So readers who want to read just the corrected 1745 edition have to accustom themselves to overlook strings in angle brackets, strings in square

brackets where single, and strings in the second angle brackets where double.

Hutcheson draws heavily on Cicero for words, sentences, and parts of sentences. In adding quotation marks and references, I have restored to Cicero most of what was his own. Finally, a few printer's errors have been silently corrected, and Greek standard characters are used instead of the original eighteenth-century abbreviations.

The English Translation

A Short Introduction to Moral Philosophy, in Three Books, Containing the Elements of Ethicks and the Law of Nature was printed in Glasgow by Robert Foulis in 1747. In the present edition, the Latin text and the text of the English translation are presented on facing pages. As we learn from the advertisement of the anonymous translator, Hutcheson would have preferred that the book had not been translated, but having found it impossible, he "therefor thought it proper it should rather be done in Glasgow." I have not been able to identify the author of the translation, but he is likely to be a person with whom Hutcheson was acquainted. Internal evidence shows that he was familiar with Hutcheson's thought as well as with the literature on natural law. Moreover, he had in his hands the manuscript of *A System of Moral Philosophy,* as many added notes and the wording of several sentences depend on it. In the advertisement the translator says also that he used "some few Latin terms of art in the second and third book," and he omitted a few sections "relating solely to some Latin ways of speaking in the civil law"; at the same time, he "inserted some short sentences, or added a note or two, to make some point clearer." Therefore in the present edition there are the following alterations:

1. Strings of text (sentences or words) *added* by the translator are enclosed in {braces}.

2. Significant strings of text (sentences or words) *omitted* from the 1747 translation are added, enclosed in <angle brackets>.

3. Cases in which the translation is significantly unfaithful: More accurate translations are added in square brackets in the text where feasible, otherwise in the notes. I kept these interpositions to a minimum, allowing

for a margin of arbitrariness, as in all translation. So readers who want to read the 1747 translation as corrected by the editor have to accustom themselves to overlook strings in square brackets where single, and strings in the second angle brackets where double, as well as strings in braces.

In both the Latin and the English text, notes by Hutcheson and by the translator are preceded by the original footnote markers (*, †, ‡, §, ||, #). Editor's notes are added to the original notes in square brackets or, when required, separately numbered.

I have made the English version with its annotation self-contained and independent of the Latin text, with only occasional, necessary references to the notes of the latter.

ACKNOWLEDGMENTS

My thanks are due in the first place to Knud Haakonssen, the general editor of this series, for the extremely valuable guidance and encouragement that he gave me at various stages in producing this edition of Hutcheson's *Institutio* and its old translation, the *Short Introduction.* I am also indebted to James Moore for many discussions on Hutcheson's views, and I have found especially helpful his notes and commentaries on the writings of Gershom Carmichael. I am grateful to my friend and colleague Giancarlo Giardina, of the Department of Classical and Medieval Philology at the University of Bologna, for discussing a few passages of Hutcheson's *Institutio.*

Finally, I wish to express my special gratitude to Dan Kirklin, managing editor of the publishing department of Liberty Fund, for the very intelligent and superlatively kind assistance he gave me in revising the proofs of this rather complicated edition.

ABBREVIATIONS

Works by Francis Hutcheson

Inquiry on Beauty	The first treatise of *An Inquiry into the Original of our Ideas of Beauty and Virtue; In Two Treatises. I. Concerning Beauty, Order, Harmony, Design. II. Concerning Moral Good and Evil.* London, 4th ed., 1738.
Inquiry on Virtue	The second treatise of the preceding.
Essay on Passions	The first part of *An Essay on the Nature and Conduct of the Passions and Affections. With Illustrations On the Moral Sense.* London, 3rd ed., 1742.
Illustrations	The second part of the preceding.
Institutio	*Philosophiae moralis institutio compendiaria, Ethices & Jurisprudentiae Naturalis elementa continens.* Glasgow, 1742, 2nd ed., 1745.
Short Introduction	*A Short Introduction to Moral Philosophy.* Glasgow, 1747.
Synopsis	*Synopsis metaphysicae, ontologiam & pneumatologiam complectens.* Glasgow, 1744.
System	*A System of Moral Philosophy.* London, 1755.

Other Works

De finibus	Cicero. *De finibus bonorum et malorum.*
De iure belli	Grotius, Hugo. *De iure belli ac pacis libri tres, in quibus ius naturae et gentium, item iuris publici praecipua explicantur.* Paris, 1625.
De officiis	Cicero. *De officiis.*
De officio	Pufendorf, Samuel von. *De officio hominis et civis iuxta legem naturalem libri duo.* Lund, 1673.

De iure nat.	Pufendorf, Samuel von. *De iure naturae et gentium libri octo.* Lund, 1672.
Notes on Puf.	Carmichael, Gershom. *Natural Rights on the Threshold of the Scottish Enlightenment: The Writings of Gershom Carmichael.* Ed. J. Moore and M. Silverthorne. Indianapolis: Liberty Fund, 2002.
Tusc. Disp.	Cicero. *Tusculanae disputationes.*
Two Treatises	Locke, John. *Two Treatises of Government.* London, 1689.

GENERAL NOTE

In both the Latin and the English texts, angle brackets < >, square brackets [ ], and braces { } have the same meanings, namely, respectively, that angle brackets enclose omitted text, square brackets enclose changed text, and braces enclose added text. Note that in the Latin text the editor had to compare the 1745 edition with the 1742 edition, whereas in the English text he had to compare the 1747 English translation with the 1745 Latin edition. That means that a reader who wants to know if a passage in the English text was added to the 1745 second edition must look for braces at the corresponding passage on the Latin facing page. Braces in the English text mean only that the translator added text that is unsupported by the Latin. Where a whole chapter or section was added, the editor noted that fact in the footnote to the English text.

To save space, the footnotes to the English sometimes begin on the left-hand page; a short rule ——————————————————— is used, when needed for clarity, to separate the footnotes to the English from the footnotes to the Latin.

PHILOSOPHIAE
MORALIS
INSTITUTIO COMPENDIARIA,
LIBRIS III.

Ethices et Jurisprudentiae Naturalis
ELEMENTA continens.

Auctore FRANCISCO HUTCHESON
in Academia Glasguensi P.P.

Editio altera auctior et emendatior.

Ο῾ ἀνεξέταστος βίος, οὐ βιωτὸς ἀνθρώπῳ.
Plat. Apol.[1]

GLASGUAE,

Typis ROBERTI FOULIS, Academiae Typographi;
apud quem venales prostant.

M DCC XLV.

1. Plato, *Apology* 38a. 5–6.
The unexamined life is not worth living.

A SHORT INTRODUCTION TO MORAL PHILOSOPHY,

IN THREE BOOKS;

CONTAINING THE
ELEMENTS OF ETHICKS
AND THE
LAW OF NATURE.

By FRANCIS HUTCHESON, LLD.

LATE PROFESSOR OF PHILOSOPHY IN
THE UNIVERSITY OF GLASGOW.

TRANSLATED FROM THE LATIN.

GLASGOW,

Printed and sold by Robert Foulis.
Printer to the University.

MDCCXLVII.

<8a>

BY THE TRANSLATOR.

The Author of this book had no inclination that it should be translated, as he wishes that all our students were much enured to the latin tongue, which for the two last centuries, (and in many preceeding, in such style as they had) was the common channel of communication among the Learned through all Europe. He was abundantly aware that such compends, wrote in the most succinct manner their authors could, and yet touching at a great variety of subjects, with hints of the principal topicks of reasoning, must appear very jejune and unpleasant to common readers: not to mention the unavoidable terms of art, which can scarce be turned into easy common language. But he found that the preventing a translation was impossible; as it <10a> was designed in London soon after the publication of the first edition. He therefor thought proper it should be rather done in Glasgow. The English reader must excuse the translator in the use of some few latin terms of art in the 2d and 3d books, and in the omission of a section or two relating solely to some latin ways of speaking in the civil law. He has sometimes inserted a short sentence, or added a note or two, to make some points clearer. He needs the readers indulgence too, if, in following the original pretty closely, he sometimes makes sentences too long, or not so smooth and easy as our native tongue would require.

In celebri apud antiquos Philosophiae divisione, quae pars moralis *appella-batur, has complexa est disciplinas;* Ethicam, *strictius dictam, quae hominum mores internos regere profitetur et emendare, et* Jurisprudentiam naturalem. *Hujus deinde tres sunt partes: prima,* Jurisprudentia privata, *quae jura docet legesque in libertate naturali vigentes: altera,* Oeconomica, *leges tradens et jura quibus regenda est domus: tertia est* Politica, *quae Rerum publicarum formas explicat, ipsarumque inter se jura. Harum omnium in hoc libello prima traduntur elementa: quibus perlectis, tyronibus facilior erit aditus, ad claris-sima, in hac philosophia, sive antiquorum* Platonis, Aristotelis, Xenophontis, Ciceronis; *sive nuperorum,* Grotii, Cumberlandi, Puffendorfii, Harring-toni, *aliorumque scripta et inventa cognoscenda.*

Nobis etiam non monentibus, perspicient Eruditi, quanta hujus libelli pars ex claris <ii> *aliorum scriptis est deprompta; ex* Cicerone et Aristotele; *atque, ut alios sileam recentiores, ex* Puffendorfii de Off. Hom. et Civis *libello; quem, vir optimus, doctissimus,* Gerschomus Carmichael *nuper in hac Aca-demia P. Professor, inter omnes ejusdem commentatores palmam ferens, ita supplevit et emendavit, ut libri* substantiâ, *quam vocant, multo pluris sint* accessiones. [*De instituto meo autem, quod*] [*Cur autem*] *post tot hu-jusmodi libellos a viris doctissimis conscriptos, hunc contexendum susceperim,* [*sic habetote*] [*haec causa est*]: *Docenti cuique suo utendum judicio, sua arridet methodus, docendi ratio, rerum series,* [*argumentorumque momenta, quae discentium ingeniis, ut juvenum captus est, optimè accommodata, atque ad sensus penitùs permanantia, sibi videntur. Quumque nostra methodus, istis quae nuper invaluerunt, non paullum discrepet; si quid ea afferat*] [*quae discentium captui accommodatissima sibi videtur. Si quid autem in nostra methodo sit*] *quod discipulis prodesse potest, eorum intererit, breve aliquod*

The [*In the*] *celebrated division of philosophy among the ancients* {*was into the* rational *or* logical, *the* natural, *and the* moral. *Their*}< *the branch that was called*> *moral philosophy contained these parts,* ethicks *taken more strictly, teaching the nature of virtue and regulating the internal dispositions; and the knowledge of the* law of nature. *This later contained,* 1. *the doctrine of* private rights, *or the laws* < *and rights*> *obtaining in natural liberty.* 2. Oeconomicks, *or the laws and rights of the several members of a family; and* 3. Politicks, *shewing the various plans of civil government, and the rights of states with respect to each other. The following books contain the elements of these several branches of moral philosophy; which if they are carefully studied may give the youth an easier access to the well known and admired works either of the ancients,* Plato, Aristotle, Xenophon, Cicero; *or of the moderns,* Grotius, Cumberland, Puffendorf, Harrington *and others, upon this branch of philosophy.*

The learned will at once discern how much of this compend is taken from the writings of others, from Cicero *and* Aristotle; *and to name no other moderns, from* Puffendorf's *smaller work,* de officio hominis et civis, *which that worthy and ingenious man the late Professor* Gerschom Carmichael *of Glasgow, by far the best commentator on that book, has so supplied and corrected that the notes are of much more value than the text. The reasons* <ii> *of my undertaking to compose anew a compend of this branch of philosophy, after so many such compends have been published by very learned men, were these; Every teacher must use his own judgment on these subjects, use his own method, and that disposition of the several parts, and those arguments which seem to him of greatest force, best suited to the apprehensions of the students, and aptest to touch their hearts on such subjects. And as the method and order which pleased me most is pretty different from what has of late prevailed; if it can be*

3

in manibus terere syntagma, quod rerum seriem, summaque disputationum capita exhibeat; ipsisque omnia vivâ voce fusius explicata, in memoriam revocet. <iii>

{Ciceronis de officiis *libros suo merito laudatissimos, viri quidam docti, tanquam Ethices totius summarium complexos absolutum, inconsideratè nuper laudarunt; quum ipse saepius testetur, totam de* virtute summoque bono *doctrinam, Ethices partem longè praestantissimam et maximè necessariam, alibi quaerendam; cujus etiam locos praecipuos, in libris* de Finibus *et* Tusculanis, *ipse antea tractaverat: quinetiam moneat, se, in libris* de Officiis, *praecepta tradidisse,* Stoicos *potissimùm secutum; quibus tantum inter* virtutes, *et* officia ex virtute, *discrimen esse placuit, ut haec in rerum mediarum, quae nec bonae sint nec malae, numero habuerint. Docent itaque hi* de officiis *libri, qua ratione, viri honesto loco nati, virtutumque cognitione satis ante instructi, vita sit instituenda, ut honestati verae is semper adhaerescens, opes, potentiam, gratiam, honores, et gloriam consequatur.*

In hoc libello denuo excudendo, quaedam addenda videbantur, et non pauca corrigenda. Cogitabam etiam claros in hac philosophia scriptores, et antiquos et nuperos passim citare, locosque librorum commonstrare. Verum <iv> *reputabam; hoc iis solùm profuturum quorum in manibus essent ipsi libri; qui*

---

1. See the Introduction, p. x.

* {As we find from *Cicero*'s first book *de finib.* that *Brutus* had wrote a book *de virtute* addressed to *Cicero;* this might be the reason why no book of *Cicero*'s bears such a title; tho' 'tis manifest to any who read the books *de finibus* and the *Tusculan questions,* that the fundamental doctrine of morals is copiously delivered in them, and presupposed in the books *de officiis,* and passed over in a section or two.}

† {See Book I. ch. i, ii. [6] and Book III. ch. iii. [14].}

‡ {Nay he also declares I. iii. c. 3. [14] that he writes only *de mediis officiis,* which might be performed both by the *wise* and the *unwise;* and yet in the latter they allowed no virtue. Besides, the antients generally delivered all the *jurisprudentia naturalis,* and their doctrine about civil government in their *politica,* or books *de legibus,* of which there's

of any advantage in education, it must be of use to the students to have in their hands an abridgement, containing the method and the principal heads of argument, to recall to their memories the points more largely insisted upon in their lectures.[1]

The design of Cicero's *books* de officiis, *which are so very justly admired by all, has been mistaken inconsiderately by some very ingenious men, who speak of these books as intended for a compleat system of morals or ethicks. Whereas* Cicero *expresly declares, that the doctrine concerning* virtue, *and the* supreme good, *which is the principal < and most necessary> part of ethicks, is to be found elsewhere. Nay in his own books* de finibus, *and* Tusculan questions, *he had previously treated these subjects more copiously.*{*} *And he tells us expressly,*{†} *that in his book* de officiis *he follows the* <iii> Stoicks, *and uses their way of treating this subject. Now 'tis well known that the Stoicks made such difference between* virtue, *which they counted the sole good, and the* officia, *or external duties of life, that they counted these duties among the* things indifferent, *neither morally good nor evil.*{‡} *The design then of these books* de officiis *is this; to shew how persons in higher stations, already well instructed in the fundamentals of moral philosophy, should so conduct themselves in life, that in perfect consistence with virtue they may obtain great interest, power, popularity, high offices and glory.*[2]

In the second impression of this book some few additions seemed necessary and several amendments. The author once intended to have made references all along to the more eminent writers, antient or modern, who treated the several subjects. But considering that this could be of no use except to those who have the cited books at hand, and that such could easily by their indexes find the

---

little or nothing in the books *de officiis;* tho' these are parts of the moral philosophy of the antients.}

2. This and the following paragraph were added in the second edition, 1745. Among the learned or ingenious men Hutcheson is referring to there were Archibald Campbell and David Hume. In his *Reflections* directed against Hutcheson's *Inquiry on Virtue* (included in *An Enquiry into the Original of moral Virtue,* Edinburgh 1733, pp. 452–53) Campbell quoted many passages from Cicero (*De officiis,* III.11, 34, 75, 83) condemning the separation of utility from virtue. In a letter to Hutcheson of 17 Sept. 1739 Hume declared that he had Cicero's *Offices* in his eye in all his reasonings on morals. See the Introduction, p. xx.

nullo fere negotio, consultis librorum indicibus, eadem sibi reperire possent: labori igitur et ingrato et parum necessario peperci. Vix ipsos latet in Philosophia tyrones, Ethices fundamenta, et generalem omnem de moribus doctrinam, apud antiquos modo laudatos, et Cumberlandum, *comitemque de* Shaftesbury, *copiose explicatam esse: nullumque de* jure naturali et gentium *locum, scriptores claros* Grotium *et* Puffendorfium, Barbeyracii *commentariis uberrimis auctos,* Harringtonium, Lockium, *et* Bynkershokium, *ne plures memorem, intactum reliquisse: apud* Barbeyracium *etiam reperiuntur nuperorum nomina, qui singulas quaestiones plenius exposuerunt: quorum libri, iis qui uberiores de locis singulis disquisitiones perspicere volunt, sedulo sunt evolvendi.*}

Vobis, Juvenes, non Eruditis, haec scribuntur elementa: quibus paulum immorati, ad majora progredimini et ampliora; ad omnis scientiae, omnis elegantiae, artiumque bonarum inventores et excultores eximios scriptores Graecos et Romanos <perlegendos>. Dumque hos exprimitis, <v> puriores sacrarum literarum, quae miseris mortalibus certam vitae beatae spem reducunt, fontes aditote; ut animos vestros omni virtute exornetis, ad omnia officia honestiora instruatis, cognitionisque sitim ingenuam et laudabilem expleatis. {Animis igitur vestris medeatur Philosophia; *inanes solicitudines detrahat, cupiditatibus liberet; pellat timores: ita morati sitis, ita animo et vita constituti, ut ratio postulat: neque hanc disciplinam ostentationem scientiae, sed legem vitae sanctissimam putetis, quam nemo sine scelere, nemo impunè spreverit; cujusque monitis parere, quantum animo conniti possumus, summa est naturae nostrae dignitas, summa sapientia, vitaeque prosperitas.*}

---

3. Hutcheson is referring to Richard Cumberland, *De legibus naturae,* London, 1672 (translated by John Maxwell, London, 1727); Anthony Ashley Cooper, Third Earl of Shaftesbury, *Characteristicks of Men, Manners Opinions, Times,* London, 1711; Hugo Grotius, *De jure belli,* Paris, 1625; Samuel Pufendorf, *De jure nat.,* Lund, 1672 (the English translations of Grotius and Pufendorf with the large annotations by Jean Barbeyrac were published, respectively, in London, 1738, and in Oxford, 1710); James Harrington,

corresponding places for themselves: he spared himself that disagreeable and unnecessary labour. All who have looked into such subjects know that the general doctrine and foundations of morals may be found in the antients above mentioned, and in Dr. Cumberland, *and in Lord* Shaftesbury: *and that scarce any question of the law of nature and nations is not* <iv> *to be found in* Grotius, Puffendorf, *especially with* Barbeyrac's *copious notes,* Harrington, Lock, *or* Bynkershoek, *to mention no more. Nay in* Barbeyrac *one finds the principal authors who have published large dissertations on particular heads. Such as want more full discussions of any such points, must have recourse to these authors.*[3]

These elementary books are for your use who study at Universities, and not for the learned. When you have considered them well, go on to greater and more important works. Go to the grand fountains of all the sciences, of all elegance; the inventers and improvers of all ingenious arts, the Greek and Roman writers: and while you are drawing from them what knowledge you can, have recourse also to yet purer fountains, the holy Scriptures *which alone give to sinful mortals any sure hopes of an happy immortality; that you may adorn your souls with every virtue, prepare yourselves for every honourable office in life, and quench that manly and laudable thirst you should have after knowledge. {Let not philosophy rest in speculation} let it be a medicine for the disorders of the soul, freeing the heart from anxious solicitudes and turbulent desires; and dispelling its fears: let your manners, your tempers, and conduct be such as {right} reason requires. Look not upon this part of philosophy as matter of ostentation, or shew of knowledge, but as the most sacred law of life and conduct, which none can despise with impunity, or without impiety toward God: and whose precepts whoever seriously endeavours to obey, as far as he is capable, shews the truest worth and excellence, and the highest wisdom; and is truly the most prosperous as to his greatest interests in life.*[4] <v> <vi>

The Common-wealth of Oceana, London, 1656; John Locke, *Two Treatises on Government,* London, 1690; Cornelis van Bynkershoek, works on international law such as *De dominio maris* (1702) and *De foro legatorum* (1721).

4. The last two sentences were added in the second edition. (From "let it be a medicine . . .")

Βίον αἱροῦ τὸν ἄριστον·· ἡδὺν δ᾽ αὐτὸν ἡ συνήθεια ποιήσει.

Pythag.[1]

Ἤδη οὖν ἀξίωσον σεαυτὸν βιοῦν ὡς τέλειον καὶ προκόπτοντα· καὶ πᾶν τὸ βέλτιστον φαινόμενον ἔστω σοι νόμος ἀπαράβατος

Epictet. Enchir.[2]

Ἄνδρας γενομένους ὁ θεὸς παραδίδωσι τῇ ἐμφύτῳ συνειδήσει φυλάττειν, ταύτης οὖν φυλακῆς μηδαμῶς καταφρονητέον, ἐπεὶ καὶ τῷ Θεῷ ἀπάρεστον, καὶ τῷ ἰδίῳ συνειδότι ἐχθροὶ ἐσόμεθα.

Ejusd. Fragment.[3]

Αἱροῦ πρότερον τὰς ἐπιθυμίας κολάζειν, ἢ διὰ τὰς ἐπιθυμίας κολάζεσθαι.

Ejusd.[4]

Ἑνὶ τέρπου καὶ προσαναπαύου, τῷ ἀπὸ πράξεως κοινωνικῆς μεταβαίνειν ἐπὶ πρᾶξιν κοινωνικὴν σὺν μνήμῃ Θεοῦ.

M. Antonin.[5]

Ἐπὶ πάσῃ ὁρμῇ καὶ σμικροῦ καὶ μεγάλου πράγματος Θεὸν ἀεί που δεῖ καλοῦσιν.

Plato, in Tim.[6]

Ἀθανάτοις τε Θεοῖς καὶ ἡμῖν χάρματα δοίης.   incerti Poetae[7]

1. Joannes Stobaeus, *Anthologium* 3.1.29.3.
2. Epictetus, *Enchiridion* 51.2.1.
3. Epictetus, *Fragmenta*. [Possibly a Christian or modern paraphrase of Epictetus].
4. Epictetus, *Fragmenta*, 113, in *Epictetae Philosophiae Monumenta*, III.
5. M. Aurelius Antoninus, *Meditationes* 6.7.1.
6. Plato, *Timaeus* 27.c.2.
7. M. Aurelius Antoninus, *Meditationes* 7.39.1.1.

Choose the best course of life, and custom will make it the most pleasant. *Pythagoras.*

Assume to yourself to live like a perfect man, or one who has made great proficiency in philosophy, and let it be an inviolable law, to act the part that appears most virtuous. *Epictetus.*

{Other animals are committed to the government of men, but} God has committed men to the government of their own natural conscience. This governor we never should disobey; for it is offensive to God, and makes us enemies to the conscience within us.
Epictet. Fragm.

Choose rather to correct your own passions, than to be corrected and punished on their account. *The same author.*

In this one thing delight and rest yourself, in going on constantly from one social action to another with remembrance of the Deity.
Marcus Antonin.

In every design, or attempt whether great or small we ought to invoke God. *Plato.*

Give joy to the immortal Gods and those that love you.
An unknown Poet in Antonin.

<i>

LIBRORUM ET CAPITUM
ARGUMENTA.
[THE CONTENTS OF BOOKS AND CHAPTERS.]

In epistola ad Juvent. *Philosophia moralis* "ars vitae ad virtutem et beatitudinem assequendam instituendae." Ejus partes *Ethica,* et *Jurisprudentia naturalis.* Hujus itidem tres partes. 1. *Jurisprudentia privata.* 2. *Oeconomica.* 3. *Politica.* [In a Letter to the youth, *moral philosophy* is the art of living to pursue virtue and happiness. Its parts are *Ethics,* and *Natural jurisprudence.* The parts of the last are three: 1. *Private jurisprudence* 2. *Economics* 3. *Politics.*] p. 3. Operis suscipiendi causa. [The reason for undertaking this work.] p. 4. Quo consilio scripti libri *Ciceronis de officiis.* [The design of Cicero's *De officiis.*] p. 5. et cohortatio ad Philosophiam. [and an exhortation to philosophy.]

LIB. I. Ethica. [*Ethics.*]

Cap. I. *De natura humana.* [*On human nature.*]

1. Philosophia moralis ars *architectonica* aliis imperans. [Moral philosophy is a superior art commanding the others.] pag. 1. Ex hominis natura eruenda officiorum notitia. [The knowledge of our duties has to be dug up from human nature.] p. 2.

2. Constat homo ex animo et corpore. In quo sita corporis praestantia et infirmitas. [Man consists of soul and body. Excellences and weaknesses of the body.] p. 3, 4.

3. Animi partes sive facultates, *intellectus* et *voluntas.* Ad intellectum referuntur *sensus:* iique *externi* vel *interni.* [The parts or powers of the soul, *understanding* and *will.* The *senses* report to the understanding and they are *external* or *internal.*] 4, 5. Sensibus prima *boni malique* notitia paratur. [Senses provide the first acquaintance of *good* and *evil.*] ibid. Quaedam perceptiones mediae. [Perceptions of a middle kind.] ib. Aliae antecedentes et *directae,* nullâ alia praeeunte; aliae *reflexae.* [Some perceptions are antecedent and *direct,* others are *reflexive.*] 6.

THE
CONTENTS
OF THE SEVERAL
BOOKS AND CHAPTERS. <vii>

In the Preface. The division of philosophy into 3 parts. The several branches of moral philosophy. 1. The Author's intention in this compend. 2. The design of *Cicero's* books *de officiis.* ib. An account of this 2d edition. 3. And an exhortation to philosophy. 4.

BOOK I. *The Elements of Ethicks.*

Chapt. I. *Of human nature and its various parts or powers.* p. 1.

1. How moral philosophy an art superior to others. 1. derived from the structure of our nature. 2. the method of treating it. *ib.*

2. The human body its dignity. 3.

3. The powers of the soul, *understanding* and *will.* 4. the senses *external* and *internal,* whence our notions of good and evil. 4, 5. Sensations of a middle kind, their use. sensations *direct* and *reflex.* 6.

In the 1747 English translation, the titles of chapters, sections, and contents differ considerably from the original Latin titles. Within the brackets in the Latin table of contents are stricter, more correct translations of these titles.

4. *Sensus interni* quales.. [Which are the *internal senses.*] ib. Sensu percipiuntur omnes ideae. [All the ideas are perceived by sense.] 7. *Vis rationis.* [The *power of reason.*] ib. Hae vires a Deo ad homines pervenerunt, Deique consilium ostendunt. [These powers are given to men by God and show his wisdom.] ib.

5. *Bona* sensu prius quam ratione percipiuntur. [Every sort of good is perceived by sense before reasoning.] 8. De voluntate. [On will.] ib. Sui in optimo statu conservandi studium cuique infixum, omniumque *appetitio* quae ad vitam faciunt beatam, et contrariorum *fuga.* [In every man is rooted the study to preserve himself in the best condition, the *desire* of all the things that make for a happy life, and the *avoidance* of the contraries.] 8, 9. *Gaudia* et *mœrores* unde nascuntur. [The causes of *joy* and *sorrow.*] 9. Quatuor voluntatis motus. [Four motions of the will.] ib.

6. Motus perturbati sive *passiones;* a voluntate diversae. [The *passions* or turbulent motions; they are different from the calm motions of the will.] <ii> 10. *Appetitus rationalis* et *sensitivus.* [The *appetite* is *rational* or *sensitive.*] ib. Hic dividitur in *concupiscibilem* et *irascibilem.* [The last one is divided into *concupiscible* and *irascible.*] ib. *Passionum* quatuor genera; cujusque partes plurimae. [Four general classes of passions. Of each class there are many subdivisions.] 11.

7. Voluntatis motus vel *gratuiti,* vel ex *philautia* orti. [The motions of the will are *disinterested* or *selfish.*] ib. Utrumque genus vel *purum,* vel perturbatum. [Each kind is calm or turbulent.] ib. Eorum partes. [Their parts.] 12. Quae propter se expetenda. [What is desired for itself.] 13. Homini naturalis est *benevolentia gratuita.* [Disinterested benevolence is rooted in human nature.] ib.

8. *Sensus reflexi,* quibus cernuntur. *Pulchritudo; Harmonia,* rerum *convenientia.* [The reflexive senses, by which we perceive *beauty, harmony,* and the *concord* of things.] 14, 15. et laeta sit *veri cognitio.* [and the *discovery of truth* is joyful.] ib.

9. *Sympathia,* sive sensus communis. [*Sympathy,* or common sense.] 15.

10. Homo ad agendum natus. *Recti et honesti sensus,* explicatur. [Man was destined by nature for action. The sense of what is right and honourable is explained.] 16–23.

11. Comprobationis *gradus varii;* unde *pietatis,* et *amicitiae* sanctitas elucet. [The different degrees of approbation; whence the sanctity of *piety* and *friendship* shines forth.] 23–26.

12. Sensus hujus *principatus,* cui in omni vita parendum. [The supremacy of this sense which we ought to obey throughout our lives.] ib.

Cap. IV.

1. *Pietatis erga Deum* partes duae; verae sententiae, cultusque iis consonus. [Two parts of piety toward God: true opinions and worship suited to them.] 77.

2. Ex pietate nascuntur virtutes purissimae, gaudiaque maxima. [From piety arise the purest virtues and the greatest delights.] 77–80. Hominibus depravatis non desperandum. [Corrupted men ought not to despair.] 80.

3. *Cultus externi* natura et utilitas. [The nature and utility of external worship.] 82.

Cap. V. *Officia erga homines.* [The duties toward other men.] 84.

1. Arctiores hominum conjunctiones et vincula naturalia. [The strongest human ties and natural bonds.] 85. In affectionibus benignis jucunditas summa. [The highest delight in kind affections.] 86.

2. Aliae aliis honestiores. [The more honourable mutual affections.] ib. Virtutum sociarum *summa.* [The sum of all social virtues.] ib.

3. Arctiorum societatum utilitas et sanctitas. [Utility and sanctity of the stronger ties.] 87. Caritates arctiores haud reprimendae. [We ought not weaken our tender affections.] ib. Indicia in vultu. [Their appearance in countenance.] 88.

4. *Amicitiae* ortus. [The source of *Friendship.*] 89. Inter solos bonos. [Only among the virtuous.] 90. Amicitiae leges, ejusque utilitas. [The laws of friendship and its utility.] ib.

5. Amor duplex, *benevolentia* et *complacentia.* Haec saepe nimia, non illa. [Love is divided into *benevolence* and *complacence.* The last is often too great, not the first.] 90, 91.

Cap. VI. *De animi cultura.* [*On the culture of the mind.*] 92.

1. Rerum cognitio necessaria; summi boni, Dei, hominisque. [The knowledge of things is necessary: of the supreme good, of the nature of God and men.] 93.

2. Pietas erga Deum, rerumque externarum despicientia. [Piety towards God and contempt of external things.] 94, 95. Usu exercitationeque opus. [The need of habit and practice.] 96.

3. *Mediocritas* inter appetituum excessus et defectus. [The middle way between the excess and the defect of our appetites.] 96. Omnes appetitus utiles esse possunt. [All the appetites may be advantageous.] 97. Mediocres venustissimi et tutissimi. [Their moderate degree is the most graceful and safest.] 99. Quod plurium exemplis illustratur. [Illustration of this by many examples.] 99–104.

BOOK II. Elements of the Law of Nature.

Cap. III. *De virtutum et vitiorum gradibus.* [*On the various degrees of virtue and vice.*]

Cap. IV. *De jure hominum naturali.* [*On the natural rights of men.*] 143.

1. Status quid: is duplex, vel *naturalis libertatis,* vel *adventitius.* [What is a state: a state is one of two: either of *natural liberty* or *adventitious.*] 144. Status libertatis non est *status belli.* [The state of *liberty* is not a *state of war.*] ib.

2. Jura *privata, publica, communia.* [*Private, publick,* and *common* rights.] 145. unde primo singulorum jura privata innotescunt. [Whence private rights of individuals first become known.] ib. Jura vel *naturalia,* vel *adventitia.* [*Natural* or *adventitious* rights.] 146.

3. Jura *perfecta* et *imperfecta.* [*Perfect* and *imperfect* rights.] ib. Jura *naturalia* perfecta recensentur. [Perfect *natural* rights reviewed.] 146–148.

4. Naturalis hominum aequalitas. [Men's natural equality.] ib.

5. Jura naturalia imperfecta. [Imperfect natural rights.] 149.

6. De *beneficentia* et liberalitate. [On *beneficence* and liberality.] 150.

Cap. V. *De jure adventitio.* [*On the adventitious rights.*]

1. Jura adventitia vel *realia,* vel *personalia.* [Adventitious rights *real* or *personal.*] 151. Realium praecipua, *rerum dominia.* [The principal real right is *property.*] ib. Jus utendi rebus inanimis. [The right of using inanimate things.] 152, 153.

2. 3. Ut etiam animatis; et carne vescendi. [The right of using animals, and of eating their flesh.] 153.

4. Dominium quid sit ejusque causae. [What is property and its grounds.] 154.

Cap. VI. *De dominii acquirendi rationibus.* [*On the methods of acquiring property.*]

1. 2. Dominium vel *primum* vel *derivatum.* [Property is either *original* or *derived.*] 156. Primum, *occupatione* constituitur. [Original property arises from first *occupation.*] 157. Quaenam jure potior. [Which methods of occupation are more righteous.] 158.

3. Quousque occupare potest quisquam. [How long anybody can occupy.] 161. <vii>

4. Quae res communes. [Which things are for perpetual community.] 163. Communio *negativa* vel *positiva.* [*Negative* or *positive* community.] 164.[1] *Res nullius,* sacrae, sanctae, religiosae. [Things sacred, holy, or religious.] ib. Res publicae. [Public goods.] 165. Usucapio. [Prescription.] ib.

---

1. In the 1745 edition these subtitles are erroneously placed in art. 3.

Cap. VIII. *De Legibus condendis et Jurisdictione.* [*On making Civil Laws and on their Execution.*] 325.

PHILOSOPHIAE MORALIS
INSTITUTIO COMPENDIARIA

 {♡} LIBER I {♡}

Ethices Elementa.

CAPUT I

De Hominis Natura ejusque Partibus.

I. Quemadmodum caeterae omnes artes et disciplinae, bonum aliquod {naturae accommodatum} consequendum tanquam finem suum respiciunt; Philosophiam moralem, quae vitae totius ordinandae ars est, finem spectare longe praestantissimum necesse est; quum se ducem profiteatur, quantum hominum viribus fieri potest, ad vitam [eam quae maximè est secundum naturam, quam docet etiam esse beatissimam] [beatam], cui inservire debent omnia quae caeteris artibus effici possunt. Suo igitur jure in caeteras imperium sibi arrogare videtur{, eatenus saltem ut praescribat quasnam quisque, et quem ad finem, excolere debeat}. Quum [vero communis haec sit anticipatio sive naturae judicium, quod in animorum affectione aliqua aut habitu, atque actionibus consentaneis] [autem constet inter omnes, in virtutibus ipsis, atque in officiorum functione], vel situm sit [esse] illud Beate vivere, vel eorundem <2> ope {parari et} obtineri; [in quo philosophorum omnium, rationibus utcunque discrepantium, consentit oratio, docentium in ipsis virtutibus officiorumque functione, summi boni adipiscendi, sive beate vivendi, spem omnem esse sitam;] [(si modo virtutem appellent "vires animi aut habitus praestantissimos," atque officia, descriptione hujusmodi rudi & generali, "actiones omnes quae ex virtutibus proficiscuntur," aut quae, secundum rectam rationem, hominis summo bono assequendo inserviunt)] in Philosophia morali <tradenda,> haec <duo> imprimis sedulo erunt investiganda, [quaenam vita sit secundum naturam; quaenam beatissima] [in quo sita sit vita beata]; quidque sit ipsa virtus.

23

∽ ❦ BOOK I ❦ ∽

The Elements of Ethicks.

CHAPTER I

Of Human Nature and its Parts.

I. As all other arts <and sciences> have in view some <natural> good to be obtained, as their proper end, Moral Philosophy, which is the art of regulating the whole of life, must have in view the noblest end; since it undertakes, as far as human reason [powers] can go, to lead us into that course of life which is most according to the intention of nature, and most happy, to which end whatever we can obtain by other arts should be subservient. Moral Philosophy therefore must be one of these commanding arts which directs how far the other arts are to be pursued.[1] <As, however, a common suggestion or natural judgment tells us that happiness, or the means to obtain it, consists in some affection or habit of the soul and in the consequent actions> [a]nd since all Philosophers, even of the most opposite schemes, agree in words at least, that "Happiness either consists in virtue and virtuous offices, or is to be obtained and <2> secured by them":[2] The chief points to be enquired into in Morals [Moral Philosophy] must be, what course of life is according to the intention of nature? wherein consists happiness? and what is virtue?[3]

---

1. This beginning on the supremacy of moral philosophy is similar to Aristotle's *Nicomachean Ethics* (1094a) and Cicero, *De finibus* V.16.

2. This is what Cicero maintains in *De Finibus* V and stresses in *Tusc. disp.* V.

3. See *Tusc. disp.* V.19. Cicero says that, whereas for the Stoics happiness and virtue are coincident, the Stoics have different books on virtue and on the highest happiness, for logical and rhetorical reasons. Hutcheson, as well as Cicero, follows the Stoics: Hutcheson in the first two chapters of the present work, Cicero, in the fourth and fifth books of *De finibus* and *Tusc. disp.* Adding the third question: "what does it mean to follow

Quicunque divina mente et ratione, cum mundum hunc universum, tum genus humanum fabricatum fuisse credit, expectabit in ipsa hominis natura et constitutione [fabrica] repertum iri indicia haud obscura, quae monstrent, quodnam sit hominis {munus et} opus proprium, ad quodnam vitae genus et officia, sit a natura provida et solertissima subornatus; quaenam denique res vitam homini beatam efficere possint. Intrandum igitur in hominum naturam, ut perspiciamus "quid simus, quidnam victuri gignamur,"[1] et quos Deus nos esse jusserit. {Dei autem naturaeque voluntas optimè innotescet anquirentibus, quaenam sint ea omnia quae sensu quovis naturali nobis commendantur, quaeque eorum praecipua; ad quaenam appetenda naturâ impellamur; quaenam denique ad vitam beandam vim habeant maximam.} In hac disquisitione leviter tantum attingenda ea quae ad alias pertinent disciplinas [scientias], ut in his praecipue moremur <3> quae ad mores regendos plurimum valent.

More omnium disciplinarum, a notioribus ad magis obscura detegenda progredimur: neque, rerum dignitate ducti, ab iis quae naturâ prima sunt, Dei nempe Op. max. voluntate <non> ordimur; sed a naturae nostrae constitutione, quae cognitu facilior [cognitione prior] est; ut eâ perspectâ colligamus, quodnam [de animorum affectionibus et actionibus nostris Dei] [circa animi nostri consilia et actiones, divini] fabricatoris sit consilium et voluntas. Neque prorsus omittenda ea officiorum indicia aperta, quae vitae humanae commoditates [commoda] atque utilitates exhibent externae; licet forte ex alio fonte fluat omnis vera virtus, quàm ex istiusmodi voluptatum aut utilitatum appetitione [appetitionibus], <quae continent res externae>.

II. Primo igitur, constat homo ex animo [anima] et corpore, quorum utrumque suas habet vires partesque naturales: corporis partes cognitionem habent faciliorem, medicis propriam; hoc <tantum> obiter attingimus, il-

---

1. Persius, *Saturae*, III.67. It is already quoted by Hutcheson in his *Essay on Passions*, pref., page [xviii], quoted and discussed by Shaftesbury in his *Miscellaneous Reflections*, III.1 (*Characteristicks of Men, Manners, Opinions, Times*, ed. by Lawrence E. Klein, Cambridge University Press, 1999, p. 406).

All such as believe that this universe, and human nature in particular, was formed by the wisdom and counsel of a Deity, must expect to find in our structure and frame some clear evidences, shewing the proper business of mankind, for what course of life, what offices we are furnished by the providence and wisdom of our Creator, and what <therefore> are the proper means of happiness. We must therefore search accurately into the constitution of our nature, to see what sort of creatures we are; for what purposes nature has formed us; what character God our Creator requires us to maintain. Now the intention of <God and> nature with respect to us, is best known by examining what these things are which our natural senses {or perceptive powers} recommend to us, and what the most excellent among them? and next, what are the aims of our several natural desires, and which of them are of greatest importance to our happiness? In this inquiry we shall lightly pass over such natural powers as are treated of in other arts [sciences], dwelling chiefly upon those which are of consequence in regulating our morals.

In this art, as in all others, we must proceed from the subjects more easily known, to those that are more obscure; and not follow the priority of nature, or the dignity of the subjects: and therefore don't deduce our first notions of duty from the divine Will; but from the constitution of our nature, which is more immediately <3> known; that from the full knowledge of it, we may discover the design, intention, and will of our Creator as to our conduct [affections and actions].[4] Nor will we omit such obvious evidences of our duty as arise even from the considerations of our present secular interests; tho' it will perhaps hereafter appear, that all true virtue must have some nobler spring than any desires of worldly pleasures or interests.

II. First then, Human nature consists of soul and body, each of which has its proper powers, parts, {or faculties}. The inquiry into the body is more easy, and belongs to the Physicians. We only transiently observe, that it is

nature" in the second edition, Hutcheson stresses his teleological and providential perspective here, as well as in many other additions. Compare the skeptical answer by Hume in his letter to Hutcheson of Sept. 17th, 1739.

4. This Aristotelian epistemic argument is used by Hutcheson against the legalistic perspective in ethics, that is, against those (Pufendorf, Locke and Carmichael) who base natural law on God's will or decrees.

lud ita formatum esse, ut longe aliorum animantium corporibus antecellat.
{Non solum enim} sensuum organis, [partibusque, aliis ad vitam cujusque,
aliis ad generis conservationem aptissimis instructum est, verum etiam iis
artificiosissime fabricatis, quae operi cuique, mentisque solertis et artificio-
sae imperiis infinitis exequendis commodissime inserviant] [instructum est,
partim ejus, aliae ad vitam cujusque, aliae ad genus humanum conservandum sunt aptissimae; aliae ad motus omnes pro mentis imperio peragendos,
infinitamque eam actionum varietatem, quam efficere voluerit mens solers
et artificiosa]. <4> Non praetereunda est forma ad dignitatem erecta, et
contemplationi idonea; membrorum motus facillimi et celeres; tot artium
ministrae manus <solertissime fabricatae>; vultusque ad omnium animi
motuum indicia exhibenda flexibilis{; quaeque ad vocis variae et orationis
usum in corpore machinata est natura:} quae omnia fusius persequuntur
anatomici.

Artificiosam [Exquisitam] hanc corporis compagem [machinam], flux-
am et caducam esse, novis quotidie egentem ciborum fulturis, et continuo
vestitu, alioque cultu, quò a malis innumeris extrinsecus irruentibus protegatur, norunt omnes: in tutelam igitur data est animo sagaci et provido,
quae altera pars hominis, eaque longe praeclarior.

III. Animi autem partes, quarum est adspectus illustrior, sunt variae{*}: ad
duas tamen reducuntur classes; quarum altera vires omnes cognoscendi continet, quae *Intellectus* dicitur; altera vires appetendi quae dicitur *voluntas*.

Intelligendi vires sunt plures, ideo hic brevius percurrendae, quod in iis
plenius explicandis versentur *Dialecticae* et *Philosophiae primae* scriptores.
Primo veniunt *sensus,* <5> quo nomine appellatur "Animi quaevis constitutio aut conformatio naturalis, cujus vi certas Ideas aut species ex certis

---

* {De natura hominis praeter *Aristotelem* in ethicis, librisque de anima, *Nemesium,*
Lockium, Malebranchium; vid. *Ciceronem* de finib. 1. v. *Arrianum* passim, et comit. de
Shaftsbury Disquisitionem de virtute, libellumque cui titulus, *Sensus communis.*}

---

* {See this explained by Dr. Cumberland, *de Lege Naturae.*} [This added note shows
the competence of the anonymous translator. The long chapter 2 of Cumberland's *De
legibus naturae* is dedicated to vindicate the supremacy of man over the other animals,
against Hobbes, using observations from a number of contemporary anatomists and
physicians (art. 22 and ff.). Both Hutcheson and Cumberland (art. 29) drew from Cicero's remarks in *De natura deorum* and *De legibus* on the dignity of the human body.]

† Concerning human nature, beside *Aristotle's* moral writings <and his books on the

plainly of a more noble{*} structure than that of other animals. It has not only organs of sense and all parts requisite either for the preservation of the individual or of the species, but also such as are requisite for that endless variety of action and motion, which a rational and inventive spirit may intend, and these organs formed with exquisite art. One cannot omit the dignity of its erect form, so plainly fitted for {enlarged} contemplation; the easy and swift motions of the joints; the curious structure of the hand, that great instrument of all ingenious arts; the countenance, so easily variable as to exhibit to us all the affections of the soul; and the organs of voice, so nicely fitted for speech in all its various kinds, and the pleasure of harmony. These points are more fully explained by Anatomists.

This curious frame of the human body we all see to be fading and perishing; needing daily new recruits by <4> food, and constant defence against innumerable dangers from without, by cloathing, shelter, and other conveniencies. The charge of it therefore is committed to a soul endued with forethought and sagacity, which is the other, and by far the nobler part in our constitution.

III. The parts or powers of the soul, which present us with a more glorious view, are of various kinds:† but they are all reducible to two classes, the *Understanding* and the *Will.*[5] The former contains all the powers which aim at knowledge; the other all our desires {pursuing happiness and eschewing misery}.

We shall but briefly mention the several operations of the understanding, because they are sufficiently treated of in Logicks and Metaphysicks. The first in order are the *senses:* under which name we include every "constitution or power of the soul, by which certain {feelings,} ideas or percep-

---

soul>, *Nemesius de homine, Locke,* and *Malebranch;* many excellent observations are made in *Cicero's* 5th book *de finibus, Arrian,* and *Lord Shaftesbury's Inquiry,* and *Rhapsody.* [Hutcheson refers to Locke's *Essay Concerning Human Understanding,* Malebranche's *Recherche de la Verité,* Arrian's *The Encheiridion* ("Manual") *of Epictetus,* and Shaftesbury's *Inquiry Concerning Virtue or Merit* and *The Moralists.* Nemesius, bishop of Emesa in Syria at the end of the fourth century A.D., is the author of *De natura homine,* a treatise of Christian anthropology that explains the middle position of man in the scale of beings, describes in detail the powers of the soul, and criticizes Stoic fatalism.]

5. See Hutcheson, *Synopsis* 2.1.2, p. 47.

accipit [recipit] rebus objectis": Suntque hi sensus vel *externi* vel *interni*. Externi a corporeis pendent organis, ita constituti, ut ex motu quovis validiore, aut mutatione in corpore, sive per vim extrinsecus impressam, sive per vim internam, confestim oriatur in animo perceptio quaedam aut informatio. Gratae sunt, aut saltem non molestae perceptiones, quae excipiunt motus, mutationes, [impulsionesque] [aut impressiones] corpori utiles aut innocuas; molestae vero et cum dolore conjunctae, quas excitant mutationes corpori nociturae.

Corporis voluptates et dolores quamvis satis valide animum commoveant, breves sunt plerumque et fluxae <admodum>: neque voluptatum {istiusmodi} praeteritarum recordatio {per se} grata est, aut dolorum molesta.

Sensibus his primam [primas] *bonorum malorumque* notitiam adipiscimur [comparamus notitias]. Quae res {sensibus externis objectae} gratas excitant perceptiones, sunt bonae, quae molestas malae. <Earum quae sensibus obiciuntur externis> Quae aliis {sensibus subtilioribus} cernuntur [percipiuntur] motum excitantes gratum, *bona* [itidem] [simili ratione] dicuntur, et quae molestum, *mala*. Beatitudo vulgò dicitur is [in universum, est] "status ubi rerum {motum} gratum <sensum> excitantium suppetit copia, dolore {omni graviori} amoto." *Miseria*, "ubi irruunt <6> dolores crebri et diuturni, omnia ferè grata excludentes."

A corpore pendent etiam Perceptiones quaedam mediae, <nulla aut> exigua cum voluptate aut dolore per se conjunctae; quae rerum externarum suppeditant notiones [ideas], earumque mutationes indicant. His corporum quorum vis magnitudines, figuras, situs, motum, aut quietem cognoscimus; quae omnia visu et tactu praecipue cernuntur [percipiuntur]; neque sensum excitant per se vel gratum vel molestum; licet nos saepe certiores faciant eventuum, ex quibus, alia de causa, cupiditatem [laetitiam] aut iram, gaudia aut moerores colligamus.

tions are raised upon certain objects presented." Senses are either *external,* or *internal* {and mental}. The external depend on certain organs of the body, so constituted that upon any impression made on them, or motion excited, whether by external impulses or internal forces in the body, a certain feeling [perception] or notion is raised in the soul. The feelings [perceptions] are generally either agreeable, or at least not uneasy, which ensue upon such impressions and changes as are useful or not hurtful to the body: but <5> uneasy feelings ensue upon those which are destructive or hurtful.[6]

Tho' bodily pleasure and pain affect the soul pretty vehemently, yet we see they <usually> are of short duration and fleeting; and {seldom} is <not> the bare remembrance of past bodily pleasures agreeable, <n>or the remembrance of past pain in it self uneasy{, when we apprehend no returns of them}.

By these senses we acquire the first notions of *good* and *evil.*[7] Such things as excite grateful sensations of this kind, we call *good;* what excites painful or uneasy sensations, we call *evil.* Other objects also when perceived by some other kinds of senses, exciting also agreeable feelings, we likewise call good, and their contraries evil. *Happiness* in general, is "a state wherein there is plenty of such things as excite these grateful sensations of one kind or other, and we are free from pain." *Misery* consists in "frequent and lasting sensations of the painful and disagreeable sorts, excluding all grateful sensations."

There are also certain perceptions dependent on bodily organs, which are of a middle nature as to pleasure or pain, having a very small degree of either joined immediately with them: these are the perceptions by which we discern the primary qualities of external objects and any changes befalling them, their magnitude, figure, situation, motion or rest: all which are discerned chiefly by *sight* or *touch,* and give us neither pleasure nor pain of themselves; tho' they frequently intimate to us such events as occasion desires or aversions, joys or sorrows.[8] <6>

6. Cf. Hutcheson, *Synopsis* 2.1.3, pp. 48–49.
7. Cf. Hutcheson, *Synopsis* 2.1.3, p. 51.
8. On pleasant, painful, or neutral sensations see Hutcheson, *Synopsis* 2.1.3, p. 49.

Corporis voluptates et dolores, nobis cum mutis animalibus communes, nonnullum ad vitam vel beatam vel miseram momentum afferunt [habent]. Perceptiones mediae, rerum externarum qualitates indicantes, magnum praebent in vita usum, in actionibus externis regendis, in rerum cognitione, et in artibus fere omnibus capiendis et exercendis.

Utrumque {hoc} perceptionum {externarum} genus dici potest *directum* et *antecedens;* quòd non alias ideas aut species praecurrentes exigat. Aliae autem sunt perceptiones, etiam earum specierum quae non sine organis corporeis ad animum perveniunt, quas, distinguendi causa, dicimus *reflexas* aut subsequentes, quia alias prius admissas subsequantur <7> ideas; de quibus mox erit agendum. Hactenus de sensibus externis.

IV. Sensus interni, sunt illae animi vires, quibus omnia quae intra se fiunt, aut ipse secum molitur, percipit; sive actiones, sive passiones, judicia, voluntates, desideria, gaudia, dolores, et agendi consilia. Hae vires, *conscientiae internae,* aut *reflexionis* nomine, apud claros scriptores appellantur; quibus omnia quae in ipsa mente fiunt cernuntur [objiciuntur], pariter ac sensibus externis res externae. Hi sensus externi et interni omnem suppeditant idearum supellectilem, [aut] [et ratiocinandi] materiam, in qua exercetur homini propria rationis vis; quae plenius forent declaranda, nisi ad logicam pertinerent.

Rationis ope, rerum *relationes,* quae dicuntur, <et> cognationes, et nexus cernere valet mens; "consequentia" et "causas, earumque progressus, et antecessiones non ignorat, similitudines comparat, et rebus praesentibus adjungit et annectit futuras, et facile totius vitae cursum videt, ad eamque degendam praeparat res necessarias."[2]

Rationis usu facilè innotescit, mundum universum Dei sapientissimi opt. max. consilio ab initio fuisse constitutum, et omni tempore administratum,[3] atque humano generi tributam esse hanc rationis, supra caetera animantia, praestantiam, una cum caeteris omnibus <8> sive corporis sive animi viribus, unde hominibus elucere poterit parentis sui, creatoris et con-

---

2. Cicero, *De officiis* 1.11.4–13.
3. Cf. Cicero, *De natura deorum* 2.75.1–3.

---

9. This paragraph refers to Locke, *An Essay concerning Human Understanding,* 2.1.3–5. Locke's distinction between external and internal sensations is different from Hutch-

Bodily pleasures and pains, such as we have in common with the brutes, are of some importance to our happiness or misery. The other class of perceptions, which inform us of the qualities and states of things external to us, are of the highest use in all external action, in the acquiring of knowledge, in learning and practising the various arts of life.

Both these kinds of external perceptions may be called *direct* and *antecedent,* because they presuppose no previous ideas <or forms>. But there's another class of perceptions employed about the objects of even the external senses, which for distinction we call *reflex* or *subsequent,* because they naturally ensue upon other ideas previously received: of these presently. So much for external sensation.

IV. Internal senses are those powers {or determinations} of the mind, by which it perceives or is conscious of all within itself, its actions, passions, judgments, wills, desires, joys, sorrows, purposes of action. This power some celebrated writers call *consciousness* or *reflection,* which has for its objects the qualities, actions or states of the mind itself, as the external senses have things external. These two classes of sensation, external and internal, furnish our whole store of ideas, the materials about which we exercise that noblest power of *reasoning* peculiar to the human species. This also deserves a fuller explication, but it belongs to Logick.[9]

'Tis by this power of reason, that the soul perceives the relations and connexions of things, and their consequences and causes; inferrs what is to ensue, or <7> what preceded; can discern resemblances, consider in one view the present and the future, propose to itself a whole plan of life, and provide all things requisite for it.

By the exercise of reason it will easily appear, that this whole universe was at first framed by the contrivance and counsel of a most perfect intelligence, and is continually governed by the same; that it is to him mankind owe their preeminence above other animals in the power of reason, and in all these excellencies of mind or body, which clearly intimate to us the will

---

eson's direct or antecedent and reflex or subsequent perceptions mentioned above, even if Hutcheson pretended them to be the same. Locke was mainly interested in the operations of the understanding, while Hutcheson wanted to expand on his theory of finer perceptive powers of the soul.

servatoris munificentissimi, ratio et consilium; quaeque hominum officia, quod vitae genus et institutio, ipsi sint grata.

V. Quum autem omne ferè bonum, quod momentum aliquod per se afferre potest ad vitam beatam, sensu aliquo proximo ratiocinationem omnem antecedente, percipiatur; rationis enim est, bona, quae sensu prius erant percepta, inter se comparare, iisque consequendis idoneas monstrare rationes et subsidia: sublimiores idcirco sensus omnes, aut percipiendi vires, sunt sedulo observandae, quippe monstraturae {quaenam naturae sint aptissima, atque} ex quibus <demum rebus> conficiatur vita beata. [Quaedam tamen antè de voluntate dicenda,] [Harum tamen explicationi praemittenda est voluntatis contemplatio;] quia et animi motus, voluntates, desideria et agendi consilia contemplantur hi sensus subtiliores, et varia inter ea cernunt discrimina.

Ubi primum igitur, ex sensu qualicunque grato aut molesto, boni aut mali cujusvis notitiam adepta est mens, sua sponte subnascuntur motus quidam, ab omni sensuum perceptione diversi, boni nempe *appetitio* seu *desiderium,* et mali *fuga* et *aversatio.* Semper etenim se prodit insita quaedam omni naturae ratione praeditae propensio aut impetus altè infixus [proclivitas altè infixa], ad omnia ea appetenda, quae <9> [ad vitam facere videntur beatam] [ipsius facere videntur beatitudinem], atque ad contraria omnia amolienda. Quamvis enim pauci serio secum examinaverunt quaenam sint ea quae ad vitam vel beatam vel miseram, vim habent maximam [maximum habent momentum]; omnia tamen appetunt homines naturâ, quae aliquod hujusmodi momentum afferre videntur ad [vitam beatam] [beatitudinem], et contraria fugiunt: quumque plura occurrunt, quae simul consectari [prosequi] nequeat mens, illa naturâ appetit, si modo tranquillo tantum motu feratur, quae caeteris plus [pollere] [habere momenti] videntur. Ubi vero, in eadem re, variae simul commiscentur bonorum et malorum species, appetit aut fugit mens, prout plus boni aut mali in re objecta inesse videatur.

Praeter hoc *desiderium* et *fugam* proprios [aversationem, primarios] voluntatis tranquillae motus, recensentur alii duo, *gaudium* et *tristitia.* Sunt vero hi novi potius mentis status, aut sensus subtiliores, quam impulsiones [motus] ad agendum. Hac autem ratione, quodammodo conficiuntur quatuor motuum classes, antiquioribus decantatae; qui omnes ad voluntatem, κατ᾽ ἐξοχὴν, sive *appetitum rationalem* referuntur. Ubi boni spectatur adeptio, oritur *desiderium;* ubi mali spectatur depulsio, *cautio* aut *aversatio.* Ubi

of our munificent Creator and Preserver; and shew us what sort of offices, what course of life he requires of us as acceptable in his sight.

V. Since then every sort of good which is immediately of importance to happiness, must be perceived by some immediate power or sense, antecedent to any {opinions or} reasoning: (for 'tis the business of reasoning to compare the several sorts of good perceived by the several senses, and to find out the proper means for obtaining them:) we must therefore carefully inquire into the several sublimer perceptive powers or senses; since 'tis by them we discover what state or course of life best answers the intention of {God and} nature, and wherein true happiness consists. But we must premise some brief consideration of the *Will,* because the motions of the will, our affections, desires and purposes, are the objects of these more subtile senses, which perceive various qualities and important differences among them.

As soon as the mind has got any notion of good or evil by grateful or uneasy sensations of any kind, <8> there naturally arise certain motions {of the *Will*}, distinct from all sensation; to wit, *Desires* of good, and *Aversions* to evil. For there constantly appears, in every rational being, a stable essential propensity to desire its own happiness, and whatever seems to tend to it, and to avoid the contraries which would make it miserable. And altho' there are few who have seriously inquired what things are of greatest importance to happiness; yet all men naturally desire whatever appears to be of any consequence to this end, and shun the contrary: when several grateful objects occur, all which it cannot pursue together, the mind while it is calm, {and under no impulse of any blind appetite or passion,} pursues that one which seems of most importance. But if there should appear in any object a mixture of good and evil, the soul will pursue or avoid it, according as the good or the evil appears superior.

Beside these two calm primary motions of the Will, *desire* and *aversion,* there are other two commonly ascribed to it, to wit, *Joy* and *Sorrow.* But these two are rather to be called new states, or finer feelings or senses of the soul, than motions of the will naturally exciting to action. In this manner however we make up these four species mentioned by the antients, all <specially> referred to the *Will,* or *rational appetite:* when good to be obtained

bonum contigit, aut malum est depulsum, oritur *gaudium;* ubi malum premit, aut bonum est amissum, *tristitia.* <10>

VI. Ab his animi {placidi} motibus purioribus, et tranquilla [tranquillo] stabilique beate vivendi [suae beatitudinis] appetitione, quae ratione utuntur duce; diversi plane sunt motus quidam vehementiores et turbidi, quibus, secundum naturae suae legem, saepe agitatur mens, ubi certa species ipsi obversatur, atque bruto quodam impetu fertur ad quaedam agenda, sequenda, aut fugienda, quamvis nondum, adhibita in consilium ratione, secum statuerat ea ad vitam facere vel beatam vel miseram. Hos motus quisque intelliget, qui, in se descendens, in memoriam revocaverit quali animi impetu fuerat abreptus, quae passus, quum {acriore} libidine, ambitione, ira, odio, invidia, amore, commiseratione, laetitia, aut metu, agitabatur; etiam ubi nihil de earum rerum, quae mentem commoverant, cursu ad vitam beatam aut miseram serio cogitarat. Quid quod saepe in partes contrarias distineantur et distrahantur homines, cum "aliud cupido, mens" vero, ejusque appetitus tranquillus, "aliud suadeat."⁴

Perturbatos hosce {animi} motus reducunt antiqui in ἐπιθυμίαν et θυμὸν; quorum utrumque a voluntate, βούλησι, est diversum; prior, voluptatis spectat adeptionem, posterior, doloris depulsionem. Utrumque continet ὄρεξις ἀλόγος, sive *appetitus sensitivus,* qui scholasticis est vel *irascibilis* vel *concupiscibilis:* <11> eorum motus *passiones* appellant. {Appetitum hunc parum aptè sensitivum vocant, nisi vox sensus, ad alias a

---

4. Ovid, *Metamorphoses* 7.19–21: "sed trahit invitam nova vis, aliudque cupido, mens aliud suadet: video meliora proboque, deteriora sequor," quoted also in *Synopsis* 2.2.4, p. 68.

---

10. Cf. Hutcheson, *Essay on Passions* 2.1, pp. 27–28, and *System* 1.1.5, vol. I, pp. 8–9 and note, where Hutcheson himself refers the division to Cicero, *Tusc. disp.,* books iii and iv.

11. This distinction between calm affections of the soul and vehement passions was criticized by Hume in his letter of Jan. 10th, 1743 (*The letters of David Hume,* edited by J. Y. T. Greig, Oxford, 1932, p. 46). Hume considered the division "vulgar and specious"

is in view, there arises *Desire;* when evil to be repelled, *Aversion:* when good is obtained or evil avoided, arises *Joy;* when good is lost, or evil befallen us, *Sorrow.*[10]

VI. But beside the calm motions or affections of the soul and the stable desire of happiness, which employ <9> our reason for their conductor, there are also others of a very different nature; certain vehement turbulent Impulses, which upon certain occurrences naturally agitate the soul, and hurry it on with a blind inconsiderate force to certain actions, pursuits, or efforts to avoid, exerted about such things as we have never deliberately determined to be of consequence to happiness or misery. Any one may understand what we mean by these blind impetuous motions who reflects on what he has felt, what violent propensities hurried him on, when he was influenced by any of the keener passions of lust, ambition, anger, hatred, envy, love, pity, <delight> or fear; without any previous deliberate opinion about the tendency of these objects or occurrences which raised these several passions to his happiness or misery. These passions are so far from springing from the previous calm desire of happiness, that we find them often opposing it, and drawing the soul contrary ways.[11]

These several passions [violent motions of the soul] the antients reduce to two classes, to wit, the *passionate Desires,* and the correspondent *Aversions;* both which they teach to be quite distinct from the Will; the former aiming at the obtaining some pleasure or other, and the latter the warding off something uneasy. Both are by the schoolmen said to reside in the *sensitive* <or irrational> *appetite;* which they subdivide into the{*} *concupiscible* and *irascible;* and their impulses they call *Passions.* The *sensitive appetite* is not a very proper name for these determinations of the soul, unless the schoolmen would use the <10> word *senses* in a more extensive signi-

---

(*A Treatise of Human Nature,* 2.1.1, p. 276 and 2.3.3), as "a calm ambition, a calm Anger . . . [which] may likewise be very strong, & have the absolute Command over the Mind" (*Letters, ibidem*). Hutcheson, here as well as in the *Essay on Passions,* follows the Cartesian, Malebranchean, and Stoic tradition.

* {ἐπιθυμία και θυμός} [Aristotle distinguishes three kinds of appetitions in the soul: in its rational part, volition ('βούλησις), in its irrational part, desire (ἐπιθυμία) and impulsiveness (θυμός) (*De anima* 432 b 5; *Nichomachean ethics* III IIII, b5ff.). Accordingly the schoolmen subdivide the irrational part in concupiscible and irascibile.

sensibus externis percipiendi vires porrigatur: etenim species quaedam nulli sensui externo obviae, motus animi turbulentiores non raro excitant; ambitionem, congratulationem, malevolentiam, gloriaeque et divitiarum libidines, offensionesque contrarias. Isti autem nomini subesse volunt, omnes appetitiones et offensiones vehementiores et improvidas, sensuque turbido conjunctas.} Istiusmodi motuum quatuor sunt genera, qui bonum spectant consequendum, *cupiditatis;* qui malum depellendum, *metus;* qui bonum quod contigit, aut malum quod depulsum est, *laetitiae,* qui bonum amissum aut malum imminens, *aegritudinis* [*doloris*] nomine notantur. Horum cujusque etiam plura sunt genera, aut partes, pro rerum varietate quam spectant variae passiones, quibus sunt nomina notissima, <libido, congratulatio, ambitio, avaritia, luxuries, superbia, ira, indignatio, invidia, ultio, aemulatio, verecundia;> quaeque ex iis quae mox sunt dicenda, satis cognosci poterint.

VII. Voluntatis motuum, sive puriorum sive turbidorum, alia est divisio, prout *sibi* quisquam expetit voluptatem aliquam aut utilitatem, aut *alteri.* Gratuitam esse aliquando hominum bonitatem, nullam suam utilitatem spectantium, ubi animo benigno et amico alteri consulunt, satis constabit si quisque <12> se excusserit, si vitae suae consilia amica et caritates, {studia denique et dilectiones quibus bonos clarosque prosequimur;} si morientium curas et studia, officiorumque in extremo spiritu conservationes perspexerit; praecipue vero clarorum virorum facta, et consilia, et mortes pro amicis, pro liberis, pro patria, praemeditatas et voluntarias.

fication, so as to include many perceptive powers of an higher sort than the bodily senses. For 'tis plain that many of the most turbulent passions arise upon certain occurrences which affect none of the external senses; such as ambition, congratulation, malicious joy, the keen passions toward glory and power, {and many others,} with the turbulent aversions to their contraries. The schoolmen however refer to this *sensitive appetite* all the vehement inconsiderate motions of the will, which are attended with confused uneasy sensations, whatever their occasions be.

Of these passions there are four general classes: such as pursue some apparent good are called {*passionate Desires* or} *Cupidity;* such as tend toward off evil are called *Fears*{, or *Anger*}; such as arise upon obtaining what was desired or the escaping evil, are turbulent *Joys;* and what arise upon the loss of good, or the befalling of evil, *Sorrows.* {[nor have we in our language words appropriated so as to distinguish between the several calm and passionate motions of the will.]}[12] Of each class there are many subdivisions according to the variety of objects about which they are employed, which <have very familiar names and> will be further explained hereafter.

VII. There's also another division of the motions of the will whether calm or passionate, according as the advantage or pleasure in view is for ourselves or others.[13] That there is among men some disinterested goodness, without any views to interests of their own, but pursuing ultimately the interests of persons beloved, must be evident to such as examine well their <11> own hearts, the motions of friendship or natural affection; and the love and zeal we have for worthy and eminent characters: or to such as observe accurately the cares, the earnest desires, of persons on their deathbeds, and their friendly offices to such as they love even with their last breath: or, in the more heroic characters, their great actions and designs, and their marching willingly and deliberately to certain death for their children, their friends, or their country.

---

12. This sentence, added by the translator, is in square brackets in the original text. Here Hutcheson follows the Ciceronian division of the passions (*Tusc. disp.* IV.11–14). See also Hutcheson, *Synopsis* 2.1.4, p. 68, and *System* 1.1.5, vol. I, pp. 7–8.

13. Cf. *An Essay on Passions* 1.3, p. 13, and *System* 1.1.5, vol. I, p. 8.

Voluntatis motus hi gratuiti, sunt vel puri vel perturbati, quales et illi quibus sibi consulit quisque{, eaque consectatur quae sibi grata videntur}. <Atque> Varii qui {in utroque genere} existunt animi motus, simpliciores aut magis inter se implicati, innumera obtinent nomina, pro variis rebus expetitis aut declinatis; atque prout vel se respicit mens, vel alios homines, eorumque mores, et fortunas; aut caritates, et conjunctiones varias, quibus nobiscum, aut inter se, colligantur; aut contra, odia, et dissidia quibus distrahuntur illi, quibus aliquid animum nostrum commovens obvenerat; aut qui suis consiliis, aut actionibus, hisce eventibus causam dederant}. Diversi longe sunt hi motus benigni a tranquillo communis foelicitatis desiderio, neque ex eo nascuntur: etenim per se suâque sponte existunt, ea specie causâve oblatâ, quae iis excitandis apta nata est. Iis explicandis commodior erit locus, postquam subtiliores animi sensus explicuerimus, citra <13> quorum notitiam plurimi voluntatis motus intelligi nequeunt.}[5]

Quae sensu quovis proximè commendantur sunt omnia propter se expetenda; in iisque, aut eorum praecipuis et maximis, situs est bonorum finis. Quumque usu rationis compertum fuerit, res per se neutiquam jucundas, comparandis rebus aliis, per se bonis et expetendis, inservire; <haec etiam> omnia quibus ea est vis expetentur, propter ea quibus assequendis inservire videntur; qualia sunt opes, divitiae, potestas.

Quemadmodum vero, praeter *passiones* eas, aut motus perturbatos, qui-

---

5. This passage replaces the following sentences, deleted by Hutcheson in the second edition, as he added two articles (xv and xvi) on the same subject: <: quales sunt benevolentia, comprobatio, amicitia, στοργὴ, pietas, gratia, congratulatio, moeror, philautia, verecundia, ostentatio, arrogantia, superbia, commiseratio, indignatio, invidia, contemptus, ἐπιχαιρεκακία, atque ejusmodi plures; quibus effuse explicandis non immoramur.

Neque tamen temerè, & pro specie tantum fortuito objecta, oriuntur omnes hae passiones. Quaedam naturali impetu moventur, ita ut nemo fere aut pauci possint esse earum immunes. Victus & amictus, fere, appetitio est naturalis, famis, sitis, aut frigoris sensu molesto excitata. Commune animantium omnium est conjunctionis appetitus procreandi causa, & in eos qui procreati sunt praecipua quaedam cura. Vi pariter naturali, at non adeo necessaria, moventur caeterae passiones, aut appetitiones, specie ea oblata, quam iis excitandis aptam constituerat ipsa natura, sensuque quodam commendaverat. Virtutis significatio amorem excitat & comprobationem; beneficia accepta, gratiam; injuriam, aut noxa, iram & ultionem: Miseria aliena, praecipue immerentium, commiserationem; omnia denique quae sensu commendantur, appetitionem aliquam movent; quae sensu reprobantur, fugam aut aversationem. Unde patebit non aliter quam explicatis omnibus hominum sensibus, satis intelligi posse voluntatis motus.>

The disinterested affections are either calm, or turbulent and passionate, even as the selfish in which one pursues what seems advantageous or pleasant to himself. And the several affections or passions, whether more simple or complicated, have a variety of names as their objects are various, as they regard one's self, or regard others, and their characters, fortunes, endearments, and the several social bonds with us or with each other; or <on the contrary> the enmities or dissentions by which they are set at variance; or as their former conduct or designs have occasioned these events which excite our passions.

[14]These particular kind passions are quite different from any calm general good-will to mankind, nor do they at all arise from it. They naturally arise, without premeditation or previous volition, as soon as that species or occasion occurs which is by nature adapted to raise them. We shall have a more proper place to explain them a little further after we have mentioned the more sublime perceptive powers; without the knowledge of which many motions of the will must remain unknown [unintelligible]. <12>

What any sense immediately relishes is desired for itself ultimately; and happiness must consist in the possession of all such objects, or of the most important and excellent ones. But when by the use of our reason we find that many things which of themselves give no pleasure to any sense, yet are the necessary means of obtaining what is immediately pleasant and desirable, all such *proper means* shall also be desired, on account of their *ends*. Of this class are, an extensive influence in society, riches, and power.

But as beside the several <natural> particular passions of the selfish kind[15] there is deeply rooted in the soul a steddy propensity or impulse

14. Not a new paragraph in the *Institutio,* but added in the second edition.
15. Latin text says: "But as beside those passions or violent motions by which our self-love looks for the things which are recommended to us by a law of nature. . . ." With "particular" and "of selfish kind" the translator succeeds in making the sentence easier, but we miss the idea that particular passions are natural.

bus certas res, naturae lege sibi commendatas, sui causa quisque exquirit, insita est homini tranquilla propensio, aut impulsio quaedam valida, cogitabundo cuivis obvia, [ad vitam ex ipsius natura beatissimam] [ad maximam quam capit ejus natura beatitudinem] appetendam; cujus appetitus ope caeteros animi motus, sui causa quicquam anquirentes, regere possit et reprimere: sic, quicunque animo tranquillo aliorum naturas, ingenia, mores, in suo conspectu posuerit, similem inveniet animi propensionem, ad communem omnium, eamque maximam, [prosperitatem et felicitatem] [beatitudinem] expetendam. Quam animi affectionem, sensu suo interno maxime comprobatam, quicunque seria meditatione excoluerit, eam adeo validam poterit efficere, ut caeteris omnibus appetitionibus, <14> sive suam, sive paucorum quorumvis utilitatem spectantibus, imperare possit, easque regere aut reprimere.

VIII. His de voluntate breviter expositis, progredimur ad alios animi sensus declarandos, quos diximus *reflexos* aut subsequentes; quibus novae cernuntur species, novae admittuntur perceptiones, ex rebus sensu aliquo, externo aut interno, praeceptis; ex aliorum etiam hominum conditione, aut eventibus etiam ratiocinatione aut testimonio cognitis, oriundae. Horum quosdam, minus ad rem nostram facientes, obiter attingemus, in aliis magis necessariis moraturi. Visu et auditu cum caeteris animalibus communi utuntur homines: apud hos vero, "aurium" et oculorum "est admirabile quoddam et artificiosum judicium,"[6] quo multa cernunt subtiliùs; in formis corporeis, *pulchritudinem, venustatem,* partium *convenientiam;* in sonis, gratum concentum et *harmoniam;* in artibus, "in pictis, fictis, coelatis,"[7] in ipso motu et actione, *imitationem:* quae omnia humaniore nos perfundunt voluptate. Huic comparandae inserviunt artes plurimae, et mechanicae et liberales; hanc consectantur homines in iis operibus, eoque instrumento omni, quae vitae usus et necessitates requirunt.

Sunt et non dissimiles perceptiones gratae, ex rei objectae *amplitudine*

6. Cicero, *De natura deorum* 2.146.1.
7. Cicero, *De natura deorum* 2.145.10.

16. The reference to the "whole system" and to the "smaller system or party" is not in the Latin text, but is truly Hutchesonian. (See *System* 1.1.6, vol. I, p. 10.) In this paragraph of the *Institutio* Hutcheson appears to emphasize that the desire of universal happiness is as ultimate in our nature as the desire of our own happiness. This goes

toward its own highest happiness, which every one upon a little reflection will find, by means whereof he can repress and govern all the particular selfish passions, when they are any way opposite to it; so whosoever in a calm hour takes a full view of human nature, considering the constitutions, tempers, and characters of others, will find a like general propension of soul to wish the universal prosperity and happiness of the whole system. And whosoever by frequent impartial meditation cultivates this extensive affection, which the inward sense of his soul constantly approves in the highest degree, may make it so strong that it will be able to restrain and govern all other affections, whether they regard his own happiness or that of any smaller system or party.[16]

VIII. Having given this summary view of the Will, we next consider these senses we called *reflex* or subsequent, by which certain new forms or perceptions are received, in consequence of others previously <13> observed by our external or internal senses; and some of them ensuing upon observing the fortunes of others, or the events discovered by our reason, or the testimony of others. We shall only transiently mention such of them as are not of much importance in morals, that we may more fully explain those which are more necessary.

[17]The external senses of Sight and Hearing we have in common with the Brutes: but there's superadded to the human Eye and Ear a wonderful and ingenious Relish or Sense,[18] by which we receive subtiler pleasures; in material forms *gracefulness, beauty* and *proportion;* in sounds *concord* and *harmony;* and are highly delighted with observing exact *Imitation* in the works of the more ingenious arts, Painting, Statuary and Sculpture, and in motion and Action; all which afford us far more manly pleasures than the external senses. These are the Pleasures to which many arts both mechanic and liberal are subservient; and men pursue them even in all that furniture, those utensils, which are otherways requisite for the conveniency of life. And the very *grandeur* and *novelty* of objects excite some grateful percep-

---

against Butler's idea that virtue is coincident with calm self-love (e.g., *Fifteen Sermons preached at Rolls Chapel,* ii. 8. Compare *System* 1.7.12, vol. I, p. 139). A more polemic paragraph against Butler is found in *System* 1.4.12, vol. I, p. 75.

17. Not a new paragraph in the *Institutio.*

18. The Latin text has "judicium." But the translator is true to Hutcheson with his "relish or sense."

subnascentes, <15> atque ex ipsa *novitate,* pro naturali cognitionis et scientiae appetitu.

In ingenuis hisce voluptatibus numeranda est ea humanissima, quae ex veri *cognitione* exsurgit; quam omnes propter se appetunt; quaeque pro ipsarum rerum dignitate, cognitionisque evidentia, laetior est et jucundior.

Quae sensibus hisce commendantur omnia sunt quidem propter se, et sua sponte, expetenda. Etenim solertissimo et benignissimo Dei opt. max. consilio, in uberiorem vitae commoditatem, ita fabricati sunt hi sensus, et appetitus, ut ea fere omnia nobis proxime et per se commendent, quae, et alia ratione, vel nobis vel humano generi sunt profutura.

IX. Sunt et subtiliores alii sensus et utiliores; qualis est ea *sympathia,* sive sensus communis, cujus vi super aliorum conditione commoventur homines, {idque innato quodam impetu, consilium omne aut rationem praevertente,} ex aliorum foelicitate, gaudium, ex infortuniis moerorem colligentes; prout et ridentibus arrident, et flentibus collachrymant; etiam ubi nulla suae conditionis habetur ratio: Unde sit {etiam} ut nemo satis beatus esse possit, ex eo solo quod sibi suppetant omnia ad vitae copiam et jucunditatem facientia: hoc etiam expetet <16> quisque, ut suppetant et ea quae aliis sibi caris vitam praestare possint beatam; quippe quorum [horum enim] miseriâ omnis vitae suae status perturbaretur.

Mira hac naturae vi, quadam quasi contagione, una cum gratuita bonitate, efficitur, ut vix ullae sint voluptates, ne corporis quidem, quae aliorum consortio non plurimum adaugeantur. Nulla est laeta aut hilaris animi commotio, quae non inter plures dispertiri et diffundi flagitet. Vix quicquam gratum, laetum, facetum, aut jocosum, quod non ex pectore exardescat, ebulliat, atque inter alios prorumpere gestiat: neque quicquam homini gravius aut tristius, quam aliorum, praecipue immerentium, spectare aerumnas, dolores, moerores, miseriam.

tions not unlike the former, which are naturally connected with and sub-servient to our desires of knowledge. Whatever is grateful to any of these perceptive powers is for it self desirable, and may on some occasions be to us an ultimate end. For, by the wise <and benevolent> contrivance of God, our senses and appetites are so constituted {for our happiness}, that what they immediately make grateful is generally <14> on other accounts also useful, either to ourselves or to mankind.

Among these more humane pleasures, we must not omit that enjoyment most peculiarly suited to human nature, which arises from the discovery of Truth{, and the enlarging of our knowledge}; which is ultimately desir-able to all; and is joyful and pleasant in proportion to the dignity of the subject, and the evidence or certainty of the discovery.[19]

IX. There are other still more noble senses and more useful: such is that *sympathy* or fellow-feeling,[20] by which the state and fortunes of others affect us exceedingly, so that by the very power of nature, previous to any rea-soning or meditation [purpose], we rejoice in the prosperity of others, and sorrow with them in their misfortunes; as we are disposed to mirth when we see others chearful, and to weep with those that weep, without any con-sideration of our own Interests. Hence it is that scarce any man can think himself sufficiently happy tho' he has the fullest supplies of all things req-uisite for his own use or pleasure: he must also have some tolerable stores for such as are dear to him; since their misery or distresses will necessarily disturb his own happiness.

By means of this sympathy and of some disinterested affections, it hap-pens, as by a sort of contagion or infection, that all our pleasures, even these of the lowest kind, are strangely increased by their being shared with others. There's scarce any chearful or joyful commotion of mind which does not naturally require to be diffused and communicated. Whatever is agreeable, <15> pleasant, witty, or jocose naturally burns forth, and breaks out among others, and must be imparted. Nor on the other hand is there any thing more uneasy or grievous to a man than to behold the distressing toils, pains, griefs, or misery of others, especially of such as have deserved a better Fate.

19. In the *Institutio* this paragraph is before "Whatever is grateful . . . to mankind."
20. The *Institutio* has "sensus communis"; see the essay *Sensus communis* 2.3.1 and note in Shaftesbury, *Characteristiks,* pp. 48–49.

X. Hominem vero ad agendum esse natum monstrant omnes ejus vires, instinctus, et desideria actuosa{; quod et sensus cuique alte infixus confirmabit. "Appetit enim animus aliquid agere semper, neque ulla conditione quietem sempiternam potest pati": "neque si jucundissimis nos somniis usuros putemus, Endymionis somnum nobis velimus dari; idque si nobis nostrisve accidat, mortis instar putemus"⁸}. Facultatis etiam [fere] cujusque in homine comes est et moderator sensus aliquis, eum ejusdem usum comprobans, qui [universis est commodissimus] [maxime est secundum naturam], vitaeque communi <17> maxime profuturus [profuturum]. Muta etiam animantia, quamvis fortè nullos habeant hujusmodi sensus subtiliores, quos *reflexos* diximus, instinctu quodam tamen, omnem voluptatis notitiam aut spem antecedente, incitantur quaeque ad ea quae sunt secundum cujusque naturam; et in iis summam sibi inveniunt foelicitatem; aut saltem optimè generis sui foelicitati inserviunt. Tales et in hominibus reperiuntur instinctus plurimi; qui rationis et in se [suaque agendi consilia introspiciendi] [reflectendi] vi instructi, variis etiam gaudent sensibus reflexis, quibus subtilius est judicium de plurimis quae sensus fugiunt crassiores; praecipue vero de omni virium insitarum usu. His {etenim sensibus} cuique {proxime et per se} commendatur is naturalium virium usus, qui maximè est secundum naturam; quique aut sibi aut humano generi est maxime profuturus: idemque in alio comprobatur, et fit per se laetabilis et gloriosus. In ipso corporis statu, et motu, cernimus aliquid sua sponte et per se gratum; quod et in alio comprobamus. Invoce et gestu; in corporis, ipsiusque animi viribus; in artibus imitatricibus, quas antea diximus; in ipsis actionibus externis, et exercitationibus, quibus vel in gravioribus negotiis, vel animi causa utimur, aliud alio cernitur magis decorum, et homine dignum; quamvis nulla virtutis moralis <18> specie commendetur. {In iis tamen quae homini propriae sunt viribus, earumque usu, praecipue elucet

---

8. Cicero, *De finibus* 5.55.3–5 and 15–17. In this chapter XX, Cicero emphasizes the tendency of men to action.

X. But further: that man was destined by nature for action plainly appears by that multitude of active instincts and desires natural to him; which is further confirmed by that deeply implanted sense {approving or condemning certain actions}. The soul naturally desires action; nor would one upon any terms consent to be cast into a perpetual state of sleep, tho' he were assured of the sweetest dreams. If a sleep like that of {*}*Endymion* were to befal ourselves or any person dear to us, we would look upon it as little better than Death. Nature hath therefore constituted a certain *sense* or natural *taste* to attend and regulate each active power, approving that exercise of it which is most agreeable to nature and conducive to the general Interest. The very brute animals, tho' they have none of these reflex senses we mentioned, yet by certain instincts, even previously to any experience or prospect of pleasure, are led, each according to its kind, to its natural actions, and finds in them its chief satisfactions or at least are subservient to their particular happiness. Human nature is full of like instincts; but being endued with reason and the power of reflecting on their own sentiments and conduct, they have also various reflex senses with a nice discernment <16> {and relish} of many things which could not be observed by the grosser senses, especially of the exercise of their natural powers.[21] By these senses that application of our natural powers is immediately approved which is most according to the intention of nature, and which is most beneficial either to the individual or to mankind; and all like application by others is in like manner approved, and thus made matter of joy and glorying. In the very posture and motion of the body, there is something which immediately pleases, whether in our own, or that of others: in the voice and gesture, and the various abilities of body or mind, in the ingenious arts of imitation <already mentioned>, in external actions and exercises, whether about serious business or recreations, we discern something graceful and manly, {and the contrary ungraceful and mean}, even without any appearance of moral virtue in the one, {or vice in the other}. But still it is chiefly in these abilities and exercises which are peculiar to mankind that grace and dignity

---

* {Who in the old fable continued to live, but never awoke out of a sleep he was cast into by Diana.} [See note 8 in the *Institutio.*]

21. Compare *System* 1.4.4, vol. I, pp. 58–59.

omnis venustas, omne decus. Quae caeteris animalibus sunt communes, eae humiles, hominisque praestantia parum dignae. Inter ea quae homini sunt propria, a voluntariis tamen virtutibus diversa, praecipua est veri cognitio. "Omnes enim trahimur et ducimur ad cognitionis et scientiae cupiditatem, in qua excellere pulchrum putamus: labi autem, errare, nescire, decipi, malum et turpe ducimus."[9]}

Quod vero attinet ad vires animi illustriores, voluntatis motus, et graviora agendi consilia; insitus est omnium divinissimus ille sensus, decorum, pulchrum, et honestum, in animi ipsius motibus, consiliis, dictis, factisque cernens. Hoc sensu certum homini ingenium et indoles, agendi genus quoddam, vitaeque ratio <quaedam> et institutio, ab ipsa natura commendatur; atque in consentaneis officiis peragendis, et recordandis, sensu mens pertentatur laetissimo; contrariorum vero omnium piget pudetque. Aliorum etiam facta aut consilia honesta favore prosequimur et laudibus; eosque in quibus est virtutis significatio, majore amplectimur benevolentia et caritate. Contraria aliorum facta, aut consilia, damnamus et detestamur. Quae hoc sensu comprobantur recta dicuntur, <19> et pulchra; et *virtutum* nomine appellantur: quae damnantur, soeda dicuntur, aut turpia aut *vitiosa.*

Comprobationem movent voluntatis motus, et agendi consilia omnia benigna, aut illae animi propensiones{, vires} et habitus, qui ex ea gratuita bonitate fluere, aut cum ea connecti videntur; {aut indolem erectiorem, sublimioribus gaudiis deditam, neque suae solum voluptati humiliori aut utilitati intentam indicare;} aut saltem qui contrariam indolem, angustam et humilem sui curam aut philautiam, suam ipsius solummodo respicientem utilitatem aut voluptatem <humiliorem>, excludere censentur. Quae damnantur sunt vel haec ipsa philautia {nimia}, vel morosae, iracundae, invidae, aut malignae animi affectiones, quibus incitantur homines ad alios laedendos; aut denique nimiae humiliorum voluptatum libidines.

---

9. Cicero, *De officiis* 1.18.2–6.

---

22. For the distinction between natural or involuntary virtues, like quick apprehension or memory, and voluntary or moral virtues see Cicero, *De finibus,* V.36. Hutcheson emphasizes the difference between natural abilities and virtues. Here, while he owns that

appear; such as we have in common with beasts appear of less dignity. And among the human pursuits which yet are different from moral [voluntary]²² virtues, the pursuits of knowledge are the most venerable. We are all naturally inquisitive and vehemently allured by the discovery of truth. Superior knowledge we count very honourable; but to mistake, to err, to be ignorant, to be imposed upon, we count evil and shameful.

But to regulate the highest powers of our nature, our affections and deliberate designs of action in important affairs, there's implanted by nature the noblest and most divine of all our senses, that *Conscience* [sense] by <17> which we discern what is graceful, becoming, beautiful and honourable in the affections of the soul, in our conduct of life, our words and actions. By this sense, a certain turn of mind or temper, a certain course of action, and plan of life is plainly recommended to us by nature; and the mind finds the most joyful feelings in performing and reflecting upon such offices as this sense recommends; but is uneasy and ashamed in reflecting upon a contrary course. Upon observing the like honourable actions or designs in others, we naturally favour and praise them; and have an high esteem, and goodwill, and endearment toward all in whom we discern such excellent dispositions: and condemn and detest those who take a contrary course. What is approved by this sense we count *right* and *beautiful,* and call it *virtue;* what is condemned, we count *base* and *deformed* and *vitious.*

The Forms which move our approbation are, all kind affections and purposes of action; or such propensions, abilities, or habits of mind as naturally flow from a kind temper, or are connected with it; or shew an higher taste for the more refined enjoyments, with a low regard to the meaner pleasures, or to its own interests; or lastly such dispositions as plainly exclude a narrow contracted selfishness aiming solely at its own interests or sordid pleasures. The forms disapproved are either this immoderate selfishness; or a peevish, angry, envious or ill-natured temper, leading us naturally to hurt others; or a mean selfish sensuality.

---

we are naturally prompted to cultivate natural abilities and especially knowledge, as a subject fit for a book written for young students, he avoids Hume's attempt to play down the distinction in *Treatise* III.3.4–6. This paragraph is a precursor to the "sense of decency or dignity" described in *System* 1.2.7, vol. I, pp. 27–28. See below, note 34.

Innatum esse homini hunc sensum, testimonio omnium gentium et se-
culorum, plurima suis suffragiis comprobantium et damnantium, [suae
utilitatis ratione omni detracta,] [quamvis nulla suae utilitatis habeatur ra-
tio] satis confirmatur. Quas utilitates astutè saepe spectari volunt, aut com-
probandi et damnandi causas callidè commenti sunt quidam non indocti,
[ex illis ipsis deprompta argumenta,] [his fere omnibus] sensum hunc esse
innatum, omnibusque his causis priorem, satis ostendunt [efficiatur:].
<20> Quae ipsi agenti obventurae sperantur [sunt] utilitates, sive apertiores
sive magis latentes, sua ipsi consilia et actiones commendare possunt, non
vero aliis, qui nullum inde capiunt fructum. Utilitates aliis ex actione quavis
obventurae, sine proximo decori sensu, eam neutiquam ipsi agenti commendabunt.[10] Quantumvis [Utcunque] ipse qui agit sua moveatur utilitate,
[ea tamen apud alios] [ejus tamen ratio abita, apud ceteros,] actionis honestatem imminuere videtur, <aut> nonnunquam omnino tollere. Beneficentiam eam praecipuè [solam] comprobant homines, quam putant gratuitam; quam fucatam simulatamque esse norunt, oderunt. Ubi utilitates
apertiores, gloria, gratia, remuneratio spectantur praecipue, exigua aut nulla
videtur esse honestas: Haec enim officiorum simulatione, sine ulla vera
bonitate, assequimur.

[11]Quid, quod et {ipsi agenti et aliis,} eo honestior videtur recta actio,
magisque laudabilis, quo majore cum labore, damno, aut periculo fuerat
conjuncta. {Non igitur consilia actionesque honestae ea specie commendantur, quod ipsi prosint qui easdem susceperat: neque magis quod nobis
spectantibus et comprobantibus prosint. Eâdem enim laude admiratio-
neque prosequimur res praeclare gestas heroum priscorum, in primis
mundi seculis, unde ad nos nihil emolumenti pervenisse arbitramur. Virtutem etiam in hoste, <21> nobis formidolosam, comprobamus: proditoris
contra, quem ob nostram utilitatem mercede corrupimus, perfidiam odi-

---

10. In the first edition this passage "Quae ipsi agenti obventurae . . . commendabunt"
succeeded the following one: "Utcunque, ipse qui agit . . . assequimur."
11. Not a new paragraph in the first edition.

---

23. Literally: "Some not unlearned men want, often cunningly, these utilities to be
considered or slyly forge them as the causes of our approbation and condemnation."

That this sense is implanted by nature, is evident from this that in all ages and nations certain tempers <18> and actions are universally approved and their contraries condemned, even by such as have in view no interest [utility] of their own. Many artful accounts of all this as flowing from views of interest have been given by ingenious men;[23] but whosoever will examine these accounts, will find that they rather afford arguments to the contrary, and lead us at last to an immediate natural principle prior to all such views.[24] The agent himself perhaps may be moved by a view of advantages of any sort [by a view of more open or more hidden utility] accruing only to himself, to approve his own artful conduct; but such advantages won't engage the approbation of others <that do not gain any profit by it>: and advantages accruing to others, would never engage the agent, without a moral sense, to approve such actions. How much soever the agent may be moved by any views of his own interest [utility]; yet this when 'tis known plainly diminishes the beauty of the action, and sometimes quite destroys it. Men approve chiefly that beneficence which they deem gratuitous and disinterested; what is pretended, and yet only from views of private interest, they abhor. When the agent appears to have in view the more obvious interests of getting glory, popularity, or gainful returns, there appears little or nothing honourable. 'Tis well known that such advantages are attainable by external actions, and hypocritical shews, without any real inward goodness.

But further, does not every good action appear the more honourable and laudable the more toilsome, dangerous or expensive it was to the undertaker? 'Tis plain therefore that a virtuous course is not approved under that notion of its being *profitable to the agent*.[25] <19> Nor is it approved under the notion of *profitable to those who approve it*, for we all equally praise and admire any glorious actions of antient Heroes from which we derive no advantage, as the like done in our own times. We approve even the virtues of an enemy that are dreaded by us, and yet condemn the useful services of a Traytor, whom for our own interest we have bribed into perfidy. Nay

24. The English repeatedly uses the word "interest" for the Latin "utilitas" or "utilitates."

25. This and the following four sentences were added in 1745. The arguments are as old as the *Inquiry on Virtue*.

mus et detestamur, ut etiam aliorum libidines sibi opportunas flagitiosi.

Neque dixeris ideo officia comprobari quod populari fama sint gloriosa, aut praemia consecutura; haec enim ei soli qui officiis fungitur eadem commendabunt.} Nemo {deinde} laudat, aut ab aliis laudem sperare potest, qui non sentit esse aliquid quod et sibi, et aliis, per se, sua sponte, et sua natura, videatur laudabile. Nemo gratiam referendam sperat, nisi qui eo ipso fatetur benevolentiam, et beneficentiam, esse per se et sua natura amabilia. Nemo praemia a Deo potest sperare, nisi qui credit esse aliquid quod ipsi Deo videtur per se amabile, et praemio dignum. Nemo poenas a Deo metuit, nisi pro meritis. Qui leges Dei laudat, ideo laudat quod ea jubeant quae per se sunt recta, justa, pulchra; vetentque omnia contraria.

{Hunc sensum a natura datum, atque ideo plurima per se, sua vi, sua sponte videri recta, honesta, pulchra, laudabilia, ostendunt et animi placidi motus, et turbidi, vi prorsus naturali excitati; qui suam cujusque utilitatem haud respicientes, ex aliorum moribus et fortunis observatis nascuntur, palamque <22> testantur quales nos esse velit natura, de his mox erit agendum. Per omnium vitas, vitae que fere partes omnes, serpit hic sensus, neque ullam fere delectationem ingenuam, aut artem, sui expertem esse sinit. Hinc omnis fere pendet Poëtica et Rhetorica, ipsaeque pictorum, eorumque qui signa fabricantur, sculptorum, histrionumque artes: in amicis, conjugibus, sodalibus eligendis plurimum valet, seque in ipsos lusus jocosque insinuat. Qui haec omnia pensitaverit, nae ille cum *Aristotele* consenserit "ut ad cursum equum, ad arandum bovem, ad indagandum canem, sic hominem ad duas res, ad intelligendum et agendum esse natum, quasi mortalem Deum."[12]

Neque verendum ne hac ratione, quae sensui cuidam, ipsi quidem animo non corpori naturâ insito, virtutum vitiorumque notitias omnes tandem acceptas refert, virtutis dignitati et constantiae quicquam detrahatur. Stabilis enim est natura, sibique semper constans: neque magis metuendum, ne hominum naturâ mutatâ, evertantur virtutum fundamenta, quam ne

---

12. Cicero, *De finibus* 2.40.2.

the very Dissolute frequently dislike the vices of others which are subservient to their own.

Nor can it be alleged that the notion under which we approve actions is their tendency to obtain applause or rewards: for this consideration could recommend them only to the agent. And then, whoever expects praise must imagine that there is something in certain actions or affections, which in its own nature appears laudable or excellent both to himself and others: whoever expects rewards or returns of good offices, must acknowledge that goodness and beneficence naturally excite the love of others. None can hope for Rewards from God without owning that some actions are acceptable to God in their own nature; nor dread divine punishments except upon a supposition of a natural *demerit* in evil actions. When we praise the divine Laws as holy, just and good, 'tis plainly on this account, that we believe they require what is antecedently conceived as morally good, and prohibit the contrary, {otherwise these Epithets would import nothing laudable}.

That this sense is implanted by nature, and that thus affections and actions of themselves, and in their <20> own nature, must appear to us right, honourable, beautiful and laudable, may appear from many of the most natural affections of the Will, both calm and passionate, which are naturally raised without any views of our own advantage, upon observing the conduct and characters and fortunes of others; and thus plainly evidence what Temper nature requires in us. Of these we shall speak presently. This {moral} sense diffuses it self through all conditions of life, and every part of it; and insinuates it self into all the more humane amusements and entertainments of mankind. Poetry and Rhetorick depend almost entirely upon it; as do in a great measure the arts of the Painter, Statuary, and Player. In the choice of friends, wives, comrades, it is all in all; and it even insinuates it self into our games and mirth. Whosoever weighs all these things fully will agree with *Aristotle* "That as the Horse is naturally fitted for swiftness, the Hound for the chace, and the Ox for the plough, so man, like a sort of mortal Deity, is fitted by nature for knowledge, and action."

Nor need we apprehend, that according to this scheme which derives all our moral notions from a sense, implanted however in the soul and not dependent on the body, the dignity <and firmness> of virtue should be impaired. For the constitution of nature is ever stable and harmonious; nor need we fear that any change in our constitution should also change the

sublata gravitate, mundi compages dissolvatur. Neque huic rationi conse-
quens est, omnia ipsi Deo a primo fuisse ita paria et indifferentia, ut aliter
constitutis hominum sensibus, alia omnia honesta aut turpia efficere po-
tuisset. Si quidem enim <23> Deus a primo fuit sapientissimus, perspicie-
bat, affectiones animi benignas iis insitas animantibus, qui sibi invicem suis
actionibus prodesse aut obesse possent, omnium saluti inservituras: con-
trariarum autem omnia contraria fore consequentia; neque aliter fieri potuisse: eum itidem sensum inserendo, qui omnia benigna et benefica com
probaret, perspexit se ea omnia cuique per se grata effecturum, quae alia
omni ratione, toti horum animantium universitati necessario profutura essent: contrarium autem sensum qui contraria probaret inserendo, (quod an
fieri poterat vix satis apparet,) ea per se grata reddidisset, quae, aliis de causis,
et singulis et universis fuissent nocitura. Deus igitur a primo bonus et sapiens, sensum hunc amica et benigna comprobantem, necessario inserere
voluit; neque virtutis natura magis est mutabilis, quam Dei ipsius bonitas
et sapientia. His quidem Dei virtutibus ab hac quaestione sejunctis, nihil
certi maneret.}[13]

XI. Comprobationis autem diversi sunt gradus, virtutumque species aliae
aliis pulchriores, ut et vitiorum, turpiores. "Inter benevolas animi affectiones aequè late patentes, magis decorae sunt stabiles et tranquillae, quam
perturbatae." "Inter animi motus pariter tranquillos et puros, aut pariter
turbatos et vehementes, illi <24> magis laudantur qui latius patent, et maxime qui latissime, ad totam scil. rerum sensu praeditarum universitatem
pertinentes."[14]

---

13. These two paragraphs were added in the second edition.
14. Quotation marks are in the original text.

nature of virtue, more than we should dread the dissolution of the Universe by a change of the great principle of Gravitation. Nor will it follow from this scheme, <21> that all sorts of affections and actions were originally indifferent to the Deity, so that he could as well have made us approve the very contrary of what we now approve, by giving us senses of a contrary nature. For if God was originally omniscient, he must have foreseen, that by his implanting kind affections, in an active species capable of profiting or hurting each other, he would consult the general good of all; and that implanting contrary affections would necessarily have the contrary effect: in like manner by implanting a sense which approved all kindness and beneficence, he foresaw that all these actions would be made immediately agreeable to the agent, which also on other accounts were profitable to the system; whereas a contrary sense (whether possible or not we shall not determine,) would have made such conduct immediately pleasing, as must in other respects be hurtful both to the agent and the system. If God therefore was originally wise and good, he must necessarily have preferred the present constitution of our sense approving all kindness and beneficence, to any contrary one; and the nature of virtue is thus as immutable as the divine Wisdom and Goodness. Cast the consideration of these perfections of God out of this question, and indeed nothing would remain certain or immutable.[26]

XI. There are however very different degrees of approbation and condemnation, some species of virtues much more beautiful than others, and some kinds of vices much more deformed. {These maxims generally hold.} "Among the kind motions of the Will of equal extent, the calm and stable are more beautiful <22> than the turbulent or passionate." And when we compare calm affections among themselves, or the passionate among themselves, "the more extensive are the more amiable, and these most excellent which are most extensive, and pursue the greatest happiness of the whole system of sensitive nature."[27]

26. These last two paragraphs were added in 1745. The subjects of the last paragraph had been debated by Hutcheson in his Letters to Gilbert Burnet and resumed in his *Illustrations* I, pp. 233–44.
27. Cf. *System* 1.4.10, vol. I, pp. 68–69.

Diximus ex virtutis comprobatione ardentiorem efflorescere amorem, in eos qui virtute videntur praediti. Quumque in omnes nostras vires, affectiones, sensus, vota, appetitiones, animum [mens] reflectere possimus, eaque contemplari; ille ipse decori et honesti sensus acrior, ardentior virtutis appetitio, et honestiorum omnium amor et caritas, omnino comprobabitur; neque ulla animi affectio magis, quam optimi cujusque dilectiones et caritates. Atque quum ipse Deus omnis boni et honesti sit fons inexhaustus, et exemplar absolutum, cui et innumeris beneficiis omnino gratuitis acceptis devinciuntur homines; nulla animi affectio magis comprobabitur, quam summa in Deum veneratio, ardentissimo cum amore, et studio illi obsequendi cui gratiam referre nequimus, conjuncta; una cum fidentis submissione animi, se suaque omnia ipsi permittentis, stabilique [ipsius virtutes] [ipsum in omni virtute] imitandi studio, quousque patitur naturae nostrae imbecillitas.

Damnantur itidem magis malignae omnes animi affectiones, et agendi consilia, quo deliberata sunt magis et obstinata. Levior <25> {paulò} est eorum turpitudo quae ex subita quadam, et brevi transitura cupiditate sunt profecta; longèque levior eorum quae ex subito metu aut ira. Damnatur maxime ea sordida et rebus suis semper attenta philautia, quae omnem humaniorem sensum excludit, omnes affectiones benignas superat, atque ad alios quoscunque sui causa laedendos incitat.

Merito inter turpissima, et naturâ ratione praeditâ indignissima, censetur omnis in Deum impietas; sive admittantur ea scelera quae Dei contemptum palam produnt; sive ea sit de Deo colendo incuria, ut nulla de eo meditatio, nulla sit ejus veneratio, nulla ei gratia habeatur. Neque quicquam affert, vel ad pietatis laudem et necessitatem minuendam, aut impietatis turpitudinem, quod Deo neque prodesse possit hominum pietas, neque obesse impietas. Etenim animi affectiones spectat praecipue, et comprobat

---

28. This sentence was criticized by Hume in his letter to Hutcheson of Jan. 10th, 1743 (pp. 46–47). Quoting from *Les caractères* of La Bruyère, Hume suggests that talents of body and mind are much more admired than benevolence. Again, as in his letter to Hutcheson of Sept. 17th, 1739 (p. 34), he states that Hutcheson has "limited too much"

It was already observed that our esteem of virtue in another, causes a warmer affection of good-will toward him: now as the soul can reflect on all its powers, dispositions, affections, desires, senses, and make them the objects of its contemplation; a very high relish for moral excellence, a strong desire of it, and a strong endearment of heart toward all in whom we discern eminent virtues, must it self be approved as a most virtuous disposition; nor is there any more lovely than the highest love towards the highest moral excellency.[28] Since then God must appear to us as the Supreme excellence, and the inexhaustible fountain of all good, to whom mankind are indebted for innumerable benefits most gratuitously bestowed; no affection of soul can be more approved than the most ardent love and veneration toward the Deity, with a steddy purpose to obey him, since we can make no other returns, along with an humble submission and resignation of ourselves and all our interests to his will, with confidence in his goodness; and a constant purpose of imitating him as far as our weak nature is capable.

{The objects of our condemnation are in like manner of different degrees.} Ill-natured unkind affections and purposes are the more condemned the more stable and deliberate they are. Such as flow <23> from any sudden passionate desire are less odious; and still more excusable are those which flow from some sudden fear or provocation. What we chiefly disapprove is that sordid selfishness which so engrosses the man as to exclude all human sentiments of kindness, and surmounts all kind affections; and disposes to any sort of injuries for one's own interests.

We justly also reckon Impiety toward God to be the greatest depravation of mind, and most unworthy of a rational Being, whether it appears in a direct contempt of the Deity; or in an entire neglect of him, so that one has no thoughts about him, no veneration, no gratitude toward him. Nor is it of any avail either to abate the moral Excellence of Piety, or the deformity of impiety, to suggest that the one cannot profit him, nor the other hurt him. For what our [conscience or moral sense] [sense of what is right

---

his "Ideas of Virtue" and presents this criticism as an opinion he has in common with many appraisers of his thought. Perhaps this is one of the reasons why Hutcheson repeatedly presents his catalogue of virtues in his *Institutio* and adds two sections.

aut damnat, hic recti et honesti sensus, non earum in rebus externis effi-
caciam. Depravatus est et detestabilis, qui benefico et optime merito non
habet gratiam, etsi eam referre nequeat; quique vel viros claros atque optimè
meritos non amat, laudat, celebrat; quamvis eos nequeat ad altiores dignitates aut opes promovere. Sponte sua prorumpit ingenium probum et
honestum, sive <26> quis potest quicquam illorum gratia quos amat et
veneratur efficere, sive non potest. Haec omnia non adeo ratiocinatione,
sed intimo potius probi cujusque sensu innotescunt.

XII. Sublimior hic sensus, quem vitae totius ducem constituit ipsa natura,
etiam atque etiam est considerandus; quippe qui de omnibus animi viribus,
motibus, et agendi consiliis judicat; inque ea omnia suo jure arrogat sibi
imperium; gravissimamque eam sert sententiam, in ipsis virtutibus, ipsoque
pulchri et honesti studio, sitam esse et hominis dignitatem sive praestantiam {naturalem}, et vitam beatissimam. Qui sensum hunc sovent exco-
luntque, ejus vi sentiunt se confirmari posse ad gravissima pericula subeunda, aut maximas rerum externarum jacturas lubenter faciendas, ne
amicorum, patriae, aut communem omnium utilitatem, ullamve officii sui
partem deserant: eâque sola ratione, suam indolem vitaeque rationem, sentiunt se penitus posse comprobare. Acri item morsu cruciantur, caecisque
verberibus caeduntur, qui hunc animi spernunt principatum, officia sua
externorum malorum metu, aut utilitatum appetitione deserentes.

Divinioris [Sublimioris] hujus sensus, qui animi affectiones gratuitas et
latissimè patentes commendat <27> praecipuè, principatus elucet cum sua
sponte, suaque vi, tum quod sibi {praecipuè} plaudat vir bonus, suum
probet ingenium, sibique vel maxime placeat, quum reprimit, non solum
eos omnes appetitus, sive humiliores, sive sublimiores, qui suae prospiciunt
utilitati aut voluptati; verum arctiores quasque στοργῆς aut amicitiae caritates,[15] ipsumque patriae amorem; quo communi et majori omnium con-

---

15. Στοργὴ or natural affection between relatives, and, even more, caritas and benevolentia are very common words in Cicero's lexicon.

and honourable] chiefly regards are the affections of the heart, and not the external effects of them. That man must be deemed corrupt and detestable who has not a grateful heart toward his benefactor, even when he can make no returns: who does not love, praise and celebrate the virtues of even good men, tho' perhaps he has it not in his power to serve or promote them. Where there is a good heart, it naturally discovers itself in such affections and expressions, whether one can profit those he esteems and loves or not. These points are manifest to the inward sense of every good man without any reasoning.

XII. This nobler sense which nature has designed to be the guide of life deserves the most careful consideration, since it is plainly the judge {of the whole of life,} <24> of all the various powers, affections and designs, and naturally assumes a jurisdiction over them; pronouncing that most important sentence, that in the virtues themselves, and in a careful study of what is beautiful and honourable in manners, consists our true dignity, and natural excellence, and supreme happiness. Those who cultivate and improve this sense find that it can strengthen them to bear the greatest external evils, and voluntarily to forfeit external advantages, in adhering to their duty toward their friends, their country, or the general interest of all: and that in so doing alone it is that they can throughly approve themselves and their conduct. It likewise punishes with severe remorse and secret lashes such as disobey this natural government constituted in the soul, or omit through any fear, or any prospect of secular advantages, the Duties which it requires.

That this Divine Sense {or Conscience} naturally approving these more extensive affections should be the governing power in man, appears both immediately from its own nature, {as we immediately feel that it naturally assumes a right of judging, approving or condemning all the various motions of the soul; as also} from this that every good man applauds himself, approves entirely his own temper, and is then best pleased with himself when he restrains not only the lower sensual appetites, but even [as well as] the more sublime ones of a selfish kind [concerning his own pleasure and utility], or [but even] the more narrow and contracted affections of love toward kindred, or friends, or even his country, when they interfere with the more extensive interests of mankind, and the common prosperity of

sulat foelicitati. Bonitatem enim eam latissimè patentem, caeteris omnibus <praeponit> animi affectionibus, sive suam spectent utilitatem, sive eorum qui arctiore quavis necessitudine sibi devinciuntur{, non praeponit solum hic sensus; verum etiam laetiore honestatis veraeque gloriae conscientia, damna omnia, gaudiaque omissa, et jacturas honestatis causa factas cumulatissimè pensabit; quippe quae ipsam officiorum honestatem et speciem praeclaram adaugent praecipue, et huic sensui commendant: cui nihil simile in alio quolibet sensu, se inferiorem reprimente, reperitur}. Qui vero secus egerit {ac monet hic sensus,} hic vere sibi plaudere nequit, si internum animi sensum exploraverit. Quum de aliorum indole, consiliis factisque judicamus, similia omnia semper comprobamus, immo ab iis flagitamus; omniaque semper damnamus contraria; quum nulla nostrae utilitatis ratione judicium depravatur. <28> {Atque idcirco quamvis omnia quae homini naturâ eveniunt, aut in hominem cadere possunt, *naturalia* quodammodo dicantur; ea tamen sola quae parti huic diviniori, cujus est in reliquas imperium naturale, se probant, *secundum naturam,* eique apta et convenientia dicenda.}

XIII. Huic conjunctus est et sensus alter, qui homini jucundissimam facit eam comprobationem, et caritatem, quam ab aliis, ipsius facta et consilia spectantibus, consequitur; molestissimas, è contrario, facit aliorum ipsius facta recolentium censuras, vituperationes, omnemque infamiam; quamvis neque ex gloria speret emolumentum quodvis aliud oriturum, neque ex infamia incommodum: haec enim propter se expetuntur, aut fugiuntur.

---

* {What the Author here intends is obvious, and of such importance as deserves a fuller explication. In a voluptuous life the more a man has impaired his health, his fortune, his character, or the more he has obstructed his progress in knowledge, or in the more elegant pleasures, the more also he must condemn and be dissatisfied with his own temper and conduct, and so must every observer. In the pursuits of honours and power, or the splendor of life; the more one has impaired his fortune or health, and the more of his natural pleasures and enjoyments he has sacrificed to these purposes, the more he

<25> all. Our inward conscience of right and wrong [This sense] not only prefers the most diffusive goodness to all other affections of soul, whether of a selfish kind, or of narrower endearment: but also abundantly compensates all losses incurred, all pleasures sacrificed, or expences sustained on account of virtue, by a more joyful consciousness of our real goodness, and merited glory; since all these losses sustained increase the moral dignity and beauty of virtuous offices, and recommend them the more to our inward sense:{*} which is a circumstance peculiar to this case, nor is the like found in any other sense{, when it conquers another of less power than its own}. And further, whoever acts otherways cannot throughly approve himself if he examines well the inward sense of his soul: when we judge of the characters and conduct of others, we find the same sentiments <26> of them: nay, this subordination of all to the most extensive interests is what we demand from them; nor do we ever fail in this case to condemn any contrary conduct; as in our judgments about others we are under no byass from our private passions and interests. And therefor altho' every event, disposition, or action incident to men may in a certain sense be called *natural;* yet such conduct alone as is approved by this diviner faculty, which is plainly destined to command the rest, can be properly called *agreeable* or *suited to our nature.*[29]

XIII. With this moral sense is naturally connected that other {of Honour and Shame}, which makes the approbations, the gratitude, and esteem of others who approve our conduct, matter of high pleasure; and their censures, and condemnation, and infamy, matter of severe uneasiness; even altho' we should have no hopes of any other advantages from their approbations, or fears of evil from their dislike. For by this sense these things are made good or evil immediately and in themselves: and hence it is that we

---

must be dissatisfied with his own measures, and be disapproved by others. But in following the dictates of conscience, in adhering to his duty and the practice of virtue, the greater sacrifice he has made of all other enjoyments, the more he himself and all others approve his conduct and temper, and he answers the more compleatly the wishes and expectations of all who love and esteem him.}

29. This sentence was added in 1745.

Unde et gloria delectantur plurimi, etiam superstite, quamvis nullum ejus sensum se sperent habituros. {Neque ideo tantum laudem appetunt homines quod ipsorum virtuti praestantiaeque testimonium ferat, ipsorumque de se judicium honorificum confirmet. Honore enim delectantur etiam viri optimi, sibique suae virtutis satis conscii.

Hunc sensum a caeteris quidem diversum, at priori, cujus est de virtute vitioque judicium, subnixum, a natura datum esse, satis docet ille animi motus naturalis, qui <29> *pudor* aut *verecundia* appellatur, vultûs rubore se prodens: quem non virtutis solum verum omnis decentiae custodem cernimus, humiliorumque appetituum praesentem et vigilem moderatorem; unde} laudis[16] hic et vituperii sensus magnum praebet in vita usum, in hominibus ad omnia praeclara incitandis, iisque ab omni inhonesto, turpi, flagitioso, aut injurioso, deterrendis.

In hoc recti honestique sensu, et altero cum eo conjuncto, laudis scil. aut vituperii, multo minus sibi invicem dissimiles reperiuntur homines quam in caeteris; si modo eadem species proxima, ab intellectu, diversis hominibus repraesentetur; eadem nempe studia et animi affectiones, dijudicanda, honesta sint an turpia. Ubi vero contrariae sunt hominum de vita beata sententiae, aut de iis quae ad vitam pertinent beatam, eamve praestare possunt; non mirum est eos, (etsi similis sit omnino de moribus omnium sensus) quum de actionibus judicant externis, in diversa omnia abire, actionesque laudare et vituperare contrarias: Aut si <diversi> homines {alii alias et} contrarias habeant de legibus divinis opiniones, hi ea credentes vetita, quae illis licita et honesta videntur; quum inter omnes conveniat, Deo esse parendum: aut denique, si contrariae foveantur de aliorum

---

16. "Laudis . . ." begins a new paragraph in the first edition.

---

* {This is suggested by Aristotle *Ethic. ad Nicom.* L. i. c. 5.} [1095b, 26–30. This sentence was added in the second edition. A parallel criticism of Aristotle and the same note is found in *System,* vol. I, p. 26. As the note is added by the translator of the *Institutio,* this is evidence that he had access to a manuscript copy of the posthumous *System,* circulating among Hutcheson's friends since 1737.]

see many solicitous about a surviving fame, without any notion [hope] that after death they shall have any sense of it{, or advantage by it}. Nor can it be said{*} that we delight in the praises of others only as they are a testimony to our virtue and confirm the good opinion we may have of our selves: for we find that the very best of mankind, who are abundantly conscious of their own virtues, and need no such confirmation, yet have pleasure in the praises they obtain. <27>

That there's a natural sense {of honour and fame[30]}, founded indeed upon our moral sense, or presupposing it, but distinct from it and all other senses, seems manifest from that natural <motion of the soul that is called shame or> modesty, which discovers itself by the very countenance in blushing; which nature has plainly designed as a guardian not only to moral virtue, but to all decency in our whole deportment, and a watchful check upon all the motions of the lower appetites.[31] And hence it is that this sense is of such importance in life, by frequently exciting men to what is honourable, and restraining them from every thing dishonourable, base, flagitious, or injurious.

In these two senses, of moral good and evil, and of honour and shame, mankind are more uniformly constituted than in the other senses; which will be manifest if the same immediate forms or species of actions be proposed to their judgment; that is, if they are considering the same affections of heart whether to be approved or condemned, they would universally agree. If indeed they have contrary opinions of happiness, or of the external means of promoting or preserving it, 'tis then no wonder, however uniform their moral senses be, that one should approve what another condemns <when they judge external actions>. Or if they have contrary opinions about the divine Laws, some believing that God requires what others think he forbids, or has left indifferent; while all agree that it is our duty to obey God: or lastly, if they entertain contrary opinions about the <natural dis-

30. In this case "shame" would be a more consistent addition by the translator.
31. Also this sentence was added in 1745. That "pudor," or modesty, is a natural principle connected with the sense of honour and shame is what Hutcheson debated also in *System* 1.5.3, vol. I, pp. 83–85.

indole, ingenio, et moribus opiniones; his eos credentibus <30> probos, pios, et benignos, quos illi censent inter saevos et improbos. His de causis in diversa omnia abibunt, quamvis, simili de moribus sensu, eaedem animi affectiones omnibus a natura commendentur.

XIV. "Quum sensuum horum ope," alia "venustâ, decorâ," gloriosâ, aut "venerandâ" specie vestiantur; alia, vili et erubescendâ; si quando uni eidemque rei, plures et sibi invicem contrariae simul inducantur species, existet novus quidam sensus, "eorum quae dicuntur *ridicula, aut ad* risum movendum idonea." Quum vero communis sit de humanae naturae dignitate, "prudentiaque quadam" majore "et solertia, opinio"; in hominum dictis factisque, ea "risum movere solent peccata turpia, quae non sunt cum gravi dolore aut interitu conjuncta": haec enim "magis commiserationem excitarent." Risus quidem est animi commotio jucunda; derideri autem, et ludibrio esse, fere cunctis est molestum, quod et homines studiose solent praecavere, gloriae nempe plerumque cupidi. Hinc non levis erit hujusce, sive sensus, sive facultatis, in moribus hominum corrigendis, usus. "Risum" etiam movere solent alia qualiacunque, "quae simul praeclaram aliquam exhibent speciem," <cum> vili tamen et despiciendae immistam; ex qua observata non levis oritur aliquando nec inutilis voluptas, nec spernendum <31> colloquii condimentum, et curarum graviorum requies et levamen.[17]

---

17. Hutcheson, *Synopsis* 2.1.5, p. 55.

positions, manners, and> characters of men {or parties}; some believing that sect or party to be honest, pious and good, which others take to be savage or wicked. On these accounts they may <28> have the most opposite approbations and condemnations, tho' the moral sense of them all were uniform, approving the same immediate object, to wit, the same tempers and affections.[32]

XIV. When by means of these senses, some objects must appear beautiful, graceful, honourable, or venerable, and others mean and shameful; should it happen that in any object there appeared a mixture of these opposite forms or qualities, there would appear also another sense, of the *ridiculous* [of those things that we call ridiculous or apt to excite laughter]. And whereas there's a general presumption of some dignity, prudence and wisdom in the human species; such conduct of theirs will raise laughter as shews "some mean error or mistake, which yet is not attended with grievous pain or destruction to the person": for all such events would rather move pity. Laughter is a grateful commotion of the mind; but to be the object of laughter or mockery is universally disagreeable, and what men from their natural desire of esteem carefully avoid.

Hence arises the importance of this sense or disposition, in refining the manners of mankind, and correcting their faults. Things too of a quite different nature from any human action may occasion laughter, by exhibiting at once some venerable appearance, along with something mean and despicable. From this sense there arise agreeable and sometimes useful entertainments, grateful seasoning to conversation, and innocent amusements amidst the graver business of life.[33]

---

32. See *Inquiry on Virtue*, IV, 3–5 and *System* 1.5.7, vol. I, pp. 92–97.

33. See Hutcheson, "Reflections upon Laughter," *The Dublin Weekly Journal*, 5, 12, and 19 June 1725, now in Hutcheson's *Collected Works*, vol. 7 (New York: Garland, 1971).

{XV. Prout hominum varii sunt sensus, varia admodum itidem cernuntur bona et mala: quorum omnium tamen triplex est ratio; alia enim *animi,* alia *Corporis,* alia *externa.* Ad animum referuntur ingenium perspicax et acutum, memoria tenax, scientiae, artes, prudentia, virtutesque omnes voluntariae: Ad Corpus, sensus integri, vires, valetudo, velocitas, agilitas, pulchritudo: Externa sunt libertas, honores, imperia, divitiae. Quumque omnia quae sensu quolibet commendantur, ad se exquirendum appetitum stimulare soleant, quaeque improbantur ea voluntas aspernetur; varii itidem erunt voluntatis motus, sive mens placide feratur sive perturbatione agitetur. Quatuor animi motus placidos antea memoravimus, *Desiderium, Fugam, Gaudium,* et *Tristitiam;* quatuor item turbidos, *Libidinem, metum, laetitiam* et *aegritudinem.* Horum vero cujusque plures sunt partes, a se invicem longe diversae, pro rerum quas sequimur aut fugimus diversitate, prout nobis aliisve prospicimus, atque prout nostris aliorumve rebus prosperis aut adversis commovemur: Inter hos ipsos motus aliorum fortunas respicientes insignia sunt discrimina, pro variis eorum moribus et ingeniis, variisque inter se <32> conjunctionibus aut dissidiis, eorumque causis.

Longum foret haec omnia persequi, variasque apud doctos passionum divisiones examinare: praecipua tantum attingemus; et motuum nomina notabimus, quae nonnunquam promiscuè sive ad perturbationes sive ad constantias notandas adhibentur.

I. Qui *cupiditati* sive *libidini* subjiciuntur motus turbidi, sui cujusque bona corporis aut externa spectantes, sunt cibi, potusque, cupediarum, et veneris appetitiones; honoris item, imperii et divitiarum, quae ambitio et avaritia vocantur. His contraria mala propulsant et adspernantur offensiones contrariae, timores, scil. et Irae, quae *fugae* aut *metui* subjiciuntur.

---

34. This and the following section were added in the second edition. On the reasons for this addition, see the Introduction (p. xiii). This account of particular passions is different from the account given in his *Essay on Passions* and, in a way, new. Hutcheson bases his catalogue on the division of Cicero's four chief passions (desire and fear, joy

XV.[34] These various senses men are indued with constitute a great variety of things good or evil; all <29> which may be reduced to these three classes, the goods of the soul, the goods of the body, and the goods of fortune or external ones. The goods of the soul are ingenuity and acuteness, a tenacious memory, the sciences and arts, prudence, and all the *voluntary virtues*{, or good dispositions of Will}. The goods of the body are, perfect organs of sense, strength, sound health, swiftness, agility, beauty. External goods are liberty, honours, power, wealth. Now as all objects grateful to any sense excite desire, and their contraries raise aversion; the affections of the will, whether calm or passionate, must be equally various. We already mentioned the four general classes [calm affections] to which they may be reduced, to wit, *desire, aversion, joy* and *sorrow*{: nor have we names settled to distinguish always the calm from the passionate, as there are in some other languages.} <and the four turbulent motions: *lust, fear, delight,* and *distress*>. But of each of these four there are many subdivisions, and very different kinds, according to the very different objects they have in view, and according as they are selfish or disinterested, respecting our own fortunes or those of others. And then among those which respect the fortunes of others there are great diversities, according to the different characters of the persons, their fortunes, and different attachments, friendships or enmities, and their various causes.

To pursue all these distinctions, and examine the several divisions made by the learned, would be tedious. We shall briefly mention the principal Passions, the names of which are also often used for the calm steddy affections of the will; {[nay the same name is often given to desires and joys, to aversions and sorrows.]} <30>

1. The several species of *desire* of the selfish kind respecting one's own body or fortune, are the natural appetites of food, whether plainer or more exquisite, lust, ambition, the desires of praise, of high offices, of wealth <that are called *ambition* and *avarice*>. Their contraries are repelled by the *aversions* of *fear* and *anger,* {and these of various kinds.}

---

and sorrow) (*Tusc. disp.* IV. 16 and ff.), but he intersects the first criterion with the division between selfish and disinterested passions and the traditional distinction between body, soul, and external goods.

Animi sui bona spectant, cognitionis, scientiarum, artium, virtutumque appetitiones, et proborum imitatrix aemulatio. Contraria aspernantur, Pudor et verecundia. motuum hujusmodi plurimis desunt nomina signata.

2. Aliorum res prosperas expetunt Benevolentia, στοργὴ, caeteraeque cognationum caritates. Probis et bene meritis res prosperas consectantur Favor, Gratia et Officiositas venerabunda. Eorum res adversas avertere student Metus, Irae, Commiserationes, Indignationes. Malorum, contra, et improborum <33> res prosperas impedire Invidentiâ et indignatione conamur.

3. Quae *Laetitiae* subjiciuntur perturbationes, sui cujusque corporis bona aut externa spectantes sunt Delectatio, Superbia, Arrogantia, Exultatio, Jactatio. Horum tamen bonorum usus diuturnior fastidium nonnunquam aut nauseam parit. Ex malis contrariis instantibus oriuntur, Aegritudo, Angor, Desperatio, apud antiquos quidem Ira dicitur; "Libido eum puniendi qui videatur laesisse injuriâ";[18] quam idcirco *libidini* potius subjiciunt quam offensioni contrariae.

Ex animi sui bonis praesentibus, virtutibus praecipuè voluntariis, oriuntur Plausus interni, praedicandi studium, honesta Superbia, et Gloriatio. Ex malis contrariis Pudor, animique morsus, Demissio et Infractio. Illa *laetitiae,* haec *aegritudinis* sunt partes.

4. Aliorum virtutes nobis obversantes excipiunt amor, favor et veneratio, consuetudineque adjunctâ, amicitia: Aliorum vitia, excipiunt offensiones contrariae, Odium, Contemptio, Detestatio, quae *aegritudini* sunt affinia.

Ex proborum et bene meritorum rebus secundis, laeta nascitur Congratulatio; ex adversis, Moeror, Misericordia, et Indignatio. Ex improborum rebus adversis ἐπιχαιρεκακία sive malevolentia, et exultatio; ex <34> eorundem rebus secundis Moeror, et Indignatio.

Qui horum omnium definitiones videre cupit, consulat *Aristotelem, Ciceronem, Andronicum,* aliosque. Quae exposuimus satis confirmant aliquid esse per se, suâ naturâ, suaque vi, rectum honestum et laudabile, ejusque

---

18. Cicero, *Tusc. disp.* 4.21.2; cf. also 4.44.2.

The goods of the soul we pursue in our desires of knowledge, and of virtue, and in emulation of worthy characters. Their contraries we avoid by the *aversions* of shame and modesty; we are on this subject often at a loss for appropriated names.

2. The disinterested *Desires* respecting any sort of prosperity to others, are benevolence or good-will, parental affections, and those toward kinsmen. The affections of *desire* toward worthy characters, are favour or good wishes, zealous veneration, gratitude. The *aversions* raised by their misfortunes are fear, anger, compassion, indignation. The prosperity of bad characters moves the *aversions* of envy and indignation.

3. The several species of *Joy* respecting ones own prosperous fortunes, are delectation, pride, arrogance, <pertness,> ostentation. And yet a long possession of any advantages of the body or fortune often produces satiety and disgust. From the contrary Evils arise sorrow, vexation, despair. *Anger* indeed by the Antients is always made a species of *desire,* to wit, that of punishing such as we apprehend have been injurious.

From our possessing the goods of the soul, especially virtuous affections [voluntary virtues], arise the internal *joyful* applauses of conscience, an honourable pride and glorying. From <31> the contrary evils arise shame, remorse, dejection, and brokenness of spirit, which are species of *sorrow.*

4. The virtues of others observed raise *joyful* love, and esteem, and veneration, and where there's intimacy, the affections of Friendship. The vices of others move a sort of *sorrowful* hatred, contempt or detestation. The prosperity of the virtuous, or of our benefactors, raises a *joyful* congratulation; their adversities raise grief, pity, and indignation. The adversities of the vitious often raise joy and triumph, and their prosperity grief and indignation.

Whoever is curious to see large catalogues of the several motions of the Will may find them in *Aristotle's Ethicks, Cicero's 4th Tuscul.* and *Andronicus* <and others>.[35] But from what is above mentioned 'tis manifest that there's some natural sense of right and wrong, something in the temper and af-

---

35. Andronicus of Rhodes (First century B.C.) was head of the Peripatetic School and editor of Aristotle's works. A little treatise on the passions (Περι παθων) was attributed to him.

sensum homini innatum; quum mores hominum sequantur horum motuum naturalium plurimi; atque in simili fortuna, mores hominum contrarii contrarios animi motus in nobis excitare soleant, nulla nostrae utilitatis specie objectâ.} [19]

{XVI. Horum motuum nonnulli ita naturali impetu incitantur, ut pauci in
ulla vitae parte eorum expertes reperiantur, victus, amictus, aliûsque cultus
appetitio, famis, sitis, frigoris, aut caloris sensu molesto excitatur. "Commune animantium omnium," ad certam aetatem, "est conjunctionis appetitus, procreandi causa, et in eos qui procreati sunt praecipua quaedam
cura."[20] Qua ex stirpe inter homines oriuntur caeterae cognationum et af-
finitatum caritates. Vi pariter naturali, licet non adeo continua aut necessaria, caeteri motus, occasione oblatâ, existunt. Virtutum significatio amorem, comprobationem et amicitiam excitat; conatus quosque honestos
favore studioque prosequimur, successus gratulamur, et frustrationes <35>
deploramus et indignamur: atque ex rebus improborum similibus motus
naturâ existunt contrarii: Beneficia accepta gratiam movent; injuria aut
noxa, iram et ultionem; Miseria aliena, immerentium praecipuè, commiserationem. Naturales itidem sunt appetitiones cognitionis virtutumque
omnium, gloriae, valetudinis, virium, formae, voluptatis; omnium denique
quae sensu quolibet commendantur.}[21]

XVII. [XV.] Neque omittendae sunt aliae quaedam naturae nostrae partes
aut vires, quae pariter ad voluntatem vel intellectum pertinere possunt;
qualis est ea cujus vi ideas quaslibet aut animi affectiones, utcunque inter
se longe dispares, quae simul acrius animum commoverant, ita in posterum
conjungimus, ut harum una deinceps in mente excitata, alias omnes, secum

---

19. The whole article XV was added in the second edition.
20. Cicero, *De officiis* I.II.7–9.
21. The whole article XVI was added in the second edition.

---

36. Literally: "Some of these motions arise with so natural an impulse that few are
found without experience of them in some stage of life. The appetites for food, clothes,
and other convenience are excited by the uneasy sensations of hunger, thirst, cold and

fections we naturally approve for it self, and count honourable and good; since 'tis from some such moral species or forms that many of the most natural passions arise; and opposite moral characters upon like external events raise the most opposite affections, without any regard to the private interests of the observer.

XVI. Some of these affections are so rooted in nature that no body is found without them. The appetites toward the preservation of the body are excited in every stage of life by the uneasy sensations of hunger, and thirst, and cold. The desire of offspring at a certain age, and parental affection is also universal; and in consequence of them the like affections toward kinsmen.[36] The other affections when the objects are presented are equally natural, tho' not so necessary <and continuous>. <32> The appearance of virtue in another raises love, esteem, friendship: Honourable designs are followed with favour, kind wishes, and zeal: their successes move joyful congratulation, and their disappointment sorrow and indignation; and the contrary affections attend the prosperity of the vicious{, even tho' we apprehend no advantage or danger to ourselves on either side}. Benefits received with a like natural force raise gratitude; and injuries, resentment and anger; and the sufferings of <others, specially of> the innocent, pity. We also justly count natural the desires of knowledge, of the several virtues, of <fame,> health, strength, beauty, pleasure, and of all such things as are grateful to any sense.[37]

XVII. There are some other Parts of our constitution not to be omitted, which equally relate to the understanding and will. Such as that natural disposition to *associate* or conjoin any ideas, or any affections, however disparate or unlike, which at once have made strong impressions on our mind; so that whensoever any occasion excites one of them, the others will also

---

heat. Common to every animal, at a certain age, are the desire of coupling and procreation, and a certain continuing care for the offspring."

37. This second added section is more connected with the *Essay on Passions* 3.3–6. In this case particular passions are secondary to or dependent on the perceptions of the reflected senses.

olim conjunctas, repraesentatura sit, idque consestim, sine ullo voluntatis imperio. Huic idearum conjunctioni accepta est referenda, rerum praeteritarum sere omnis revocatio et memoria, et facilis sermonis usus. Ex incauta tamen idearum conjunctione et complicatione, plurimum saepe adaugentur humiliores omnes cupiditates; quum voluptatibus humilioribus conjunctae sunt species omnino alienae, at longe magis praeclarae, ita ut haud facile divelli possint. Hinc <36> ex elegantiae cujusdam, aut artis ingenuae, aut prudentiae, immò liberalitatis et beneficentiae, opinione, aut specie conjuncta, sortiuntur voluptates quaedam, et res externae, miram quandam, at minime naturalem vim, desideria hominum commovendi, et magnum videntur habere ad vitam beatam momentum. {Plurimum igitur intererit qualis cujusque sit institutio, quales familiaritates, consuetique eorum sermones quibuscum vivitur: horum enim omnium vis magna, sive ad mores emendandos, sive ad depravandos.}

Huic affines sunt *habitus.* Ita enim nata sunt et mens et corpus, ut omnes eorum vires consuetudine, et exercitatione, augeantur et perficiantur. Usu quidem frequentiore voluptatum imminuitur jucunditas, et dolorum itidem molestia: consuetae verò ubi desunt voluptates, molestius oritur desiderium. Unde, ad omnes sive actiones sive voluptates consuetas magis sumus proclives, et difficilius ab iis cohibemur.

Quae propter se sunt expetenda, sensu aliquo, diximus, proximè commendari. Homo autem animal acutum, sagax, memor, ratione praeditum et consilio,[22] alia quaevis expetet, quae rerum per se expetendarum copiam consicere valent: quales sunt divitiae, et potentia, quae cunctis hominum <37> studiis et desideriis, sive honestis, sive flagitiosis, benevolis aut malevolis, inservire possunt; unde et ab omnibus expetuntur.

---

22. Cf. Cicero, *De legibus* 1.22.4.

constantly attend it, and that instantly, previous to any desire. To this association is owing almost wholly our power of memory, or recalling of past events, and even the faculty of speech.[38] But from such associations incautiously made {we sometimes are hurt in our tempers.} The meaner pleasures of sense, and the objects of our lower appetites, acquire great strength this way, when we conjoin with them some far nobler notions, tho' not naturally or necessarily allied to them, so that they cannot easily be separated. Hence by some notions of elegance, ingenuity, or <33> finer taste, of prudence, <even of> liberality and beneficence, the luxurious ways of living obtain a much greater reputation, and seem of much more importance to happiness than they really are. Hence 'tis of high consequence in what manner the young are educated, what persons they are intimate with, and what sort of conversation they are inured to; since by all these, strong associations of ideas are formed, and the tempers often either amended or depraved.[39]

Of a like nature to these are *Habits,* for such is the nature both of the soul and body that all our powers are increased and perfected by exercise. The long or frequent enjoyment of pleasures indeed abates the keenness of our sense; and in like manner custom abates the feelings of pain.[40] But the want of such gratifications or pleasures as we have long been enured to is more uneasy, and our regret the keener. And hence men are more prone to any pleasures or agreeable courses of action they are accustomed to, and cannot so easily be restrained from them.

We have already shewed that whatever is ultimately desirable must be the object of some immediate sense. But as men are naturally endued with some acuteness, forethought, memory, reason, and wisdom, they shall also naturally desire whatever appears as the proper *means* of obtaining what is immediately desirable; such means are riches and power, which may be subservient to all our desires whether virtuous or vitious, benevolent or malitious; and hence it is that they are so universally desired. <34>

38. See *Synopsis* 2.1.6, p. 57.

39. This sentence was added in 1745. If we assume that at the time Hutcheson was opposing Hume's candidature to the chair of moral philosophy in Edinburgh, the addition on the subject of the association of ideas has a certain irony since it was dangerous in Hutcheson (see *Essay on Passions* 4.3 and ff.), but was positively treated by Hume.

40. See *Synopsis* 2.1.8, pp. 58–59.

Ad fabricam hominum, qui tanta rationis vi, tot sensibus praeclaris sunt instructi, tot societatis vinculis et caritatibus inter se devincti, absolvendam, adjunxit Deus opt. max. orationis et eloquendi vim:{*} "quae primum efficit ut ea quae ignoramus, discere, et ea quae scimus, docere possimus. Deinde hac cohortamur, hac persuademus, hac consolamur afflictos, hac deducimus perterritos a timore, hac gestientes comprimimus, hac cupiditates iracundiasque restinguimus: haec nos juris, legum, urbium societate devinxit: haec a vita immani et fera segregavit."

Quamvis vero hae omnes quas recensuimus naturae nostrae vires, aut partes, sint hominibus ita communes, ut haud fere cuiquam <mortalium> quaevis earum prorsus deesse videatur; mira tamen est ingeniorum inter homines diversitas, cum aliae <atque diversissimae> naturae partes, apud alios, <caeteris partibus> longè praepolleant viribus, et vitae regant tenorem. Apud multos [alios] vehementiores sunt voluptatum humiliorum appetitus; aliis humaniorum et elegantiorum acrior est sensus et appetitio: apud alios eminent cognitionis studia; apud alios <viget> praecipue <38> ambitio, aut futuri provida nimis avaritia: vigent apud alios benignae animi affectiones, miserorum commiseratio, benevolentia, et beneficentia, et harum comites et fautores, virtutis amor et honestatis studium; alii ad iras, odia, et invidiam sunt proniores. In hac vero hominum conditione, quam cernimus depravatam esse et degenerem, humiliores, fere ubique, et minus honestae libidines dominantur; quaeque purior monstraret ratio maxime esse appetenda, ea plurimi parum norunt, aut parum in iis cognoscendis versantur; parciusque igitur in iisdem anquirendis occupantur.

Hanc ingeniorum diversitatem, ab ipsis incunabulis aliquando conspicuam, mirum in modum augent et confirmant mores, instituta, disciplinae, consuetudines, habitus, et exempla dissimilia et contraria: ne de corporum constitutione varia, cujus explicatio medicorum est, agamus{: Quinetiam in moribus hominum corrumpendis eadem vim habent haud exiguam. Non tamen inde solum satis explicari posse videtur ea communis omnium imbecillitas aut pravitas; quae tanta est ut sine morbis vitiisque, quorum

---

* {Cicero De nat. deorum. lib. II} [2.148.5–11].

To finish this structure of human Nature, indued with such powers of Reason, such sublime perceptive powers, such social bonds of affection, God has also superadded the powers of speech and eloquence, by which we are capable of obtaining information of what we were ignorant of, and of communicating to others what we know: by this power we exhort, by this we persuade, by this we comfort the afflicted, and inspire courage into the fearful; by this we restrain immoderate foolish transports, by this we repress the dissolute desires and passionate resentments; this power has conjoined us in the bonds of justice and law and civil polity, this power has reclaimed Mankind from a wild and savage life.

Altho' all these several powers and faculties we have mentioned are so common to all mankind, that there are scarce any entirely deprived of any one of them; yet there is a wonderful variety of tempers: since in different persons different powers and dispositions so prevail that they determine the whole course of their lives. In many the sensual appetites prevail; in others there's an high sense of the more humane and elegant pleasures; in some the keen pursuits of knowledge, in others either ambition or anxious avarice: in others the kind affections, and compassion toward the distressed, <benevolence> and beneficence, with their constant attendants and supporters, an high sense of moral excellence and love of virtue: others are more prone to anger, envy, and the ill-natured affections.[41] In the present state of mankind which we plainly see is depraved and corrupt, sensuality and mean selfish pursuits are the most universal: <35> and those enjoyments which the higher powers recommend, the generality are but little acquainted with, or are little employed in examining or pursuing them.

This diversity of Tempers, sometimes observable from the cradle, is strangely increased by different customs, methods of education, instruction, habits, and contrary examples; not to speak of the different bodily constitutions, which belong to the art of Medicine. The same causes often concur to corrupt the manners of men, tho' our depravation in our present state cannot wholly be ascribed to them. For such is the present condition of mankind, that none seem to be born without some weaknesses or dis-

41. See *System* 1.7.2, vol. I, p. 119.

tamen longe alii apud alios sunt gradus et genera, nemo nascatur: In se quisque formam et notionem viri boni reperiet, <39> quae mortalium nemini ab omni parte conveniet; immo plurimos officii sui numeros se praeteriisse fatebuntur optimi quique; quamvis haud spernendos dederit natura igniculos, ingeniisque nostris innata sint quaedam virtutum semina, quae quidem raro adolescere patimur.[23] Sed de morborum causis et medicina, ut de omnis mali origine, variae fuerunt neque improbabiles philosophorum conjecturae: de causis tamen eorundem, et de medicina salutari, nemo, nisi Deo monstrante, quod satis liqueat quicquam affirmare potest}. Qui vero seriò operam dederit in veris et praecipuis bonis cognoscendis, iisque a fallacibus, et falsis secernendis, atque in partibus animi nobilioribus excolendis, poterit hic perturbatos animi motus reprimere, atque ingenium, sive naturale sive adventitium, non parum immutare, et in melius emendare.

XVIII. [XVI.] Qui multiplicem sensuum horum perspexerit varietatem, quibus res adeo dispares hominibus commendantur appetendae; animique propensiones pariter multiplices, et mutabiles; et inter se saepe pugnantes appetitus, et desideria, quibus suam quisque consectatur utilitatem, eamque variam, aut non minus variam voluptatem; eam etiam ingenii humanitatem, affectionesque benignas multiplices; humana <40> huic natura prima specie videbitur chaos quoddam, rudisque rerum non bene junctarum moles, nisi altius repetendo, nexum quendam, et ordinem a natura constitutum, et principatum deprehenderit, aut ἡγημονικὸν aliquod, ad

23. Cf. *Tusc. disp.* 3.2.8.

eases of the soul, or one kind or other, tho' in different degrees. Every one finds in himself the notion of a *truly good man,* to which no man ever comes up in his conduct. Nay the very best of mankind must acknowledge that in innumerable instances they come short of their duty{, and of that standard of moral goodness they find within them}. And altho' nature has given us all some little sparks as it were to kindle up the several virtues; and sown as it were some seeds of them; yet {by our own bad conduct and foolish notions} we seldom suffer them to grow to maturity. <On the causes of these diseases of the soul, and on the origin of evil, various and not unlikely were the conjectures of philosophers.> But a full and certain account of the original of these disorders, and of the effectual remedies for them, {in all the different degrees in which they appear in different persons,} will never be given by any mortal without a divine revelation.[42] And yet whosoever will set himself heartily to inquire into the true happiness of human nature, to discover <36> the fallacious appearances of it, and to cultivate the nobler faculties of the soul, he will obtain a considerable power over the several turbulent passions, and amend or improve in a great degree his whole temper and disposition, whether it be what nature first gave him, or what his former conduct and circumstances have made it.

XVIII. The consideration of all that variety of Senses or tastes, by which such a variety of objects and actions are naturally recommended to mankind, and of a like multiplicity of natural desires; and all of them pretty inconstant and changeable, and often jarring with each other, some pursuing our own interests or pleasures of one or other of the various kinds mentioned, and some pursuing the good of others; as we have also a great many humane kind affections: This complex view, I say, must at first make human nature appear a strange chaos, or a confused combination of jarring principles, until we can discover by a closer attention, some natural connexion or order among them, some governing principles [principle] nat-

---

42. The last seven sentences (from "The same cause often concur . . ."), which were added in 1745, strengthen the moral pessimism of these paragraphs, an attitude rather unusual in Hutcheson.

modum caeteris ponendum idoneum. Philosophiae munus est hoc investigare, atque monstrare qua demum ratione haec sint ordinanda; miro enim
artificio

Hanc Deus, et melior litem natura diremit.[24]

Quod aliquatenus perspici poterit ex iis quae diximus, decori et honesti
sensum explicantes. Neque longa opus est disputatione, aut conquisitis argumentis, quum in se descendendo quisque inveniet, se, illa honestum a
turpi discernendi facultate, {ad imperandum, totamque vitam regendam
natâ,} esse praeditum, cujus ope cernere licebit, eum vitae tenorem atque
ordinem, quem solum poterit comprobare, {quique igitur est maxime secundum naturam;} ubi scil. vigent benevolae omnes et gratuitae animi affectiones, simul et communi omnium consulimus utilitati; amicorum, ne-
cessariorum, aut nostro privato duntaxat consulentes commodo, ubi majori
omnium non obstat foelicitati: omnemque ubi morum excolimus mansuetudinem, bonitatem, pietatem, easque <41> animi, corporisque vires,
quibus Deo hominibusque inservire possimus. Quae insuper animi vis,
recti et honesti jucundissimo sensu, et bonae spei pleno, mentem perfun-
dens, nos ad officia quaevis, etiam laboriosa et periculosa, suscipienda poterit obfirmare, eaque peracta munificentissime remunerare.

Quin et ipsa ratio, perlustrans ea veri indicia, quae nobis exhibet nostra
aliarumque rerum constitutio, ostendet foelicitatem maximè stabilem et
homine dignissimam, eodem vitae tenore, quo communi consulitur utilitati, cuique parari; et eam plerumque rerum externarum copiam, quae alias
praebet voluptates, in suo genere laetissimas. Haec etiam monstrabit, Dei
opt. max. providentia omnia administrari; unde nova elucebit spes et laetissima. Hinc colliget, ea dogmata de officiis, quae ex mentis humanae re-

24. Ovid, *Metamorphoses* 1.21.

43. Also, this paragraph was criticized by Hume in his letter to Hutcheson of Jan.
10th, 1743: he argued that Hutcheson had embraced "Dr Butler's opinion in his Sermons
on Human nature; that our moral Sense has an Authority distinct from its Force and

urally fitted to regulate all the rest.[43] To discover this is the main business of Moral Philosophy, and to shew how all these parts are to be ranged in order: and we shall find that with wonderful wisdom

God and kind nature has this strife composed.

Of this we may have some notion from what is above explained about that moral Power, that sense of what is becoming and honourable in our actions. Nor need we long dissertations and reasoning, since by inward reflection and examining the feelings of our hearts, we <37> shall be convinced, that we have this moral power {or Conscience} distinguishing between right and wrong, plainly destined and fitted to regulate the whole of life; which clearly discovers to us that course and conduct, which alone we can entirely approve <and therefore which is most in accordance with the intention of nature>; to wit, that in which all kind affections are cultivated, and at the same time an extensive regard maintained toward the general happiness of all; so that we pursue our own interests, or those of our friends, or kinsmen, no further than the more extensive interests will allow; always maintaining sweetness of temper, kindness, and tender affections; and improving all our powers of body or mind with a view to serve God and mankind. This same moral sense also filling the soul with the most joyful satisfaction and inward applauses, and with the most cheering hopes, will strengthen it for all good offices, even tho' attended with toil and dangers, and reward our efforts with the most glorious recompense.

Nay our reason too reviewing the evidence exhibited to us in the whole order of nature, will shew us that the same course of life which contributes to the general prosperity, procures also to the agent the most stable and most worthy felicity; and generally tends to procure that competency of external things which to a good mind is in its kind the most joyful. The same reason will shew us that the world is governed by the wisest and best Providence; and hence still greater and more joyful hopes will arise. We shall thence conclude that all these practical truths discovered from reflec-

---

Durableness, & that because we always think it *ought* to prevail" (*Letters,* p. 47). The word ἡγεμονικὸν (the governing self or principle) suggests the influence of the emperor Marcus Aurelius, whose *Meditations* Hutcheson translated in 1742.

rumque aliarum fabrica observatâ eruerat, legum divinarum habere vim, monstrantium quaenam Deus a nobis exigat, quaenam ei grata, quibusque ejus comprobationem et favorem simus consequuturi. Hinc melioris, post corporis interitum, vitae exsurget spes, atque in omni honesto officio animi obfirmatio et fiducia; hinc divina pietatis et religionis gaudia animum percipient; omniaque laeta et gloriosa, sub <42> numinis benigni auspiciis, bonus quisque, non sibi solum, verum bonis omnibus, rerumque omnium universitati, poterit polliceri. {His etiam constitutis et perspectis, amico foedere conspirabunt omnia naturae principia, quae suae cujusque, quaeque aliorum utilitati prospiciunt.}

tion on our own constitution and that of Nature, have the nature and force of divine Laws pointing out what <38> God requires of us, what is pleasing to him, and by what conduct we may obtain his approbation and favour. Hence the hopes of future happiness after death, and a strength and firmness of soul in all honourable designs. Hence the soul shall be filled with the joys of Piety and Devotion; and every good mind shall expect every thing joyful and glorious under the protection of a good Providence, not only for itself but for all good men, and for the whole universe. And when one is persuaded of these Truths, then both our social and our selfish affections will harmoniously recommend to us one and the same course of life and conduct.

CAPUT II

De Summo Bono et Virtute.

I. Pleniore naturae humanae, ejusque partium, exposita descriptione, progredimur anquirere de finibus bonorum et malorum, sive de hominis summo bono, et vitae degendae ratione.

Non multum morabimur in quaestionibus illis decantatis, de *intellectus* imperio in *voluntatem,* aut voluntatis in intellectum, quae potius ad pneumatologiam pertinent. Haec obiter monenda, ignoti nullam esse cupidinem; menti tamen a primo insitas esse plures propensiones ad certas res, ubi primum aliquam earum adepta fuerit notitiam, appetendas, atque ad contrarias propulsandas; quam *velleietatem simplicem* dicunt scholastici. Quae ubi ita valida fuerit, ut mentem ab aliis rebus praesentibus exquirendis aut perfruendis, possit avocare, ipsiusve <43> inertiam excutere, studium excitabit rei expetitae consequendae subsidia et rationes omnes cognoscendi; perspiciendique quaenam earum sint maxime idoneae: quibus exploratis, permovebit etiam, secundum Stoicos, ad ea consilia exsequenda, sive ad stabile agendi propositum; quam *volitionem,* dicunt scholastici, *efficacem.* Haerent in hac parte Peripatetici quidam, negantes voluntatem necessario sequi vel ultimum intellectus judicium practicum, licet plerumque sequatur. Vim sui impellendi flectendique voluntati tribuunt, quae, "positis his omnibus ad agendum *praerequisitis,* quae dicuntur, agere potest, vel non agere, (addunt quidam etiam) hoc agere, vel huic contrarium."[1] Haec *philosophiae primae* scriptoribus permittimus dijudicanda. In univer-

---

1. Quotation marks in the original text.

Concerning the Supreme Good.

I. Having in the former chapter premised a pretty full description of human Nature and its several powers, we proceed to inquire into <the ends of Goods and Evils, or> the Supreme Good or Evil{, and wherein the chief Happiness of mankind consists}, with the proper plan of life in order to obtain it.

We shall lightly pass over certain celebrated questions about the mutual powers of the *understanding* and *will* over each other, which properly belong to Pneumaticks {or Metaphysicks}. We only suggest in passing, 1. That what is wholly unknown cannot be the object of desire, and yet there are certain natural propensities {or instincts in each species} toward certain objects or actions, as soon as it obtains any notion of them, and aversions to their contraries. These the schoolmen call the *first simple motions of Will.* When these are so strong as to call off the mind from any other objects it may have been employed about, and surmount its sloth, {or any dispositions to rest,} it raises also a desire of searching out the proper means <and reasons> of obtaining the objects desired, and of discovering which of them are most eligible: and when this point is settled, then, according to the *Stoicks,* we are determined to execute these means, or there arises the *effectual purpose* of action [that steddy purpose of action that Schoolmen call *effectual volition*].[1] Many [Some] of the *Peripateticks* deny that the Will is certainly determined to follow even the last *practical* <40> *judgments,* tho' it generally does so. They alledge that it has an inherent power, notwithstanding any judgments or desires about the proper ends or means, of determining it self to act or abstain; nay some add, that it can determine it self to either of the contraries, to pursue good, or to pursue evil even under that notion. Let Metaphysicians determine these points. This in gen-

1. See *Synopsis* 2.2.2, pp. 62–63.

sum vero videtur, potestatem aliquam, vel imperium, improprie admodum tribui posse intellectui; cujus quippe munus solum est verum cernere: velle autem, jubere, aut imperare, voluntatis.

Voluntatis in intellectum imperium non aliud est quam quod potest quisque, [prout voluerit] [pro suo arbitrio], animum ad hanc vel illam partem examinandam convertere; atque ubi summa non occurrit evidentia, assensionem cohibere et *amplius* pronunciare. Representatis vero certis indiciis, assensionem cohibere <44> nequit, aut contrariae inhaerere sententiae; immo ubi speciosiora ab una parte occurrunt argumenta, <pro> voluntatis imperio nequit homo eam partem non existimare probabiliorem. Atque haec hactenus.

II. Neque magis moramur in quaestionibus plurimis theoreticis, de generalibus *boni finisque* ideis, aut divisionibus; utpote facilibus, et ad pneumatologiam pertinentibus. Haec sunt in promptu axiomata. 1. Rerum aliae propter se expetuntur; aliae quod aliis rebus comparandis inserviant; aliae denique ob utrumque. 2. Omnia propter se expetita, vi quadam aut sensu proximo, aut instinctu, et naturali quadam commendatione, nulla ratiocinatione praeeunte, nobis conciliantur. Rationis {enim} est, ea investigare quorum ope res hujusmodi parari possint: aut, si {inter varios fines} contentio quaedam aut comparatio fiat, [cernere qui] [quinam fines] sint maxime expetendi; quaeque iis assequendis optimè inserviant. 3. Triplici sub specie res nobis commendantur, *jucundi, utilis, et honesti*. Jucunda dicuntur, omnia quae sui causa quisquam expetit, ut aliqua voluptate fruatur; rarò tamen in hoc genere ponuntur sublimiores ex {rerum cognitione et} virtute voluptates. Utilia sunt, quae propter alia, non propter se appetuntur. Honesta sunt ipsae virtutes, quae sua propria specie ac dignitate animum

eral seems true that we cannot properly ascribe any active <ruling> power to the *understanding*, about our conduct in life. 'Tis its business only to discover *Truth;* whereas *willing, ordering, commanding, purposing*, are acts of Will.[2]

The *will* again seems to have no other power over the *understanding* than this, that a man may as he wills turn his understanding to consider all the evidence on either side, and where the highest evidence does not occur, he can suspend any {peremptory} assent, and resolve upon a further hearing of the cause. But wherever full, certain evidence appears, he cannot at pleasure withhold his assent, or assent to the other side. Nay where on one side he sees superior probabilities [better reasons], he cannot avoid judging that side to be more probable.

II. We also pass over some speculative questions about the general notions of Good, and Final Causes or Ends, and their divisions; as they are easy and belong to other sciences. These maxims seem evident. 1. The objects of desire are pursued either ultimately for themselves, or as means to something further, or on both accounts. 2. Whatever is ultimately desirable is either recommended by some immediate sense or some natural instinct or impulse, <and approbation> prior to all reasoning. 'Tis <41> the business of reason to find out the *means* of obtaining what we desire: or if various objects of desire interfere, to inquire which of them is of most importance to happiness, and what the best means of obtaining such objects. 3. Things are recommended to our pursuit, under one or other of these three forms or notions, either as *pleasant, profitable,* or *honourable.* Under the notion of pleasure are such things pursued in which we have only in view some grateful sensation to ourselves; and yet moral writers seldom include under this branch of *pleasant,* either the moral virtues, or the sciences and ingenious arts. These things are called *profitable* which are desired as means of somewhat further. The *honourable* are the several virtues {either intellectual or moral,} which recommend themselves by their own peculiar dignity,

2. Here and in section II, second maxim, below, Hutcheson emphasizes that reason or understanding does not have the power to determine us to action; this is aimed at his rationalist adversaries. Compare *Essay on Passions* 2.2, pp. 30–31n., and *Illustrations,* I, pp. 219–20.

<45> commovent. 4. Boni cujusvis ad vitam beatam momentum, pendet ex ipsius et *dignitate* et *diuturnitate* [duratione]. In bonorum enim dignitate magna est varietas. Quae sensibus ejusdem generis percipiuntur, quales sunt omnes {ferè} voluptates corporis nobis cum beluis communes, eorum digniora sunt quaeque majora et gratiora, quae et *intensiora* vulgo dicuntur. Quae altioribus percipiuntur animi viribus, suam propriam habent dignitatem, quae proxime et per se elucet, omniumque ita movet comprobationem, ut laudentur hi, beatique censeantur, recteque egisse, qui hisce delectationibus omnem corporis posthabuerunt voluptatem. Quod de iis cernere licet, qui artibus elegantioribus, doctrinae studiis, et praecipue ipsi virtuti et officiis honestis, se totos dediderunt.

Naturae igitur sagaci et providae, hoc summum est bonum, "quod propter se expetendum est; quo referuntur fere omnia, ipsum vero nusquam; quod summam habet dignitatem; quod stabile est, et vitam beatam potest praestare."[2]

III. In vita beata quaerenda, quae vel omnibus, vel plurimis et praecipuis, debet esse bonis cumulata, monendum est, neminem omnis voluptatis usum copiosissimum sibi posse polliceri, aut omnium malorum amotionem. Ut fluxae sunt et instabiles res <46> humanae, ita omnis quae ex rebus externis pendet voluptas est itidem incerta. Mutantur et intereunt subinde res ipsae; mutabile est hominis ingenium; mutabilis et incerta ea valitudo, quae ad voluptatem fruendam exigitur. Externa omnia, non in nostra potestate, sed in fortunae posita esse videntur temeritate; aut verius, divina reguntur providentia, quae nemini, quod ad res attinet externas, [ab instabili et variâ] [de stabili & inconcussa] cavit fortunâ.

---

2. Quotation marks in Hutcheson's text. Cf. Cicero, *De finibus* 3.21.15.

{very different from the lower sorts of pleasures}. 4. The importance or moment of any good toward our felicity depends on its dignity and duration. There's a great difference among the several sorts of good in point of dignity. When we compare together the goods corresponding to senses of the same order, such as those relating to the external senses [those pleasure of body that we have in common with beasts], the dignity is just the intenseness of the pleasure in the sensation. But the objects of the superior senses have their own peculiar excellence, {not to be compared with the lower pleasures,} appearing of it self, and raising the desires of such as know them; so that we approve and praise, and count the persons happy, and wise in their conduct, who despise all bodily pleasures in comparison with them. 'Tis thus we plainly judge of the man who prefers the joys < of refined arts, > of knowledge, and of < 42 > virtue and virtuous action to all others, and devotes himself entirely to them{, in opposition to even the highest sensual enjoyments}.[3]

To a rational being therefor who is indued with forethought these must be the characters of his supreme Good: "It must be something ultimately desirable to which most other things are referable < while it is not a means to anything else >; which has the highest dignity, which is stable {or durable}, and sufficient to satisfy or make happy."

III. In our enquiries after happiness, which must either consist in the full enjoyment of all sorts of good, or at least in that of the principal sorts, we must observe, that 'tis impossible for one to ensure to himself the full enjoyment of all sorts of pleasure, and an immunity from all evil. According to the uncertain fleeting nature of human affairs, all external enjoyments must be uncertain. The objects themselves are perishable; and our own tastes and relishes are changeable; our health of body on which many enjoyments depend is very unstable: external objects depend not on our power, but {as 'tis commonly said}, are the Gifts of Fortune, or more properly, depend upon the Divine Providence, which has ensured no man in the constant possession of them.

3. See *System* 1.7.[1], vol. I, p. 117.

Quid, quod et inter se pugnant ipsae voluptates; neque potest idem, omnibus simul conquirendis strenuam navare operam, aut conquisitis jucunde
frui: immo etiam, sublimiorum voluptatum dignitas istiusmodi consor-
tium aspernatur; earumque pulchritudo, {sensusque laetissimus} non
parum ex eo pendet, quod ob eas, humiliores plurimas omisimus et sprevi-
mus, labores etiam et aerumnas forti animo pertulimus.

Quum igitur datum non sit bonis omnibus copiose frui, aut omnia effugere mala; inquirendum est deinceps, quae bona sint praecipua, maximeque ad vitam beatam facientia? quaeque mala gravissima, vitaeque statum tranquillae maxime turbantia? Inter se comparanda sunt, igitur, ea
bona quae diversis hominum sensibus commendantur, eorumque et dignitas spectanda, et {diuturnitas <47> sive} duratio. Malorum pariter comparanda inter se sunt genera, ut videamus quodnam sit extremum, aut
gravissimum.

IV. {Hic obiter monendum; quod quamquam *Hieronymo Rhodio,* aliisve
ejusdem sententiae patronis, largiundum sit, ipsam doloris omnis vacui-
tatem consecutionem afferre voluptatis cujusdam; atque statum hunc non
dolendi (adeo benigna est naturae nostrae conformatio) jucunditatem
quandam laetamve constantiam comitari; dummodo nulla interea cupiditate aut metu mens agitetur; ita ut qui malo omni careat verè sit in bonis:
nobis tamen tot sensibus atque appetitibus actuosis a natura instructis, ea
indolentiae jucunditas haud quaquam satis est ad bene vivendum; quum
neque magna sit, neque homine dignissima, neque eum habeat ictum quo
pellat animum, ut inde petantur initia agendi. Aliis igitur bonis judicanda
est vita beata, quae sensu aliquo percipiuntur.}

Need we also mention that there are many inconsistencies among the several enjoyments, so that one cannot vigorously pursue or enjoy them all: nay such is the dignity of the superior enjoyments, that they scorn such conjunction with the lower; their beauty and highest joy arises from our having despised and sacrificed <43> to them the lower pleasures, and even resolutely exposed our selves to toils and distresses on their account.

Since then there's no obtaining a full enjoyment of all sorts of good, or avoiding of all evil, we must carefully enquire which sorts of good are the most important to happiness, and what evils are the most grievous, and most eversive of tranquillity and happiness. We must therefor compare together the several goods which affect the various senses, and that both in respect to dignity and duration: and in like manner compare the several evils to discover which of them are most grievous and destructive.[4]

IV. We may here transiently notice, that tho' we grant to *Hieronymus* of Rhodes, and some others of antiquity, that upon the mere removal of all pain there naturally ensues a state in it self grateful and pleasant: and that a stable sort of tranquillity and joy accompanies an intire immunity from uneasy sensations, so kind is the constitution of our nature, provided the mind is not disturbed by any keen desires or fears; so that their maxim is true, that wherever there's freedom from all evil there must be the possession of some good: yet 'tis plain that beings endued with so many senses and active appetites and desires, cannot be made happy by mere indolence.[5] This pleasure is but of a low kind, nor has it any dignity; much less can it have such force upon the soul as to be the spring of our actions and conduct in life. Happiness therefor must depend upon other sorts of goods suited to our perceptive powers. <44>

---

4. There is a chapter on the supreme good or happiness in Hutcheson's *Inquiry on Virtue* (chap. VI), as well as in *Essay on Passions* (chap. V), and in his *System* (chap. VII). Whereas the present chapter of the *Institutio* and chap. VII of the *System* are similar, with parallel consideration of the order of the pleasures, the details of each section are rather different.

5. Hieronymus of Rhodes (III century B.C.) is often cited in Cicero's *De finibus* (e.g., II.19.7).

Et primo, patet corporis voluptates nullam habere dignitatem[3] ob quam
laudari possint. Sit quamvis grata earum titillatio, aut motus jucundi; humiles tamen sunt sua natura omnes, et plurimae [prae pudore celandae]
[erubescendae]: cito etiam fluunt; praeteritarumque insuavis erit recordatio, nihil secum ferens laetabile aut gloriosum, quod graviora vitae <48>
incommoda, aut aerumnas, lenire possit aut compensare.

Neque dixerit quisquam, communi hominum suffragio eas maxime
comprobari, ideo quod hominum bona pars iis solis ferè inhiet. Enimvero
hoc a vero adeo est alienum, ut pauci admodum reperiantur, qui, sedato
paulum brevi libidinis fervore, non fatebuntur, eas voluptates vitam beatam
praestare non posse. Mortalium etiam nequissimi, imperfectis quibusdam
aut fucatis virtutum speciebus plurimum capiuntur, et delectantur; ami-
citiis, scil. et officiis benignis, erga eos quos sibi vel natura devinxit vel consuetudo, quosque pro temerario judicio maximi faciunt. Neque omnino
cessando, aut hisce solis voluptatibus fruendo, se foelices autumant: his
{etenim} adjungunt saepe actiones plures et officia, quae sibi videntur honesta. {Atque vigeant quamvis appetitiones humiliores, viribusque polleant;
ea tamen animi pars cujus est in reliquas omnes imperium naturale, quae
divinior est, atque cujus monitis praecipuè judicandum quid Deus postulet
et natura, voluptates corporis tanquam homine parum dignas aspernatur,
atque potius a vita beata semovendas arbitratur.}

Quid memorem, voluptates corporis furtivis coloribus amicitiae, commoditatis, beneficientiae, <49> saepe esse [vestitas et ornatas] [coopertas],
atque elegantiorum artium voluptatibus conditas, quae cunctis {alioquin}
viles essent et erubescendae. Quid? quod rarius iis fruendis repugnare videatur decori, et honesti sensus; quia saepissime, pro mira perturbationum
fallacia, videntur hae voluptates innocuae. At contra, virtutes, propriâ sua
et vera dignitate se bonis commendant, eosque faciunt beatos. Neque enim

---

3. Cf. Cicero, *De finibus* 2.75.1.

In the first place 'tis plain that bodily pleasures have none of that dignity which is the object of praise. Were the sensations never so intense, yet they all are plainly mean, and many of them shameful: they are transient too and fleeting; nor does the remembrance of past enjoyments give any such pleasure, or yield any such matter of joy or glorying, which could allay any sorrows or distresses in life, or support us under them.

Nor can it be justly alledged, that the common sentiments of mankind seem to make these the highest of all, because we see the greater part of men much devoted to them alone. This is so far from truth, that there are few to be found, who, when the fervor of their passions is a little cooled, won't own, that such pleasures are quite insufficient to happiness. The most worthless characters have some imperfect <and artificial> notions of virtues almost continually influencing them; some friendships, some kind offices towards such as either nature or acquaintance hath attached to them, and whom they rashly happen to esteem. Nor can any one deem himself happy in constant inactivity or sensual enjoyments: they must conjoin with them frequent actions and offices, which according to their notions are virtuous. But, how strong soever the lower appetites may be {in proportion to the nobler}, yet still that diviner faculty naturally destined to govern the rest, and from whose dictates we are chiefly to judge of the intention of God and nature, rather scorns and rejects sensual enjoyments, as below the dignity of the rational nature, and will not allow them to make a part of the true happiness.[6] <45>

Need we further insist that sensual pleasures are almost continually recommended by some borrowed colours of a moral kind, of friendship, humanity, beneficence, or an elegant taste; otherways they would be despicable and shameful. Nay our {conscience or moral} sense <of what is right and honourable> seldom appears in opposition to them; since by the strange deceit of the passions, we generally persuade ourselves of their innocence.[7] But on the other hand the virtues charm and make us happy by their own native beauty and dignity: nor are we to imagine that happiness is found only in mirth, gayety, lasciviousness or diversions, the amusements

6. See *System* 1.7.4, vol. I, p. 126.
7. See *System* 1.7.4, vol. I, p. 125.

lascivia, et lusu, et joco comite levitatis, sed saepe etiam tristes, sua bonitate, firmitate, et constantia sunt beati.

A luxuriosorum {etiam} judicio provocare licet, qui ventribus dediti, nunquam delectationes homine digniores, et honestiores, ex stabili probitatis et constantis virtutis sensu oriundas, experti sunt. Malè verum hi corrupti judices examinant: nobiliores apud eos hebescunt sensus. Animi autem gravitas et constantia, virtutesque omnes, sensus haud obtundunt externos. Sentiunt viri boni omnem in voluptate corporis jucunditatem, eâque spreta, virtuti adhaerescunt; omne, aut longe longeque maximum, sentientes in ea positum esse momentum ad vitam beatam. Honestis hominum istiusmodi studiis non se immiscet voluptas; neque ea commendat, quod sint efficientia voluptatum. <50> Immo ab ipsis potius laboribus, molestiis, periculis, commendatur virtus,

> *Per damna per caedes, ab ipso*
> *Ducit opes animumque ferro.*[4]

Quin et luxuriosorum haec comprobantur suffragiis. Quotusquisque enim adeo perditi est ingenii, qui non praeclara aliqua virtutis specie, magis quam ulla corporis voluptate, commovebitur? qui amici causâ non omittet voluptatem; aut ad famam tuendam, et contumeliam repellendam, non etiam labores suscipiet et pericula? Quotusquisque solis hisce corporis voluptatibus solitariis, se totum dare poterit, sine socia ulla aut amica hilaritate? Qui rari reperiuntur, eos caeteri omnes, tanquam hominum monstra, oderunt, et detestantur. Quam brevis est harum voluptatum sensus? qui nempe omnis ab ipso appetitus pendet vigore; quo cessante, cessat voluptas, longa relinquens intervalla ingrata, et taedii plena futura, nisi honestioribus studiis repleantur.

---

4. Horace, *Carmina* 4.4.59–60.

of weaker minds. There's an higher happiness to the grave who are intent on serious business, from their own goodness, strength of mind, and steddiness.

There's just cause too of appealing from the judgment of the voluptuous, who given up to sensuality, seldom experience the joys of a virtuous sort most becoming the rational nature, and never feel the pleasures of entire stable integrity and goodness. They are corrupt judges, having the nobler senses of the soul much stupified. But the external senses are never imagined to be any way impaired by the greatest dignity and steddiness of soul in all the moral virtues.[8] The good man knows all the good in sensual pleasures, and despises it that he may adhere to virtue; finding upon full knowledge of both, that in virtue consists the supreme good.[9] These honourable enjoyments are never blended with sensual pleasures, or recommended to us as the means of obtaining them; on the contrary, <46> they are chiefly recommended by the labours, troubles and dangers incurred;

> *Midst losses, deaths, deriving force*
> *And spirit from the hostile sword.*   HOR.

Nay we have in this cause frequent testimonies from the voluptuous themselves. How few are such abandoned wretches as not to be much more affected with the beauty of some virtues, than with any bodily pleasures? Who won't sometimes in serving a friend, or maintaining their own moral characters, or refuting certain calumnies, expose themselves to toils and danger, and forego pleasures?[10] How few are devoted to mere solitary sensuality without any social friendly affections and joys? The few who are so, the world looks upon as monsters, and detests them. And then how transient and fleeting are these pleasures, since they depend entirely upon the continuance of the appetite? when the natural craving is sated, all pleasure is gone; and there must be long, tedious and disagreeable intervals, unless they are filled up with more honourable pursuits.

---

8. See *System* 1.7.2, vol. I, p. 121.
9. See Shaftesbury, *An Inquiry concerning Virtue or Merit*, II.II.I; *Characteristicks*, pp. 202 and 211.
10. See *Essay on Passions* 5.2, p. 131.

Monstrat etiam ratio, quod observasse in hac quaestione multum profuerit, vitam temperati, et modesti, honestis studiis occupatam, donec naturales recurrant et vigeant appetitiones, saepe admittere eum, qui et tutis-
simus est, et laetissimus, humiliorum <51> voluptatum sensum, quas
nempe rarior semper commendat usus. Adeo commoda, igitur, est naturae
nostrae ratio, tanta virtutis bonitas, tam lene imperium, ut non ab eo voluptatum humiliorum usu, sibi addictos cohibeat, qui, ratione rite subductâ,
erit jucundissimus: licet hoc quidem imperet, ut vegeti conserventur sensus
animi nobiliores, reprimendisque cupiditatibus, ubi virtuti obstiterint, pares. At contra, dominante libidine, exiguus est aut nullus virtuti locus; ex-
ulat omne gaudium illud longe maximum, quod ex recti et honesti sensu
oritur, et bene merendi memoria: immo plerumque exulant humaniores ex
artibus ingenuis voluptates.

V. Veniat deinceps in medium ea delectatio, quae ex vitae cultu, ornatu, et
elegantia, oritur; quae, quamvis beluinis voluptatibus longe anteponenda,
neque tamen est aut magna aut diuturna. Exigua haec praebere potest so-
lamina malorum, quae vitam maxime vexant humanam; quales sunt corporis morbi; aut animi, iis saepe molestiores; metus, scil. angores, solicitudines, moerores. Res ad vitae ornatum et splendorem spectantes, donec
videntur novae, sunt etiam gratae; jucunditatem autem imminuit usus et
consuetudo. Consuetorum saepe nos satietas capit, et taedium; novaque,
pro mira in hac re <52> ingenii mutabilitate, confestim expetimus, innumeris nos objicientia curis, quorum etiam mox poenitebit.

Quid? quod omnia haec amicam postulant cum aliis conjunctionem.
Liberalitatis, commoditatis, et bonitatis, in foelicitate cum aliis communi-
canda, specie quadam haec ornata, laeta nobis fiunt et gloriosa. Horum
etiam fere omnia, pessimis mortalium et miserrimis, cum optimis esse possunt communia.[5]

---

5. In the first edition this paragraph was after the following one: "Spectetur etiam . . .
avocatur."

A little reflection too will shew us, what is of high importance in this matter, that in a temperate <and restrained> course of life, filled up with the most virtuous pursuits, till the natural appetites recurr, there is generally that enjoyment of the lower pleasures which is both safest and most delightful; since moderation and abstinence heightens the enjoyment. With such goodness is our nature constituted {by God}, so gentle is the reign of virtue, that it restrains not its subjects from that enjoyment of bodily pleasures, which upon a right estimate will <47> be found the sweetest: altho' this she demands, that we should still preserve so lively a sense of the superior pleasures, as may be sufficient to controul the lower appetites, when they make any opposition.[11] But on the other hand under the empire of sensuality there's no admittance for the virtues; all the nobler joys from a conscious goodness, a sense of virtue, and deserving well of others, must be banished; and generally along with them even the rational manly pleasures of the ingenious arts.

V. Let us next consider that pleasure which arises from the elegance and grandeur of life: this no doubt is of a far superior kind to brutal sensuality, and yet is neither very great nor durable. Such things can give small alleviation to any of the important evils of life, such as bodily diseases, or those of the mind, which are often more severe, our own <fears,> anxieties, sollicitudes, sorrows. While these matters of ornament, elegance or grandeur are new to us, they are pretty agreeable; but being a short while enured to them puts an end to their pleasure: we are soon cloyed; and if the taste continues, we fall a hunting after something new, with a strange caprice and inconstancy; exposing ourselves to innumerable chagrins and sollicitudes, to obtain what again we shall presently be cloyed with and nauseate.

Need we insist further that all these things require also some friendly society: their principal charm is in some notions of liberality, kindness, good-will, and sharing of pleasures with others: by these chiefly they are made joyful to us and matter of glorying. And <48> then such things may be enjoyed by the very worst and most wretched of mankind as well as by the most worthy.

11. See *System* 1.7.4, vol. I, p. 127.

Spectetur etiam quae ex artibus ingenuis percipitur voluptas; eaque humanissima, quae veri cognitionem comitatur. Eam quidem cuilibet corporis voluptati longe anteferendam, testatur ingenui cujusque sensus: stabilis etiam est magis et diuturna. Libero igitur quovis tempore, quum nulla
nos avocant officia honestiora, quicquid curae aut operae huic comparandae impenditur, jure laudabitur; ejusque laeta erit recordatio. {Hic proprius
humanitatis cibus, haec homine digna delectatio; haec partis divinioris exercitatio et perfectio; purior est haec voluptas, et honestior, et jucundior,
virtutibusque voluntariis amica.} Hanc [Haec] tamen <omnia> vitam beatam non posse praestare, facile intelligitur; quum neque dignissima sit
<quae ex his oritur> delectatio; et, majori cuidam et digniori, quae ex vir-
tute, officiisque exsurgit honestis, et humano generi <53> aut amicis profuturis, sua natura, inserviat omnis in artibus aut scientiis peritia. Unde et
sensu omnium comprobabitur is, qui rerum vel praestantissimarum studia
abjecerit, aut distulerit, ubi amicis, aut patriae laboranti, est succurrendum;
aut quum officio quovis amico et benigno abiis studiis avocatur.

Finge homini haec omnia quae ad vitae ornatum spectant, una cum corporis voluptatibus, virgulâ divina esse suppeditata, eundemque saepe in rerum maximarum contemplatione otiosè occupari; quum, tamen, is nec
quemquam amet, nec ab ullo ametur; nullusque apud eum locus sit officiis
ullis amicis aut benignis: aut finge naturales eum habere animi erga alios
affectiones; omnes tamen ipsi propinquos, aut caritate conjunctos, esse miseros: quis eousque hominem ex homine exuit, ut talem sibi optaret conditionem, eamve putet invidendam; et non potius aut miserrimam, aut de-
testandam? Quid si etiam subnascantur motus animi tetrici, invidentia,
odium, suspicio, metus; quae mentem benignis affectionibus vacuam plerumque occupant, quamvis in summa degatur rerum aliarum copia: omnino
miserrima erit haec vitae conditio, omnis liquidae voluptatis expers, et

Let us subjoin to these the pleasures of the ingenious arts, and that most truly manly sort which we enjoy in knowledge and the sciences: these the sense of every one who has any tolerable genius or gentlemanly taste, must indeed prefer far above any bodily pleasures; and they are also far more durable and stable. Whenever therefor we have leisure from the honourable offices of life, what study or pains we employ about them is truly laudable, and the remembrance of it will be agreeable. This is the natural food of the rational nature, and a pleasure suited to it; this is the proper exercise and improvement of that diviner part: these pleasures are of a purer kind, and more honourable and joyful, and friendly too to the voluntary virtues. And yet we may easily see that they alone are not sufficient to happiness: they are not absolutely the highest; and are plainly in their own nature destined for something further, even for these honourable offices by which we may serve our friends or our country.[12] And hence it is that all men must approve one who would throw aside even the most delightful studies about the most important subjects, when he were called to succour his friends or his country, or to perform any kind or friendly office.

Let us imagine with our selves a person possessed of every ornament and elegance of life, along with all the means of bodily pleasures, and this by some miraculous providence [by a magic wand]; and that he were employed <49> in the noblest contemplations with uninterrupted leisure, and yet void of all social affection, neither loving any nor beloved, without any opportunities of friendly offices: or imagine him retaining the natural affections toward others, but that all his kinsmen, all the objects of his love are {calamitous and} miserable: Is there any man so divested of humanity as to wish for such a lot to himself, or think it desirable?[13] must not every one look upon it as miserable and detestable? Imagine further, that the morose unkind affections also arise, envy, hatred, suspicion, fear; passions which generally fill up the vacancy of the kind affections in our hearts, even when we live in the greatest affluence: surely this state of life must be deemed most miserable, void of all true pleasure, and more to be dreaded

12. Literally: "and every skill in arts or sciences naturally serves the interests of something more important and excellent arising from virtue, honourable offices and profiting our friends or mankind."

13. See *Essay on Passions* 5.4, pp. 138–39.

morte vel saevâ magis metuenda. <54>

At contra, amica vitae societas, amor mutuus, et fiducia, et honesta officia, vitam laboriosam, et aerumnosam, exoptandam efficere possunt, et laudabilem.

VI. Progrediamur ad alium beatitudinis aut miseriae fontem, sensum nempe communem, aut sympathiam; per quam ex aliorum conditione foelici aut misera, gaudia colligimus aut moerores; atque fatebuntur fere omnes, magnam admodum [ejusdem vim esse ad vitam vel beatam vel miseram] [hinc hauriri posse vel beatitudinem, vel miseriam]. Quis est enim, Deum testor et homines! qui non longè praetulerit liberorum suorum, propinquorum, amicorum, civium, libertatem, foelicitatem, virtutem, omni non solum corporis jucunditati, verum et omni, quae ex artibus, aut rerum cognitione, oriri potest? Quis non omnia haec lubens projiceret, potius quam eos videat in conditione vitae vel misera, vel erubescenda? Ubi vigent et excoluntur animi affectiones homini naturales, vix quicquam majus afferre potest, ad vitam vel beatam vel miseram, momentum, quam aliorum hominum status, et fortunae. Quanta malorum nostrorum aderit levatio, ex eorum foelicitate qui nobis sunt carissimi? Quantaque omnis nostrae vitae disturbatio, ex eorum miseria?

Hanc animi sympathiam omnino comprobamus: aliorum dolere infortuniis honestum <55> est; neque hanc indolem nostram immutatam volumus, quamvis nobis moerores et luctus creet graves, licet haud erubescendos. Durum, contra, et ferreum ingenium, etsi hiscuris et moeroribus immune, damnamus; immo miserum censemus, quia turpissimum.

Diuturna etiam esse possunt haec gaudia et moerores, prout eorum quos amamus, permanet vita beata aut misera. Immo amicorum infortunia praeterita, longo post tempore, in memoriam non sine gravi dolore possumus revocare. Hac etiam de causa, magnum affert hic sensus momentum, ad vitam beatam vel miseram.

Quae ex hoc fonte hauriri potest foelicitas, non est in nostra potestate, a providentia nempe pendens divina: hanc igitur nemo magis sibi praestare potest, quam humiliorem istam quae corpore percipitur. Neque quicquam refert observasse, plurimos suo vitio aut culpa esse miseros, quamvis nihil ipsis externum desit. Etenim hoc ipsum est miserrimum, et praecipue deplorandum, quod sua culpa tot sint miseri, vel quod omnem vitae beatae

than even a painful death. And yet on the other hand, friendly society in life, mutual love and confidence, and virtuous offices, can make a laborious toilsome life, even amidst distresses, desirable and glorious.

VI. Let us proceed to another source of happiness or misery, our sympathy or social feelings with others, by which we derive joys or sorrows from their prosperity or adversity. And this all must allow to be of great importance <for our happiness or misery>. For, in the name of all that's sacred! who would not prefer beyond all comparison the liberty, virtue, and felicity of his children, his kinsmen and friends, his countrymen, not only to sensual pleasures, but to the noblest pleasures {of a selfish sort} in the arts and sciences? who would not rather forego them all than behold all such as are dear to him in a condition either miserable or shameful? While there's any life or <50> vigour in the natural affections of the social kind, scarce any thing can more affect our happiness or misery than the fortunes of others. What powerful relief under our own misfortunes arises from seeing the prosperity of such as are dear to us! and how is all our enjoyment of life destroyed and beat to pieces by seeing their misery!

This social sympathy we naturally approve: to be touched deeply with the misfortunes of others is honourable; nor can we wish to be divested of this sense even when it occasions to us severe <even if not shameful> distresses and sorrows: and the contrary temper, the hard insensible heart, tho' free from such cares and sorrows, we naturally detest, and deem it miserable because it is odious and base.

The joys or sorrows of this class may also be very lasting, according as the prosperity or adversity of the persons we love continues. Nay we have deep sorrow in reflecting upon the distresses or deaths of friends for a long time after these events: this duration of these sensations adds exceedingly to their importance.

What happiness we derive from this source is plainly independent of us, and is determined by Providence. No man can insure it to himself any more than external pleasures. Nor is it of consequence to prevent sympathetick pain, to think that men are generally the guilty causes of their own miseries <although no external good fails them>. Nay this very thing is chiefly deplorable and most pityable, that men are made miserable by their own

spem, in rebus vilioribus et caducis collocent. Qui se miseros putant, omnes sunt miseri; quamvis mutato ingenio, rebus externis non immutatis, beatis esse liceret.

Non aliud horum malorum datur perfugium, non aliud tranquillitatis, aut stabilis gaudii <56> fundamentum, animo vere benigno, quam ut Deum opt. max. mundi rectorem semper respiciat; solidis argumentis sibi persuasum habens, omnia, consilio ipsius benignissimo et sapientissimo, in communem omnium foelicitatem administrari; omniaque quae conspiciuntur mala, {multa quidem et varia,} non plura aut majora esse, quam quae, in mundi universi salutem et perfectionem, exigit optima divini imperii ratio; quorum plurima tandem foeliciter cadent iis etiam ipsis quorum calamitates deploramus.

VII. Sequitur alius decori et honesti sensus huic affinis, cujus est in vita momentum maximum: quod quisque perspiciet, qui aliquid in aliorum utilitatem strenuè, amicè, piè et fortiter gestum, in animum revocare potest; atque observaverit quanto gaudio mentem perfundat ejus recordatio? Quo sensu spectet alios? quanta caritate, quo benevolentiae ardore eos prosequatur, qui in istiusmodi officiis occupantur? quamque beatos eos esse existimet, in ipsis laboribus et periculis; immo quum mortes subeunt pro amicis aut patria, {aut} pro vera in Deum pietate propaganda, voluntarias? Quae sibi somnia vigiles fingunt homines otiosi, integram pro se aut suis, depingentes vitae rationem, quam putant foelicissimam, satis ostendunt, nullam {animo} concipi posse vitae beatae <57> rationem, sine omnium fere virtutum officiis continuis et fortibus, inter labores et pericula inlustratis. Haec a primis puerorum aetatibus menti alte infixa haerent. Testatur tota naturae nostrae fabrica, nos ad agendum esse natos; atque in agendo ex virtute, [vitam reperturos beatissimam] [beatitudinem reperturos summam] prae qua sordent voluptates.

Quanto deinde gaudio, summa cum tranquillitate et fiducia conjuncto, expletur vir bonus, qui Deo se similem praestare, quantum fieri potest, conatus, eum sibi propitium habet, rectorem, patremque, et remuneratorem

faults, placing their hopes of happiness in such mean perishing objects. All who deem themselves miserable are truly so, even altho' a <51> change in their own tempers would, in the same external circumstances, make them happy.

There's plainly no other refuge from these evils, no other foundation for tranquillity or stable joy to a kind heart, but a constant regard to the Deity and his wisdom and goodness governing this world; with a stable persuasion that all is ordered in the wisest and best manner for the universal felicity; and that all that variety of evil we behold is yet no more or greater than what is requisite <by the perfect wisdom of God> for the prosperity and perfection of the universe, and may at last also frequently tend to the real good of these very persons whose misfortunes we bewail.

VII. The next source of happiness or misery naturally connected with the former, is that {*conscience* or} *sense* of what is right and honourable, which is also of great importance in life. This any one may perceive who can recollect any offices he has done for others with vigour, friendliness, an high sense of duty, or fortitude; and observes with what joy the remembrance must fill his soul. What are our sentiments of others? with what endearment, what ardent good-will do we embrace such as are engaged in such offices? and how happy do we deem them even amidst their toils and dangers; nay when they are voluntarily exposing themselves to certain death for their friends, their country, or for the propagation of true religion? The very resveries of men at leisure, when they are imagining to themselves, or those they love, a whole plan of life of the greatest dignity and happiness they can conceive, sufficiently shew that they can have no notion of an happy <52> course of life without a continued course of steddy virtue, display'd amidst toils and dangers. These sentiments appear rooted in our hearts from our childhood. The whole frame of our nature shews that we are destined for action, and that in virtuous action alone we can find the highest happiness, in comparison with which all sensual pleasures appear despicable.

And then, with what joy, with what tranquillity and confidence must a good man be filled, who endeavouring to resemble the Deity as far as he can, is persuaded that he has the Deity for his propitious kind Ruler, Father,

munificentissimum: qui omnia benignissimo illius numine regi vertique credens, lubens fidensque amplectitur omnia quae eveniunt; ea optimo esse consilio destinata, atque sibi etiam profutura, compertum habens; qui summam novit et amat bonitatem, in eaque delectatur contemplandâ et imitandâ.

Huc accedit, quod diuturna sunt, et permanentia gaudia, quae ex recti conscientia oriuntur, et officii prudenter gnaviterque peracti. Labores honestos, et molestias brevi transituras, excipit recordatio gloriosa, et laetissima. Officiorum honestorum nunquam taedebit virum bonum; immo ejus accenditur magis quotidie animus, ad nova ejusmodi officia peragenda, et clariora. Accedat et gaudium haud leve, quum de eorum foelicitate <58> gratulamur, quibus profuerunt nostra officia; proborum omnium comprobationes et laudationes, pro meritis sperandae; laetaeque spes, omnia a Deo hominibusque consequendi, quae ad securitatem faciunt aut prosperitatem. Neque ulli deesse possunt honestiorum officiorum opportunitates, si quisque pro sua conditione ei rei unice studeat. Ubi inopi et imbecillo bene de hominibus, in rebus externis promerendi, occasio deest; potest hic, hominibus optima quaeque precatus, atque verae pietatis, et humillimorum officiorum exemplo, pro virili profuturus, pia cum fiducia et gaudio[, ingenuae suae honestatis veraeque probitatis, Deum judicem aequissimum, et hominum sapientiores quosque, comprobatores fautoresque fore, sibi tuto promittere] [divinae se providentiae curandum permittere].

VIII. Hunc sensum consequitur laudis et vituperii sensus acerrimus. Laus quidem et gloria, ubi antecesserat honestas, accessione haud spernendâ complebit vitam beatam: per se autem parum efficiet. Vanum enim et leve est ingenium, quod falsus honor juvare poterit. Vera quidem gloria radices agit et propagatur; falsa vero omnia tanquam flosculi decidunt. De falso honore nemini exploratum esse potest eum in vesperam duraturum. Veritatis tanta est vis, ut saepe supra hominum opinionem, {sive ad personam <59> speciosam mendacibus et malitiosis eripiendam,} sive ad infamiam refellendam mendacem, virtutemque calumniis oppressam vindicandam et

and munificent Rewarder; who, being assured that all events are governed and disposed of by his Providence, willingly embraces whatever befals him, firmly trusting that it is ordered with perfect wisdom, and shall tend to his good: one who knows and loves the Supreme-excellence, and is frequently employed in the contemplation and imitation of it.

Add to all this, that these joys are the most stable and durable which arise from a consciousness of our good dispositions, and of having acted according to them. The honourable toils and troubles are soon over, and are succeeded by joyful and glorious reflections. The {taste is not changeable or inconstant; the} practice of virtue is never cloying; nay it rather whets anew our appetite for further good offices of the same or a nobler kind. To this are joined these further pleasures, when we congratulate with those we have served effectually; when we justly expect the approbation and praises of mankind; when we have the joyful hopes of obtaining from God and men whatever is <53> requisite for our safety and felicity. Nor need any one fear the want of opportunities for exercising his virtues in good offices, if he is heartily set upon them, according to the condition of life allotted him. The indigent or weak may not be capable of important services to others in external things. But such a one, having most ardent wishes for the prosperity of mankind, and resolved to profit them at least by his example of piety, and by such mean offices as are in his power, may with an humble confidence and joy approve this goodness of his heart, these honourable affections to God the most equitable judge, and to the wisest of mankind, and expect their favour, approbation and protection.

VIII. What naturally ensues upon this sense, is that of *honour* and *infamy*, which is a very keen and lively one. Praise and glory when they are founded upon virtue, make no small accession to happiness; but without this foundation they are of little consequence. That must be an unfair and trifling mind which can be delighted with praises it knows not to be due to it. True glory like a lively tree spreads its roots deep, and diffuses its branches: but false glory like the blossoms, must soon fall. No man can be assured that groundless honours can remain with him even for a day. Such is the power of truth, that it frequently prevails beyond all expectation, either in the unmasking of ostentatious hypocrites or in vindicating the injured char-

illustrandam, mirum in modum valeat. Quumque actiones solum honestas laus naturâ insequatur, bene sanum suadebit et impellet omnis ea famae et gloriae appetitio, ad vitam ex virtute degendam atque ad omnia officia honesta obeunda.

IX. Ne denique silentio transeamus eam foelicitatem qualemcunque, quae in leviore quadam est sita laetitia aut hilaritate, ex jocis, ludisque, et risu orta: hoc obiter monendum; nisi mentis omnino hebescat acies, projiciaturque omnis homine digna ratio et meditatio, atque summa subnascatur rerum maximarum incuria turpissima; non alia ratione quam per virtutis et officiorum omnium conservationem, hominem sibi vel tranquillitatem vel hilaritatem posse polliceri. Ubi enim vel turpitudinis suae conscientiâ ulceratus est animus, vel vigent maligni et tetrici animi motus, virtutibus contrarii; aut metus et suspiciones, vitiorum comites assidui; nullam is liquidae voluptatis cujuscunque partem gustare valebit. Non abs re in hoc negotio dixeris,

Sincerum est nisi vas, quodcunque infundis acescit.[6] <60>

Stabilis tum demum et vera erit animi hilaritas, omni ingenuo joco, ludoque perfruendo idonea, ubi comitem habuerit ingenii humanitatem, morum mansuetudinem, mentem sibi recti consciam, et amicam cum bonis vitae societatem. Quicquid igitur est in his rebus expetibile, illud omne etiam ad virtutes omnes excolendas cohortabitur, et ad omnia vitae officia conservanda.

X. Quod ad opes attinet et potestatem; quicquid in illis est aestimabile [expetibile], ad eadem omnia sanum quemque incitabunt; quùm aliorum gratiâ et benevolentiâ, eaque fide, quam nobis apud alios comparamus, et parentur opes facillime, et conserventur. Neque opes quamvis magnae, contra hominum odia et invidiam quemquam [possessorem] tueri poterunt. Haec autem cum non propter se appetantur, verum ad alia quaedam referantur, ex iis quae de praestantissimis diximus voluptatibus, de vera rerum utilitate, et vitae foelicitate, constabit, eos potentiae aut divitiarum fructum capere tutissimum, {laetissimum} et simul honestissimum, qui ad liberalitatem eas referunt et beneficientiam.

6. Horace, *Epistulae* 1.2.54.

acter, and rescuing virtue from calumnies. And since the true object of praise is virtue alone; that natural strong passion for praise should excite every <54> wise man to regulate his whole life according to the rules of virtue, and employ himself continually in some truly honourable offices.

IX. That we may not quite omit another source of enjoyment tho' of a lower kind; that which consists in mirth and gaiety, amidst sports, diversions and jesting; we shall only briefly suggest, that unless the nobler powers be much stupified, and we cast aside all manly thought and reflection, indulging a base negligence about the most important concerns, we can no other way than by virtue and a careful regard to the duties of life, promise to ourselves either tranquillity or chearfulness. For when the soul is galled and ulcered either with remorse, or with the ill-natured envious passions opposite to virtue, or with fears and suspicions, {constantly attendants of vices,} there can be no undisturbed enjoyment of any satisfaction. In this matter the common similitude holds, "whatever is poured into a sour cask must soon grow acid." 'Tis then alone we can be truly easy and cheerful, fit to relish all manly pleasantries and mirth, when we are possessed of a courteous, humane, sweet temper, with a good conscience, and maintaining a friendly social intercourse with good men. Whatever therefore is valuable in gayety and mirth, should also excite us to cultivate all kinds of virtue, and persuade us to activity in discharge of all the duties of life.

X. As to wealth and power; whatever good is in them, should naturally lead a wise man into the same virtuous course: since it is by obtaining the favour and good-will of others, and maintaining credit in society, that wealth and power are easiest obtained and preserved: <55> nor can the greatest wealth or power secure its possessor against a general hatred or resentment. But as wealth and power are not desired for themselves, but for further purposes; from what we have shewn to be the noblest pleasures of life, and our highest advantage and happiness, it must appear, that they alone reap the true fruits, and have the safest and sweetest and most honourable enjoyment of wealth or power, who employ them in liberality and beneficence.

Quum autem omni animanti hic imprimis a natura datus sit appetitus, ut se vitamque suam conservet, de eo pauca hic dicendum; qui quidem, ut plerique alii, nimius esse potest. Neque enim ipsum vivere <61> adeo per se expetendum est, ac beatè vivere. Constat etiam vitam aliquando minime esse exoptandam; ubi scil. cum gravi turpitudine aut ignominia, et scelerum atrociorum conscientiâ est conjuncta, aut cum gravioribus corporis cruciatibus. Mortem sibi carissimi exoptaret amicus, ubi non aliter haec illi effugienda forent mala. Moriendum est omnibus; et id incertum, an eo ipso die: prudentis igitur saepe est, et sibi consulentis, vitam gravibus periculis ultro objicere, quum hoc postulet sanctum aliquod vitae officium, ne propter vitam vivendi solam perdere velit causam. Obfirmandus igitur est animus contra mortis terrores; qui enim mortem semper impendentem timet, quî poterit animo consistere? hac autem praecipue ratione est obfirmandus, si ab adolescentia sit seriò meditatum, post mortem, si modo eâ deleantur animi, sensum fore nullum; certè igitur non molestum: at si non deleantur; quod spondet et Dei benignissimi providentia, et ipsa animi natura pene divina; bonis omnibus sensus erit optandus: atque hanc vitam caducam et aerumnosam, excipiet ea quae sola vita est nominanda.

In eo igitur conspirant omnia quae diximus, ut doceatur vitam beatam esse sitam in ipsa virtute, aut in agendo ex virtute <62> praestantissima; quae tamen complenda est ex modicis saltem corporis et fortunae bonis {, ita ut sanitas saltem adsit, earumque rerum modica copia quibus sibi negatis doleat natura humana}. Sufficit per se virtus ad vitam beatam; quae tamen est cumulanda vitae perfectae prosperitate, ut fiat beatissima.

XI. Confirmabitur etiam haec sententia uberius, si contentio fiat et comparatio malorum, quae variis hisce bonis contraria, diversos hominum sen-

But since one of the first and strongest principles in all animals is the desire of self-preservation, we must offer a few thoughts on this head. 'Tis plain this desire like most others may be too strong: nor is mere living so much the object of it, as an happy life: and 'tis certain that in some circumstances life ceases to be desirable: as for instance, when we cannot preserve it without great baseness, ignominy and remorse; or must continue it under grievous bodily pain. The most friendly heart would wish for the death of his friend, when he cannot otherways escape these evils. Death is a certain event to all, and no man knows how soon it may happen. It must therefor often be wise conduct for for one's own interest to expose his life to the greatest dangers when any sacred duty requires it, that he may not for the preservation of life lose all that makes it worth retaining. We ought therefor to fortify our minds against the terrors of death: for one who dreads an evil always impendent{, and that may surprize us every moment}, can retain no tranquillity. And this strength of mind is to be obtained by deep meditation from our youth, that after death, if it destroys the <56> mind as well as the body, 'tis impossible there can be any evil, or any uneasy sensation. But if our souls perish not in death, which we justly conclude both from the goodness of God and the divine powers of the soul it self; then all good men may hope for a joyful state, and that this <wretched[14] and> fading mortal life shall be succeeded by a new life of a nobler kind, which alone deserves that name.

The whole former reasonings unite in this conclusion, that happiness consists in the virtues of the soul, and in the continued exercise of them in good offices: to the completion of which however some moderate advantages with respect to the body and fortune are requisite, at least that we enjoy health, and such a competence of external things as may satisfy the painful cravings of nature. From the possession of virtue alone life is to be counted happy: but to make it compleatly so there must be a moderate degree of external prosperity.

XI. The same conclusion is further confirmed by comparing the several evils contrary to the several sorts of good already compared. And here in the first

---

14. Hume observes rightly in his letter to Hutcheson of Jan. 10, 1743, "I fancy you employ the Epithet *aerumnosam* more from Custom than your settled Opinion" (*Letters,* I, p. 47).

sus afficiunt. Atque primo, licet corporis dolores majores habeant impetus, quam ejusdem voluptates, ut ad se conservandos acriori stimulo incitentur homines; extremum tamen malorum non sunt censendi. In errorem inducuntur homines, quod saepe turpitudinem aliquam leviorem, ipso periculi imminentis metu quodammodo imminutam, comparare soleant cum corporis cruciatibus gravissimis. Quorundam tamen facinorum tanta est turpitudo, tanti sunt aliquando conscientiae semet damnantis cruciatus, tamque saeva verbera; tanti etiam moerores et luctus ex eorum qui nobis sunt devinctissimi miseria subnascentes, ut omnes longe superent corporis dolores, et statum efficiant longe miserrimum.

Quod ad diuturnitatem [durationem] attinet, breves fere sunt corporis dolores, ut et ejus voluptates. <63> Si longus sit dolor, aut levior est, aut pluribus intervallis dolore vacuis plerumque distinctus. Gravissimi dolores nequeunt esse diuturni, quia morte delentur.[7] Praeteritorum, ubi nihil simile in posterum timetur, haud molesta, immo potius suavis est recordatio,[8] quandoque etiam gloriosa.

Voluptatibus elegantioribus, ex formarum specie perspecta, ex sonorum harmonia, et imitationibus artificiosis, iisque quae ad vitae ornatum referuntur et elegantiam, ortis, nulli sunt naturâ dolores contrarii. Voluptatis enim, non doloris, hi sensus nati sunt praebitores et ministri. Ubi quidem acriora sunt harum rerum desideria, aut ubi ex iis gloria captatur, molestum erit homini despe sua decidere; grave erit absentium desiderium. His vero rebus plane carere, non necessariò affert molestiam; cum multis sit vitae status tranquillus et foelix, qui ea non habent; unde neque curant habere.

{Quod vero praecipuè ad rem attinet: corporis doloribus aut damnis neutiquam per se nos objiciunt virtutes, eave invehunt: avertunt potius, iisque medentur. Si quidem casu incurrant dolores aut damna, (de quo haud magis improbis quam probis cautum esse potest;) aut si ipsius virtutis causa dolores aut damna sint perferenda, (quod etiam incidere potest; in graviora tamen et <64> foediora, longè saepius homines conjiciunt flagitia et sce-

---

7. Cf. Cicero, *De finibus* 1.40, 41, 49.
8. Cf. Cicero, *De finibus* 2.105.9.

place, 'tis plain that the strength and force of bodily pain is greater in proportion than that of bodily pleasures; and this wisely ordered, that we may be the more strongly excited to our own preservation: and yet they are not to be looked upon as the greatest of evils. Men are often led into this mistake by comparing some smaller kinds of moral turpitude, even when they are excused in some measure or alleviated by the greatness of the temptation [by the fear of some incumbent danger], with the highest bodily tortures. <57> But some crimes are so detestable, and must occasion such self-abhorrence, and torturing remorse, and some sorrows and distresses occasioned by the misery of persons very dear to us are so deep, as to occasion misery superior to any bodily torments.

And then as to duration, the pain of the body, as well as its pleasures, can seldom be very durable. Such pain as is lasting must generally be of a lighter sort, or admit of frequent intervals of ease. The severer kinds must generally soon end in death: and the remembrance of past pain when we dread no returns of the like, has nothing uneasy in it, nay is sometimes sweet, and matter of glorying.[15]

The more elegant pleasures of the arts, from beauty, harmony, and ingenious imitation, and all these things which relate to the ornament or grandeur of life, have no proper pain opposite to them. These more sublime senses are the avenues of pleasure and not of pain. Where indeed men have indulged strong desires of such gratifications, or affect glory and eminence by them, it may be very uneasy to be disappointed, and we may regret much the want of them. But an absolute want of them is not a natural necessary cause of any misery. Nay we see that the greater part of men are abundantly easy without them, and therefor have no solicitude to procure them.

But 'tis of the highest use to observe, that virtue of it self has no natural tendency to expose us to any of these external losses or pains: nay it rather prevents or removes them. But if it should be our fortune to incurr such losses or pain, from which surely the vitious <58> are no more secured than the virtuous; or if sometimes on account of virtue we should be exposed to such evils, which is sometimes the case, (tho' men are much more frequently involved by their vices in such evils, and that in a more shameful

15. See *Essay on Passions* 5.11, p. 163.

lera:) ea fortiter sustinere aut obterere docebit virtus, multoque et vario solatio sublevabit: monstrabit enim sapientia, ea esse virtutum clarissimarum
materiam, campumque in quo se exerceant, sibique novas adsciscant vires:
quodque iis fortiter ferendis nostra in Deum pietas, patientia, et magnanimitas illustrabuntur, firmabuntur et tandem munificentissimè remunera-
buntur.}

Gravior saepè est ea quae ex aliorum infoelicitate oritur miseria, cui
neque ulla voluptatum, aut rerum externarum, copia, levamen afferre potest. Nec gravis solum, verum etiam diuturna solet esse ea moestitia; quum
omnis de amicorum aut dilectorum graviore infortunio aut dedecore cogi-
tatio, semper futura sit molesta. Non alia hujus aegritudinis saepe restat
consolatio, quam quae depromitur ex stabili in Deo opt. max. omnia gu-
bernante, fiducia{, qua solâ probi bonique animos suos erigere possunt}.

Omnium tamen malorum gravissimum est animi depravati, scelerisque
sui sensu vexati, turpitudo; quae nempe hominem ipsum sibi odiosum facit,
suumque ingenium, quod sibi maxime est intimum, vile sibi reddit, et pudendum, {immo probrosum} et detestandum. Diuturna etiam est ea aegritudo <65> miserrima; quum omnis scelerum suorum aut flagitiorum
recordatio, homini sit gravis et erubescenda; eamque molestiam vix, ac ne
vix quidem, morum emendatione, aut damni dati reparatione, possit tandem exuere. Hanc comitantur solicitudines, metus, angores: atque prout
pessime de aliis fuit meritus, vigebit continua de Deo hominibusque suspicio, ne pro meritis sibi rependant.

Huic naturâ conjuncta est infamia, quae si modo vera, graviter etiam et
diu excruciat animum, omnemque excludit verae amicitiae, aut gratiae
apud alios consequendae, {eorumque studia in nostram utilitatem adscis-
cendi} spem.

Haec omnia ostendunt, non sine causa placuisse veteri Academiae et Pe-
ripateticis, [vitam beatam] [beatitudinem] sitam esse {in} Ενέργεια χατ'

base way) Virtue can teach us to bear such evils with resolution, or to conquer them; or will afford us a variety of strong consolations under them.
Just reflection will shew us that such events are the proper matter of exercise
for the most glorious virtues, the course in which they must run, and train
themselves, acquiring daily new force: that it is by bearing them with patience that our resignation to God, our submission, and magnanimity must
be display'd, strengthened, and at last gloriously rewarded.

The miseries of the sympathetick kind from the distresses of others are
often more severe, nor can they be allayed by any sensual pleasures or any
external objects. Such distresses are also very lasting: since all remembrance
or reflection upon any grievous misfortune or infamy of any person dear
to us must always be matter of great uneasiness. There is scarce any consolation under such distress except what must be derived from resignation
and trust in the Deity; by which alone it is that good men can support their
spirits in all events.[16]

But still the most grievous of all evils is the moral turpitude of a depraved
heart conscious of its own baseness. This makes a man odious to himself;
and makes his own temper, what's most essential and intimate to him, appear base and shameful, nay ignominious <59> and detestable. This evil
too is of the most lasting nature; since the remembrance of our past crimes
or impieties must ever be grievous and shameful. Nor can we shake off this
uneasy tormenting feeling unless by an entire alteration of temper, and
reparation of any injuries we have done; nor will this it self do it effectually.
It's common attendants too are solicitudes, fears, anxieties; and, as such
persons have deserved ill of God and mankind, they must live in a perpetual
dread that they shall be repaid according to their demerits.

Along with these inward causes of misery, comes also infamy; which
when justly deserved gives severe and lasting torment, excludes all hopes
of true friendship or favour with others, and of obtaining their faithful
assistances for our advantage.

From all this we see that it was with the justest reason the old Academy
and the Peripateticks placed happiness in "a constant activity according to
the highest virtue in a prosperous course of life." This the schoolmen call

16. See *System* 1.7.15, vol. I, p. 145.

ἀρετὴν ἀρίστην ἐν βίῳ τελείῳ.[9] Quod summum bonum est *formale,* quod dicitur.[10]

Eadem igitur vitae beatae summa, quae et virtutum. Ut nempe Deum toto amemus animo, et homines stabili prosequamur benevolentia, omnesque animi corporisque vires quae communi inservire possint utilitati, studiose excolamus{: in quibus sita est ea vita quae maxime est secundum naturam}.

XII. Ex animis autem nostris hoc nunquam excidere debet, nos totos a Deo pendere, <66> omniaque [omnesque] et animi et corporis bona [perfectiones], ipsasque virtutes omnes, a Deo ad nos pervenisse; et sola Dei provida tutela conservari posse et foveri. Quumque honestum omne ingenium {foras spectet}, aliorum prospiciens et consulens foelicitati, quae omnis a Deo pendet, quamque nullae hominum vires praestare possunt; nullum certè laetae spei, tranquillitati stabili, aut solido gaudio, potest substerni fundamentum, praeter solam, in Deo, quem optimum novimus et maximum, fiduciam; quâ nosmet, nobisque caros, immo mundum universum ipsius permittimus providentiae, de omnium rerum benignissimâ administratione securi. Recte igitur dixerunt philosophi scholastici ipsum Deum esse summum hominis *bonum* quod vocant *objectivum;* ex quo cognito, amato {et redamante,} exsurgit bonis omnibus summa foelicitas.

---

9. Aristotle, *Ethica Nichomachea* 1.8.1098a.16–18.
10. In the first edition there follow five paragraphs that form art. 1 of chapter III in the second edition.

the *supreme formal good*. The same therefor is the summary notion of happiness and of virtue: to wit, "that we should love and reverence the Deity with all our soul, and have a stedfast goodwill toward mankind, and carefully improve all our powers of body and mind by which we can promote the common interest of all"; which is the life according to nature.

XII. But we ought always to keep this in our thoughts, that we entirely depend on God; that all the goods either of mind or body, all our virtues, have <60> been derived from him, and must be preserved or increased by his gracious Providence: and since every good temper must always extend its views abroad, studiously pursuing the happiness of others, which also entirely depends on the will of God, and cannot be ensured by human power: there can be no other stable foundation of tranquillity and joy than a constant trust in the goodness, wisdom and power of God, by which we commit to him ourselves, our friends, and the whole universe, persuaded that he will order all things well. The schoolmen therefor justly call God the supreme object of happiness, or the *supreme objective good*,[17] from the knowledge and love of whom, with the hopes of being favoured by him, our supreme happiness must arise.

17. On the distinction between formal and objective good or end, see *Synopsis*, 2.2.2, p. 63.

CAPUT III

De variis Virtutum Divisionibus.

I. Quum igitur vitam secundum virtutem actuosam, ostendimus esse summum bonum; inquirendum est accuratius quaenam sint virtutes, quae ex virtute actiones, et erga quos sint exercendae. <67>

In recti et honesti explicatione, docuimus animi virtutes praecipuas esse benevolos voluntatis motus, et consilia agendi ex propensa in alios voluntate: praestantiores deinde esse eas animi affectiones benignas, quae tranquillae sunt; eamque praestantissimam quae patet latissime: in praestantissimarum numero etiam posuimus ardentem virtutis ipsius amorem, summam animi in ea delectationem, ejusque excolendi studium; cui conjunctus est erga omnes virtute praeditos amor ardentior, et erga honestissimum quemque ardentissimus; unde pietatis in Deum elucebat honestas summa, et quantopere ad eam sanctissime colendam teneamur.

Inter virtutes mediocres aut infimas, recensentur et caritates arctiores, quas vel natura constituit vel consuetudo: clariores tamen illae, quas "morum" excitavit "bonorum similitudo":[1] unde et amicitiae, quam gignit conservatque virtutum significatio, elucet sanctitas. Laudabilis etiam et decora est erga quosvis comitas, moresque mansueti et benigni.

1. Cicero, *De officiis* 1.56.5.

Concerning the Chief Divisions of Virtue.

I. [1]Having shewn that our chief good consists in virtuous activity, our next Inquiry must be, what are the several virtues? and what actions flow from them? and toward what objects?

In explaining our natural {conscience or} sense of what is good and honourable, we shewed that the chief virtues of the soul are kind affections and beneficent purposes of action: and that of these the calm {and stedfast} are more excellent than the passionate, and that the most extensive are the most excellent. Amongst the most excellent too we placed an ardent love of moral excellence, < the highest delight of the soul in it, > an earnest desire of increasing it in ourselves, and an high esteem and love toward all who are possessed of it, with the highest love toward the supreme excellence. Whence appeared our duty of loving God with the highest veneration, and the sacred obligations we are under to cultivate such affections.[2]

In the middle or lower classes of virtues we placed these narrower affections which either nature or acquaintance have excited: of these the more lovely are such as arise in a virtuous heart upon observing in others the like virtuous dispositions: and hence such friendships as virtue has begot and nourished must appear very lovely.[3] There's also something very engaging in a general courtesy, and sweetness of deportment toward all we have any intercourse with. <62>

---

1. In the first edition of the *Institutio*, the first five paragraphs of this chapter were located before the last paragraph of chapter II, section 11. The fact that this catalogue of virtues was part of the chapter entitled "De summo bono et virtute" suggests that the present chapter was a late addition to the first edition. See Introduction, p. xiv.

2. See above, I.11, pp. 21–22.

3. See above, I.12, p. 24; Hutcheson is more explicit on different kinds of benevolence and their degree of moral excellence in the *Inquiry on Virtue,* III.6, pp. 177–78.

Virtutibus etiam annumerantur illi habitus qui nobiliores animi vires perficiunt; qui cum benigno ingenio sunt natura conjuncti, eique inserviunt; aut qui denique libidines aut perturbationes quascunque virtutibus obstantes reprimunt, cohibent [superant] aut excludunt; <68> hosque omnes, tanquam per se honestos, comprobamus. Solertissimo enim consilio, ita a Deo fabricata est mens humana, ut animi vires et affectiones eo magis comprobet, idque proximè et per se, quo majorem vim [majus momentum] habent ad totius humani generis foelicitatem. Hinc [non solum] [etiam] comprobantur arctiores benevolentiae affectiones et caritates, in vita admodum necessariae, ubicunque majori plurium non obstant utilitati; [verum etiam] [comprobatur] animus simplex, ingenuus, et fallere nescius; abstinentia etiam, continentia, et fortitudo; quae scil. animum ostendunt honesti sensu acriore imbutum, atque voluptatum, dolorum, et utilitatum externarum despicientia confirmatum. Quaedam etiam decori species cernitur in eo corporis motu et statu, qui virtutum exhibet indicia: contrariae autem omnes sive animi sive corporis affectiones displicent, odioque dignae censentur.

Quid, quod sensu quodam, a jam memorato quidem diverso, at non prorsus dissimili, comprobantur et animi et corporis vires habitusque, a virtutibus voluntariis omnino diversi. Quas homini dedit Deus vires, earum usum qui maxime est secundum naturam, vitaeque humanae utilissimum, nobis etiam natura commendavit. Unde et comprobantur studia cognitionis, atque artium elegantiorum; diligentia item et industria, et <69> in laboribus perferendis patientia. Hominem etiam magis decere videntur exercitationes illae, quae vel ingenium ostendunt acrius, et sublimius; vel corporis vires augent et confirmant. [Voluptatum, contra, humiliorum consectatio ardentior, animique aut corporis mollities, honestis laboriosisque officiis inutilis, quaeque eam produnt omnia, ea hominis praestantia parum digna, parumque decora.][: quae, contra, animi, corpisve mollitiem produnt, honestis, & laboris officiis inutilem, eae parum decorae.]

We reckon also among the virtues all these habits {or dispositions}, which tend to improve the nobler powers of the soul, or are naturally joined with or subservient to generous affections; and all such too as tend to restrain the meaner sensual appetites, the ordinary obstacles to virtue, and gives us a power to controll them: all these we immediately esteem for themselves. For by the wise contrivance of our Creator, our natural taste [human mind] is so formed, that we immediately approve and esteem all such affections or powers, the more in proportion as they are of greater importance to the general good. And hence it is that we not only approve {and love} the kind affections of a more contracted kind, which are so necessary in the several relations of life, while they are not opposite to any more extensive interest; but we also immediately approve a *sincere, ingenuous, candid temper;* we praise *abstinence* or contempt of {wealth and} pleasure, and *fortitude:* as all these naturally evidence a mind possessed of an high taste for moral excellence, confirmed by an indifference about, or contempt of sensuality, and external advantages, or disadvantages. Nay we immediately relish such a state or motion in the body as carries natural indications of virtue; and all the contrary dispositions whether of mind or body appear disagreeable and offensive.[4]

Need we mention again some natural sense, different from the moral one, but not unlike it, by which we relish and value some powers of the mind and the body quite different from any of the voluntary virtues. To all the powers God has given us there's conjoined some sort of sense or relish, recommending that exercise <63> of them we call natural, which is also the most subservient to the general good. Hence we highly approve the pursuits of knowledge and the ingenious arts, a capacity of application, industry, and perseverance. Nay even in bodily exercises {and recreations}, we most approve these which either shew something of ingenuity or strength, or tend to encrease them.[5] <On the contrary, the eager seeking after lower pleasures, the effeminate softness of body and soul, useless for honourable and industrious offices, and all those conveniences that foster that softness, are not worthy and suitable to human excellence.>

4. See *System* 1.4.9, vol. I, pp. 66–68.
5. See above I.10, pp. 15–16.

{II. Generali hac virtutis informatione exposita, profuerit etiam varias ejus partes et genera recensere, ut eorum quodque lumen suum ostendens nos magis ad se alliciat.}

²Virtus, voce laxius acceptâ, omnem notat in re quacunque vim, quae naturae sentientis foelicitati inservire potest: arctius accepto vocabulo, notat habitum aliquem vires animi perficientem: quo sensu[. Hoc modo] dividuntur virtutes in *intellectuales,* quae omnem in artibus et scientiis ingenuis animi culturam continent; et *morales,* quae κατ᾽ ἐξοχὴν virtutes vocantur, et voluntatem perficiunt; quae praecipùe sunt ethici fori. {Ethico tamen haud praetereundae virtutes intellectuales, non ideo solum, quod ex iis oritur homine dignissima voluptas, cui animus assuetus, sensumque nactus sublimiorem, humiles et vitiosas spernet voluptates; quare <70> et scientiae ψυχῆς καθάρματα jure censeantur: verum etiam quod virtutibus voluntariis plurimum auxilii afferant. Ex altiore enim naturae totius mundique cognitione, elucebunt Dei conditoris virtutes, accendetur pietas, rerumque humanarum parabitur despicientia; quaeque virum bonum plurimum ornabit et perficiet, sive modestia, sive ταπεινοφροσύνη, quae ex tenuitatis et imbecillitatis humanae conscientia oritur: neque sine multiplici rerum vulgarium peritia, rebus gerendis necessaria prudentia adesse poterit. Ad alias tamen disciplinas haec omnia pertinent. De toto genere monemus, haec "duo vitia" esse fugienda, "unum, ne incognita pro cognitis habeamus, iisque temere assentiamur." Quocirca "ad res considerandas et tempus, et diligentia," et animus praejudicatis opinionibus et perturbationibus vacuus est adhibendus. "Alterum" est "ne nimis magnum studium in res obscuras et difficiles, easdemque non necessarias," conferamus.³

2. In the first edition chapter III begins here.
3. Cicero, *De officiis* 1.18.7–19.4.

II. Having given this general {rude} draught of the virtues, 'tis proper to consider their several kinds, that each of them displaying its beauty to us, may more allure us to pursue them.[6] Virtue in the largest acceptation, may denote any power or quality which is subservient to the happiness of any sensitive being. In its stricter acceptation it denotes any habit or disposition which perfects the powers of the soul; and thus virtues are divided into the *intellectual,* which include all improvements of the mind by ingenious arts and sciences; and *moral,* which are chiefly counted virtues, being perfections of the *will* {and *affections*}[7]; and these are the chief object of Ethicks.

And yet the intellectual virtues are not to be altogether omitted in Morals; not only because they afford a noble branch of happiness, pleasures exceedingly becoming our rational nature; to which whosoever is enured, and has got an high taste for them, is enabled to contemn the meaner enjoyments which lead to vice; whence the sciences have justly been deemed *purifications of the soul:* * but because they give a more direct aid to the moral virtues. For from a deeper enquiry into nature and the universe, the perfections <64> of the great Creator are displayed, our dutiful veneration toward him increased, the mind led into a just contempt for the low worldly pursuits of mankind; and that *humility,* or deep consciousness of our own weakness and manifold imperfections, is obtained, which is a chief ornament and perfection in a good character. Nay, without a great deal of knowledge in the lower and ordinary affairs of life, we must be deficient in that practical prudence which is always necessary in our conduct. But these virtues or accomplishments belong principally to other branches of philosophy, or arts. This we suggest only in general, that in the pursuits of knowledge these two faults are to be cautiously avoided, the one that of rash precipitate assenting<, taking as known what is unknown>; and for this purpose we must both take time and make vigorous application, and bring along a mind free from prejudices and prepossessions, or any passionate attachments. The other fault is employing too much keenness upon subjects, perhaps <obscure and> difficult, but of small use or necessity in life.

6. This sentence was added in 1745.

7. The division between intellectual and moral virtues is in Aristotle's ethics and in Cicero's *De finibus* V.36.

* Pythagoras and Plato called them καθάρματα ψυχῆς.

Quod ad virtutes Ethicas et voluntarias attinet: earum alii alias tradiderunt divisiones.} Aristotelici hoc praecipue spectantes quod variis animi perturbationibus, sive passionibus immoderatis, a recto tramite abripiamur, quum interea hi omnes naturae impetus sive instinctus, provido Dei consilio, in aliquam vitae utilitatem insiti fuerint; virtutem <71> definiverunt "habitum deliberativum in mediocritate situm, secundum rectam rationem."[4] Ex hoc virtutis haud levi officio, quod ab extremis excessuum aut defectuum, animi motus, qui saepe solent esse immodici, cohibeat; in virtutibus explicandis percurrerunt varias passiones, earumque varios gradus, justo vehementiores, aut languidiores; medios monstrantes esse tutissimos et utilissimos, et maxime decoros; quos volunt esse virtutes. [Habitus autem qui eam conservant mediocritatem, celebrem apud antiquos partitionem persequentes,] [Has autem omnes, prout sunt internae animi affectiones] ad quatuor reducunt capita, quae *cardinales* appellantur virtutes; *prudentiam, justitiam, temperantiam,* et *fortitudinem:* ex quibus animi affectionibus praestantissimis, tanquam ex fontibus, manare voluerunt reliquas omnes virtutes.

III [II]. Prudentiam volunt esse attentum et sagacem dijudicandi habitum, inter ea quae in vita prodesse possunt aut nocere, rerum usu et meditatione comparandum, et conservandum; qui quidem ad omnia fere officia rite obeunda est necessarius{; in intellectualium potius quam moralium numero habendus. Veram tamen solidamque prudentiam assequetur nemo, nisi cui animus virtutibus voluntariis excultus est, rectique et honesti sensu acriori imbutus, "pectusque <72> generoso honesto incoctum."[5] Caeteros decipit prava quaedam solertia aut astutia, verae prudentiae imitatrix, quae ab ea tamen abest distatque plurimum. Huic virtuti contraria sunt *temeritas, imprudentia, ingenii confidentis arrogantia, astutia*}.

---

4. Quotation marks in Hutcheson's text. Cf. Aristotle, *Ethica Nichomachea* 1106b, 36–1107a, 1 and 1114b, 26–29.
   5. Persius, *Saturae* 2.74.

As to the moral virtues seated in the will; the divisions given of them by different authors are very different. The followers of Aristotle, having this principally in view, that 'tis by immoderate ungoverned passions that we are led into vice, while yet all these passions have been wisely implanted in our nature by the Deity for necessary purposes, they define virtue, "a considerate habit of the soul preserving a mediocrity according to right reason";[8] as indeed it is a great part of the office of virtue to keep the several affections, which are frequently disorderly, from both <65> the extremes of *excess* and *defect*. In this view, to explain the several virtues they go through the several natural passions, and their several degrees, when they are either too languid or too vehement; and shew that the middle degrees are the safest, the most advantageous, and the most graceful; and these they count virtuous. Now the several habits by which this mediocrity is preserved, according to a celebrated division among the Antients, they reduce to four classes, which are called the *Cardinal Virtues; Prudence, Justice, Temperance* and *Fortitude:* from which they derive all the several branches of virtue.[9]

III. Prudence they describe "a cautious habit of consideration and forethought, discerning what may be advantageous or hurtful in life"; which must be acquired and preserved by experience and frequent meditation. This habit no doubt is necessary in all the business of life. But one would think prudence were rather to be ranked among the intellectual than the moral virtues: and yet no man can attain to the true solid prudence, whose heart is not improved by the moral virtues, with an high sense of moral excellence; and who has not deeply imbibed the more generous sentiments of goodness. Others may have a sort of crafty sagacity in worldly affairs, which assumes to it self the title of Prudence and Wisdom, but yet is very remote from it. The vices opposite to this virtue are *rashness, inconsiderateness, a foolish self-confidence,* and *craft.*

8. This definition is from Aristotle. See note 4 in the Latin text.
9. This division is introduced by Plato in *Respublica* IV and generally resumed afterward in ethics.

Fortitudinem dicunt virtutem animum contra omnes in officio obeundo labores et pericula obfirmantem;[6] quaeque metus omnes aut vanos aut nimios reprimit; rerumque humanarum parit despicientiam, perspectâ earum natura; omnes scil. utilitates externas prae ipsa honestate, et laeta recti conscientia, cujus Deus testis erit et comprobator, sordere: nihilque hominem tantum timere aut fugere debere, quam vitia omnia, et animi depravati turpitudinem: quumque omnibus brevi sit moriendum, mortem, vel immaturam, cum honestate conjunctam, esse vitae inhonestae et ignominiosae longe anteponendam: unde et excelsus dicitur animus, et magnus, nulla re externa concutiendus.[7]

{Hic animus magnus et excelsus in tribus praecipue cernitur, in honesti amore studioque eximio; in ea "rerum humanarum," quam diximus, "despicientia"; atque "animi" ab omni "perturbatione"[8] liberi tranquillitate. Fortitudinis igitur laudem neutiquam assequitur qui vitia, turpitudinem, aut justam non <73> metuit infamiam. Fortis est potius et prudentis, haec omnia studiosè declinare, pericula item qualiacunque quae nulla officii ratio subire suadet. Quoniam vero duplex est appetitus ἀλογός, ἐπιθυμία et θυμός: atque huic modum ponere volunt fortitudinem, illi Temperantiam;[9] fortitudinis partes, praeter *magnanimitatem, constantiam, tolerantiam, patientiam,* recensent etiam *lenitatem* et *clementiam,* ita tamen ut reipub. causa adhibeatur *severitas,* et *nemesis* justa, vitia omnia et injurias expellens et coërcens.

Fortitudini adversantur hinc *timiditas, ignavia,* earumque comes *saevitia;* illinc *audacia* et *temeritas;* quacum saepe conjuncta est superba *"pertinacia"* et *ambitio,* "sive nimia cupiditas principatus,"[10] aequo civium juri contrariae.}

6. Cf. Cicero, *Tusc. disp.* 5.41.8, *De finibus* 5.67.6.
7. Cf. Cicero, *De officiis* 1.66–67.
8. Cicero, *De officiis* 1.66.
9. Cf. Aristotle, *Ethica Nichomachea* 1117b, 23–25.
10. Cicero, *De officiis* 1.64.3.

Fortitude they define to be "that virtue which strengthens the soul against all toils or dangers we <66> may be exposed to in discharge of our duty":[10] 'tis this virtue which represses all vain or excessive fears, and gives us a superiority to all the external accidents of our mortal state; grounded on a thorough knowledge of their nature, that no external advantages are to be compared in point of happiness with the possession of virtue, and gaining the approbation of our own hearts, and of God, to whom our tempers must be perfectly known; and that nothing ought so much to be dreaded <or shunned> as vice and the moral deformity of the soul: and consequently, since death must soon befal us in all events, that an early death with virtue and honour is highly preferable to the longest ignominious life. On such principles as these must be founded that true greatness and elevation of mind which is not to be disturbed by external accidents.[11]

This true grandeur of mind is discovered in these three things; in an high relish and love of moral excellence; in that superiority to and contempt of external accidents just now mentioned; and in a tranquillity free from passion.[12] There is therefor no true fortitude in not dreading moral turpitude or just infamy: the truly brave and wise avoid these things above all; as they will also decline any dangers to which no virtuous offices call them. Now as our passionate motions are of two kinds; one, that of passionate desires, the other that of aversions, fears or anger;[13] and fortitude regulates these latter, as Temperance does the former; among the branches of Fortitude, are reckoned beside Magnanimity, Constancy, Hardiness, and Patience, *Lenity* also of temper and *Clemency;* and, <67> when the publick interest requires it, *Rigour* and *Severity,* with such just Resentment as is requisite to repell or restrain injuries.

The vices opposite to Fortitude on one hand, are *Pusillanimity* and *Cowardice,* and their common attendant *Cruelty;* on the other hand, furious *boldness* and *Temerity,* which is often attended with *obstinacy* and *ambition,* or too keen desires of eminence, inconsistent with that equality of right which should be maintained in every free state.

10. See Latin text, note 6.
11. See Latin text, note 7.
12. See Latin text, note 8.
13. See above, I.6, p. 9, note *.

Temperantiam <autem> describunt, virtutem quae humiliores omnes appetitus, corporis voluptatem consectantes, cohibet et regit; quibus nempe voluptatibus, tanquam esca, ad turpia plurima alliciuntur homines, honestaque officia deserere coguntur. Huic praecipue adjungunt decori et pulchri in dictis, factis, consiliisque, conservandi studium, cui maxime obstant humiliorum voluptatum illecebrae. {Temperantiae partes sunt *Modestia, verecundia, castitas, frugalitas,* ἐντέλεια, sive animus tenui et simplici victu cultuque <74> contentus, atque in omni morum spurcitie coercenda *severitas.* Huic virtuti adversantur *luxus, ingluvies, temulentia, impudentia, lascivia, obscoenitas, mollities,* et delicatum in victu cultuque *fastidium.*} <Atque prout motus perturbatos, sive ὄρεξίν ἀλόγον, dividunt in ἐπιθυμίαν & θυμὸν; huic imperare & modum ponere volunt fortitudinem, illi temperantiam.>

Omniúm vero virtutum principem, cui inserviunt caeterae, volunt *justitiam;* quae est "habitus animi, communi utilitate conservatâ, suam cuique tribuens dignitatem."[11] Hujus ambitu includunt omnes animi affectiones benignas, quibus amica conservari potest hominum consociatio; aut aliquid conferri in aliorum hominum utilitatem: quales sunt *liberalitas, beneficientia, magnificentia, amicitia,* bene merentium *grata memoria, comitas, mansuetudo,* {*veritas, fides, hospitalitas,*} *patriae caritas,* [*pietasque omnis, praecipue erga Deum,*] [Atque ipse in Deum pietas] qui civitatis antiquissimae et sanctissimae, cujus caeterae sunt partes, rector est et parens. Priorum trium virtutum natura, ex iis quae de summo diximus hominum bono,{*} et earum rerum quas appetimus comparatione, innotescet: justitiae natura, ex iis quae de vario hominum jure sunt dicenda.

<III.> Has quanquam virtutes volunt esse inter se necessario conjunctas, in gradu etiam *temperantiae,* sive medio, aeque ac in *heroico;* ex singulis

---

11. Cicero, *De inventione* 2.160.7. Quotation marks in Hutcheson's text.
* {Lib.I. Cap. 2}

Temperance is that virtue which restrains and regulates the lower appetites toward sensual pleasures; as 'tis by them that men are most frequently
ensnared into all manner of vices, and into a neglect of every thing honourable. In this virtue most remarkably appears the grace and beauty of
manners [of words, actions and purposes], which is quite destroyed by sensuality [by the allurements of lower pleasures].

The several branches of Temperance are {*Moderation of mind*}, *Modesty*,
Chastity, *Frugality*, a *Contentment* with, or Relish for plain simple fare, and
a *Severity* of manners in opposition to all obscenity and lewdness. The opposite vices are *Luxury*, *Gluttony*, *Drunkenness*, *Impudence*, *Wantoness*, *Obscenity*, effeminate *Softness*, and *Delicacy* as to food and other cares about
the body.

But *Justice* they make the sovereign virtue to which all the rest should
be subservient: this they define "an habit constantly regarding the common
interest, {and in subserviency to it,} giving or performing to each one whatever is due to him upon any natural claim."[14] Under it they include all the
kind dispositions of heart <68> by which a friendly intercourse is maintained among men, or which leads us to contribute any thing to the common interest. Such as *Liberality*, *Beneficence*, *Friendliness*, *Gratitude*, *Magnificence*, *Courtesy*, *Humanity*, *Veracity*, *Fidelity*, *Hospitality*, *Love of our
Country*, *Dutiful affection* in the sacred relations of life, and principally *Piety*
toward God, who is conceived as the Ruler and Father of that most venerable and sacred political Body, the Rational Creation, of which our several
countries are but small parts. The nature of the three former cardinal virtues
may be known from what was said above about the supreme Good, and
the comparisons made of the several objects of our natural desires: and the
nature of Justice will be more fully explained in the second Book,* where
we treat of the several rights of mankind.

These {four} virtues they maintain to be naturally connected and insep-
arable not only in their highest degree, which they call the *Heroic;* but in
the middle degree, called that of *Temperance,* {when the lower appetites are
easily governed: altho' they may be separated in the first weaker disposition

14. See Latin text, note 11.
* See book ii, Chap. 2 and Chap. 4.

tamen quaedam propria deducunt <75> officia, idque non inconcinne. <alia tamen videtur ratio & facilior & magis a natura.> Sed haec hactenus.

{IV. Suboritur hic quaestio subdifficilis, de virtutis origine, an scil: naturâ hominibus obveniat, an consuetudine et institutione, an instinctu quodam divino. Qua de re breviter monendum; quae naturâ eveniunt ea omnia Deo accepta referenda: neque minorem benefico gratiam habendam, ideo quod, pro larga ipsus bonitate, eadem quamplurimis dederat beneficia; vel quod stabili quadam ratione, certaque naturae lege ab ipso constituta, ex ea eventuum serie, cujus ipse moderator fuerat et dispensator, haec commoda nobis obvenerint; vel etiam interventu aliorum, quibus ipse usus est ministris aut legatis. Ob ipsas igitur virtutes omnis Deo gratia habenda. Neque incredibile videatur, Deum mundi universi moderatorem suo numine homines ad honesta et praeclara ducere et instigare; incredibile potius, eum in bonis praecipuis largiundis, quam in vilioribus, esse restrictiorem. Cunctis quidem quae a fortuna pendent opportunitatibus plus pollet natura, atque multo magis instinctus divinus. Vires tamen insitas plurimum promovebit doctrina, institutio, et exercitatio. Ut omnes hae causae conspirent praecipuè optandum. Sine doctrina non nunquam valebit ipsa natura instinctusque <76> divinus: sine aliqua ἐυφυία,[12] sive naturali virtutis indole,

---

12. "good nature." Aristotle, *Ethica Nicomachea* 1114b, 12.

called the degree of *Continence.*} And yet from each of them some peculiar duties are derived which they dilate upon very agreeably. But so far for this subject.

IV. There arises here a question of some little difficulty about the original of virtue, whether it arises from the very constitution of our nature, or from instruction and habit, or by some divine influence or power. On which subject we briefly suggest, that whatever <69> flows from any natural principles is as much owing to God, {and we are as much indebted to him for it, as if it had in an extraordinary manner been effected by his power}. Nor ought our gratitude to be less for any benefit, on this account that the liberal Donor has diffused the like goodness amongst many, or that these benefits have been bestowed upon us in a certain regular method, according to some fixed laws, in consequence of a stable series of causes determined at first by the goodness and wisdom of the Author of nature; or because he has used other voluntary agents as his ministers and instruments, {whom he has inclined or excited to do us such good offices}. Any virtues therefor {which we find in ourselves} should be the chief matter of thanksgiving and praises to God. And yet there's nothing incredible in this that the universal Governor of the world should also by his power inspire and excite men to whatever is glorious and honourable: nay 'tis rather improbable that he who had displayed such goodness in bestowing external advantages on us, should not also exert the same goodness and power in bestowing the more noble benefits. {*} <Nature has a great power, and providence much more, concerning the circumstances that depend on fortune. But instruction, education and discipline would advance the internal powers a great deal>. The concurrence of these {three} causes to be sure [must undoubtedly make men virtuous] [should be desiderable]. We sometimes see an happy natural disposition, with something like a divine impulse, produce great matters without much aid from instruction {or discipline}: but without some tolerable natural disposition, <70> at least without a natural taste

---

* {This cannot appear strange to those who ascribe to the constant operation of God those forces in the material world by which its frame is preferred. See Antoninus B.I, c. 17 and B. ix. c. 48.} [The translator refers to the *Meditations* of Marcus Aurelius Antoninus, but there is not a chapter 48 in book IX.]

quae saltem virtutes capere possit, (quam nemini ferè prorsus negatam videmus,) nihil valebit disciplina: sine qua tamen rarius in ulla arte quicquam praeclari sperare licebit.}

Neque moramur in Aristotelis mediocritate examinanda, quae quamvis cognitione haud indigna sit, primariam tamen virtutis aut honesti notionem non attingit. Atque licet non solum in appetitionibus humilioribus, aliisve nobilioribus, quibus quisque suam tantum spectat utilitatem, verum etiam in arctioribus benevolentiae vinculis, mediocritas quaedam, ab extremis excessûs aut defectûs utrinque reducta, sit laudanda; nullus tamen potest esse excessus in iis animi propensionibus quae sunt honestissimae; amore nempe et veneratione Dei opt. max., caritate illa quae totum complectitur humanum genus, aut in ipso {verae} virtutis amore<, si modo verae adsint de virtute sententiae>.

V.[IV.] Utilior forte, et magis a natura petita, et facilior, alia videbitur divisio, pro eorum erga quos virtutes sunt exercendae diversitate, in *pietatem erga Deum,* et *bonitatem erga homines:* tertium adjungi potest genus, earum virtutum quae suam cujusque respiciunt perfectionem. Atque licet nihil sit in ipsa philautia praeclari aut honesti; [hominisque] [Neque aliter hominis] erga se officia {ita} sint venusta et <77> laudanda, [si] [quam quatenus] vel ad pietatis vel ad bonitatis officia referantur; horum tamen consideratio non est omittenda, cum, aliis omnibus officiis peragendis, homines magis reddant expeditos et idoneos.

Hanc divisionem persecuturis, prima se offert pietas erga Deum; quae consideranda est, ut ipsius innotescat et natura, et ad vitam beatam momentum: proxime veniunt virtutes erga homines alios: et denique, ea sui cultura quae et pietati et humanitati exercendae inserviet.

or capacity for virtue (which however scarce any one wants altogether) instruction {or custom} would be of little or no effect. {Of these two a good
natural disposition seems of greater consequence, as nature is a more stable
principle. And yet instruction and habit wonderfully improve the natural
disposition;} and 'tis but seldom that without their aids we can expect to
see any thing great and eminent.

We shall not dwell further upon that mediocrity insisted on {so much}
by *Aristotle:* for tho' it well deserves our consideration, yet 'tis plain that
the primary notion of virtue does not consist in it. And however it may
hold not only as to our lower appetites, and some of the more sublime ones
by which we are pursuing more manly enjoyments of a selfish kind, but
even in the more narrow affections of good-will, that a middle degree,
equally removed from both the extremes of excess and defect, is the most
laudable; yet there can be no excess in these affections in which virtue chiefly
consists, to wit in the <reverence and> love of God, and in that extensive
good-will toward all, or in the love of moral excellence, {provided we have
just notions of it}.[15]

V. There's another division more obvious and perhaps more natural, according to the several objects toward whom our virtues are to be exercised,
into *Piety* toward God, and *Good-will* toward Men: to which a third branch
may be added of such virtues {as immediately relate to *ourselves*}, by which
a man immediately aims at his own perfection. And altho' there be nothing
morally lovely in mere self-love, and it <71> must be some reference to our
duty to God, or to that toward men, which must make a man's duties toward himself appear venerable or amiable; yet this third branch must not
be omitted, since it is by means of a proper self-culture that we must be
<fit and> prepared for any honourable services to God or mankind{; and
with this reference they are exceedingly amiable}.

In pursuit of this last division, we first explain the duties of Piety, both
to shew their true nature, and their importance toward our happiness; next
we consider our duties toward our fellows; and lastly that self-culture which
is subservient to Piety and Humanity.

15. Added by the translator, but present in the 1742 edition.

De Virtutibus et Officiis erga Deum.

I. Duabus partibus absolvitur omnis erga Deum pietas, ut scil. [vera de Deo sentiamus] [veras foveamus de Deo sententias], et cultum praestemus veris [hisce] sententiis consonum. Veras de Deo sententias docet [philosophia prima] [metaphysica], aut ea pneumatologiae pars, quae theologia dicitur naturalis. Deum nempe esse Ens primum, et a nullo alio pendens; omni perfectione absolutum <et infinitum>; potentissimum, sapientissimum, et optimum sive benignissimum; mundi universi creatorem, fabricatorem, moderatorem, omnisque boni fontem inexhaustum. His, in ethicis utimur ut concessis, anquirentes <78> de iis animi affectionibus, et cultu sive interno sive externo, qui sint his sententiis consoni.

Monstrabit cujusque sensus, tantam naturae primae praestantiam, et amplitudinem infinitam, omni admiratione, et celebratione, summaque animi submissi veneratione, esse accipiendam. Quumque nulla homini sit appetitio magis naturalis illâ veri cognoscendi, rerumque causas perscrutandi maximarum, et cognitione dignissimarum; nullum erit hominis opus, Dei cognoscendi studio, virtutumque divinarum venerabunda contemplatione, aut honestius aut jucundius. Neque quidem, sine ea naturae praestantissimae cognitione, eximiae intelligendi vires, a natura datae, satis exerceri possunt aut expleri.

CHAPTER IV <72>

Our Duties toward God.

I. Piety consists in these two essential parts, first in just opinions {and sentiments} concerning God, and then in {affections and} worship suited to them.[1]

The just opinions concerning God are taught in <that part of pneumatology that is called> natural Theology or Metaphysicks: to wit, that the Deity is the original independent Being, compleat in all possible perfection, of boundless power, wisdom and goodness, the Creator, Contriver and governor of this world, and the inexhaustible source of all Good. We take these principles as granted in treating of Morals, and inquire what affections of soul, what worship internal or external is suited to them.[2]

The inward sense {of the heart}[3] must shew at once, that this preeminence and infinite grandeur of the original cause of all, ought to be entertained with the highest admiration and praise and submissive veneration of soul: and since there's no desire more becoming the rational nature than that of knowledge, and of discovering the {natures and} causes of the greatest subjects, no occupation of the mind can be more honourable, or even delightful, than studying to know <God and reverently surveying> the divine perfections: nor indeed without ascending to the knowledge of the supreme Excellency, can these honourable intellectual powers we are endued with find a proper object fully to exercise and satisfy them. <73>

1. Cf. Pufendorf, *De officio* 1.4.1.
2. For a detailed account of God's attributes, see *Synopsis* 3.2–4, pp. 97–114 and *System* 1.9, vol. I, pp. 168–208.
3. This sense is the internal sense explored in the *Inquiry* on beauty (V. 18–21).

II. Quod ad attributa attinet quae *moralia* dicuntur: numen omnium primum et benignissimum, quod pro infinita sua vi, bonitate, et sapientia, omnia solertissime fabricavit, suam rei cuique dans naturam, vires, sensus, appetitus, rationem, ipsasque virtutes; largaque manu suppeditans quibusque, ea omnia quae {secundum suam cujusque naturam}, ad voluptatem, [beateque vivendum] [aut beatitudinem, naturae ipsorum accomodatam] facere possunt; animo agnoscendum est gratissimo, amore gratuito, comprobatione et laudatione, laetaque spe et fiducia, <79> ab omni arrogantia et superbia purgata.

Si plenior habeatur bonitatis divinae et sanctitatis ratio; quòd omni virtute et bonitate delectetur; quod bonos omnes comprobet et amet; omnibus hinc effulgebunt bonis spes laetiores, major et laetior fiducia, cum ardentiore virtutis et Dei ipsius amore; stabilique securitate et tranquillitate, animi se suaque omnia divinae permittentis providentiae. Existet etiam Dei imitandi studium, iisque qui in Deo sunt similes sovendi animi affectiones; et stabile simul consilium ea omnia pro virili agendi, quibus explere valeamus munus quod nobis imposuit Deus et natura, sive cadat fortuna secunda, sive adversa.

Haec Dei ob omnem virtutem et bonitatem gratuitam venerandi colendique, contemplatio, quem {bonus quisque} testem animo intuetur, et comprobatorem, [nos] [virumque quemque bonum] perducet ad καταληκτικὸν illud, summum purissimae virtutis apicem, ut in ipso Deo imitando et amando, munusque nobis assignatum obeundo; in ipsa denique virtute, et officiis, omnem, aut longe praecipuum, officiorum fructum petendum censeamus. Neque sine ea Dei agnitione, eoque in Deum animo, poterit vir bonus et benignus quicquam fidenter sperare, vel de se, vel de suis quos <80> habet carissimos, aut de rerum universitate. Neque satiari potest aut expleri ipsa virtus, omni hominum generi benigne prospiciens, aut ipse honestissimus virtutis amor et comprobatio, nisi aliqua natura reperiatur, virtute omni perfectissima; in qua cognita, amata, et redamante, possit vir

II. As to the moral Attributes of God: that original and most gracious Power which by its boundless Force, Goodness, and Wisdom has formed this Universe <with the greatest skill>, granting to each being its proper nature, powers, senses, appetites, or reason, and even moral excellencies; and with a liberal hand supplying each one with all things conducive to such pleasure and happiness as their natures can receive; this Power, I say, should be acknowledged with the most grateful affections, with generous love, and the highest praises and thanksgiving; and with a joyful hope and confidence, purified from all {vanity,} pride, or arrogance, {since we are such dependent creatures, who owe to it all we enjoy}.

If we more fully consider the divine Goodness and moral Perfection; that the Deity must delight in all virtue and goodness; that he must approve and love all good men: this will suggest to all such still more joyful hopes, with an higher and more delightful confidence and trust, and more ardent love of virtue and of the Deity. Hence will arise a stable security and tranquillity of the soul, which can commit it self and all its concerns to the divine Providence. Hence also a constant endeavour to imitate the Deity, and cultivate in ourselves all such affections as make us resemble him; with a steddy purpose of exerting all our powers in acting well that part which God and nature has assigned us, whether in prosperity or adversity.

Such contemplations of the venerable and adorable Excellency and gratuitous Goodness of God, whom <74> every good man regards as the witness and approver of his actions, will lead us to an ultimate resting in virtue: that highest purity of it, by which we look upon [conformity to the divine Will] [the imitation and love of God], the discharging the duty assigned us by him, and performing our part well, as [the chief good, the chief] [the whole or the most important and desirable] fruit of virtue. Nor without this knowledge of the Deity, and these affections, can a good benevolent heart find any sure ground of hope and security, either as to it self or the dearest objects of its affection, or as to the whole state of the universe. Nor can the virtuous mind, which extends its affectionate concerns to all mankind, or the love <and praise> of moral excellence it self, ever be satisfied and at rest, unless it be assured that there's some excellent Being complete in every perfection, in the knowledge and love of which, with a prospect of being beloved by it, it can fully acquiesce, and commit it self and the

bonus conquiescere; seque, suos omnes, et totum hominum genus, illius providentiae benignae securus committere.

{Atque quamvis nemo sit qui imbecillitate animi varia, morbisque et vitiis non laboret; quique vitae suae actae tenorem examinans, plurimis gravissimisque erroribus se implicatum, plurima turpia et foeda in Deum hominesque admisisse, non inveniet, unde et poenas haud leves sibi irrogandas jure metuet: tanta tamen Dei conspicitur bonitas et clementia; tantâ lenitate mitique indulgentia, in homines imbecillos et depravatos, per tot secula imperium exercuit; ut iis quibus ipsum pie colere, ejusque praeceptis, quantum hominum infirmitas contendere potest, parere cordi est, haud quaquam desperandum videbitur, quin seriâ poenitentia, virtutisque studio conantibus, Deus futurus sit propitius et placabilis; quippe qui pro sapientia sua immensa, eam clementiam, et imperii sui legumque majestatem, inter se amicè conciliandi, rationem aliquam <81> excogitare potest. Idque nemini dubium esse potest, quod nobis satis est, in pietate perfecta vim ad beate vivendum esse maximam, ejusque assequendae studia sincera, vel ad foelicitatem consequendam, vel ad miseriae levationem plurimum valitura.}

Ad Deum suâ naturâ referuntur sublimiores animi vires: a Deo ortae, ad Deum nos revocant et retrahunt rationis vires egregiae, animi affectiones et caritates omnes latius diffusae, ipse etiam decori et honesti sensus et amor. His vinculis ad Deum aptatur et alligatur natura omnis ratione praedita,

dearest objects of its cares, and the whole of mankind to his gracious providence with full security.[4]

And altho' there's none of human race who are not involved in manifold
weaknesses<, vices,> and disorders of soul, none who upon reflection won't
find themselves intangled in many errors and misapprehensions about matters of the greatest importance {to the true happiness of life}; and in the
guilt of manifold crimes committed against God and our fellow-creatures;
on account of which they may justly dread {the divine justice, and appre-
hend} some impendent punishments: yet such is the divine goodness and
clemency; with such long-suffering and mercy has he continued for many
ages to exercise his gracious providence about weak corrupted <75> mortals, that such as sincerely love [worship] him, and desire, as far as human
weakness can go, to serve him with duty {and gratitude}, need not entirely
lose hopes of his favour. Nay they have some probable ground to expect,
that God will be found propitious and placable to such as repent of their
sins and are exerting their utmost endeavours in the pursuits of virtue; and
that his infinite wisdom {and goodness} will find out some method of exercising his mercy toward a guilty world, so as not to impair the authority
of his laws and the sanctity of his moral administration, {tho' human wisdom should never particularly discover it}. And further, what is sufficient
for our purpose in the present question can admit of no debate; that the
perfection of virtue, must constitute our supreme felicity; and that the ardent desires, and sincere efforts to attain it, cannot fail of a most important
effect, either in obtaining compleat felicity, {or at least some lower degree
of it,} or a great alleviation of misery.[5]

The sublimer powers of the soul of their own nature lead us to the Deity:
as they are derived from him, they powerfully draw us back to him again.
Our high powers of reason, our benevolent affections of the more extensive
kinds, and our natural sense and love of [moral excellence] [what is right
and honourable], have all this natural tendency. By these bonds all rational
beings are as it were connected with and affixed to the Deity, if they have

4. See *System* 1.10.4, vol. I, pp. 215–16.

5. This paragraph was added in 1745 and bears witness to Hutcheson's rather anti-
calvinistic attitude toward grace and election.

cui nobiliores animi sui partes curae est excolere. Neque Deum tantum ideo amat, quod ex eo sibi speret foelicitatem: ex ipsa enim virtutis omnisque praestantiae comprobatione, sensuque quem homini inseruit natura, per se, et sua sponte, gratuitus efflorescit amor et veneratio eorum in quibus conspiciuntur virtutes, nulla suae utilitatis habita ratione.

Quum vero voluntatis motus, et propensiones omnes vegetiores, sua sponte se exerant, atque vicissim exercitatione vigeant et augeantur; saepius, et statis temporibus, exercenda est pietas, in officiis honestissimis et laetissimis, Deum contemplando, et laudando, gratias ei agendo, {delictorum veniam obnixè <82> rogando,} nos nostraque ipsi secura cum fiducia permittendo; ejus et auxilia implorando, ut animos virtutibus excolere, et mores emendare, omniaque honesta vitae officia obire valeamus. Quin etiam perfectissimum illud omnis virtutis exemplar saepius recolendo, accendetur omnis honestatis studium ardentius.

{Cavendum autem ne vana quadam opinione abrepti, pietatem nostram cultumve, Deo utilitatem aliquam afferre putemus, eumve sui causa cultum a nobis flagitare. Nostra in eo praecipue vertitur utilitas; nostri causa eum Deus exigit, ut summa fruamur foelicitate et virtute, purissimisque animi gaudiis. Qui hanc de praeceptis religiosis fovet sententiam, ab utroque extremorum pariter abhorrebit; *impietate* scil: quae in religiosi cultus omnis neglectu aut contemptione sita est; et *superstitione,* quae saevum quoddam, immane, aut morosum horret quod sibi finxit numen, cultu ritibusque inanibus aut inhumanis placabile.}

III. Hactenus de cultu Dei interno. Natura autem nihil amat solitarium; sua sponte coram aliis prorumpunt animi motus, et quasi contagio alios afficiunt. Non secretò solum, verum palam etiam, et publice colendus est Deus, ut magis vigeat nostra pietas; similisque in aliis sensus excitetur; <83>

any care to cultivate these higher powers. Nor is the spring of this divine love the mere prospect of our own felicity to be found in him: for from our natural <76> sense and approbation of moral excellence, wheresoever it is discovered, there must arise a disinterested love and veneration, detached from all considerations of our own interests.

And further since all the more lively affections of the soul naturally display themselves in some natural expressions, and by this exercise are further strengthned; the good man must naturally incline to employ himself frequently and at stated times in some acts of devotion, contemplating and adoring the divine excellencys; giving thanks for his goodness; humbly imploring the pardon of his transgressions; expressing his submission, resignation, and trust in God's Providence; and imploring his aid in the acquisition of virtue, and in reforming his temper, that he may be furnished for every good work. For the frequent meditation upon the supreme and perfect model of all goodness must powerfully kindle an ardent desire of the same {in every ingenuous heart}.

But here we must avoid any imaginations that our piety or worship can be of any advantage to the Deity, or that he requires it of us, for any interest of his own. 'Tis rather our own interest that is promoted by it, and 'tis for our sakes that God enjoins it; that we may obtain the truest felicity, and excellence, and the purest joys. By entertaining these sentiments concerning the worship of God, we shall be secured from both the extremes, of *impiety* on one hand, which consists in a neglect and contempt of all religious worship; and *superstition* on the other, which is an abject dread of <77> a cruel or capricious Dæmon men form to themselves, which they conceive appaisable by savage or fantastick rites.[6]

III. Hitherto we have treated of internal worship. But our nature scarcely relishes any thing in solitude; all our affections naturally discover themselves before others, and infect them as with a contagion. This shews that God is not only to be worshipped in secret, but [openly] in publick; which also tends to increase our own devotion, and to raise like sentiments in

---

6. This paragraph was added in 1745. See *System* 1.10.5, vol. I, p. 218.

eamque beatitudinem et perfectionem cum aliis communicemus.

Commendantur et haec officia sua utilitate: cuique prosunt, quod suam cujusque augeant pietatem; ex communi vero omnium pietate, omnes ad omnia vitae munera obeunda promptiores longe fiunt et alacriores, et ab omni improbo et iniquo coërcentur. Atque inde est quod semper apud homines invaluit haec persuasio, ad homines in officio continendos, atque ad eorum conjunctionem et consociationem tuendam et conservandam, plurimum posse religionem.

Quum {Dei} cultus omnis externus sit piorum animi affectuum declaratio; patebit, in his cultum eum praecipue versari, ut Dei laudes celebremus, easque aliis illustremus; ut gratias palam agamus, nostramque in eo fiduciam profiteamur; ut precibus in solemni hominum coetu invocantes, ejus potentiam, providentiam, et bonitatem agnoscamus: ut delictorum confessione, misericordiam imploremus et veniam; nos denique totos ipsi ducendos, regendos, et emendandos permittamus. {Ubi pia foventur istiusmodi dogmata quae memoravimus, iisque convenientes voluntates, accendetur etiam studium anquirendi de omnibus quae dederit Deus suae voluntatis documentis; cujus quaecunque eluxerit significatio, sive per <84> ipsam rerum naturam, sive alio quovis miro et clariori, supra vulgarem naturae sortem, indicio, quod sperasse videntur philosophorum principes, eam vir bonus, laetus amplexabitur.}

others, and makes them thus partakers of this sublime enjoyment.[7] This social worship {is not only the natural result of inward piety, but} is also recommended by the many advantages redounding from it; as it has a great influence in promoting a general piety: and from a general sense of religion prevailing in a society all its members are powerfully excited to a faithful discharge of every duty of life, and restrained from all injury or wickedness. And hence it is that mankind have always been persuaded, that religion was of the highest consequence to engage men to all social duties, and to preserve society in peace and safety.[8]

The external worship must be the natural expressions of the internal devotion of the soul; and must therefor consist in celebrating the praises of God, and displaying his perfections to others; in thanksgivings, and expressions of our trust in him; in acknowledging his power, his universal Providence and goodness, by prayers <in solemn assemblies> {for what we need}; in confessing our sins, and imploring his mercy <and forgiveness>; and finally in committing <78> ourselves entirely to his conduct, government, and correction, with an absolute resignation.[9]

Where such devout sentiments [doctrines] are cherished, and affections suitable to them, there must be kindled an ardent desire of inquiring into all indications of the Divine will. And whatever discoveries we find made of it, whether in the very order of nature, or by any supernatural means, which some of the wisest of the Heathens [the best philosophers] seem to have expected, the good man will embrace them with joy.

7. See *System* 1.10.4, vol. I, pp. 217–18.
8. This short paragraph is a substitute for Pufendorf's long discussion on the absolute necessity of religion for the security of the state.
9. See *System* 1.10.4, vol. I, p. 218.

CAPUT V

De Officiis erga alios Homines exercendis.

I. Quae erga homines exercendae sunt virtutes et officia, eodem recti honestique sensu cernuntur et commendantur; atque ad eas virtutes fovendas et exercendas, variis impulsionibus naturalibus incitamur. Insita sunt cuique benigniorum plurima affectionum genera, pro diversis hominum conjunctionibus et necessitudinibus, a natura constitutis. Maribus et foeminis mutuos inseruit natura amores, {animos miris modis accendentes;} neque [non] tam beluinam respicientes voluptatem, quam amicam vitae societatem, summa ea caritate devinctam, quam virtutum opinio utrinque accenderat; quarum indicia edere solet et ipsa corporis pulchritudo. Insitum est sobolis procreandae desiderium, et procreatae praecipua cura, et amor eximius et singularis: haec subsequuntur fratrum, sororumque <85> {germanorum et patruelium}, consobrinorum, sobrinorumque, quin [et] etiam affinium, caritates.

Quin et subtiliora quaedam sunt societatis vincula. (1) Boni bonos, "moribus" inter se "similes" necessario diligunt, quasi propinquitate "conjunctos" et natura.[1] (2) "Beneficiis ultro citro datis acceptisque," magis inter se "devinciuntur" homines.[2] (3) Serpit etiam latius benevolentia in familiaritatibus et viciniis, ubi <ulla est> virtutum vel vulgarium {facta est} significatio. (4) Porrigit se etiam ad cives; ubi plures, ratione monstrante, communis utilitatis causa, sub uno imperio sunt conjuncti. (5) Atque tandem complexu suo totum continet genus humanum, et siqua sunt alia animantium genera superiora. (6) Hisce conjuncta est miserorum commiseratio,

---

1. Cicero, *De officiis* 1.55.5.
2. Cicero, *De officiis* 1.56.10–57.1.

81

Our Duties toward Mankind.

I. The <virtues and> duties to be performed toward others are in like manner pointed out to us by our natural sense of right and wrong [by the same sense of what is right and honourable]; and we have many natural affections exciting us to <to cherish and practise> them. There are many sorts of kind affections in the several relations of life, which are plainly implanted by nature. Thus nature has implanted in the two sexes a strong mutual affection, which has a wonderful power, and has in view not so much the low gratification common to us with brutes, as a friendly society for life, founded upon that endearment which arises from a mutual good opinion of each others moral characters, of which even beauty of form gives some evidence. There's also implanted a strong desire of offspring, and <a special care and> a very tender peculiar affection toward them. In consequence of this, there are also natural affections among brothers, sisters, cousins, and remoter kindred, and even such as are allied by marriages.[1]

But there are still more subtile social bonds. Good men who know each other have a natural affection not unlike that among kinsmen. 2. Men are still further bound by an intercourse of mutual offices. 3. But benevolent affections still spread further, among acquaintance and neighbours, where there's any measure even of the commonest virtues. 4. Nay they diffuse themselves even to all our Countrymen, members of the <80> same polity, when multitudes are once united in a political body for their common interest. 5. And {in men of reflection} there's a more extensive good-will embracing all mankind, or all [higher kinds of] intelligent natures <if there are any>. 6. Along with these, there's a tender compassion toward any that

---

1. Cf. Cicero, *De officiis,* I.54. This chapter is parallel to Pufendorf, *De officio* I.8, and, as Carmichael suggests in his *Notes on Puf.,* p. 76, Hutcheson follows Cicero's *De officiis* I, 42–60, and *Lelius, de amicitia.*

et sublevandi studium; atque cum foelicioribus, ubi nulla intervenerat si-
multatis causa, laeta congratulatio.

Per se et sua sponte comprobantur hi motus benigni; in iis quisque sibi
placet; lubens iisdem, tanquam naturae accommodatis, indulget; et similes
quosque in aliis comprobat et veneratur. Contrarii autem motus, qui saepe
in homines cadunt, ira, odium, invidentia, ultionis appetitio, et malevolentia omnis, sunt proximè et per se molesti; in iis recordandis nemo sibi
placere, aut <86> similes in aliis comprobare potest; saepe sunt erubescendi
et detestandi: quumque videntur et justi et necessarii, nihil in se continent
aut laetabile, aut gloriosum.

{II}. Satis docuimus quantum hae affectiones benignae, cum officiis quae
ex iis fluunt, ad vitam beatam conferant. Norunt omnes, qui non exuta
humanitate induerunt beluae feritatem, sine mutuo amore, benevolentia et
beneficientia, vix ullam percipi posse foelicitatem: neque vitam solitariam,
quantumvis copiosam, homini esse vitalem. Stabiliores etiam et latius patentes quasque animi affectiones benignas, diximus esse honestiores. Neque
tamen ad vitam beatam sufficient, sine actione, voluntates ignavae, quamvis
benignae: vires enim insitas excolere et exercere est laetissimum; propen-
samque voluntatem naturâ sequuntur actiones et officia benigna.

Haec igitur est virtutum sociarum summa, ut quisque humani generis
fovens caritatem, communi omnium pro viribus consulat prosperitati [foe-
licitati]: atque interea, arctiores omnes, in variis vitae necessitudinibus, propensiones foveat, singulorum quorumvis, quod patitur communioris ratio,
inserviens utilitati et foelicitati.

{III.} Quum autem paucis, communi omnium utilitati propius inserviendi,
vires <87> et occasiones suppetant; quisque tamen aliquid in propinquorum, amicorum, vicinorum, aut civium utilitatem, afferre [conferre] queat;

are in distress, with a desire of succouring them; and a natural congratulation with the prosperous, unless there has interveened some cause of aversion or enmity.

These kind affections [motions] are immediately approved for themselves: every one feels a complacence in them, and applauds himself in indulging them as some way suited to his nature <and approves and honours like affections in others>: but the contrary affections [motions] which are occasionally incident to men, such as anger, hatred, envy, revenge, and malice, are of themselves uneasy; nor can any one applaud himself in remembring them, or approve like passions in others: they are often matter of shame and remorse; and even when they seem justifiable and necessary, yet they contain nothing joyful, nothing glorious.

II. We have abundantly shewn how much these kind affections with the suitable virtuous offices contribute to our happiness. All men who have not quite divested themselves of humanity, and taken up the temper of savage beasts, must feel that without mutual love, good-will and kind offices, we can enjoy no happiness: and that solitude, even in the greatest affluence of external things, must be miserable. We also shewed that the calm, steddy [that the more stable and more extensive] affections were more honourable {than the turbulent}. But we must still remember, that mere kind affection without action, or slothful wishes <81> will never make us happy. Our chief joy consists in the exercise of our more honourable powers; and when kind affections are tolerably lively they must be the spring of vigorous efforts to do good.

This therefore is the sum of all social virtues, that with an extensive affection toward all, we exert our powers vigorously for the common interest, and at the same time cherish all the tender affections in the several narrower relations, which contribute toward <the utility and> the prosperity of individuals, as far as the common interest will allow it.

III. But as there are very few who have either abilities or opportunities of doing any thing which can directly and immediately affect the interests of all; and yet every one almost can contribute something toward the advantage of his kinsmen, his friends or his neighbours, and by so doing plainly

(qua ratione etiam communi humani generis inserviet foelicitati;) in arctioribus hisce officiis rectè versamur, ubi communiori non adversantur utilitati, neque officiorum latius patentium adest opportunitas. Immo in eo naturam sequimur et Deum, qui arctioribus hisce naturae vinculis, alios aliis fecit nobis longè cariores, nostraeque curae et benevolentiae praecipuae commendavit.

Haud igitur reprimendi, aut imminuendi, arctiores hi diligendi sensus, in vita, et jucundi saepe, et necessarii. Immo omnes fovendi potius et augendi, ut cujusque est momentum ad communem omnium utilitatem. Quae tamen latissime patet benevolentia, ea praecipue fovenda; ipse etiam honesti amor, atque stabile Deo in omnibus obsequendi studium; quibus moderatoribus subjectae caritates arctiores, virtutis carmen optime absolvent. Hoc etiam sua cujusque utilitas postulat: quum, ut plenius mox docebitur, ita nati sint homines, ut sine aliorum ope et auxilio, sine mutuo officiorum commercio, singuli {neque} suae saluti, nedum vitae foelicitati aut jucunditati, consulere valeant [nequeant]. Atqui, amicis praecipue < 88 > officiis et beneficientia, concilianda est aliorum benevolentia; eorumque studia, ad nostram utilitatem amplificandam, adsciscenda. Contrario autem animi habitu, sordidâ philautiâ, multoque magis vi et injuriis, alienantur a nostra utilitate vicinorum animi; nascuntur odia, et dissidia; mala insuper omnia ab omnibus nobis infensis merito metuenda. Immo existunt in animis nostris affectus tetrici et molesti, continuae vigent suspiciones, et metus non vani: quum, ad injurias propulsandas et ulciscendas, incitentur non solum hi quos injuriae proxime tetigerunt, verum intacti, quibus super conditione communi est cura.

{Neque alia praetereunda quae, mirâ solertia, hominum conjunctioni amicae tuendae, injuriisque et damnis avertendis, machinata est natura. Quanta enim vultui venustas accedit ex amica laetitia et hilaritate moderata, laetâque sympathia et gratulatione! Quanta pulchritudo ex animo con-

promotes the general good; 'tis plainly our duty to employ our selves in these less extensive offices, while they obstruct no interest more extensive, and we have no opportunities of more important services. In doing so we follow nature and God {its author}, who by these stronger bonds has made some of mankind much dearer to us than others, and recommended them more peculiarly to our care <and benevolence>.

We must not therefor, {from any airy views of more heroic extensive offices,} check or weaken the tender natural affections, which are great sources of pleasure in life, and of the greatest necessity. Nay 'tis our duty rather to cherish and encrease them, in proportion to their importance to the common interest. But at the same time we should chiefly fortify the most extensive <82> affections, the love of moral excellence, and the steddy purpose of conformity to the divine will. While these nobler affections have the controll of all the rest, the strengthning the tender affections in the several narrower attachments of life will rather tend to compleat the beauty of a moral character, and the harmony of life. The interest too of each individual should lead him to this cultivation of all kind affections; since, as we shall presently shew, so are we formed by nature that no man {in solitude}, without the aids of others and an intercourse of mutual offices, can preserve himself in safety or even in life, not to speak of any pleasure or happiness. Now 'tis plain, that 'tis only by kind offices and beneficence that we can procure the good-will of others, or engage their zeal to promote our interests: whereas by contrary dispositions, by a sordid selfishness, and much more by violence and injuries, we incur the hatred of others; wrath and discord must arise, and we must live in perpetual dread of the evils which the resentments of others may occasion to us. Nay further from such conduct there naturally arise in our own minds all the sullen, uneasy passions of suspicion, {jealousy,} and too well grounded fears: since not only the persons immediately injured, but all others who have any regard to the common interest, are roused {by a just indignation} to repell and revenge any injuries attempted against their neighbours.

Nor should we omit some other wonderful contrivances in nature to preserve a social life among men and avert injuries <and damages>. What a manifest accession of beauty <83> is made to the countenance from friendly mirth, and cheerfulness, and an affectionate sympathy and con-

stante, sibique recti conscio, atque ex interna sui comprobatione! In amici, ejusve qui grato beneficii sensu movetur, vultu, quae gratia, quamque mitis flamma ex benignis emicat oculis! Intentatâ autem injuria aut noxa, ubi ejusdem propulsandae spes est, in vultu torvo se prodit ira, trucibus ex oculis ignes existunt terribiles. Ubi, contra, nulla mali <89> avertendi spes est, quanta eloquentiae vi instruxit natura, non homines solum, verum et muta penè animantia, premente tristitia, dolore, metuque graviore? Qualis illa vox flebilis et querula! Qualis vultus oculique moesti et dejecti, suspiria, lachrymae, gemitus! Quanta eorum omnium vis ad commiserationem apud omnes excitandam, quò promptius opem ferant, maturiusve ab incoepta injuria abstineant?}

{IV.} Amicitiam hoc loco indictam transire, vetat et ipsius honestas et utilitas: quam admirabilem benevolentiae magnitudinem qui ab indigentia ortam volunt, ut quod quisque minus per se consequi possit, id accipiat ab alio, humilem illi tribuunt et minimè generosum ortum, et fundamentum parum firmum: quum, commutatâ utilitate, tolleretur omnis ex hoc fonte profluens amicitia: quae omnis etiam fucata foret simulatio, non vera benevolentia.

Oritur igitur amicitia ex naturali ea honestatis, quam saepius memoravimus, comprobatione: cujus ubi fit significatio, inter eos quibuscum vivimus, per se efflorescit summa caritas et benevolentia. Sua enim sponte "bonos boni diligunt adsciscuntque sibi, quasi propinquitate conjunctos et natura."[3] Quae caritas, {studio perspecto,} "beneficiisque ultro" "citro datis acceptisque,"[4] ita <90> augetur, ut nulli naturae conjunctioni cedat; atque ea omnia quae nobismet, amicis etiam, ipsorum causa, exoptamus.

3. Cicero, *Laelius de amicitia* 50.5.
4. Cicero, *De officiis* 1.56.10.

gratulation with others? How much grace arises from a resolute conscious virtue, and the inward applauses of a good heart? What charms in the countenance, what gentle flames sparkle in the eyes of a friend, or of one who is full of gratitude for any kindness received. On the other hand, when an injury is received or apprehended, and there's hope of {avenging and} repelling it, in what storms of countenance does resentment discover it self, and what wrathful flames flash from the eyes? But when there's no hopes of repelling the injuries intended, with what powerful eloquence has nature instructed even the dumb animals, as well as mankind, under any oppressive sorrow or pain, or any great terror? How moving is that mournful wailing voice, that dejected countenance, weeping and downcast eyes, sighs, tears, groans? How powerfully do they move compassion in all, that they may <promptly> either give succour in distress, or desist from the intended injuries?[2]

IV. In this place we must not pass by the virtue of *Friendship,* which is so lovely and so useful in life. To alledge that this ardent affection of such admirable force, arises merely from a sense of our own {weakness and} indigence, that so what one cannot obtain by his own power, he may by the aids of others; is ascribing to it a mean and despicable original, and a very unstable foundation: since at this rate any change of interest, {so that we apprehended trouble or inconvenience by our friendlyness,} must at once destroy all affection or good-will: nay indeed there could be no <84> real love, but a mere hypocritical profession of it, from such views of interest.

The true spring of friendship therefor must be that natural approbation and love of moral excellence already mentioned. For whensoever virtue appears in the manners of those with whom we are acquainted, there must arise immediately{, without views of interest,} an high esteem and love toward them. For the Good, as a sort of kindred souls naturally love and desire the society of each other. This love when it is strengthened by seeing each others friendly zeal, and by an intercourse of mutual services, becomes at last as strong as any tyes of blood; so that we have the same ultimate concern about our friends that we have about our selves.

2. See Nicolas Malebranche, *De la recherche de la verité,* V.III.

Quum autem mali, naturâ mobiles et varii, neque aliis, neque sibi diu
placere possint; solos inter bonos stabilis esse potest amicitia; quippe quam
sola virtus aut gignere potest aut continere. Unde constabit, honesta tantummodo ab amicis postulanda, aut amicorum rogatu facienda; ne sub-
ducto fundamento, corruat amicitia. Est igitur amicitia, "animorum moribus et honestate similium, mutua cum caritate arcta conjunctio";[5] quae,
cui contigit, ei est optimus et jucundissimus, ad virtutem et vitam beatam,
comitatus. "Quid" enim "dulcius," quid utilius, "quam habere" virum
probum et prudentem, "quicum omnia audeas sic loqui ut tecum?" Quis
"esset tantus fructus in prosperis rebus, nisi" habeas "qui illis, aeque ac tu
ipse, gauderet? Adversas vero ferre difficile esset, sine eo, qui illas gravius
etiam quam tu ferret": et in utrisque, prudentia sua et consilio tibi opitu-
letur. "Amicitia quoquo te verteris praesto est: nullo loco excluditur, nunquam intempestiva est aut molesta": "nam et secundas res facit splendidi-
ores; et adversas, partiens communicansque, leviores."[6]

{V.} De benignis autem omnibus animi <91> affectionibus sedulò observandum, quod, quamvis nimia esse nequeat, quae latissime patet erga omnes, benevolentia; neque nimius Dei opt. max. aut verae virtutis amor;
amores tamen arctiores, quos vel accendit sanguinis conjunctio, vel consuetudo, quantumvis per se venusti, nimii aliquando esse possunt, neque
viro bono penitus probandi. Duplex est amor, alter *benevolentiae,* quo aliis
bene esse volumus; alter comprobationis aut dilectionis; quae dicitur *complacentia;* quo moribus aliorum delectamur, et eorum frui cupimus consortio. In priore, non adeo facile extra oleas vagamur; si modo semper adsit
debita divinae providentiae animi submissio, et justa in Deo fiducia; atque
si, pro dignitate suâ, magis vigeat ea quae ad omnes pertinet benevolentia;
ita ut nunquam amici utilitati, majorem plurium, aut digniorum, aut om-

---

5. Quotation marks in Hutcheson's text. Cf. Cicero, *Laelius de amicitia* 20.7.
6. Cicero, *Laelius de amicitia* 22.5–22.

But as vitious men are naturally inconstant and variable, with such opposite passions as hinder them from either pleasing themselves long, or being agreeable to others; stable friendship is only to be found among the Good: since it must both be produced and preserved by virtue. And hence flows the grand rule of friendship, that we neither ought to desire our friends concurrence in any thing vitious, nor concurr in it at his request; least we undermine its only foundation. Friendship therefor is "the affectionate union of minds resembling each other in virtuous manners."[3] Which whosoever enjoys, will find it the most agreeable companion in the road to virtue and happiness. What can be sweeter, what more useful than to have a wise worthy friend with whom we may converse as freely as with our own soul: what enjoyment <85> could we have of prosperity without the society of one who as much rejoices in it as we do ourselves? and for adversity, 'tis hard to bear it without the Society of such as perhaps suffer more by sympathy than we do. In both fortunes we need exceedingly the wise counsel of friends: friendship which ever way we turn us will be a present aid; no station excludes it; 'tis never unseasonable or troublesome. 'Tis the chief ornament of prosperity, and exceedingly alleviates our adversities by bearing a share in them.

V. We may further observe in relation to the kind affections, that tho' the most extensive good-will toward all can never be too great, nor can our love of God and virtue admit of any excess; yet all the more contracted affections, arising either from the tyes of blood, or acquaintance, however lovely of themselves, may sometimes be excessive, and beyond that proportion which a good man would approve. Love is often divided into that of *benevolence* or good-will, and that of *complacence* or esteem, by which we are pleased with the tempers of others and desire their society.[4] In the former branch there's less danger of exceeding the just bounds, provided we retain a just submission to, and trust in the divine Providence, and preserve the more extensive affections in their proper superiority, so as not to sacrifice the interest of our country, or of the larger societies, or of persons of su-

---

3. Cf. Cicero, *Lelius, de amicitia* 20.7. See the Latin text, notes 3–6.
4. Cf. Hutcheson, *An Inquiry on Virtue* II.2, pp. 134–36.

nium communem, posthabeamus. De complacentia vero, qui locus magis lubricus, et amicitiae vicinior, sedulo cavendum ne in indignos feratur; ne ad turpia nos alliciat; nevè ita totum occupet hominem, ut amico amisso, aut gravioribus calamitatibus implicito, concidat planè animus, caeterisque omnibus humanitatis aut pietatis officiis fiat ineptus. Praecaventur autem optimè haec incommoda, non reprimendo amores <92> hosce sanctos, etsi arctiores; sed potius summam erga Deum venerationem et amorem fovendo, spemque praecipuam in eo locando, et fiduciam; simul et curas cogitationesque, animo aequiore, porrigendo, ut in aliis etiam similes cernamus virtutes, iis haud inferiores, quas in amicis tanta cum delectatione admirabamur.

periour worth, to that of our friends, or favourites. But the love of complacence which comes nearer to friendship, stands on more slippery ground. We ought to be very cautious that this affection be not employed about unworthy <86> objects; or allure us to any thing vitious; nor so engross the whole man, that if these beloved persons be removed from us, or be involved in any calamities, our souls should sink entirely, and become unfit for all offices of piety and humanity. The best preventive of these evils, is not a restraining and checking all the tender affections of a narrower kind; but rather the cultivating the highest love and veneration toward the Deity, placing our hope and confidence in his Providence; and enlarging our views and concerns with more equitable minds toward the rest of mankind, that we may also discern what real excellencies are among them, perhaps equalling or surpassing those we had with such fond admiration beheld in our peculiar favourites.

CAPUT VI

De Officiis cujusque erga se, et de Animi Cultura.

I. Quum pleraque erga se officia, suae cuique utilitatis ratio commendet, ea non aliter honestam et laudabilem induunt speciem, quam si ad Dei cultum, aut aliorum utilitatem referantur: quod si fiat, nulla erunt sanctiora aut magis laudanda.

Animi cultura in his praecipue vertitur, ut mens veris imbuatur sententiis circa res ad officium pertinentes; atque quam maximam sibi comparet rerum digniorum scientiam; quae omnis est frugifera, conferens aliquid ad bene beateque vivendum, cùm sua jucunditate non levi, tùm quod ducat ad virtutes divinas illustrandas, et faciliorem officiorum cognitionem et functionem. Species enim ab intellectu repraesentatas <93> sequuntur fere voluntatis motus. {Uberiori igitur scientiae parandae, ab iis opera danda quibus adsunt ingenii vires et opportunitates; omnium vero officium est, studio et diligentiâ prudentiam vitae moderatricem parare.} Addiscendum igitur, recte ea aestimare quae appetitus stimulare solent; perspiciendumque quid quaeque "ad bene beateque vivendum"[1] afferant, et qui sint "fines bonorum et malorum";[2] quibus cognitis, inventa est totius vitae ratio. Altè igitur infigendum, quod supra attigimus, summum hominis bonum esse situm, in ipsa pietate erga Deum, et erga homines benevolentiâ et beneficientiâ.

Natura idcircò divina, omnesque ejus virtutes immensae, pro viribus explorandae; praecipuè quae venerationem nostram, amorem, fiduciamque

---

1. Cicero, passim, e.g. *De finibus* 1.14.10.
2. Cicero, passim, e.g. *De finibus* 5.17.9.

Concerning our Duties toward Ourselves,
and the Improvement of the Mind.

I. As {powerful} motives of private interest naturally excite us to our several Duties toward ourselves; to give them something venerable and laudable they must be {ultimately} referred either to the service of God, or some advantages to be procured to others. With this reference they become highly virtuous and honourable.[1]

The culture of our minds principally consists in forming just opinions about our duty; and in procuring a large store of valuable knowledge about the most important subjects: as indeed all branches of knowledge have some use, and contribute in some measure to happiness, either by the immediate pleasure, or by discovering more fully to us the divine perfections, or enabling us better to know and discharge our Duty; since the affections of the will naturally follow the judgments formed by the understanding. All therefor who have abilities and proper opportunities, ought to apply themselves to improve their minds with an extensive knowledge {of nature} in the sciences; and 'tis the duty of all to acquire by diligent meditation and observation that common prudence which should constantly govern our lives. We ought therefor to make just estimates of all things which naturally raise our desires, consider thoroughly <88> their importance to happiness, and find out wherein consists our supreme good; the discovery of which must also discover the true plan of life. <As we observed before> We should therefor deeply impress this on our minds, that our chief good is placed in devout affections toward God, and good-will and beneficence toward mankind.

The divine nature therefor and its boundless exellencies should be matter of our most careful inquiry; especially those attributes which excite our

1. See *System* 1.4.8, vol. I, p. 65.

alliciunt. Delendaeque omnes opiniones aut suspiciones voluntatis cujuspiam aut consilii in Deo, quae summae ipsius sapientiae, aut bonitati humano generi consulenti, adversentur.

Sedulo etiam discendum est, quid homines simus, quos Deus esse velit,
quod munus, quam personam, communem aut cuique propriam, imposuit; ut Deum sequamur, et naturam, unicum ad vitam beatam ducem.

Intrandum est in naturam humanam; aliorum <94> etiam indoles,
agendi principia, et consilia, perspicienda; ne deteriora fingamus aliorum
ingenia, quam recta monstrabit ratio. His enim perspectis, praecidentur
plurimi motus animi tetrici et maligni, ira, odium, et invidia; fovebitur
humanitas, commiseratio, placabilitas denique omnis, et clementia.

{II.} Profuerit etiam saepius hoc reputare, quod ex animo excidere nunquam debet, Dei providentiâ, vel efficiente, vel sanctissimè permittente,
omnia evenire: quaeque aspera videntur et injuriosa, aut contumeliosa, ea
materiam esse virtutibus bonorum divinioribus objectam, in qua se exerceant et augeant: in ipsis autem virtutibus summum est bonum.

"Rerum" autem aliarum "adhibenda est despicientia";[3] quam compara-
bit quicunque sedulo perpenderit, quam viles, sordidae, fluxae, et caducae,
sint corporis voluptates, quaeque res iis inserviunt, atque ipsa quidem corpora! Quam exigua sint gaudia, quam parum necessaria, quae ex vitae cultu
et splendore percipiuntur; quamque etiam incerta; quot curis paranda {et
servanda}, et quam cito satietatem aut nauseam allatura! Deinde, quam im-
perfectae sint omnes scientiae, ad novas obscuritates, "ancipitesque cogi-

---

3. Cicero, *De officiis* 1.72.7.

pious veneration, love, and trust in him. And we are to extirpate all imaginations or suspicions, of any purposes in God which are inconsistent with
the perfection of wisdom, goodness, and love to his creatures.

We ought also carefully to study our own nature and constitution; what
sort of beings God requires we should be; what character* either more general, or more peculiar to each one, God requires he should support and act
up to in life: that thus we may follow God and nature as the sure guide to
happiness.

We ought therefor to enter deeply into human nature; observing both
in ourselves and others the true principles of action, the true tempers and
designs: least we rashly form worse notions of our fellows than just reason
would suggest. By a thorough view of these things, we should often prevent
or suppress many of the harsher and ill-natured passions, anger, hatred,
and envy; <89> and cherish humanity, compassion, lenity, forgiveness and
clemency.[2]

II. This should also continually be in our thoughts, that all things fall out
according to the divine counsel, either directly ordering them, or at least,
permitting them with the most perfect purity, {for some excellent purpo-
ses}: and that consequently what appears to us harsh, injurious, or ignominious, may be designed to afford occasion for exercising and strength-
ening the most divine virtues of the Good; and in them consists their chief
felicity.

The soul should be inured to a generous contempt of other things; and
this we may acquire by looking thoroughly into them: by observing how
mean, sordid, fading, and transitory are all bodily pleasures, all the objects
that afford them, and our very bodies themselves! by observing how small
these joys are and how little necessary, which arise from the external elegance and grandeur of life; and how uncertain they are; what cares they
cost in acquiring and preserving; and how soon they cloy and give disgust!
{as to speculative knowledge;} how uncertain and imperfect are many sci-

---

* {See a full explication of these characters, the *general* including all integrity and
probity of manners, and the *particular,* suited to each one's genius, explained in *Cicero
de Offic.* B. i. 30, 31, 32, *&c.*} [*De officiis,* I. 105–21].

2. Cf. *Essay on Passions* 6.4, pp. 191–93.

tandi curas," et tenebras, animum <95> subinde ducentes impeditum; nostramque, de rebus fere cunctis, detegentes caecitatem aut hebetudinem! Quantula {itidem} res sit gloria, ab ignaris saepe immerito collata; aevi brevis et incerti spatio fruenda, per exiguam terrae partem permeans, cum omni laudatorum et laudantium memoria, aeterna nocte mox obruenda! {Eadem etiam brevis aevi memoria et meditatio, animum ad aspera omnia et adversa ferenda aut spernenda confirmabit: praecipue hoc adjuncto, animum fortiter perpetientem et perferentem, vires suas amplificaturum; atque ad instar ignis validi, omnia conjecta in suam naturam convertentis, aestuque ardentiore prorumpentis; se ea ipsa mala in insignioris laudis virtutisque materiam convertere posse.} Ut brevi praecidamus; humana omnia fluxa, incerta, putida, brevis dieculae spatio interitura, in immenso et utrinque porrecto aeternitatis oceano, mox absorbenda. Quid enim est in hominis vita diu? "cedunt et dies et menses et anni": cuique "moriendum" "est; et illud incertum, an hoc ipso die":[4] quumque advenerit supremum tempus, omne quod praeteriit effluxit: tantum remanet quod virtue et recte factis consecutus sis; beatae immortalitatis spem praebens laetam, quae sola animum vera fortitudine confirmare, et divini imperii <96> justitiam et bonitatem illustrare potest.

[5]Quemadmodum autem in caeteris artibus, praecepta percepisse parum est, neque quicquam magna laude dignum, sine usu et exercitatione, consequi possumus; in ethica, quae est ars vitae, multo magis, rei magnitudo usum quoque exercitationemque desiderat. Suum igitur arrogent sibi justum imperium mens et ratio, viresque animi paene divinae, in appetitus omnes humiliores; eosque regere et reprimere assuescant. Quod quidem continuam ferè, in degenere hoc humani generis statu, flagitat meditationem, attentionem, et disciplinam interiorem; cui plurimum conferent

4. Cicero, *Cato Maior de senectute* 69.9, 74.6.
5. Not a new paragraph in the first edition.

ences, leading the embarassed mind into new obscurities and difficulties
and anxious darkness; and discovering nothing more clearly than the blind-
ness {and darkness}, or the small penetration of our understanding <into
almost everything>. Again how poor an affair is glory {and applause}! which
is ordinarily conferred by the ignorant, who cannot judge of real excellence;
our enjoyment of which is confined within the short space of this life;
which can be diffused through but a small part of this earth; and which
must <90> soon be swallowed up in eternal oblivion along with all the
remembrance either of these who applaud or of the persons applauded.
This [thought too of] [recollection and meditation on] the shortness of
life, will equally enable the soul to bear or despise <hardness and> adversity;
taking this also along, that the soul who bears it well, will obtain new and
enlarged strength; and like a lively fire, which turns every thing cast upon
it into its own nature, and breaks forth superiour with stronger heat, so may
the good man make adverse events matter of new honour and of nobler
virtues. To sum up all briefly, all things related to this mortal state are fleeting, unstable, corruptible; which must speedily perish, and be presently
swallowed up in that boundless ocean of eternity. For what can be called
lasting in human life? Days, months, and years are continually passing
away; all must die, nor is any sure that death shall not surprise him this very
day: and when that last hour overtakes him, all that's past is lost for ever;
nor can there remain to him any enjoyment, except of what he has acted
virtuously; which may yield some joyful hope of an happy immortality.
This hope alone can be the foundation of true fortitude[; this prospect
alone can fully satisfy the mind as to] [and exalt] the justice and benignity
of the divine administration.

But as in other arts, the mere knowledge of the precepts is of little consequence, nor can any thing laudable be obtained without practice and exercise; so in moral philosophy, which is the art of living well, the importance
of the matter requires habit and continual exercise. Let our <Mind and>
Reason therefor, and the other divine parts [powers] in our constitution,
assume to themselves <91> their just right of commanding the inferiour
faculties [desires], and enure them to a constant subjection. And this in our
present degenerate state must require almost continual <meditation,> attention and internal discipline; to the success of which it will contribute

officia pietatis erga Deum, adoratio, preces, delictorum confessio, et pia
vota.

{III.} Ad virtutes plenius intelligendas, et a vitiis secernendas, atque ad animum virtutibus exornandum, haud parum conferet virtutes recensere, earumque characteres et nomina signata; atque ostendere vitia illis opposita,
ubi peccatur in appetituum naturalium vel excessu vel defectu, inter quos
mediocritatem servant virtutes. *Passionum* sive perturbationum explicatio
ad pneumatologiam pertinet. Singulas enumerare, earumque diversos gradus laudandos aut vituperandos, eorumque characteres <97> praecipuos et
signa, longam exigeret disputationem et variam. Quin etiam optime coletur
omnis virtus, ubi verae foventur, quas diximus, circa res omnes humanas,
quae appeti solent, [opiniones;] [sententiae] eaeque crebra meditatione alte
sunt infixae; atque usu et disciplinâ, partes animi praestantiores humilioribus [imperare assuescunt] [imperant].

Hoc interim monemus de appetitibus sive perturbationibus, earum nullam esse, simpliciter et in toto genere damnandam; nullam esse, quae non
insignem aliquando vitae hominum afferat utilitatem; quum saepè ipsius
cui inest, saepe aliorum ad quos forte attinet, inservire possit commoditati
{, foelicitati, aut virtuti augendae et conservandae}. Fieri quidem potest, ut
naturae praestantiori, cui majores sunt animi vires, inutiles essent futuri
motus istiusmodi perturbati; hominibus tamen saepe sunt necessarii. Est
cujusque appetitûs status quidem medius, saepe et utilis et venustus. Qui
ad eam mediocritatem non perveniunt, homini ipsi, hominumve societati
minus sunt utiles. Qui verò exultantes, "sive cupiendo sive fugiendo," "finem et modum transeunt,"[6] sunt ipsi homini cui insunt, et molesti et turpes, vitaeque hominum inimici, et saepè pestiferi. {Mediocritates autem

6. Cicero, *De officiis* 1.102.7.

much that we be frequently employed in the offices of Piety {and Devotion} toward God, in adoration {of his perfections}, prayers, confession of sin, and pious {desires, and} vows of obedience.

III. To apprehend more fully the nature of virtue and vice, and to adorn the soul with every moral excellency, it may be of use to run over the several species of virtue, with their characteristicks, and established names; and observe the several opposite vices, whether in the excess or defect of some natural desire <whereas virtue preserves a middle degree between them>.[3] The explication of the several Passions <or perturbations> belongs to [another branch of Philosophy] [pneumaticks]. To count them all over, and mark their several degrees whether laudable or censurable, with their several signs or characters, would require a very long discourse, with great variety of matter: but what's of most importance to lead us to virtue, is the forming just estimates of all {human affairs, all} the objects of the natural desires; and by frequent meditation deeply infixing in our hearts just impressions of their values [them], and habituating the superior parts of the soul to a constant command over the inferior.

This however must be remembered concerning our natural desires and passions, that none of them can be pronounced absolutely evil in kind: none of them which may not sometimes be of great use in life, either to the person in whom they reside, or to others of mankind: <92> in <preserving and> promoting either their Advantage, pleasure, or {even their} virtue. Superior orders of intelligence who have the superior powers more vigorous, may perhaps stand in no need of such violent motions or instigations; but to mankind they seem often necessary. And there is a moderate degree of each of them which is often advantageous, and often laudable. Such affections as don't come up to this moderate degree are not sufficient for the purposes either of the individual, or those of society; and such as are too luxuriant and vehement, whether in pursuit of good or repelling of evil, and pass over the proper bounds, become uneasy and dishonourable to the person in whom they are, and are hurtful or pernicious

3. This paragraph follows Aristoteles, *Nichomachean Ethics* II, 1107a, 28–1108b, 10.

plurimas non solum innocuas, verum et virtutum ministras <98> et satellites, virtutumque authores, ad officia plurima honestissima instigantes, immo ipsas esse virtutes merito arbitramur. His animi impulsionibus motibusque, sive cupiendo sive fugiendo, vitâ sensuque fruimur pleniore, augentur animi vires, cursusque incitatur: unde easdem *animae alas*, aut *quadrigas*, appellavit Plato.

Neque dubiis signis monstravit natura quid velit postuletque. Dum enim moderati sunt hi motus, ratione in consilium adhibita, omnia manent venusta et decora. Quum vero motu turbido et effraenato abripimur, nihil mente agitare, nihil ratione, nihil cogitatione consequi possumus; atque a proposito saepius aberrare necesse est, neque interea ulla decori conservatio. "Licet ora ipsa cernere iratorum, aut eorum qui libidine aliqua, aut metu commoti sunt, aut voluptate nimia gestiunt: quorum omnium vultus, voces, status, motusque,"[7] a natura recedunt.}

Mediocribus igitur appetitionibus, et ab extremis utrinque reductis, honesta virtutum nomina sunt imposita, ut et extremis, vitiorum inhonesta. Mediocribus tamen quibusdam, desunt signata nomina; unde incautè statuerunt quidam, quosdam esse animi [motus toto genere] [affectus prorsus] malos, et per se damnandos. His tamen vitiosis affectibus <99> respondent et innocui quidam ejusdem generis gradus, et necessarii.

Modicum, exempli causa, vitae conservandae studium, est et necessarium, et haud molestum. Ubi hoc deficit, existit ingenium audax, temerarium et incautum, ipsi homini saepè inquietum, saepe pestiferum, et hu-

---

7. Cicero, *De officiis* I.102.11–14.

to Society.[4] The moderate degrees of several passions we justly deem not only innocent, but exceedingly subservient to virtue, as its guards or ministers; nay as the springs of many honourable actions, and as real virtues. By means of these better passions whether in pursuit of good or warding off of evil, we enjoy a more lively sense of life, the force of the soul is enlarged, and its activity invigorated: whence *Plato* calls these passions the *wings* or *chariot-horses* of the soul.[5]

Nature has given us the clearest indications of what she requires in this matter. For while these passions are kept moderate under just government, and directed by reason, the whole deportment is graceful and lovely. But when we are hurried away by any furious unbridled passion, we are utterly incapable of exercising our reason, or finding out what is wise and becoming us; we quite miss the very aim of the passion it self, <93> and our whole deportment is disagreeable and deformed. Observe the very countenances of persons enraged, or of such as are transported with any ardent enflamed desire, or distracted with terror, or fluttering with joy. Their whole air [countenance and voices], the whole state and motion of the body becomes {deformed and} unnatural.

We therefor give the honourable titles of *virtues* to these moderate passions, equally confined from the two extremes; and call the extremes *vices*. But we have not appropriated names for the moderate and just degrees of several passions; and hence some have rashly imagined, that some of our natural passions are wholly and absolutely evil. And yet 'tis plain that there are also certain moderate degrees of these passions both innocent and necessary.

To illustrate all this by examples. A moderate desire of *self-preservation* is both necessary and easy. Where this is awanting, men shew a desperate audacious disposition without any caution. This temper is generally restless, turbulent, and destructive both to the person himself and to the society

---

4. On the necessity of passions, see *Essay on Passions* 2.6, pp. 48–55. Hutcheson refers to Simplicius's commentary on Epictetus's *Manual* (Simplicius, *Commentaire sur le Manuel d'Épictéte,* critical edition by I. Hadot, Leiden: Brill, 1996), chapter 35, and to William King's *De Origine Mali* (London, 1702), III.4.

5. See Henry More, *Enchiridion Ethicum,* I.VI.11, p. 27, and Plato, *Phaedrus,* 246a–d.

manae etiam societati. Ubi nimium est hoc studium, existit metus, et pusillanimitas, et ignavia; {qui mentis habitus} et hominum societati {sunt} inutiles <affectus>, et ipsi cui insunt molestissimi; eum omnibus injuriis, et contumeliis, et dedecori objicientes.

Modicae voluptatum appetitiones sunt et utiles et necessariae, neque homini molestae. Ubi existit ἀναισθησία,[8] parum vitae jucunditati prospicitur: rarius tamen ab hac parte peccatur. Ubi nimia est cupiditas, quae *luxuries* aut intemperantia dicitur, excluduntur fere omnia vitae gaudia honestiora; neque famae et honestati, neque sanitati, aut rei familiari, aut ipsi vitae conservandae, consulitur; ipsaque haec indoles tantum non continuis obnoxia est molestiis.

In rebus utilibus duae versantur virtutes; *frugalitas* nempe, quae prudens est rei familiaris cura; et *liberalitas,* quae nos ad bene faciendum faciles efficit [facit proclives]. Illa huic omnino est necessaria: utraque est jucunda, et utilis, et honesta; prior tamen utilitati magis <100> inservit, posterior honestati. Prioris excessus, et posterioris defectus, est *avaritia;* qua vix ullum est animi vitium aut foedius aut molestius; rerum copiam appetens neque necessariam, neque unquam utendam; summis saepe malis comparandam, curaque majore et metu servandam. Frugalitatis defectus et liberalitatis excessus, est *profusio* aut *prodigalitas;* rei familiari pestifera, neque vitae jucunditati, aut saluti consulens, neque ipsi, quam praecipue appetere solet, famae.

Liberalitatis apex est *magnificentia,* ubi prudenter, honesta de causa, magni fiunt sumptus. Ab hac deficit parci et avari, sibi ingrata, et molesta, liberalitatis affectatio. Modum superat, hominum parum elegantium aut ornatorum omnia profundens ἀπειροκαλία,[9] et inutilis et indecora.

Fortitudinis, ad eundem modum, apex est *magnanimitas;* sive animus altus, constans, et rebus externis inconcussus, solam in omnibus spectans honestatem. Cui ab una parte opponitur audax superbia et arrogantia; ani-

8. Aristotle, *Ethica Nicomachea* 1109a, 4.
9. Aristotle, *Ethica Nicomachea* 1122a, 31.

he lives in. Where this care of self-preservation is excessive, it appears in Timidity and cowardice; dispositions quite useless to the publick, and tormenting to the person, exposing him to all injuries and affronts <and dishonour>.

A moderate relish for *sensual pleasures* is useful, nay necessary <and easy>. An entire insensibility would deprive one of a great deal of innocent pleasure; but seldom meet we with any thing wrong on this side. Where the taste is too high, which we call luxury or intemperance, it generally excludes all the more manly enjoyments, <94> neither consulting reputation nor honour; nor even health or fortune, or the preservation of life. This turn of mind too must frequently expose a man to continual chagrin and uneasiness.

About our *estates* or *worldly goods* two virtues are employed, *frugality,* which consists in a wise management of them family estates {for honourable purposes}, and *liberality,* which excites us to acts of kindness to others. The former is absolutely necessary to the exercise of the later: both are pleasant, advantageous, and honourable: the former more peculiarly subservient to our advantage, and the latter to our honour. The excess of frugality and defect of liberality is *avarice,* which is among the most deformed and most uneasy vices, pursuing stores quite unnecessary, and which it never intends to use; stores that must be obtained with much toil and uneasiness, and need rather more <trouble and anxiety> to preserve them. The defect of frugality and excess of liberality is *prodigality,* destructive to our fortunes, little subservient to the pleasure or safety of life, or even to fame, which it seems chiefly to have in view.

The highest pitch of liberality is called *magnificence,* where great expences are wisely employed for some honourable purposes. The defect of this is seen in an affectation or shew of magnificence with an unwilling narrow heart. The excess is sometimes seen in the inelegant boundless profusion of persons who have no just notion of decency and elegance.

The highest pitch of fortitude is in like manner called *magnanimity;* or an elevation and firmness of soul, which no circumstances of fortune can move, aiming <95> solely at moral excellence in all its conduct. The extreme in excess often appears in a desperate audacious ambition, stopping

mi affectio homini ipsi molestissima; neque aliorum, neque suae, aut saluti, aut libertati, aut famae satis consulens: ab altera, opponitur *pusillanimitas,* aut formidolosum ingenium, inutile et molestissimum. <101>

De potentiae appetitione, eadem fere omnia dicenda; modicam utilem esse viro bono, minimèque molestam; nimiam autem, molestissimam et turpissimam; sibique et aliis periculosam. Ubi justo languidior est, opportunitatibus oblatis, deseritur et honestatis locus, et virtutis.

Laudis appetitus modicus, nihil ferè dicere attinet, quantam praestet utilitatem, si simul major sit virtutis. Nimius tamen est inquietus et molestus, omnemque ipsius virtutis veram imminuit gloriam et inquinat: ubi abest omnis, deest etiam stimulus, ad officia honesta suscipienda, saepe haud inutilis.

Neque ira omnis et iracundia damnanda; licet nulla admodum sit venusta. Injuriarum, quae rarior esse solet ἀναισθησία, satis foret homini incommoda, eum nempè contumeliis et petulantiae objiciens; neque suae prospiciens famae, neque suorum saluti. Iracundia quae nimia, est et ei cui inest molestissima, et saepe pestifera; neque ullus est animi affectus hominum societati perniciosior.

Justa quaedam, et homine libero digna est *indignatio,* cum ad opes aut honores provehuntur indigni. Cui nulla inest hujusmodi affectio, parum sibi, aut suis, aut patriae est prospecturus: ubi tamen est nimia, <102> aut non justa de causa, (quae *invidia* dicitur, unde nascuntur odia inveterata;) deterrima est animi rubigo, ei cui inest et molestissima, et turpissima, omnia saepe miscens divina et humana.

De his autem omnibus quae irae sunt affines, aut malignae videntur, animi affectionibus, hoc omninò tenendum, iis non amplius indulgendum quam exigit sui aut suorum conservatio, aut communis utilitatis cura: qui-

at no dangers<, and arrogance>. Such a temper must be dangerous and uneasy to the possessor, and inconsistent with his safety, as well as that of others; as also destructive of the liberty and dignity of all around. The other extreme is pusillanimity or cowardice, rendering a man useless and miserable.

The like holds as to the *desire of power* and promotion in the world: a moderate degree is useful and sits easy on a good man: when it grows excessive, 'tis both uneasy and restless, and very vitious, and dangerous to it self and all around. Where it is too faint and weak even when just occasions offer, men abandon the proper station or opportunities of virtue and honour.

So also a moderate *desire of fame* is manifestly of great use, if we have yet higher desires of virtue. The excess of this desire is restless and uneasy, and often defiles and debases the true beauty of virtuous actions. Where men want this desire, or have it very languid, they want a very potent incitement to all virtuous offices.

Nor can all *anger* or *resentment* be condemned, altho' there's little lovely in any degree of it. An entire insensibility of all injuries, of which there are but few instances, would be a very inconvenient disposition; exposing a man to the contumelies and petulance of others; nor well consistent with his own character, or the safety of such as he is bound to protect. Excessive anger on the other hand is a most tormenting passion, <96> and often destructive to the person in whom it is found; nor is there any passion more dangerous to society.

There's a certain just *indignation,* becoming a good man, when the worthless are promoted to power or dignity. One void of such sentiments would be too little solicitous about the interests either of his friends or his country. But where this passion is excessive, or rises without just cause (which we call *envy,* the common spring of inveterate malice) it is the most destructive poison [rust] to the soul, tormenting to the breast where it resides, and extremely vitious, leading into the most horrid crimes.

This is to be observed of all the unkind passions which partake of anger, that they should be indulged no further than is plainly necessary for our own preservation or that of our friends [and country] [or concern for com-

bus quidem, si absque irâ satis consuli possit, nihil in ira erit laudabile aut
venustum. Contra, lenitate et mansuetudine, placabilitate et clementia,
nihil amabilius, nihil honestius.

{Inter} virtutes quae *homileticae* dicuntur {prima est *veritas,* animique
candor: de quibus fusius alias.* His contraria sunt mendacia, fallaciae, fraudes; simulatio itidem dissimulatioque omnis malitiosa.

In eodem genere sunt virtutes aliae, eorum quibuscum vivitur voluptati,
aut gratiae apud eos ineundae inservientes,} *comitas, urbanitas, concinnitas,
suavitas,* εὐτραπελία,[10] *facetiae;* <sunt> omnino laudandae et decorae,
hominum conjunctioni conservandae aptissimae, his opposita sunt utrinque vitia. Ab una parte, servile scurrae ingenium, omnia ad voluptatem
aliorum loquentis, et <103> assentantis, atque ad obscoenos aut illiberales
descendentis jocos; ab alterâ, gravis, inconcinna, et agrestis rixantium as-
peritas, quae nullam iis, quibuscum vivitur, exhibet reverentiam, quaeque
inani libertatis specie commendatur. Horum vitiorum incommoda non attinet dicere; quum sint et per se invenusta, et saepe pestifera{: omniumque
una cautio est, ut cum mores nostri puri sint et emendati, eos quibuscum
vivimus et vereri et diligere videamur}.

De *verecundia* breviter monendum, eam ex ipso recti et honesti sensu
acriore subnasci; et in junioribus spem dare ingenii foelicioris, ad omnem
virtutem optime subornati. Ubi nimia tamen est in aetate matura, hominem ab officiis honestis capessendis saepe cohibet: ubi aut exigua est aut
nulla, deest virtutis et honesti custos potentissimus.

---

* {Lib. II, cap. 10.}
10. Aristotle, *Ethica Nichomachea* 1108a, 24.

mon interest]. If we could without these passions ensure their safety, there would be nothing desireable or laudable in them: nay on the other hand, nothing is more lovely <or honourable> than lenity, mercy, placability and clemency.

Among the virtues of social conversation, the first and chief is *veracity* and candour, of which we shall treat more fully in* another place. The opposite vices are all as it were defects: lyes, deceit, fraud, crafty hypocrisy and dissimulation.

In the same class are some other virtues tending to give pleasure to and oblige all we converse with; such as *courtesy, good-manners, complaisance, sweetness, pleasantry, wit:* all which are laudable and graceful, and promote friendliness and good-will in society. There <97> are opposite vices on both hands: on the one, a *servile fawning,* and flattery, and scurrility; having no other view than insinuating by any sort of pleasure into the favour of those it makes court to, and stooping into the most ungentlemanly or obscene jests: on the other, a troublesome, unmannerly *rusticity* and roughness, shewing no respect or deference to company, but pleasing it self with a shew of liberty and boldness. 'Tis needless to dwell upon the inconveniences arising from these vices, as they are always mean and indecent, and often lead to the greatest mischiefs. The true preservative against both extremes is first to take care to attain a truly virtuous temper; and then, to maintain both a real good-will and a respect for those with whom we live in society.

As to *modesty* {and *bashfulness*}, 'tis worth our notice that this passion plainly arises from a lively sense and solicitude about what is decent [right] and honourable, and hence gives in our youth hopeful prognosticks of a fine genius, well formed by nature for every thing virtuous. But where it is excessive in maturer years it often retards or withholds men from acting an honourable part: where this sense is very weak or wholly awanting, men want a powerful guardian to every virtue.

* Book ii. c.10.

Qui haec omnia uberius explicata legere cupit, consulat Aristotelem, et Aristotelicos{*}. Hoc obiter monemus, quum tot verae virtuti utrinque immineant fata, summa opus esse cura, attentione, et disciplina; ut cohibeantur aut regantur hi animi motus perturbati; ut vigeat semper decori <104> et honesti sensus, et recta ratio; nobiliores etiam et tranquillae voluntatis affectiones, quae et suam cujusque, et humani generis communem spectant foelicitatem.

{IV.} Neque corporis omittenda est cura, cujus vires et valetudo, temperantia et exercitatione conservandae atque augendae; ut rationi obedire possit, in omni labore perferendo, quem exigunt officia honesta.

Quumque parum humano genere prodesse possunt hi, qui non artem aliquam maturè didicerunt, in qua se exerceant; eligenda cuique est ars ingenio apta, aut vitae institutum licitum, et humano generi profuturum. Neque hoc munere eximendi sunt illi, quibus tantae suppetunt facultates, ut quaestus faciendi causa hoc non sit necessarium. Enimvero illorum praecipuè est, publicae consulere utilitati, juris legumque peritiam, aut politicam prudentiam comparare, aut eam rerum humanarum notitiam, quibus, vicinis omnibus, consilio, opibus, gratia, et auctoritate prodesse possint; ne inutilia sint terrae onera, frugibus tantum consumendis nati.

Artium autem quaeque, quo major ei inest prudentia et ingenii solertia, et quo major ad vitam communem quaeritur utilitas, eo est honestior. Ob

* {Utilissima congessit vir sanctissimus *Henric. Morus,* in enchiridio ethico; virque non magis genere quam ingenio nobilis, *Comes de Shaftsbury* in sua *de virtute disquisitione,* et *Rhapsodia.*}

* <Very useful observations have been collected by Henry More, a most virtuous man, in his *Enchiridion Ethicum,* and by the Earl of Shaftesbury, a man not less noble in capacity than in birth, in his *Inquiry on Virtue* and in his *Philosophical Rhapsody.*> [Nei-

A more copious explication of all this subject may be found in *Aristotle* and his followers:<*> we may however suggest {before we quit it}, that since such fatal dangers threaten virtue as it were on both hands, we should certainly apply the greatest care and attention and self-discipline, in governing our several passions, in maintaining a lively and vigorous sense of moral excellence, <98> and cultivating our rational powers [right reason] and the nobler and more extensive calm affections, [whether toward our own true interests or those of mankind] [that look at our own or at the common happiness of mankind].

IV. There's also some care to be taken of our bodies. Strength and health is to be acquired or preserved chiefly by temperance and exercise; that so our bodies may be enabled to obey the commands of the soul, in enduring all toils we may incurr in discharge of our duty.

And since men can do little service to society who have not in their younger years been trained to some useful art or occupation: every one should timeously choose some one, suited to his genius, lawful in its nature, and of use to mankind.[6] Nor ought such as are born to estates, who therefor need not for their own support any lucrative profession, think themselves exempted from any such obligation. For it seems more peculiarly incumbent on them{, as Providence exempts them from other cares,} to contribute to the publick interest, by acquiring a compleat knowledge of the rights of mankind, of laws, and civil polity; or at least such acquaintance with all the common business of mankind, that they may be able either by superiour wisdom, or by their interest<, favour,> and influence, to serve {their country or} their neighbours; and not be useless loads of the earth, serving only to consume its products.[7]

As to the several professions or occupations [arts], we deem them reputable on these two accounts, as they either require a finer genius and greater wisdom, or as they are of greater use in society. On both accounts the oc-

---

ther Henry More, nor Shaftesbury were exactly "followers of Aristotle"; More, however quotes extensively from Aristotle's *Nichomachean Ethics*. On virtue as a middle between opposite vices, see *Enchiridion Ethicum*, II.9, pp. 59–62].

6. Cf. Pufendorf, *De officio* V.2. But Pufendorf's chapter on duty to oneself is mostly concerned with the rights of self-defence.

7. See Carmichael's *Notes on Puf.*, pp. 66–67.

utramque causam <105> commendantur doctrina rerum honestarum, jurisprudentia, medicina, studia militaria, et caeterae elegantiores.[11] Ob utilitatem, et non levem ingenii solertiam, commendatur mercatura copiosior, et artes quaedam mechanicae. Agriculturâ vero, nulla innocentior, nulla dulcior, nulla homine, nulla libero dignior.[12]

In arte eligenda, totâque vitâ constituenda, "ad suam cujusque naturam" et ingenium, "consilium est omne revocandum."[13] "Ad hanc autem rationem, quoniam maximam vim natura habet, fortuna proximam, utriusque omnino ratio est habenda, in deligendo genere vitae, sed naturae magis; multo enim est firmior et constantior."[14]

---

11. Cf. Cicero, *De officiis* 1.115 and 151.

12. Cf. Cicero, *De officiis* 1, 151: [. . .] Nihil est agri cultura melius, nihil uberius, nihil dulcius, nihil homine, nihil libero dignius.

13. Cicero, *De officiis* 1.119.6.

14. Cicero, *De officiis* 1.120.1–5.

cupation of teaching others the grand principles of piety <99> and virtue, {or even the more ingenious arts,} is reputed honourable; so are also the professions of law, medicine, and war, and some others of the more elegant arts. The more extensive merchandise, and even some mechanick arts, are justly reputable both on account of their great utility, and the considerable abilities of mind requisite in them. {Agriculture has been the chief delight of the finest spirits, as} no manner of life is more innocent, none affording sweeter amusements, none more becoming a rational creature, or a person of genteel taste in life <than agriculture>.

In the choice of our occupation or profession for life, our chief regard should be to our natural genius. But as our success in any occupation depends in the first place upon our genius, and next to it upon favourable circumstances of fortune, regard is to be had to both, but chiefly to our natural genius: for nature is a much surer and steddier principle.[8]

8. See in the Latin text, notes 11–14.

¹{CAPUT VII

De Virtutis Studio excitando et retinendo.

I. Virtuti strenuam operam esse navandam, vix opus est ut pluribus doceamus. Cognito enim et persuaso, in ea praecipue sitam esse vitam beatam, caeteraque omnia incerta, infirma, fragilia, caduca, hominisque praestantia parum digna; ea vitae via ingrediunda videbitur, quam <106> intimus cujusque sensus ratioque monstrabit esse maxime secundam naturam, quaeque ad veram hominique propriam ducit foelicitatem: quo pacto etiam quod in homine summum est maximeque divinum exercebitur et perficietur, munusque a Deo impositum explebitur.

Quorsum enim animos nobis largitus est Deus tot virtutibus capiendis exercendisque aptos? Quorsum tributae tot egregiae vires, tantumque ad optimas artes instrumentum; rationis orationisque facultates eximiae, cognoscendi studia, "rerum innumerabilium memoria," "conjectura consequentium non multum a divinatione differens," humiliorum appetituum "moderator pudor,"² tot propensiones benignae aliorum utilitati prospicientes, sensusque honestum turpi aequum iniquo secernens, atque in laboribus perferendis animi robur et magnitudo? Quorsum ea veri investigatio quae ad coelum ipsum penetravit, Deum mundi rectorem, ejusque

---

1. The chapter is added in the second edition.
2. Cicero, *De finibus* 2.113.3–6.

Some Practical Considerations to Excite and Preserve the Study of Virtue.

I. We need not now spend many words in shewing the necessity of <stren-uously> pursuing virtue. For if we are sufficiently persuaded that in it con-sists our chief felicity, and that all other things are uncertain, weak, fading and perishing, nor sufficiently adapted to the dignity of the rational nature, we must deem it necessary to enter upon that course of life which our {con-science or} inmost sense, as well as {right} reason recommends, as most suited to our nature, and which leads to the peculiar happiness of rational beings: by which means also we exercise and improve these powers which are supreme and most God-like in our constitution, and discharge the office imposed upon us by God {and nature}.[1]

With what other view has God given us souls so well fitted for the knowl-edge and practice of so many virtues? To what purpose so many noble pow-ers, such furniture of soul for most excellent arts {and offices}; the powers of reason and speech, {the powers of invention,} the desires of knowledge, an almost boundless retention and memory of things past, a provident sa-gacity about futurity resembling divination, a sense of what is honourable and shameful as the controller of our lower appetites; so many kind affec-tions consulting the good [interests] of others, a {conscience or} sense dis-tinguishing the right <101> from the wrong, the honourable part from the vitious and base: along with a strength and grandeur of mind for enduring dangerous toils? To what purpose that penetration into nature which reaches even to the heavens, discovers the Deity presiding in the universe,

---

1. The whole of chapter VII was added to the second edition of the *Institutio*. The first section might be seen as an answer to Hume's question in his letter to Hutcheson of Sept. 19th, 1739: "For pray, which is the End of Man?" Hutcheson's answer increases the quotations from Cicero's philosophical works. See the notes of the Latin text.

virtutes immensas agnovit, vitaeque aeternae post corporis interitum spem laetam ostendit?

Quid loquor de sapientiae studiosis? Quae est enim gens, aut quod genus hominum, apud quos de numine aliquo, officioque ipsis praescripto, personâque aliqua imposita, et de animorum immortalitate, pro ipsorum <107> meritis, beata aut misera, non maneat firma omnium consensio? Haec igitur naturae judicia merito existimamus, naturae apta, firmisque et apertis rationibus subnixa, quae "una cum seculis aetatibusque hominum inveterarunt," quum "ficta" omnia et "vana diuturnitate extabuerunt."³

Aliae ex philosophia prima petantur rationes; hoc sedulo monemus: Quae validissima docent argumenta, ex solertissima mundi structura petita, naturam sagacem et artificiosam hunc mundum corporeum in initio constituisse, omnique tempore regere et movere; iis prorsum simillima pariter ostendere, *qualitatum moralium,* virtutum vitiorumque, habitam fuisse rationem; naturasque omnes rationis participes justo regi imperio, ita ut tandem bonis omnibus benè sit, malis male. Quumque in hac vita non raro aliter eveniat, alia speranda est totius divinae administrationis explicatio, Deo op. max. usquequaque digna. Quod uberius confirmabit ipsa animi natura penè divina: "tanta enim animorum celeritas," "tanta memoria praeteritorum, futurorumque prudentia, tot virtutes, tot artes, tot scientiae, tot inventa," vetant "eam naturam, quae res eas continet," putare "esse mortalem":⁴ Immortalitatis autem spes, gravissima suggeret virtutum <108> invitamenta, atque ab omni turpitudine maxime deterrebit.

II. Quo autem alacrius virtuti operam demus, haec semper in promptu sint; quod animum studiis rebusque honestis intentum vires raro deficient: ad-

---

3. Cicero, *De natura deorum* 2.5.5–7, with slight alterations.
4. Cicero, *Cato Maior de senectute* 78.8–11.

discerns his infinite perfections, and raises us to the hopes of immortality after the dissolution of the body?

Do we speak only about Philosophers? what nation or clan is there where there has not always prevailed an universal and firm persuasion, that there is a Deity, that he enjoins certain duties upon mankind, appoints them a certain moral character they must maintain; and that their future state after death shall be happy or miserable according to their conduct in this world. These therefor are the dictates of nature, sentiments adapted to our frame, and supported by obvious reasons, which continue coeval with mankind; whereas the credit of ill-founded <and vain> fictions by length of time has always decayed, and at length vanished away.

Metaphysicians suggest many other arguments for the immortality of the soul; we only suggest here, that as the ingenious and artificial structure of the universe affords the strongest arguments for the existence of artificial intelligence, [the Creator][, the forever mover and ruler] of this material frame, so arguments exactly parallel to them{, from the structure of our souls,} shew that God has also a regard to the moral qualities, the virtues and vices {of rational creatures}; and that he exercises a just moral government over them, under which happiness must be secured at last to the virtuous, and misery alloted to the <102> vitious. And since we see that this does not hold universally in the present state of this world, we may reasonably expect another display or unfolding of the divine administration in a future state, in every respect worthy of God. This too is confirmed by the very nature of the soul it self. For that wonderful life and activity of our minds, that extensive remembrance, that sagacious foresight, those noble powers and virtues, those ingenious arts and sciences and inventions, make it incredible that substances [natures] containing such excellencies can perish {along with these despicable bodies}. Now such prospects of immortality must suggest the most potent motives to all virtue, and the strongest dissuasives from vice.

II. And that we may with greater resolution endeavour to cultivate all virtue, let us have always at hand these thoughts; (1.) That where there's an hearty inclination to what is honourable and good, we seldom want strength in execution, and have ground to hope for the divine assistance. {We even see

erit opitulator Deus: vigilando, agendo, bene consulendo, prospere omnia cedent: novas in dies vires mens adipiscetur, humilioribus appetitibus reprimendis pares: quaeque primo dura et difficilia videantur, ea usus facillima faciet et jucundissima: laboris cujusque honesti, brevi effluxerit omnis molestia, laetaque semper manebit memoria.

2. Ne autem a virtutis studio, rerum externarum avidae cupiditates, aut voluptatum illecebrae nos avocent, solida et stabilia quae honestatem comitantur gaudia et spes laetissimae saepius pensitandae. Multum etiam profuerit, res humanas attentius introspicere, earundemque despicientiam, saepius antea memoratam adhibere, vitaeque brevitatem, mortemque omnibus instantem saepius intueri.

3. Sed quoniam utilitati externae et voluptati, cujus modus quidam est et naturalis et necessarius, aliquid dandum; dummodo meminerimus alia longe esse praestantiora: ne illi omni bellum indicendum videatur, singulas virtutes animo percurramus, <109> ut videamus quantum earum quaeque ad vitae prosperitatem ipsamque voluptatem afferat.

Prudentia, eaque animi vis, qua motus inconsultos et improvidos regere valet, in omni pariter vitae institutione est necessaria, ut finem qualemcunque expètitum assequamur, neque in ea quae praecipue aversamur libidinibus occaecati praecipites feramur.

Quae *justitiae* partes sunt, ad pacem colendam, ad offensiones declinandas, ad incolumitatem, gratiam, famam, fidem, opes, authoritatem parandam plurimum valent, atque etiam amicitiam "et caritatem, vitae sine metu degendae praesidium firmissimum."[5] Eae enim virtutes semper alunt aliquid, tum "vi sua" et "natura, quod tranquillet animos; tum spe, nihil earum rerum defuturum quas natura non depravata desideret."[6] Cujus, contra, "in mente consedit" vis et injustitia, "hoc ipso quod adsint, tur-

---

5. Cicero, *De finibus* 1.35.7–8.
6. Cicero, *De finibus* 1.50.6–9.

---

2. Hutcheson returns to the cardinal virtue, as in Chapter III, and in the Conclusion

in the ordinary course of things, that} by vigilance, activity, and wise deliberation, all matters generally succeed prosperously: men daily increase in
ability; their superiour powers acquire new strength and command over the
lower appetites; and what at first appeared hard and difficult, by custom is
made easy and even delightful. The toil and trouble of any honourable
offices will soon be past and gone, but the remembrance of them will remain perpetual matter of joy.

(2.) But least the keen desires of the external advantages, and the alluring
pleasures of this life should abate <103> our virtuous pursuits; we should
frequently consider with the deepest attention what stable and solid joys
and hopes accompany virtue: we should consider also the nature of all
worldly enjoyments, and obtain that just contempt of them we often mentioned; and ever keep in view the shortness of this life, and that death must
soon overtake us all.

(3.) And yet since there's a certain measure of external pleasures and
enjoyments natural and necessary, we must have some regard to them; provided we still remember that there are others much more important. That
we may not therefore seem obliged as it were to declare war against all the
conveniences or pleasures of this life, let us run over the several virtues, and
see how much each of them generally contributes to our present prosperity
and pleasure.[2]

Prudence which restrains the inconsiderate foolish impulses of the passions, must be alike necessary in every course of life whatsoever, that we
may effectually pursue any end we propose, and not blinded by lust run
headlong into the objects of our strongest aversions.

The several branches of *Justice* are of the greatest consequence to maintain peace, to avoid offending {and provoking} others, to obtain safety, favour, reputation, credit, wealth, extensive influence, and friends, which are
the surest defences against all dangers in life. These virtues in their own
nature preserve the soul easy and calm, and yield a joyful hope that we shall
always obtain such things as are [naturally necessary and desirable] [desired
by a uncorrupted nature]. On the other hand, where designs of violence

---

to the book on ethics in *System*. But here the point of view is different and considers the
contribution of these virtues to the pleasures of life; it is the same in Cicero's *De finibus*
V (especially 65 and ff.).

bulenta" non potest non fieri; suspicioneque, "solicitudine," metuque, "noctes atque dies exesa."[7] Quid loquar de pietate? qua propitius fit Deus mundi rector, omnisque fortunae dispensator; qui piis et bonis si non jucunda, aptissima cuncta dabit et optima; unde etiam vitae beatae et aeternae spe laeta, mortalium animi erigentur. <110>

Quae *temperantiae* subjiciuntur virtutes reliquarum omnium fautrices fidissimae, corporis sanitati et viribus inserviunt; quinetiam pulchritudini; quum animi sedati, ut fere omnium virtutum, insit in ipso vultu significatio. Bonis externis etiam augendis, manifesto utiles sunt frugalitas, victus cultusque tenuis, diligentia et industria: hisque omnibus adversatur luxuria omnis et intemperantia; corporis vires, valetudinem, formam, labefactans, infamiae et contemptui objiciens, animi aciem obtundens, omnesque appetitus humiliores effraenatos reddens et intractabiles.

Nostrae et nostrorum saluti prospiciunt *fortitudo,* virtutesque fortitudini affines. Ignaviâ autem et timiditate non solum virtutis locum deseremus, verum in ea nosmet nostrosque saepe conjiciemus pericula, unde facile eripuisset fortitudo, animusque praesens. Hujus virtutis expertem, penes alios erit, malorum graviorum comminatione, impium efficere et sceleratum: qua servitute nihil saevius aut turpius. Si quis autem gravioribus malis sit obnoxius, iisve virtutis ipsius causa objiciatur; illi "magnum illud et difficile certamen" inituro, et "cum capitali adversario dolore" depugnaturo, "omnes patientiae et fortitudinis rationes" excitandae,[8] legesque in memoriam revocandae, <111> quae vetant effoeminari virum, "debilitari, dolore frangi, succumbere."[9] Praecipue vero reputet, nunc esse certamen honestissimum; adesse Olympia; omnia Dei numine evenire: Deum certaminis esse spectatorem, judicem, et remuneratorem; ignavumque et stolidum, propositâ laude et honestate, vitae caducae, morborum vi alioqui, et saepe cum sae-

7. See Cicero, *De finibus* 1.50.12 and 51.4–5.
8. See Cicero, *De finibus* 4.31.8–11.
9. Cicero, *De finibus* 2.95.7–8.

and injustice <104> possess the heart, as they are turbulent and uneasy in their own nature, so they devour the breast with perpetual suspicions, solicitudes, and fears. Need we speak of {the highest branch of justice,} Piety towards God? this secures to us the favour of the supreme Governour of the world, the sovereign Arbiter of our fortunes, who will always provide for the virtuous, if not the things at present most pleasurable, yet such as are truly fittest for them, and most advantageous and pleasant at last. And from piety will arise the hope of immortality which can always support the soul {in every circumstance of fortune}.

The several parts of *Temperance,* as they faithfully cherish all other virtues, so they tend to preserve and improve our health, strength, and even the beauty and grace of our persons; as the tranquillity and inward ease of the soul shews it self in the countenance. And frugality, a sparing simple way of living, diligence, and industry, are plainly subservient to wealth and affluence: which luxury and intemperance tend to destroy; as they also impair our health, strength, and beauty, and expose us to infamy and contempt; stupifying the nobler parts of the soul, and making all the lower appetites outragious and intractable.

Fortitude and all its parts are a safeguard to ourselves and our friends. Whereas by cowardice <and timidity> we not only quit our station of honour and virtue, but often involve ourselves in such dangers as we might easily have escaped by fortitude and presence of mind. The person void of this virtue must be in the power of others to make him what they please, by the threats of evil; <105> even to involve him in the most impious and basest vices; which is a state of miserable servitude. If any good man is threatned with great dangers, or exposed to them even on account of his virtues; as on such occasions he is entering on the most difficult combat, encountering with our most capital adversary, pain; 'tis his business to rouse up all the forces of fortitude and patience and resignation, to recollect the sacred laws of these virtues, which prohibit any effeminate weakness, prohibit our sinking or losing spirit, or crouching under this load. Let him think with himself, now he's ingaged in the most honourable combat, more glorious than the Olympicks; God presides the witness, judge, and rewarder; 'tis cowardly and foolish when the prize is so glorious, to spare a life that must soon perish however, and perhaps in a more tormenting man-

viori cruciatu, et sine honore periturae, quin etiam rediturae, parcere. Virtutis, magnitudinis animi, pietatis, patientiae fomentis hujusmodi, dolores mitigari, mortisque terrores imminui solent.

III. Virtutes omnes a Deo ad homines pervenisse, saepius dictum. Ipsorum igitur Philosophorum monitis, Deus precibus supplicibus obnixe invocandus, ut divinis illis donis nos exornet; nobisque strenuam dantibus operam vires animosque sufficiat: neminem enim censuerunt virum magnum sine afflatu divino unquam fuisse. Quid quod et per se, suaque vi, virtutum immensarum quae in Deo sunt venerabunda contemplatio, gratiarum actiones, laudationes, delictorum confessiones, preces, non solum pietatem erga Deum augent foventque, verum etiam omnem morum probitatem et bonitatem. Ad Deum igitur in omni περιστάσει[10] confugientes, ejusque auxilio freti, animis <112> praesentibus, honestoque et decoro retinendo semper intentis, in memoriam revocemus, quibus virtutibus exercendis nunc adsit occasio? quibus animi viribus nos instruxerit Deus et natura, ut cum istiusmodi casibus conflictemur? Quam laeta et gloriosa futura sit victoriae, officiique conservati memoria? quamque pudendum, si levi aliqua dulcedine aut dolore victi, nosmet turpitudine et dedecore conspurcemus?

Omnia virtutis colendae praecepta fusius exponere, ab instituto nostro alienum. Consulantur Philosophi Graeci, Romani, aliique qui eam materiam copiosius tractarunt: atque de singulis vitae officiis, quicquid ἀψικάρδιον,[11] animumque excitans occurrerit, condatur componaturque, ut in vitae usus depromatur.* "Extruamus denique animo magnitudinem excellentiamque virtutum, atque non dubitabimus quin earum compos"[12]

---

10. Arrianus, *Dissertationes* 2.6.17 *passim* and Marcus Aurelius Antoninus, *Meditationes* 9.13 and 9.41.

11. Marcus Aurelius Antoninus, *Meditationes* 9.3.2.2.

* Ciceronis Tuscul. II [This reference is wrong].

12. Cicero, *De finibus* 5.71: "Age nunc, Luci noster, extrue animo altitudinem excellentiamque virtutum: iam non dubitabis, quin earum compotes . . ."

ner, <without honour,> by the force of some disease; a life too that does not extinguish the soul, but shall return to us again. 'Tis by {such representations made to ourselves of the honourable forms of} virtue, {fortitude,} magnanimity, duty to God, and patient resignation, that such pains are abated, and the terrors of death in some measure taken away.

III. It was formerly observed that 'tis from God we have derived all our virtues.[3] The Philosophers therefor{, as well as Divines,} teach us to have recourse frequently to God by ardent prayers, that, while we are exerting ourselves vigorously, he would also adorn us with these virtues, and supply us with new strength. They taught that no man ever attained true grandeur of mind without some inspiration from God. Need we add, <106> that the very contemplation of the divine perfections, with that deep veneration which they excite, thanksgivings, praises, confessions of our sins, and prayers, not only increase <and cherish> our devotion and piety, but strengthen all goodness of temper and integrity. We ought therefor to have recourse to the Deity in all difficulties, trusting in his aid, with firm purposes of acting that part which is most honourable; and recall to our thoughts, what virtues this emergence gives opportunity to exercise, what furniture or armour has God and nature given us for encountering with such dangers? how joyful shall the remembrance be of our conquering such temptations, and discharging our duty well? and how shameful to be conquered by the allurements of some trifling pleasure, or the terrors of a little pain, and thus debase ourselves by a vitious and ignominious behaviour.

'Tis not our present purpose to unfold at length all the precepts and motives to virtue. They may be found in the Greek and Roman Philosophers and [modern authors] [and others that managed this subject more plentifully): {in perusing whom} it may be proper to collect and keep ready for our use all the more lively and affecting sentiments which occurr: "and let us form and settle in our minds a lively notion of the grandeur and excellence of the several virtues, so that we mayn't question but that such as are possessed of them" {must be the truly wise and completely happy

3. See above, IV.2, p. 75.

"quisquis est," "sibique ipse placatus, ut nec tabescat molestiis, nec frangatur timore, nec sitienter quid expetens ardeat desiderio, nec alacritate futili gestiens deliquescat, is sit sapiens quem quaerimus, is sit beatus: cui nihil humanum aut externum intolerabile ad dimittendum animum, aut nimis laetabile ad efferendum videri potest." "Nam quid aut in studiis <113> humanis, aut in tam exigua brevitate vitae, magnum sapienti videri potest, qui semper animo sic excubat, ut ei nihil improvisum accidere possit, nihil inopinatum, nihil novum."[13]

IV. Quandoquidem vero, hoc viro bono praecipue propositum est, ut vitam agens secundum naturam, in communem aliquid afferat prosperitatem, quae citra varias plurium conjunctiones et consociationes conservari nequit: studiose etiam anquiret de omnibus rectae rationis praeceptis, quibus singulae vitae partes ad naturam conformentur, quibusque servatis, hominum conjunctionem munifice pro virili tueri possit et conservare.[14] Haec praecepta verò collecta et composita *Jus Naturale* conficiunt: quae altera Philosophiae moralis pars est vitae regendae utilissima.}

13. Cicero, *Tusc. disp.* 4.37.10.
14. Cf. Cicero, *De finibus* 5.65.

characters}.* "Such a man must be satisfied with himself, neither pining and fretting under troubles, nor broken with any terrours, nor tormented with any impatient ardent desires, nor <107> dissolved in trifling pleasures and joys: to him no accidents of this mortal state appear so intolerable as to sink his spirits, nor so joyful as to give him high transports. And what is there in the pursuits of this world, and in this short transitory life, that can appear of great consequence to a truly wise man, whose soul is so constantly upon the watch, that nothing happens to him unforeseen or surprizing, nothing unexpected, nothing new."

IV. Now as 'tis the grand view of the good man, that according to the intention of nature he should always be employed in contributing something to the general interest and happiness, which plainly requires that large numbers of mankind should be joined in an amicable society; he ought also carefully to enquire into all the rules or dictates of right reason, by which every part of life is to be regulated, and by observing which he may on his part preserve this social union among mankind: and these precepts or conclusions of right reason collected together make what we call the *Law of Nature;* which is the next branch of Moral Philosophy, of great use in the conduct of life. <108>

* Cicero's *Tuscul. Questionae,* Book IV. [See notes 13 and 14 in the Latin text.]

<114>

PHILOSOPHIAE MORALIS

INSTITUTIO COMPENDIARIA

ᗢᏯ LIBER II ᗢᏯ

Jurisprudentiae Naturalis Elementa.

CAPUT I

De Lege Naturali.

I. Quo melius {ad naturam conformentur singulae vitae partes,} hominumque inter se officia et jura intelligantur, prius exponenda est doctrina generalior, complicatas quasdam, in ethicis, notiones evolvens et explicans; quam [breviter exhibemus] [proxima tria capita exhibent].

Primas honesti et turpis notiones, in libro superiore, ex hominis conformatione deduximus; ex quibus constiterit, ea omnia *recte* {sive *jure*} fieri, possideri, aut ab aliis postulari, quae vel ad communem omnium faciunt utilitatem, vel singulorum propriam, <115> nemini nocentem, communique utilitati non repugnantem. Unde dicitur quisque *jus* habere, ad ea omnia agenda, habenda, aut ab aliis consequenda: quique {alium quemvis} impediret ita agere aut habere, aut quod ita postulatur praestare recusaret, *injuriam* facere diceretur.

Altius verò rem repetenti patebit, hanc naturae nostrae fabricam, clara continere indicia voluntatis Dei, alias hominum actiones jubentis, alias ve-

✺ BOOK II ✺

Elements of the Law of Nature.

CHAPTER I

Of the Law of Nature.

I. That we may shew how all the several parts of life may be brought into a conformity to nature, and the better discern the several Rights and Duties of Mankind, we shall premise the more general Doctrine in Morals, <unfolding and> explaining some pretty complex notions {and terms constantly occurring}; and this is "the subject of this and the two following chapters."[1]

In the preceeding book we shewed, how from the very structure of our nature we derived our first notions of right and wrong{, virtuous and vitious, in our affections and actions}: and that it was then *right* and *just* that any Person should act, possess, or demand from others{, in a certain manner}, "when his doing so tended <110> either directly to the common interest of all, or to the interest of {some part or} some individual, without occasioning any detriment to others."[2] And hence we say in such cases that a man *has a right* thus to act, possess or demand: and whoever would obstruct or hinder him thus to act or possess, or would not comply with such demand, is said to do an *injury* or *wrong*.

But resuming this matter a little higher; 'tis plain that this structure of our nature exhibits clear evidences of the will of God {and nature about

---

1. The sentence inserted in braces translates the text of the 1742 edition and is identical to *System* 2.1.[1], vol. I, p. 227.
2. See *System* 2.3.1, vol. I, p. 253.

tantis. {Atque licet *legis* notio, cui congruant aut non congruant voluntates aut actiones, sit *artificialis* et factitia; ita tamen ubique gentium et in omni tempore hominibus familiaris et facilis fuit, ut meritò naturalis etiam dicatur. Etenim *justae potestatis* cognitio facillima est, ex ea quam in liberos immaturos, ipsis utilissimam, parentibus natura tribuit.} Idque usu {etiam omnibus} compertum, homines {adultos} non semper suo marte, sed aliorum monitis saepius scire quae sint vitae profutura aut nocitura; (prudentiorum enim judicio et monitis, cognitionis et prudentiae humanae bona pars innititur:) quumque hominum quosdam caeteris multò esse 30 lertiores, fatebuntur et ipsi qui minus sapiunt; jubebit semper ἡγεμονικὸν illud cuique infixum, ut coetus hominum numerosiores, in communem conjuncti utilitatem, prudentioribus quibusdam <116> rectionem omnium permittant, cogantque renitentes, ut eorum jussis obsequantur qui hoc legitimum nacti sunt imperii jus. Hinc [pervulgata] [omnibus nota] est *justi imperii* notio [justa imperandi potestas]; ubicunque scil: ex ipsa imperii delati forma et modo satis constat, nulla fore imperantibus ad peccandum invitamenta, aut spem saltem nullam aut exiguam, imperio sibi permisso in populi perniciem impunè abutendi. Cuique notissima igitur est *legis* vis et natura, quae est "jure imperantis voluntas, subditis declarata, actiones alias jubens, alias vetans, praemiis propositis et poenis."

II. Quum autem constet, Deum esse et optimum et maximum, constabit etiam, ad omnium communem, et cujusque propriam pertinere foelicitatem, ut omnes Deo, sive jubenti, sive vetanti, pareant; cui sanctissime de-

our conduct}, requiring certain actions and prohibiting others.[3] The notion of a *law* to which our <wills or> actions may be compared, is, no doubt, *artificial,* formed upon observation: and yet it has in all ages been so obvious and familiar to men that it may also be called natural. For the notion of a *just power,* or *right of governing* others, is obviously intimated, from that power nature has invested the Parent with, over his children, so manifestly tending to their good. And this too is known to all by constant experience, that the bulk of mankind don't by any nice reasonings or observation of their own discover what is advantageous or hurtful in life; nay that the greater part of the practical sagacity and wisdom of the generality depends upon the discoveries and instructions of a few, who have had greater penetration and sagacity: and since {'tis commonly known, and} even the men of less sagacity acknowledge it, {that there are great diversities of genius,} and that some few have superior abilities to the common herd: that moral [ruling] principle implanted in all must also recommend it as advantageous to all, that large societies of men united for <III> their common interest, should commit the administration of their common concerns to {a council of} a few of the wiser sort, and compell any who may thereafter be refractory to submit to their orders, who have thus obtained a just right of governing. Hence the notion of *just power,* or of a *right of governing,* is among the most common and familiar with mankind, when from the very plan and model of power constituted, there's tolerable precaution taken that the Rulers shall have either no inducements to abuse it to the detriment of the whole body, or no hopes of doing so with impunity. Hence the notion of [the force and nature of] *law* too is obvious to all, to wit, "The will of those vested with just power of governing, declared to their subjects, requiring certain actions and forbidding others with denunciations of rewards or punishments."[4]

II. Now since 'tis generally agreed among men, that the Deity is endued with the highest goodness, as well as with wisdom and power; it must obviously follow that an universal compliance with the will of God must tend

3. See *System* 2.3.7, vol. I, p. 265.
4. See *System* 2.3.8, vol. I, pp. 267–68.

vinciuntur ab ipso creati, conservati, bonisque plurimis munificentissimè cumulati. Constabit ibidem, omnia jussis Dei adversantia, communi etiam adversari foelicitati, animumque prodere ingratissimum. Unde et manifestum est, Deum jure pleno, virtutibus suis perfectissimis innixo, imperium sibi in omnes vindicare.

Sed quum homo, nè suae quidem prudentiae, nedum stabilis et sincerae bonitatis, fidem {satis firmam} apud alios facere queat; <117> quippe quam saepe imitaretur obscura malitia, nullo certo indicio a verâ bonitate secernenda, siquidem ea ratione ad imperia ascendere daretur: quumque nullum imperium suspectum et formidatum, populo de sua salute dubio, utile aut laetum esse possit; non ex prudentiae suae aut bonitatis opinione eximia, recte imperium sibi arrogabit homo, si absit eorum consensus qui imperio subjiciuntur, neque ipsis satis cautum sit, ne potestas assumpta in populi perniciem convertatur.

III. Quumque porro [rerum omnium rector et] [hominum] fabricator Deus, eum recti et honesti sensum nobis inseruit, easque rationis vires, quarum ope, observatâ nostra rerumque aliarum naturâ, facile intelligimus quaenam communi omnium, et propriae cujusque inserviant utilitati, quaenam eidem obsint; et simul perspicimus, benigna vitae officia, ipsi qui iis fungitur, fore plerumque utilia, contraria vero inutilia; obtinebunt haec omnia rectae rationis praecepta,{*} sive *dictata practica,* vim *legis* a Deo jussae, sancitae, et promulgatae.

---

* {Hac de quaestione totâ legantur *Cumberlandi* prolegomena, et caput I. libri *De lege naturae,* contra *Hobbesium.*}

both to the general good, and to that of each individual; to which compliance also we are most sacredly bound in gratitude, as we were created
<and preserved> by him, and are constantly deriving good from his mu-
nificent hand: it must also in like manner follow, that all disobedience to
the will of God must be opposite to the common felicity, and shew a base
ungrateful mind.[5] Now these considerations plainly shew that it is perfectly
just and right in the Deity to assume to himself the government of his
rational creatures, and that his *right* is founded upon his own *moral excellencies.* <112>

But since no man can give sufficient evidence to the satisfaction of all,
that he is possessed even of superiour wisdom, and much less of his stable
inflexible goodness; since ambitious dissimulation would always make the
greatest shew of goodness, if this were a sure step to ascend to power; nor
can men search into each others hearts to detect such hypocrisy: and since
no power generally suspected and dreaded can make a people, who are dif-
fident of their most important interests, easy or happy; no man can justly
assume to himself power over others upon any persuasion of his own superior wisdom or goodness, unless the body of the people are also persuaded
of it, or consent to be subjected to such power, upon some reasonable security given them, that the power intrusted shall not be abused to their
destruction.

III. And further since it was God our Creator <and ruler> who implanted
this sense of right and wrong in our souls, and gave us these powers of
reason, which observing our own constitution, and that of persons and
other things around us, discovers what conduct tends either to the common
prosperity of all, or that of individuals, and what has a contrary tendency;
and shews also that all sorts of kind offices generally tend to the happiness
of the person who discharges them, and the contrary offices to his detriment: all these precepts or practical dictates of *right reason* are plainly so
many *laws,** enacted, ratified by penalties, and promulgated by God {in the

---

5. On this section see *System* 2.3.7, vol. I, pp. 265–67.
* On this subject see Cumberland's *Prolegomena,* or introduction, and Ch. 1. Concerning the law of nature. [See also *System* II.3.8, vol. I, p. 268.]

In omni lege duae sunt partes *praeceptum* et *sanctio:* illud. jubet aut vetat; haec monstrat praemia iis tribuenda qui legi paruerint, <118> poenasque eos manentes qui eam violaverint. In legibus civilibus, praeter praemia quibusdam propria, hoc commune est, ut qui paruerint, omni civium jure, et communibus vitae civilis commodis, fruantur. Poenae verbis disertis plerumque sunt annexae. Legum naturalium sanctiones innotescunt, quo modo et praecepta. Omnia nempe animi gaudia, spesque laetae, quae virtutes suâ natura comitantur; omnes item utilitates, sive sponte ab honestis officiis nascentes, sive ab hominum comprobatione et benevolentia, sive ab ipso Deo sperandae; sive in hac vita, sive in illa quae insecutura est, sunt legum naturalium praemia. Poenae sunt, mala omnia interna aut externa, ex vitiis sua sponte nascentia, animi morsus, inquietudines, ipsique metus molestissimi; omnia denique quae a Deo hominibusque infensis, recta docet ratio esse metuenda.

IV. Lex etiam divina, pro varia promulgandi ratione, vel est *naturalis,* vel quae *positiva* dicitur. *Naturalis,* per rationem rerum constitutionem observantem innotescit; *positiva,* signis institutis, voce nempe aut scripto, promulgatur.

Leges voce promulgatae aut scripto, sunt ratione materiae, vel *necessariae,* vel *non necessariae.* Utilitatem {quidem} aliquam communem spectare debet, et solet, omnis <119> lex: Aliae tamen leges monstrant ejus consequendae rationes unicas et necessarias, adeo ut contrariae leges inutiles essent aut pestiferae; aliae {contra} inter diversas rationes, quarum nulla omnino incommoda, optimas eligunt; aut inter aequè commodas, unam; ubi

---

6. Square brackets by the translator, to notice his own comment.
7. Pufendorf, *De officio* 1.2.7. See *System* 2.3.8, vol. I, p. 268.

very constitution of nature}. [As words or writing <113> are not essential
to the nature of a law, but only the most convenient way of notifying it.]⁶

In every law there are two parts, the *precept* and the *sanction*.⁷ The precept
shews what is required or forbidden; and the sanctions contain the rewards
or punishments abiding the subjects, as they observe or violate the precept.
In Civil Laws, beside the peculiar rewards or *premiums* proposed in some
of them, there is this general reward understood in them all, that by obedience we obtain {the defence and protection of the state}, with the other
common advantages of a civilized life, and [all] the rights of citizens. The
penalties of human laws are generally expressed. The sanctions of the law
of nature are known and promulgated in like manner with the preceptive
part. The *rewards* are all those internal joys and comfortable hopes which
naturally attend a virtuous course; and all these external advantages whether
immediately arising from good actions, or generally obtained by the good-
will and approbation of others, or of the Deity, whether in this life or in a
future state. The *penalties* are all those evils internal or external, which naturally ensue upon vice; such as remorse, solicitude, and distressing fears and
dangers: in fine, all these evils which right reason shews may probably be
expected to ensue through the just resentment of the Deity or of our fellow-
creatures.

IV. The divine laws according to the different manners of promulgation
are either *natural* or *positive*.⁸ *Natural* laws are discovered by our reason
observing the natures of things. *Positive* laws are revealed only by words or
writing. Laws <revealed by words or writing> may again be divided according <114> to the matter of them into the *necessary* and the *not-
necessary*.⁹ Every sort of law indeed should have in view some real benefit
to the state: but some laws point out the sole and necessary means of obtaining some great benefit{, or of averting some great evil}; so that contrary
{or even different} laws could not answer the necessary purposes of society:
while others only fix upon the most convenient means, where many others
might have tolerably answered the end; or, where there's a variety of means

8. Pufendorf, *De officio* 1.2.16.
9. See *System* 2.3.9, vol. I, pp. 269–70.

{hoc} exigit vita communis, ut in unâ quadam plures conveniant.{*} Quod usu venit in locis, temporibus, aliisque ejusmodi constituendis, ubi pluribus commune negotium simul est obeundum. Hae dicuntur etiam, ratione materiae, *positivae;* illae *naturales.*

V. Leges fere omnes, praecipue naturales, totum respiciunt populum, vel omnes ex certo ordine. Inter homines nonnunquam feruntur *privilegia;* eaque vel in gratiam, vel in odium. Est *privilegium,* "lex privata, unum aut paucos respiciens." Si ob merita praeclara, in gratiam feratur privilegium, neque communi obsit utilitati, est justum. Incidere potest {etiam}, licet rarius, ut in odium scelerati et malitiosi, justum irrogari possit privilegium.

Aequitas, sive *Ἐπιείκεια,* est "legis correctio et emendatio, ubi verba legum causis non sunt adaequata"; magis, utpote, aut minus quam par est porrecta. Locum habet hoc aequitatis genus, tantum in legibus quae <120> verbis enunciantur. Lex {enim} naturalis, non verbis, sed [ast] ratione duce, omnia ex aequo et bono determinat.

VI. *Dispensationes,* quas vocant, invexit *jus canonicum,* quibus aliquis legibus solvitur. Harum varia sunt genera; dantur enim *exemptiones,* sive immunitates, vel a praecepto, vel sanctione. Ubi quidem ita delicti admissi

---

* {Illae, ratione materiae, *necessariae* dicuntur leges; hae *non necessariae.*}

---

10. Here the translator cancels an unnecessary note of the Latin text.
11. See *System* 2.3.9, vol. I, pp. 269–70, for some examples.
12. See Pufendorf's, *De iure nat.* 1.6.18 and *De officio* 1.2.16.

equally apposite, yet fix upon one set of them, when 'tis necessary that multitudes should agree in using the same means.[10] Such is the case in appointing *set times* and *places,* and other *circumstances,* where matters of common concern are to be transacted jointly by many.[11] These latter sort of laws are also called *positive* as to their matter, and the former *natural,* in the same respect.[12]

V. Laws generally respect alike a whole people, or at least all of a certain class or order; this holds as to all natural laws. But sometimes civil laws are made in singular cases, respecting only one person; these the Romans called *privilegia;* which were either out of singular favour, or singular resentment. If such *privileges* are granted for extraordinary merits, and have no pernicious tendency toward the body, they are very justifiable. Cases may happen too, tho' seldom, in which it may be just to bring to punishment some very artful dangerous criminal by a special law{, which is not to be made a precedent in the ordinary procedure of justice}.

Equity is {sometimes understood as something distinct <115> from *strict law,* being} "the reasonable wise correction of any imperfection in the words of the law, [by their being either not sufficiently extended, or too extensive in regard to the true reason or design of the law.] [when they are not adequate to the circumstances.]" This equity has place only as to laws promulgated in words; for the law of nature determines all points, not by words but, by right reason, and what is humane and good.[13]

VI. The doctrine of the <so called> *dispensations* was brought in by the Canon-law. A dispensation is "the exempting one {out of special favour} from the obligation of a law."[14] Dispensations <or immunity> are either from the preceptive part, or from the sanction, in remitting the penalty. Where the penalty is remitted or altered in such a manner as consists with

---

13. See *System* 2.3.2, vol. I, p. 274.
14. The translator draws from Pufendorf's definition in *De officio* 1.2.9. Cf. *System* 2.3.12, vol. I, p. 275. Hutcheson enlarges on the subject in pp. 275–80.

datur venia, aut tollitur sanctio, ut communi interea satis consulatur utilitati, legumque conservetur vis et majestas, nihil est in eo iniqui. Istiusmodi
dispensationes nonnunquam largiendi potestas, summis plerumque permittitur civitatum rectoribus. <Praecedens> A praecepti verò justi vinculo
immunitas, aegerrimè admittenda.

At (1.) nulla intelligitur esse *dispensatio,* si quis eo usus jure quod ipsi
leges tribuunt, aut potestate quavis sibi per leges permissâ, vicini perimat
obligationem, aut novam ipsi imponat. Ut si creditor debitum remittat; aut
civitatis rector ea agat quae jure potest, per se, vel per alios suo mandato
instructos.

(2.) Legibus aliquando minimè iniquis, sive divinis, sive humanis, datur
quibusdam immunitas a poenis externis, quas actionibus parum honestis
promeruere; ubi pro populi hebetudine, vel moribus pravis, non <121> alia
ratione, graviora praecaveri possunt mala. At neque hoc volunt esse
dispensare.

(3.) Nulla rectoris cujusvis permissione, aut jussu, vel pravi animi motus
fieri possunt boni, vel ex bonis mali: neque magis immutari potest actionum, ex animi virtutibus aut vitiis manantium, natura. *Dispensationes*
igitur a praeceptis, quas volunt canonici, tantum sunt justae, quando leges
ipsae sunt aut improbae aut stolidae: quarum ingentem farraginem invexit
jus canonicum.

VII. Jus naturale, quum legum multitudinem in corpus quoddam com-
positam sonat, aliud dicitur *primarium,* aliud *secundarium:* hoc mutabile,
illud immutabile volunt. Non tamen ex propositionibus evidentibus et noe-

---

15. Here the translator cleverly follows either the first edition of the *Institutio* or the
System (see 2.3.2, vol. I, pp. 275–76), or both.

* See *Vinnius*'s comment on the Instit. lib. i. 2. II. The same distinction is variously
explained by other authors; but scarce any of them so explain it as to make it of im-

the common safety, and does not weaken the authority and influence of the law, it is not to be blamed. Such a dispensing power {for singular important reasons} is frequently vested in the supreme Rulers or Magistrates of States. But for {previous}[15] exemptions from the preceptive part of any wise law they can never be reasonable.

But first, we don't count it a dispensation when any one, using his own right and the ordinary power vested in him by law, frees another from some legal obligation, or imposes a new one. As when a creditor remits a debt; or the supreme Governor <acts or> commissions subjects to act in his name what he has a right to execute, {tho' without such commission these subjects had acted illegally in doing so}.

Again, sometimes by laws, whether divine or human, an external impunity may be justly and wisely granted <116> to such conduct as is very vitious and culpable; if either through the stupidity or depravity of the people such vices could not be restrained without much greater inconvenience than what arises from the permission of them. But this comes not up to the notion of dispensation.

But in the third place, no grant or permission of any governor, human or divine, can make evil malevolent affections become morally good or innocent, or benevolent ones become evil: nor can the moral nature of actions flowing from them be any more altered by mere command or permission. The *dispensations* therefor, the *Canonists* intend, are then only justifiable, when the laws themselves are bad or imprudent, of which the Canon-law contains a great multitude.

VII. The *Law of nature* as it denotes a large collection of precepts is commonly divided into the *primary* and *secondary;* the former they suppose immutable, the latter mutable. This division is of no use as some explain it,* that the primary consists of self-evident <and noetic> propositions, and

---

portance. [Here the translator, referring to Arnoldus Vinnius (*In quattuor libros Institutionum imperialium Commentarius academicus et forensic,* Amsterdam 1692), as well as Hutcheson, adopts Carmichael's criticism of the distinction between primary and secondary laws. See *Notes on Puf.,* p. 203.]

ticis, constat prius; neque ex dianoeticis solis, posterius: quaeque etiam ex certis sequuntur praemissis conclusiones, pariter sunt certae et immuta- biles. Neque alio sensu est utilis haec distinctio, quam si praecepta, quae ad vitam tolerabilem sunt omnino necessaria, dicantur primaria; quae au- tem ad vitae ornatum, et uberiorem foelicitatem faciunt, secundaria. Neque in foro Dei, sunt haec prioribus mutabiliora; quamvis violantibus saepius detur immunitas a poenis externis.

Ex iis quae in libro superiore sunt dicta, patebit officia nostra omnia, prout lege quadam <122> naturali a Deo praecepta {sunt}, duabus mon- strari legibus primariis: quarum prima est, *Deum esse colendum;* cum quo conjunctum est, quod ei in omnibus sit obsequendum.

Altera est, *communi omnium utilitati et foelicitati, et singulorum quorum- vis, dummodo ea communiori aut majori non adversetur, esse prospiciendum.*

the secondary of such as require reasoning.[16] Many of those they count primary require reasoning <and the other way round>: nor are just conclusions more mutable than the self-evident premises. The only useful sense of this distinction is, when such precepts as are absolutely necessary to any tolerable social state are called the *primary;* and such as are not of such necessity, but tend to some considerable improvement or ornament of life <117> are called *secondary.* But these latter in the sight of God and our own consciences are not mutable, {nor can be transgressed without a crime, more than the primary;} altho' there may be many political constitutions where the violation of these secondary precepts passes with impunity.

From the doctrine of the former book it must appear, that all our duties, as they are conceived to be enjoined by some divine precept [natural law ordered by God], are included in these two general [primary] laws, the one that "God is to be worshipped {with all love and veneration}": and in consequence of it, that "he is to be obeyed in all things."

The second is, that "we ought to promote {as we have opportunity} the common good of all, and that of particular {societies or} persons, while it no way obstructs the common good, or that of greater societies."

16. Hutcheson, as well as Carmichael, contrasts *noetic* and *dianoetic* propositions, according the common Aristotelian and Scholastic distinction between Nous, i.e., the intellect that knows the first principles, and Dianoia, or discursive thought, i.e., the intellect that makes use of argumentation.

CAPUT II

De Juris Natura et divisionibus.

I. Quum communi omnium saluti et prosperitati conservandae,] [Quod ut fiat,]¹ amica hominum societas conjunctioque sit omnino tuenda et conservanda, [quod per se satis patet; atque simul haec sit officiorum erga homines summa ut omnium saluti et foelicitati prospiciamus, constabit] [ut ex mox dicendi patebit. Hac autem de causa] actiones omnes, quibus quisquam sibi, aut suis ita benefacit, ut aliorum utilitati non obsit, esse omnino licitas; quum, qui uni prodest parti, caeteris inviolatis, toti etiam prosit societati. Deinde, quum sint utilitates plurimae et voluptates; quas, {nemine laeso}, sibi aut suis, in certo rerum statu, comparare possunt homines, {studioseque appetere solent,} quasque iis salvas praestari, nec ab aliis hominibus <123> impediri, auferri, aut intercipi, humanae interest societatis; quum id {et ad singulorum foelicitatem, et} ad amicam hominum conjunctionem conservandam pertineat; ad has utilitates aut voluptates capiendas, censentur homines habere *jura,* eâ altera, quam diximus; lege naturali planè constituta, aut munita: quippe quae jubeat et confirmet {omnia} quae quicquam ad communem omnium, aut singulorum, ubi nemini nocetur, conferunt utilitatem: haec igitur omnia jurè fieri dicuntur. {Quinetiam quae cujusque sunt erga alios officia honesta, ea et cuique sensus animi sublimiores commendant; eademque isti, in amica vitae conjunctione, suo merito, aut *jure* aliquo, postulare possunt, et expetere atque expectare solent:} vix igitur commodius {*officiorum praecepta,* aut} *naturae Leges,* quae dicuntur, *speciales,* {sive jurisprudentia naturalis,} tradi poterunt, quam explicando omnia quae vel singulis hominibus, hominum coe-

---

1. Neither a new chapter, nor a new paragraph in 1742 edition.

Of the Nature of Rights, and Their Several Divisions.

I. Since it is manifestly necessary to the common interest of all that large numbers of men should be joined together in amicable societies, and as this is the sum of all our duties toward men that we promote their happiness {as we have opportunity}; it must follow that all actions by which any one procures to himself or his friends any advantage, while he obstructs no advantage of others, must be lawful: *since he who profits one part without hurting any other plainly profits the whole.* Now since there are many enjoyments and advantages naturally desired by all, which <in safe circumstances> one may procure to himself, his family or friends, without hurting others, and which 'tis plainly the interest of society that each one should be allowed to procure, without any obstruction from others, (since otherways no friendly, peaceable society could be maintained:) [since it is relevant to the preservation of a friendly society as well as to the happiness of individuals] we therefor deem that each man has a *right* to procure and obtain {for himself or his friends} such advantages and enjoyments; which Right is plainly established and secured to him by the second general precept above mentioned, enjoining and confirming whatever tends to the general good of all, or to the good of any part without detriment to the rest. In all such cases therefor men are said to act according to their *right*. <119> [1]And then, as the several offices due to others are <also> recommended to us by the sense of our own hearts [by our higher senses]; so others in a social life have a claim to them, and both desire, and naturally or justly expect them from us, as some way due to them: in consequence of this it must appear, that the several rules of duty, or special laws of nature [or laws of nature called *special*], <or *natural jurisprudence*>, cannot be delivered in a more easy manner than by considering all the several *claims*

1. Not a new paragraph in the *Institutio*.

tibus, aut denique humano generi competunt, aut competere possunt *jura;*
ea quippe omnia lege aliqua speciali muniri censentur.

{Varia igitur hominum jura monstrant primò sensus appetitionesque
naturales, ea exposcentes quae ad suam cujusque aut suorum utilitatem faciunt, aut officia erga alios amica commendantes: quae tamen omnia, <124>
secundum rectam rationem, communi utilitate ita dirigenda, ne quid contra eandem admittatur aut ab aliis postuletur.}

[Haec altera est *juris* notio praeter eam modò explicatam, quando legum
collectionem sonat: notat enim saepius][2] [Praeter eam juris significationem,
quam memoravimus, alia est ejus acceptio;] *qualitatem quandam moralem*
[, aut facultatem homini rectè concessam.] [homini competentem notans.].
Qua autem ratione, ex recti et honesti sensu, ortatur haec juris notio, nulla
legis cujuslibet habita ratione, satis est dictum.{*} Cognita autem legis naturalis, quae omnia continet rectae rationis praecepta, sive *dictata practica,*
notione, expeditiores erunt, et breviores rerum moralium definitiones,
quum ad legem referuntur; atque eundem praestabunt usum, si modo hoc
teneamus, leges omnes naturales, communem omnium utilitatem, et singulorum, communiori utilitati non adversantem unicè spectare.

Jus igitur est, "Facultas homini lege concessa, ad aliquid agendum, habendum, aut ab alio consequendum." Non tamen, {quod antea docuimus,}
juris omnis notio prima includit vel legis concedentis rationem, vel communis utilitatis ab eo proventurae. Recti enim et honesti sensu, atque sensu
cujusque communi, comprobabitur, quicunque, nemine laeso, vel sibi vel
suis prodest, sive agendo, sive occupando, ante legem <125> ullam, aut

---

2. Here was the beginning of chapter II—with the same title—in 1742 edition.
* {Lib. I. Cap. 1, 12. et Cap. praecedente Lib. II.}

or *rights* competent either to individuals, to societies, or to mankind in general as a great body or society; all which are the matter of [deemed granted by] some special laws.

The several rights of mankind are therefor first made known, by the natural feelings of their hearts, and their natural desires, pursuing such things as tend to the good of each individual or those dependent on him: and recommending to all certain virtuous offices. But all such inclinations or desires are to be regulated by right reason, with a view to the general good of all <so that nothing is allowed or claimed against the common interest>.

Thus we have the notion of *rights* as [This is another notion of right besides the one just explained referred to the collection of laws, usually meaning some] moral qualities, or *faculties,* granted by the law of nature to certain persons.[2] We have already sufficiently explained how these notions of our *rights* arise from that *moral sense* of right and wrong, natural to us previous to any consideration of law or command.<*> But when we have ascended to the notion of a {divine} natural law, {requiring whatever tends to the general good, and} containing all these <precepts or> practical dictates of right reason, our definitions of moral qualities may be abridged by referring them to a law; and yet they will be of the same import; if we still remember that the grand aim of the <120> law of nature is the general good of all, and of every part as far as the general interest allows it.

A Right therefor may be defined "a faculty {or claim} established by law to act, or possess, or obtain something from others"; tho'<, as we explained before,> the primary notion of right [is prior to that of a law, nor does it always include a reference to the most extensive interest of the whole of mankind][has a reference to a law granting it or to the common interest coming forth from this right]. For by our natural sense of right and wrong, and our sympathy with others, we immediately approve any persons procuring to himself or his friends any advantages which are not hurtful to others, without any thought either about a law or the general interest of

2. See *System* 2.3.1, vol. I, p. 253.
* <Book I. Chap. 1.12. and previous chap., book II.> [This note is left out by the translator, perhaps with good reason: neither the previous chapter, nor Book I, chap. I, sect. xii, explains why our notions of *rights* arise from *moral sense.*]

communiorem utilitatem spectatam. Ex singulorum foelicitate exsurgit communis omnium foelicitas: {atque} in suam cujusque, et suorum utilitatem, cuique inseruit Deus naturales appetitus et caritates; comprobantur etiam, aut saltem non damnantur, conatus ex his orti, idque per se; ubi nec alterius adversantur utilitati, neque sensui aut appetitui nobiliori obstare videntur. Hinc et jure suo quisque ea agere aut occupare censetur, ex quibus nullum aliis oritur damnum; ipsi vero qui agit aut occupat, iisve quos caros habet, nascitur emolumentum.

Hoc tamen omnino tenendum; nullum esse jus privatum ad quicquam agendum, habendum, aut consequendum, quod communi omnium utilitati est contrarium: haec enim omni sive singulorum, sive coetuum juri, modum ponere debet.

II. Quumque hominum saluti, ne de vita dicamus copiosa et jucundâ, necessaria sit plurium conjunctio, ubi vigeant commercia, et mutua auxilia; (quod quidem satis notum est omnibus, neque disputatione eget;) quae ad hominum conjunctionem amicam, et consociationem, tuendam sunt necessaria, ea lege naturali omninò jubentur: quaeque societatis tuendae ratio exigit, ut cuique permittantur agenda, habenda, aut <126> ab aliis consequenda, ea dicitur quisque *jure suo* agere, tenere, aut postulare.

{Ut} juri omni respondet lex quaedam, jus illud constituens aut confirmans, ita etiam *obligatio*. Dicimur obligari ad aliquid agendum, aut alteri dandum faciendum, cum internus cujusque sensus eas actiones aut praestationes esset comprobaturus, omniaque contraria, tanquam turpia et foeda, improbaturus. Eâdem ratione intelligitur *obligatio* ad abstinendum: atque hoc sensu, [separatâ legis notione] [ante legem latam] intelligitur obligatio. Alia vocis acceptione, omnis referenda est ad legem obligatio, et praecipuè ad divinam; quum scil. notat "gravissimum, ex suae utilitatis ratione, invitamentum, ad aliquid agendum, aut omittendum, homini propositum": quod legibus praecipue fieri potest divinis. Atque huc recidunt

all. For as the general happiness is the result of the happiness of individuals; and God has for the benefit of each individual, and of families, implanted in each one his private appetites and desires, with some tender natural affections in these narrower systems: actions flowing from them are therefor naturally approved, or at least deemed innocent, and that immediately for themselves, unless they should appear hurtful to others, or opposite to some nobler affection. Hence every one is conceived to have a *right* to act or claim whatever does no hurt to others, and naturally tends to his own advantage, or to that of persons dear to him.

And yet this we must still maintain, that no private right < to act, possess, or demand from others> can hold against the general interest of all. For a regard to the most extensive advantage of the whole system ought to controll and limit all the rights of individuals or of particular societies. < 121 >

II. Now since a friendly society with others, and a mutual intercourse of offices, and the joint aids of many, are absolutely necessary not only to the pleasure and convenience of human life, but even to the preservation of it; which is so obvious{*} that we need not reason upon it. Whatever appears necessary for preserving an amicable society among men must necessarily be enjoined by the Law of Nature. And in whatever circumstances the maintaining of peace in society requires, that certain actions, possessions, or claims should be left free and undisturbed to any one, he is justly deemed to have a *right* so to act, possess, or claim from others.[3] As some law answers to each right < establishing and enforcing it>, so does an *obligation*. {This word has two senses,} 1. We are said to be *obliged* to act, or perform to others, "when the inward sense {and conscience} of each one must approve such action or performance, and must condemn the contrary as vitious and base": in like manner we conceive an obligation to omit or abstain. This sort of obligation is conceived previous to any thought of the injunction of a law. 2. Obligation is sometimes taken for "a motive of interest superior to all motives on the other side, proposed to induce us to certain actions or performances, or omissions of action." Such motives indeed must arise

* {See Cicero's Offices, B. ii. 3, 4, 5, &c.}
3. A new paragraph in the *Institutio*.

fere omnes obligationis definitiones, quas afferunt illi, qui eam omnem ex legibus ortam volunt: neque aliud sonant metaphorica illa, *vinculum juris, necessitate astringens;* aut, *necessitas absoluta homini imposita.*

III. Jura, pro diversa ad societatem tuendam et excolendam necessitate, dividuntur in *perfecta,* et *imperfecta:* illorum tanta est necessitas, ut iis communiter spretis et violatis, disturbanda foret omnis hominum societas et conjunctio. Sunt igitur <127> hujusmodi jura omnibus per vim conservanda et defendenda; eorumque violatio poenis gravissimis est coercenda.

Imperfecta quae dicuntur jura, ad societatem excolendam et ornandam, plurimum nonnunquam conferunt; atque [eorum] [ad ea praestanda] quae jure imperfecto exiguntur, sanctissima saepe est obligatio: sunt tamen ejusmodi, ut graviora sequerentur incommoda, nisi cujusque pudori et honestati ea permittantur praestanda, aut negligenda; in iis cuique religiose <observandis &> praestandis, elucent illae bonorum virtutes, quibus praecipue laus et gloria comparatur.

---

4. Literally: "According to another meaning, obligation has always a reference to a law and, particularly, to a divine law, denoting 'a solemn inducement imposed upon men, for reason of its utility, to perform or to omit certain actions.' Such inducements can be brought about especially by divine laws." See *System* 2.3.6, vol. I, p. 264.

* {These are the definitions of *Puffendorf,* and of *Barbeyrac* in his notes on *Grotius,* as also in his animadversions on a *Censure upon Puffendorf,* ascribed commonly to Mr. *Leibnitz,* published with the French Translation of the book *de Officio Hominis et Civis.*} [The translator rightly refers to Samuel Pufendorf, *De iure nat. libri octo,* Lund, 1672, I.1.21 and I.6.5, Hugo Grotius, *Les Droit de la guerre et de la paix,* trans. Jean Barbeyrac, 2 vols., Amsterdam, 1724, I.1.9–10 and notes by Barbeyrac, p. 47, note 5 and pp. 48–49, note 4, and Pufendorf's *Les Devoirs de l'homme, et du citoien,* ed. J. Barbeyrac, Amsterdam, 1718, published with [Gottfried Wilhelm von Leibniz's] *Jugement d'un anonyme sur l'orginal de cet abrégé* [De officio]: *avec des réflexions du Traducteur* [Barbeyrac], pp. 429–

from the laws of an omnipotent Being.[4] This latter meaning seems chiefly intended in these metaphorical definitions of great authors, who would have all obligation to arise from the law {of a superior},{*} *"a bond of right binding us by a necessity* <122> *of acting or abstaining"* or an *"absolute necessity imposed upon a man, to act in certain manner."*[5]

III. Rights according as they are more or less necessary to the preservation of a social life are divided into *perfect* and *imperfect.* Perfect rights are of such necessity that a general allowing them to be <disregarded or> violated must entirely destroy all society <and union>: and therefor such rights ought to be maintained <and preserved> to all even by violence: and the severest punishments inflicted upon the violation of them.[6]

Imperfect rights {or claims} are sometimes indeed of the greatest consequence to the happiness and ornament of society, and our obligation to maintain them, and to perform to others what they thus claim, may be very sacred: yet they are of such a nature that greater evils would ensue in society from making them matters of compulsion, than from leaving them free to each one's honour and conscience to comply with them or not.[7] 'Tis by a conscientious regard to these imperfect rights or claims of others, {which are not matters of compulsion,} that virtuous men have an occasion of displaying their virtues, and obtaining the esteem and love of others.

---

95. Hutcheson has likely in mind also Richard Cumberland, *De legibus naturae disquisitio philosophica,* London, 1672, V, 11, for Cumberland criticizes the metaphorical [i.e., circular] use of the word vinculum (bond) in the common definition of the obligation drawn from Justinian's *Institutes,* III, XIV, quoted by Pufendorf as well as by Hutcheson here.]

5. For a parallel but shorter, and in some details different, account of obligation, see *System* 2.3.6, vol. I, p. 264: referring the reader to "Leibnitz's censure on Puffendorf and Barbeyraque's defence of him," Hutcheson says that "ingenious men have contradicted each other with keenness; some asserting an obligation antecedent to all view of interest, or laws; others deriving the original source of obligation from the law or will of an omnipotent Being." See the introduction, pp. xiv–xvi.

6. See *System* 2.3.3, vol. I, p. 257.

7. See *System* 2.3.3, vol. I, p. 258.

Non vero facilè definiuntur limites inter jura omnia perfecta et imperfecta. Sensim enim, et per innumeros gradus, ascendimus a levissimo quoque jure imperfecto, per graviora et sanctiora, ad ea quae a perfectis vix secerni possunt; prout varii sunt hominum necessitudines, et merita, et dignitates, quibus innituntur jura imperfecta. Debentur viro cuivis innocenti, licet alienigenae, quaedam humanitatis officia; quae sanctiore jure postularet civis, aut vicinus; multò sanctiore propinqui, amici, fratres, parentes; haec tamen omnia censentur jura imperfecta.

Tertium addi potest juris, fucati potius quam veri, genus; quod dicitur *externum;* quum scil. utilitatis cujusdam remotioris ratio <128> exigit, ne impediantur homines quaedam agere, possidere, aut ab aliis deposcere, quae tamen parum honeste, aut non sine turpitudine, in ea causa, agi, possideri, aut flagitari possunt. Hae juris species inanes, nulli viro bono placiturae, saepe oriuntur ex contractibus temerariis, aut ex legibus nonnunquam civilibus minime damnandis.

Patet interea, nullam esse posse pugnam inter vera jura, sive perfecta, sive imperfecta: saepe tamen juri imperfecto obstare potest jus externum: imperfecta autem non sunt per vim asserenda, aut vindicanda; {cumque juris tuendi tantum causa suscipienda sint bella,} nequit <igitur> esse bellum utrinque justum.

IV. In duo etiam genera dividuntur jura, prout *alienari possunt,* aut *non possunt.* Prioris generis sunt ea, quae et verè transferre valemus, quaeque translata aliquem praebent in vita usum. Ubi alterutra deficit conditio, alienari nequeunt jura. Patet igitur internas animi, de religione et cultu Dei,

Yet the boundaries between perfect and imperfect rights are not always easily seen. There is a sort of scale or gradual ascent, through several almost insensible steps,[8] from the lowest and weakest claims of humanity <123> to those of higher and more sacred obligation, {till we arrive at some imperfect rights so strong that they can scarce be distinguished from the perfect,} according to the variety of bonds among mankind, and the various degrees of merit, and claims upon each other. Any innocent person<, even a stranger> may have some claim upon us for certain offices of humanity. But our fellow-citizen or neighbour would have a stronger claim in the like case. A friend, a benefactor, a brother, or a parent would have still a stronger claim, even in these things which we reckon matters of imperfect obligation.

There's also a third kind of Right, or rather an external shew of it, which some call an *external right:* when some more remote considerations of distant utility require that men should not be restrained in certain actions, enjoyments; or demands upon others, which yet are not consistent with a good conscience, or good moral dispositions.[9] These external shews of Right, which will never satisfy a good man as a foundation of conduct, often arise from imprudent contracts {rashly entered into by one of the parties}, and often even from the wisest Civil Laws.

'Tis plain here, that there can be no opposition either between two perfect rights or two imperfect ones. But imperfect rights may be contrary to these called external. Since however the imperfect rights are not matters of just force or compulsion; wars, which are violent prosecutions or defences of some alleged rights, cannot be just on both sides. <124>

IV. Rights are also divided into the *alienable,* and such as *cannot be alienated* or transferred. These are alienable, where the transfer can actually be made, and where some interest of society may often require that they should be transferred from one to another.[10] Unless both these qualities concurr, the Right is to be deemed unalienable. 'Tis plain therefor, for instance, that for

8. See, *System* 2.3.5, vol. I, p. 262.
9. See, *System* 2.3.3, vol. I, p. 259. On rights perfect, imperfect, and external see also, *Inquiry,* II.7.6, pp. 278–81.
10. See, *System* 2.3.4, vol. I, p. 261.

sententias, et affectus internos, quum utraque deficiat conditio, ab omnibus pactis et legibus esse immunes: suo enim cuique judicio necessario utendum; neque utile esse potest, quemquam contra animi sui sententiam quicquam profiteri; aut in Deo colendo ea agere, quae ipse putat esse impia aut vana. <129> Ex generali hac de jure doctrina, efficitur duo esse primaria in societate tuenda praecepta. (1.) "Nequis alterum laedat"; aut dolorem aliquem vel molestiam, hominum societati neque necessariam neque utilem, alteri creet. Dein (2.) "ut quisque pro virili, in communem utilitatem aliquid conferat"; suorum saltem, aut vicinorum utilitati consulens. Atque qui societatis aut systematis parti cuivis prodest, nullo aliis illato detrimento, toti etiam prodest societati.

defect of both these qualities, our opinions in matters of Religion <and worship> are unalienable; and so are our internal affections of devotion; and therefor neither of them can be matters of {commerce,} contract, or human laws. No man can avoid judging according to the evidence which appears to him; nor can any interest of society require one to profess hypocritically contrary to his inward sentiments; or to join in any external worship which he judges foolish or impious{, and without the suitable affections}.

From the general account given of the nature of Right, these must be the two fundamental precepts of a social life; first, that "no man hurt another" or occasion any loss or pain to another which is neither necessary nor subservient to any superior interest of society. The second is "that each one on his part, as he has opportunity, should contribute toward the general interest of society"; at least by contributing toward the interest of his friends or family. And he who innocently profits a Part, contributes also in fact to the good of the whole.

De Virtutum et Vitiorum Gradibus,
inter se comparatis{; iisque
quae speciem moralem afficiunt}.

I. Conscientiae nomen decantatum, primariò denotat ipsum honesti et turpis sensum; aut saltem [in omni conscientiae notione includitur necessariò hic sensus,] [hunc ei sempre antecessione sensum, necesse est;] sine quo nulla cerneretur honesti aut turpis species. Hoc autem posito, ratio monstrabit, quaenam sint actiones externae, quae laudandas aut damnandas indicant animi affectiones. Vulgo definitur conscientia, "judicium hominis de actionibus suis, quod ad moralem attinet speciem," sive de actionibus <130> ad legis praescriptum examinatis. Dicitur vero actio homini *imputari,* sive laudi aut vitio verti, quia ex ipsius voluntate orta, ingenium ejus indicat esse honestum aut turpe.

Conscientia est vel *certa,* vel *probabilis; dubia,* vel *scrupulosa;* quae ex ipsis vocabulis satis innotescunt. Quum de agendo deliberamus, dicitur *antecedens;* quum de praeteritis est judicium, dicitur *subsequens.*

Viri boni conscientia antecedens, anquirit de momento quod habet actio quaevis, ad omnium, aut singulorum utilitatem; quae *bonitas* dicitur *materialis.* Ea enim ratione materiae est bona actio, quae lege praecipitur, aut communi inservit utilitati, quocunque demum animo fuerit suscepta. *Conscientia subsequens* spectat etiam quo animo, quo consilio, actum erat; in quo sita est *bonitas,* quae dicitur, *formalis.* Actio enim legi in adjunctis om-

---

1. See *System* 2.1.5, vol. I, p. 234.

2. See *System* 2.1.1, vol. I, p. 228.

3. In the first four sections of this chapter, it is clearly Hutcheson's intention to treat such themes as imputation, voluntary and necessary actions, vincible and invincible

Concerning the Various Degrees of Virtue and Vice, and the Circumstances on which They Depend.

I. That inward power called *Conscience,* so much talked of, is either this very moral sense {or faculty} we have explained, or includes it as its most essential part; since without this sense we could discern no moral qualities. But when this is presupposed, our reason will shew what external actions are laudable or censurable according as they evidence good or evil affections of soul. *Conscience* is commonly defined to be a "man's judgment concerning the morality of his actions"; or his judgment about his actions as to their conformity or contrariety to the law.[1] And an action is then said to be *imputable,* <or matter of praise and censure> when by its proceeding from his will it evidences his temper and affections to be virtuous or vitious.[2]

The common divisions of conscience, into *certain, probable, doubtful,* or *scrupulous,* need no explication. When we deliberate about our future actions 'tis called *antecedent:* when we judge of past actions, 'tis called *subsequent conscience.*[3]

The antecedent conscience of a good man{, or his previous deliberations,} turn upon the tendencies of actions to the general good of all, or to the innocent enjoyments of individuals, {or of parts of this system}: and this tendency makes an action *materially good.* For <126> actions are called good *materially,* by their having this tendency, or their being required by the law, whatever were the motives or views of the agent. The *subsequent conscience* regards chiefly the motives, design, and intention <of past actions>, on which depends what is called *formal goodness.* For such actions

---

ignorance, conscience and erroneous conscience, discussed by Pufendorf in *De officio* 1.1. However Hutcheson does not follow Pufendorf in his argument; nor is there great similarity between these sections and the corresponding chapter 1, book II, of *System.* On antecedent and subsequent conscience, see Pufendorf, *De iure nat.* 1.3.4.

nibus consentanea [conformis], vel quae ex honestis animi affectionibus profecta est, *formaliter* est *bona.*

II. Quae in virtutibus et vitiis comparandis spectantur adjuncta, vel ad *intellectum* referuntur, vel ad *voluntatem,* vel {ad} *rei ipsius* quae agitur momentum, una cum *agentis viribus* pensitatum.

Hic autem ante omnia constat, eas solas actiones laudi verti aut vitio, sive imputari, <131> quae ab homine fiunt sciente et volente, quaeque si nollet, non fierent: easque tantum omissas imputari, quae si studium non defuisset, fieri poterant: [cujusmodi omnes] [quae] etiam *liberae* dicuntur, et solae ingenii vel honesti vel turpis sunt indicia. Necessaria igitur, quae nobis vel insciis, vel nolentibus, eveniunt, non imputantur: neque *impossibilia,* quae dicuntur, omissa: quae, nempe, etiamsi quis maxime voluisset, fieri non poterant. Non tamen idem de iis dicendum, quae ipsum tantum hominis ingenium, aut animi motus vehementiores, fecerunt necessaria; aut quae ideo tantum impossibilia sunt, quod ea sit hominis indoles, ut ea neutiquam velle possit. {In ipsa enim voluntate, animique habitibus praecipue sita est honestas aut turpitudo: quinetiam suam sibi indolem moresque sponte sibi homines effingunt; aut ea saltem plurimum immutare valent.}

Quae inviti [agere dicuntur] [agunt] homines, ea vel *vi adacti,* ubi valentior renitentis membra impellit vel *ignorantiâ* et *errore* inducti agunt, ubi non norunt quid agitur: quaedam denique sunt *mixta;* ubi quod minime per se gratum est, ad gravius aliquod malum avertendum suscipitur. Quae ab invitis vi adactis [fieri dicuntur] [fiunt], {ea} soli cogenti imputantur:

are called formally good as agree with the law in all respects, and flow from good affections.[4]

II. The circumstances regarded in comparing the morality of actions are of three sorts, as they relate either to the *understanding*, or to the *will*, or to the *importance* of the action itself considered along with the abilities of the agent.

But here 'tis previously certain, that such actions alone are matter of praise or censure, or can be *imputed*, which are done with knowledge and intention, and which had not happened if we had seriously resolved against them. And that in like manner no omission can be imputed where the most hearty inclination would have been without effect. Such actions or omissions are called *free* or voluntary, and such alone carry any evidence of the goodness or depravity of the temper. Necessary events therefor, which would happen even without our knowledge, or against our will, are no matter of imputation; nor is the omission of an [a so called] impossibility, which no desire of ours could have accomplished, any matter of imputation. But this is not the case with such actions as are only called necessary on this account, that the agent's inclination and turn of temper that way, or his passions, were so strong, that during that temper of his he could not will otherways.[5] Nor is it <127> the case in omissions of such actions as are therefor only called impossible, because such was the person's depravity of temper that he could have no inclination to them. Virtue and vice are primarily seated in the temper and affections [habits] themselves; and 'tis generally in our own power in a considerable degree to form and alter our tempers and inclinations.

There are three classes of actions called involuntary, to wit, such as we are compelled to by superior *external force;* such as we do *ignorantly* <or erroneously>*;* and such as are called *mixed*, when we do what of it self is very disagreeable in order to avoid some greater evil. What men are driven to by external force is imputable only to him who uses the violence. What

---

4. On the distinction between formal and material goodness, see Pufendorf, *De iure nat.* 1.7.4 and *System* 2.3.1, vol. I, pp. 252–53.
5. See *System* 2.1.2, vol. I, p. 229.

quae ab ignaris, tunc tantum <132> imputantur, quum ignorantia est culpanda. Mixta omnia imputantur; sunt enim libera, quippe ab agentis voluntate profecta. Imputantur autem in malam partem, aut bonam prout
quae ex actione nascuntur mala, sunt iis quae avertuntur majora, aut minora. Mala verò turpia, malis physicis sunt multo graviora.

III. Quamvis autem in ipsa voluntate, ejusque moribus, praecipuè sita sit
omnis honestas aut turpitudo; ipsius tamen rei, quae agitur, ignorantia, actionis speciem moralem afficiet. Licet enim mala appeteret vir optimus,
siquidem ipsi bona videantur, et honesta; error tamen aut ignorantia saepe
haud culpâ vacat, siquidem *voluntaria* sit, et *vincibilis;* quum, nempe, diligentiâ, ut a viris probis fieri solet, adhibitâ, verum innotuisset. Quae quidem *involuntaria,* et invicta est ignorantia, ab omni culpa vacat.

Voluntaria, deinde, vel est *affectata,* quam dicunt, [sive sponte arcessita,
ubi licet erroris adsit suspicio, de industria tamen] [ubi animo destinato]
verum exquirere nolumus; vel *supina,* ubi socordes, et de officio praestando
improvidi et incauti, animum ad eam rem non advertimus. Prior turpitudinem neque tollit neque imminuit: posterior paulum imminuit; idque
prout major minorve fuerat socordia <133> et negligentia; faciliorque, aut
minus facilis officii cognitio.

Involuntaria est ignorantia, vel *in se, sed non in sua causa,* vel *et in se, et
in sua causa.* Prioris generis est ubi verum inter agendum scire nequit homo;
poterat tamen scivisse, si debitam antea adhibuisset diligentiam, qualem
solent viri probi: posterioris, quum ne eâ quidem adhibita, verum scire poterat. Haec autem sola, non illa, ab omni crimine excusat. Quamvis, enim,
in eo nulla sit turpitudo, quod ea nunc agat homo, quae sibi recta videntur;

is done through ignorance is imputed differently according as the ignorance is culpable or not. But the actions called *mixed* are all imputed, as they are truly free, and proceed from the will: but they are imputed as innocent or as criminal, according as the evil avoided was {in its whole effect} greater or less than the evil done to avoid it. Now moral evils{, and such as hurt the common interest,} are greater than the natural evils{, and such as hurt only the agent}.

III. {As to the circumstances relating to the understanding:} altho' all moral virtue and vice is primarily seated in the will, yet frequently our ignorance or error about the nature of the things we are employed about may affect the morality of actions. And altho' the best of men must intend what is in fact evil, if it appear to them to be good <and honourable>; yet such mistakes are frequently blameable, if the error or ignorance was any <128> way voluntary<, and vincible>, what could have been avoided by such diligence as good men commonly use in such cases. That ignorance indeed which is wholly involuntary and *invincible* excuses from all blame.

Voluntary or vincible ignorance is either *affected,* when men directly design to avoid knowing the truth with some apprehensions of it: or what arises from gross *negligence* or sloth; when men have little solicitude about their duty, and take little thought about their conduct. The former no way diminishes the guilt of the action. The latter may be some alleviation of guilt, and that more or less, according as the sloth was greater or less, or the discovery of the truth was more or less difficult.

Ignorance truly involuntary is so either *in it self but not in its cause,* or it is involuntary in both respects. The former is the case when at present, and in the midst of action, men cannot discover the truth{, tho' they earnestly desire it}; but had they formerly used the diligence required of good men they might have known it. The latter is the case when no prior culpable negligence occasioned our ignorance: and this sort excuses altogether from guilt, but not the former.[6] There is indeed no moral turpitude at present shewn by a man's acting what at present appears to him to be good; but

6. See *System* 2.1.4, vol. I, p. 233.

hic tamen error, eum antegressae arguit negligentiae, quae ingenium prodit parum honestum.

Ignorantia est vel *juris,* vel *facti.* Quae divisio in legibus positivis prae-cipuè locum habet: prout ignota est aut lex, aut rei quae agitur natura. In lege naturali, ipsa rei naturâ probè perspectâ, cum effectis, et eventuum consecutione, utilibus aut nocituris, lex ipsa innotescit.

IV. Quaestionibus, quae de conscientia errante moveri solent, hinc respon-deri poterit.

(1.) Ipse error, aut legis naturalis ignorantia, non rarò est culpanda; variè [diversissimè] tamen, pro variâ hominum perspicacia, et solertia; diver-sisque veri cognoscendi opportunitatibus; <134> et perinde ut facilior est, vel minus facilis, ipsarum legum cognitio.

(2.) Quae turpia credimus, reclamante conscientia agere, aut quae vi-dentur honesta omittere, quia pravum indicat ingenium, in quo non domi-natur honesti amor, semper est damnandum; variis tamen gradibus, pro delicti admissi turpitudine varia, aut officii omissi dignitate, rationum in-super, quae ad peccandum impulerunt, gravitate aut dignitate. Saepe enim gravissimorum malorum metus, saepe amicitia, et parentum amor, στοργὴ dicta, saepe ipsa patriae caritas, homines ad iniqua impellunt; quae omnia non parum actionis turpitudinem imminuunt.

(3.) Quanquam qui conscientiae erranti morem gerit non in eo peccat quod id faciat; non tamen est a crimine penitus immunis; quum ipse error saepè sit culpandus. Culpa tamen gravior est aut levior pro ipsa errorum natura. Alii enim errores per se animum produnt turpem, odio, superbia, aut saevitia agitatum: alii vero negligentiam solùm, aut honestiores animi propensiones haud satis valuisse, indicant.

(4.) Magis plerumque peccat qui conscientiae renititur erranti, quam qui ei obsequitur. Uterque erroris culpâ tenetur; prior vero, etiam prodit ho-nesti curam exiguam, <135> et magnam legum divinarum incuriam. Ubi

ignorance or error, tho' at present invincible, may be a strong evidence of a prior culpable negligence, which may discover a depravity of temper.

Ignorance is either about matter *of law* [right] or matter *of fact.* This division takes place chiefly in positive <129> laws <according as the law or the nature of the fact is unknown>: for in the law of nature if the fact, or natural tendency and consequents of actions, beneficial or pernicious to society, are known [carefully examined], this it self makes the laws known.

IV. From these principles we may answer the chief questions about an erroneous conscience. 1. Error or ignorance of the law of nature is generally culpable; but in very various degrees, according to the different degrees of natural sagacity in men, and their different opportunities of information and inquiry, and as the laws themselves are more or less easy to be discovered.

2. To counteract conscience in doing what we deem vitious, or in omitting what we take to be our duty, must always be evil; as it shews such depravation of the temper that a sense of duty is not the ruling principle. But this guilt too is of very different degrees, according to the sanctity of the several duties omitted, or the turpitude of crimes we commit; and the different sorts of motives, more or less favourable, which excited us to this conduct. For sometimes 'tis only the terrour of the most formidable evils which almost enforce us, sometimes lovely principles of friendship, gratitude, filial duty, parental affection, or even love of a country, which induce us to act against our consciences; now in such cases the guilt is considerably alleviated.

3. In following an erroneous conscience, the guilt consists not in thus following it, or doing what we deem to be our duty; but it lies rather in something culpable in the error it self, or in the causes of it, and this in various degrees. For some errors of themselves shew a base temper, influenced directly by malice, pride, or <130> cruelty: others shew only negligence and inattention, or that the nobler affections of heart are too weak.

4. 'Tis generally true that counteracting even an erroneous conscience is worse than following it. In both cases the guilt of the error is equal; and he who counteracts his conscience shews also <a poor concern for what is honourable and> a new contempt of the divine law. And yet where some of

vero humaniores animi motus, conscientiae obstabant erranti, imperia aliorum, non veram rei honestatem aut bonitatem spectanti, confusâque et fallaci ejus umbra deceptae; ingenium nonnunquam videbitur minus depravatum ex eo quod egerat homo, contra quam istiusmodi conscientia monuerat, quam si ei paruisset.

V. Quae ad voluntatem pertinent adjuncta, in actionibus inter se comparandis spectanda, ex supra dictis intelligi possunt: quum honesti sint animi motus benigni; turpes, maligni; immo nimia philautia, aut nimiae humiliorum voluptatum appetitiones: interque affectiones benignas, laudabiliores sint stabiles magis et tranquillae; et tranquillarum honestissimae, quae patent latissimè.

1. Officia igitur deliberata, consilioque stabili suscepta, iis quae ex perturbato quovis, et brevi amoris aestu nascuntur, sunt honestiora.

2. Turpiora pariter sunt delicta et injuriae, quae destinato consilio, aut odio fiunt inveterato; quam quae ex ira, metu, aut vehementiore fluunt cupiditate. {De ira metuque observandum, quod, quia ad beate jucundève vivendum hoc imprimis exigatur, ut antè amoveantur dolores ferè <136> omnes, atque virtus prima sit vitia fugisse; idcirco et acriores sunt animi motus omnes mala adspernantes, iis quae bona consectantur.} Actionum

---

7. See *System* 2.1.5, vol. I, p. 235.
8. About this general premise, see *Inquiry on Virtue*, III, 9, and *System* 2.2.2, vol. I, pp. 239–40. The estimation or computation of the morality of actions is not a subject of Pufendorf's *De officio* and is only slightly treated in Pufendorf's *De iure nat.* 1.8. This subject is peculiar to Hutcheson and is largely treated in his *Inquiry on Virtue*, Section III, especially Art. 8–12, and Section VII, Art. 9, as well as in the whole chapter II of *System*. However, while there is substantial concord between the main rules of this evaluation, the order and the details of Hutcheson's account are in many ways different in the three works. The *Inquiry* deals with the moral evaluation according to (1) the quantity of good or evil produced and (2) the kind of affections involved in Section III, and

the more humane and lovely dispositions carry it against the commands of an erroneous conscience, guided rather by authority, and some confused <and deceitful> notions of duty, than any distinct view of moral excellence {in what it commands}, the disobeying it may be a better sign of the temper [a sign of a better temper] than following its dictates. {As in the case of one who deems it his duty to persecute for Religion, and yet is restrained from it by humanity and compassion.}[7]

V. The circumstances affecting the morality of actions which relate to the Will must appear from what was said above; that all kind affections of soul are amiable [honourable], and the contrary vitious; as is also excessive self-love, and a keen desire of sensual pleasures; that the calm stable affections of a friendly sort are more lovely{, than the turbulent passions}; and that the more extensive are the more honourable.[8]

1. Such duties therefor as are done deliberately, and from steddy purpose of heart, are more lovely than those which proceed from some sudden gusts of kind passions.[9]

2. And in like manner such injuries as are done deliberately and with premeditation, or from inveterate ill-will, are much worse than those which arise from <131> sudden anger, fear, or some passionate bent toward pleasure.

As to all motions of anger and fear{, which aim at the repelling some impendent evil,} we may observe; that as the first step, and most necessary one, toward happiness and ease, is the warding off of pain, and the first office of virtue is the avoiding vice; the passions of *aversion from evil* are naturally stronger in their kind, than those pursuing positive good; and as

---

applies this evaluation to juridical matters in Section VII. The *System* generally follows the same order, and its Section V coincides in many points with Section VII, Art. 9, of the *Inquiry*, but some matters are redundant, and in Sections III and IV the tension between the excellency of calm and extended benevolence and the duty (and usual practice) of cultivating the limited affections becomes problematic. In the *Institutio*, the four points of Section V are pretty general, the moral evaluation is the last treated in Section VII, and Section VI shows the difference between moral and juridical evaluations of our actions rather than their agreement.

9. See *Inquiry on Virtue*, III.14, p. 194.

{igitur} turpitudinem plerumque {magis} imminuunt vehementiores istiusmodi perturbationes{, quibus haud facile obsistitur}; non tamen {om-
nem} penitus tollunt: quum, cui cordi est honestas, quique serió hoc ageret,
motus {etiam} hosce reprimere possit, eousque saltem ne in actiones pro-
rumpant externas.

3. Eadem benefaciendi studia, aut aeque late patentia, ab omnibus,
quamvis virtute paribus, non sunt expectanda: quum adeo diversa sint
hominum ingenia, vires, opportunitates, otia, aut negotia.

4. Inter arctiores animi affectiones benignas, non leve est discrimen, pro
variis amoris causis, quarum aliae aliis multo sunt honestiores. Quae ex
nostrâ cum alterius utilitate conjunctâ, oritur benevolentia, quamvis turpitudine vacet, nihil tamen habet praeclari; quum cadere in hominem turpissimum, et erga turpissimos exerceri queat. Neque {per se} praeclara est
ea caritas quae inter sanguine conjunctos, aut amantes, intercedit. Perturbati fere sunt hi motus, arctisque limitibus inclusi: atque ita nati sunt homines, ut qui nihil altius sapiunt his non careant. Nihil tamen magis <137>
contra naturam, nihil turpius, quam ut haec inter necessarios omnino de-
siderentur. Durus sit omnino et ferreus oportet, qui ne ex causis quidem
hisce naturalibus, omniumque validissimis, concipit animum benignum.

Praeclarior paulo ea quae ex beneficiis acceptis oritur benevolentia, et
gratiae referendae studium, ubi abest fucata omnis novis beneficiis captan-
dis <destinata> amicitiae simulatio. Huic affinis est miserorum commiseratio, et sublevandi studium. Arctiores tamen sunt et hae animi propensiones:
qui validis hisce causis non commovetur nemo est, nisi omnem simul
exuerit humanitatem. In hujusmodi officiis vulgaribus non admodum
elucet virtus; in iis tamen neglectis aut detrectatis, summa turpitudo.

Praeclarior longe est ea benevolentia et caritas, quam morum similitudo

'tis harder to resist their impulses, they are greater alleviations of guilt, in vitious actions, tho' none of them can wholly take it away; since it is always in one's power, who has an hearty concern about virtue, and sets himself to it, to restrain these passions in a great measure, and prevent their breaking out into external actions.

3. We cannot expect the same degrees of beneficence, or a like extent of it, in all equally good characters, considering the different tempers of men, their different abilities, opportunities, leisure, or hurry of business.

4. There are great differences in point of moral excellence among the several narrower sorts of kind affections, according to their different springs or causes, some of which are far more honourable than others. That good will which arises from some conjunctions of interest, {so that we wish well to others only for our own interest arising from their prosperity,} tho' it may be free from any moral turpitude, yet has nothing morally amiable; since such affection may be found in the worst of men, and may have the worst for its object: nor is there much moral beauty in the affections merely <132> founded on the tyes of blood, or in the passions of lovers. These motions are generally turbulent and are all of a narrower kind: and such is the constitution of our nature, that they are often found among such as shew scarce any other virtues. And yet the want of such affections in such relations, would shew a great depravity. That heart must be singularly hard and insensible to kind affections which cannot be moved to them by these strong natural causes.

There is an higher moral beauty in that good-will and gratitude which arises from benefits received, where it is {truly sincere,} without any shew or ostentation designed to obtain further favours. In a like class we may reckon pity and compassion, with a desire of giving relief to the distressed. And yet these two are of a narrower nature: and such is the frame of the human heart, so strong are these impulses, that none but monsters are void of all degrees of such affections. In the common offices of these kinds there's no eminent virtue; but in neglecting or omitting them{, contrary to such strong natural impulses,} there must be evidenced great depravation.

That <benevolence and> love arising from a conformity of virtuous dis-positions{, which we call friendship,} is far more lovely: as it shews an high

bonorum allexit. Ostendit enim acriorem honesti sensum, et amorem; {qui etiam} sua sponte ad plures pertineret, in quibus similis virtutum esset significatio. Huic autem praestat amor patriae alte infixus. Omnium tamen pulcherrima, ea stabilis animi prudentis affectio, quae universum benevolentia complectitur humanum genus; et singulis oblatâ occasione consulit.

Exigit autem, quod facile patet, communis <138> utilitatis ratio, animi appetitionibus et naturae instinctu commendata, ut quisque, quantum patitur communis utilitas, sui, eorumque quos sibi commendarunt necessitudines arctiores et naturales, curam habeat praecipuam; utque in officiis huic curae consentaneis plerumque occupetur: quibus nempe solis {fere}, hominum pars longe maxima, communi utilitati inservire possint.

VI. Haec in universum tenenda; quo arctiore et validiore naturae vinculo adstringimur ad officia quaevis, eo minor erit in iis servatis honestas, et major in neglectis turpitudo. Quo sanctiore juris vinculo tenemur, quo pleniore jure postulatur officium, eo minus laudabile est praestitisse, magisque vituperabile praetermisisse, aut detrectasse. Quo debiliore jure postulari poterat officium, eo minus est flagitiosum detrectasse, eo honestius ultro praestitisse; si modo adsit sanctiora officia praestandi cura major, pro eorum sanctitate.

In actionibus et consiliis damnandis, minor, caeteris paribus, erit turpitudo, quo speciosiores causae ad peccandum impulerunt. Patriae amori posthabuisse eam justitiam, quae et exteris omnibus consulit; aut patriae utilitatem, amicorum aut bene de nobis meritorum utilitati posthabuisse, non perinde foedum, ac si quis suae haec utilitati <139> posthabuisset, aut voluptati; quae causa est omnium infima.

relish for moral excellence, and an affection which would extend to many in a considerable degree, if like virtues appeared in them. A strong love for one's country, is yet more excellent. But of all social affections that is most amiable, which, conjoined with wisdom, is stedfastly set on promoting the <133> most extensive happiness of all mankind, and doing good to each one as there is opportunity.

And yet the common interest of the whole, which both the nobler desires of the soul, and our moral sense [natural instinct] chiefly recommend to our care, plainly requires that each one should more peculiarly employ his activity for the interest of such whom the stronger ties of nature have peculiarly recommended, or entrusted to his care, as far as their interests consist with the general good, and that his ordinary occupations should be destined for their benefit. The bulk of mankind have no ability or opportunity of promoting the general interest any other more immediate way.

VI. These seem to be general rules of estimation in this matter. The stronger that the natural impulse is in any narrower ties of affection, the less there is of moral beauty in performing any supposed offices; and the greater is the moral deformity of omitting them. The stronger the moral obligation is to any performance, or the *right* by which others claim it, the less laudable is the performance, and the more censurable and injurious is the omission or refusal of it. And the weaker the *right* or claim of others is, 'tis the less vitious to have omitted or refused any office, and 'tis the more honourable to have readily performed it; provided we shew a readiness proportionably greater in performing such offices as others have a more sacred claim to.

In comparing [condemning] vitious actions or designs, other circumstances being equal, the turpitude is the less, the greater or the more specious the motives were which <134> induced us to it. To have violated the laws of universal justice out of zeal for our country, or to have neglected the interest of our country from zeal for our friends, or from gratitude to our benefactors, is not so base and deformed, as if one had neglected or counteracted these more extensive interests for his own gain, or for any sensual gratification; this last excuse is indeed the meanest of all.

Quantum ad actionem simpliciter bonam hominem incitaverit suae utilitatis appetitio, tantum praeclarae speciei deteritur; et nulla alia re expetitâ, nulla manet laus, licet actio sit licita.

Ubi suae utilitatis ratio, quae ejusmodi est ut virum etiam bonum non parum commoveret, hominem ad peccandum incitaverit; turpitudo, eâ de causa imminuitur. Animi autem motus perturbati, quos excitare solent mala graviora, {nobis nostrisve} imminentia, virum bonum magis concutiunt, quam qui spectant utilitatum novarum aut voluptatum adeptionem: multo igitur magis delicti turpitudinem elevant. Voluptatum quidem appetitiones nimiae sunt per se turpissimae, indicantes levissimam et vilissimam animi partem caeteris prorsus dominari.

Quae suscipimus officia praeclara, si nobis damnosa sint, aut multo cum labore et periculo conjuncta, ea tanto sunt honestiora. Quum vero aliorum utilitatem praecipuè spectent {viri boni} virtutes praeclarae, {non ea gaudia interna ex suae virtutis opinione eximia, aut gloriâ, oritura;} ad suae voluptatis, aut utilitatis, aliorsum spectantes illecebras spernendas, animum suum confirmare <140> conabitur vir bonus: quod optime fieri potest, ubi haec altè menti insident, Dei opt. max. providentiâ mundum administrari, bonisque omnibus optimè consuli; unicamque, ad vitam beatam et immortalem, per virtutem patere viam. Has igitur spes eximias, ex animo minimè ejiciet {vir bonus}: eas vero fovebit et confirmabit, ut in omni virtute sit perfectior et constantior.

VII. Quod ad rei quae agitur naturam, agentisque vires, attinet; haec vera videntur. (1.) Pro ratione momenti, quod actio quaevis ad communem affert utilitatem, quamque expetebat agens, eam, caeteris paribus, esse honestiorem.

---

10. See *Inquiry on Virtue,* III.11, point 4, p. 189, VII.9, point 2, pp. 288–89, and *System* 2.1, point 2, vol. I, p. 238 and 2.3.5 point 3, p. 246.

11. See *Inquiry on Virtue,* VII.9, point 3, pp. 289–90, and *System* 2.3.5, point 4, vol. I, p. 246.

As far as any views of one's own advantage have excited a man to such actions as are in their own nature good, so far the moral beauty is abated:[10] and when there was no other affection moving him, there remains no moral beauty, tho' the action may still be innocent, or void of any vice.

Where any such views of interest as must exceedingly move even the best of men, have excited one to what is culpable, the moral turpitude is diminished on that account. The passions excited by the present apprehension of some great evil <for us or those that are dear to us> make a much greater impression upon the best of men, than such as arise from prospects of any new advantages or pleasures; and therefor they are much stronger alleviations of guilt.[11] Keen {selfishness, or} love of pleasures, are of themselves <very> dishonourable; and shew that the meaner parts of the soul have usurped a base tyranny over its nobler faculties.

The honourable offices we undertake, if they are expensive, toilsome, or dangerous to ourselves, they are on this account the more honourable.[12] And yet since the grand aim of the good man is the promoting the publick good, and not the pleasing himself with an high <135> admiration of his own virtues; he must also endeavour to fortify his soul, as much as he can, to surmount all allurements or temptations tending a contrary way: and this is most effectually done by a deep persuasion that a perfectly just and wise Providence governs the world, will take care of the interests of the virtuous; and that the only path to an happy immortality is by virtue: the good man therefor will be far from excluding out of his counsels these glorious hopes, nay he will cherish and confirm them; that he may thus become the more inflexible and steddy in every virtuous design.

VII. As to the *importance* of actions and the *abilities* of the agents, these general rules seem to hold. 1. That, other circumstances being equal, the moral goodness of actions is proportioned to their importance to the common interest, which the agent had in view.[13]

---

12. See *Inquiry on Virtue,* III.11, point 4, p. 189; VII.9, point 4, vol. I, p. 290; and *System* 2.3.3, point 4, vol. I, p. 241.

13. See *Inquiry on Virtue,* III.11, point 2, p. 187, and *System* 2.3.1, point 1, vol. I, p. 238.

(2.) Caeteris item paribus, posito quovis actionis momento, ejus honestas, pro virium ratione *inversa* quae dicitur, major erit aut minor: id est, majorem ostendit is virtutis indolem, qui in re tenui, opibusque exiguis, beneficientiâ opulentos aequat.

(3.) Eadem ferè de actionum malarum turpitudine dicenda: eam scil. caeteris paribus, servare rationem detrimenti secuturi *directam,* et virium *inversam.* Id est, turpiora sunt quae graviora post se trahunt damna; quaeque ab imbecillioribus, contentis tamen nervis omnibus, perpetrata, animum produnt ad nocendum obfirmatum.

(4.) In aestimando autem actionis momento, <141> spectanda est omnis eventuum consecutio, qui provideri poterant, quique citra actionem non evenissent; idque sive sua sponte et consecutione naturali sequantur; sive intervenientibus aliorum actionibus, quas elicuerat haec actio, aut provocarat. Prospiciet enim vir bonus ea omnia, quae ex actionibus suis evenire possunt; cavebitque, ne quid temerè agat, contra communem utilitatem, aut quod ad damnum publicum aut privatum inferendum, ansam est praebiturum, aut irritamentum non necessarium.

De actionum eventibus haec tenenda: Commodum publicum, etsi provisum, nisi etiam inter agendum expetitum {fuerat}, neutiquam actionem honestare, aut laudi verti posse; quum honestam non indicet voluntatem. Damnum vero publicum, quod provideri [praevideri] poterat, quamvis neque expetitum erat, neque provisum [praevisum], actionis turpitudinem augere; quum ipsa de publicis commodis aut incommodis incuria et negligentia sit turpis, debilesque ostendat fuisse affectiones animi benignas.

(5.) Neque tamen mala est omnis actio unde damna oritura praevidentur; neque mala omnia quae ex actione eveniunt, quamvis praevisa, eandem turpem reddunt, nisi et propter se expetita fuerant. Ex bonis <142> quippe et malis eventibus, mixtum est omnium ferè actionum externarum momentum. Nullum est vitae institutum, quod non sua habeat et commoda

---

14. See *Inquiry on Virtue,* III.11, point 3, pp. 187–88, and *System* 2.3.1, point 1, vol. I, p. 238.

15. See *Inquiry on Virtue,* III.12, p. 191, and *System* 2.3.1, point 3, vol. I, pp. 238–39.

2. When other circumstances are equal, the virtue of an action is *inversely* as the abilities of the agent: that is, when the importance of two actions is equal, he shews the greater virtue who with smaller abilities <and poorer resources>, equals the more potent in his beneficence.[14]

3. The like observations hold about the vice of evil actions, that it is *directly* as their importance to the publick detriment foreseen, and *inversely* as the abilities of the agents: or that these are worst which have the worst tendency; or which undertaken by persons of little power, shew that they have maliciously exerted all their force in doing mischief.[15]

4. In estimating the importance of actions, we must take in that whole series of events, which might have <136> been foreseen to ensue upon them, and which without these actions would not have happened; whether these events be the natural direct effects of the actions, or happened by the intervention of other agents, who by these actions have been provoked or incited to take certain measures.[16] For every good man will consider all that may ensue upon any steps he takes; and will avoid doing any thing contrary to the common utility, or which may without necessity give an occasion or temptation to any publick <or private> detriment{, either more or less extensive}.

As to the events or effects of actions, this holds; that any publick advantage ensuing, tho' it had been foreseen, yet if it was not intended and desired, adds nothing to the virtue of the action, nor is it matter of praise; as it shews no goodness of temper. But publick detriment which might have been foreseen, tho' it was not directly desired, nor perhaps actually foreseen, may add to the moral turpitude. Because that even a negligence and unconcernedness about the publick interest is of itself vitious, shewing either an entire want, or a great defect in goodness of temper.

5. But we must not pronounce every action to be evil from which some evil consequences were foreseen to ensue;[17] unless these evils were directly desired for themselves. The consequences of most external actions are of a mixed nature, some good, some bad. There's no course of life which has

16. See *Inquiry on Virtue*, III.8, pp. 181–82, and *System* 2.1.3, vol. I, pp. 230–31.

17. <neither all the evils consequent to any action, though foreseen, make it evil> The translator rightly dropped this pleonastic sentence.

et incommoda; quae omnia ad calculos vocanda. Eae igitur actiones ratione momenti sunt bonae, ubi commoda, quae sine istiusmodi incommodis parari non poterant, haud parum praeponderant: Eaeque malae, unde incommoda oriuntur commodis plura et majora; aut ubi haec sine illis parari poterant.

(6.) In foro Dei tamen, et conscientiae, imputantur haec omnia, non prout re verà eveniunt; verum prout [eorum spes erat probabilis] [probabiliter sperari poterant eventura]. Non enim in ipsis eventibus sita est honestas aut turpitudo; sed in animi consiliis, et voluntate. Unde pari saepe sunt in culpa hi, quorum alter casu, aut aliorum cura impeditus, nemini nocuit, alter verò gravissime. Neque minus laudandus qui honesta pro viribus, etsi frustrà, conatus est, quam quibus omnia ex voto contigerunt.

VIII. Inter ea quae voluntatem et agendi vires afficiunt numerantur habitus, et consuetudines: quae licet *praesentium voluptatum* sensum imminuant, absentium tamen augent desiderium molestum, hominesque ad eas insectandas propensiores reddunt, agendique dant facilitatem. Habitus hi, ut sponte fuerant adsciti; sic actionum <143> intermissione, cautioneque et diligentiâ, reprimi potest eorum vis, et penitus deleri. Quomodocunque igitur, actionis rectae honestatem minuant virtutum habitus, hominis tamen et ingenii laudem augent. Habitus, contra, pravi, utcunque actionis cujusque turpitudinem minuant, hominem tamen ipsum turpiorem faciunt, magisque damnandum.

not its own advantages and disadvantages; all which are indeed to come into computation. These actions therefor alone are good, on account of their importance, whose good consequences <137> foreseen overballance their evil consequences; and when the good could not have been obtained without these or equal evils: and those actions are evil in this respect, where the evil consequences overballance all the good; or where the good might have been obtained without such evils{, or with a smaller degree of them}.[18]

6. But in the sight of God and Conscience these events are imputed not as they actually happen, but according as there was a probable prospect that they might happen. For the moral good and evil consists not in the external events, but in the affections and purposes of the soul. And hence two persons may be equal in guilt, tho' one of them, restrained by accident or the prudence of others, has done no damage, and the other has done a great deal. And he is equally laudable who has made noble attempts, to the utmost of his power, tho' unsuccessfully, with those to whom all things have succeeded according to their wishes.[19]

VIII. Amongst the circumstances which affect both the will and the abilities of the agents, may be reckoned *custom* and *habit:* which tho' they rather abate than increase the pleasure of particular enjoyments, yet increase the regret and uneasiness in the want of what we have been enured to, make us more inclined to pursue like enjoyments, and give us greater facility and readiness in any course of action. As the acquiring of such habits was voluntary, so it still remains in our power to abate their force or take them away altogether by cautious abstinence or frequent intermission of such actions and enjoyments. However therefor an habit <138> of virtue, {making each office less difficult,} may seem to abate a little of the excellence of each particular office, yet it plainly adds to the beauty and excellence of the character: and on the other hand habits of vice, however they may a little abate the deformity of each particular vitious action, yet plainly shew the character to be the more deformed and odious.[20]

18. See *Inquiry on Virtue,* III.8, p. 181, and *System* 2.1.3, vol. I, p. 231.
19. See *Inquiry on Virtue,* VII.9, point 1, p. 288, and *System* 2.2.5, point 2, vol. I, pp. 245–46.
20. On habit or *consuetudo,* see Pufendorf, *De officio* I.I, point 13.

Homini denique laudi dantur aliorum actiones, quin et causarum naturalium et inanimarum effectus exoptati; quatenus, actionibus suis honestis, aliquid ad eos attulit. Imputantur et damna, ex aliorum vitiis, aut rerum etiam inanimarum moribus orta; quatenus, vel faciendo, vel non faciendo, secus quam debebat, ad ea quicquam attulit.

Sometimes it may happen that one is justly praised on account of the good actions of other men, nay that even the desirable effects of natural inanimate causes are imputed to him as honourable, when by some honourable actions of his own he has contributed to these events. And in like manner the damages or injuries immediately done by other men or inanimate causes, are imputed as crimes, when one has occasioned them by any action or omission contrary to his duty.[21]

21. See Pufendorf, *De officio* 1.1, point 18.

CAPUT IV

De Jure Privato Naturali.

I. ‹Ex dictis constat› Propria singulis officia, {jam diximus,} vix [non] expeditius declarari posse, quam percurrendo diversa quae hominibus competunt *jura,* una cum iis quae cuique respondent *obligationibus;* pro diverso hominum statu, variisque vitae necessitudinibus. ‹144›

Status est, "Hominis conditio permanens, varia jura, et longam obligationum seriem includens": Estque vel *solutus et liber* quem constituit ipsa natura; vel *adventitius,* ab aliquo hominum instituto ortus.

Libertatis solutae et naturalis status est, "eorum qui nulli communi hominum imperio subjiciuntur." Qui quidem primus erat inter adultos, parentum potestate solutos: quem et quoddam hominum genus semper retinebit; summi saltem civitatum diversarum rectores, ipsaeque {inter se} civitates.

Denominatur {autem} status a jure et legibus in eo vigentibus, non ab iis quae, pro hominum pravitate, contra leges fiunt. Est igitur libertatis naturalis status, amicus et pacatus; innocentiae et beneficientiae status, non rapinae, violentus et hostilis. Quod recti et honesti sensus, et suae utilitatis ratio, cuique satis monstrabunt. Etenim [Enim][1] absque plurium consortio, (quod observasse profuerit estque in promptu,) absque plurium auxiliis, officiorumque amicorum commercio, neque nasci poterant homines, neque conservari, nedum ulla vitae commoditate aut jucunditate frui. Con-

---

1. A new paragraph in 1742 edition.

---

1. *System* 2.4, vol. I, p. 280.
2. See *System* 2.4.2, vol. I, p. 283.

Concerning the Natural Rights of Individuals.

I. We have already shewn that the several duties of life may be naturally explained by explaining the several *rights* belonging to men, and the corresponding obligations, in all the several states and relations they stand in to each other. By a *state* we understand "some permanent condition one is placed in, as it includes a series of rights and obligations."[1] Our state is either that of the *<unbound> freedom in which nature placed us;* or an *adventitious* state, introduced by some human {acts or} institution.

The state of *natural <and unbound> liberty,* is "that of those who are subjected to no human power": which plainly obtained at first in the world, among persons adult and exempt from the parental power. This state too must always subsist among some persons, at least among the sovereign Princes of independent states, or among the states themselves, with respect to each other.[2]

The character of any state is to be taken from the rights and laws which are in force in it, and not from what men may do injuriously contrary to the laws. 'Tis plain therefor {from the preceeding account of our nature and its laws}, that the state of nature is that of peace and good-will, of innocence and beneficence, and not of violence, war, and rapine: as both the immediate <140> sense of duty in our hearts[of what is right or honourable], and the rational considerations of interest must suggest to us.{*}

For let us observe what's very obvious, that without society with a good many of our fellows, their mutual aids, and an intercourse of friendly offices, mankind could neither be brought to life or preserved in it; much less could they obtain any tolerably convenient or pleasant condition of life.

---

* {This suffices to overturn the fallacious reasonings of *Hobs* upon the state of nature as a state of war of all against all.} [The reference to Hobbes is more explicit in *System* 2.4.1, p. 282.]

stat etiam, nemini eas esse vires, ut sibi polliceri possit, se alios quosvis de-
victurum, quos laedere cupiverit, <145> aut spoliare; quosve injuriis inten-
tatis, pro eorum super conditione communi curâ, sibi hostes concitaverit.
Vix fere quisquam est cui ad ulciscendum [laedendum] desunt vires, ubi
indignatione justa commovetur: hominumque vires sunt ad laedendum
plerumque {longè} efficaciores, quam ad alios beatos conservandos. Quae
in rebus externis sita est prosperitas [beatitudo], a corporis, ejusque partium
omnium, valetudine pendet; quae infirma et fragilis, vi quantulacunque
facile turbatur; resque exigit complures, quae laedi, interverti, aut corrumpi
possunt. Perspecta haec hominum conditio infirma, et incerta, bene sano
cuique monstrabit, pacem et amicitiam, quantum fieri potest, cum omnibus esse colendam.

II. Jura, prout lege naturali proximè constituta {sunt} vel in utilitatem singulorum, vel *universitatis* aut populi, vel in omnium communem, dividuntur in *privata, publica,* et *communia.* Jura cujusque privata primò indicant ipsi cujusque appetitus naturales, et sensus, ea seligentes quae ad
cujusque faciunt foelicitatem: recti etiam honestique sensus, animique
motus benigni, {satis docent hanc} facultatem, sibi utilia aut jucunda pa-
randi, cuique permittendam; eamque defendendam omnibus commendant.
<146>
Primò, igitur, spectanda sunt naturae cujusque principia:* deliberatio
dein revocanda, secundum rectam rationem, ad aliorum majores quasque
utilitates, et omnium communem: ut, his non repugnantibus, cuique ea

---

* Vid. Grot. de J. B. et P. I. 2. 1.

---

3. See *System* 2.4.5, vol. I, p. 290.
4. *System* 2.4.5, vol. I, p. 292.
5. *System* 2.4.3, vol. I, p. 284.

'Tis plain too that no one has such strength that he could promise to himself to conquer all such as he may desire to wrong or spoil, and all such enemies as he may raise up against himself {by an injurious course of life}; since an honest indignation at wrongs will make many more enemies to him than those he immediately injures: and there are few who won't find considerable strength to avenge themselves {or their neighbours}, when they have conceived a just indignation.[3] And then men have it generally in their power much more certainly and effectually to make others uneasy and miserable, than to make others easy and happy. External prosperity requires a perfectly right state of the body, and all its tender and delicate parts, many of which may be disturbed and destroyed by very small forces; it requires also a considerable variety of external things, which may be easily damaged, taken away, or destroyed. A just consideration of this infirm, uncertain condition of mankind, so that their prosperity may so easily be disturbed, must engage every wise man rather to cultivate peace and <141> friendship with all, as far as possible{, than to provoke any by unnecessary enmity or injury}.[4]

II. The rights of men according as they immediately and principally regard either the benefit of some *individual,* or that of some *society* or body of people, or of *mankind* in general as a great community, are divided into *private, publick,* and *common to all.*[5] The *private* rights of individuals are pointed out by their senses and natural appetites, recommending and pursuing such things as tend to their happiness: and our moral faculty {or conscience},[6] <and the kind motions of the soul> shews us, that each one should be allowed full liberty to procure what may be for his own innocent advantage or pleasure, nay that we should maintain and defend it to him.

{To discover therefor these *private rights*} we should first attend to the several natural principles or appetites in men,* and then <according to right reason> turn our views toward the general interests of society, and of all around them: that where we find no obstruction to the happiness of others,

---

6. *System* 2.4.4, vol. I, p. 285.
* See *Grotius* de Jure Belli, &c. I. c. 2. 1. See also Sect. 1. of the preceding chapter. [In *De iure belli,* I.2.1 Grotius connects "ius naturae" with Cicero's "prima naturae": cf. *De finibus,* passim, but particularly III.21, IV.15, and IV.16].

agere, habere, exigere, permittatur, quae nemine laeso, ipsi sunt commoda aut grata.

Singulorum jura sunt vel *naturalia,* vel *adventitia.* Naturalia, nullo hominum facto aut instituto praeeunte, cuique tribuit natura. *Adventitia,* ex aliquo hominum facto aut instituto nascuntur.

III. Singulorum jura naturalia, sunt vel *perfecta,* vel *imperfecta.* Inter jura cujusque naturalia et perfecta, haec sunt praecipua: (1.) Jus ad *vitam,* et corporis integritatem; (2.) Jus *pudicitiae* conservandae; (3.) et *existimationis,* quae dici solet, *simplicis* sive famae viri probi et hominum societate non indigni. (4.) Jus ad libertatem; sive jus [suo arbitratu] [pro suo arbitrio] agendi quaecunque nulla lege prohibentur. (5.) Jus etiam in vitam suam, eo usque ut possit quisque se non solum periculis quibusvis, verum et certae morti objicere, ubi id exegerit sanctum aliquod officium, unde major humano generi, aut praestantioribus quibusvis, orietur utilitas, quam quae ipsius vitam compensabit; <147> quod et recti honestique sensus, et virtutis amor, cuique commendabit.

{(6.)} Est etiam cuique jus, cujus sensus altè a natura est infixus, suo utendi judicio, quod sine ulla alteri illata injuria [fiat] [fieri potest], in omnibus quae ad officium, praecipue vero ad Dei cultum [de deo colendo], spectant. Contra suum de officio judicium, nemo quicquam recte agit: neque in simulatione, aut dissimulatione, ulla est virtus; immo saepe maxima turpitudo. Non igitur in commercia veniunt, animi, de religione aut virtute, sententiae. Nullus est ejusmodi commercii usus: neque fieri potest, ut ea judicet quisquam quae alter voluerit. Patet igitur alienari non posse hoc jus; {eosque} nihil agere, qui sententias pacisci velint, easve aliorum arbitrio permittere. Finge aliquem temerè judicasse, falsasque fovere de religione sententias: is, dummodo nemini noceat, suo utitur jure externo;

{or to the common good, thence ensuing,} we should deem it the *right* of each individual to do, possess, or demand and obtain from others, whatever may tend to his own innocent advantage or pleasure.

Private rights are either *natural* or *adventitious*. The former sort, nature itself has given to each one, without any human grant or institution. The adventitious depend upon some human deed or institution.[7]

III. The private natural rights are either *perfect* or *imperfect*. Of the perfect kind these are the chief.[8] <142> 1. A right to life, and to retain their bodies unmaimed. 2. A right to preserve their chastity. 3. A right to an unblamished character for common honesty, so as not to be deemed unfit for human society. 4. A right of liberty, or of acting according to one's own judgment {and inclination} within the bounds of the law of nature. 5. A right over life, so far that each one, in any honourable services to society or his friends [to more important men], may expose himself not only to dangers, but to certain death, when such publick good is in view as overballances the value of his life. This our {conscience, or} moral sense, and love of virtue will strongly recommend to us in many cases. 7. [6.] There's also a sense deeply infixed by nature, of each one's *right of private judgment,* {or of judging for himself in all matters of duty,} especially as to religion; for a {base} judgment or opinion cannot of itself be injurious to others: and 'tis plain no man can without guilt counteract his own conscience; nor can there be any virtue in dissimulation or hypocrisy, but generally there's great guilt in it. Our sentiments therefor about religion and virtue cannot be matter of commerce {or contract, so as to give others a right over them}. Such commerce is no way requisite for any good in society; nor is it in ones power to judge or think as another shall command him. All engagements or contracts of this kind are null and void. <It is therefore evident that this right can not be alienable and that the acts of those that would impose contracts to opinions and leave them to the power of anybody are null and void.> Suppose one has judged amiss and has false opinions <as to religion>: yet while he injures no man, he is using his own *external right;* that is, {tho' he

---

7. *System* 2.5.1, vol. I, p. 293.
8. On the same private perfect rights see *System* 2.5.1, vol. I, pp. 293–99.

id est, graviora longe sequerentur incommoda, si alteri illum poenis coer-
cere, aut malorum metu ut contrariam profiteatur sententiam cógere,
permitteretur.

{(7.)} Est etiam jus cuique naturale, rebus communibus communiter
utendi; atque, ut is ipsi pateat aditus, qui caeteris, ad jura adventitia ac-
quirenda; utque cum aequalibus aequaliter excipiatur. {(8.)} Est etiam jus
connubia ineundi, cum omnibus qui volunt, <148> si modo sui sint juris,
nulloque priore contractu, [aliove justo impedimento prohibeantur] [im-
pediti]: neque est tertio cuivis, aut homini aut coetui, prohibendi jus.
Neque cuiquam qui nullum nactus est imperium in alios, jus est volentes
prohibendi, ne societates quasvis, sui commodi causa ineant, aut commercia {exerceant} innoxia.

Haec cuique competere jura perfecta, monstrabit sensus cujusque, et naturae prima: neque iis violatis constare posset vita inter homines socia et
pacata. Ea etiam confirmabit communis utilitatis ratio, animique affectiones omnes honestiores.

{IV.} Hoc vero sunt omnes pares et *aequales,* quod adultis omnibus jura
haec naturalia pariter competant, et lege naturali muniantur; quae jubet ut
cuique consulamus, quantum communis patitur utilitas: utque tenuioribus
et hebetioribus sua tueamur exigua; aequè ac ampliora sua, potentioribus
aut solertioribus. Communis etenim hoc exigit utilitas, idque sanctissimè,
ne quis mortalium ratione praeditus, nisi sponte sua, aut ob delictum, alienae subjiciatur voluntati, nulla suae utilitatis habita ratione: dummodo

acts amiss, yet} much greater evils would ensue if any power were vested in others to compel him by penalties or threatnings of <143> tortures, either to a change of his sentiments, or to a profession of it [to a profession of contrary opinions].

<7.> Each one also has a natural right to the use of such things as nature intended to remain common to all; that he should have the same access with others,[9] {by the like means,} to acquire adventitious rights; and that he should find equal treatment with his equals. <8.> Men have likewise rights to marriage with such as are willing to inter-marry with them, provided they be under no prior bonds of marriage, or hindred by any other just impediment: nor can any third person or society which has not acquired any just power over the parties, pretend a right to obstruct their designs of inter-marriage; or to hinder any who are not their subjects from entering into any other innocent associations or commerce of any kind for their own behoof.

The sense of every one's heart, and the common natural principles, shew that each one has these perfect rights; nor without maintaining them can there be any social <and peaceful> life: so that they are also confirmed by considerations of common utility, and our more extensive [honourable] affections.

IV. In this respect all men are originally *equal,* that these natural rights equally belong to all, at least as soon as they come to the mature use of reason; and they are equally confirmed to all by the law of nature, which requires that we should consult the interest of each individual as far as the common utility will allow; and maintain to the feeble and weak their small acquisitions or advantages, as well as their greater acquisitions or advantages to the ingenious and active.[10] For 'tis <144> plainly for the common good, <and most sacredly> that no mortal endued with reason {and forethought} should without his own consent, or crime, be subjected to the will of his fellow, without regard to his own interest, except in some rare cases, that

9. Here, as in many other cases, the translator uses almost the same words used by Hutcheson in *System* 2.5.1, vol. I, p. 298, suggesting that he had access to a copy of Hutcheson's posthumous work.

10. See *System* 2.5.2, vol. I, p. 299 and ff., and cf. Pufendorf, *De officio* 1.7.

magna aliqua populi utilitas, in casu quodam rariore, id non flagitet. Nemo enim adeo est hebes, aut de suis suorumque rebus adeo securus et improvidus, cui non sit <149> mortis instar, se suosque ex aliena pendere voluntate, et alterius inservire libidini, gravissimis contumeliis semper obnoxios. Naturâ igitur nemo est servus, nemo dominus. His tamen non obstantibus, plura sunt prudentioribus et melioribus jura imperfecta, quae aliis non competunt; majorque iis cultus debetur, et officia praestantiora.

Quum vero nulla sint indicia certa, aut criteria, quorum ope inter omnes convenire possit, quinam hominum sint caeteris solertiores et meliores; quumque et hebetiores, praestantem sibi saepe arrogent prudentiam; omniumque pessimi malitiosè saepe simulent probitatem et bonitatem, a verâ haud facilè secernendam; patet, nullo prudentiae aut probitatis obtentu, posse quemquam, jure, in alios invitos imperium sibi arrogare. Hoc enim communi maxime obesset foelicitati.

V. Omni singulorum juri imperfecto, respondet obligatio aliqua aut officium, recti et honesti sensu, et communi omnium utilitate, saepe sanctissime commendatum. Haec sunt praecipua. Cuique jus est exigendi ea ab aliis officia, quae accipienti prosunt, danti vero neque sunt molesta nec damnosa. Est et cuivis innocuo jus ad humaniora ea officia, quae ipsi multo magis sunt profutura, quam praestantem gravatura. Quae causa praecipuè est calamitosi cujusque, <150> aliorum egentis auxilio. Honestioribus, licet non calamitosis, jus est ad aliorum officia majora, ad suffragia, praesertim, quibus ad honores altiores promoveantur. Jus etiam est cuique, non suo merito infami, ut legibus aequis, in societates aut civiles aut religiosas, ad vitam commodiorem, aut magis piam degendam, recipiatur. Jus denique est cuique innoxio, ut humanis et benignis, pariter cum paribus, excipiatur

the [some great] interest of a society may make it necessary. None of mankind are so stupid and thoughtless about their own interests, as not to count
it next to death to have themselves and all that's dear to them, subjected to
another's pleasure or caprice, and thus exposed to the greatest contumelies.
Nature makes none masters, none slaves: and yet the wiser and better sort
of men have many imperfect rights superior to those of others, and superior
offices and services of humanity are due to them.

But as nature has set no obvious or acknowledged marks of superior
wisdom and goodness upon any of mankind; and often weak men may
have high notions of their own wisdom; and the worst of men may make
the greatest shews of goodness <and virtue>, which their fellows cannot
discover to be hypocritical; 'tis plain that no pretences of superior wisdom
or goodness will justify a man in his assuming power over others without
their own consent; this would be plainly eversive of the common interest
[happiness]{, and the source of perpetual wars}.

V. To every imperfect right of individuals there answers a like *obligation* or
duty which our conscience [sense of right and honourable] <and the common utility of all> plainly enjoins, and in some cases most sacredly. These
are the chief imperfect rights: each one may justly claim such offices as are
profitable to him, and no burden or expense to the performer. Nay every
innocent <145> person has a right to such offices of others, as are of high
advantage to him, and of small burden or expence to the performers.[11] This
is particularly the case of men under great calamities, needing the charitable
aids of others. Men of eminent characters, tho' under no calamity, have a
right to some higher offices from others, as particularly to their friendly
suffrages for their advantage or promotion. Each one whose vices have not
made him infamous has a right to be admitted on equitable terms into any
societies civil or religious, which are instituted in his neighbourhood, for
his more convenient subsistence, or his improvement in piety. And lastly
each one, who has not forfeited by some crime, has a right to be treated on

11. See Pufendorf, *De officio* 1.8.4. On imperfect rights see also *System* 2.5.4, particularly p. 304.

officiis; atque cum imparibus, pro ratione dignitatis.

VI. De beneficientia et liberalitate constat, beneficii momentum ad accipientis utilitatem, esse pro ipsius beneficii ratione, accipientisque indigen-
tiâ, majus vel minus: danti vero graviora esse, aut leviora, beneficia, pro
eorundem pretio, dantisque inopia. Unde accipienti egeno saepe sunt utilissima, quae danti opulento sunt minimé gravia.

Beneficientia, quae virum bonum maxime decet, et in qua praecipue
elucet virtus, has "habet cautiones": (1.) "ne obsit benignitas et iis ipsis,
quibus benigne videtur fieri, et caeteris." (2.) Deinde "ne major" "sit quam
facultates," suumque fontem exhauriat. (3.) "Tum ut cuique pro dignitate
tribuatur."[2] In dignitate aestimanda "spectandi sunt" 1. "Mores" hominum;
2. "Animus erga nos"; <151> 3. Vitae communitas et conjunctio; 4. Et denique "officia ante in nos collata."[3] Horum nullum est negligendum; minime quod ultimum posuimus, quum "nullum" sit "officium gratiâ referenda magis necessarium," aut vitae hominum magis utile;[4] ingrato autem
animo nihil turpius aut inutilius. Gratiae igitur referendae, ubi simul caetera praestari nequeunt, cedunt pleraque liberalitatis officia.

2. Cicero, *De officiis* 1.42.
3. Cicero, *De officiis* 1.45.
4. Cicero, *De officiis* 1.47.

an equal footing of humanity with his equals, and with others in proportion to their merits.

VI. Concerning beneficence and liberality, these general maxims are evident,{*} that the importance of any benefit to the receiver, is proportioned jointly to the quantity of the benefit and his indigence: and that benefits are less burdensome to the giver the smaller their value is and the greater his wealth. Hence liberality may be exceedingly advantageous in many cases to him [the needy man] that receives it, and yet of small or no burden to the giver.

Beneficence, which is peculiarly becoming a good man, and eminently displays the goodness of his heart, ought to be practised with these cautions; first, that it don't hurt the persons it is employed about or the community. 2dly. That it be proportioned to our fortunes, <146> so as not to exhaust its own fountain. 3dly, That it be proportioned to the merits or claims of others. Among these claims we regard, first, the moral characters of the objects, and next their kind affections towards us, and thirdly the social intercourses we have had with them, and lastly the good offices we formerly received from them. None of these considerations are to be neglected, and least of all the last one; since there's no obligation more sacred than that of gratitude, none more useful in life; nor is any vice more odious than ingratitude, or more hurtful in society. When therefor in certain cases we cannot exercise all the beneficence we desire, offices of gratitude should take place of other offices of liberality.

---

* {This is taken from *Cicero de Officiis* Lib. I. 14, 15, &c.} [See *Institutio*, the front page, notes 2–4. However Hutcheson has also in mind Pufendorf, *De officio* I.8.]

CAPUT V

De Jure Adventitio reali, et Rerum Dominio.

I. Adventitia, quae ex hominum instituto aliquo aut facto oriuntur, jura, sunt vel *realia*, quae dicuntur, vel *personalia*. Illa "rem aliquam certam et definitam proxime spectant": haec vero "certum hominem sive personam": {de his plenius alias}.

Inter jura realia, prima veniant in medium *rerum dominia:* quorum origo et causae declarandae. Monstrant primò externi hominum sensus et appetitus, certas res in victum et amictum exposcentes; mutorumque animalium sensus similes, et appetitus, (ad quos regendos aut cohibendos, <152> nullam aliam habent facultatem superiorem,) monstrant, res inanimas, animalium causâ, a Deo benigno fuisse fabricatas, ut vita foret ipsis laeta et copiosa: animalium autem terrestrium praecipui sunt homines. Hoc etiam confirmabit ratio, docens, quae gignuntur è terra, citò sua sponte interitura, non in alium usum, divinâ bonitate et sapientia digniorem, destinata esse, quam ut animalium, praecipue vero hominum, utilitati inserviant aut foelicitati.

II. Quamvis autem, homini innata quaedam bonitas, et commiseratio, ad ipsas pertineat beluas, ab omni in eas retrahens saevitia, quam non exigit gravior hominum utilitas, quorum cuique major longe erit cura, et commiseratio: cernent tamen homines, vitam sibi duram omnino et laboriosam futuram, nisi jumentorum laboribus subleventur. Cernent etiam, jumenta

---

1. "Curious" is not in the *Institutio,* but in *System* 2.6.2, vol. I, p. 310, inside a sentence almost identical; cf. note 9 to Chapt. IV.

Of Real Adventitious Rights and Property.

I. The adventitious rights constituted by some human deed or institution are either *real* or *personal.* The real terminate upon some certain definite goods: the personal terminate upon some person{, not peculiarly respecting one part of his goods more than any other}. <About these we will say more elsewhere.>

The principal real right is *property;* the spring [the source and cause] of which is this [we have to explain.], First the external senses and appetites of men naturally lead to the use of external things for the preservation of life: and the like senses <and appetites> in brute animals (who have no superior faculties which could controll these senses and appetites) lead to the same: this sufficiently shews that God has graciously created things inanimate for the use of <a pleasing and rich> animal-life: now man is plainly the chief animal in this earth. Reflection confirms the same; since all these {curious}[1] vegetable forms must soon perish of their own accord, and therefor could be intended for no other use, so worthy of the divine goodness <and wisdom>, as that of supporting animal life agreeably, and chiefly human life.

II. There's indeed implanted in men a natural kindness and sense of pity, extending even to the Brutes, which should restrain them from any cruelty toward them which is not necessary to prevent some misery of mankind, toward whom we must still have a much <148> higher <concern and> compassion. But men must soon discern, {as they increase in numbers,}[2] that their lives must be exceedingly toilsome and uneasy unless they are assisted by the beasts fitted for labour. They must also see that such beasts of the

---

2. This addition by the translator is justified by what Hutcheson says in *System* 2.6.3, vol. I, p. 312.

omnia, atque animalium mitiora, quorum hominibus praecipuus est usus, sine hominum provida curâ, conservari non posse; hiberna nempe fame, et frigore, aut ferarum vi peritura: neque hominibus, in se conservandis semper occupatis, siquidem nullum a jumentis accederet auxilium, mutis animalibus conservandis aut protegendis vacaturum. Monstrat igitur ipsa ratio, animalia mitiora, praecipue quae laboribus ferendis sunt idonea, <153> hominum fidei et imperio esse permissa, ut hominum solertiâ conservata, curae hujus et custodiae, laboribus suis, persolvant, mercedem: atque hac ratione communitatem quandam, aut societatem, in communem utriusque generis utilitatem, esse constitutam; ubi imperant animalia ratione praedita, et serviunt rationis expertia.

Quae laboribus ferendis inutilia sunt animalia muta, ab iis, alia ratione, hominibus persolvenda est merces defensionis et custodiae, cum haud levi hominum labore conjunctae; quibus nempe silvestres agri sunt in pascua mitigandi, atque ferae et rapaces beluae abigendae. Lacte nempe aut lana, hominibus persolvenda est ea merces, qui, aliâ lege, labores, iis conservandis necessarios, perferre nequirent.

III. Quin et si victûs, pro hominum numero, ita maligna esset copia, ut plurimis fame pereundum foret, nisi mutorum animalium carne vescerentur; monstrabit ratio, illa animalia haud graviore morte perire, inopinatò in hominum cibum mactata, quàm omnibus, ab hominum tutela exclusis, pereundum esset: immò fame, frigore, aut ferarum vi, immaturiùs pleraque perirent et saeviùs. Non igitur iniquè aut crudeliter, at potius prudenter et benigne, agitur, ubi homines hanc leonum, ursorum, <154> luporum, canum aut vulturum praedam, saevius perituram, in suos usus intervertunt.

Videmus insuper mutorum animalium genera debiliora, in fortiorum et sagaciorum cibum a natura esse destinata. Quo eorum usu hominibus

---

3. In *De iure nat.* 4.3.2–6 (Barbeyrac translation, vol. I, pp. 484–89), Pufendorf condemns any cruelty toward animals and does not take for granted man's right to kill and eat animals, just as most ancient philosophers believed. The defense of this human right is based on the idea that there is not any right or obligation common to men and

gentler kinds and easily tameable, whose services men need most, cannot be preserved without the provident care of men; but must perish by hunger, cold, or savage beasts: nor could men unassisted by work-beasts, and over-burthened in supporting themselves, employ any cares or labour in their defence. Reason therefor will shew, that these tractable creatures fitted for labour are committed to the care and government of men, that being preserved by human care, they may make a compensation by their labours. And thus a *community* or society is plainly constituted by nature, for the common interest both of men and these more tractable animals, in which men [animals endowed with reason] are to govern, and the brute animals to be subject.[3]

Such tractable [speechless] animals as are unfit for labours, must make compensation to men for their defence and protection some other way, since their support too requires much human labour; as they must have pastures cleared of wood, and be defended from savage creatures. Men must be compensated by their milk, wool, {or hair,} otherwise they could not afford them so much of their care and labour.

III. Nay, if upon the increase of mankind they were so straitened for food, that many must perish by famine, unless they feed upon the flesh of brute animals; Reason will suggest that these animals, slaughtered speedily by men for food, perish with less pain, <149> than they must feel in what is called their natural death; and were they excluded from human protection they must generally perish earlier and in a worse manner by hunger, or winter-colds, or the fury of savage beasts. There's nothing therefor of un-justice or cruelty, nay 'tis rather prudence and mercy, that men should take to their own use in a gentler way, those animals which otherways would often fall a more miserable prey to lions, wolves, bears, dogs, or vultures.

Don't we see that the weaker tribes of <speechless> animals are destined by nature for the food of the stronger and more sagacious? Were a like use

---

beasts; see also Carmichael, *Notes on Puf.,* pp. 91–92. Hutcheson does his best to show that men and animals form a community, or "a well ordered complex system" (*System* 2.6.5, vol. I, p. 313).

negato, et pauciora istorum generum propagarentur et conservarentur; eorumque animalium vita minus foret tuta aut copiosa. Exigit etiam universorum animalium utilitas, ut conservetur et augeatur genus ratione praeditum, nobilioris foelicitatis aut miseriae, et diuturnioris, capax; quamvis
generum [animalium] inferiorum imminutionem exigeret {ea} praestantiorum conservatio. Haec omnia satis docent et confirmant jus illud humani
generis commune, ad omnem ex rebus inferioribus, etiam animatis,
fructum capiendum. Omnis tamen in bruta animalia saevities, hominibus
inutilis, est omninò vituperanda.

IV. Dominii vero privati alia est ratio. Dominium primum et integrum
[illibatum], "Jus omnem rei usum capiendi, eamque domini arbitratu alie-
nandi," notat. Insitae sunt cuique solertia quaedam et vires, ad res aliquas
occupandas idoneae; atque ad agendum proclives sunt homines. Arctiores
animi affectus benigni, una cum philautia, quemque incitant, ad res, sibi
et suis <155> necessarias, anquirendas et occupandas: in istiusmodi solertia
et industria delectatur gnavus quisque, et strenuus; et in eo sibi plaudit,
quod suo labore, amicorum officiorum materiam comparavit. Docet etiam
recti honestique sensus, inhumani esse et maligni, alteri, res ejus labore partas aut excultas eripere, cum possit quisque suo se labore sustentare. In
promptu est, fructus sponte nascentes ne vel centesimum quemque alere
posse: omnium igitur labore et diligentia conservandum est humanum genus. Quod igitur est diligentiae fovendae necessarium, est et humano generi
conservando necessarium: citra vero dominium, ex labore in rebus occu-
pandis et excolendis impenso, oriundum, non amplius philautia, aut arctioris caritatis stimuli, homines ad labores perferendos incitabunt; neque
quidem ipsa quae latissimè patet benevolentia: quum omnium intersit, ut

of inferior animals denied to mankind, far fewer of these animals fit for human use would either come into life or be preserved in it; and the lives of these few would be more exposed to danger and more miserable. And then, the interest of the whole animal system would require that those en-dued with reason and reflection, and consequently capable of higher <and more lasting> happiness or misery, should be preserved and multiplied, even tho' it occasioned a diminution of the numbers of inferior animals. These considerations abundantly evidence that *right* of mankind to take the most copious use of inferior creatures, even those endued with life. And yet all useless cruelty toward the brute animals is highly blameable.

IV. The grounds of *property* among men are of a different nature. Compleat unlimited *property* is "the right of taking the full use of any goods, and of alienating them as we please." Some degree of ingenuity and strength for occupying certain things, is granted by nature to every one; mankind also naturally are <150> prone to action. Our desire of self-preservation and our tender affections excite us to occupy or acquire things necessary or useful for ourselves and those we love: every man of spirit naturally delights in such exertion of his natural powers, and applauds himself in the acquisition of what may be matter of liberality and friendliness. Our sense of right and wrong also shews, that it must be inhuman and ill-natured, for one who can otherways subsist by his own industry, to take by violence from another what he has acquired or improved by his {innocent} labours. 'Tis also obvious that the spontaneous fruits of the uncultivated earth are not sufficient to maintain the hundredth part of mankind; and that therefor it is by a general diligence and labour that they must be maintained. Whatever method therefor is necessary to encourage a general industry must also be necessary for the support of mankind;[4] now without a property ensuing upon labour employed in occupying and cultivating things {fitted for the support of life}, neither our self-love, nor any of the tender affections, would excite men to industry; nay nor even the most extensive benevolence toward all; since the common interest of all requires that all should be

4. See *System* 2.6.5, vol. I, p. 320; *Inquiry on Virtue* 7.8, pp. 284–86.

omnes, pro virili, labores vitae necessarios ferant. Nemo autem impenderet labores, nisi ipsi proprius esset rerum suo labore partarum usus; aliter enim, ignavis et nebulonibus, operum patientes omnes et strenui, praedae essent et ludibrio.

Neque quidem alia ratione jucunda erit hominum vita, aut vigebit omnium diligentia et patientia, quam cuique permisso omni, <156> rerum, quas suo labore paravit et excoluit, usu; et facultate libera, iis quos habet carissimos, de eo quod ipsi superest, gratificandi. Hinc et jucundi fient labores et honesti; vigebunt amicitiae, et mutua bonorum officia; atque suâ inopia, et {ipsi} ignavi, ad labores perferendos cogentur. Neque sperari poterit in vita civili, ea continua magistratuum cura et fides, quae cunctos, ad labores debitos in commune conferendos, adigat, atque res communes, cuique, pro indigentia et meritis, sine gratia aut odio, distribuat. Neque, si ita se res haberet, in imperantium fide et prudentiâ ea esse posset civium fiducia, quae aeque jucundos redderet labores, ac si cuique, [suo arbitratu,] [pro suo judicio] res suo labore partas, suis impertire permittatur.

obliged by their own necessities to some sort of industry.[5] Now no man would employ his labours unless he were assured of having the fruits of them at his own disposal: otherways, all the more active and diligent would be a perpetual prey, and a set of slaves [laughing-stock], to the slothful and worthless.

Without thus ensuring to each one the fruits of his own labours with full power to dispose of what's beyond <151> his own consumption to such as are dearest to him, there can be no agreeable life, no universal diligence and industry: but by such ensurance labours become pleasant and honourable, friendships are cultivated, and an intercourse of kind offices among the good: nay even the lazy and slothful are forced by their own indigence, to bear their share of labour. Nor could we hope, in any plan of polity, to find such a constant care and fidelity in magistrates, as would compell all impartially to bear their proper shares of labour, and make a distribution of the common acquisition in just proportion to the indigence or merits of the several citizens, without any partial regards to their favourites.[6] And could even this be obtained in fact, yet the citizens could scarce have such confidence in their magistrates wisdom and fidelity, as would make their diligence and labour so agreeable to them, as when they are themselves to make the distribution of their profits, according to their own inclinations, among their friends or families.

5. See *System* 2.6.5, vol. I, p. 321.
6. See *System* 2.6.6, vol. I, p. 323, where Hutcheson refers to Plato's and Thomas More's "Schemes of community."

CAPUT VI

De Dominii Acquirendi Rationibus.

I. Dominium est vel *primum,* vel *derivatum.* Primum, quod ex rerum antea communium occupatione oritur et culturâ. Derivatum, quod a priore domino, ad novum est translatum. <157>

Qui res sua sponte, sine culturâ, homini utiles aut jucundas, sive pro naturali sui conservandi appetitu, sive animo in alios benevolo, primus occupavit, primus eas oculo cernendo, manu aut instrumento quovis mox arrepturus; vel sua solertia et labore includendo; aut quacunque ratione, humanis usibus propius admovendo; ideo censetur earum dominus, quoniam si alius quispiam, qui suo se labore sustentare posset, res ita occupatas huic eriperet, ipsiusque spes et conatus redderet irritos, ab omni humanitate recederet, societatem vitae abrumperet, et perpetuis contentionibus materiam esset praebiturus. Si quis enim, huic aliquid occupanti, illud rectè nunc posset eripere; simili jure poterit et aliud denuò. Quodque huic eripienti est jus, alii cuivis, in simili competet causâ: qua ratione omnis occupantium labor irritus fieri posset, ipsique ab omni rerum usu excludi, nisi perpetuis se bellis defenderent.

Nugantur illi, qui somniantes rerum dominia physicas quasdam esse qualitates, aut vincula inter res et dominum, in eo disputant, non tantam esse primò videndi, tangendi, feriendi, aut includendi vim, ut sancta con-

---

1. See *System* 2.7.1, vol. I, pp. 324.

2. Literally: "Those are trifling who imagine that property . . . and thence dispute . . . or debate. . . ." Pufendorf criticizes the same idea in *De iure nat.* 4.4.1–2. Cf. Hume, who connected the idea of property to some rules of association of ideas "fix'd by the imagination" (see the long notes to *A Treatise of Human nature* 3.2.3). In his letter to Hutcheson of Jan. 10th, 1743 (*Letters of David Hume,* pp. 47–48), Hume criticizes

The Methods of Acquiring Property.

I. Property is either *original* or *derived.* The original property arises from the first occupation <and culture> of things formerly common. The derived is that which is transferred from the first [former] Proprietors.[1]

Whosoever either from a desire of preserving himself, or profiting any who are dear to him, first occupies any of the spontaneous fruits of the earth, or things ready for human use on which no culture was employed, either by first discovering them with intention immediately to seize them, or by any act or labour of his catching or enclosing them so that they are more easily attainable and secured for human use, is deemed justly the proprietor for these reasons; that if any other person, capable of subsisting otherways, would wrest from him what he had thus acquired, and defeat and disappoint his labours, he would plainly act inhumanly, break off all friendly society, and occasion perpetual contention. What this person pretends to now, he may attempt anew every hour: and any other person may do the same with equal right: and thus all a mans pains in acquiring any thing may be defeated, and he be excluded from all enjoyment of any thing unless he perpetually defend his acquisitions by violence.

'Tis trifling to imagine[2] that property is any physical quality or bond between a man and certain goods, and thence to dispute that there's no such force or virtue <153> in first espying, touching, striking, or inclosing

---

Hutcheson for ascribing "the Original of Property & Justice" "sometimes to private Benevolence," and "sometimes to public Benevolence" and for "condemn[ing] Reasonings, of which I [that is Hume] imagine I see so strongly the Evidence." Hutcheson here follows Locke and connects property right with labour, while Hume, as well as Pufendorf, though in different ways, cannot understand the origin of property without a convention (Hume, *Treatise* 3.2.2, p. 489 ss., and Pufendorf, *De iure nat.* 4.4.4).

stituat dominii jura; quique quaestionem movent, quaenam harum rationum vim habeat maximam. Etenim dominii causas <158> investigantes, non aliud quaerimus, quam ut cognoscatur, in quibus causis et adjunctis, {quove rerum statu,} humanum sit, et erga singulos aequum, et simul hominum consociationi tuendae idoneum et necessarium, ut uni permittatur omnis quarundam rerum usus, caeterique ab eo arceantur; quo ipso cognito, munitur via facilis, ad dominii acquirendi rationes et regulas cognoscendas.

II. De diversis occupandi rationibus, ita statuendum videtur; inhumanum esse et iniquum, nulla premente necessitate, aliorum innocuos labores, inchoatos, nec dum intermissos, impedire; eorumve fructus, praematura nostra occupatione, intervertere. Si quis igitur res sibi anquirens necessarias, rem aliquam prior vidit, confestim arrepturus, aut persecuturus; qui in simili non fuerat causa, inique ageret et inhumaniter, si celerius currendo rem prius arriperet, quam antea non quaerebat. Si plures simul, res sibi necessarias anquirentes, eandem rem viderint, {quam eorum quisque facile capere posset,} ea erit his omnibus communis, quamvis unus primus {attigerit vel} arripuerit, nisi legibus civilibus, aut moribus, aliter sit constitutum. Si unus prior viderit, confestim arrepturus, alter vero prioris consilii gnarus, similes tamen ipse res anquirens, rem <159> prior arripuerit, ea res videtur communis. Nullae enim stant ab una parte causae magis humanae, quam quae ab alterâ. Si quis suo labore aut solertia feras incluserit, irretiverit, aut captu faciliores fecerit, eas huic eripere, nulla premente graviore necessitate, iniquum esset et inhumanum; licet neque primus eas vidisset, neque attigisset. Si pluribus innotuerit rem quandam esse dominio vacuam, et cuivis occupaturo patere; pluresque, non hujus consilii sibi mutuo conscii, eam occupare simul statuerint, et conati fuerint; eo quidem more, qui communi hominum consensu invaluit, dominus erit qui primus advenerit: ubi autem nihil in mores est inductum, {istiusmodi} res omnibus citius aut serius occupantibus, erit communis, aut communiter habenda, aut inter hos plures,

anything, as to constitute a sacred right of property; or to debate which of all these actions has the greatest virtue or force. For in all our inquiries into the grounds or causes of property, this is the point in question, "what causes or circumstances <and what conditions of goods> shew, that it is human and equitable toward individuals, <fit> and requisite also to the maintainance of amicable society, that a certain person should be allowed the full use and disposal of certain goods; and all others excluded from it?" and when these are discovered, our road is cleared to find out the causes and rules about property.

II. Thus therefor we should judge about the different methods of occupation: that 'tis inhuman and unjust, without the most urgent necessity, to obstruct the innocent labours others have begun and persist in, or by any speedier attempt of ours to intercept their natural profits. If therefor any person in search for things requisite for himself, first discovers them with intention immediately to seize or pursue them; one who had employed no labour about them, nor was in search for them, would act injustly and inhumanly, if by his greater swiftness he first seized them for himself. If severals at once were searching for such things, and at once discover them by sight <easy to be seized>, they will be common among them, even altho' one swifter than the rest first touched them; unless by civil laws or custom such points be otherways determined. If one first espies them, and another conscious of his design, but also in search for such things for himself, first seizes them, the things will be common to both, or in joint property: for there are <154> no more potent reasons of humanity on one side than on the other. If one by his labour or ingenuity incloses or ensnares any wild animals, or so wearies them out in the chase that they can now easily be taken; 'tis a plain wrong for another <unless pressed by a more grievous necessity> to intercept them, tho' the former had neither seen nor touched them <first>. If it is known to many that certain lands or goods lay common to be occupied by any one; and severals, not conscious of each others designs, at once are preparing to occupy them, and set about it: by the custom which has obtained, he that first arrives at them is the proprietor. But, abstracting from received customs {and laws}, such things should be common to all who without fraud or imprudent negligence employed their

pro ratione operarum et impensarum, quas prudenter et bona fide, in ea occupanda singuli contulerunt, dividenda; siquidem eorum nulli defuit bona fides, aut justa diligentia. Immo, etsi plures consilii hujus mutuo sibi conscii fuerant, recte tamen omnes occupant, et dominium obtinent commune. Neque tardioribus citra culpam; aut iis qui strenuam navantes operam, casu quodam impediebantur, aditus ad rem communem est praecludendus.

In causis hujusmodi spectandum, primo, <160> si quae humaniores suadeant rationes, ut uni prae caeteris faveatur; haec imprimis, ne innocuorum aut honestorum laborum fructus intervertantur, aut probi et industrii spes et conatus fiant irriti. Si omnibus faveat haec ratio, res debet esse omnibus communis. Si qui casus rariores ancipiti ansam praebeant disceptationi; atque res quaedam neque communiter haberi, neque sine dispendio dividi, aut commode distrahi possint, hominum conventione aut <pro> more instituto, dominium illi assignandum, cui favent istiusmodi adjuncta, quorum ea est vis, ut lites inextricabiles et bella praecavere valeant. Atque ideo tantus ubique favor comitatur prius occupantem, aut qui rem palam emerat, et cui palam fuit tradita: atque haec publica exigit utilitas.

Si inter se plures pacti fuerint, rem fore illius qui primo occupaverit; et de occupandi modo etiam pacisci oportebat: de quo si nihil convenerat, plures occupandi rationes censeri possunt pares, et commune erit dominium. Haec ad pacem tuendam sunt aptissima.

{De eo quidem quod in variis istiusmodi causis, singuli summo jure sibi arrogare possint, lites fortè incident inextricabiles: semper tamen qui virtuti student, quid postulet aequitas et humanitas, quidque viro bono <161> dignum, nisi se nimium amaverint, facile perspicient. Neque querendum, quod in his aliisque causis quibusdam, non satis clare docuerit natura, quam propè ad injurias et fraudes, sine tamen turpitudine et infamia accedere

labours in occupying them, whether they came earlier or later; and should either be held in common, or divided among them in proportion to expence and pains prudently employed by each of them for this purpose. Nay tho' each of them were aware of the designs of the rest; 'tis right that each should proceed and acquire a joint title with others. Nor should those who without any fault of their own came too late, or such whose wise and vigorous attempts have been retarded by accidents, be precluded from their share.

In such disputable cases we should first inquire what reasons of humanity give the preference to any one above the rest; and this chiefly, "that the natural fruits of no man's honourable or innocent labours should be intercepted; or any honest industrious attempts defeated." If this plea belongs alike to all, the goods should be deemed in joint property of all. <155> If some accidents or circumstances make the point very doubtful; and some sorts of goods can neither be held in common, nor divided or sold without great loss; we should follow some implicite conventions of men, appearing by the laws or customs which prevail; and assign the property to him who has on his side such circumstances the regarding of which prevents many inextricable disputes and violent contentions. Hence it is that law and custom so generally favour the first seizer, the publick purchaser, and the person to whom goods have been publickly delivered. And this conduces to [requires] the common utility.

If different persons intending to occupy agree that the whole should fall to him who first occupies; they ought also to specify the manner of occupation; otherways different methods may be deemed equally valid, and constitute a joint property. These rules seem the most conducive to peace.

No doubt inextricable questions may arise about what the several parties insisting on their utmost rights may do, without being chargeable with injustice. But such as sincerely aim at acting the virtuous part, will always easily discern what equity and humanity require, <what is worthy of a good man,> unless they are too much influenced by selfishness. Nor have we reason to complain, that, in these and such like cases, nature has not precisely enough fixed the boundaries, to let us see how very near we may approach to fraud or injury, without actually incurring the charge of it;

possimus; quum tam clarâ voce nos ad omnem honestatem, liberalitatem, et beneficientiam cohortetur.}

III. Quum autem homo sit naturâ sagax et futuri providus, non solum in praesentem sui aut suorum usum, recte res occupabit, verum et in futurum, ubi alii gravi non premuntur necessitate. Quumque res plurimae, ut hominum usui uberius et diutius inserviant, longa egeant et laboriosa cultura; ut ad eam adhibendam incitentur homines, ipsis perpetuus earum rerum permittendus est usus, sive dominium perpetuum, laboris et solertiae naturale et justum praemium. Quâ in causa sunt arva, pascua, vineae, oliveta, pomaria, horti, jumenta, et his similia plurima.

Inchoatur autem dominium, inchoatâ rerum prius communium cultura; plenum est, quum designavit occupator quousque, per se, vel per alios sibi adsciscendos, excolere et velit et possit. Iniquum enim est aut impedire labores innocuos, aut eorum fructus intervertere.

Terminatur vero dominium, aut occupandi <162> jus, occupantis, eorumque, quos sibi adsciscere potest, excolendi viribus. Neque primo appulsu in vastam insulam, plurium familiarum capacem, pluriumque cultura egentem, fieri potest unus paterfamilias totius insulae dominus. Quisque recte occupat quantum poterit excolere: inculta manent communia. Neque primo classis suae appulsu domina sit civitas vastae continentis, plurium civitatum capacis, cui excolendae unius civitatis coloniae neutiquam sufficerent. Recte occupat haec civitas quantum spes est se posse modico et justo tempore excolere; suosque jure porrigunt coloni limites, ultra id quod possunt quinquennio primo aut decennio mitigare; neutiquam vero ultra

---

3. This paragraph is much longer than the parallel one in *System* 2.7.2, vol. I, p. 325–26. This is an exception and perhaps also a clue that Hutcheson did not like Hume's long notes on the association of ideas just mentioned.

when we are so loudly exhorted to every thing honourable, liberal and beneficent.[3] <156>

III. But as man is naturally endued with provident forethought, we may not only justly occupy what's requisite for present use, but may justly store up for the future; unless others be in some extraordinary distress. There are also many things requiring a very long course of labour to cultivate them, which after they are cultivated yield almost a perpetual and copious use to mankind. Now that men may be invited to such a long course of labour, 'tis absolutely requisite that a continual property be allowed them as the natural result and reward of such laborious cultivation. This is the case {in clearing woody grounds} for tillage or pasture; {preparing} vineyards, olive-yards, gardens, orchards{; in rearing or breaking} of beasts for labour (and many others similar).[4]

Property is deemed to begin as soon as one begins the culture of what before was unoccupied; and it is compleated when the cultivator has marked out such a portion as he both can and intends to cultivate, by himself or such as he can procure to assist him. As 'tis plainly injust to obstruct any innocent labours intended, or to intercept their fruits.

But the abilities of the occupier with his assistants must set bounds to his right of occupation. One head of a family, by his first arriving with his domesticks upon a vast island capable of supporting a thousand [many] families, must not pretend to property in the whole. He may acquire as much as there's any probability he can cultivate, but what is beyond this remains common. Nor can any state, on account of its fleets first arriving on a vast continent, capable of holding several empires [states], and which its colonies can never sufficiently <157> occupy, claim to itself the dominion of the whole continent.[5] This state may justly claim as much as it can reasonably hope to cultivate by its colonies in any reasonable time: and may no doubt extend its bounds beyond what it can cultivate the first ten or twelve [fifteen] years; but not beyond all probable hopes of its ever being

---

4. See *System* 2.7.1, vol. I, pp. 324–25.
5. See *System* 2.7.3, vol. I, pp. 326–27.

[quam ulla est excolendi spes] [omnem regionis occupatae excolendae spem]. Justum autem excolendi tempus, primis occupantibus concedendum, virorum prudentium arbitrio definiri debet, vicinarum, aeque ac hujus civitatis, habita ratione, prout numerosiores sunt, novisque magis indigentes sedibus; aut minus numerosae, civesque laxius habitantes. Ubi novis plures indigent sedibus, rectè istius continentis partes incultas, a cultis remotiores, occupabunt aliae civitates, ea inconsultâ, aut invitâ, quae prima partem occupaverat. Neque ea exigere potest, ut hi advenae civili ipsius imperio se subjiciant. Satis est si <163> aequae pacis legibus consentiant. Veruntamen prout in libero populo justae aliquando sunt leges agrariae, paucorum opes nimias, et civitati periculosas, cohibentes; civitatibus ita vicinis jus est, mature praepedire eas unius occupationes, ex quibus, ipsi earum libertati aut majestati, periculum imminere videatur; nisi alia ratione satis sibi cavere poterint. Communi enim utilitati adversatur quam maximè, ut unius civitatis superbiae, avaritiae, ambitioni, aut luxui, aliarum jura, majestas, libertasque, permittantur pessundanda.

Singulis tamen hominibus, ut et hominum coetibus, permittenda sunt rerum quarundam dominia jure acquisita, supra eum modum, quem exigit ipsorum usus; quum eae commerciis praebeant materiam, cum aliis rebus quibus indigent commutandae.

IV. Ex his dominii causis patebit, *res usus inhexausti,* ita occupari non posse, ut ab earum usu alii arceantur; praecipue etiam, quod nullo hominum labore res istiusmodi meliores fieri possint. Si quidem ad tutiorem earundem usum, sumptus exigantur aut labores, recte hoc exigunt hi, qui utiles eos sumptus aut labores impenderant, ut iis compensandis caeteri, pro rata

able to cultivate. The just reasonable time to be allowed to the first occupiers, must be determined by prudent arbiters, who must regard, not only the circumstances of this state, but of all others who may be concerned, according as they are more or less populous, and either need new seats for their colonies, or have already sufficient lands for their people. If many neighbouring states are too populous, they may justly occupy the uncultivated parts of such a new discovered continent, leaving sufficient room for the first occupiers; and that without the leave of the first discoverers. Nor can the first discoverers justly demand that these colonies sent by other states should be subjected to their empire. 'Tis enough if they agree to live amicably beside them as confederated states [under a few common laws]. Nay as in a free democracy [nation], 'tis often just <by agrarian laws> to prevent such immoderate acquisitions of wealth by a few, as may be dangerous to the publick{, even tho' these acquisitions are a making without any private injuries}: so neighbouring states may justly take early precautions, even by violence if necessary, against such acquisitions of any one, as may be dangerous to the liberty and independency of all around them; when sufficient security cannot be obtained in a gentler way.[6] Nothing can be more opposite to the general good of mankind than that the rights, <158> independency, and liberty of many {neighbouring] nations should be exposed to be trampled upon by the pride, luxury, ambition, or avarice of any [only one] nation.

'Tis plain however, that both individuals and societies should be allowed to acquire stores of certain goods far beyond all their own consumption; since these stores may serve as matter of commerce and barter to obtain goods of other kinds they may need.

IV. From these principles about property it appears, that such things as are inexhaustible by any use, are not matters of occupation or property, so that others could be excluded from them: for this further reason too, that such things can scarce be improved by any human labour. If indeed for the more safe use of any of them labour or expences are requisite; those who wisely employ labour or expence for this purpose, may justly require that all others

6. See *System* 2.7.3, vol. I, p. 327.

parte, aliquid conferant. Aer igitur, lumen solis, aqua profluens, et oceanus, omnibus <164> manent communia; quin et freta. Transeuntibus autem recte imponi potest tributum aliquod, ab ea civitate, cujus propugnaculis, aut navibus armatis arcentur piratae, tutumque omnibus per ea freta munitur iter: quod tamen tributum non est augendum, ultra rationem sumptuum, omnibus transeuntibus utilium. Cunctis autem permittendus omnis rerum communium usus, qui non etiam vicini soli, ab aliis occupati, usum includit.

Hinc constat, res a Deo hominibus fuisse relictas, in ea communione quae dicitur *negativa,* non *positiva.* Illa est "status rerum in medio positarum, ut occupationi pateant": haec vero "status rerum quae sunt in plurium dominio indiviso," ad quas nempe sibi sumendas, sine dominorum omnium consensu, nemini jus est. Recte igitur quivis, caeteris inconsultis, res prius {*negative*} communes occupabit; neque in dominio primo constituendo, omnium de rebus dividendis conventionibus opus fuit.

Quae *nullius* dicuntur res, occupationi tamen non patentes, neque omnibus communes, sunt in dominio coetus, aut *universitatis:* ut res *sacrae,* <et> *sanctae,* [et *religiosae;* quarum nonnullae quidem sunt] [Religiosae sunt aliquando inter] res familiares; quamvis legibus quibusdam superstitiosis, <165> prohibeatur aliquando, ne quis res istiusmodi ad alios usus convertat. Neque enim res istae usum aliquem Deo praestare possunt; neque ipsius jus dominii in omnia, ullo hominum facto augeri potest, vel imminui.

---

7. See *System* 2.7.5, vol. I, pp. 329.

8. See *System* 2.7.5, vol. I, pp. 330–31. Also, Pufendorf emphasizes this distinction between negative and positive community, to reach the opposite conclusion, that the origin of property is by convention (*De iure nat.* 4.4.2 and 4).

9. The fifth section in the *Institutio* does not begin here, with the treatment of *res nullius,* but afterward, with the treatment of the accessions.

who use them should in a just proportion contribute to make compensation. The *air,* the *light, running water,* and *the ocean* are thus common to
all, {and cannot be appropriated:} the same is the case of *straits* or *gulphs.*
And yet if any state is at the expence to build fortified harbours or to clear
certain seas from Pyrates for the behoof of all traders, they may justly insist
on such taxes upon all traders who share the benefit as may proportionally
defray the said expences, as far as they really are for the benefit of all traders,
but no further.[7] Now no man should be excluded from any use of things
thus destined for perpetual community, unless this use requires also some
use of lands which are in property.

These reasonings also shew that all things were left <159> by God to men
in that community called *negative,* not *positive. Negative community* is "the
state of things exposed to be appropriated by occupation." Positive community is "the state of things in the joint property of many": which therefor
no person can occupy or acquire without the consent of the joint proprietors. At first any one might justly have occupied what he wanted, without
consulting the rest of mankind; nor need we have recourse to any old conventions of all men, to explain the introduction of property.[8]

V.[9] The goods called by the Civilians *res nullius,* which, as they say, are not
in property, and yet not exposed to occupation;{*} such as temples, the
fortifications of cities, and burial-places [sacred, holy or religious buildings
or places], are truly the property either of larger societies, or of families;
altho' this property is often so restricted by superstitious laws, that it can
be turned to no other use.[10] 'Tis vain to imagine that any such things afford
use to the Deity, or that his supreme right over all can be enlarged or diminished by any human deed.

* {Of these there are 3 classes, *sacrae, sanctae, religiosae,* Of which follow three examples in order.} [The three examples picked up by the translator are drawn from *System*
2.7.6, vol. I, p. 331].
   10. The "superstitious laws" Hutcheson is referring to are clearer in *System* 2.7.6,
pp. 332–335, where he enlarges on "some wild notion of consecration or sanctity infused
into stones, timber, metals, lands" and against "the Popish religion."

Res publicae, quamvis extra singulorum patrimonia et commercia, veniunt tamen in populorum commercia, sive inter se, sive cum privatis: ut *theatra, porticus, viae, balnea.*

Res olim occupatae, communes fieri possunt, si a domino sint projectae, aut postquam vindicare eas poterat diu neglectae; quod etiam animum abdicandi satis indicare potest. Diuturna earum possessio quemvis constituet dominum. Ubi dominus rei, invitè licet amissae, non apparet, cedit possessori. Sunt autem aliae causae, haud iniquae, cur alia *usucapio,* legibus civilibus, in communem utilitatem, et ad fraudes praecavendas constituatur.

Cum solo occupato, occupantur et ea, quorum nullus aliis potest esse usus, sine usu soli; ut *lacus, stagna,* et *flumina* ripas occupatas interfluentia: immo et ea, quorum ex usu promiscuè permisso, rebus nostris periculum immineret; ut sinus, longius a mari in agros occupatos recedentes, partesque maris littoribus propiores, unde bellicis tormentis <166> laedi possint res nostrae. Non tamen occupantur fera animalia, quae sponte se subducere possunt, et in quibus custodiendis, aut includendis, nullus est impensus labor. Licet recte alios ab aucupio, venatione, aut piscatu, in solo nostro, possimus arcere.

V. Accessiones appellantur, omnes *fructus, incrementa, alluviones, commixtiones, confusiones, specificationes,* quae dicuntur, et *meliorationes:* de quibus hae regulae facillimae.

1. Rei nostrae *accessiones* omnes, quae nullam alterius rem aut operam includunt, sunt nostrae; nisi quis alius jus aliquod recte acquisivit, nostro derogans aliquid dominio.

---

* {*Res publicae,* or *res populi.*}

† {*Usucapio*} [on Prescription see *System* 2.7.7, vol. I, pp. 335–36; Pufendorf, *De officio* I.12.15.]

The goods belonging to states{*} are not in the property or patrimony of any individuals, nor come into their commerce. But they are the property of the community, which may transfer them as it pleases. Such are publick theatres, high-ways, porticos, {aqueducts,} bagnios.

Things formerly occupied may return into the old <160> state of community if the proprietor throw them away, or abandon his property; and this intention of abandoning may sometimes sufficiently appear by a long neglect of claiming it, when there's nothing to obstruct his recovery. A long possession in this case will give another a just title. Goods unwillingly lost fall also to the fair possessor, when the proprietor cannot be found. There are also other reasons why civil laws have introduced other sorts of *prescription*{†} for the common utility, and to prevent inextricable controversies.

In the occupying of lands, a property is also constituted in such things as cannot be used without some use of the ground; such as lakes, <pools,> and rivers as far as they flow within the lands in property; nay such parts also of things otherwise fit for perpetual community, as cannot be left open to promiscuous use without indangering our property; such as *bays* of the sea running far into our lands, and parts of the ocean contiguous to the coast, from whence our possessions might be annoyed. But by occupying lands we acquire no property in such wild creatures as can easily withdraw themselves beyond our bounds, and are no way inclosed or secured by our labour. And yet the proprietor may justly hinder others from trespassing upon his ground for fouling, hunting, or fishing.

All {natural, accidental, or artificial} improvements, {or adventitious increase}, are called accessions, such as fruits of trees, the young of cattle, growth of timber, and artificial forms [such as fruits, increases, floods, mixtures, fusions, specifications].{‡} About which these general [very easy] rules <161> hold, 1. "All accessions of our goods which are not owing to any goods or labours of others, are also our property; unless some other person has acquired some right which limits our property."

---

‡ {*Fructus, incrementa, alluviones, commixtiones, confusiones, specificationes.* The explication of all these may be found in any compend of civil law, or law dictionary.} [On the accessions see *System* 2.7.8, vol. I, pp. 337–38.]

2. Ubi citra dolum malum, aut culpam, plurium res aut operae, ad rem aliquam conficiendam, aut conflandam concurrerunt, aut rem fecerunt meliorem; dominium est hisce pluribus commune, pro rerum aut operarum quas singuli contulerunt ratione. Res igitur ipsa est his communiter, aut vicibus alternis, in eadem ratione, utenda; aut inter hos ita dividenda, si sine dispendio hoc fieri possit.

3. Quorum si nullum possit fieri, qui minore cum incommodo, re communi carere possunt, eam cedere debent magis indigenti, <167> acceptâ compensatione, a viro probo definiendâ.

4. Ubi *dolo malo,* aut *culpa lata,* res aut opera aliena rei meae est immista, unde mihi sit minus utilis; ejus pretium ab eo, qui dolo aut culpâ, rem meam contrectavit, est mihi praestandum; immo praestandum quod mea interesset, salvam habuisse rem meam et intactam: atque rem meam mihi inutilem ipse sibi habeat. Si vero res mea mihi facta fuerit utilior, mea erit; tantumque illi à me praestandum, quantum ipsius opera factus sum locupletior.

Plenum igitur Dominium continet haec quatuor. (1.) Jus rei possidendae. (2.) Jus omnem ejus usum capiendi. (3.) Jus alios ab eo arcendi. (4.) Jus, prout domino libuerit, eam transferendi, vel absolutè, vel sub conditione quavis licita, et in quemcunque eventum; sive totam, sive mutilam; aut quemcunque ejus licitum usum, alteri permittendi. Jure saepe civili imminuuntur dominii jura, saepe priorum dominorum factis aut contractibus. <168>

2. When without the fraud or fault of any of the parties, the goods or labours of different persons have concurred to make any *compound,* or have improved any goods, "these goods are in joint property of all those whose goods and labours have thus concurred; and that in proportion to what each one has contributed." Such goods therefor are to be used by them in common, or by turns for times in the said proportion, or to be thus divided among them, if they will admit division without loss.

3. But if they admit no such common or alternate use, or division, they to whom they are least necessary should quit their shares to the person who needs them most, for a reasonable compensation, to be estimated by a person of judgment and integrity.

4. When by the fraud or gross fault of another, his goods or labours are intermixed with my goods, so that they are less fitted for my purpose; the persons by whose gross fault this has happened is bound to compensate my loss{*} or make good to me the value of my goods, nay{†} all the profit I could have made had they been left to me entire as they were; and let him keep to himself the goods he has made unfit for <162> my purpose. But if by the intermedling of others my goods are made more convenient for me, my right remains; and I can be obliged to compensate to them no further than the value of the improvement to my purposes, or as far as I am enriched.

Full property originally contains these several rights: first, that of retaining possession, 2. and next, that of taking all manner of use. 3. that also of excluding others from any use; 4. and lastly, that of transferring to others as the proprietor pleases, either in whole or in part, absolutely, or under any lawful condition, or upon any event or contingency, and of granting any particular lawful use to others. But property is frequently limited by civil laws, and frequently by the deeds <or contracts> of some former proprietors.[11]

---

* {This *pensatio damni,* which is often due when there was no fraud in the case.}

† {*Pensare quod interest,* which always includes the former, and often extends much further.}

11. See *System* 2.7.9, vol. I, pp. 338–39.

CAPUT VII

De Jure Derivato, ejusque Causis.

I. Derivata jura adventitia sunt vel *realia* vel *personalia*. Juris realis materia, sunt ipsa rerum dominia; personalis materia est libertas naturalis, jus scil. cujusque pro sua voluntate et judicio agendi, suasque res administrandi. Hujusmodi juris parte aliqua, ad alterum translata, subnascitur eidem jus personale.

Ad hanc distinctionem, cui et in lege naturali est locus, explicandam, primo monendum, quod mutua officia, et junctos plurium labores, saepe communis exigat utilitas: quodque, aucto hominum numero, multò foelicius suppetent cunctis res utiles, ubi quisque sibi artem aliquam eligens, in ea se exercet; ejusque peritus, magnam comparat rerum quarundam copiam, quas rebus aliorum, diversas artes exercentium, commutare poterit; quàm si quisque, per vices, omnes artes utcunque exerceret, in earum nullâ ad insignem perventurus solertiam.

Constat etiam, post homines multiplicatos, agros omnes ferè, brevi ita fuisse occupatos, ut non paucis, unde se alere possint, nulli restarent occupandi. Illis igitur <169> relictae erant vires suae et artes, ut suis operis, vulgaribus aut artificiosis, pro aliis rebus commutatis, sibi res compararent necessarias. Locupletiores vero aliorum operis et artificiis, plerumque maxime indigent; quae salvo pudore, ab aliis gratis expectare haud possunt:

Of Derived Property.

I. The derived <adventitious> rights are either *real* or *personal*. The materials whence all real rights arise is our property. Personal rights are founded on our natural liberty, or right of acting as we choose, and of managing our own affairs. When any part of these original rights is transferred to another, then a personal right is constituted <to him>.

To apprehend this distinction, which has place in the law of nature, as well as in civil law, 'tis to be observed, that the common interest of all constantly requires an intercourse of offices, and the joint labours of many: and that when mankind grow numerous, all necessaries and conveniences will be much better supplied to all, when each one chooses an art to himself, by practice acquires dexterity in it, and thus provides himself great plenty of such goods as that art produces, to be exchanged in commerce for the goods produced in like manner by other artisans; than if each one by turns practised every necessary art, without ever acquiring dexterity in any of them.[1]

'Tis plain too, that when men were multiplied considerably, all lands of easy culture must soon have been occupied, so that {there would none remain in common; and that} many could find none to occupy for their support, such persons therefor would have no other fund <164> than their own bodily strength or ingenuity, that by <exchanging> their common or artificial labours <with the goods of others> they might procure necessaries for themselves: the more opulent too{, for their own ease,} would more frequently need the labours of the indigent, and could not with any conscience expect them gratuitously. There must therefor be a continual course

---

1. This first section has its parallel in *System* 2.8.1, vol. I, pp. 340–43. However in the *System* there is no reference to the advantages of the division of labour, nor to the scarcity of unoccupied lands and the need of the "labours of the indigent" by the proprietors.

crebris igitur {semper} opus erat *pactis,* (quorum natura deinceps plenius explicanda,) quibus et *dominia* {sive *jura realia*} transferrentur; et *jura personalia,* ad certam mensuram aut *quantitatem* ab aliis exigendam, sive *debita,* constituerentur.

Conveniret autem non raro inter paciscentes, ut dominus, omni rei suae dominio neutiquam translato, eam creditori ita subjiceret, ut nisi ad diem praestitutum aliunde solutum fuerit debitum, ex ea re distracta, aut vendita, solveretur: hac ratione constituebatur creditori *jus reale.* Aliquando patrifamilias assiduo et industrio, ita fidem haberet creditor, ut nullam posceret *hypothecam,* contentus jure personali, non unam aliquam debitoris rem, prae alia, respiciente. Ex damno item dato, simile oriretur jus tantummodò personale. Commerciorum vero gliscentium fides sanctissimè servanda, formulas quasdam semper exigebat solennes et publicas; quibus adhibitis, plena intelligebatur dominii fieri translatio, <170> contractu nullo priore, qui latuerat, eludenda. Quod nisi obtineretur, nemo quicquam emere vellet, sibi forte, ex contractu aliquo latente, cum tertio quodam prius inito, mox eripiendum. Obligationes suas quascunque, vir bonus sanctissime spectabit, etiam personales: commerciorum autem fides necessario servanda hoc exigit, ut pactis, bona fide et publicè, ad jura realia transferenda initis, jura cedant personalia, quamvis priora.

II. Jura *realia derivata,* sunt vel pleni dominii partes quaedam, a reliquis separatae, vel ipsa dominia [ab uno ad alterum translata] [nova]. Partes quae

---

2. Scot. for "notorious."

* {Whatever may be determined by human laws or courts, there is no natural foundation in justice for preferring the pledge or mortgage as to any loans made after he knew

of contracts among men, <the nature of which has to be explained afterward> both for the transferring of property or real rights; and the constituting claims to certain services, and to certain quantities or values, to be paid in consideration of these services; which are personal rights.

Now it would often happen that a proprietor without entirely transferring his property in lands or other goods, would yet consent so to subject them to certain claims of his creditor, that unless the debt be discharged at the time agreed, the creditor by the possession or sale of such lands or goods might secure himself: by a transaction of this kind a *real right* is constituted <to the creditor>. Sometimes the creditor would have such confidence in the wealth and integrity of his debtor, that he would demand no such *real* security as {a pledge or} mortgage, but accept of a personal obligation, which had no more peculiar respect to any one piece of goods or property of the debtor than another. In like manner; from any damage done there would arise only a *personal right.* But further, when it was found absolutely necessary to maintain the faith of <swelling> commerce, certain publick and notour[2] forms have been received, to make full translation of property: which must have always been deemed so valid and sacred, that no prior latent contracts with others could defeat them. Were not <165> such *forms* thus agreed upon, no man would buy any thing; since he could have no security that it would not be wrested from him by a third person upon some prior latent contract. A good man no doubt will sacredly regard all his {contracts and} obligations personal or real{; and avoid what may defeat any right of another of any kind}. But there's such a necessity of maintaining the faith of publick commerce,{*} that all contracts entered into publickly and without fraud, in order to transfer real rights, must take place of {latent contracts and} personal rights, tho' prior in time.

II. Derived real rights are either certain parts of the right of property, subsisting separately from the rest; or compleat property transferred. The

---

the debts due to others, and suspected that they were in danger of losing them.} [This note added by the translator is grounded on what Hutcheson says in the parallel passage of *System* 2.8.1, vol. I, p. 343.]

separatae solent manere, sunt quatuor; scil. 1. Jus possidendi rem alienam, quae sine vi aut dolo, ad aliquem pervenerat. 2. Jus haereditarium, 3. Jus pignoris aut hypothecae, (4)[1] et servitutes.

Qui rem alienam, sine vi aut dolo possidet, vel novit eam esse alienam; vel ex causa probabili, credit eam esse suam: atque hic proprie dicitur *bonae fidei possessor.*

Qui vi aut dolo, sine justa causa rem alienam possidet, ei nullum est jus: quum domino, aut ejus nomine reposcenti cuilibet, jus sit eam possessori injusto eripiendi, ut domino reddatur. Qui tamen sine vi aut dolo possidet quod novit esse alienum; ut qui res <171> amissas aut naufragas invenit; ei jus est eas retinendi, quod valebit contra omnes praeter dominum, [per se, aut per alium,] [ad ejus mandatarium] reposcentem. Qui si nullus vindicet, res cedit possessori. Tenetur autem possessor publicè denunciare, res eas apud se esse, domino repetenti reddendas: eas enim celasse, crimen habet furti. Recte tamen a domino exigit impensas, in iis conservandis aut denunciandis, prudenter erogatas.

Bonae fidei possessor, primo, rem tenetur cum fructibus extantibus domino reddere. 2. Dein si res, ejusve fructus sint consumpti, tenetur domino praestare quantum ex rei alienae usu factus est locupletior, quòd rebus suis interea pepercerat; vel quantum, pro sua conditione, ipsius interfuit tam diu lautius vixisse. Iniquum enim est hominem, hominis non consentientis incommodo, suum augere aut commodum aut voluptatem.

3. Ubi res ipsae, earumve fructus periere; ea praestare non tenetur bonae

---

1. (1742 edn. more correct.)

parts which often subsist separately are four, the *rights of possessing* what [the goods of another that] one obtains without force or fraud; the *rights of heirs in entail* [hereditary rights]; the rights of the *pledge* or *mortgage;* and *servitudes.*

[1.] He that possesses the goods of another without fraud or violence, either knows that they are the property of others; or upon probable ground believes them to be his own. And this latter is the *bonae fidei possessor,* or the presumptive proprietor.[3]

Whosoever by fraud or violence possesses the goods he knows belong to others, has no manner of right. The proprietor, or any other honest man for the proprietor's <166> behoof, has a right to demand and take them from him by force, to restore them to the proprietor. But when we get possession of any goods without fraud or violence, which we know belong to others, (as when one finds goods lost at land, or wrecks at sea), these we may detain till they are claimed by the proprietor, or some person commissioned by him; and if no such person ever appears, the goods fall to the possessor. But in such cases the possessor is bound to give publick notice that he has found such goods, and is ready to restore them to the owner: to conceal them would be equal to theft. But he may justly insist to have all his prudent charges in the keeping or advertising them refunded to him.

The obligations on the presumptive proprietor are, first to restore to the owner the goods, with all their unconsumed fruits{, profits and increase}.

2. If the goods or their increase be consumed, to refund to the value of what he is inriched by the use of them, in sparing so much of his own property; or as much as it can be deemed valuable to him to have so long lived with more elegance or pleasure, considering his circumstances. For 'tis a just maxim, that "no person should derive to himself any pleasure or advantage at the expence of another without his consent."

3. If both the goods and their increase have perished by accident, the presumptive proprietor {who holds no profit by them} is not obliged to

---

3. See *System* 2.8.3, vol. I, pp. 344–49, and Pufendorf, *De officio* 1.13, for similar lists of duties incumbent upon presumptive proprietors. In *De iure nat.* 4.13.7 Pufendorf says that he draws his catalogue from Grotius (*De iure belli* 2.10, 3–13).

fidei possessor, aut fructus quos percipere neglexerat; utebatur enim rebus tanquam suis. Cessat autem bona fides, ubi primum possessori innotuit probabilis suspicandi causa, rem esse alienam: eaque cessante, omnia *latâ culpa,* neglecta aut omissa, praestare tenetur. <172>

4. Quum rem oneroso partam titulo, domino reddit bonae fidei possessor, pretium ab auctore suo recte reposcit.

5. Ubi auctor solvendo non est, haud aequior est domini causa, quam bonae fidei possessoris. Neque enim sanctius est domini jus, quam quo res emptione, successione, testamentis, aut donationibus {partae} tenentur; quippe quibus plerumque constituuntur ipsa dominia. Quumque certum alteri aut utrique damnum sit ferendum, neque ulla publicae utilitatis ratio, uni prae altero faveat; nisi quid aliter suadeant humanitatis aut liberalitatis rationes, {damnum} inter eos dividendum videtur: {idque eo magis, quod saepè bonae fidei possessor rem alienam sibi parando, domino negotium gesserat utile, quippe cui aliter nulla rei suae vindicandae fuisset copia}. Si quis dixerit hoc esse utile, ut caveant emptores, ne res emant furtivas. Res suas, contra, diligentius custodiant domini; ne in eas, ipsorum negligentia amissas, aut raptui expositas, incidant viri probi, tanquam in laqueos.

6. Rem suam, a bonae fidei possessore alteri donatam, a donatario recte vindicat dominus, neque illi ullum est repetendi jus.

make good the value: nor is he accountable for such profits as he neglected to take: for he used these goods {believing them to be his own, even} as he would have used <167> his own. But one ceases to be deemed presumptive proprietor as soon as he has any probable intimation that the goods are not his own{, by any plausible claim put in by another}: and whatever is culpably lost, squandered or grosly neglected thereafter he is bound to make good.

4. When the presumptive proprietor restores to the true owner any goods he bought or obtained for valuable consideration; he may justly insist to have the price or consideration restored to him by his *author,* or the person from whom he obtained them.

5. Where this person is bankrupt, {or can't be found,} the cause of the presumptive proprietor is as favourable as that of the true one. Nor does the true proprietor hold by any title more sacred than by purchase, succession, testament, or donation, which are the ordinary foundations of the true property, as well as of the presumptive. And since a certain loss must fall upon one or both parties, nor is there any reason of publick interest pleading for one more than the other; the loss should be equally divided between them, unless some reasons of humanity <and liberality> recommend a different decision; especially since it often happens, that the presumptive proprietor has done a most valuable service to the proprietor, in purchasing his goods, which otherways might have been lost to him for ever. If one pleads the general advantage of making purchasers look well to their titles, that they may not purchase goods injuriously obtained: 'tis on the other hand an equal publick advantage that the proprietors be made more vigilant about their <168> goods, least when they are lost or stollen through their negligence, fair purchasers may be involved in losses by their means.

6. Where the presumptive property has been obtained [bestowed to another] gratuitously, and the goods are claimed by the true owner, they must be restored. Nor has the person who got them gratuitously in this case any recourse for their value.

III. De jure *haereditario* certum est, eum qui pleno jure est dominus, posse rem suam ad quemvis, in quemcunque eventum, <173> et sub conditionibus quibusvis licitis transferre. Haeredis igitur cujusque substituti non minus sanctum est jus, quam donatarii. Neque minus inhumanum est, cohibere dominum, ne ad haeredem substitutum, sibi carum, rem suam in certum eventum transferat; quam prohibere ne amico vivus donet, aut ad haeredem proximum, in mortis eventum transferat. Non minus inhumanum est, haeredis secundi aut tertii spem, sine justa causa praecidere, quam amici dona intervertere. Rectè tamen leges civiles, in communem utilitatem, [vetant in infinitum porrigere] [vetare possunt, ne in infinitum porrigantur] haec jura, possessoribus fortè gravia futura, aut ipsae civitati: prout prodigae et inconsultae donationes, aequi judicis sententia, rescindi possunt.

IV. Ad eorum jura quibus aliquid debetur confirmanda {et munienda} dantur *pignora,* ea lege, ut res oppignorata, nisi ante statum diem solutum fuerit debitum, cedat creditori; quae est *lex commissoria,* nihil iniqui continens, si modo debitori reddendum sit quod superest pretii, ex re vendita, post solutionem illius quod debebatur. Saepe vero non traditur res creditori; sed ipsi in eam, per formulas quasdam publicas, constituitur jus reale, quod *hypotheca* dicitur. Quod cum sit, huic creditoris juri, cedunt omnia jura adversus debitorem personalia, <174> quamvis priora, quae ante hypothecam constitutam non publice innotuerant. Neque recte queruntur isti, quorum jura personalia juri cedunt reali subsequenti: sibi enim imputent quod posthabeantur <ipsi>, minore cautione contenti, iis quos prioris sui juris non monuerant, quique majorem impetrarunt cautionem, citra quam, fidem debitoris haud fuissent sequuti.

---

4. More literally: "hereditary right," but the context makes clear that Hutcheson is referring here, as well as in *System* 2.8.4, vol. I, pp. 349–50, to the special institution of leaving an estate to a line of heirs in such a way that none of them can sell or mortgage it.

* {This clause is called *lex commissoria,* or the clause of entire forfeiture.}

III. Concerning the right of heirs in entail,[4] these points seem clear; that one who has full property may transfer his goods to any person upon any contingency, or under any lawful conditions. The right therefor of persons in remainder is as sacred as any right founded in donation: nor is it less inhuman to hinder the proprietor to convey his property to a person dear to him, upon any contingency, than to hinder a friendly immediate donation, or conveyance to his first heir upon the event of his death. It is no less inhuman to defeat the hopes of the second or third in remainder, without any demerit of theirs, than to intercept other donations to friends. And yet there may be prudent reasons why civil laws should prevent making such perpetual entails as may be very inconvenient to the several successors in their turns, or pernicious to the community; even as courts of equity often make void prodigal and inconsiderate donations.

IV. For further security to creditors pledges {and mortgages} were introduced, or goods so subjected to the power of the creditor{*} that, if the debt is not discharged <169> at the time prefixed, the goods should become the property of the creditor. In this there would be no iniquity, if the creditor in such cases were also obliged to restore to the debtor whatever surplus of value there was, upon a just estimation of the goods, beyond the sum of the debt.{†} <Yet often the goods are not transferred to the creditor, but by some public forms a real right is conferred on him, called *hypotheca* or mortgage>. Where such real security is given, it takes place of all prior debts, which have not been publickly intimated before the mortgage. Nor can prior creditors justly complain <that their personal rights yield to the following real right>: let them blame themselves that they insisted not on higher security, and thus are postponed to creditors who using more caution insisted on higher, <without which they would have not trusted the debtor,> and who had no notice of their prior claims.

---

† {Here no mention is made of the difference between the *pignus,* and *hypotheca* as in the original. Our words *pledge* and *mortgage* don't fully express it. *Pignus* is like a mortgage with possession, and *hypotheca,* one without possession, whether of lands or moveables.}

V. Inter jura realia, denique, sunt *servitutes:* "jura scil. certi usus ex re aliena percipiendi"; quae ex contractu nascuntur; aut ex eo quod, in dominio transferendo, haec sibi prior dominus retinuit; aut denique ex lege civili. Servitutes omnes sunt jura realia, definitam rem spectantia; pro variis tamen, ut vocantur, *subjectis* quibus competere videntur, non *objectis* quae spectant, dividuntur *in reales* et *personales.* Hae in certi hominis gratiam constituuntur, eo defuncto interiturae. Illae in praedii vicini commoditatem constitutae, cuicunque ejus domino competent. Personales sunt, *ususfructus, usus, habitatio,* et similes quaedam aliae. Reales sunt vel *urbanae,* vel *rusticae.* Urbanae sunt *oneris ferendi, tigni immittendi, altius tollendi,* aut *non tollendi, luminum, prospectus,* &c. Rustica, contra, spectant praedia, *iter, actus, via,* &c. de quibus jureconsulti uberius. <175>

‡ {The several servitudes mentioned in the original could not have been explained to an English reader without a very tedious and useless discussion, as the Roman servitudes differed much from ours. They are found in every compend of the civil law.} [However this section is more or less parallel to Pufendorf, *De officio* 1.12.8.]

5. The translator has described only usufructus. "Use" is "when a Man receives from a Thing belonging to another, only the daily and necessary Service, the Substance remaining as before." "Habitatio" or Dwelling "is a Right by which a Man receives all the Advantages commonly proceeding from the letting out the Houses of others." Pufendorf, *De iure nat.* 4.8.12, English translation, London 1703, pp. 359–60.

6. The translator has described roughly only some of the servitudes or services. "Altius tollendi or not tollendi" is the service of raising or not raising a building higher than the

V. The last class of real rights are *servitudes* that is "rights to some small use of the property of others"; which generally arise from contracts; or from this that in the transferring of property they have been reserved by the granter; or sometimes from civil laws. All servitudes are real rights, terminating upon some definite tenement. And yet with regard to the *subject* they belong to, and not the *object* they terminate upon, they are divided into *real* and *personal*. The *personal* are constituted in favour of some person, and expire along with him: the real are constituted for the advantage of some <near> tenement, and belong to whatever person possesses <170> it.{‡} An instance of the former is tenantry for life impeachable for waste <usufructus, usus, habitatio and similar others>.[5] The real servitudes are either upon *town-tenements*, or *farms* in the country. Instances of the former are the rights of putting beams or rafters into a neighbouring gable or wall; a right that our windows shall not be obstructed by any building in the adjacent tenement; and such like.[6] The rural servitudes, are chiefly that of roads for passage or carriages, or of little channels for rivulets, brought through a neighbouring farm [The rural servitudes consider founds, as *iter, actus, via* and others more copiously treated by jurists].[7]

---

nearby houses; "prospectus" is the service "by which my Neighbour is bound to let me freely look into his Estate, [. . . or] of not *hindring* Prospect; by which a man is tied up from doing any Thing in his Estate, which might interrupt a free Prospect on any side, especially towards any delightful place." Pufendorf, *De iure nat.* 4.8.12, English translation, London, 1703, p. 361.

7. Respectively: "Passage; *the* Right of a Path *for* Men, to *walk* through my Neighbour's Ground into mine for the benefit of the latter. Carriage; the Right of driving Beasts or Wains. Road, or Way; the Right of going, walking, driving; *as likewise* of carrying, leading bearing and drawing any Thing which makes for the advantage of my estate." Pufendorf, *ibidem*.

CAPUT VIII

De Dominii transferendi Rationibus, per Contractus, Successiones, aut Testamenta.

I. Ab uno ad alterum transit plenum dominium, vel *facto domini voluntario;* vel absque eo, *vi legis* naturalis aut civilis. Atque utroque modo transit, vel *inter vivos,* vel in *eventum mortis.*

Facto prioris domini inter vivos voluntario, transit dominium, vel gratis, *donationibus;* vel ex causa onerosa, in *commerciis,* ubi pro re datur res pretio aequalis, aut jus aliquod remittitur. Hoc transferendi [donandi] jus in dominio includi antea monuimus. De pactis erit posthac agendum.

II. Facto prioris domini {voluntario}, in eventum mortis, transit dominium per *testamentum,* quod jure naturali, est "quaevis voluntatis domini, de bonis suis, in eventum mortis transferendis, declaratio, quae dilucidè probari potest"; de iis enim quae probari nequeunt, et de iis quae non sunt, idem est judicium.

Aequum esse ut testamenta valeant, quum nihil continent iniqui, ostendit ipsum dominii jus, et commune omnibus ferè consilium, <176> in rebus ultra suos usus comparandis; ut iis, nempe, gaudeant illi quos quisque habet carissimos. Durum esset et inhumanum, atque industriae inimicum, prohibere ne [suo arbitratu] [pro suo arbitrio] quisque res suo labore innocuo partas, ad quos velit, in quemcunque eventum, transferre possit. Grave <foret>, atque admodum incommodum, homines vivos et validos {eo} adigere, ut jus aliquod in res suas, ad cognatos aut amicos <transferant>, ple-

The Methods of Transferring Property,
Contracts, Succession, Testaments.

I. Property may be transferred, either by the *voluntary deed* of the former proprietor, or without any deed of his, by *appointment of law* either natural or civil: and in each of these ways it is transferred either *among the living*, or upon *the event of death*.

By the deed of the proprietor among the living, property is transferred either *gratuitously* in donations; or for *valuable consideration* in commerce, wherein a price, or goods of equal value, or rights, are transferred in consideration of it. This power of alienating, we formerly shewed, is included in the right of property. We treat of contracts and commerce hereafter.

II. By the deed of the proprietor upon the event of death property is transferred in *testaments* or *last-wills*. According to the law of nature "any declaration of a man's will how his goods should be disposed of upon the event of his death," is a valid testament; provided there be sufficient documents or proof made of this will. For that of which no proof can be made must be deemed as if it were not.[1]

The nature of property itself, and the known intention of mankind in their acquiring goods beyond their own use, that they may contribute to the happiness of <172> such as are dearest to them, shew that the wills of the deceased which contain nothing iniquitous should be observed. 'Tis cruel and inhuman, and destructive to industry to hinder men to transfer as they incline what they have acquired by their innocent labours, and that upon any contingency. It would be disagreeable and often highly inconvenient to oblige men while they are living, and perhaps in good health, to make irrevocable conveyances of their property to their kinsmen <or

---

1. On the first three paragraphs, see *System* 2.8.7, vol. I, p. 352.

num et irrevocabile {ipsis sit transferendum}: crudele foret, morientibus illud qualecunque cognatis aut amicis benefaciendi solatium praeripere; crudele et iniquum <amicis> superstitibus, haeredibus institutis aut legatariis, amicorum morientium beneficia, ipsis destinata, intervertere. Spreta igitur *metaphysicorum* subtilitate, dicentium, absurdum esse *hominem tunc velle aut agere, quum amplius velle aut agere nequeat;* testamenta recte censentur jure naturali confirmari.

Quum vero ex bonis nostris plurima sint praestanda, quae alii jure perfecto, vel perfectis proximo, postulant; aes {scil:} alienum dissolvendum, {damna sarcienda,} soboles conservanda, parentes egeni alendi; irrita erunt testamenta juri istiusmodi contraria. Immo, ubi desunt parentes et liberi, par est ut propinquis inopia laborantibus, nisi manifesta obstet causa, detur testamenti inofficiosi <177> querela. Leges naturales, non minus quam civiles, <recte> etiam prospiciunt, ne quid testamento contra communem utilitatem sanciatur: atque jubent eas, quibus falsariorum artes praecaveantur, in testamentis, ubi fieri potest, adhiberi formulas solennes; citra quas testamenta confirmari nequeunt.

III. Legis *naturalis vi,* vel invito priore domino, inter vivos transfertur dominium, ad id praestandum quod alter suo jure postulare poterat, quodque dominus praestare detrectaverat. Haec plenius erunt explicanda, ubi dicemus de jure quod ex contractu oritur, aut ex damno, sive injuriâ dato, sive absque injuriâ.

Legis item naturalis vi, sine facto prioris domini, in eventum mortis transit dominium, in *successionibus ab intestato.* Cujus sunt hae causae apertissimae; quod certum sit homines, in bonis ultra suos usus congerendis,

---

2. In the corresponding page of *System* (2.8.7, vol. I, p. 354), Hutcheson adds a note referring to "some improper use of metaphysicks in this subject" and to the notes on Pufendorf, *De iure nat.* 4.10, by Jean Barbeyrac.

friends>: It would also be cruel to deprive the dying of this satisfaction that their acquisitions should be of advantage to their <kinsmen or> friends: it would be inhuman <and unjust> toward the surviving friends, the heirs or legatees, to frustrate or intercept the kindnesses intended them by the deceased. Without regard therefor to the metaphysical subtilities of such as object, that *'tis absurd men should then be deemed to will and act when they become incapable of will or action,* we conclude that the law of nature grants this power of disposing by will.[2]

But as many obligations both of a perfect kind, and such as are pretty near of equal sanctity, must be discharged out of our goods, all just debts must be paid, <damages repaired,> our children, or indigent parents maintained: wills are therefor justly made void as far as they interfere with these obligations. Nay tho' there were no surviving parents or children, 'tis reasonable that other near indigent kinsmen, who have given no just cause for their being thus neglected, should be admitted to certain shares of the fortune of the deceased, even contrary to an inhuman capricious will. The law of nature too as well as civil laws invalidate any thing in wills <173> which may be detrimental to the community; and enjoin that wills be made with such solemn forms {and circumstances} as may be necessary to prevent forgeries: and, where these forms are omitted without necessity, deems the will to be void.

III. Property is transferred *among the living,* even against the will of the proprietor, by appointment of <natural> law, for the performance of whatever the proprietor was strictly bound to perform, and yet declined. This branch will be more fully explained when we treat of contracts, and the rights arising from damage done either injuriously or without a crime{, and the manner of prosecuting our just rights*}.

Upon *the event of death,* without any deed of the proprietor, property is transferred *by the law* in the *successions to the intestate.*[3] The natural grounds of which are these: 'tis well known that the intention of almost

---

* {Chap. XV of this book.}
3. See the corresponding section of *System* 2.8.8, vol. I, pp. 355–57.

semper hoc spectare, ut iis prosint quos maxime diligunt. Hoc hominum propositum omnibus notum, continua est voluntatis testatio, ubi nihil contrarium disertè sunt testati. Liberi autem et cognati, pro communi hominum ingenio, caeteris fere omnibus sunt multo cariores: atque his praecipue comparare student, non solum necessaria vitae praesidia, verum et quae ad vitae <178> copiam, et ornatum pertinent. Quin et liberis et cognatis egenis, ab ipsa natura, quae sanguinis junctionem benevolentiae et caritatis vinculum esse voluit, tributum est jus, si non perfectum, certe perfecto proximum, ad necessaria vitae praesidia, et ad ea etiam quae faciunt ad uberiorem copiam, et vitae prosperitatem, a parentibus et cognatis consequenda, nisi justam iis dederint offensionis causam. Durum est igitur, hominibus eripere hoc mortis inopinae, quam nemo satis cavere potest, qualecunque solatium, quod soboli et cognatis profutura sint, quae suâ industria paraverunt. Haec liberorum et cognatorum, ex sanguinis conjunctione, atque ipsa naturâ orta jura violare, et aequissimas, ex cognatorum benevolentia, spes intervertere, durum est et iniquum.

Quid; quod, ubi certus de cognatorum successione mos invaluit, recte colligitur, defunctum, si modo nihil contra testatus sit, bona eo more descendere voluisse: ea igitur succedendi ratio eodem nititur juris fundamento quo et testamenta.

Ubi nulli sunt liberi aut cognati propinquiores, eadem fere argumenta humaniora suaderent, ad successionem vocandos esse amicos, si qui fuerant defuncto caeteris longe cariores. Ubi tamen, more aut lege, cognati vel remotissimi, amicis praetermissis, <179> {semper} vocantur; ex <praesumenda> defuncti voluntate {satis manifesta}, illorum jus est potius; nisi ostendi possit, cognatos hosce defunctum fuisse perosum. Moris {hujus} a majoribus traditi, hae praecipuae sunt causae, quod natura plerumque caros faciat cognatos: quod cognationis facillimè cernantur gradus, amicitiae vero difficillimè: quodque videamus eos, qui vitam habuerant victumque communem, cum amicis, magis quam cognatis, his tamen prae illis, bonorum haereditates testamentis plerumque relinquere.

Cognati ad succedendum recte vocantur pro cognationis gradibus, et gradu pares pariter. Primo veniunt liberi, inter quos rectè vocantur nepotes,

all mens acquisitions beyond their own use, is to profit those whom they love. This universally known intention of mankind is a continual declaration of their will <where nothing opposite is clearly testified>: now according to the general temper of mankind, our children and near kinsmen are dearest to us, and 'tis for them we universally endeavour to obtain not only the necessary supports, but even the pleasures and ornaments of life. Nay {God and} nature, by making these tyes of blood bonds also of love and goodwill, seems to have given our children and kinsmen if not a perfect {claim or} right, yet at least one very near to perfect, to obtain not only to the necessary supports, but even the conveniencies of life from their wealthy <174> parents or kinsmen, unless they have forfeited it by their vitious behaviour. 'Tis therefor cruel to deprive men of this general consolation upon the event of sudden death, against which no man can take certain precautions, that the fruits of their industry shall fall to their children or kinsmen. And 'tis plainly cruel and unjust to defeat these rights of children and kinsmen which {God and} nature have given them <and cheat the just expectations of benevolence from kinsmen>.

Nay where the custom has prevailed of admitting children and kinsmen to succeed; 'tis justly presumed that this was the very intention of the deceased <if there is not any witness against it>. And this right of succession has the same foundation in justice with testaments.

Where there are no children or very near relations, like arguments of humanity would plead for friends, if it were known that any such had been singularly dear to the deceased. But where by custom or law the remotest kinsmen are preferred to friends; 'tis presumable that this was the intention of the person deceased, unless proof can be made of his hatred to his kinsmen. The causes of this law or custom prevailing every where, are these; that nature almost universally endears our kinsmen to us; that 'tis easy to compute the degrees of kindred, but impossible those of friendship; and that we so frequently see that men who seemed most to delight in the company of friends and not of kinsmen, yet when they declare their own will about their goods, they leave them almost always to kinsmen.

Kinsmen should succeed according to their proximity, those of equal degrees equally. First our children, <175> among whom grandchildren by a child deceased should be admitted, at least to the share their parents would

saltem *secundum stirpes;* humanitas et aequitas aliquando vocarent *secundum capita,* ubi gravi plures orphani premuntur inopia. Una cum liberis rectè vocarentur parentes egeni, ad necessaria saltem vitae praesidia; non inique una cum his vocarentur fratres probi et egeni. Ubi desunt liberi parentesque, vocandi sunt fratres et sorores {superstites}; <una> cum {quibus} defunctorum liberi in *stirpes* vocandi, si non aliquando in *capita:* qui ubi desunt, consobrini recte vocantur sobrinique; iisque non superstitibus, eorum liberi, atque ita deinceps.

IV. Quamvis vitae civilis ratio non raro exigat, ut bonorum intestati pars melior <180> maribus deferatur, quam quae foeminis, in eodem gradu; aut inter mares, seniori, major, quam quae juniori: haud tamen inter gradu pares, ingens, his de causis, ponet discrimen. Jus autem naturale, <nullum facit discrimen> inter gradu pares, [sexu aut aetate] [sexus causa aut aetatis] {antecedentibus nihil praecipui tribuit}: neque novit successionem *linealem;* ubi uni, prae reliquis gradu paribus, defuncti persona est gerenda, eique bonorum longe pars maxima tribuenda. Ea successio est tota juris civilis, a natura et humanitate saepius longissime recedens. In primo enim gradu, sexus praestantiae cedunt omnia alia; in secundo gradu et remotioribus, et ea {sexûs et aetatis inter gradu pares} praestantia, et sanguinis etiam proximitas posthabetur; [idque ante omnia spectatur, cujusnam parens defunctus sexu primum, deinde aetate antecesserit] [de defunti olim parentis aetati, aut sexui]. Nepti enim, pronepti, aut abnepti infanti, ex filio seniore defuncto, posthabebitur non solum nepos aut pronepos ex filio juniore; verum et ipse filius secundus, annis et prudentia maturus. Atque similia omnia fiunt inter fratrum et sororum liberos, ad successionem vocandos. <181>

have had: nay sometimes humanity would appoint them a greater share, where many such orphans are in straits. Along with children some share is due to indigent parents, at least as to the necessaries of life; nay <good> brothers in distress should have some share. When there are no children or parents surviving, brothers and sisters <surviving>, with the children of any such deceased, at least for their parents share, should be admitted: and when none such survive, cousin-germans by brothers or sisters, and their posterity.

IV. The constitution and civil laws and customs of some states may require that a far larger share of the goods of persons deceased should go to sons or other heirs male, than what goes to daughters, or to females in the same degrees with the males, and to the eldest of males beyond what goes to the younger. And yet there can scarce be any reason for that vast difference made on these accounts in many nations. The law of nature scarce makes any difference among persons in equal degrees on account of sex or seniority: nor does it establish the lineal succession, where some one must always as it were sustain the person of the deceased and succeed to his real estate. This succession is wholly a{*} human contrivance, often absurd and iniquitous. In the first degree all other differences yield to that of the sex. But in the second and remoter degrees, both the preeminence <176> of sex in the successors themselves and seniority, <and even the closeness of relationship> give place to the preeminence of sex and the seniority of the deceased parent, so that an {infant-} grand-daughter or great granddaughter <or even the infant daughter of the latter> by an eldest son deceased takes place of a grandson <or of a great grandson> {of mature years and wisdom} by a second son, nay of the second son himself <of mature years and wisdom>.[4] And the like happens among nephews and nieces and their children, in succeeding to the fortunes of their uncles{: and in the successions of cousins-germain or more remote}.

---

* {This lineal succession to private fortunes has manifestly been introduced by the Feudal laws of the *Lombards*.}

4. Here the translator follows *System* (p. 357) more closely than the Latin text.

CAPUT IX

De Contractibus.

I. Quum ad hominum salutem, ne de vitae jucunditate dicatur, necessariae sint rerum permutationes et mutua auxilia; data est iis a Deo benigno, non ratio solum, sed et oratio, sive usus sermonis, quo sententias, desideria, voluntates, consilia, proposita, possint aliis declarare. Facultatis hujus comes est et moderator sensus quidam subtilior, ex veri etiam cognoscendi appetitione naturali non parum confirmatus, quo vera omnia, simplicia, fidelia, comprobamus; falsa, ficta, fallacia odimus. Veritas autem et fides, non solum suâ propriâ nobis se commendant pulchritudine; mendacia vero et fraudes, sua nos turpitudine offendunt; verum et manifesta communis utilitatis ratio ad veritatem et fidem, tanquam communi saluti necessarias, bene sanos invitabit; atque mendacia et fraudes ostendet esse hominum generi pestifera.

In operis aut rebus permutandis, in rebus communi plurium opera gerendis, sententiae, voluntates, consilia, sunt mutuò declaranda: atque ubi alteri affirmamus nos aliquid [ideo daturos, facturos,] [praestituros, daturus eo fine] ut ille vicissim <182> aliquid det aut praestet, pacisci dicimur. Est enim *pactum,* "duorum aut plurium consensus in idem placitum, obligationis constituendae aut tollendae causa datus." Quod et *contractus* dicitur, jure enim naturali non distinguuntur.

---

1. See *System* 2.9.[1], vol. II, p. 1. In his definition Hutcheson seems to join Ulpian's definition of agreement (*pactum;* Justinianus, *Digestum* II.14.1.2) and Titius's definition in his *Observationes in* [. . .] *Pufendorf* [. . .] *De officio* quoted by G. Carmichael, in his *Supplements and Observations* upon Pufendorf's *De officio* (cf. *Notes on Puf.,* p. 80).

* {The difference between *contractus* and *pactum* is found in any Civil-law-

155

CHAPTER IX <177>

Of Contracts in General.

I. Since a perpetual commerce and mutual aids are absolutely necessary for the subsistence of mankind, not to speak of the conveniencies of life, <the goodness of> God has indued men not only with reason but the powers of speech <and language>; by which we can make known to others our sentiments [opinions], desires, affections, designs, and purposes. For the right use of this faculty we have also a sublime <and ruling> sense implanted, naturally strengthened by our keen desires of knowledge, by which we naturally approve veracity, sincerity, and fidelity; and hate falshood, dissimulation, and deceit. Veracity and faith in our engagements, beside their own immediate beauty thus approved, recommend themselves to the approbation and choice of every wise and honest man by their manifest necessity for the common interest and safety; as lies and falshood [frauds] <not only displease us by their ugliness, but> are also manifestly destructive in society.

In an intercourse of services, in commerce, and in joint labour, our sentiments, inclinations and designs must be mutually made known: and "when we affirm to others that we will pay or perform any thing, with that professed view, that another shall pay or perform something on his part" then we are said to {promise or} contract. A covenant or contract is the "consent of two or more to certain terms, with a view to constitute or abolish some obligation."[1] Nor does <178> the law of nature distinguish between{*} *contracts* and *pactions*.

---

dictionary.} [According to the jurists contracts are those agreements that allow people to take legal action. In *De iure nat.,* 5.2.2–3, Pufendorf argues against this distinction and in paragraph 4 says that contracts are agreements which "deal with things and actions of commercial significance." Carmichael says that Pufendorf's "distinction is not of much use itself" and Hutcheson follows him. Cf. *Notes on Puf.,* pp. 106–8.]

Pactorum usus est omnino necessarius; nec minus necessaria rerum contractarum fides. Egent et locupletiores rebus tenuiorum et operis, quas
gratis poscere nequeunt. Colloquiis igitur et pactis opus est, ut de rebus aut
operis mutuo praestandis conveniat. Fingantur omnes ad mutuam opem
vicinis amicè praestandam vel paratissimi; sine pacto tamen non potero
mihi cujusvis opem polliceri. Quum enim ego vicini cujusdam opera in-
digeo, fieri potest ut ille aliis officiis sanctioribus, alii praestandis, distinea-
tur; aut operâ iis praebenda, qui sibi commodius paria [vicem] rependere
possunt.

Sanctissima esse fidei servandae jura, non solum ostendit fidei lumen per
se elucens, verum et gravissima quae vitam humanam vexant mala, ex perfidia orta. Fidem enim datam fallere, caeteris paribus, magis est contra naturam, graviorque injuria, et turpior; quam par officium < humanum >, alia
debitum ratione, omittere aut denegare. Fide quippè violatâ, aliorum rationes ea innixae, gravissime <183> turbantur; ipsique damno afficiuntur
[datur] et contumelia, quod fidem nostram fuerint secuti, quum alia ratione
sibi prospicere [cavere] potuissent, Ex commerciorum necessitate patet,
jura quae ex pacto aut contractu oriuntur, esse perfecta, et per vim asserenda. Perfidus quantum in se est, omnia socia hominum officia è vita tollit.

II. Praeterea, quamvis vir bonus nullum sibi ex alterius inscitia aut temeritate, commodum captaret; immo, {saepe alium} quemvis a pacti, magis illi
incommodi, quam sibi commodi, obligatione liberaret, si modo damnum
sibi datum sarciatur; tanta tamen est fidei in commerciis conservandae necessitas, atque cavillationes excludendi, quae sub levioris cujuslibet incommodi obtentu nascerentur; ut, circa res quae sunt commerciorum materia,
hominumque prudentiae et potestati lege naturali subjectae, pactis quamvis
temerariis constituantur jura quaedam externa; quibus etsi uti nollet vir
bonus, communis tamen utilitatis causa, ea sunt eousque confirmanda, ut,
ubi in iis persequendis perstat is cui quid inde debetur, vim etiam adhibi-
turus, nemo ei recte vim opponere possit. De pactis hisce tenet haec regula;

Contracts are of absolute necessity in life, and so is the maintaining of faith in them. The most wealthy must need the goods and labours of the poor, nor ought they to expect them gratuitously. There must be conferences and bargains about them, that the parties may agree about their mutual performances. Suppose all men as just and good as one could desire, nay ready for all kind offices: yet without contracts no man can depend upon the assistance of others. For when I need the aid of a neighbour, he may be engaged in some more important services to a third person, or in some services to those who can give him a recompense more requisite in his affairs.

The sacred obligation of faith in contracts appears, not only from our immediate sense of its beauty, {and of the deformity of the contrary,} but from the mischiefs which must ensue upon violating it. 'Tis plainly more contrary to {the social} nature, and frequently a <more serious and> baser injury, to break our faith, than in other equal circumstances to have omitted or declined a duty we owe another way. By violating our faith we may quite defeat the designs of such as trusted to our integrity, and might have otherwise obtained the aid they wanted: and, from the necessity of commerce, it must appear, that the rights founded on <pactions and> contracts are of the *perfect* sort, to be pursued even by force. The perfidious for his part breaks of all social commerce among men. <179>

II. And further; tho' a good man would not take any advantage of another's weakness or ignorance in his dealings, nay would frequently free another from a bargain which proved highly inconvenient to him, and not very necessary to himself, provided any loss he sustained were made good; yet there's such a manifest necessity of maintaining faith in commerce, and of excluding the cavils which might be made from some smaller inconveniences to one or other of the parties, that in the proper matters of commerce, the administration of which the law of nature commits to human prudence <and power>, our covenants tho' rashly made must be valid, and constitute at least such external rights to others, as must for the common utility be maintained, tho' perhaps a good man would not insist on them. But if the person who claims them persists in his claim to the utmost, we can have no right to oppose him violently; but ought to observe our cov-

"Plurima fieri non debent quae facta valent."

Commerciorum *materia* sunt operae nostrae, <184> aut res illae, quarum commutationes crebras exigit vitae communis ratio, quibusque commutatis, neque violatur reverentia quae Deo debetur, neque cujusquam jus perfectum; quarum denique administratio, nulla lege speciali nobis praeripitur.

III. A pactis diversae sunt nudae propositi nostri declarationes, quae neque in alterum jus transferunt, neque ad perstandum in eo consilio nos obligant. Ad pacta propius accedunt quae dicuntur promissa imperfecta; ubi intelligitur, vel ex verbis, vel ex more instituto, nullum nos cogendi jus in alterum transferri; solâ verò probitate, aut pudore nos obligari; atque ea solum lege, nisi is cui promissum est, suâ culpâ, nobis mutandi consilii causam dederit, ita se gerendo, ut beneficio destinato fuerit indignus. Qua etiam de re judicium sibi reservasse intelligitur promissor; tantumque teneri ad damnum sua inconstantia datum sarciendum, quamvis sine causa consilium mutasse videatur.

IV. In contractuum obligatione, et exceptionibus legitimis explicandis, tria sunt spectanda; *intellectus*, nempe, et *voluntas*, actionum humanarum duo principia interna; atque ipsa *materia* in qua versantur.

De intellectu patet, communem hoc exigere utilitatem, atque ipsam humanitatem, <185> ne cui fraus inferatur, ex ipsius circa res suas inscitia quae culpa vacat. Unde contractus [juniorum, qui *minores* dicuntur,] [minorum] quique ob judicii imbecillitatem, negotiorum suorum naturam nondum intelligunt, rarius [neutiquam] obligant: quod de mente captorum, aut delirantium pactis est dicendum; atque etiam de pactis ebriorum, {quamdiu omnis consilii et prudentiae expertes sunt}. Quamvis enim ebrietas, non

---

2. See *System* 2.9.2, vol. II, p. 4.

3. The translator mixes up the "bare declaration of our future intentions" and the "imperfect promise." Here Hutcheson draws this distinction from Grotius, *De iure belli,*

enants; according to an old rule, that "what ought not to have been done, yet in many cases when done is obligatory."[2]

The proper *matters of commerce* are our labours and goods, or in general, all such things as must be frequently interchanged among men for the interest of society; and by a commerce in which we neither directly violate that pious reverence due to God, nor the perfect right of another; and about which no special law {of God} deprives us of the right of transacting.

III. We must distinguish from contracts *the bare declarations of our future intentions;* which neither transfer any right to others nor bind us to continue in <180> the same purpose. What come nearer to contracts are {these} *imperfect promises,*[3] in which from <received words or> custom 'tis understood, that we convey no right to others to oblige us to performance, but only bind ourselves in honour and veracity; and that too only upon condition, that the person to whom we make such promises so behave as to be worthy of the favour designed him, and don't by his bad conduct give us just cause of altering our intentions: and in this point the promiser reserves to himself the right of judging; nor does he bring himself under an higher perfect obligation, than that of compensating any loss the other may sustain, even tho' he should without cause alter his purpose.

IV. The circumstances to be considered in explaining the nature of contracts and the just exceptions against their obligation, <are three and> relate either to the *understanding,* or the *will,* the two internal principles of action, or the *matter* about which they are made.

As to the *understanding;* the common interest, as well as humanity, requires, that no person should sustain any damage on account of any ignorance in his own affairs which is no way faulty. And hence the contracts of minors <unwary and> unacquainted with the nature of the business, are not obligatory; nor of those seized with madness or dotage, nor of ideots, nor even of men quite disordered by drunkenness so as to have lost

---

2.11.2–4, as is clear in the correspondent section of *System* 2.9.3, vol. II, pp. 5–6. See also Pufendorf, *De officio* 1.9.4–7.

sine gravi culpa, poenis coercenda, arcessatur; dolosis tamen, ea occasione lucrum sibi captare, haud permittendum. {De ebriorum criminibus aut injuriis dissimilis est ratio: licet enim non teneantur homines, se semper rebus suis curandis et administrandis idoneos conservare, se tamen semper praestare tenentur innocuos et justos.} Ubi alterum latuerat alterius ebrietas; tenebitur ebrius, discussa crapula, damnum, sua culpa alteri datum, praestare. Ebrietatis vero plures sunt gradus: quorum quidam, licet homines magis solitò incautos, aut temerarios faciant, non tamen eos omni rationis usu spoliant. Si quidem ex his omnibus darentur exceptiones, incertum foret omne inter homines commercium. De hisce vero causis, non aliter quam viri probi arbitrio interposito, sigillatim judicari poterit.

De immaturo juniorum [minorum] judicio, ante legis <186> civilis definitionem, idem <foret> dicendum: cum aliis citiùs, aliis feriùs, efflorescat commerciis idonea prudentia. Ne vero pacta omnia aut pleraque maneant dubia, et cavillationibus obnoxia; certa aetas, in omni hominum coetu est determinanda, ad quam qui pervenerit, is sui juris censendus est, et idoneus rerum suarum administrator. Haec aetas ita est definienda [determinanda], ut quam paucissimi animo maturi, a rebus suis gerendis cohibeantur, et quam paucissimi improvidi ad eas gerendas admittantur. Non malè ex jure civili receptum est, ut ante annum quartum decimum exactum, in maribus, et duodecimum in foeminis, impuberes, qui et pupilli vocantur, a rebus gerendis arceantur; sintque in naturali parentum tutela; aut, his defunctis, in eorum tutela quos vel testamento parentes, vel leges civiles tutores constituerunt, ad aetatem usque pupillarem [finitam: atque dein] [qua elapsa] ad annum vicesimum primum, aut vicesimum quintum, ut olim jure civili, ita sint sub curatoribus, ut sine eorum consensu nihil paciscendo agere pos-

the use of their reason.[4] And altho' there may be a great crime in drunkenness which may justly be punished; yet this is no reason why the fraudulent and covetous should be allowed to make a prey of them. The case is
very different as to crimes or injuries done by men intoxicated. <181> For
tho' we are not bound with respect to others to preserve ourselves always
in a condition fit for transacting of business, yet we are bound to preserve
ourselves innocent continually, and to avoid doing injuries. If one of the
parties was not aware that the other was intoxicated; this later will be bound
to make good any loss the other sustained by his nonperformance of the
contract. But there are many degrees of intoxication, some of which tho'
they may abate our caution and prudence, yet don't deprive us of the necessary use of reason. If all these degrees also made contracts void, there
could be no sure transactions among men. Questions concerning these degrees, must be decided in the several cases by the judgment of prudent
arbitrators.

The same might be said concerning the imprudence of youth, previous
to civil laws: since the degree of prudence requisite for commerce appears
in different persons at very different ages. That therefor commerce may be
ascertained, and such endless evasions prevented, 'tis absolutely necessary
that in every society some certain age be agreed upon, to which whosoever
attains must be deemed his own master, and capable of managing his own
business. This age must be determined with this view, that as few as possible
of ripe judgment be excluded from the administration of their own affairs,
and yet as few as possible admitted before the maturity of judgment. The
medium fixed by the Roman law is as good as any; that minors, <also called
wards,> before fourteen years of age in males, and twelve in females, should
have no management of their affairs, but be under the natural guardianship
of their parents; or, if <182> they are dead, under that of the guardians
their parents or the law has appointed: and after these years, till twenty-
one, or as it was in their earlier times, till twenty-five, they should be so
subjected to curators, that no deed of theirs intended to bind themselves

---

4. In *System,* Sections 6 and 5 of Chapter 9 correspond to this section. See also Pufendorf, *De officio* 1.9.10–11.

sint *minores,* unde alteri jus nascatur, aut res ipsorum obligentur.

Contractu quidem *minores* non sunt laedendi; neque tamen aliorum damnis sunt locupletandi. Ubi [tamen quicquam] [quid] cum iis pactum fuerit, atque ab altera parte praestitum, <187> si ipsorum intersit ut pactum confirmetur, tenentur postquam adoleverit ratio, promissa et conventa praestare: si non intersit; quicquid ex pacto ab altero acceperant, aut ejus pretium reddendum; aut denique quantum ulla ratione eo facti sunt locupletiores; aut quantum ipsorum interfuit, pro sua conditione, id olim accepisse. Non raro quidem, ante annos legitimos, res suas satis commodè administrare possunt *minores;* [quumque ita se res habet, neque ab altera parte] [atque, ubicunque nullus] intervenerat dolus malus, aut culpa, in foro Dei et conscientiae, quod actum est, aeque ac inter adultos, valet.

Ubi quidem adsunt parentes, tutores, aut curatores publicè constituti; iis inconsultis vix sine culpa aut dolo, de re graviori, cum *minoribus* poterit quisquam pacisci: qui nempe vehementi feruntur impetu et improvido, ad promittendum faciles, cupidi, utilium tardi provisores [provisiores], liberales, spei pleni, et diffidere nescii.

V. Qui ad paciscendum permotus fuerat *errore* aliquo circa rem ipsam, ejusve *qualitates aestimabiles,* quarum {scil.} plerumque praecipua in pactis istiusmodi habetur ratio, pacto non tenebitur; eique, errore deprehenso, quicquid ex pacto solverit reddendum. Non tamen ita censetur errasse, qui alias expectabat qualitates quam prae <188> se tulerat, quaeque in rebus istiusmodi reperiri non solent. Si vero tantum erratum fuerat de re alia, aut eventu diverso, quo tamen errore aliquis ad paciscendum permotus erat: deprehenso errore, debet alter, ex humanitate, poenitendi locum dare ei qui erraverat, si is omne damnum inde oriturum, praestare sit paratus. Non vero hoc pleno jure postulandum; nisi is qui erravit, illud de quo erratum fuit tanquam pacti conditionem diserte pronunciaverit.

Rei, de qua initur pactum, natura, ejusque *qualitates aestimabiles,* earumque defectus quarum causâ pacta {istiusmodi} solent iniri, pacti *essentiam,* ut dicitur, attingunt. Ubi de his erratum est, errore deprehenso, non tenebitur qui erraverat. Ubi tantum de pretio erratum est; deceptus jure suo

or their fortunes, should be deemed valid without the consent of their curators.

'Tis on one hand unjust that minors should sustain losses in contracts; but 'tis on the other hand unjust that they should be enriched at the expence of others. If therefor any contract has been made with them, and something paid or performed by the other party, if it is not detrimental to them to confirm the contract, they ought to do it when they come to maturity: if it be found detrimental, they should restore or compensate what was received on that account, or as far as they were profited. Minors before the legal years often have sufficient judgment in certain matters; and when it is so, nor was there any thing fraudulent or faulty on the the other side, they are bound before God and their own consciences by their contracts, even as the adult.

When parents or curators are at hand, one can scarce without a gross fault enter into any important contracts with a minor without their consent. As generally the passions of the young are impetuous and incautious; they are rash in promising, keen in their desires, improvident, liberal, full of hopes and void of all suspicion.

V. He who was engaged into a contract by any mistake or error about the very nature of the object or goods, or these qualities which are chiefly regarded in <183> them, is not bound: and<, when the mistake is discovered,> whatever he has paid on that account should be restored. But no man has this plea who was engaged only by a secret expectation of such qualities as he did not openly insist on, or of such as are not commonly expected in such goods. If the mistake was about some different matter or event, which moved him to the bargain; when the mistake is discovered, humanity may require it of the other party to set him free, especially if he is ready to compensate any damage occasioned by his mistake. But this is not a matter of perfect obligation, unless the person in the mistake made it an express condition of the bargain.

The nature of the goods, and the qualitys upon which their value depends, and the defects of such qualitys, are, as they speak, *essential points* in contracts. Where one of the parties has been in a mistake about them he is not bound. Where the mistake has been only about the current price;

exigere potest, ut quod sibi deest suppleatur; aut quod ultra pretium dederat, reddatur: aut, altero hoc nolente, ut pactum sit nullum.

Qui culpa sua, aut temeritate, de rebus pacti praecipuis erravit, causamve alterius errori dedit, alteri damnum datum tenetur praestare. Qui vero dolum malum adhibuit, tenetur praestare quantum alterius interest ut pactum bona fide expleatur. {Neque eorum quae, dolo decepti, isti qui dolum adhibuit promisimus, ulla est obligatio: quia istius dolo, nobis defuit ea rei quae agitur notitia, <189> quae ad paciscendum aut promittendum est necessaria; atque iste ad damnum injuria datum sarciendum tenetur.}

Ubi tertius aliquis dolum adhibuit, eo non colludente, sed inscio, quo cum paciscor; pactum erit ratum. Ab eo tamen, qui dolum adhibuit, exigendum est quantum mea interfuisset, non deceptum fuisse.

VI. In pactis semper intelligitur, *voluntatem* adesse se obligandi, ubi ejus sit significatio. Neque ulla esset fides, si valeret exceptio ex arcana voluntate, sermoni aut signis editis contrariâ.

Vocibus et scriptis paciscendi animus commodissimé declaratur; sufficit tamen signum quodcunque, de quo inter paciscentes convenit, aut quod pro more consueto consensum indicat. Immo et actionum quarundam ea est natura, ut nemo nisi insanus aut improbus eas suscipiat, qui non certis pacti legibus etiam consentit. Ex hisce igitur, quemvis consensisse merito colligitur, [nisi cunctis quorum interest praemonitis, contrarium testatus fuerit] [si non contra intervenerat praemonitio, aut aperta testatio]. Ubi per eas actiones consensus indicatur, *pactum* dicitur *tacitum.* Quod eo indicio

---

5. Compare the first two paragraphs of Section 5 with *System* 2.9.9, pp. 14–15, and Pufendorf, *De officio* 1.9.12.

* {The Civilians thus distinguish between *pensare damnum,* and *praestare quod interest:* obliging those who wrong others through negligence or inadvertence to the former

the person deceived {and sustaining the loss} has a perfect right to have the price reduced to equality; which if the other party refuses the bargain may be made void.[5]

Whoever by any fault or rashness of his caused the mistake of the other party, or fell into a mistake himself, is bound to compensate any loss the other thereby sustains: but he that dealt fraudulently, is bound further to make good any profit the other could have made, had the bargain been executed with integrity.{*} <184> Any promises or contracts obtained from us by the fraud of the person with whom we contracted, are plainly void; because through his fraud we wanted the due knowledge requisite in contracting, and he is bound to compensate our damage occasioned by his fraud{, which is easiest done by making the bargain void}.

Where the fraud of a third person has moved us to a contract without any collusion with the other party; the bargain is valid. But we have a right of demanding compensation of any loss from that third person who deceived us.[6]

VI. We always deem that all such voluntarily consent who voluntarily use such signs of consenting as by custom import it. Nor could there be any faith maintained, if we allowed exceptions from a secret dissent contrary to our expressions.

Words and writing are the fittest methods of declaring consent: but any other sign agreed upon by the parties, or received by common custom is sufficient. Nay some actions in certain circumstances are justly deemed to declare consent, when they are such as no man of common sense or equity would do, unless he also consented to certain terms. From such actions therefor we justly conclude a person's consent, unless he timously premonish all concerned of the contrary. Covenants or contracts founded on consent thus declared are called *tacit:* which are distinguished from another

---

only, but in case of fraud or more gross negligence obliging always to the later.} [Cf. *System* 2.9.12, vol. II, p. 23 and notes.]

6. Cf. Pufendorf, *De officio* 1.9.13, points 1 and 2.

secernitur ab *obligatione quasi ex contractu* orta, de qua alias, quod in hac, nulla obligationem tollere potest denunciatio [praemonitio] contraria, in illo potest.

Primariis et expressis pacti legibus, ex <190> rei natura {saepe} intelligitur, leges et conditiones tacitas esse adjectas [tacitae saepe adjici], quales negotiis istiusmodi adjici, ex rei natura, aut more, intelligunt omnes sanâ mente praediti.

Ad rerum dominia aut alia jura transferenda, sive gratis, sive ex *causa onerosa,* exigitur et accipientis et dantis consensus. Quum rem transferendi, aut amico donandi animus, haud indicet, aut rei suae projiciendae, aut alteri nolenti obtrudendae, voluntatem. Levioribus tamen indiciis colligitur, adesse rei utilis accipiendae voluntatem; et semper quidem ex praecedente rogatione, si quod oblatum est ei respondeat.

Quum autem in pleno dominio includatur jus, rem, sub licita quavis conditione, aut in quemvis eventum, transferendi, aut amicorum fidei committendi, donec de sperato eventu constiterit; de haereditatibus et legatis patet, valere testatoris voluntatem, eo usque ut manere debeant haereditates, et res legatae, apud *fidei-commissarios,* donec de haeredum eas adeundi, aut legatariorum accipiendi voluntate constiterit. Quin et recte servantur res in eorum gratiam qui nondum sunt nati. Iniquum enim est impedire testatorem, ne res suas {cognatorum aut} amicorum soboli, si qua suscepta fuerit, conservet. Iniquum est, beneficia, a parentibus, cognatis, aut amicis destinata, nascentibus <191> praeripere. Haeredi tamen aut legatario nolenti, nihil recte obtrudi potest. Infantium [item, perinde ac] [vero et] nondum natorum, habenda est omnino ratio, et res haereditariae, quamvis nullus sit *fidei commissarius,* iis, ab humano genere, aut a quovis occasione oblata, sunt conservandae.

set of obligations, to be presently explained, said to arise{*} *after the manner of contracts,* by this, that in tacit contracts the obligation is prevented by an express <185> declaration to the contrary; but not in the others.

Beside the principal expressed articles in contracts, there are frequently others plainly understood as adjected from the very nature of the transaction, or from the prevailing custom among all who are engaged in such business.

The consent of both parties, of the receiver as well as the giver, is necessary in all translation either of property or any other rights, whether gratuitous or not. For from one's intention of bestowing any thing on a friend, we cannot conclude any design of throwing it away in case he don't accept, or of forcing it upon him. But a lower sort of evidence will serve to prove a consent to accept any thing valuable; and we may always presume upon it, if the thing was previously requested; provided the offer answer the request.

But as in full property there's included a right of disposing under any lawful conditions, or upon any contingency; and of giving in trust to a friend, till some future event happens: inheritances and legacies may thus be left with trustees, till it be found whether the heirs designed, or the legatees are willing to accept. Nay goods may thus be kept in favours of persons not yet existing; as it is unjust to hinder the proprietor to appoint his goods thus to be reserved for the offspring of his <kinsmen or> friends if they shall happen to have any: and 'tis injurious toward such offspring to have defeated or intercepted any benefits destined for them by their deceased parents, kinsmen, or friends. And yet no heir or legatee can be forced to be proprietor of any thing thus left to him without his own consent. Mankind <186> however, and each one as he has opportunity, when no special trustee is appointed, ought to take this care of infants, or persons unborn, to preserve such inheritances or legacies for their behoof{, till they can accept them}.

---

* {Chap. xiv.} [The distinction between contracts, tacit conventions and obligations *quasi ex contractu* is better explained, with examples, in *System* 2.9.4, vol. II, pp. 6–8.]

VII. Pendet contractuum vis ex contrahentium voluntate aut consensu; qui si tantum *sub conditione* dabatur, eâ deficiente, nulla erit obligatio. Debet autem de conditione adjecta utrinque constare, ne commercia omnia fiant incerta. Solae igitur valent conditiones, quas aut alteruter diserte pacto adjecerat, aut ex negotii natura, utrinque intellectum iri, bona fide putaverat; non eae quas tacite alter in animo fovebat, in hujusmodi negotiis non semper intelligendae. Si quid alter inter paciscendum, praestare susceperit, aut alteri affirmaverit, quo ad paciscendum alliceretur, id quidem conditionis vim habere censebitur.

Quum contractus dividuntur in *absolutos* et *conditionales;* conditio propriè est "eventus quidam, alteri, aut utrique paciscentium, incertus, atque a pactis praestationibus diversus; qui si non accidat, nullus erit contractus." Conditio apertè *impossibilis* adjecta, ostendit nihil actum esse. De rebus illicitis, (quae aliquando dicuntur <192> *moraliter impossibilia,*) ab alterutra parte praestandis, sive de facinore turpi, mox erit dicendum. Facinus quidem turpe, a tertio quopiam, sine ulla [ullo] paciscentium conspiratione [concursu] peragendum, potest esse justa conditio; si modo nullae ex pacto proponantur facinoris illecebrae.

Conditiones, si sint penes alterum paciscentium, dicuntur voluntariae, sive *potestativae;* si non sint, dicuntur fortuitae, sive *non potestativae;* sunt et quaedam *mixtae.* Ad voluntarias aut mixtas praestandas, neuter obligari censetur.

VII. As the obligation of contracts plainly depends on the consent of the parties{, and without it is void}; so when it was only given under certain conditions, if they don't exist, there's no obligation. But such conditions must be known as such on both sides, otherways there could be no faith in our transactions. These conditions therefor alone are {of such force as that their non-existence makes the transaction void} <valid>, which were either expresly made conditions by one or other of the parties, or which the person who insists on them did in conscience believe the other party understood as adjected from the nature of the affair; and not every one which one of the parties might secretly expect would exist, tho' the like is not ordinarily expected in such transactions. Whatever indeed one party has undertaken for to the other, or positively affirmed to him to engage him to the bargain, *that* the other party may justly be deemed to have made a condition of his consenting.

In the known division of contracts into *absolute* and *conditional,* by a condition is understood "some event yet uncertain to one or both the parties, distinct from the prestations covenanted, upon the existence of which the validity of the contract depends."[7] A condition known to be naturally impossible, shews that there's no engagement. We shall presently speak of <187> another sort of impossibility <sometime called *morally impossible*> from the prohibition of law, or moral turpitude. But a vitious action of any third person, to be done without any aid of the parties contracting, may be a just condition; provided nothing in the contract give any invitation to such actions.

Conditions in the power of either party are called *voluntary;* others are *involuntary;* and some are of a mixed nature. But neither side is understood to be obliged to make these conditions called voluntary or mixed to exist,{*} {for then they would be absolute covenants of the bargain}.

---

7. See *System* 2.9.8, p. 13.
* {A voluntary condition is of this sort: "If I shall retire to live in the country, I agree to set my city-house at such a rent." By this I don't bind myself to live in the country. "I promise, if I incline to sell certain lands, that such a man shall have them at a certain price."} [This distinction between conditions potestativae, fortuitae and mixed was in the Justinian's code and is discussed by Pufendorf, *De iure nat.* 3.8.4.]

VIII. Consensum voluntarium impedire potest *metus:* cujus duplex est natura. {Vel} enim est suspicio probabilis, alterum, postquam meam partem explevero, me decepturum: vel [alias] denotat timorem ex gravi malo intentato ortum. De priore haec tenenda videntur. 1. Qui cum improbis et sceleratis, quorum mores antea noverat, sponte paciscitur, omnino tenetur. 2. At ubi post contractum innotescit alterius improbitas aut scelus; non quidem eo ipso abrumpitur contractus; quod tamen a me praestandum est tantisper differre licebit [potero], donec contra istius perfidiam, mihi, pro viri prudentis arbitrio, satis sit cautum. Omnis quidem fides tolleretur, si nulla cum improbis et sceleratis, {iisve qui diversa tenent de <193> religione dogmata,} esset servanda; [quum nullae sint notae manifestae, aut signa satis certa, quibus honestos a turpibus secernere queamus;] [cum nulla sint de moribus & virtute hominum indubitata criteria] atque pro mentis humanae caecitate, [adeo diversae, immo contrariae semper fuerint de religione, atque etiam de hominum] [, diversissimae, de aliorum] moribus, apud diversos, sententiae.

De secundo metus genere, ubi metu mali mihi injuste intentati, ad paciscendum impulsus fui, duplex est quaestio, prout intentatum fuit malum ab eo quocum paciscor, vel ab altero. Ubi ab altero, atque pacto inito contra mala mihi intentata, viri cujusquam probi auxilium arcesso; pactum omnino valebit nisi alia de causa, aliquid iniqui contineat. Auxilium enim in periculis avertendis praestitisse, officium saepe utilissimum est, et mercede dignissimum.

Si quidem {ab altero} mihi immerito malum intentatum fuerat, ni cum tertio non colludente quiddam paciscar, ego verò ei tertio metum meum celare cogar: pactum irritum erit, postquam ostendero, metu injustè incusso, mihi ademptam fuisse libertatem, negotiis gerendis necessariam; omne tamen damnum huic tertio a me datum, ut a me avertantur pericula,

VIII. The due freedom of consent may be taken away by fear.[8] But of this there are two sorts, one denoting a suspicion that when one party has fulfilled his part of the bargain, the other party won't fulfil his: the other denotes a terror occasioned by some great evil threatened. As to the former sort these observations seem just: 1. He that voluntarily contracts with openly unjust and impious men, whose characters he previously knew, is plainly obliged by his contract{, as he must have tacitly renounced any exception from their character, which was previously known}. But 2ly. If he only comes to the knowledge of their characters after the contract, 'tis not indeed void; but he may justly delay performing on his part, till they give such security for the performance of theirs as a wise arbiter <188> judges sufficient. To maintain that all contracts entered into with the unjust, or heretical or impious, are void, would destroy all faith among men; since there are no such obvious characteristicks to distinguish the good from the bad as all will agree in: and considering the weaknesses of mankind, they have always had the most opposite opinions about the moral and religious characters of men around them{; as in all ages there have been the greatest diversities and contrarieties of opinions}.

As to the second sort of fear; when I have been forced into a contract by fear of evil threatened; there are two cases, according as the evil is unjustly threatened either by him I contract with, or by a third person {without any collusion with the person I contract with}. In the later case when by contract I obtain the aid of an innocent man against dangers threatened by another, no doubt I am bound; unless there be something very exorbitant in the terms. For the giving aid in such perils is no doubt a most useful service well deserving compensation.

If indeed I am threatened unjustly with some great evil by any man unless I enter into a certain bargain, or make a promise, to a third person, who is in no collusion with him who threatens me, while yet I am forced to conceal from him the terror I am under; the bargain or promise is void, because by this terror I am deprived of that liberty which is necessary in commerce. But any damage this innocent person sustains by the disap-

8. This and the following section are very similar to Sections 10 and 11, Chapter 9, of *System,* pp. 16–23. See also Pufendorf, *De officio* 1.9.13 and 14.

praestare teneor. Idem etiam dicendum, ubi, pro mea timiditate, <194> metus nimius erat et temere conceptus.

Quae quispiam promittit aut paciscitur legitimae potestatis metu, ea etiam praestare tenetur: quum huic potestati jure subjectus esse intelligatur.

IX. At ubi metu mali injustè intentati, aliquid illi qui metum incusserat promissum est; hoc omnino spectandum utrum sub juris specie aliqua probabili, qua vir caetera probus aliquando decipi potest{, malum fuerit intentatum}; an contra, nulla juris specie obtentâ, quae hominem istiusmodi fallere posset. In priore causâ, quamvis qui metum incussit, nullum re vera jus acquirat, quo recte uti possit; remotiore tamen communis utilitatis ratione habita, quod actum est jure externo nonnunquam valebit. De jure suo aliquando errare humanum est. Hinc et inter homines haud improbos saepè nascuntur bella, quae aut pactis, aut alterius internecione, finienda {sunt}: ut pactis finiantur longe satius est: eorum tamen nullus esset usus, si semper valeret vis injustae et metus exceptio, quae utrique parti semper pateret. Contra foedera igitur pacem reducentia, non admittenda est haec exceptio, ubi speciosae utrinque fuerant bellandi causae, et bellum sub juris tuendi specie {probabili} susceptum erat. Si quidem foederis <195> leges sint omnino iniquae, humanitati omni contrariae, parti devictae, vitae conditionem miseram omnino et servilem redituræ; haec, nulla juris specie munita, non valent; justa manebit exceptio.

Sin autem, nullâ juris specie, vis scelerata ad pacta extorquenda intentetur; pacta nihil valent. Vi enim istiusmodi adhibitâ, omnia hominum jura

pointment, I am bound to make it good, as it was occasioned by me for my own safety. The same holds, <189> when through my cowardice I have been excessively afraid without cause.

Any contracts entered into from fear of a just magistrate, {or the sentence of a judge,} are plainly valid, since we are deemed subjected to such civil power.

IX. But when I am forced to contract through fear of evils unjustly threatened by the very party I contract with, we must distinguish whether these evils are threatened under some such plausible shew of right as might possibly impose upon an honest man, or on the other hand, by openly avowed injustice, without any such shadow of right. In the former case, tho' the author of such violence acquires no right by it, which he can use with a good conscience; yet on account of some more distant interests of mankind, he may have a sort of *external right*{, with which the other party may be bound to comply}. Nothing is more incident to mankind than to mistake about their rights; and hence arise wars too frequently, while yet neither side is sensible of the injustice of their cause. These wars must either be composed by treaties and contracts, or must end with the ruin of one side. Now 'tis highly eligible that they should be ended rather by some treaty: and treaties could be of no use if they still lay open to this exception of unjust force, which either side might plead {whensoever they inclined to renew the old controversy}. This exception therefor must not be allowed against treaties of peace, when there were any plausible pretences on both sides for the preceeding war.[9] If indeed the terms of peace are manifestly iniquitous and oppressive, contrary to all humanity, making life quite miserable <190> and slavish to the less fortunate side; such treaties have no plausible shews of justice, and lay open to the exception.{*}

But where violence is used or threatened, without any pretence of right, to extort promises or contracts, they cannot be obligatory. By such violence the author of it plainly abdicates or forfeits all the rights of men; all the

---

9. The idea that the "exception of unjust force" should not be allowed against treaties of peace is shared by Carmichael. See *Notes on Puf.,* pp. 85–86 and note 11.

* {See Book II. Ch. xv. 8. and Book III. Ch. vii. 8. 9.}

abdicantur: omnia quae ex lege naturali, aut hominum aequitate, poterant a quopiam flagitari, repudiantur et remittuntur. Qui {istiusmodi} vim adhibet, se humani generis hostem profitetur, nullaque juris societate devinctum. Postulat {igitur} communis utilitatis ratio, ut haec hominum monstra, quacunque ratione exscindantur. {Fingamus insuper haec promissa obligare. Quantumcumque tamen ei qui vim adhibuit ex promisso debeatur, tantundem et ipse damni injuriâ dati nomine alteri debebit: per *compensationem* igitur, promissi obligatio tolletur.} Neque dixeris promissorem, ex ipsâ negotii naturâ, huic vis et metus exceptioni tacito pacto renunciasse{: nam ipsum id *renunciasse* coactum, in damnum deputandum esset}. Tacitonè insuper pacto, is acquiret jus, qui ne pacto quidèm, diserte enunciato, in ea causa acquirere poterat; quique hìc ea agit, quae omnis humani juris abdicationem planissime continent?

Quamvis autem istorum hominum, in omni <196> aliorum jure pessundando, nulla habenda sit ratio; ubi tamen ad saniorem mentem redituri videntur, praeteritorum veniam petentes, ex locis munitis descensuri, arma tradituri, atque in posterum satisdare volentes; et ubi non sine innocentium strage, aut sanguine multo, coerceri aut deleri possunt; communis aliquando exigit utilitas, ut pacta cum iis inita, [malis gravioribus avertendis] [hisce finibus] inservientia, sanctissime serventur: civibusque, quibus damnorum pensationem ab iis exigere, aut res suas vindicare, non permittitur, publicè praestandum est damnum.

X. Ut pacta aut promissa valeant, ipsorum *materia,* aut res utrinque praestandae, intra paciscentium vires esse debent. Unde ad ea, quae a nobis volentibus fieri non possunt, quae dicuntur *impossibilia,* nulla est obligatio. Si quid promissum fuerat, quod postea casu, aut sine paciscentium culpa existit *impossibile,* omnia istâ causâ data, sunt reddenda, aut pensando [compensanda]. Ubi alterutrius dolus, aut *lata culpa,* in rei *impossibilitate*

benefits to be claimed from the law of nature, or the humanity of his fellows; as he openly professes himself a common enemy to all, free from any social tye. The common safety therefor requires that such monsters should be cut off by any means. Suppose that such {extorted} promises were valid, yet whatever upon such a promise is due to the author of the violence, he is always indebted at least as much to the person thus compelled, upon account of damage done him unjustly: these two claims therefor extinguish each other by *compensation*. Nor can one here allege that by the act of promising under this terror the promiser tacitly renounces this exception of unjust force previously known; for this forced renounciation alleged is one part of the damage: and what pretence is there of alleging an obligation by tacit compact, to one who in such a cause is incapable of acquiring a right by the most express contract, and who in this very affair abdicates or forfeits all human rights?

But, however that no regard is to be had to such persons in thus trampling upon all the rights of mankind, yet when they sufficiently appear to be returning to a soberer mind, asking pardon of what's past, offering to <191> quit their fastnesses, to deliver their arms, and to give security for their future conduct; and when such {confederacies} cannot be otherways destroyed without shedding much innocent blood of our citizens; the common interest may sometimes require to enter into such treaties with them, and to observe them faithfully <in order to avoid greater evils>: and as to any of our citizens who by this means are excluded from prosecuting them for reparation of damages, they ought to obtain it from the community.

X. Contracts or promises cannot be of force unless the matter of them be *possible* to the parties: and therefore no man can be obliged to{*} what he cannot accomplish tho' he seriously desired it. If one has promised any thing, which by some subsequent accident without his fault becomes impossible, he is only obliged to restore or compensate the value of any thing he received in consideration of it. Where the fraud or other gross fault of one party either made the matter impossible, or concealed the impossibility,

* {Book II. Ch. iii. 2.}

celanda, aut efficiunda, intervenerit, hic quod interest praestare tenebitur.

Debet etiam pactorum *materia* esse licita; id est, de iis tantum rebus aut operis {paciscendum} quae, commerciis aptae, alienari possunt, quarumque administratio humanae committitur prudentiae, neque lege <197> speciatim homini praeripitur. Ad ea enim praestanda quae vel reverentiam Deo debitam, vel alterius jus perfectum, violant, quaeve lege prohibentur *speciali,* neque nostrae subjiciuntur potestati, nulla ex pacto nasci potest obligatio.

1. Si igitur paciscentium uterque, rem esse ita illicitam noverat, aut nosse debuerat, nulla erit pacti obligatio: conductori, ante facinus patratum poenitenti, quicquid ex pacto dederat reddendum est. Facinore autem patrato, neque patratori dandum est praemium, neque datum conductor reposcere poterit: ab utroque poenae gravissimae expetendae.

Si post pactum initum, facinoris turpitudo, quae inter paciscendum latuerat, alterutri innotescat; ei, facinore nondum patrato, poenitentiae locus est: qui conductus est acceptam mercedem reddere tenetur. Neque facinore patrato, mercedem exigere poterit patrator, nisi ipsius ignorantia culpâ caruit: si modo ipsi, aequè ac conductori, turpe fuit facinus. Sin autem conductori soli adhaerebat turpitudo, patrator rectè mercedem exigit. Humani generis interest, ut nulla sint {ex pactis} scelerum invitamenta; nullaque in istiusmodi pactis fides.

Sin autem, eo tantum illicita sit rei cujuslibet {promissae} praestatio, quod aliquis incautè, <198> et contra viri prudentis officia, res suae potestati permissas administravit; rerum contractarum fides adeò sancte est servanda,

---

* {*Praestare quod interest.*}
10. This is a mistake by the translator.

he is obliged to make good{*} the profit which would otherways have arisen to the other.

The matter of contracts must also be lawful: that is, our contracts or promises should be only about the natural matters of commerce, which can be alienated, the administration of which is committed to human prudence, and not prohibited by any special law. No obligation therefor can arise from any promise, to violate directly the reverence due to God, or the perfect rights of others, or to do what any special law prohibits, or what is not committed to our power. <192>

1. If therefor both parties know the unlawfulness of the terms of any contract, or ought to have known it; the contract is void. The one who employed another to commit a crime, may redemand what he gave to the person hired, before he has committed the crime. And if the crime be previously committed, the executor ought not to have the hire; nor if he previously received it, can the person who hired him redemand it. Both equally deserve the highest punishments; {nor should either hold any advantage by such engagements}.

If after the contract the iniquity of it appears to either side, which they had not formerly considered; before execution either of them may free himself from it: and any reward given should be restored. Nor after execution can the person employed claim his reward, unless the moral turpitude affect only the hirer and not himself [if the moral turpitude affects himself as well as the person who hired him];[10] {or} unless his ignorance was no way culpable. But where the turpitude only affects the person who employed him, then he may justly claim his hire. 'Tis the general interest of mankind that there should be no allurements to such crimes, nor dependence upon such contracts.[11]

But if the vice in any performance of covenant only consist in this, that a man has managed imprudently and contrary to the duty of a discreet cautious man, in these matters which naturally fall under commerce; 'tis of such importance to maintain the faith of commerce, that in this case,

---

11. This paragraph is not very clear, nor is the conclusion. A more coherent account is in *System* 2.9.12, vol. II, pp. 25–26.

ut "quae fieri non debebant, facta saepe valeant."

Quod de re *impossibili* dictum est, tenet de re aut actione aliena, si quis de iis quae potestati suae non subjiciuntur pactus fuerit. Qui in istiusmodi pactis, aut promissionibus, dolo usus est, quod interest praestare tenebitur: qui culpa quemvis decepit, illi damnum praestandum.

XI. Qui de re sua quavis aut opera pactus est, non omnem circa eam confestim amisit potestatem; nisi istiusmodi pactum fuit, quod totum rei dominium transtulit, jus alteri constituens *reale* et plenum, omnemve de operis suis in posterum paciscendi, facultatem sibi adimens. Unde, licet pactum jus tantum *personale* constituens antecesserat, tertio cuivis, prioris pacti inscio, constitui poterit *jus reale,* contra jus prius personale valiturum. Interveniente verò hujus tertii haud inscii dolo, pactum erit irritum. Dolis enim confirmandis, pacto* itidem qualicunque, ad eludenda quaevis officia humana, planè excogitato, quum id neutrum contrahentium latere poterat, lex naturalis maxime adversatur. In aliis <199> autem causis, "pactorum, quae cum eodem ineuntur, priori posterius derogabit." In pactis autem quae eadem de re cum diversis conficiuntur, "quae jura tantum personalia constituunt, iis cedent quae jura constituunt realia"; si modo abfuerat illius dolus, aut *lata culpa,* ad quem transferendum erat jus reale. In pactis denique uniusmodi quae cum diversis ineuntur, "qui tempore prior, jure potior."

---

* Matth. 15.5. Mark 7.11.

too "our transactions and covenants are obligatory, tho' we were faulty in entering into them."

Covenants about the goods or actions of others which <193> are not subjected to our power, are in the same case with those about impossibilities. Whoever has acted fraudulently in such covenants is lyable to make good all the profit would have accrued from the faithful performance of them: and he who has deceived others by any culpable negligence is obliged to compensate the damages.

XI. Every sort of contracts about one's goods or labours does not immediately divest him of all moral power of transacting about them in a different manner with others. This is the case only in such as convey the intire property at once, or a real right; or such as give another the whole right to one's labours for a certain time, or during life, so as to preclude his contracting with others about the same. But when one has only made a contract constituting a *personal right* against himself, he may thereafter convey a valid *real* right, to such as knew nothing about the former contract, which will take place of the personal right tho' prior.[12] Where indeed this new grantee has acted fraudulently, being apprized of the former contract; the subsequent one should be void. For the law of nature can never confirm frauds, or any* contracts plainly contrived and designed to elude any obligations of humanity, when this design must be known to both parties in the contract. But in other cases, "of two covenants entered into with the same person, the later derogates from the former." But of contracts entered into about the same thing with different persons, "such as convey a real right take place of those which only <194> convey a personal"; provided there has been no fraud on his part to whom the real right is transferred. And lastly in contracts of the same nature entered into with different persons, "the prior takes place of the posterior."[13]

---

12. See above 2.7.4, p. 169.

* Matth. xv. 5. Mark vii. 11. [Hutcheson refers to the two passages where Jesus blames the Pharisees for refusing to relieve their old parents by declaring sacred to God their own goods.]

13. See Pufendorf, *De officio* 1.9.19 and 1.9.21 for the next section.

XII. Paciscimur etiam per legatos et internuncios, sive *mandatarios*. Ubi {plena ipsis permissa potestas, neque} ulla [nulla] sunt mandata mutuò declaranda, legatorum potestatem ejusque potestatis fines monstrantia; ad ea obligari censemur, quae legati pro sua prudentia gesserint: nisi ostendi possit legatos dolosè egisse, aut praemii spe fuisse corruptos; aut pactum adeò manifestè iniquum sit, ut, viro prudente arbitro, doli mali det indicia. Quas leviores, legati culpa, patimur injurias, eae in ipsum legatum vindicandae. Potestatis autem legato permissae finibus apertè declaratis, quod ultrà a legato actum fuerit neutiquam obligabit. <200>

XII. We may contract by *factors* or *agents,* or persons commissioned for that purpose, as well as in our own persons. Where full powers are given, and no special instructions to be shewn to all he deals with, expressing the extent of our agent's commission, and how far we subject our rights to his transactions; we are deemed to be obliged to ratify what he does in our name, unless we can make proof that he acted fraudulently, or was bribed by the other party; or the manifest iniquity of his deeds satisfy a prudent arbiter that he must have been corrupted. As to any smaller injuries we sustain, we must impute them to our agent, while we ratify what he has done with others.

But when the powers of the agent are specially declared to all concerned, what he transacts beyond these bounds does not oblige his constituent.

CAPUT X

De Sermocinantium Officiis.

I. Doctrinae de contractibus affinis est illa quae de usu sermonis versatur. Quum caeteris animalibus eo praestent homines, quod non rationis solum, verum et orationis facultate ornantur, qua praecipuè hominum societas continetur, vigentque commercia, atque officia omnia amica; eo Dei dono eximio ita utendum est, ut exigit officii nostri, communisque utilitatis ratio.

Qua de re haud sanè levi, in ipsa naturae nostrae structura, non desunt divini consilii indicia. Sensu enim cujusque proxime commendatur is sermonis usus, quem communis exigit utilitas. In prima et tenella aetate, proclives sunt pueri ad omnia quae norunt palam declaranda. Simulationi omni et dissimulationi natura repugnat; donec rerum usu, incommoda non levia sequi observantur simplicem eam et apertam, omnium quae animo insunt, declarationem, quam proxime et per se essemus comprobaturi. Suadebit quidem recta ratio, communis utilitatis cura, eaque quâ sibi quisque consulit prudentia, ut nonnulla tegamus, <201> taceamus, eumque primum animi impetum cohibeamus: hoc vero stabile consilium, eo tantum utendi sermone, qui cum animi sententia congruit, quique alios non decipiet, {non solum} animi sensus per se <& utilitatis communis ratio> comprobat [comprobant], sive de nostris, sive de aliorum moribus judicemus{; verum etiam recta ratio, communisque utilitatis cura, idem ab omnibus postulat}.

Quum enim non solum cognitionis nostrae pars magna, aliorum sermonibus innitatur; verum etiam vitae negotia et consilia, eâ regantur rerum humanarum notitia, quam ex aliorum sermonibus comparamus, [etiam eorum qui] [quorum plures] nullo proprio juris vinculo, animi sui his de rebus sententias, nobiscum communicare tenebantur; [non aliter quam servatâ in sermone fide et veritate,] [nisi in sermone servavetur fides et veritas, omnia] haec vitae sociae commoda <tollerentur>, omnisque ea <vitae> jucunditas, quae ex mutua in aliorum verbis fiducia oritur, {conservari potest}.

169

Our Obligations in Speech.

I. Our duties in the use of speech have a near affinity to those in contracts. Mankind enjoy this preeminence above other animals, that they have the powers of reason and speech, by which chiefly a social life, commerce, and an intercourse of kind offices are maintained. 'Tis in general plain that we are bound to use these excellent gifts of God in such manner as is most conducive to the general good, and suitable to our several obligations in life.

In this important matter we have very manifest indications of what God requires of us, in the very structure of our nature: an immediate sense seems to recommend that use of speech which the common interest requires. In our tender years we are naturally prone to discover candidly all we know. We have a natural aversion to all falshood and dissimulation, until we experience some inconveniency from this openness of heart, which we at first approve. Reflection [Right reason], a regard to the common good, and a prudent care of our own safety, will often persuade us to conceal or be silent about certain things; and to restrain the first impulse of our mind. But {when we resolve to speak to others, then} both the immediate sense of our hearts, and a rational [right reason and a] regard to the common interest, will recommend and enjoin upon us this steddy rule or purpose, of speaking <196>nothing contrary to the sentiments of our heart, or which will deceive others. These are our natural sentiments whether we are judging of our own conduct or that of others.

For as a great share of the most useful knowledge in the affairs of life, as well as that of a more speculative kind, is acquired from the conversation of others who are under no special obligations of communicating to us their sentiments; this advantage of a social life, not to mention the pleasures of conversation with mutual confidence, must be entirely lost, unless men maintain truth and fidelity in all their discourse with each other.

Quae de sermone sunt dicta, ad alia etiam signa pertinent, quae ad animi sententias declarandas adhibentur; scripturam, nempe, vel vulgarem, vel hieroglyphicam, aut symbola.

II. Signorum autem, quorum significatio sive ex ipsorum *natura,* sive ex *instituto* aut consuetudine pendet,* duplex est <202> usus: unus, ubi is qui signis utitur, neutiquam profiteri intelligitur, se animi sui sententiam cum aliis communicaturum; {iste verò} qui ea signa cernit, pro sua solertia, quaedam colligit esse vera, quamvis nihil causae sit cur credatur, alterum eo animo signa dedisse, ut se rei cujusvis faceret certiorem. Alter signorum usus eam in se habet vim, ut justam det causam colligendi, istum qui signa dederat, eo fecisse animo, ut nobis rem aliquam indicaret: quod et ipso signorum usu, prae se ferre videtur.

In signorum usu prius memorato, nulla propria est obligatio: ne quis enim, sine justa causa, alterum laedat, est obligatio communis. Ubi tamen justa est laedendi causa, ut in bello justo, nihil prohibet, quo minus his utamur dolis, quae {consilia imperatoria, sive} *strategemata* dicuntur. Immo, si nemini noceatur, hoc signorum usu, vel amicissimum fallere licebit.

De altero signorum usu longe aliter statuendum: nullo enim sive inter omnes, sive inter eos qui colloquuntur, praeeunte pacto, hic signorum usus, pacti taciti vim {in se} continet. Qui enim ea alteri dat signa, cum eo recte intelligitur pacisci, se animi sui sententiam, per haec signa, ei declaraturum, secundum interpretandi modum, vel naturalem, vel usu institutum, nisi

---

* Vid. Grot. de J. B. et P. l. III. 1. 8.

---

* See *Grotius de Jure belli, &c.* L. III. 1. 8. [The reason of this reference to Grotius is not very clear. We find the same reference and a very similar paragraph in *Illustrations,* sect. IV, p. 264–65, where Hutcheson argues against Wollaston's thesis that a bad action is equivalent to a lie. The distinction between the two usages of signs is more clearly expressed by Pufendorf in *De iure nat.* 4.1.7 and 10 and in *De officio* 1.10.3 and 4]

What we say of speech holds also concerning other signs used for the same purpose of communicating our sentiments, viz. common writing, or hieroglyphicks[, or symbols].

II. We must also observe here that there's a twofold use of signs, whether natural, or artificial and [or customary or] instituted:* one in which the person who causes the appearance is never imagined to make any profession, or to have any intention of communicating his sentiments to others. The spectator according to his own sagacity concludes from the appearances some fact or other, without imagining that the person who occasioned these appearances did it with a view to give him any information. The other use of signs is of such a nature [has such a strength] that it plainly contains this profession, or gives the observer just ground to conclude that such signs were made designedly to intimate something to him<, which the same use of the signs seems to reveal>.

In the former way of making signs, there's no peculiar <197> obligation: we are only under that obligation common to all parts of life, to do no hurt to our neighbour without a just cause. But when there is just cause, as in the case of a just war, we may without blame use such arts of deceiving, which are called < commander's in chief plans or> *stratagems.* Nay provided we do no hurt to any innocent person, there's no crime in deceiving{†} by such sort of signs our very best friends.

But we are under very different obligations as to the other use of signs. For without presupposing any old covenant or formal express agreement, the very use of signs in certain circumstances may plainly contain the nature of a *tacit convention,* and he who exhibits them is justly understood to covenant with the other to communicate his sentiments, according to that interpretation of these signs which is either natural or customary, unless there

---

† {Thus an army intending to decamp in the night, yet keep all their fires burning in the old places, to conceal their motions. A studious man to avoid interruption, keeps his doors shut, and his street-windows darkened, whence we conclude that he is abroad.} [The first example appears in *Illustrations,* Sect. IV, p. 264 as well as in *System* 2.10.3, vol. II, p. 29; the second *ibidem,* p. 31.]

subsit causa <203> aliqua utrinque cognita, cur ab eodem deflectat. Si enim nulla istiusmodi subsit pactio, frustra quisquam alterum alloqueretur, frustra alloquenti auscultaret. {Atque idem de aliis signis tenendum, sive naturalibus sive institutis, quorum similis est usus.}

Hae igitur de sermone scriptisque leges. 1. Prima; "Ubi aliis est jus qualecunque, veras loquentium sententias sciendi, non solum vera sunto quae dicuntur, verûm nihil celanto." Quae testium in judiciis est causa, eorumque qui artem aliquam totam, aliis tradere sunt polliciti.

2. Altera lex est. "Quamvis aliis nullum sit jus proprium, ubi tamen eos alloquimur, nihil dicendum, quod non animi sententiis [congruat] [sit consonum], secundum interpretandi modum, qui apud probos et prudentes invaluit." A mendacii igitur crimine non est immunis, qui sermonem ab animi sententia discrepantem [sententiae dissonum] profert, quamvis insolita quadam interpretandi ratione, aut per adjectionem quandam in mente suppressam, [inter se congruere possint] [consonus effici possit]. Permissâ enim artium istiusmodi licentia, omni dolo et fraudi patebit via.

III. Quo plenius cernatur hac in re officium, haec sedulò observanda: 1. Signa omnia, verba praecipue et scripta, ea ratione quae in morem abiit, adhibenda esse, <204> non spectata etymologia, aut antiqua quavis significatione, et inusitata. Verborum formulis, honoris aut urbanitatis causa vulgò usurpatis, nemo decipitur; neque enim ea significare intelliguntur, quae in aliis rebus adhibita significarent.

2. Si omnibus quorum interest innotuerit, in quibusdam rebus concessam esse fallendi licentiam; neque eum qui decipitur, ubi verum resciverit, de injuria queri solere; [quae in iisdem versantur] [plurimae sunt] simulandi, aut dissimulandi artes, <quae> omni vitio carent. Quod non solum

be some special reason{*} in the case, known on both sides, why we should depart from the ordinary interpretation. For did we not universally understand such an agreement as to speech, it would be a ridiculous action either to address speech to another or to listen to it. And the same holds as to{†} other signs natural or instituted, used in this manner. <198>

These therefor are the laws of speech and writing. 1. "Where others have a right to know the whole sentiments of the speaker, he is obliged not only to speak truth but to reveal the whole truth." This holds as to witnesses in courts of justice, and such as have engaged to communicate the whole mysterys of any art.[1]

The second law is. "Tho' others may have no peculiar right to know our sentiments, yet when we speak to them, we should say nothing but what agrees with our sentiments according to the common interpretation which obtains among men of understanding [honest and prudent]."[2] One is therefor guilty of falshood or lying who speaks what is thus contrary to his sentiments, altho' by some unusual way of interpreting the words, or by some mental reservation, it might agree with them. If such arts were allowed, a gate would be opened to all deceit and fraud.

III. That our duty in this point may the better appear, we must <carefully> observe, 1. that all signs, especially <spoken or written> words should be used in the customary manner, without regard to antient obsolete meanings or etymologies. Expressions of civility and courtesy, or titles of honour, deceive no body. They are known not to signify what the same words do on other occasions.

2. If 'tis known to all concerned that in some affairs certain persons are allowed to deceive; nor does the person deceived, when he comes to discover it, complain of it as an injury; what artifice or false-speaking is used in these affairs is not deemed criminal. This is the case in many diversions; and

---

* {A cypher agreed upon, for instance.}

† {Thus sending wings or spurs to a friend at court, intimates to him that we imagine he is in danger, and contains this profession.} [This example appears in *Illustrations,* Sect. IV, p. 265.]

1. *System* 2.10.4, point 5, vol. II, p. 37.

2. See *System* 2.10.3, vol. II, p. 32.

in rebus ludicris, verum et seriis quibusdam, obtinetur; ubi nos aliorum prudentiae regendos permisimus; ut medicis, aegroti; imperatori, milites.

3. Quin etiam, si mos inductus fuerit, ut hostes fictis sermonibus se invicem, ubi possunt, decipiant; neque decepti ea de causa querantur, jura gentium humaniora, fuisse ab hoste violata; censeri potest, nova quadam pactione tacita, remissum esse jus illud ortum ex pactione ea tacita, quam in se continet ipsum alloquium. Haud tamen, sine causa gravissima, vir animi candidi et probi, ea arte uti vellet; quum turpitudinis non levis speciem habere videatur.

4. Pactis autem vel foederibus quibusvis hostem decipere, neque unquam receptum fuit, nec recipi debet. <Non> Absque foederibus <205> enim, {neque} conservari possunt mitiores et humaniores belli gerendi rationes; nec [aut] maxima hominum saevitia praecaveri; nec [aut] denique, sine alterutrius partis internecione, vel miserrima servitute, pax bello mutari potest.

5. Haec vero, in sermone, verborum obligatio, ut et caeterae omnes in conventione tacita fundatae, tempestivè omnes quorum interest praemonendo, tolli potest aut praecaveri.

6. Praeter exceptionem vis et metus, antea memoratam, aliam dandam volunt nonnulli, hinc ortam, quod nonnunquam non alia ratione quam mendacio, a viris innocentibus et optimis, aut a populo fortè universo, averti possunt mala gravissima. Qualiscunque sit hujus exceptionis vis, patet eam non huic loco soli convenire, quum in aliis fere cunctis legibus, quae dicuntur speciales, ut postea{*} docebitur, ei itidem sit locus.

7. Ubi insidioso et maligno consilio, explorantur hominis cujusquam de certa re sententiae, easque captiosis quaestionibus eliciunt inimici, nullo suo utentes jure; ubi et ipsum silentium totam rem aperiret, et malis gravioribus causam praeberet; si quidem homini occurrat istiusmodi responsio, <206> quae viris probis, nullo praejudicio aut affectu pravo in ea interpretanda occaecatis, veram indicaret sententiam, quae tamen responsio aliud longe

* {Lib. II. Cap. 16.}

sometimes in serious <199> business, when we commit ourselves entirely to the conduct of others, in whose wisdom and fidelity we confide; as patients do to physicians, and soldiers to their commanders in chief.

3. Nay if the custom has prevailed in war, that enemies deceive each other by false narrations when they can, nor do the deceived complain of it as a violation of the laws of civilized nations: one may judge that by a new tacit convention enemies have remitted to each other that right otherways founded in the general convention contained in the addressing of speech to others. But a candid mind would not without the most urgent causes use such methods, since they have a strong appearance of moral turpitude.

4. But the deceiving of enemys by any pretence of a treaty or covenant, never was nor can be allowed. As it is by treaties alone that we can maintain the more human methods of carrying on war, and prevent the most savage cruelties; or restore peace again without the destruction of one side, or reducing them to miserable slavery.[3]

5. But this obligation about speech, as all others founded in tacit conventions may be prevented or taken away, by a{*} timely premonition of all concerned.

6. Beside the above mentioned exception of unjust force in matters of contracts, some plead for another exception from some grievous and extraordinary necessities; when without false-speaking we cannot preserve the innocent, or the most worthy perhaps of mankind, or even a whole nation, from ruin. Whatever <200> force there is in this exception, 'tis plain it is not peculiar to this subject; since it seems, as we shall† hereafter shew, that this exception takes place in most of the other special laws {of nature}.

7. Where men with malicious intentions, and without having any right to demand it, are endeavouring to discover a person's sentiments by captious and insidious questions; when even his silence would discover all they want to his ruin: if there occurr to him such answers as to good unprejudiced men would bear a true signification according to his sentiments, while yet they will appear to these insidious enemies to signify something very

---

3. See *System* 2.10.4, point 3, vol. II, pp. 33–34.
* {See the preceding Chap. § 6} [2.9.6, p. 184].
† Ch. xvi. [sect. II] of this Book.

insidiosis hisce significare videbitur; eâ licebit viro bono uti, quamvis inimicos ea ratione deceptum iri praevideat.

8. Quum fides in omni sermone conservata, tantam hominum vitae afferat utilitatem, haud levioribus de causis, quales saepe occurrunt, mendacio uti licebit: veluti ad iratos demulcendos, moestos consolandos, aut levius aliquod commodum consequendum, aut malum, minimè gravissimum, effugiendum. Alia enim ratione, verâ nimirum et simplici, istiusmodi bona comparari, eaque mala vel averti, vel fortiter ferri, plerumque possunt. Atque licet semel prosperè cedere potest mendacium, quum nondum innotuit, nos {in istiusmodi causis} nulla sermonis religione teneri; ubi tamen hoc palam factum est, passimque vagatur haec mentiendi licentia, nemini ulla erit auctoritas, omnisque tolletur fiducia. Hactenus de fide in verbis servanda.

IV. Alia autem sunt sermonis sanctissima officia. Illud inprimis, ut quisque sermone aliis prodesse studeat, verâ virtute laudanda et fovenda, vanisque hominum de foelicitate, et vitae prosperitate, opinionibus <207> et somniis corrigendis: utque docendo, monendo, hortando, consolando, quandoque et objurgando, benefaciendi amicam exerceat voluntatem. Inter quae officia sunt haec honestissima, aversos componere amicos, inimicitias praecavere, et dissidentes {inter sese} conciliare. Neque quicquam cautiùs vitabit vir bonus, quam alterius cujusquam famam laedere. Immo non solum a falsis abstinebit criminibus; verum, ubi nulla major utilitas, aut innocentium ne a recto tramite seducantur cura, contrarium exegerit, arcana aliorum celabit vitia. Famâ enim amissâ, difficilius ad meliorem revocantur frugem, quo-

---

* {Of this there are instances in very great characters; as also of many expressions which the speaker abundantly knew that the hearers would understand in a very false sense.}

different;{*} he may use such evasive answers, tho' he foresees that his unjust enemies will be deceived by them.

8. Since maintaining veracity in all our conversation is of such importance in society, 'tis plainly unlawful to use false-speaking from any of those smaller motives which frequently occurr in life; such as, to pacify men in a passion of anger, or to comfort the sorrowful; or in general to obtain any advantages or avert any evils which are not of the very highest kinds.[4] For we may by other means consistent with all candour and sincerity generally obtain these ends more effectually, and either prevent these evils, or assist men to bear them with fortitude. And however such false-speaking may at first have some effect, before it becomes known <201> that we make no conscience of speaking truth in such cases; yet, when this is once known, and when men generally take this liberty, they lose all credit in such cases with others, and mutual confidence is destroyed. So much concerning veracity.

IV. But there are other sacred duties in the use of speech; and this in the first place, that we study to make our speech profitable to others, in recommending and cherishing sincere virtue, in correcting the vain imaginations of men about the true happiness of life; in teaching, admonishing, exhorting, comforting, and sometimes reproving sharply, and all these shewing an hearty intention of doing good. These too are among the most honourable offices, to reconcile friends who have been at variance, to prevent animosities, or to compose them. Nor is there any thing a good man will more conscientiously avoid than hurting the characters of others. Nay he will not only avoid the spreading of false calumnies, but will conceal the secret faults of others, unless he be forced to divulge them to prevent the seducing the innocent{, or to avert some publick evil}. For men who have lost their characters and are publickly infamous, are on this account far

---

4. Here Hutcheson contradicts what Pufendorf says in *De officio* 1.10.9 and in *De iure nat.* 4.1.15, even if he agrees with Pufendorf that a kind of false-speech is allowed to physicians or commanders, but in these cases, by a preventive tacit convention (see above point 2 and *System* 2.10.4, point 2, vol. II, p. 33).

rum vita vitiis est mendosa: et quo plures vitiis conspiciantur cooperti, eo aliorum flagitia fiunt impudentiora.

Observarunt grammatici, plurima rerum nomina, praeter rem primario loco denotatam, adsignificare etiam loquentis affectus: inde sit ut res plurimae triplici notentur nomine; uno medio, rem nudam exhibente; altero, loquentis etiam delectationem, amorem et cupidinem, notante; tertio denique, contrarios odii et offensionis motus. Hinc constabit, quamvis nullum sit Dei aut naturae opus viri boni cognitione et sermone indignum, magna tamen in ipso sermone prodi posse animi vitia, ubi de hominum agitur vitiis et libidinibus; quum scil. adhibentur <208> voces quae loquentis indolem flagitiosam produnt, atque in audientium animis, similes incendunt libidines. Hic vero est sermo obscoenus et detestandus.

harder to be reclaimed to virtue; and the more that vice appears to abound in the world, the vitious grow the more impudent.[5]

Criticks have observed that many words, beside their primary meaning, have also an additional signification of the dispositions of the speaker: and hence there are often three sorts of names for the same things, or actions. One of a middle nature, barely denoting its object; <202> another denoting the speaker's delight in it, or his keen passion for it; the third denoting his aversion and hatred of it.[6] And from this we see {how to answer the reasonings of the old *Cynicks,* against supposing any crime in obscenity of language;}[7] that tho' it be true, there's no work of God, or natural action, which may not be a proper subject of inquiry and speech to a good man, {on some occasions,} yet we may evidence [give birth to a] great depravation and turpitude of mind in speaking about the dissolute actions of others: to wit, by using such words as betray a like dissolute temper in ourselves, and a delight in such vices, and kindle like vitious passions in the minds of the hearers. And in this consists obscenity, which is hateful and detestable in conversation.[8]

5. See *System* 2.10.5, vol. II, p. 41.

6. Cf. *System* 2.10.5, vol. II, p. 42.

7. This added reference to the Cynics is drawn from *System* 2.10.5, point 5, vol. II, p. 42.

8. Cf. *System* 2.10.5, vol. II, p. 43.

CAPUT XI

De Jurejurando et Votis.

I. Ad hominum pacta, promissa, et testimonia de rebus gravioribus confirmanda, accedit jusjurandum. Est autem jusjurandum "actus religiosus
quo ad rem dubiam confirmandam, Deus testis et vindex invocatur." Tanta
quidem est in omni pacto et sermone, viri boni fides, ut eum jurejurando
adstringere non sit opus, apud eos quibus est notus: sed ubi res aguntur
eorum, quibus viri probitas non est perspecta; illius et promissa et testimonia <apud eos> jurejurando sunt confirmanda; quum {in} jurejurando
nulla insit in Deum impietas, sed potius pietas. Qui enim religiose jurat,
Dei omnia intuentis, et regentis, providentiam simul et justitiam agnoscit.

Quum autem apud omnes gentes semper invaluit haec persuasio, justa
Dei providentia mundum administrari, et improbis supplicia irrogari; Dei
testis et vindicis invocatio, sensum officii hominum animis altiùs <209>
infigit, eosque poenarum metu a fraude deterret. Neque enim censendum
est, ea invocatione Deum magis attentum fieri, aut acriorem perfidiae vin-
dicem; aut consensu nostro novum puniendi jus illi tributum. Longè quidem gravius est perfidiae scelus, ubi quis promissum aut pactum juratum
violaverit; aut alios testimonio juratus deceperit.

De re leviore jurare, aut nulla de causa, omnino impium est: quum numinis reverentiam, quae bonis debet esse perpetua, imminuat, summaeque
majestatis contemptum prodat. Ubi autem crebra in civitate sunt perjuria,
eorum crimine premuntur et rectores, si jusjurandum levibus de causis, et

Of Oaths and Vows.

I. Oaths are deemed a natural confirmation of ‹pactions,› promises or testimonies, in the more important affairs: an *oath* is "a religious act in which for confirmation of something doubtful, we invoke God as witness and avenger{, if we swerve from truth.}" A truly good man indeed will so strictly regard veracity, that such as know him well need not require his oath. But when the interests of those are at stake who know not his character, they may justly demand his oath, in confirmation either of his testimony or his promise. Since the using of oaths in such cases contains no impiety toward God; but is rather an expression of pious reverence; as we acknowledge in swearing his universal knowledge, and government, ‹providence,› and justice.

And since this persuasion has obtained, in all nations and ages, that God exercises a just government over the world, inflicting punishments on the wicked; this invocation of God as witness and avenger must raise in mens minds an higher sense of their obligations, and ‹by fear of punishments› deter them from falshood. But we must not imagine that our invocations make God more attentive in observing, or more keen in punishing of perfidy; or that by our voluntary consent, we give him any new right of punishing he had not before.[1] Our own guilt indeed is made much greater when, after the confirmation of ‹204› an oath, we either violate our promises, or falsify in our testimony.

To swear about trifling matters, or without any cause, is very impious; as it plainly tends to abate that awful reverence which all good men should constantly maintain toward God; and is a plain indication of contempt. Where perjuries in serious matters grow frequent in any state, the magistrates or legislators are generally chargeable with much of the guilt, if they

---

1. See *System* 2.11.1, vol. II, p. 44.

quum minime est necessarium, saepius exigatur: aut ubi de eo praestando quod a juratis postulamus, jurejurando caveri nequit; vel quia res ipsa fieri non poterit, vel quia juratis nonnunquam illicita videbitur: aut si exigatur ubi gravia sunt perjurii invitamenta, una cum spe homines impunè fallendi. Pessime etiam de religione merentur, qui gravem aliquam et solennem verborum formulam, ad animos hominum religionis sensu percellendos [afficiendos] idoneam, in jurejurando non adhibent.

II. Quamvis in jurejurando, frustra invocetur aliquid divina potestate destitutum, <210> tanquam testis et vindex; sunt tamen jurandi formulae {quaedam}, non quidem satis commodae, at haud plane illicitae, ubi Dei nomine non adhibito, qui jurat, [sibi suisque aut rei alicui sibi carae admodum aut necessariae, dira quaedam a Deo precari] [in rem aliquam sibi caram admodum aut necessariam, Dei vindictam imprecari] intelligitur; aut ubi Deus ipse, per metonymiam invocatur.

Frustra autem adigeretur aliquis ad jurandum, per eum quem neque divina potestate praeditum, neque exercere in homines imperium credit. Sunt tamen Dei veri descriptiones omnibus communes, quibus utendum erit, quum a pluribus diversa de Deo sentientibus, exigendum est jusjurandum.

In jurejurando, ut de pactis dictum, is rite censetur jurasse, atque perjurii poenis, si fidem fefellerit, esse obnoxius, qui jurandi animum prae se ferens, ea quae a jurantibus solent, signa adhibuit.

---

* {Thus engagements by oath to adhere to certain schemes of religion, which may afterwards appear false; or to a government which may appear an unjust usurpation.} [This added footnote is derived from *System* 2.11.[1], vol. II, pp. 45–46.]

† {Thus *purgatory oaths* as to capital crimes, or very secret matters of scandal, or injustice, or about a man's secret opinions, generally have no good effect.} [Cf. below, p. 207, and *System* 2.11.4, vol. II, p. 49.]

either frequently exact oaths without necessity in smaller matters, or when the oaths give no security in the point in view;{*} when the engagement designed may either be impracticable, or appear to the persons concerned to be unlawful; or if oaths are required{†} where there are great temptations to perjury, with hopes of impunity from men. They also do bad service to religion who don't appoint an awful solemn form of words, fit to strike the minds of men with reverence in such an action.

II. 'Tis no doubt vain {to exact from others, or} to swear by any being whom the swearer judges not invested with divine power, so as to invoke that being as witness and avenger. And yet there are some forms of oaths {truly valid and} not unlawful, tho' not the most convenient, where without expressing the name of God, the swearer either names something very dear or necessary <205> to himself{‡} upon which he is understood to imprecate the divine vengeance{, or that he may be deprived of it if he should act perfidiously}; or truly invokes God under some{§} metonymical expression.

Tho' it be idle to exact an oath from any one by any being whom he conceives not as endued with divine power, nor exercising any providence; yet there are certain general descriptions of the Deity in which men {of the most opposite religions} agree: such therefor ought to be used, when persons of different religious sentiments are required to swear.

As in covenants, so in oaths, he is justly deemed to have sworn, and to be liable to the penalties of perjury should he falsify, who professing an intention of swearing makes such signs as ordinarily signify to others that one swears.[2]

‡ So we understand swearing by one's *head,* his *life,* his *soul,* his *children,* his *prince* or *patron,* the *earth,* the *light,* the *sun.* [See *System* 2.11.2, vol. II, p. 46.]

§ {'Tis thus men swear by their *faith,* viz. the object of it; or by the *heavens,* the *temples,* or *altars;* for the Divinity residing in them, or to whom they are dedicated.} [See Matth. 23.20–23. It is a footnote by Hutcheson in *System* 2.11.2, vol. II, p. 46, that suggests this footnote to the translator.]

2. See Pufendorf, *De officio* 1.11.5.

Quamvis jusjurandum una cum promisso aut testimonio, in eadem sententia includi possit, est tamen jusjurandum actus ab omni pacto aut nar-
ratione diversus; Dei nempe testis et vindicis invocatio, si quid contra officium egerimus, unde patet, hominum officia jurejurando neutiquam
immutari; novamve quod ad *materiam* attinet, obligationem constitui; nec
promissum pactumve <211> justa de causa irritum, ratum fieri, aut justam
excludi exceptionem; nec *conditionalia* mutari in *absoluta;* nec ratum fieri
quod contra jus alterius perfectum, aut de re aliena, potestati nostrae non
commissa, factum est; neque quod pietatem Deo debitam violat, legesve
definitas, quas vocant *speciales,* certas actiones omnino prohibentes, et paciscendi de iis omnem nobis adimentes potestatem. In rebus vero nostrae
potestati permissis, ut simplici pacto, sic multo sanctiùs [magis] eo quod
jurejurando confirmatum est, obligamur; etiam ubi temere, et contra prudentiae et humanitatis officia, jurati promisimus: nisi paciscentium intervenerit dolus, ad eludenda officia quaedam humaniora.

III. Sine acceptione autem, nulla erit promissionis obligatio; quin et iste
cui promissum est, de suo jure cedere, et promissorem liberare potest. Quod
fiet etiam, tempestive declarato ejus dissensu, cujus consensus priùs erat
necessarius, quam possit vel is qui promisit se ad rem quamlibet praestandam adstringere, vel alter rem oblatam accipere.

Ubi jusjurandum quisquam suo jure a nobis exigit, {verborumque formulam praescribit}; si de ipsius sensu constet, eo sensu nobis est jurandum;
si ex animi sententia fieri possit: sin minus, a jurejurando est abstinendum.
<212> Neque delegati, qui aliorum nomine, eorum forte qui summo im-
perio praesunt, jusjurandum exigunt, formulam praescriptam interpretandi jus habent.

Jusjurandum, pro vario usu, est vel *promissorium* quod vocant, vel *as-
sertorium.* Hoc, judice exigente, dicitur *necessarium;* et litigantium alter-

Altho' an oath and a promise, or an assertion, may often be expressed by one and the same grammatical sentence; yet the act of swearing is plainly a distinct one from that of promising or asserting; as it consists in the invocation of God <as witness> to avenge if we violate our faith. This shews therefor that mens duties are not altered as to their matter by an oath; nor any new matter of obligation produced; nor any covenant or promise otherways void confirmed; nor just exceptions <206> excluded; nor conditional contracts made absolute; nor any obligation imposed to act contrary to the perfect rights of others, or about matters not subjected to our power, or what would be a direct piece of irreverence and impiety toward God, or a violation of any special prohibition, by which we are precluded from transacting in certain affairs.[3] But in matters naturally subjected to our power {and committed to human prudence}, as we may bind ourselves by a common contract, so much more by one confirmed by oath, even when we have entered into it imprudently and rashly, contrary to the rules of discretion; unless when there has been a plain obvious fraudulent design of defeating some obligations of humanity.{*}

III. A promise {tho' confirmed by oath} can produce no obligation, unless it has been accepted by the other party, who also after his acceptance may remit to us his right, and free us from the promise. A promise in like manner is void, upon the declared dissent of a person whose consent was necessary before the promiser could oblige himself, or the other party accept of it.

Where one requires of us an oath by his just authority, and prescribes to us the form of words; if we understand his sense of the words, and can sincerely swear in that sense, 'tis well; if not, we should not take the oath. No inferior magistrate deputed to take an oath in the name of the state has a right to give explications of the *formula* prescribed by the supreme powers.

Oaths according to their different purposes are divided <207> into *promissory* and *assertory.* Oaths of this later sort when required by a judge

---

3. Cf. *System* 2.11.2 and 3, vol. II, pp. 47–48; Pufendorf, *De officio* 1.11.6 and *De iure nat.* 4.2.6.
* {Mark vii. 11, 12, 13.} [Compare above, 2.9.11, p. 193.]

utro, coram judice, alteri id deferente, dicitur *judiciale.* Si extra judicium sponte juretur, dicitur jusjurandum *voluntarium.* Quod in actionibus *criminalibus,* ad probationem imperfectam refellendam exigitur, dicitur *purgatorium.*

Ubi autem de capite agitur aut fama, quum tanta sint ad pejerandum invitamenta; minime commoda videtur aut justa quaestionis exercendae ratio, jusjurandum exigere purgatorium. Hac enim ratione absolventur perjuri et scelerati; convincentur illi soli, quibus tanta est pietas, ut ne vel ad famam aut vitam tuendam, se perjurio sint adstricturi: quos, viro bono satius videbitur, incerti criminis (cujus homines tali indole praeditos, mox serio plerumque poenitet,) poenas effugere <mallet>, quam ut sua ipsorum pietate teneantur.

IV. Votum est "promissio religiosa [promissum religiosum] qua ipsi Deo, ad certas res aut operas praestandas, nos adstringimus." In votis, <213> non intelligitur jus ad homines esse translatum, nisi et pactum intercesserit.

Votorum unicus est usus, ut Deum sanctissimum, justissimum, omniaque intuentem verentibus, pia omnia et honesta agendi consilia fiant constantiora; eoque magis officium deserere vereamur, ne nosmet etiam atroci perjurii crimine implicemus.

Quum autem sine illius consensu cui promissum est, nulla sit promissi obligatio, constetque Deum opt. max. quae quisquam contra officium quodvis, temerè, incautè, aut timidè, promiserat, accipere nolle; quumque homines incautos, meticulosos, iracundos, aut superstitiosos insidiosè captare; aut contra communem utilitatem, aut humanitatem, certis hominum ordinibus favere, et in eorum opibus augendis, se procuratorem ostendere vafrum, omnia undique corradentem, Deo minimè sit dignum; hinc satis efficitur votum non obligare, ad ea facienda aut praestanda, quae non piè

are called *necessary:* and when one party in judgment refers the cause to the oath of the other, 'tis called *judicial.* If this be done, not in judgment, but by the private deed of the parties, 'tis called *voluntary.* When an oath is demanded from the person accused in a criminal action, to refute imperfect proof; 'tis called a *purgatory oath,* or *oath of purgation.*[4]

But in such cases where a person's life or character is concerned, as there are very high temptations to perjury; this way of exacting purgatory oaths in tryals is highly improper and unjust. By this means the impious and wicked will always be absolved; and those only convicted who retain such a sense of piety that they won't even for preservation of life or character perjure themselves. A good man surely would rather choose that such persons should escape punishment for a doubtful crime, (of which{, if they have really been guilty,} they will probably soon repent sincerely), than that they should be brought to suffer by their very sense of religion.

IV. A vow is a religious promise made to God about something to be done or performed. In vows we don't conceive a right transferred to men, unless they have been also attended with a contract. The main use of vows is this, that by a serious consideration of a just and holy Deity beholding all our actions, we may further confirm all our pious and virtuous resolutions; and be the more cautious of neglecting our duty, lest <208> we should also involve ourselves in the horrid guilt of perjury.

But as no promise not accepted by the party to whom 'tis made can be obligatory; and as we are sure God will not accept any promises made to him rashly, out of any sudden fear, or other passion, which is contrary to the mans duty; and 'tis most unworthy of the Deity to imagine him as it were insidiously watching to catch advantages of the incautious, timorous, wrathful, or superstitious; or that, contrary to the <humanity or> common interest of all, he has some favourite orders of men for whose advantage he is acting the part of a sharping agent, snatching at all opportunities of gain to them; hence it must appear, that vows can produce no obligation to such

4. See *System* 2.11.4, vol. II, pp. 48–49.

et humaniter, citra votum fieri poterant aut praestari. Multo minus valent vota, quae ex odio, invidia, aut ira injusta aut nimia; aut contra cujuslibet jus perfectum, aut ipsa aequitatis et humanitatis officia, suscipiuntur. Neque igitur nova obligationis *materia,* per vota constitui poterit. <214>

actions or performances as would not antecedently have been pious, humane, and prudent.[5] Much less are vows of any avail which men take on
themselves from hatred, envy, groundless or excessive anger, or contrary to
either the perfect rights of others, or even any obligations of <equity and>
humanity.{*} Vows therefor produce no new matter of obligation.

---

5. Cf. *System* 2.11.5, vol. II, pp. 51–52, where these arguments against the vows in use
in the Catholic Church are developed at length by Hutcheson.

* {Mark vii. 11, 12.} [Compare above, 2 9.11, p. 193 and *System* 2.11.5, vol. II, p. 52.]

CAPUT XII

De Rerum Pretio.

I. Quo facilius res et operae inter homines permutari possint, earum *pretia* sunt aestimanda. Nemo enim res insignis et diuturni usus aut voluptatis, mutare velit iis, quarum exigua est utilitas aut voluptas: neque res quae multo parantur labore, rebus parabilibus.

Rei cujusvis pretium huic nititur fundamento, quod res ipsa ad usum aliquem aut voluptatem ministrandam est apta; absque hoc, nullum erit pretium. Hoc autem posito, rerum pretia majora erunt, prout magis [iis homines indigent] [major est hominum indigentia], ipsaeque res difficiliùs parantur. *Indigentia* erit major, pro ambientium numero, et majore rerum necessitate, aut usu gratiore. Acquirendi *difficultas* ex plurimis oritur causis; nempe ex ipsius materiae penuria; ex acquirendi labore; ex casibus iis qui proventum aliquando faciunt minus uberem; ex ingenii rarioris elegantia, quae in artibus quibusdam exigitur; ex artificum dignitate, eorumque honestiore et lautiore, pro nostratium moribus, vivendi conditione; hujus enim <215> sumptum suppeditare debent artificiorum pretia.

Rerum autem utilissimarum saepe nullum, saepe exiguum est pretium. Ubi enim earum tanta est copia, ut ubique nullo fere labore reperiantur, nullum erit pretium: ubi labore facili et minime artificioso comparantur, exiguum. Pro insigni enim Dei bonitate, quae res sunt utilissimae, et maxime necessariae, illae copiosae sunt et parabiles.

Concerning the Values or Prices of Goods.

I. To maintain any commerce among men in interchanging of goods or services, the values of them must be some way estimated: for no man would give away things of important and lasting use or pleasure in exchange for such as yielded little of either; nor goods which cost much labour in acquiring, for such as can easily be obtained.

The ground of all price must be some *fitness* in the things to yield some use or pleasure in life; without this, they can be of no value. But this being presupposed, the prices of things will be in a compound proportion of the *demand* for them, and the *difficulty* in acquiring them. The *demand* will be in proportion to the numbers who are wanting them, or their <agreeableness or> necessity to life. The *difficulty* may be occasioned many ways; if the quantities of them in the world be small; if any accidents make the quantity less than ordinary; if much toil is required in producing them, or much ingenuity, or a more elegant genius in the artists; if the persons employed about them according to the custom of the country are men in high account, and live in a more splendid manner; for the expence of this must be defrayed by the higher profits of their labours{, and few can be thus maintained}.[1] <210>

Some goods of the highest use, yet have either no price or but a small one. If there's such plenty in nature that they are acquired almost without any labour, they have no price; if they may be acquired by easy common labour, they are of small price. Such is the goodness of God to us, that the most useful and necessary things are generally very plentiful and easily acquired.

---

1. See *System* 2.11.1, pp. 53–54, and Pufendorf, *De officio* 1.14.4.

Rebus quibusdam utilissimis, nullum est pretium, quia sunt sua natura communes; aliis, quia in commercia non aliter veniunt, quam tanquam aliarum rerum appendices, quarum pretia quidem augere possunt, non vero ipsae per se aestimari; aliis denique, quia lege, vel naturali vel positiva, prohibetur earum emptio venditio, cujusmodi sunt res {sacrae, munera item,} aut officia, aut jura sacra; eaque stipendia, quibus alendi sunt viri, his officiis obeundis destinati; aut quae illorum fidei committuntur, ut sint eleemosynarum materies. Horum emptio venditio, ex nota satis historia, *simoniae* nomen est consecuta.

II. Quum vero saepe incidere soleat, ut mihi suppetat quarundam rerum, ultra meos usus, copia, desint autem aliae, quarum est apud alium copia, iste vero nulla re <216> mea indigeat: quumque ego rem mihi non necessariam, pro re alterius mutare velim, mea tamen alterius rem pretio longe superet; nec tamen, sine gravi dispendio, in partes secari possit: ad commercia expediunda, constituendum est pretium aliquod *eminens:* id est, res quaedam, aliarum rerum omnium mensura, ad quam earum pretia exigantur, est constituenda; cujus tanta [sit oportet] [est] indigentia, ut quisque res suas cum ea mutare velit, quoniam ejus ope res quasvis sibi comparare potest. Etenim ejus rei, ob id ipsum quod aliarum sit mensura, existet maxima indigentia.

Huic rei, quae aliarum sit mensura, hae debent esse qualitates; inprimis, ut sit pretiosa, ita ut ejus pondus exiguum, et ad portandum facile, majorem aliarum rerum molem, aestimatione aequet. 2. Ut sit aliquid stabile, neque sua sponte brevi periturum, neque multum usu deterendum. 3. Ut sine dispendio quasvis admittat divisiones. Ea verò omnia, solis metallis rarioribus, auro nempe, et argento conveniunt; quae igitur omnis pretii mensurae, apud gentes cultiores, sunt constituta.

Other things of great use have no price, either because they are naturally destined for community, or cannot come into commerce but as appendages of something else, the price of which may be increased by them, tho' they cannot be separately estimated;{*} or because some law natural or positive prohibits all buying or selling of them. Of this last sort are all religious offices, actions, or privileges; and even the salaries of religious offices, which are either deemed only what is necessary for the support of persons in such offices, or are committed to their trust as funds of liberality and charity toward the indigent. Buying and selling of such things from a well known piece of history is called *simony.*

II. But as it may often happen that I want some goods of which my neighbour has plenty, while I have plenty of other goods beyond my own use, and yet he may have no need of any of my superfluous stores; or that the goods I am stored with beyond my occasions, may be quite superior in value to all I want from my neighbour, but my goods cannot be divided into parcels without great loss: for managing of commerce there <211> must some sort of standard goods [outstanding price] be agreed upon; something settled as the measure of value to all others; which must be so generally demanded, that every one will be willing to take it in exchange for other goods, since by it he may obtain whatever he desires. And indeed as soon as any thing is thus made the standard of all values, the demand for it will become universal{, as it will serve every purpose}.

The goods which are made the standard, should have these properties; first, they should be of high value, that so a small portable quantity of them may be equal in value to a great quantity of other things; again, they should not be perishable, or such as wear much in use; and lastly they should admit of all manner of divisions without loss. Now these three properties are found only in the two more rare mettals, silver and gold; which therefor have been made the standards of commerce in all civilized nations.[2]

---

* {Examples of these sorts are the air, the light of the sun, wholesome air in certain situations, fine prospects.} [These examples are derived from Pufendorf, *De officio* 1.14.3.]
2. See Pufendorf, *De officio* 1.14.8, and *System* 2.2.2, vol. II, p. 56.

III. Ad praecavendam vero omnem in laminis accurate dividendis molestiam, atque ut cautum sit de metallorum puritate, inventi sunt *nummi;*
quorum excudendi <217> potestate, viris fidis commissâ, et de metalli puri
et non adulterati, quod singulis nummis inest, justo pondere cautum erit;
et quaevis, de qua conventum est, summa, sine molestia persolvi poterit.

<III.>[1] Vera metallorum, quin et nummorum, atque rerum ferè om-
nium aestimatio, pro majore eorum copia, imminuitur, pro minore augetur. Res per se ad vitam necessariae, pretia retinent stabiliora; quae tamen,
pro majore aut minore anni cujusque ubertate, non parum immutantur.
Ad stipendia igitur perpetua, aut reditus certos constituendos, quibus homines semper in eadem vitae conditione ali possint, certae earum rerum
mensurae, quae simplici hominum labore non artificioso comparantur,
sunt potius definiendae{; qualia sunt frumentum, quaeque alia simpliciori
victui aut cultui inserviunt}.

{IV.} In civitate cui sunt cum vicinis commercia, nullo imperantium decreto
immutari possunt vera nummorum pretia, earumve aestimatio pro ratione
quam ad merces habent. Non enim nummorum nomina apud nos legitima
curant exteri, metallorum {puriorum} tantummodo spectantes quantitates;
iis igitur mercium pretia respondebunt. Veruntamen, post nummorum
nomina lege constituta, multorumque cum multis res rationesque <218>
contractas, et pactiones, de pecuniae his nominibus definitae summis nu-
merandis; nummorum pretio lege nova aucto, fraudantur creditores; et im-
minuto, fraudantur debitores.

1. (In 1742 edn. there are two arts. III.)

III. {At first they have dealt in them by* weight;} but to prevent the trouble of making accurate divisions of the several barrs or pieces of mettal, and to prevent frauds by mixing them with baser mettals, *coinage* has been introduced. For when the coining of money is committed under proper regulations to trusty hands, there's security given to all for the quantities of pure mettal in each piece, and any broken sums agreed upon can be exactly paid without any trouble.

But the real value of these mettals and of money too{, like that of all other goods,} is lessened as they are more < 212 > plentiful; and increase when they grow scarcer{, tho' the pieces keep the same names}. The common necessaries of life have a more stable natural price, tho' there are some [not] little changes of their values according to the fruitfulness of the several seasons. Were one to settle perpetual salaries to certain offices, < or secure revenues, > which should support men perpetually in the same station in respect to their neighbours, these {salaries} should be constituted in certain quantities of such necessary goods as depend upon the plain inartificial labours of men, such as grain, or other necessaries in a plain simple way of living.

IV. No state which holds any commerce with its neighbours can at pleasure alter the values of their coin in proportion to that of goods. Foreigners pay regard, not to the names we give, but to the real quantities of pure mettal in our coin, and therefor the rates of goods must be proportioned to these quantities. But after a legal settlement of the denominations of coins, and many contracts and obligations settled in these legal sums or denominations, a decree of state raising the nominal values of the pieces will be a fraud upon all the creditors{, and do much gain to the debtors}; and the lowering their nominal values will have just the contrary effects [will be a fraud upon the debtors].³

---

* {This appears both by history, and the Roman word *impendere, expendere,* &c.} [This added sentence and footnote are derived from *System* 2.2.2, p. 56 and note.]

3. Hutcheson is much more detailed on the bad effects of any artificial change to the value of money by government in *System* 2.2.4 and 5, vol. II, pp. 58–62.

Quin etiam eveniet, ut metallorum inter se aestimatio nonnunquam immutetur, si aut alterutrius major solito effodiatur copia; aut si alterutrius, tantum, magnus sit in vitae cultu et ornatu usus; aut si magna ejusdem vis exportetur. Et nisi in eadem ratione immutentur nummorum pretia legitima, exportabuntur nummi, quibus, pro vera metalli aestimatione, justo minus imponitur pretium, et invehentur illi quibus nimium; non sine gravi civitatis incommodo.

Sicubi pro hujusmodi nummis, fiant alii ex metallis vilioribus; quod dignitate deest pondere pensandum [compensandum]; aut secus, cessabunt cum exteris commercia. Quae nummorum vice funguntur chirographa <quaedam>, aut tesserae, eam vim ideo tantum obtinent, quod de veris nummis solvendis idoneam faciant fidem. <219>

The values too of these two mettals may alter their proportions to each other; if an extraordinary quantity of either of them be brought from the mines; or a great consumption made only of one of them in the ornaments of life, or great quantities of it exported. And unless the legal denominations or values of the pieces be changed in like manner, such coin as is valued with <213> us too low in proportion to the natural value of the mettal, will be exported; and what is valued with us too high will remain, or be imported, to the great detriment of the country.

Wheresoever a coinage is made in baser mettals, the quantities in each piece must be made so much the greater; otherways the trade with foreigners must be lost. When notes or tickets pass for money, their value depends on this, that they give good security for the payment of certain sums of gold or silver.

De variis Contractuum Generibus Post Pretia Rerum constituta.

I. Dividuntur contractus in *beneficos* et *onerosos*. Benefici, ubi intelligitur, contrahentium alteri commodum aliquod gratis afferri: onerosi, ubi {utriusque pariter spectatur utilitas, atque} hoc agere profitentur paciscentes, ut res vel operae pretio aequales mutuo transferantur.

Beneficorum tria sunt genera decantata, *mandatum, commodatum,* et *depositum;* quibus accenseri potest *mutuum gratuitum.*

Mandatum est "contractus ubi quis alterius negotia sibi commissa, gratis obeunda suscipit." In quo si rei expediundae ratio fuerit praescripta, eam observare tenetur *mandatarius;* aut suo periculo ab [eadem discessum erit] [ea recesserit]. Si vero negotium ipsius prudentiae permissum fuit; non perfectae obligationi aut officio defuisse censebitur, si eam adhibuit diligentiam, quam istiusmodi negotiis, et suis, adhibere solent viri probi et diligentes. Neque ad damnum culpâ quavis levissima datum, praestandum tenebitur; nisi vel summam pollicitus fuerat diligentiam; eamve plane exigat negotii natura; <220> aut ultro se obtruserat, ubi aptiorum aderat copia.

De omni verò contractu benefico tenendum, eum qui in alterum contulit beneficium, non graviorem subire obligationem, quam vel disertè suscepit, vel suscipiendam plane monuit ipsa res: Eum autem in quem confertur beneficium, pro gratiae referendae officio, ad summam adstringi

---

* {There are no precise technical words in English to answer the three Latin words *mandatum, commodatum* and *depositum.* And therefor the formal definitions are omitted.}

Of the Several Sorts of Contracts.

I. Contracts are divided into the *beneficent* and *onerous:* in the former some advantage is gratuitously designed for one of the parties; in the later the interest of both is equally regarded, and the parties profess to transfer mutually things [good or labours] of equal value [price].

There are three species of beneficent contracts,{*} <*mandate* or> *commission* undertaken gratuitously, <*commodatum* or> gratuitous *loan for use,* and <*deposit* or> gratuitous *custody* of the goods of others <among which we may count *mutuum gratuitum*>.

<In mandate, that is> "in undertaking gratuitously to manage the business of others by their commission," if they have prescribed a particular manner of executing it, we are obliged to follow their orders; or if we depart from them we are liable to compensate what damage thence arises. Where the matter is left to our prudence; we are deemed bound to use such care as a wise man uses in like matters of his own, nor are we liable for every accident which might possibly have been prevented by the utmost care; unless we have expressly undertaken for the utmost diligence, or the high nature of the business plainly required it; or we have obtruded ourselves officiously, when others more capable might have been obtained.[1] <215>

We must observe this about all beneficent contracts, that he who intends a favour to others, is not deemed to undertake an higher obligation than he expressly consents to, or than the nature of the business commonly requires: but the person on whom the favour is conferred, out of gratitude should deem himself more strictly bound, and make good all losses occa-

---

1. On the three gratuitous contracts see Pufendorf, *De officio* 1.15.5–7 and *System* 2.13.[1]–3, vol. II, pp. 64–68.

diligentiam, atque ad omne damnum culpa datum praestandum; ne quem suae beneficientiae poeniteat.

II. *Commodatum* est "contractus quo quis rei suae usum alteri gratis concedit." Tenetur *Commodatarius.* 1. Ad summam diligentiam, et damnum vel levissimâ culpa datum praestandum. 2. Ad omnem etiam casum, cui res commodata apud dominum non fuisset obnoxia, praestandum; nisi commodator humaniter de jure suo cesserit. 3. Neque alium recte capit ejusdem usum quam qui est concessus. 4. Exacto [Elapso] deinde tempore, reddenda est res salva, neque magis detrita, quam usu concesso voluisse censendus est commodator. 5. Humanitas etiam juberet, ante tempus praestitutum [elapsum] rem domino magis ea indigenti reddere, aut damnum ex eo quod non reddatur ortum praestare.

Tenetur contra *commodator,* sumptus <221> omnes in rem suam factos commodatario praestare, praeter eos qui ad rei habilis usum sunt plerumque necessarii; aut saltem persolvere quantum res sua sibi facta est utilior, et ipse ideo locupletior. A commodato distinguitur *mutuum gratuitum,* quod hoc in rebus constituatur *fungibilibus,* quae non in *specie* sed in *genere* redduntur: i. e. in aequalibus mensuris, ponderibus, aut quantitatibus.

III. *Depositum,* quod est mandati genus, est "contractus, quo quis rem alienam, a domino commissam, gratis custodiendam suscipit." *Depositarius* ad mediam viri prudentis diligentiam tenetur, et ad damnum lata culpa datum, praestandum. 2. Neque re deposita, sine domini consensu, uti licet. 3. Eam domino reposcenti debet reddere, nisi ad facinus aliquod patrandum

sioned by any {the lightest} fault of his; that none may have occasion to repent of their intended favours to him.

II. < *Commodatum* or gratuitous *loan for use* is a contract by which one gratuitously allows another the use of any of his goods. It> {The gratuitous loan for use where the very same goods are to be restored} binds the borrower (1) to the highest care and to make good all losses occasioned by any negligence of his: (2) nay also to make good such accidents as the goods had escaped had they remained with the lender, except he generously remit his claim: nor (3) can the borrower take any other use than the lender granted: and (4) he ought to restore them in good order at the time agreed, no further impaired than they must be by the use allowed. (5) Nay humanity would oblige to restore them sooner if the owner needs them; or {if we need them more and keep them,} to make good the loss he sustains by wanting them.

The gratuitous lender is to refund any expences made upon the goods lent, except such as are ordinarily requisite in the use of them; or at least to refund the value of any improvements made upon them as far as they are bettered for his purposes, and so he is inriched. The civilians distinguish between this contract and < *mutuum gratuitum* or> a *loan for consumption,* in which the same individual goods are not to be restored, but equal quantities, weights or measures <of goods of the same kind, called *res fungibiles*>.[2] <216>

III. <Deposit, which is a sort of mandate, is "a contract, by which one undertakes gratuitously to keep the goods of another, by his commission." It> {Depositing of goods for gratuitous custody,} obliges the keeper to such diligence as a wise man uses in keeping like goods of his own, and to make good any losses by any gross negligence of his. He ought to make no use of them without the owner's consent, and restore them when demanded; except it be for such purposes [crimes] wherein he might have a right by

2. Cf. *System* 2.13.2, vol. II, p. 65, footnotes.

reposcat, quod depositarius jure suo per vim prohibere potest. 4. Depositarius ab omni sumptu et impensis in re custodienda prudenter erogatis, immunis est servandus.

In his contractibus, ut etiam in tutela et negotiis gestis, ad illud consequendum quod primo et praecipue spectabatur, datae erant *actiones directae;* ut contra mandatarium, ad res rationesque reddendas; contra commodatarium et depositarium, ad res reddendas. His autem dabantur *actiones contrariae,* <222> ut damna sibi et sumptus praestentur.

IV. In contractibus onerosis, profitentur contrahentes, se res *corporales,* aut *incorporales* quae dicuntur, sive jura, mutuo transferre aestimatione aequales. Atque idcirco inter bonos nihil simulandum aut dissimulandum: omnes mercium aut rerum *qualitates aestimabiles,* earumve defectus et vitia sunt declaranda: et ubi temere ab aequalitate recessum est, minus habenti quod deest, viri prudentis arbitrio supplendum; idque jure perfecto iste exigere potest. Quamvis, ne fatigentur praetores, nisi ob injurias graviores non dantur in foro actiones.

A contractibus onerosis, eo secernitur *donatio reciproca,* quod in hac rerum datarum non spectetur aequalitas.

Ex dictis de pretio constat, in mercium pretiis aestimandis, habendam esse rationem, non solum pecuniae in iis emendis, apportandis, custodiendis, erogatae, atque usurae cessantis; verum et laboris ab ipso mercatore impensi; cujus pretium pro hominum istiusmodi conditione honestiore est aestimandum, et mercibus imponendum. Hoc vero laboris pretium et curae, est vulgaris et quotidiani mercatorum lucri fundamentum. Quumque insuper merces invectae aut exportatae variis sint periculis obnoxiae,

force to resist the owner. And he justly insists to be indemnifyed as to all expences wisely employed for preservation of the goods.{*}

< In these contracts, as also in guardianship and in managing business, the primary objective is obtained by distinguishing between *actiones directae*, such as legal actions against the person undertaking a commission to get compensation for damages arising from his undertaking, or against the lender or the custodian for restoration of goods loaned or kept; and *actiones contrariae* for compensation for damages and expenses borne by mandatarius, lenders or keepers. >

IV. In the *honorous contracts*, or these for valuable consideration, the parties profess or undertake to transfer mutually goods < corporeal or uncorporeal things, as civilians say> or rights of equal value. And therefor honest men should conceal nothing, or give no false representations about the qualities estimable in such goods, or their defects: and when they inadvertently have departed from equality, according to the judgment of a wise arbiter, he who had less value than he gave, should have something further paid him till the contract be brought to equality; and this he has a perfect right to demand; tho' no courts of justice could have time to give redress to every little iniquity in such matters.

Mutual donation is not to be reckoned among onerous contracts, as in it there is no regard had to equality between the things mutually given.

From what we said about the grounds of price, 'tis plain that in estimating the values of goods {in any <217> place}, we are not only to compute the disbursment made in buying, importing, and keeping them safe, with the interest of money thus employed; but also the pains and care of the merchant; the value of which is to be estimated according to the reputable condition in which such men live, and to be added to the other charges upon the goods. This price of the merchant's labour <and care> is the foundation of the ordinary profit of merchants. But as goods exported or imported are subject to many accidents, by which they may even perish

* {The Translator omits the next paragraph in the original, explaining the *actiones directae et contrariae* of the civilians.} [This paragraph has been translated. "Actio directa" and "actio contraria" are names still in use for actions in the civil law.]

<223> ad ea praestanda, mercium servatarum pretium, pro periculorum ratione, non injuriâ augetur. Quumque etiam damnis obnoxii sint mercatores, ex eo quod, mercium, quarum copiam invexerant, pretium, insperata apud alios copia imminuatur; ad haec etiam praestanda, lucrum justum sibi captant ex mercibus copiosius convectis, quum insperatâ earundem apud alios penuria pretium augetur.

V. Contractuum onerosorum haec sunt genera. 1. *Permutatio,* quum res re mutatur. [1]2. *Emptio venditio,* quum "res pecunia mutatur." Hujus forma simplicissima est cum merces traduntur, pecuniâ soluta. Si vero de mercibus ad certum diem tradendis conveniat, pretiò vel soluto, vel de eo solvendo cautione data, quae venditori idonea videtur; ante diem, merces venditoris periculo manent; post diem <elapsum>, si nulla tradendi fuerat in ipso mora, in depositarii loco erit venditor; ut et ab initio fuisset si ab initio merces obtulisset paratas.

Emptioni venditioni plura adjici solent pacta aut leges; *addictio* scil. *in diem,* ubi pretii in diem differtur solutio; ante quem licet aut emptori, aut venditori, meliorem accipere conditionem: quae si non offeratur, [obligabit] [validus erit] contractus. Adjicitur etiam *lex commissoria,* ut si pretium ante statum <224> diem solutum non fuerit, pactum sit irritum. Lex item *retractûs,* sive redemptionis, satis nota. Jus denique *protimesios,* ut si emptor rem rursum vendere voluerit, prior dominus pretium aequale soluturus, caeteris emptoribus praeferatur. Quae res *auctione,* aut *sub hasta* venduntur, plurimô licitanti cedunt.

---

1. In 1742 edn. this is a new paragraph.

---

3. In *System* the paragraph parallel to this one is not in chapter 13, on contracts, but at the end of Chapter 12 on Value, vol. II, pp. 63–64.

4. Also on the onorous contracts Hutcheson follows Pufendorf, *De officio* 1.15.9–15 (but omits § 12 on partnership). The same order and the same items are in *System* 2.13.4–10, vol. II, pp. 68–77.

altogether; this is a natural reason for advancing the price of such goods as are safe. And as merchants are liable to losses when the prices of such goods, as they are well stored with, by any unexpected plenty happen to fall; to make good such casual losses they have a right to take a larger profit, when the goods they are well stocked with happen by any accidental scarcity of them to rise in their prices.[3]

V. These are the principal onerous contracts.[4] 1. *Barter* or exchanging goods for goods. 2. *Buying* and *selling* <or exchanging goods for money>; the simplest form of which is at once paying the money and receiving the goods. If 'tis agreed that the goods are to be delivered on some future day, the price being previously paid, or such security given for it as the seller accepts; before the day fixed the seller must run the hazard of what accidents befal the goods; but after the day, if the seller was ready then to deliver them, he is only in the case [position][5] of one with whom they were deposited; as he would have been from the first if he was then ready to deliver them.{*}

<Many agreements and conditions may be added to buying and selling; such as *addictio in diem* or a provisional sale, in which payment is delayed until some future day; before the fixed day the buyer or the seller has the right to accept any better offer; if there is none, they are bound by the contract. Another is *lex commissoria* or the forfeiture clause, by which, if the price is not paid before the fixed day, the contract is void. Likewise lex item retractus or agreement about return[6] is well known. Finally jus *protimesios,* by which if the buyer wishes to re-sell the good, the former owner has the precedence over other buyers at equal prices. Goods sold *sub hasta* or in auction are given to the best bidder among many>. <218>

5. That is, the seller runs the same hazard as a keeper, as explained in paragraph iii above.

* {The Translator here omits a paragraph explaining some terms of the Roman law not necessary to an English reader. Such as *addictio in diem, lex commissoria, lex retractus, protimesios,* &c.}

6. On these additional agreements see Pufendorf, *De officio* 1.15.9 and Hutcheson, *System* 2, 13.5, vol. II, p. 70 and footnotes.

Venduntur aliquando non res certae, sed earum spes incertae. Quibus contractibus non deerit aequalitas, in omni contractu oneroso conservanda, si verum rei ipsius <consequendae> pretium, ea ratione spei pretium superet, quâ metus pretii frustra perituri, spem superat rei consequendae.

VI. *Locatio conductio* est "contractus, in quo pro certa mercede, rei nostrae usus aut opera alteri addicitur." Locator rem usui idoneam praestare tenetur et conservare: conductor, ea uti, ut rebus similibus et suis solent viri probi; et quicquid sua culpa lata periit praestare. Ubi nullâ conductoris culpa, res locata periit; non ulterius solvenda erit merces. Aut si casu imminuatur usus, eadem ratione imminuenda est merces. Ubi rei proventus est incertus; ut uberior conductoris lucro, ita malignior istius damno cedit: exceptis casibus rarioribus et calamitosis, quorum aleam conductorem <225> suscepisse non [putandum] [est aestimandus]; quales sunt bella, diluvia, pestilentiae.

Qui opus faciundum conduxit, traditâ sibi materia aliena; ad eam diligentiam tenetur, quam viri probi adhibere solent; et ad damnum lata culpa datum praestandum. Qui ad certum aliquod opus brevi peragendum, conductus est; mercedem exigere nequit, si quo casu ab opere peragendo impediatur. Qui vero continuam alicujus operam conduxit, videtur breviorum morborum operas impedientium, quibus etiam robustiores obnoxii sunt, pericula subire; ita ut nihil ea de causa pensioni detrahere possit.

---

7. Cf. Pufendorf, *De officio, ibidem* and *De iure nat.* 5.5.6. This is the case when fish or crops are purchased in advance. The whole section 5 runs parallel to Pufendorf, *De officio* 1.15.9. See also *System* 2.13.4, vol. II, pp. 68–70.

Sometimes men purchase no certain goods but an hazard, or some advantage upon a contingency [but an expectation of goods uncertain]. In such contracts <the necessary> equality may be preserved if the price is abated below the real value of the advantage in a just proportion to the hazard of our gaining no advantage at all.[7]

VI. In *location,* or setting to hire, for a certain price we allow one the use of our goods, or our labour. The setter should make the goods fit for use, and uphold them so; and the hirer is bound to use them as discreet men use like goods of their own, and to make good any losses occasioned by any gross negligence of his. If the goods perish without any fault of his, he is no longer liable for the price of the hire than he had the use of them: or if without his fault they become less fit for use, he may insist on an abatement of the price or rent. But as in lands all the profits of a plentiful year fall to the tenant, so he must bear the casual losses of a less fortunate one. Indeed the rarer cases of extraordinary calamities, such as of wars, inundations, pestilence, seem to be just exceptions; as the tenant cannot be presumed to have subjected himself to rents in such cases.{*} {And in most of contracts the agreements of parties alter the obligations.}

<One who has contracted for a piece of work and received another's material, is bound to such diligence as a wise man uses in keeping like goods of his own, and to make good any losses by any gross negligence of his.> One who is hired for a certain piece of work, if he is hindered from it by any accident, has no claim for <219> the hire. But when one hires a person by the year, or for a longer time, the hirer seems bound to bear the loss occasioned by any such short fits of sickness as the most firm constitutions are subject to, nor can he on that account make any deduction from the price agreed upon.

---

* {A part also of the following section is omitted for the same reason, about the *locatio operis* and *locatio operae.*} [The part omitted by the translator, in angle brackets, is the case of locatio operis faciendi "when materials are given out to be manufactured or wrought by an artist at certain price" (*System* 2.13.5, vol. II, p. 70 and footnote), further evidence that the translator had a copy of Hutcheson's *System*.]

VII. Mutuum est "contractus, ubi datur alicui res *fungibilis,* ea lege, ut tempore convento reddendae sint aequales rerum similium quantitates." Si non sit gratuitum, danda etiam est usura. Res maxime *fungibiles* sunt nummi.

Quamvis autem nummi non sunt per se frugiferi, neque aliae fere res fungibiles; nummis tamen emi possunt res frugiferae, eorumque ope in commerciis lucrum potest esse multo uberius: foenoris igitur aliquid, pro lucri hujus ratione, ob pecuniam mutuo datam, exigere minime est iniquum. Neque in civitatibus ubi vigent commercia, sine gravi incommodo prohiberi possunt istiusmodi <226> pacta; licet in agricolarum [rusticorum] republica populari, {qualis Hebraeorum fuit,} non sint necessaria.

Foenoris aequi mensura major erit aut minor, prout minor est aut major nummorum qui in commerciis exercendis locantur copia. Quum major est, {atque ideo apud nostros carius emuntur merces exportandae,} minus ex data quavis summa lucrum orietur; minus igitur debet esse foenus: ubi minor est pecuniae copia, {viliùsque ideo emuntur merces exportandae;} ex data quavis summa majus orietur lucrum; majus igitur persolvi poterit foenus. Horum omnium, in legibus civilibus foenus definientibus, ratio habenda; neque aliter vim poterunt obtinere.

In *societatis* contractu, jura et obligationes ex sociorum conventione et arithmeticorum regulis notissimis innotescunt.

VIII. Diximus {jam antea, non omnes} contractus quibus aleae aliquid inest, <non esse omnes> inaequalitatis nomine damnandos. Immo istiusmodi quidam sunt omnino probandi, et hominum societati utilissimi; praecipue qui de naufragii, latrocinii, aut incendii periculis avertendis aut praestandis fiunt. Per hos enim strenuis plurimis et gnavis salva conservatur sors, quae aliter periisset. Continent hi contractus publici, societatis magnae

VII. In *loans for consumption,*{*} we don't expect the same individual goods, but equal quantities by weight or measure.[8] If the loan is not designed as a favour, there's a right to demand *interest.* <Money is the most fungible thing.> {Nor is it necessary to make interest lawful that the goods lent be naturally fruitful: for} tho' money {for instance} yields no natural increase; yet as by it one may purchase such goods as yield increase; nay by employing it in trade {or manufactures} may make a much higher gain; 'tis but natural [not unjust at all] that for such valuable advantages accruing to us by the loan, we should give the owner of the money some price or recompence proportioned to them. The prohibition of all loans for interest would be destructive to any trading nation, tho' in a democracy of farmers, such as that of the Hebrews was, it might have been a very proper prohibition.

The just interest of money is to be determined according to the quantity of wealth employed in trade. Where there's a small quantity of money in a nation, and consequently all goods very cheap, a great profit is made by any small sums employed in trade with foreigners. And therefor a great interest may well be paid. But where much money is employed in trade, a smaller profit is made on each sum thus employed, as <220> the prime cost of goods is high; and therefor a smaller interest can be afforded for it. If civil laws settling interest don't regard these natural causes, they will not have their effect.

The <rights and> obligations in the contracts of *partnership* are abundantly known by <the agreements of the partners and> the rules of arithmeticians.

VIII. We said above that contracts about hazards may maintain the just equality: and some of them are of great use in society, these particularly which ensure against shipwreck, robbery, or fire: as by their means many active industrious hands have their stocks preserved to them, which otherways had perished. These contracts seem of the same effect with a hu-

---

* {*Mutuum.*}

8. Literally: Mutuum or loan for consumption is "a contract by which <res fungibilis>, a fungible thing, is given to another on the condition that at a time agreed upon equal quantities of a good of the same kind are returned" Cf. *System* 2.13.2, vol. II, pp. 65–66 and footnote.

<227> de damnis communicandis initae, vim humanam et salutarem: ex mercedibus enim, ab iis solutis quorum salvae sunt merces, praestantur minus foelicium damna.

Neque reprehendendum, si plures, rem collatâ pecunia, animi causa emptam, sortium arbitrio permittant: si modo nemo tantam his periculis objecerit facultatum suarum partem, ut ejus jacturâ, sibi aut suis, vitae praesidia aut ornamenta praeripiantur.

Idem de sponsionibus, et variis ludorum generibus statuendum. Neque sunt haec ideo vituperanda quod aleam contineant; neque sunt omnia iniqua. At primo, nihil viro bono et prudente est indignius, quam, nulla premente necessitate, res sibi et suis necessarias aut utiles, incertae subjicere aleae; aut lucrum ex aliorum temeritate, immeritò sibi captare. Improbandi sunt igitur istiusmodi contractus, nisi in rebus versentur levioribus, quas locupletioribus animi causa projicere licet. Quin etiam, nihil a viro bono alienius quam se totum rebus ludicris dare, iisve multum temporis impendere; aut ita nugis se assuescere, ut ad seria minus habilis minusve propensus [proclivis] reddatur.

Quod attinet ad istiusmodi contractus celebriores quibus alea inest, quibusque plures res suas implicare solent; quum in communem <228> utilitatem nihil conferant, paucos tantum temerè ex plurium dispendiis locupletantes; quumque ad eos ineundos proclives admodum sint homines, pro opinione vana quam de sua foelicitate fovere solent; legibus civilibus omnino sunt coercendi: ne opes, quae in opificiis aut mercatura occupatae, rei publicae prodessent, inutiliter ad haec parum honesta, et fraudibus innumeris obnoxia, convertantur; aut insociabilis, stolida, et ignava foveatur avaritia.

mane and salutary partnership among multitudes to share among them any losses may happen; since 'tis by the premiums paid by those whose goods are safe that the ensurers are enabled to make good the losses of the unfortunate.

Nor is there any thing blameable in this that a large number for diversion contribute to purchase any piece of goods, and then cast lots who shall have it: provided none of them expose to such hazards so large a portion of their goods that the loss of it would occasion any distress to themselves or families.

The same may be said of wagering, and of various games in which there's hazard; which are not always blameable on the account of the hazard, or of any inequality. But then there is nothing more unworthy of a good man than, without necessity, to expose to uncertain hazard such a share of his goods, as the loss of it would distress his family; or to be catching at gain from the foolish rashness of others, so as to distress them. <221> All such contracts therefor are to be condemned, unless they are about such trifles as men of wealth can afford to throw away upon their amusements. And besides, 'tis highly unbecoming a good man to give himself up entirely to diversions, or waste much time upon them; or so to enure himself to amusements, as {to contract habits of indolence and trifling,} making him less fit or inclined for serious business.[9]

As to these more publick projects of lottery in which great multitudes may be concerned; as they bring in no new wealth to a state, and only enrich some few of the citizens by the losses of others; and as men thro' some vain opinions of their own good luck are generally very prone to them; they should be every where under the restraint of laws; lest that wealth, which were it employed in manufactures or commerce would be adding new strength to the state, should be turned into this useless and dishonourable channel, exposed too to innumerable frauds, and an insociable, foolish, and slothful avarice be encouraged among the citizens.

---

9. Hutcheson seems to share the opposition of Carmichael to gambling and public lotteries (*Notes on Puf.,* p. 110, where Carmichael quotes Arnauld and Nicole in support).

IX. Ad contractus firmandos accedunt *fidejussiones* et *pignora.* Fidejussor is est qui subsidiariam subit obligationem debiti praestandi, si ipse debitor solvere detrectaverit, aut non sit solvendo. Quumque creditor illi magis quam ipsi debitori saepe fidat; non minus sancta illius est obligatio. Neque ullae subterfugiendi artes fidejussori sunt licitae, quae non fuissent, si sua ipsius causa debitum contraxisset: neque recte quidem solutionem differt, nisi fraudulenta existat, inter creditorem et debitorem, contra se collusio.

Potest fidejussor vel pignore dato, vel jurejurando, firmius adstringi quam ipse debitor: ast prout est fidejussor, neque re, neque loco, tempore, aut causa, plus debere potest. *Ordinis* beneficium recte exigit fidejussor, <229> ut prius nempe [debitor excutiatur, quam ipse appelletur] [cum ipso debitore lis discutiatur]; et beneficium *divisionis,* ubi plures fuere fidejussores; nisi hisce renunciaverit.

Qui in causa *criminali* subsidiariam subeunt obligationem, *vades* dicuntur. Ad poenas vero corporales subeundas vix recte admittuntur, nisi sceleris fuerant fautores. Jure tamen ad pecuniam, multae nomine, praestandam teneri possunt.

De pignore jam diximus{*} quaedam, et de hypotheca: ubi oppignorata est res fructuosa, a mercede aut sorte deducendi sunt fructus; neque justa est in pignoribus *lex commissoria,* nisi quod ex pignoris distracti pretio superest debito soluto, debitori reddatur. Custodiendum est pignus ea diligentia media, qua res suas custodit bonus paterfamilias; quum utriusque partis hac in re spectetur utilitas. A pignore differt *hypotheca,* quod haec, re non tradita, sed debito solvendo subjectâ, constituatur. In utroque est jus reale, cui cedunt et priora jura personalia. <230>

---

* {Cap. VII.4. hujus libri.}

IX. In confirmation of contracts men often give bail or sureties, and pledges. The bail or surety is bound to make good what is due, in case the principal fails. And as the creditor frequently trusts more to the surety than to the principal, his obligation is equally sacred: nor may he use any evasive arts more than if the debt were wholly his own: nor can he justly even delay the payment; unless he finds a fraudulent collusion between the creditor and the principal to distress him.

The obligation of the surety may be stricter than <222> that of the principal, if he has given either a pledge or an oath for performance; but as he is surety he cannot be bound in a different sum or different goods, or payable at a different time or place, or upon a different foundation. He may justly insist that a suit be first commenced and judgment given against the principal; and where more than one are sureties, each one may insist that the loss be divided either equally among them{, or in the proportion in which they bound themselves} <unless he renounced these benefits>.

Sureties were sometimes given in criminal actions <and called *vades*>. They may be justly liable to pay the fines. But it would be inhuman to allow them to be subjected to any corporal punishments for the crimes of others <unless they favoured crime>.

We formerly touched at the subject of pledges and mortgages.<*> If the things pledged yield increase, this is to be deducted annually from the interest or principal of the debt. The *clause of forfeiture* at the day fixed has no iniquity in it, provided any surplus of value in the pledge be restored to the debtor after the debt is thus discharged. The pledgee is bound to keep the pledge with such diligence as a discreet man keeps like goods of his own, and not answerable for any thing further; as this contract equally regards the utility of both parties.[10] <A *hypotheca* or mortgage differs from a pledge as the good is not delivered to another but simply subject to the payment of debt>. Pledges and mortgages constitute real rights not to be defeated by any prior personal rights.

---

* <Chapter VII.4 of this book.>
10. See above 2.7.4 p. 169 and footnote and Pufendorf, *De officio* 1.15.15.

De Obligationibus quasi ex Contractu ortis.

I. Has praeter obligationes et jura, sunt et alia, quae nascuntur ex facto aliquo licito ejus adversus quem valent. De iis quae ex facto illicito oriuntur, in capite sequente agendum. Ex factis licitis [jura orta fundantur] [ortum jus omne, fundatur] vel in ipso dominii jure, vel in manifesta societatis amicae conservandae ratione. Quae hujusmodi juri respondent obligationes, ne actionum multiplicarentur formulae, eas ex contractu ortas fingunt jureconsulti. Sunt vero a pactis *tacitis* diversi, quod in tacitis ex facto quodam consensus vere indicari intelligitur; in his vero, propter manifestam rei aequitatem fingitur. In illis, denuntiatione [praemonitione] contraria, praecaveri [praepediri] potest quae ex solo consensu {aliàs} oriretur obligatio: in his neutiquam; quippe in aliâ fundata causâ aequissima{, neque ab illius qui obligatur consensu pendens}.

Obligationum quae *quasi ex contractu* oriuntur, duo sunt genera; alterum earum quae hinc oriuntur, quod quispiam rebus alienis, aut alteri quocunque modo obligatis, <231> sine contractu se immiscuerit: alterum, quum quisquam aliquod sibi commodum, alteri nec donanti nec consentienti damnosum aut sumptuosum, derivaverit. Ad priorem classem refertur ejus obligatio qui sine vi aut dolo rem possidet alienam, ut eam cum fructibus reddat. {Huc etiam} refertur et ejus qui *negotium utile gesserat,* <; qui scil.> res <tractavit> alterius, vel absentis et nescii, vel ob rationis et prudentiae idoneae defectum, consentire non valentis, {tractando}: qui

CHAPTER XIV

<223>

*Obligations Resembling those from Contracts.

I. Beside these obligations and rights already mentioned, there are others which arise from some lawful action of the person bound: of such as arise from unlawful actions we treat in the next chapter. These rights arising from lawful actions, arise either from the nature [right] of property, or from some manifest interest of society, and common social laws. The obligations answering to them the civilians feigned to arise from contracts, that the forms of the actions might be the same. They are quite different from those of *tacit conventions,* as in tacit conventions we truly conclude consent from some action; but in those 'tis plainly feigned, {tho' we know there was no consent,} as the matter itself is equitable.[1] The obligation by a tacit convention is quite prevented by a previous contrary declaration of the party: but not so in these we now speak of; as they have another just foundation, independent of the consent of the person obliged.

Of these there are two classes, one arising from this, that a person intermeddles without any contract with the goods of others, or such upon which others have a just claim: the other, from a person's taking to himself and holding some valuable advantage at the expence and loss of others, who consented not to sustain <224> such loss gratuitously. In the former class is included the obligation of such as possess the goods they know belong to others, to restore the goods with their profits; as also his obligation† who without commission manages any business for an absent <and unaware> person, or for a minor [for someone who, wanting the fit reason and prudence, can not consent]. All these are bound to account, and to

---

* *Obligationes quasi ex contractu.* [This chapter is entirely modeled on Carmichael's *Supplement* IV on "quasi contracts." See below the last note but one of this chapter.]

1. See Carmichael, *Notes on Puf.* II.2.2, p. 113.

† *Negotii utilis gestor.*

{scil}: tenetur ad rationes et res ipsas cum emolumentis reddendas. Quod spectatur in negotiorum gestorum et tutelae *actionibus directis.*

Ad hanc etiam refertur classem haeredis testamento instituti obligatio, defuncti creditores et legatarios respiciens; quae nempe oritur ex haereditatis aditione [ereditate adita]. Omnia enim defuncti bona, aeri alieno dissolvendo, et omni, quod quisquam jure suo pleno postulare potest, praestando subjiciuntur. Qui haereditatem adit, unicam unde ea praestari possunt materiam, ea omnia, quousque [sufficiunt] [pertinere possunt] bona haereditaria, deductis impensis in iis tractandis, praestare tenetur. Justum autem est *inventarii* beneficium{; ne ultra haereditatem haeres obligetur}. Neque, ad haec jura explicanda, opus est haeredem <232> fingere eandem esse cum defuncto personam.

II. Quod ad alteram attinet classem, ubi [scil: quis aliquam utilitatem,] [quicquam sibi commodum] alteri nec donanti, nec gratis damnum perferre volenti damnosam, sibi [damnosum, aliquis] adscivit: ad eam referuntur ejus obligationes, cujus absentis et inscii, aut, ob rationis et prudentiae necessariae defectum, consentire non valentis, *negotia* sunt *utiliter gesta,* aut res administratae; ut eum qui negotia gesserat, aut tutorem, indemnem praestet, et labores omnes utiles compenset, eorumque contractus, bona fide, ipsius nomine initos, confirmet. Huc spectant negotiorum gestorum, et tutelae *actiones contrariae.* Impensarum etiam, quae in pupillis alendis, educandis, aut arte quavis imbuendis, prudenter factae sunt, eadem est ratio.

Quae quidem in liberis suis alendis erogarunt parentes non egeni, ex communi parentum affectione [affectu], donandi animo erogasse censentur, ubi contrariae voluntatis nulla fuit significatio. Quin et tenentur parentes, pro sua conditione, liberis necessaria praebere vitae praesidia, et ornamenta; et quod ex bonis superest iis potissimum relinquere. Premente

restore the goods with their increase and profits <and that is considered in actiones directae concerning the management of others' business and of guardianship>.[2]

The like is the obligation of the heir or executor, toward the creditors or legatees of the deceased; and it arises from his entering heir{, or undertaking the execution of the will}. For 'tis plain, all the effects of the deceased are naturally chargeable with his debts, and with whatever others have a perfect claim to. He therefor who takes possession of the effects, the only fund whence these debts are to be paid, is bound to pay them, as far as the effects go, deducting for himself the necessary expences of management. The heirs or executors however may always claim the benefit of an *inventary*, that they may not be bound further than they find effects of the deceased. Nor need we feign {any contracts} to explain the just grounds of these obligations, {nor} that the heir {or executor} is the same person with the deceased.[3]

II. As to the second class; where a man is bound by deriving to himself some advantage at the expence of others, who did not consent that it should be gratuitous: under this is included the obligation of those on the other hand whose business was managed by others without commission, and that of minors [or that of those who, wanting the fit reason and prudence, were not able to consent] toward their guardians, to indemnify them, and compensate their <225> labours in all useful services, and to ratify any contracts prudently made for their behoof; and refund any prudent expences in their education <and instruction. That is considered in *actiones contrariae* of managing other's business and of guardianship>.[4]

What parents <who are not in straitened circumstances> expend in educating their own children, we conclude from the tender parental affection, that 'tis intended as a donation, when the parent has not declared the contrary. Nay parents are naturally bound to support and educate their children suitably to their condition, and to convey to them at death what remains

2. See *Notes on Puf.* 11.2.3–4, p. 114.
3. *Ibidem,* 11.2.5.
4. *Ibidem,* 11.2.6, pp. 114–15.

vero egestate, aut si cui forte ex liberis aliunde suppetant facultates, non iniquum foret parentem liberos <233> ad calculos vocare, ut sibi persolvantur quae erogaverit; sive ad ipsum in senectute alendum, sive ut caeteros liberos eo melius alere possit.

{III.} Si quis verò alienum aluerit inopem, id gratis factum fuisse non temerè est judicandum: immo potius eo jus esse constitutum in alumnum, ut omnia in ejus utilitatem prudenter erogata, ipsius laboribus compensentur; haud vero ea quae ad familiae altoris [herilis] ornatum pertinebant. Quumque insuper, {quae} in prima alumnorum aetate [erogata sunt omnino] [, quaedam sint erogata, quae] perirent, si immaturi obirent alumni; amplius aliquid exigere poterunt altores, pro hujus periculi ratione: quo jure ipsis concesso, haec humanitatis officia alacrius suscipient. Decrescit vero post primos alumni cujusque annos hoc periculum, atque primas tantum impensas graviore foenore onerare potest. Est igitur alumnus inops in causa debitoris, nullo suo crimine obaerati, a quo exigi saepe possunt operae, donec per eas dissolvatur aes alienum; qui tamen omnia alia retinet hominum jura: et simul ac vel laboribus suis, (quorum sibi utilissimos et maxime quaestuosos, ad viri probi arbitrium, ipsi est eli gendi jus,) vel amicorum liberalitate, debitum fuerit solutum, tollitur omne altoris jus. Ratione vero subducta pateret, neminem <234> esse alumnum, sit {modo} ei mens sana et corpus sanum, qui [quin] ante annum trigesimum, laboribus suis, omnia quae altori debuit, praestare {non} posset: neque ex hac causa recte oriri posse servitutem haereditariam, quamvis altori, pro periculi ratione, in

of their goods. But if a parent is in great straits, or if any child has some other way obtained a plentiful fortune, a parent in these cases may justly charge a child with the whole expence of its support and education, and exact it for his own maintainance in old age, or to support his other children.

III. But if one maintains and educates the <poor> child of another; there's no presumption here that it was done as a donation; 'tis more presumable that a debt is hereby constituted, to be discharged by the {goods or} future labours of this child, as far as the expence was truly made for the behoof of the child; but not what was intended for the splendor of his family who maintained it.[5] Nay further, as generally all this expence upon an indigent orphan would be lost entirely if it died before it were capable of labour; the maintainer might perhaps, in the rigour of justice, be allowed to charge something more on account of this hazard; and by this allowance men will be more encouraged to such necessary care of indigent orphans. But then this hazard continually decreases as the child advances in years, and cannot increase considerably the charge, except <226> for a few of the first years. An indigent orphan thus maintained is therefor in no worse case than that of any indigent person who without any fault of his is involved in a great debt, from whom the creditor may justly demand payment by his labours, while the debtor retains all the other natural rights of mankind, and whensoever either by his labours, (of which, he may justly choose to turn himself to such as may be most beneficial to him, and soonest discharge the debt), or by the liberality of any friend, he can discharge it, he can no longer be justly detained in service. Now were an account of all the necessary charge of maintainance, and of the value of labour, justly stated, it would appear, that such an orphan sound in body and mind could always fully discharge such debt by his labours before he were thirty years of age: and consequently that this can never be a foundation for perpetual hereditary slavery; even allowing an extraordinary interest were charged upon the expences because

5. *Ibidem,* II.2.7, pp. 115–16.

modum foenoris nautici, amplius esset solvendum: quod tamen exigere haud sineret humanitas, ab iis qui gravi aliqua premuntur necessitate; nulla autem gravior esse potest quam infantis inopis, omni parentum auxilio destituiti.{*}

Ad hanc etiam refertur classem ejus obligatio, qui favore necessitatis usus, alteri damnum dedit; qua de re postea erit agendum: atque ejus qui indebitum accepit tanquam debitum; aut aliquid ex pacto quovis aut promisso, cui legitima opponi poterat exceptio; aut ob rem aut operam, a se praestandam, quam non praestitit.

Quum res plurium communis, unius opera aut impensis est conservata aut exculta; caeterorum erga hunc obligatio ad posteriorem hanc classem, hujus erga caeteros, ad priorem est referenda.

Obligationes alium tenentes ab eo qui contraxerat, sunt veri contractus, ubi alterius <235> mandato aut jussu res contractae sunt: sin secus, sunt in causa negotiorum gestorum.

---

* {Vid. *Carmichael.* supplem. IV. ad *Puffendorfium* De officio Hominis et Civis p. 281, ejusque annotationes ad lib. II. cap. 4.}

of the hazard, as is done upon contracts of bottomry in trade.⁶ And yet this charge must appear pretty inhuman upon persons in any grievous distress: nor can any distress be conceived greater than that of an indigent child destitute of all aid from its parents.<*>

Under this branch too is included the obligation of him who using the plea of *necessity,* (of which hereafter) has done damage to others; and of one who received what appeared due, but afterward 'tis found was not due; or what was paid upon a contract against which there lay a just exception making it void; or received any price, in consideration of something which is <227> not paid or performed by him{: who are all obliged to indemnify and restore}.

When one partner in a company has preserved or improved at his own expence any of the common goods of the company; the obligation of the other partners toward him is of the later class; and his to them of the former.

The obligations contracted for us by others, if they are done by our commission, are manifest contracts; if not, they come under the case of *business managed without commission* already mentioned.⁷

6. *Ibidem,* 16, p. 144. The parallel chapter in *System* (2.14, vol. II, pp. 77–86) is not very different from the present one. Hutcheson is only more detailed in arguments on the rights of orphans adopted and against slavery (pp. 80–85).

* <See Carmichael's *Supplement* IV ad Pufendorf's *De officio hominis et civis,* p. 281 and his *Annotations* to the book II, chapter 4.> [Cf. *Notes on Puf.,* pp. 112–17 and 138–45 and the comments by the editors. It is rather surprising that here the Translator omits the note where Hutcheson clearly acknowledges his debt toward Carmichael, on the duties of children to their parents, of orphans to their adoptive parents, and on his polemic against slavery.]

7. On these three last paragraphs see *Notes on Puf.,* II.2.8–10.

CAPUT XV

Jura ex Damno dato, atque ex aliorum Injuriis orta. Jura Belli.

I. Ex iis quae saepius sunt dicta constabit, teneri quemque damnum, alteri non consentienti, a se datum praestare. Incidunt autem [Incidere possunt] causae, in quibus vir optimus ea agere possit, et debeat, quae aliis damno erunt: ubi scil. aut res suae longe pretiosiores conservari, aut mala graviora, sibi suisque imminentia, aliter averti nequeant, quam ea agendo quae aliis levia quaedam damna sunt allatura. Suo forte jure ea aget vir bonus, suscepto tamen hoc onere, damni omnis, sui aut suorum causa aliis dati, pensandi: quum et communis utilitatis et juris aequi ratio hoc exigat, ne quis ob suam utilitatem aliorum immerentium imminuat utilitates; aut si quid istiusmodi necessario factum fuerit, ut ubi primum fieri potest damnum resarciatur.

Quod et de damno injuriâ magis est manifestum. Conservari enim nequiret hominum conjunctio et societas, nisi necessaria <236> cuique foret damni abs se injuriâ dati praestatio; quae igitur per vim recte exigetur. Frustra ferrentur leges, vim omnem vetantes et injurias, si tamen iis violatis, lucrum injustum improbi obtinere possint.

Quin et societatis humanae salus hoc exigit, ut malorum graviorum metu ab injuriis improbi coerceantur, ne perpetuam iis praedam et ludibrium se praebeant omnes probi. Quamvis igitur benevolentiam omnem, clementiam et mansuetudinem, etiam erga improbos, nobis commendet Deus et natura; majorem tamen innocuorum et proborum commendant curam et commiserationem. Citra odia etiam et malevolentiam, improbi ab injuriis per vim et poenas coerceri, atque ab iis damni pensatio, cautioque ne in

Of Rights Arising from Damage Done,
and the Rights of War.

I. From the former principles 'tis plain, that each one is obliged to repair any damages he may have done to others, if they desire it. But cases often happen when a good man justly may, and ought to do, what may occasion some damages to others; if, for instance, some goods of his of incomparably greater value cannot be preserved, or some of the greatest evils threatening him or his friends be prevented, otherways than by doing what may occasion some small loss to others. He has a perfect right to act thus; and yet he always in such cases becomes liable to make good their losses sustained for his safety or that of persons dear to him. Since this is a sacred social principle of equity [Since common interest as well as a principle of equity requires], that "no man for his own advantage should impair the advantages of others; or if any necessity force him to it, that he make good their loss as soon as possible."

The same is more manifest in damages done injuriously. Human < union and> society cannot be maintained unless men are obliged to compensate all such damages, <that therefore are rightly claimed by violence>. Laws prohibiting <all violence> and injuries would have no effect, if after they were done, the injurious could enjoy their gain with impunity.

Nay the safety of society further requires that the <229> injust should be restrained from injuries by the terror of severe punishment; lest the good should be continually exposed as a prey <and a laughing-stock> to them. And therefor altho' God and nature require of us good-will, clemency and lenity, even toward the evil, yet surely they require a superior degree of these affections toward <the innocent and> the good. And the injust may be restrained by violence and punishments, and obliged to compensate the injuries done and give security for their innocent behaviour for the future,

posterum laedant, exigi poterint{: quae potius in beneficiis habenda}.

II. Damni nomine intelliguntur, non solum rerum nostrarum direptiones, corruptiones, detentiones injustae; verum et fructuum sive naturalium sive civilium interceptiones; atque omnia etiam incommoda quae ex primo damno promanarunt; *lucrum* scil. omne *cessans,* non minus quam *damnum emergens.*

Qui vel per se, vel per alios, vel faciendo vel non faciendo, secus quam obligatione perfecta tenebatur, damno causam dedit, <237> aut occasionem citra quam non evenisset, is damnum intulisse censetur. Qui malis laetantur alienis, qui injurias laudant, aut ad eas hortantur, improbum quidem produnt animum: quum tamen citra ea, saepe eaedem illatae fuissent injuriae; ea, ut poenis coercenda sunt, rarò tamen homines, per se, [ad damna pensanda obstringunt] [damno praestando obnoxios reddunt]. Ubi plures communi consilio, injuriam intulerunt; singuli pro omnibus, et omnes pro singulis, ad damnum pensandum [compensandum] tenentur. Ubi vero unus aliquis totum compensaverit; nihil amplius eo nomine laesus a caeteris exigere potest. Is tamen, qui totum pensavit [compensavit], recte divisionis contra socios postulabit beneficium. Poenarum causa est diversa {: quippe quae communis utilitatis causa irrogandae sunt.} Inter damni auctores praecipuus habetur qui caeteros imperio adegerat. Hic igitur, ubi fieri potest, primo est appellandus: ubi non potest, a patratoribus rectè exigitur damni praestatio; quandoquidem nullam hic ab ea obligatione immunitatem, iis dare poterat. Et quantumvis patratores, {qui} ad graviora, quae ipsis imminebant, mala declinanda, damna aliis dederant tantummodò leviora, necessitatis favore ab omni [culpa sint] [vitio] excusandi; non tamen cessabit damni sarciendi obligatio; quum non teneantur <238> vicini immerentes, mala illis imminentia, suo damno redimere.

1. Cf. Pufendorf, *De officio* 1.5.17.
2. This section corresponds to *System* 2.15.1, vol. II, pp. 86–88.
3. See Pufendorf, *De iure nat.* 3.1.4.

without any malice or ill-will toward them; nay 'tis doing them rather a
good office, to restrain them thus from further crimes.[1]

II. By damage is understood not only "the depriving men of their goods,
and spoiling or detaining them injuriously; but any intercepting or preventing their natural or artificial profits; with all those inconveniencies which
ensue upon the first wrongs; all gain prevented, as well as losses occasioned."[2]

Whoever by himself or by others, whether by acting or omitting contrary to his duty [what he was obliged to by a perfect right], has occasioned
any damage, which otherways would not have happened, may be deemed
an author of the injury. Such as only rejoice in the injuries done and praise
them, <and encourage them> may indeed shew {such} perverseness of temper {as deserves punishment}; but as it cannot be discerned whether the
same injuries might not have deen done without such congratulations or
applauses, men are not made liable to compensation on these accounts
alone.[3] Where an injury has been done by many in concert, they are bound
to compensation jointly and severally.[4] But if one has compensated the
whole, the sufferer can demand <230> nothing further on this account from
the rest; but he who repaired the whole damage may oblige his partners to
bear their shares with him. The case of punishments is quite different; for
punishment may be justly inflicted on all for the common safety.

[5]Among the authors of damage, he is deemed the principal, who having
authority over others, commanded them to do it. He therefor is first to be
called to account, if it can be done; if not, we may demand reparation from
the rest; since he could not by any orders of his give them any immunity
from this obligation. And tho' the executors may be free from any guilt,
having had the plea of necessity, in avoiding the far greater evils threatened
them {if they had not obeyed orders} <by occasioning only lighter damage
to others>; yet they are notwithstanding bound to make compensation:
since their innocent neighbours must not suffer, to free them from the evils
they were threatened with.

---

4. On this and the following paragraph see Pufendorf, *De officio* 1.6.8.
5. Not a new paragraph in the Latin text.

III. Qui citra culpam, damnum casu dedit fortuito; ad id sarciendum non pleno tenetur jure. Immo ex officio communis utilitatis causa honeste suscepto, praecipue in rebus trepidis, ubi difficile est satis cavere, quamvis viri strenui incuriâ leviore damnum acceptum sit, id publicè sarciendum.

Damna data a mercenariis, sine heri mandato, ipsos solos onerant. A mancipiis data, dominum obligant, ad mancipium ea lege distrahendum, qua hominis obaerati facultates; quae cum omni aeri alieno solvendo non sufficiunt, inter creditores pro rata dividendae sunt. Hinc, mancipii pretium, quod domini jus est; et illinc, damnum datum est aestimandum, quod laesi jus est; et pro eorum ratione, mancipii pretium est dividendum, aut pensatio a domino praestanda. Quod et de *pauperie* a quadrupede facta, tenendum. Si quid aliter in laesorum gratiam definiverunt [determinarunt] leges* civiles, hoc secutae sunt, ut domini, in servis suis et animalibus coercendis, fiant diligentiores.

Qui sine dolo damnum dedit, se paratum ostendere tenetur ad ea danda facienda, quae viro probo videbuntur aequa; et laeso sponte testari, dolum <a se> nocendique animum <239> abfuisse. Quem damni malo animo dati vere poenitet, hic damnum ultro sarcire, et veniam petere debet, et cautionem offerre, ad viri probi arbitrium, de non in posterum laedendo. Injuriae enim neminem verè poenitet, immo in ea perstat, qui non ad haec praestanda paratus est, aut qui lucrum injuria partum detinet. His autem oblatis, laesus veniam petenti dare, et in gratiam cum eo redire tenetur. Quod eo alacrios praestandum, quod saepius sibi quisque, si non hominum

---

* Exod. XXI.28–30. Institut. IV.t.8.9.

III. If one without any fault, by mere accident does damage to another; he is not strictly bound to repair it.[6] Nay if one engaged in any important services to the community, in any dangerous emergence, where 'tis scarce to be expected that men can use the greatest caution, happens by some negligence to do damage to his neighbour, it should be rather repaired by the community.[7]

Damage done by hired servants without their master's orders, should be repaired by themselves. What is done by a slave binds the master to divide the price of the slave in the same manner as the effects of a bankrupt are divided among the creditors; computing on <231> one hand the value of the slave, which is the claim of the master, and on the other that of the damage done, which is the claim of the sufferer; and in proportion to these two the price of the slave is to be divided.[8] In the same manner the owner is bound to compensate damage done by his cattle, without any fault or negligence of his. If civil laws* have been more rigid upon the owners, it has been with this view, that the owners may be made more careful in guarding well their slaves and cattle{, which are kept for their own behoof}.

If one without any malitious design has done damage, he ought to shew himself ready at first to do or perform whatever any wise arbiter shall judge reasonable, and to declare the innocence of his designs. If one has had an evil intention, and truly repents afterwards of it; he ought also to offer compensation, to beg pardon, and give whatever security against future injuries a prudent arbiter shall think sufficient. No man truly repents of any injury he has done, nay he persists in it, while he declines to do these things, and detains the gain of his injustice. But when the injurious offer all these things voluntarily, we are bound to be reconciled and to pardon them: which all of us should do the more readily and heartily, that each

---

6. Cf. Pufendorf, *De officio* 1.6.10.

7. Cf. this and the following paragraph with *System* 2.15.1, vol. II, pp. 88–90.

8. According to Pufendorf, the owner is obliged either to repair the damage or to surrender the slave (*De officio* 1.6.11, *De iure nat.* 3.1.6). Hutcheson's solution, rather surprisingly—as is clear from the examples given in *A System*—makes the reparation the smaller, the bigger the damage compared with the value of the slave.

* Exod. xxi. 28, 30. Institutes. iv. title 8, 9. [Exodus xxi, 28–30 prescribes stoning for the negligent owner of a goring bull that kills somebody.]

vicinorum, Dei saltem opt. max. clementiâ eget et veniâ.

IV. Quum vero animo obstinato vicinus injuriam intentat, neque monitus
a proposito dimoveri potest; aut damnum a se injuriâ datum sarcire negat;
aut denique quae jure nostro postulamus, praestare pertinaciter renuit: exigit non solum nostra, verum et omnium communis utilitas et salus, ut per
vim depellatur injuria intentata; damnique pensatio, et quicquid nobis debetur, extorqueatur; eaque etiam {ut} improbo irrogentur mala, quorum
terrore et ipse in posterum, et caeteri, ad injurias tardiores reddantur.

Haec juris violenta defensio aut vindicatio, est *bellum:* quod "status est
per vim certantium juris tuendi causâ." Quum autem in civitatibus constituendis praecipuè <240> spectatum fuit, quod omnibus notum, ut civium lites ab arbitris aequis dirimantur, et praecaveantur mala ab hominum
infensorum iracundia metuenda; apparebit, longe aliter juris nostri defensionem et vindicationem, in vita civili, ac in libertate naturali esse insti-
tuendam.

Bella sunt vel *publica* vel *privata.* Publica, quae a civitate aut populo
suscipiuntur: privata, quae apprivatis. Publica sunt vel *solemnia,* vel *minus
solemnia.* Solemnia (quae et *justa* vocant Romani, qualicunque de causa,
nisi planè nefaria suscepta fuerint,) "quae populi nomine, eorumque jussu
qui [reip. Praesunt] [summo sunt in imperio] utrinque, sub aliqua juris
specie geruntur." Publica quae minus solemnia, ab altera tantum parte, aut
populi, aut rectorum jussu geruntur. Qualia praedonibus, aut civibus se-
ditiosis et turbulentis inferuntur; vel quae *civilia* dicuntur, ubi de populi,
aut de regni jure aliquo, inter diversas civium factiones decertatur.

one so often needs to be pardoned, if not by his fellow-creatures, yet by our merciful creator.[9]

IV. When one obstinately persists in his injuries and won't desist from his designs upon admonition, nor repair damages done; or refuses to perform what we <232> have a perfect right to demand; not only our private interests, but the common interests, and safety of all requires, that the injuries intended should be repelled by violence, and reparation of damage and whatever else is due to us by a perfect claim should be obtained; and even some further evil inflicted on him, by the terror of which both he and others be restrained from the like practices.

This violent defence or prosecution of our rights is war. <War is "the state of those who are in violent conflict in order to defend a right."> But as one grand view of constituting civil power was this, as 'tis known to all, that the controversies of citizens should be decided by impartial judges, and thus the mischiefs prevented which might arise from mens redressing themselves under fresh impressions of injuries; very different rules of violent defence or prosecution must obtain according as men are either in natural liberty or under civil government.[10]

Wars are divided into *publick* and *private*. The former are such as are undertaken by a *state*, or in the name of a body of people: *private* wars are those among private persons. The publick wars are divided into the *solemn*, <called also *justa* by the Romans, whatever was the occasion, even an obviously wicked action> or these authorized on both sides by the supreme powers of states, upon some specious shews of right; and <less solemn, or> those so authorized only on one side: such as the wars made upon bands of pyrates or robbers, or citizens making insurrections; or what are called *civil wars,* between different parties in the same state contending about some rights of the people, or of the government.

9. See Pufendorf, *De officio* 1.5.16.

10. In *System,* the items relating to war in Sections 4–8 are not in the chapter on injuries and damages in Book II, but treated in Chapter X of the third book, "on the laws of peace and war," Sections i–iv, vol. ii, pp. 347–352. Here Hutcheson seems closer to Grotius than to Pufendorf.

De singulorum in libertate degentium privatis bellis nunc dicendum: quae tamen de his statuuntur, simili de causa, tenent in bellis publicis; quum in pari libertatis statu, inter se constituantur ipsae [diversae] civitates liberae, earumque rectores summi.

V. Bella et publica et privata nonnunquam <241> esse licita, immo communi saluti saepe necessaria, ex dictis fatis constat: neque omnia prohibent sacrae literae; quippe quae imperii civilis jura confirmant, magistratibus *jus gladii* tribuunt,{*} et bellatores quosdam egregios laudant {et celebrant}.

In utroque belli genere, tria spectanda; {quaenam scil.} *causae justae;* quodnam belli *inchoandi tempus,* et {qui} petendi *fines;* (quae, terminus a quo, et terminus ad quem, dicuntur:) quae omnia, ubi de singulorum bellis agitur, variè definienda, prout bellantes vel in vita degunt civili, vel in libertate naturali.

Ante omnia monendum; injuriam quamvis atrocem, ab altero nobis illatam [non obstare, quo] [nihilo tamen] minus, adversus eundem colenda sit benevolentia: quinetiam ejusdem foelicitas expetenda est, quantum patitur hominum meliorum, omniumque communis utilitas. Quam haec patitur clementiam, erga vel pessimos, boni cujusque sensus comprobabit. Intentatâ igitur, aut illatâ injuriâ, ad eam avertendam, damnive pensationem, cautionemque in posterum consequendam, cuncta leniora prius tentanda. Neque omne jus suum amittit hostis quamvis injustus; neque contra eum datur licentia <242> infinita; sed ea sola, quae vel injuriae repellendae, vel damno sarciendo, vel melioribus in posterum protegendis est necessaria. Quae horum nulli commodè inservit saevitia, turpis est et detestanda {: quum sine necessitate, hominibus quibusdam gravia invehat mala, caeteris inutilia, et saepe exemplo cunctis nocitura}.

---

* {Vid. Epist. ad *Roman.* XIII.I. &c. et ad Hebraeos. XI.32, 33, 34. I. Petri II.13, 14.}

We first treat of the *private wars* of men in natural liberty. And the same reasonings hold in *publick* <233> *wars;* since sovereign states and princes are with respect to each other in the same condition of natural liberty.

V. We have already shewn that wars both publick and private are sometimes lawful, nay necessary for the common safety. Nor do the scriptures prohibit them in all cases: as they plainly authorize civil power, give to magistrates the* *power of the sword,* and praise some eminent heroes in war.

In both kinds of war three points are to be settled: the *just causes,* the *term of commencing,* and the *term of ending them,* or the sum of our demands in war <which are called *terminus a quo* and *terminus ad quem*>. When we speak of these three in the wars of particular persons, they are to be differently determined according as the parties live in natural liberty or under civil government.

But we must always remember, that tho' we have received the very greatest injuries from any person, yet we ought to maintain good will toward him, and even desire his happiness, as far as it is consistent with that of better men and of the community. All clemency consistent with these ends, toward even the most injurious, is what every man's heart must approve. When therefor any injury is designed or done to us, we should try first all gentler methods, either to prevent it, or obtain reparation of damage and security for the future. Nor should we judge that an unjust enemy has <234> forfeited all his rights, or that every outrage against him is justifiable. That violence alone is just which is necessary, or naturally conducive, to repell the injury, repair the damage, or obtain security for the future. Any cruelty not requisite for these ends is plainly criminal and detestable; as it occasions grievous sufferings to some of our fellows, without any necessity for the interests of others; and is a precedent to like cruelties on other occasions{, even toward those who have a just cause in war}.

---

* {The *jus gladii* is well known to include both the power of capital punishment, and of defending a country by arms, among the Romans to whom the apostle writes, Ch. xiii. 4.} See also Hebr. xi. 32, 33, 34. 1 Pet. ii. 13, 14. [Saint Paul, as well as Saint Peter, recommends obedience to the magistrates. In Hebr. xi. 32–34, Saint Paul praises some famous heroes of the Hebrews.]

VI. {Belli} in libertate naturali {suscipiendi} *causa* justa, est juris perfecti quaevis violatio. Nullum enim erit jus tutum, nulla vitae securitas, nisi contra injurias inferentem ad vim confugere liceat, ne quis injurias a se illatas impunè ferat. Levioribus injuriis nobis saepius illatis maximae collabentur opes: neque innocuis tolerabilis foret vitae conditio, improborum petulantiae inultae semper obnoxia. Injurias leviores ferendas suadebit humanitas, si modo damna reparari possint, et a viris caetera probis, per brevem iram, cujus mox eos poenitebit, inferantur: hanc tamen patientiam, ab altero nemo suo jure postulare poterit. Quae rariores et insolitae sint bellorum causae haud improbandae, nondum {aut} illatâ aut intentatâ injuriâ,* alias docebitur.

Ubi igitur violatum est jus, sive rebus nostris ereptis aut laesis, sive quae nostro <243> petimus jure denegatis; aut ubi vicino cuivis par sit injuria; licet, immo saepe honestum est, eos quoscunque, qui juri nostro, aut vicini cujusvis, tuendo aut vindicando se opponunt, per vim cogere, ut ab injuriis desistant, nobisque et vicinis quae debentur, praestent. Res *in specie* debitas per vim occupare licet: aut si harum non sit copia, res quaslibet hostiles, quae iis omnibus quae debentur praestandis sufficient. In jure nostro aestimando, labores omnes et damna, quibus causam dederat injuria hostilis, sunt computanda. Immo poenae nomine, aut cautionis de non laedendo, res hostiles jure occupantur, quantum arbitro prudenti necessarium videbitur.

In statu quidem civili ea injuria sola, a cive qui in jus vocari potest, intentata, vi privata recte propulsatur, quae damnum minitatur irreparabile. Aliarum depulsionem, damnique pensationem, tutius magistratui permittimus. Quae nullo ejusdem auxilio praecaveri possunt aut reparari, illas vi omni necessaria aut commoda jure propulsamus. Si quis etiam [civium] [jure civis], civilem exuerit, conditionem, aut ita occultè injurias inferat, ut

* Vid. Lib. III.9.2.

VI. The *just causes* of beginning war in natural liberty are any violation of a perfect right. There could be no security in life, none of our rights could be safe, were we prohibited all violent efforts against the injurious, and they allowed to pass with impunity. By a frequent repetition of even smaller injuries the greatest wealth must soon be exhausted: and life must become intolerable to innocent men if they are thus exposed to the perpetual insults of their petulant or insolent neighbours. Humanity may often persuade a good man to overlook lighter injuries, which can easily be repaired; if especially, they proceeded from some sudden gust of passion in men who in the main parts of their character are good, and will soon repent of it. Yet no man can justly claim such patience toward himself from others. There are some more rare cases in which perhaps it may be just to make war before any injury is done or attempted: but of these hereafter.*

When therefor any of our perfect rights are violated, either by destroying or damaging our goods, or <235> refusing what we have a perfect right to claim; or when a like injury is done to any innocent neighbour; 'tis lawful, nay often honourable by force to compel those who oppose us or our neighbour in obtaining our rights, to desist from these injuries, and to perform whatever is due to us <and to our neighbour>. We may seize the particular goods we have a claim upon; or if we cannot find them, seize any goods of the enemy sufficient to compensate all that's due to us. And in computing this, we should include all our labours, and losses or expences occasioned by the injury. Nay we may proceed further <in seizing the goods of the enemy> by way of punishment, or obtaining security for the future, as far as a wise arbiter will judge necessary: [but of this presently].[11]

In civil society indeed, these injuries alone justify the violence of private persons against any fellow subject who is amenable to laws, which may occasion an irreparable damage. The warding off, or the repairing of others should be obtained in a more prudent way by the aid of the magistrate. But such as can neither be prevented nor remedied this way, we justly may repell with <any necessary or suitable> violence. But if any one, who is as to right a citizen or subject, renounces this bond; or makes his attempts so

* Book III. ix. 2.
11. Square brackets in the original text.

vix in jus vocari possit; contra eum* vigent omnia quae in libertate jura: quales sunt praedones furesque nocturni. <244> Contra alios cives, juris vindicatio judicibus permittenda.

VII. *Terminus a quo* {in libertate} inchoanda est juris violenta defensio aut vindicatio, est, ubi alter vel denuntiatione, vel actione hostili, aliove indicio certo, nosmetipsos, aliumve innocuum laedendi consilium declaraverit, nec monitus desistat. Neque enim primus ictus est excipiendus; quippe qui lethalis esse potest: neque expectandum donec inferatur injuria, quae forté reparari nequiret; cujusve illatae pensationem infoelicius exegeris, quam nondum illatam propuleris. Injurias igitur tardius molientem maturè opprimere licebit.

In statu civili, vim cum graviore aliorum periculo conjunctam, haud recte prius adhibemus, quam aggressor nos ad eas redegerit angustias, ut neque sine periculo fugere liceat, neque a civibus, aut magistratibus auxilii sit copia.

VIII. Terminus sive finis, ultra quem in statu libero non recte producitur bellum, hic est; quum *aggressor,* aut injuriae auctor, vel poenitentia ultro permotus, vel vi coactus, a laedendo abstinuerit, omnisque damni a se dati pensationem, cautionemque in posterum, ad viri probi arbitrium, obtulerit. Haec si pertinaciter detrectaverit, per vim jure extorquentur. Quin et humani generis <245> interest, ut ei qui atrocius sine ulla juris specie deliquerit, aliisque exemplo suo injuriarum et scelerum auctor fuerit, ejusmodi supplicia irrogentur, quibus non solum ipse, sed et alii omnes ab ejusmodi delictis deterreantur.

Quae causae ostendunt poenas in vita civili jure irrogari, eaedem omnes statui libero conveniunt: quamvis in eo neque adeo facilè irrogari, aut pru-

---

* Exod. XXII.2, 3. Leg. XII. Tab.

secretly that there's small hope of bringing him to justice; we have the same
rights against him as if we were in natural liberty.* Such are all robbers and
thieves in the night. Against other citizens our remedy must be obtained
from judges or magistrates.

VII. The term of commencing violence [the violent defence or prosecution
of rights] in liberty, is when one either by express declaration or any <236>
hostile action <or other certain evidence> has discovered a fixed purpose
of hurting us or any innocent neighbour; and won't desist upon admonition. We are not obliged to receive the first assault; as it may perhaps prove
fatal to us: nor need we wait till the injury is executed; which may perhaps
prove irreparable: and 'tis generally easier to prevent than to remedy. We
may therefor justly prevent and surprize such as have formed and declared
sufficiently their injurious designs of hostility.

The proper term of commencing in civil life any violence that may be
dangerous to others, is when the aggressor has brought us into such straits
that we can neither retire without danger, nor obtain any aids from magistrates or our fellow-citizens.

VIII. The term or bounds beyond which we ought not to continue violence
in natural liberty, are when the aggressor or the author of the injury either
voluntarily repenting, or compelled by force, desists from injuring, and offers compensation of all damages done, and such security for the future as
any prudent arbiter shall judge necessary. If he obstinately refuses these
things we may justly obtain them by force. Nay the common interest of
mankind requires that such as without any plausible shew of right, have
done gross injuries, and given such dangerous example to others, should be
punished in such a severe manner as may probably deter not only themselves, but all others from like crimes.

The same reasons which justify the inflicting of punishments in civil
life, justify it also in natural liberty; tho' in this state we cannot expect that

* Exod. xxii. 2, 3 and some fragments of the 12 tables. [Exodus, xxii, 2–3 and Digest
IX. Tit. 1 declare that there is no crime in killing thieves during the night. The issue is
discussed by Grotius in *De iure belli* 2.1.12–14.]

denter temperari possint. Neque vel poenarum causae, easve expetendi rationes, imperium civile exigunt in eo qui irrogat, neque ut is qui punitur imperio sit subditus.

In statu civili, periculo praesente depulso, non producendum est bellum. Damni enim pensatio, omnisque in posterum cautio, in judiciis, non hominum infensorum vi, est exigenda. Omnis quae jure adhibetur vis, vel jus nostrum tuendum, vel utilitatem aliquam communem, spectare debet. Quae horum neutrum spectat, quaeque cum odio et malevolentia est conjuncta, ea est *vindicta,* quae et lege naturali damnatur et Christiana.

Quum porro jura nostra non solum rem aliquam habendam, quam recte vi defendimus, verum et quaedam ab aliis consequenda spectent; in libertate, quae ab aliis jure sed frustra flagitavimus, per vim vindicare <246> aut persequi licet. In vita civili {contra}, ea vindicatio omnis, actione intentata, sive de debito, sive de damno, etiam infecto, magistratuum prudentiae et judiciis est permittenda. De jure nostro in statu libero persequendo, {ubi} de belli causis agebatur [agentes] satis {ante} diximus.

IX. Hinc etiam [Ex dictis] patet, condicta privatorum certamina, quae nunc *duella* vocantur, ubi provocans et provocatus se ultro in loco sistunt condicto, extrema omnia invicem inferre parati, nulla {satis probabili} juris specie, vel inter homines liberos, vel cives, defendi posse. Juris nostri defendendi aut persequendi modum longe commodiorem, ostendet recta ratio; ut nempè vel arbitris compromisso <constitutis> permittatur litem dirimere; vel, ubi hoc alter detrectaverit, ut cum eorum auxiliis, quos nobis causae nostrae aequitas, aut rei communis cura, socios adjunxerit, bello aperto jus nostrum persequamur. Quod ad opprobria attinet [verbaque contumeliosa] [& calumnias], {et falsa crimina;} ea per duellum refellere,

punishments <237> shall be so effectually executed, or so prudently regulated. Neither the grounds of punishments, nor the reasons of inflicting
them, presuppose civil power in the inflicter, nor civil subjection in the
sufferer.

Under civil government subjects ought not to continue violence after
they are secured from present danger. The reparation of injuries and precautions for the future are to be obtained by the sentence of a judge, and
not by the violence of the enraged parties. All just violence should be with
a view either to the defence of our rights, or to some publick advantage.
What has not such intention; and is accompanied with hatred of the person, and joy in his misery, is that criminal *revenge,* which is condemned
both by the natural and christian laws.

And further as rights respect not only our holding or possessing, but also
our obtaining sometimes from others some goods or services: in natural
liberty we may use violence in pursuit of what is due to us from others,
when they refuse to perform voluntarily what we justly demand. But in
civil life all such prosecution of our rights should be made by actions in
law, either for debts, reparation of damages, or precautions against damages
apprehended; and these matters decided by the wisdom of magistrates and
judges:[12] as must appear from what was said about the causes of war in
natural liberty, and the ends of civil government.

IX. From these principles it must follow that such duels as are often practised among us, where the challenger and the person challenged meet in a
place appointed, intending the death of each other, or what <238> may
occasion death, cannot be justified <by any form of reasonable right> either
in natural liberty or civil society. <Right> Reason would always teach a far
better method of defending and prosecuting our rights; first, by committing any disputed point to arbiters in natural liberty; and if either side declined to submit to them, the other should obtain the assistance of such
neighbours as the equity of his cause or regard to the common safety can
engage to his side, and make open war in prosecution of his right. As to
any reproaches or contumelies <or false reports>; the duel is often a foolish,

12. Cf. Carmichael, *Notes on Puf.,* p. 70.

et ineptissimum est, et saepe saevissimum. Quum caeca omnino sit martis hujusmodi alea; et poena saepe major quam delictum. Si quis alterius famam falsis laeserit criminibus, aut etiam arcana ejus vitia inhumaniter divulgando, nullo hoc exigente officio: in statu libero, <247> quo dignus est supplicium, ad viri prudentis arbitrium, ei est irrogandum; qua in re ab humanioribus vicinis auxilia petenda. Si quis in eo statu, nullâ injuria lacessitus, animum erga nos declaraverit hostilem, is quidem tutissima {potius} ratione improvisò videretur [est] opprimendus; aut, quantum exigit nostra aliorumque incolumitas, poenis {palàm} coercendus. Neque vel in vita civili, si hostilem civis contra me ostendat animum; hominum fugere congressus, aut omissis officiis quae sunt foris peragenda, intra aedes me continere teneor, nisi quatenus humanitas, aut salutis meae cura, id moneat. Atque si quis in me versantem in rebus licitis, injuste impetum fecerit; recte me cum istius caede defendero. Immo, procaces istiusmodi et petulantes occidere, officium est hominum vitae amicissimum. Haec omnia sine condicto certamine fieri possunt.

Sin autem tanta rectores civitatum ceperit rei maximae incuria, ut ad civium famam, contra opprobria aut falsa crimina, defendendam, nullae sint idoneae leges, nulla judicia; atque si invaluerit mos, a barbaris et superstitiosis deductus seculis, ut infamis, novisque semper injuriis dignus habeatur, iisque sit obnoxius, qui propter opprobria quaedam [aut maledicta in se conjecta] [accepta], <248> auctorem ad certamen condictum non provocaverit, aut ab altero qui se laesum putat provocatus, certamen detrectaverit: Certaminum ejusmodi crimen, in civitatis rectores praecipuè est conferendum; quamvis non prorsus immunes sint ipsi qui decertant; is praecipuè qui alterum provocavit. Alia enim plerumque ratione vir bonus famam tueri, et fortitudinem {etiam} ostendere poterit, [si qua aut bellum publicum ingruerit, aut] [ubi scil.] alter ipsum per vim aggressus fuerit.

and often too cruel a method of refuting them. The fortune of the combat is often as blind and capricious as any: and death is too grievous a punishment for opprobrious words. If one has hurt the character of others, either by false reports, or even by divulging inhumanly, without any necessity, their secret vices; in natural liberty we may justly, with the assistance of friendly neighbours, inflict such publick punishment as any wise arbitrators shall deem proper for the crime. And if in this state any one, <unprovoked,> has given full evidence of an hostile intention to destroy us; we should rather take the safest way to prevent by surprize, or to restrain him, in such manner as our own and the common safety requires. Nay under civil government, we are not bound to avoid publick places, or neglect any business which requires our appearing abroad, because we know that one designs to assault us; unless either humanity or a regard to our safety move us to it. And if we are unjustly attacked while we are employed in our own lawful business, we may justly defend ourselves even by killing the aggressor: and doing so [and killing in this way petulant and insolent men] is often a <239> very useful service to mankind. All this may be done without any concerted duels.

But if the legislator has been so negligent of a most important matter, as to appoint no suitable <laws, nor> legal redress for the citizens when injured in their characters by calumnies or reproaches; and if that custom prevails, which took its rise in the most barbarous and superstitious ages, that a man is deemed infamous, and always exposed to new insults, and these generally approved too, if upon certain reproaches or contumelies uttered against him, he does not challenge the author of them; which will be the case too with one who declines to accept a challenge from any who imagine they are injured by him.[13] The larger share of this guilt is chargeable on the civil governors themselves; tho' the parties are not excusable, especially the challenger. For a good man may generally find a better way of vindicating his character, and even of shewing his fortitude, if either there arise any publick wars, or if he is first attacked by violence.

13. Hutcheson shares with Carmichael (*Notes on Puf.*, pp. 68–69) a rather strict censure against the practice of dueling. On duels cf. *System* 2.15.6, vol. II, pp. 97–98 and 100–101.

Unica forte de causa* justum esse potest, ab altera saltem parte, certamen sponte susceptum; ubi scil. hostis publicus potentior, προμαχοῦ cujusdam virtute fidens, foedus de pace conditionibus aequis reducenda, ea solum lege, nobiscum inire velit, si hic a nostrae gentis πρόμαχῳ in certamine victus fuerit. Res quidem graviores, quae solae bellorum justae sunt causae, duelli istiusmodi aleae committere dirimendas, saevum est et stolidum: quippe quae per arbitros melius dirimi poterant. Si vero hostis potentior in istiusmodi praelii eventum controversiam conjicere, neque eam leniore ratione dirimere velit; {is} maxime laudandus, qui ad majorem innocentium stragem praecavendam, patriam suo periculo defendere <249> ea ratione conatur, quae spem ostendit maxime probabilem.

* Grot. de J. B. III.20.43.

There is indeed one case in which concerted duels may be lawful on one side:* if a publick enemy of our country, of superior power, trusting to the valour of some champion on his side, offers to grant us reasonable terms of peace only upon the event of this champion's being defeated by one of our side; or will have the controversy decided according to the fate of such a combat. 'Tis no doubt foolish and inhuman to decide controversies <at least the serious ones that only are cause for a just war> this way, when it might be done <240> by arbitration. But if a more potent enemy will not consent to any other way [will cast the controversy in the result of such a combat and will not decide it in a milder way]; 'tis a glorious action on our side, if one to prevent much blood-shed exposes himself for his country to this hazard, in which his country has better hopes of success than any other way.

* Grotius D. Jure B. &c. iii. 20. 43. [Here Hutcheson agrees with Grotius, *De iure belli*, 3.20.43. 4.]

CAPUT XVI

De Jure extraordinario ex Necessitate,
omniumque Jure communi.

I. Officia ferè omnia sensu proximè, cuique monstrari et commendari, saepius jam dictum: inter varias item honesti species, naturalem esse ordinem;
aliasque, quamvis per se pulchras, aliis pulchrioribus, et ad communem
utilitatem momentum majus afferentibus, in contentione cedere: honestique praecipuam venustatem, in iis animi affectionibus et consiliis, quae
maximae omnium utilitati inserviunt, elucere. Hinc efficitur, omnia privatorum jura, omnesque leges speciales, majori plurium utilitati, aut omnium communi, posthabendas. Quam vis igitur rationis {rectae} dictata,
leges speciales appellatae, quasque libero quovis tempore migrare turpissimum, officia viro bono fere semper digna jubeant; tempore tamen mutato,
nonnunquam commutatur officium; casusque quidam rariores, in ipsis legibus excepti intelliguntur.

Non igitur, premente necessitate, violandae <250> leges naturales, aut
iniqua et improba facienda. Immo qui exceptione utitur legitima, sibique
concessa, aut legi paret sanctiori quae minus sanctae aliquid derogat, is eo
ipso legi paret. Legum aut socialium ea sanctissima, quae singulorum, aut
pauciorum saluti et utilitati, omnium communem anteponit.

Extraordinary Rights in Cases of Necessity,
and the Common Rights of Mankind.

I. It has been already frequently shewn that an immediate sense generally points out and recommends our several duties; and that there are different degrees of them, in a certain subordination, some more, some less honourable; that the later should give place to the former, when they are inconsistent [some, though amiable for themselves, should give place to such as are more amiable and conducive to a greater amount of publick good]; and that the supreme beauty appeared in these affections of soul which are most extensive{, which should therefor controul the narrower}: and that in consequence of this, all the rights of individuals, and all the special rules of life [laws] should be postponed to the universal interest of all.[1] Altho' therefor these practical conclusions <of right reason> called the *special laws* of nature, which we are sacredly bound in all ordinary cases to observe, point out what is almost continually the virtuous part; yet by an extraordinary change of circumstances, it may become our duty to act in a different manner; and such singular cases are to be deemed excepted in these special laws.[2] We never should speak thus, that in cases of singular necessity, we may justly violate the law of nature, or act unjustly or vitiously{: such expressions are contradictions}. But it is truly obeying the law to take the benefit of any exceptions appointed in it; or to follow the more sacred law when it derogates any thing from <242> one of less importance. Now of all the social laws that is the most sacred, which prefers the general interest and safety to that of individuals or small parties.

1. Cf. *System* 2.17.1, vol. II, pp. 117–19.
2. A new paragraph in the Latin text.

II. Quum vero hominis cujusque probi sensus, legum specialium vim et majestatem conservandam moneat; ab iis levi de causa minimè discedendum: neque levis est necessitas quae iis quicquam derogare [putanda est] [debet]. Non solum igitur, quae incommoda ex iis servatis continuò sequerentur, quaeque commoda praesentia ab iisdem deflectere suadeant, cautissimè circumspiciendum; verum praecipuè, sintne quaedam incommoda graviora, ex ea in causis similibus licentia omnibus permissa, <forent> in posterum metuenda. Ponamus, exempli gratia, aliquid quod latius pateat: quum tanta sit fidei et veritatis, sive in sermone, sive in commerciis rebusque contractis, religiosè observatae utilitas; et tanta pariter, ex conservato dominii jure, liberâque rerum suarum possessione et administratione cuique permissâ, oriatur vitae securitas et mutua fiducia; oportet gravissimae sint causae, ingentia mala avertenda, aut bona consequenda, quae justitiae <251> regulis hisce quicquam derogabunt. Neque ad causas leviores extendi debet necessitatis favor: {etenim} prospicienda {etiam} graviora longê incommoda, quamvis remota, quae ex earum legum auctoritate de causa quavis leviore imminuta, sunt tandem nascitura. Excipiendi igitur casus tantùm gravissimi, ubi mala his omnibus incommodis graviora sunt avertenda; quibus casibus, qui leviores et magis consuetos annumeraret, improbus planè sit oportet et sceleratus.

Frustra dixeris, nullius utilitatis causâ facienda turpia et inhonesta. Nemo negat. Sed quaerimus, num casu quodam rariore, haec turpia sint et inhonesta? [Neque deliberandum,] [Non] an propter utilitatem deserenda sit honestas; sed, an non magnam utilitatem honestas nonnunquam sequatur? Neque magis attinet dicere, legi divinae semper adhaerendum; caetera, {rerum} eventus nempe, casusque futuros, judicii nostri non esse, eaque Deo permittenda. Haec {Philosophi} quidam minime mali, sed non satis acuti. Quaerimus enim, an in ipsa Dei lege hi casus excipiantur? et numnam exceptiones, eadem ratione, qua ipsae leges innotescant? Si nostri

II. But as the sense of every good man must shew it to be of high importance to preserve the authority of all the special laws {and that they should
be religiously regarded}; we cannot be justified in departing from their appointment upon any light causes: the necessity must be great and manifest
which will justify it. We must < therefore > not only consider cautiously
what present advantages may ensue in this case from such a singular step;
or what present inconveniences from following the ordinary law; but much
more what greater and heavier {and more general} evils may follow from
such a liberty allowed to all. Let us take an example or two, which may
illustrate other cases. As the maintaining of veracity and faith in our conversation and dealings is of the highest importance to society; as is also the
maintaining the rights of property, and leaving to each one the free administration of his own, for the mutual confidence and security of men in
society: the causes must be of the highest nature, some terrible evils to be
avoided or exceeding great advantages to be obtained which can be allowed
to make exceptions from these important rules. Nor ought this plea of necessity to be extended to lighter matters: for we should consider all the < far
heavier evil> consequences, even of a remoter kind which must ensue upon
diminishing the deep reverence men should have for these laws. No cases
therefor but those of the highest nature are to be deemed excepted; when
evils superior to all these evil consequences are to be < 243 > averted: and
none will reckon among these, any ordinary ones of a lighter nature, unless
he is plainly wicked and impious{, void of any conscience of duty}.

    'Tis to no purpose to argue here, that we are to do nothing vitious < and
dishonourable> for any prospects of advantage. In this all agree. But the
question is, whether such extraordinary conduct be vitious in these circumstances, or not? It should not be matter of hesitation, whether we may
abandon the conscientious part for the advantageous: but whether some
great utility to ensue don't make some extraordinary steps lawful or honourable? Nor is it more to the purpose to allege, that we should always
adhere to the divine laws, and that we are no judges of future events, but
should commit them to providence. Such things are pleaded by some very
good men [some philosophers], tho' not very acutely in this point. For the
very question is, are not these cases to be deemed exceptions in the divine
laws? and made known to us by the same use of reason by which the law

judicii non sint rerum eventus; neque sunt ipsae leges; quippe quas rerum eventus vitae hominum amicos aut inimicos prospiciendo indagamus. Primos <252> enim animi impetus quosque, non esse solos vitae duces, inter omnes constat.

Hoc {quidèm} necessitatis obtentu, <forte> abutentur homines improbi, utilitati inhiantes, aut voluptatibus unicè dediti: non tamen sine ea morum pravitate et nequitia, quae nulla legum religione contineri posset. Homines itidem iracundi, ultionisque cupidiores, omni de violenta sui defensione doctrina abutentur. Non tamen idcirco vituperanda est omnis violenta sui defensio; neque magis vituperanda {igitur} omnis, a legum{, quibus plerumque parendum,} normâ, {in casibus rarioribus} declinatio. Temporibus saepius cedunt dominii privati jura: re alienâ, domino inconsulto, aut invito, uti licet, vel abuti, quum id exigit plurium conservatio; ut in jacturis faciendis, aedibusque incendii sistendi causa diruendis. Temporibus etiam nonnunquam cedunt jura sanctiora. Civibus fortissimis rectè imperatur ut, ad patriam tutandam, certae morti se objiciant. Ponte dejecto, aut portâ clausâ, quibus plerumque defendendi sunt omnes cives, hosti vel saevissimo objiciendi cives hectoridae. Splendido reique Romanae salutari mendacio nobilis est rex Hostilius. At plurimas habet lubrica haec doctrina cautiones.

III. {1.} In legibus duabus primariis de <253> Deo colendo, et communi omnium utilitate promovenda, nullae sunt exceptiones. Immo quae in legibus specialibus valent exceptiones, in hac altera generali fundantur. Dei

itself is made known? If we are no competent judges of future tendencies, we are no judges about the ordinary natural laws; which are no otherways discovered than by our reasoning upon the tendencies of certain methods of action, as they appear conducive to the publick interest or detrimental: for no man can allege that our sole rule of life are the impulses of each particular passion {which we may generally approve in ordinary cases}.[3]

No doubt wicked selfish men devoted wholly to their own interests or pleasures will abuse this plea; but not without such impiety and unfairness of mind as would <244> break through any bonds of laws. The passionate and revengeful often abuse the doctrine of self-defence{, and that about prosecuting the injurious}: but we don't therefore {quit this doctrine, and} prohibit [condemn] all violence in defence or prosecution of our rights. Nor should we any more condemn all departure in singular cases from what the special laws of nature require in ordinary ones. Men seem agreed that the common rules of property yield to some singular exigences. One may use or destroy the goods of another without his consent, when 'tis necessary for the preservation of multitudes, as in the lightening of ships in a storm, or blowing up of a house to stop a raging fire. Nay some higher laws give way to singular necessities. The bravest and best citizens are exposed [are rightly ordered to expose] to certain death for their country{, in services where there can be no hopes of their escaping}. By drawing a bridge or shutting the gates, by which all the citizens have a right to be protected, the bravest men are sometimes [the bravest Romans were] exposed to the most cruel enemies. *Tullus Hostilius* is renowned to all ages for presence of mind in delivering a false account, by which the Roman people were preserved.[4] But this doctrine so liable to misapplication needs always the following cautions.

III. First of all: the two general laws about loving God and {our neighbour, or} of promoting the general good of all, admit of no exceptions: nay in this later are founded all the exceptions which lye against any of the more

---

3. See *System* 1.17.6, vol. II, p. 128.

4. In his *History of Rome* (I.27) Titus Livius tells how during a battle the Roman king Tullus Hostilius makes his enemies and his own troops believe that the Albans, his treacherous allies, are not fleeing but going to attack the enemy from behind.

quidem cultus externus, nulli certo tempori necessariò alligatur.

2. Quo honestius èst cujusque ingenium, eo minus ad exceptiones in leviore quavis causa sua admittendas, aut necessitatis veniam sibi arrogandam, erit proclivis.

3. Omnium quae ex juris hujusmodi insoliti usu, sive consecutione naturali, sive ex hominum pravitate et temeritate nascuntur, ratio habenda. Non tamen ut hominibus denegentur omnia jura, quorum speciem fallacem opponent improbi. Verum haec ipsa mala, ab hominum improbitate metuenda, ad calculos sunt vocanda: causisque tantum gravissimis exceptiones dandae; quibus, in rebus levioribus abutetur nemo, nisi ea sit pravitate et nequitia, ut legem quamvis notissimam violaturus esset.

4. Quo sanctior, vitaeque hominum utilior est lex, eo graviores oportet esse causas, ob quas danda exceptio.

5. Causae quae ex aliorum utilitate, aut omnium {communi} petuntur, iis quas quisquam ex sua aut suorum utilitate petit, longe sunt honestiores. De sua utilitate suoque jure aliquid remittere, viro bono saepe licet, <254> saepe honestum est: communem vero utilitatem deserere non licet. "Temporibus igitur prudenter parendum."

6. Nulla necessitas tanta est, ut cuivis, mala sibi imminentia, in alios immeritos conjicere, iisve avertendis, alios paribus aut gravioribus malis implicare liceat: huic enim adversatur utilitas communis.

7. Quaecunque damna, ad mala graviora a nobis nostrisque avertenda, in alios non consentientes conjicimus [damus], ea omnia praestare sanctissimè tenemur. Juri huic {mala nostra graviora aliorum levioribus redimen-

special laws. But the external acts of worship are not necessarily annexed to any one time{, and therefor yield to urgent exigencies}.[5] <245>

2. The more honourable any person's temper is, the less apt will he be to allow to himself exceptions for any smaller interest of his own, or to claim any privileges of necessity.[6]

3. We must bring into account all the effects probably to ensue from any extraordinary steps, whether by natural consequence, or from the unfairness or rashness of others. Not that men are to be excluded from every right which unjust persons may make a pretence of in improper cases: but even these bad consequences are to come into the general account, to prevent our allowing exceptions in any but the most weighty cases. So that no man can plead exceptions in lighter ones, without that depravity of mind which would break any acknowleged law{, without any such pretence}.

4. The more sacred and important any law is, the greater must the causes be which can found any exception.

5. Causes of a publick nature [seeking the interest of others or of all] are far more honourable than those of a man's own <and of his friends'> advantage. A good man often may quit part of his own <and his friends'> right; and 'tis often honourable not to take the advantages he might. But he is not thus master of the publick interests, and must act according to what the exigence of the times require.

6. No plea of necessity will justify a man in freeing himself from any threatening evil, by casting the like or greater upon any innocent person. This is plainly not subservient to any publick utility.

7. Whatever smaller damages we cast on others who do not consent to suffer them gratuitously, in <246> order to free ourselves from any great danger, we are sacredly bound to repair. To this right in natural liberty, of warding off some great danger by actions detrimental to others, there cor-

---

5. Here Hutcheson repeats what was said by Carmichael at the beginning of his comment on Pufendorf's exposition of "the case of necessity" in *De officio* 1.5. 18 (*Notes on Puf.*, p. 71).

6. For the same points established in this section, see *System* 1.17.9, vol. II, pp. 136–40.

di} in libertate, extra ordinem singulis competenti, respondet in vita civili, *imperii jus eminens;* de quo aliàs.

IV. Ex communi hominum cognatione et caritate, jura quaedam communia nascuntur, quae non unius aut paucorum, sed omnium communi utilitati inserviunt [prospiciunt]: haec igitur, occasione datâ, cuique tuenda sunt et persequenda. {Ante} *juris publici* [explicationem haec ideo exponenda] [explicationi, horum explicatio ideo praemittenda], quod haec in libertate, ante civitates constitutas, {aequè} vigeant. Eorum pauca ponemus exempla quae latius pateant.

1. Cuique, occasione oblata, totique adeò humano generi, jus est prohibendi ne quisquam, sine justa causa e vita excedens, officia, humano generi, ejusve parti cuivis, <255> debita defugiat. Prohibendum igitur [item], ne quis se ipse interimat; aut corpus mutilando vitae muneribus ineptum reddat.

2. Jus {omnium commune} est, perniciosos pessimique exempli mores coercendi [prohibendi], quamvis nemo quisquam, prae aliis, iis laedatur. Coercenda venus naturae repugnans et nefanda; partuum etiam abactiones, artesque omnes humano generi inimicae.

3. Impediendum {item}, ne quis res suas, quae vitae hominum plurimum prodesse possunt maligno perdat animo, aut inutiles perire sinat.

4. Omnibus et singulis jus est, injuriam alii cuivis inferendam propulsandi, illatamque vindicandi: poenas item in eos qui injuriam intentarunt irrogandi, quarum terrore isti, caeterique omnes, ad injurias tardiores reddantur.

5. Humano generi jus est prohibendi, ne, qui arcanum aliquod hominibus salutare invenerit, ejus notitiam secum interire sinat; eumque vel poenâ proposita cogendi, ut aequis legibus id cum aliis communicet, cunctisque quibus sit opus ejusdem usum impertiat.

responds in civil society an *eminent right in the supreme powers,* of which hereafter.{*}

IV. From the common bond of all with all, by which all mankind are constituted by nature one great society, {with some common laws binding them,} there arise certain common rights, not specially regarding the utility of any one, or a few, but that of all in general; which therefor every one as he has opportunity should maintain and prosecute. These rights as they obtain also in natural liberty, should be considered previously to those of civil societies. We shall give a few instances, which will also lead us to others.[7]

1. Mankind as a body, and each one as he has occasion, have a right to hinder any one to quit life without a just cause, or thus desert the duties incumbent on him. Suicide should therefor be prevented, or such self-maiming as may make one unfit for the duties of life.

2. There's also a common right of all, to prevent certain vitious practices of most pernicious example, which yet cannot be said to injure any one person more than another: such as monstrous lusts, procuring abortion, or any other practices which are hurtful to mankind in general.

3. We are likewise to hinder any man to destroy such goods of his own as may be very useful in life, <247> out of any caprice or ill-nature: nay they should not be allowed to perish of themselves without being used.

4. There's also a like common right of one and all, to prevent injuries, and to punish such as are done; so [and to inflict such evils to the offender] that by the terror of the punishment, others also may be restrained from like attempts.

5. Mankind have a right also to compell any person, who has discovered any secret of great use in life, to divulge it upon reasonable compensations, and not suffer it to perish with himself; that such as need it may also enjoy the benefit.

---

* {Book III. Ch. v. 4.} [In the much larger chapter on "the rights of necessity" in *System* (2.17.5, vol. II, pp. 124–25), however, Hutcheson admonishes that "were there no justifying pleas of necessity in natural liberty, there is no accounting for this eminent right of magistrates in civil polity."]

7. The same points are treated in *System* (2.16.1–6, vol. II, pp. 104–10).

6. Hoc etiam abs quovis hominum, cui vires suppetunt, jure exigit humanum genus, nisi ipsi suppetat etiam rerum copia; ne se ignaviae dedat, liberalium et munificorum <256> eleemosynam, iis qui se alere nequeunt, in suos usus iniquè praerepturus. Ad victum et amictum, arte aliqua licita, aut laboribus, parandum, istiusmodi fuci cogendi.

Perfecta videntur haec {quae diximus} jura, quae humano generi tanquam populo aut *universitati* competunt. Alia sunt imperfecta; quibus quae respondent officia, pudori cujusque et honestati permittenda; quae satis intelligi poterunt, ex iis quae de virtutibus diximus.*

* {Vid. Lib. I. Cap. III et V.}

6. Mankind in general, and every society, may justly require it of all such as enjoy ordinary health and strength, unless they otherways have a fund for their support, that they should maintain themselves by their own labour, and not intercept the liberality or charity of good men; which is due only to the weak who cannot support themselves. Such slothful wretches are to be compelled to labour <or to any lawful art for supporting themselves>.

The instances we have given are rights of the perfect kind belonging to mankind as a body. Imperfect rights of this class answer to the general duties of humanity and beneficence (above explained in treating of the nature of virtue) which must be left free to the honour and conscience of men.<*>

* <See book I, chapters iii and v.>

De Juris < abolitione sive> interitu. De Litibus in
Libertate dirimendis, et Interpretatione.

I. Tribus modis tolluntur obligationes: *solutione* illius quod debebatur; *cessione* in debitoris gratiam, idque vel gratis, vel ex causa onerosa; et *conditionis defectu.*

Rectè solvit vel ipse debitor, vel alius quilibet ipsius mandato, ipsiusve nomine, ita ut ipsius manifestè intersit, dummodo loco et tempore constituto fiat. Ubi {quidem} debitoris non interest; creditor alteri cuiquam, fortè inhumano, solvere volenti, actionem < 257 > suam adversus debitorem cedere neutiquam tenetur. Haec tenenda [obtinent] ubi vel res certa, vel pecunia numeranda, vel opera quaevis vulgaris debebatur: quippe in quibus creditoris haud interest quis solvat. In iis autem, quae honoris causa praestantur operis, aut in quibus ingenii spectatur elegantia, secus se res habet.

In rebus item *fungibilibus,* iisve quarum pretia ad certam rei istiusmodi mensuram rediguntur, si [quidem utriusque] [modo] solutionis dies adest aut praeteriit, *compensatio* admittenda, ubi ad aequalem summam duo sibi mutuo creditores sunt{: immo pro concurrentis summae ratione, ex majore deducendum; ut tantum id quod reliquum est deberi censeatur}.

How Rights and Obligations Cease:
How Controversies are to be Decided in Natural
Liberty: and the Rules of Interpretation.

I. Obligations cease by three several ways: by the *paying* or *performing* what was due; by *remission* in favour of the debtor <whether gratuitous or for onerous cause>; and by the *failing of the condition*.[1]

Payment may be made either by the debtor himself, or any commissioned by him, or acting in his name and for his behoof; but it must be at the time and place agreed on. Where payment is offered not by appointment of the debtor, nor for his behoof; the creditor is not bound to transfer his right against the debtor to the person thus offering payment, who may have some malitious intention against the debtor. What is here said relates only to the delivery of common goods or money, or performing common labours or services, in which 'tis no matter to the creditor who pays him. The case is otherways in homages of honour, or such labours as are valued on account of singular ingenuity.[2] {In these no substitution can be made without the consent of the person to whom they are due.}

In money, or goods only regarded by weights, measures, or quantities [In res *fungibiles,* or in goods the values of which are reduced to a certain measure]; if two persons be mutually indebted to each other in equal sums, and the days of payment <249> on both sides come, the debts mutually destroy each other: and this is peculiarly called *compensation*. Nay tho' the sums are not equal, yet the debts should be deemed abolished as far as the sums concur, and the surplus only to remain due.

---

1. Cf. Carmichael, *Notes on Puf.,* p. 121.

2. Here and in the followings paragraphs Hutcheson touches on all the points treated by Pufendorf in *De officio* 1.16. Cf. also *System* 2.15.8, vol. II, pp. 103–5, a rare case of a shorter parallel section in the *System.*

2. Ad cessiones pertinent *transactiones* omnes, et obligationes quibus lites tolluntur: *delegationes* item, ubi vice sua debitor alium dat reum creditori consentienti, aut cui is jusserit: *Condonationes* etiam expressae vel tacitae; *acceptilationes* itidem; *dissensus* que mutuus.

3. Ob conditionis defectum, tollitur obligatio alterius partis perfidiâ; si modo pactum irritum fieri mallet altera, quam perfidum cogere ut promissis maneat. *Mutato* item *statu,* quae in eo fundata erat obligatio tollitur. Tempore dein exacto [elapso], dissolvuntur <258> obligationes ad certum temporis terminum constitutae. *Morte* denique solvuntur obligationes, quae certos quosdam homines aut personas solùm respicientes, neque ad haeredes erant transmittendae, neque adversus haeredes valiturae. De quibus omnibus ex rei natura, aut ipso contractu, facilè constabit.

II. In libertate lites amica litigantium disceptatione optime dirimuntur; amicorum deinde communium, aut vicinorum officiis; puro denique sive absoluto compromisso, quo res viri probati arbitrio permittitur; idque vel secundum partium jura perfecta; vel ex aequo et bono, *ut inter bonos benè agier.*[1] Hac posteriore via vir bonus suas cum vicinis controversias dirimi volet.

Viri cordati, nulla necessitudine arctiore contendentium alterutri devincti, quibusque nihil lucri accessurum est, quoquo modo lis dirimatur, arbitri eligendi. Qui, quum nulla ipsorum utilitate, neque gratiâ aut odio, ab aequo et bono abripiantur, quamvis ipsis contendentibus neque prudentiores sint neque aequiores, facilius tamen quae vera et aequa perspicere poterunt. Eorum arbitrio litigantibus standum, nisi doli {fortè} comperta sint indicia; pactum nempe aliquod de lite in alterutrius gratiam dirimendâ;

---

1. Legal form used, e.g., by Cicero (*De officiis* 3.61.9 and 12, 3.70.3).

To the second way, to wit, of some remission; are reducible all these *transactions* {or bargains} agreed to for extinguishing disputed claims: as also *delegations;* by which the debtor with consent of the creditor transfers to him < or to anyone appointed by him > an equivalent debt due to himself: as also < *condonationes* or releases, explicit or tacit>, the forgiving of debts and accepting any thing in lieu of them; < likewise *acceptilations*>[3] and lastly mutual dissent of the parties; by which the mutual obligations of a bargain are taken away.

3. Under the head of the failure of the condition, is included the *perfidy* of one party in a bargain; which sets the other free, if he chooses it, rather than to compel the perfidious to performance: as also a *change* of *state;* by which all obligations are made void which were plainly founded upon it: as also the *expiration of the time;* which takes away obligations which were to endure no longer: and lastly *death* takes away such as only respected the persons, and were not designed to subsist to the heirs of the creditor, or affect the heirs of the debtor: and these points are generally known from the nature of the business, or the terms of the contract.

II. In natural liberty controversies are best decided by friendly conferences of the parties, or the interposal of common friends; or by an absolute *compromise* or submission to arbiters of approved characters; and <250> this either as to the strict point of right [as perfect right], or as to the equitable and humane part on both sides. Every good man would always choose to make submissions of this later sort{, and not insist upon the strictest point of right}.[4]

The proper arbiters are persons of wisdom, under no special attachment to either side, and who can gain nothing by the decision of the cause in favour of either party. Such men influenced by no interest or passion, tho' they be neither wiser nor better men than the parties contending, yet will more easily discern what is just and equitable. The parties are bound to stand to their decision, unless they find evidence of corruption, such as some secret contract with one party; or unless there be such manifest in-

---

3. "Acceptilation" is a release from debt or obligation without payment.
4. On this section see *System* 2.18.2, vol. II, pp. 142–45.

aut adeo manifesta arbitrii iniquitas, ut <259> dolum plane prodat: qualis arbitrii Romani inter *Nolanos* et *Neapolitanos*.{*} Levior enim iniquitas [si quae existat] [quaeque], probabili juris specie sussulta, compromissi obligationem neutiquam solvit.

Quod si arbitri neque ex litigantium [partium] confessione, syngraphis, aliisve istiusmodi documentis, verum eruere valeant; citandi testes, et jurisjurandi religione astringendi. De testibus primo videndum *Cassianum* illud, *cui bono;* et duo minimùm exigendi. Quamvis enim pro testium numero non augeatur fides, uiiusque probi et spectati multum valeat testimonium; unus tamen, modo malitiosus, versutus, animique fidens, narrationem falsam ita callidè contexere poterit, ut nulla judicis arbitrive solertia adduci possit, ut secum discrepet, dolumque prodat. Duo vero aut plures, de iis omnibus rei judicandae adjunctis, quae neminem qui interfuit latere solent, (qualium ingens judici solertiori occurret numerus,) seorsum interrogati, si vel contraria plura testentur; vel eadem omnia aut recordari, aut oblivisci, prae se ferant; manifesta dabunt fraudis fallaciaeque indicia.

III. In vera promissorum, contractuum, testamentorum, legumque scriptarum sententia eruenda, interpretandi regulis opus <260> est, ex arte grammatica, aut critica praecipuè depromendis.

---

* {Cic. de offic. I. 10.}

---

5. Cicero, *De officiis*, 1.33. The Roman arbiter Quintus Fabius Labeo persuaded the opponents separately to accept narrower boundaries and gave the residue to Rome.

6. Cf. Cicero, *Pro Milone*, 32.5, for the use of this phrase.

iquity in the decision as must plainly evidence some fraud or unfairness < as was the case of the Roman arbiters between the inhabitants of Nola and Naples[5]>. But if it is only some smaller inequality or mistake in the decision, upon some shew of right, {by which one party thinks he is wronged,} he is notwithstanding bound to submit to the award.

The arbiters should proceed as judges do, to find out the truth by the acknowlegements of the parties, or by signed deeds, or other such documents: and next to cite witnesses, and interrogate them upon oath; regarding always this < rule of *Cassianum* *"cui bono"*>,[6] whether the witnesses be not engaged by interest on one side; and they should demand two at least to proceed upon. For tho' the credibility does not at all increase in proportion to the numbers of witnesses, and sometimes the testimony of one wise honest man gives full satisfaction; yet it would be dangerous to proceed upon the testimony of <251> one: as a person of great hypocrisy and art and presence of mind may contrive such a consistent story, that no interrogatories put to him can detect the falshood of it, or make him contradict himself. But when two or more witnesses, are separately examined, without hearing each others testimonies, about all such circumstances as might have been observed by persons really present, (of which a vast multitude may occur to a sagacious judge); if they either frequently contradict each other; or both always remember the same circumstances, and both always pretend to have forgot or overlooked the same circumstances, they give plain evidence of a concerted fraud. [A compleat consistency therefor of two thus examined, gives abundant evidence.][7]

III. For discovering the true intent and meaning of promises, contracts, testaments, and written laws, the proper rules of interpretation are often useful. But they belong rather to < the grammatical art, or to> the art of criticism than to morals{; as they are not peculiar to these matters}.[8]

---

7. Square parenthesis in the translation.
8. This is the reason why a parallel section is missing in *System,* as explained by Hutcheson at p. 147 note. Even in the *Institutio* Hutcheson, while following Pufendorf's section on 'interpretation' (*De officio* 1.17) tries to simplify Pufendorf's rules.

Imprimis monendum; qui paciscentis speciem prae se ferens, ea dedit signa, quae dare solent qui quicquam promittunt, eum ad id praestandum teneri, quamvis alia secretò secum tunc temporis agitantem. Neque aliter ulla esset commerciorum fides.

2. Verborum popularium et usitatorum ea est significatio quam usus confirmat, omissis causis aut vocum originibus; nisi adsint insuetae significationis [acceptionis] indicia.

3. Artium vocabula et nomina signata, ex peritorum definitionibus interpretanda.

4. Ubi orationis, aut scripti ejusdem, partes diversae sibi invicem lucem praeferre possunt, obscuriora [et dubia perspicuis aperienda] [per magis perspicua sunt explicanda].

5. Ubi absurdi aliquid aut secum pugnantis, verba sensu simplici et figura nudato [continere videntur] [continerent], [neutiquam verò si figurata habeantur] [quod tamen tolleretur, si figurat haberentur]: figurata omnino habenda.

6. In scripto istiusmodi, cujus partes priores nullum jus transferunt, in illum qui non et posterioribus consenserit, "posteriora prioribus derogant": quod in testamentis, pactisque, quae cum eodem contrahuntur, obtinetur.

7. Ex *materia, adjunctis, effectibus,* et <261> *consequentibus,* ad veram verborum sententiam dijudicandam indicia promuntur. Verus enim est sensus qui cum materia et adjunctis convenit, quique nihil absurdi secum trahit.

8. Ex paciscentium fine aut scopo cognito, atque ex legum ratione unicâ aut integra, optima petuntur ad pacta legesque interpretandas adjumenta [criteria].

9. Perinde etiam ut est materia *favorabilis* aut *odiosa,* porrigitur vel coarctatur verborum interpretatio.

IV. Ubi vero contendentium alter, aut uterque, suis fretus viribus, aut adversarii apud vicinos gratiam, aut astutiam metuens malitiosam, litem arbitris dirimendam permittere recusat; non aliud restat perfugium, quam ut jura sua [uterque cum amicorum auxilio] [quisque] per vim tueatur aut persequatur. Unde crebra in libertatis statu oriri bella necesse est, cum magno vicinorum incommodo et periculo saepe conjuncta. Quae ut prae-

1. We must still remember that such as profess to contract with others, and use such signs as commonly express contracting, are to be deemed bound, what ever way their mind was then employed: nor otherways could there be any faith in commerce.

2. The sense of common *popular words* is to be determined by custom, without regard to original meanings or etymologies; unless there appears evidence that they were taken in an unusual sense.

3. *Terms of art* are to be understood according to the definitions of the artists. <252>

4. Where the different parts of any deed relate to the same thing; the ambiguous or obscure are to be cleared up by the more plain and distinct.

5. If words taken in their simple and unfigured sense import something contradictory and absurd, but not when interpreted as figurative; they are to be deemed figurative.

6. In deeds which convey no right in their prior parts to such as don't also consent to the subsequent; the subsequent limit the preceeding. This holds in the different parts of testaments, and in different deeds made between the same parties.

7. There are also just conjectures of interpretation to be derived from the *subject-matter,* the *circumstances, effects,* or *consequents.* For that is probably the true interpretation which suits the subject-matter and circumstances, or which involves no absurd consequences.

8. Contracts are best explained from knowing the views of the parties; and laws in like manner from the reason or design of them.

9. We are also to regard whether the matter be of a *desirable* or favourable nature, or on the contrary undesirable or odious; for accordingly we give a larger or more confined sense to the words.

IV. But where all or any of the contending parties in natural liberty, trusting to their own strength, and each dreading the interest or art of his adversaries in influencing any arbiters they might choose, declines to compromise; there remains no other remedy than that each defender prosecute his right by violence, <253> with what aid he can get from his neighbours: and by this means multitudes must often be involved in great inconveniences and dangers. Now 'tis probable, that in order to avoid these mischiefs, and to

caverentur mala, [utque] [hominum coetus] multi sub prudentiorum imperio, ad lites dirimendas, et exterorum vim ingruentem efficacius repellendam conjungerentur, credibile est homines ad civitates et imperia civilia constituenda confugisse.

get large societies regulated by the authority of a few of the wiser sort, in the decision of their debates, and the exerting their united force for the common safety of all [and in order to reject more effectually the violence and the attacks of foreigners], men have had recourse to a political union and a civil power.[9]

9. See *System* 2.18.4, vol. II, pp. 146–47.

<262>

PHILOSOPHIAE MORALIS

INSTITUTIO COMPENDIARIA

꒯꒯ LIBER III ꒯꒯

Oeconomices et Politices Elementa.

CAPUT I

De Conjugio.

I. Status liberi, ab ipsa natura constituti, obligationes et jura, in superiore libro explicata sunt: ad *status adventitios,* hominum facto aliquo aut contractu constitutos, nunc progredimur.

Status hi sunt vel *domestici,* qui paucorum, unius nempe familiae respiciunt utilitatem; vel *publici,* qui multorum utilitati inserviunt, civium nempe omnium in republica, aut plurium etiam civitatum.

De statu omni et necessitudine domestica agit ars *Oeconomica;* cujus elementa, tribus percurremus capitibus. Sunt et alii quidam status adventitii, eorum nempe qui ad arctiorem aliquam communitatem, in *universitate,* <263> civili imperio subjecta, sunt consociati; quorum genera sunt infinita, neque in philosophia explicanda.

II. [Non ultra unius animalis aetatem, duraturum erat quodque animantium genus] [Unius tantum aetatis essent omnia animantium terrestrium genera], nisi hoc machinata fuisset natura, ut in omni genere mares forent et foeminae, procreandi vi et appetitu instructi, et praecipuâ quadam in procreatos curâ in eum finem donec se ipsi conservare possint. Mutis quidem animalibus conservandis nihil amplius {ferè} machinata est natura; quippe quae brevi et facili matrum cura conservari possunt et educari, neque ulla ab vivendum arte indigent; quum ab ipsa natura vestiantur, quaedam etiam armentur; pastumque iis copiosè, qui cuique aptissimus est, sponte submittat ipsa terra. Hominum autem vitae conservandae et exco-

ᘛᐦᘚ BOOK III ᘛᐦᘚ

The Principles of Oeconomicks and Politicks.

CHAPTER I

Concerning Marriage.

I. We have in the former book treated of the rights and obligations of that *state of liberty constituted by nature.* We proceed to the *adventitious states,* founded upon some human deed or institution.

These states are either *domestick,* regarding the utility of a few, so many only as can subsist in one family; or *publick,* respecting the utility of a whole nation or state, or even of many states.

Oeconomicks treat of the rights and obligations in a family; the chief points of which are delivered in <256> these first three chapters. There are many other adventitious states of persons united in some narrower communities or corporations included within some political body, and subject to it; of which there are innumerable multitudes, which are not under the cognisance of philosophy.

II. All kinds of terrestrial animals must have subsisted only for one age, if nature had not consulted their preservation by a difference of sex, a desire of offspring, and a tender care of it till it can subsist by itself. In the brute [speechless] animals nature has done little more; as their young can be sufficiently preserved and reared by the care of their dams, since they need scarce any instruction for their simple ways of life. Nature finds all the clothing and armour they need; and the earth of itself sends up their food in abundance. But for the improvement and even preservation

lendae, artes exiguntur plurimae et inventa. Delicatiora enim sunt hominibus corpora, exquisitiore victu et cultu tuenda; animique artium jucundissimarum capaces. Provido igitur naturae consilio, diutius manet eorum soboles tenera et invalida, adultorum sedulâ egens et continua curâ; ut eo facilius ab adultis regatur, atque prius, artibus variis, et disciplinis, ad vitam commode degendam inservientibus, imbuatur, quam vires intractabiles adipiscatur. <264>

Gravi huic et necessario muneri explendo, quod etiam per στοργὴν insitam utrique parenti natura imposuit, quum impares {plerumque} sint matres; utriusque labores, et curae diuturnae exiguntur: quae tolerabiles non erunt, nisi parentibus mutuo amore et stabili amicitia conjunctis: quum et nova subinde iis nascitura erit soboles, {quae} eadem curâ per magnam vitae partem prorogatâ, conservanda erit. Muneri huic pergravi alacrius procurando et obeundo, maribus et foeminis miros inseruit natura amores; quos magis accendit virtutum in moribus, atque ipsa forma, significatio, quam illa caeca, et cum mutis animalibus communis, corporum miscendorum libido. Monstrant hi amores non aliter sobolem humanam esse propagandam, quam a parentibus fida et constanti amicitia, <conjunctis> et firmo {etiam} de continua vitae consuetudine et communis sobolis curâ, foedere conjunctis [devinctis]. Omnis enim fida amicitia perpetuitatem expetit: quaeque a certo temporis termino pendet, aut ab eventis quae conjuges fidissimi nequeunt praestare, nulla est.

[III.] Conjugum hi amores, et στοργὴ; a natura insita, ostendunt notandum esse *Platonem* et alios quosdam minime malos; quibus, a naturâ, et communi etiam utilitate, audacius recedentibus, placuit, per prolem, neutri

of human life a multitude of arts and inventions are necessary; as their bodies are more delicate, needing nicer food, and clothing, and other care; and their minds capable of many delightful arts. Their offspring therefor, by the wise order of nature, continues far longer tender and infirm, needing the constant <and attentive> care of the adult; that thus they may be more easily governed and instructed in the various arts <and disciplines fit for the conveniences> of life, before they acquire untractable strength.

Now as the mothers are quite insufficient alone for this necessary and laborious task, which nature also has plainly enjoined on both the parents by implanting in both that strong parental affection; both parents are bound to concur in it, with joint labour, and united <257> cares for a great share of their lives: and this can never be tolerable to them unless they are previously united in love and stable friendship: as new children also must be coming into life, prolonging this joint charge.[1] To engage mankind more chearfully in this laborious service nature has implanted vehement affections between the sexes; excited not so much by views of brutal pleasure [by that blind lust of corporal union that they have on common with speechless animals], as by some appearances of virtues, displayed in their behaviour, and even by their very form and countenances.[2] These strong impulses plainly shew it to be the intention of nature that human offspring should be propagated only by parents first united in stable friendship, and in a firm covenant about perpetual cohabitation and joint care of their common children. For all true friendship aims at perpetuity: there's no friendship in a bond only for a fixed term of years, or in one depending upon certain events which the utmost fidelity of the parties cannot ensure.[3]

III. This natural love of the sexes, and equally natural love of offspring, shew that *Plato* and some other excellent writers are justly censurable, for departing too audaciously from nature, in appointing their states to be sup-

---

1. The same stress on instruction of the offspring as the chief aim of marriage and on the duties of both parents is found in Carmichael (*Notes on Puf.*, pp. 128–29).

2. See Hutcheson, *System* 3.1.2, vol. II, pp. 151–52, and *Inquiry on Virtue* 6.3, pp. 251–52.

3. Apart from the following section (see the following note), the chapters on marriage in the *Institutio* and *System* give the same arguments in the same order.

<265> parentum agnoscendam, civitates suas esse reficiendas; ut {scilicet} avertantur incommoda quaedam, viâ multò leniore et gratiore praecavenda. Nullae quippe leges, nulli mores eousque valere poterunt, ut in parentibus de sua sobole incertis, omnique στοργή; vacuis, idoneam communis sobolis curam excitarent. Quod etiam si fieri possit, gravatissime tamen ab iis praestarentur haec officia, in sobole {incerta} conservanda et educanda, molestissima, quae in sobole certâ, per στοργὴν, fiunt levia et jucunda. [Incognita] [Sublata cognitione] insuper sobole, tollitur gravissimum omnis diligentiae et industriae invitamentum. Quin et in civitate sua Plato, ob causam non satis idoneam nec ad intelligendum facilem, civium paucorum tantum et praestantiorum habuit rationem, caeteris longe pluribus neglectis, et miserae servituti subjectis.

Quid, quod etiam incommoda, ex [eo quod cuique nota sit sua soboles] [sua cujusque sobolis cognitione], metuenda, per leges de juniorum educatione accuratiore, de testamentis, et successionibus, melius praecaveri poterant. Neque cognitae sanguinis junctioni adscribendae sunt hae seditiones, et factiones crebrae, quibus civitates saepe videmus vexatas. Tollenda pariter foret et omnis amicitia; aut major {certè} in amicis aut Reipub. partibus eligendis, <266> prudentia hominibus tribuenda, quam, in liberis et cognatis educandis, aut haeredibus instituendis, iisdem tribuit *Plato.*

De multorum imbecillitate, quos tamen haeredes instituendos suaderet στοργή, metus est inanis. Invalidis saepe valida est soboles; validisque, invalida; sive animum spectes sive corpus. Neque ut omnes cives vel robusti vel solertes sint, ulli civitati opus est: saepe etiam ingenio et virtute pollent, quibus exiguae sunt corporis vires.

---

* {See Plato's scheme in his books *de Republica.* The evils avoided by his scheme, are avarice, and injustice; vast estates, and the attendant power and influence, descending to worthless heirs; the employing mens affections upon the contracted system of a family or two, which otherways might be extended to the whole state: and thence many dis-

plied in new subjects by children unknown to both the parents; and this in order to prevent some evils{*} which may be prevented in a much more easy <258> and gentle manner. For never could any laws or institutions have such influence, that persons quite uncertain about their offspring, and hence not influenced by the natural affection, would take a proper care of the young. Or if they were compelled effectually, the labour <for preserving and educating a doubtful progeny> would be most disagreeable to them, which to parents assured of their own offspring is light and delightful. And further while their offspring is unknown, men want one of the strongest incitements to all diligence and industry. Nay further Plato's scheme, without any sufficient reason or criterion that one can understand, is only calculated for the happiness of the few finer spirits; while the plurality are <neglected and> subjected to a miserable slavery.

Nay further; these inconveniences he dreads so much from each one's knowing his own children, might be prevented another way, by proper laws {and publick institutions} about <a more careful> education, testaments, and successions. Nor can we ascribe the factions <and seditions> which often tear states to pieces to our knowing the tyes of blood; as one may easily see in all nations. He should also have prevented all particular friendships; or shewn that men have much superior sagacity in the choice of friends or of state-parties, than he allows them about the education of children, or the love of kinsmen, or in making their testaments.

As to the apprehension of danger from this, that many very weak men by means of the tender parental affections come into great wealth, 'tis without ground. The offspring of the weak is frequently very vigorous; and that of the vigorous weak, both in mind and body. <259> Nor is it necessary for any state that all its members should be either robust or ingenious. And sometimes the finest genius <and virtue> is lodged in an infirm body.

---

sentions and factions.} [In *System* 3.1. Plato's plan in Book V of *Republic* is criticized at the end of the chapter on marriage (Section XIV, pp. 184–87), beginning with a summary of the evils Plato wanted to avoid. This is likely the reason why the translator added this note.]

IV. Non igitur hujusmodi malorum metu, tot et tantae ipsius naturae commendationes negligendae: sed potius rectae rationis dictata omnia et praecepta, monstrantia qua demum ratione fida in conjugio amicitia, ad sobolem educandam necessaria, conservari possit, naturae leges censeri debent. Coërcenda igitur non solum venus nefanda, in Deum naturamque contumax, hominumque generi pestifera; verum et concubitus vagi, quos nullum de amica vitae consuetudine antecesserat foedus, quippe qui promiscuè permissi, juniorum et animos perderent et corpora; sobolem incertam, omnique patrum cura destitutam, propagarent; matresque incautas ab omni honesta vitae conditione exclusas, ad infamiam, inediam, omniaque flagitia projicerent. Atque <267> utinam patribus, talium flagitiorum auctoribus, eadem inureretur infamia.

Matrimonium inire tenentur adulti, quibus ad familiam, pro ipsorum conditione, alendam, facultates suppetunt; quique ea sunt prudentiâ quae familiae, regendae, sobolique educandae, est necessaria; nisi officiis honestioribus et hominum generi utilioribus distineantur. Turpe quidem est cuivis, sine gravi causa, curas et officia humano generi, pro suis partibus praestanda, detrectasse.

V. Foederis conjugialis [ineundi] leges hae sunt praecipuae. Prima, "ut foemina viro castum servet cubile": quum nihil magis nefarium sit, aut injuriosum, quam foetum viro supponere adulterinum [spurium], bonorum haeredem; et στοργὴν, verae tantum soboli debitam, dolosè intervertere.

2. Altera est lex, "ut parem uxori vir servet fidem." Iniquissimum enim foret, ut uxoris amores conjugiales, et curae omnes, {unà cum dote,} uni viro ejusque soboli devoveantur, quum {interea} viri amores, uxori primae

---

4. Cf. Pufendorf, *De officio* 2.2.2.
5. Cf. Pufendorf, *De officio* 2.2.3.

IV. We must not therefor through fear of a few inconveniences counteract what nature has so strongly recommended: but rather look upon all such <precepts and> deductions of <right> reason, as shew how a faithful friendship may be maintained in wedlock, for the proper education of off-spring, as so many sacred laws of nature. Men ought to restrain not only all monstrous lusts, as outrages against God and nature, <destructive of mankind,> but also all dissolute procreation without any proper covenant about a friendly society for life.[4] For if such indulgence were allowed to all, it must destroy both the bodies and minds of the youth, produce a race destitute of all paternal assistance, and expose the incautious mothers to infamy, poverty and a perpetual course of debauchery, without any hopes of ever attaining any reputable state in life. It were to be wished that an equal infamy attended the other sex, the common authors of or solicitors to such vices.

Such adult persons as have a sufficient stock both of wealth to support a family in their condition of life, and of prudence to govern it <and to educate the offspring>, seem obliged to marry, unless they are hindered by some important offices <and ones more useful to mankind> {inconsistent with the cares of a family}.[5] It would be dishonourable for one without a weighty cause to decline his share of the cares and services requisite for the preservation of the human race.

V. The chief articles in this covenant are these. 1. "That the woman be faithful to the man in cohabiting <260> with no other"; as it must be the greatest injury to impose upon him an adulterous offspring, for heirs to his fortune, and objects of that <tender> affection which is naturally due only to his own.[6]

2. The second is, "that the husband should be equally faithful to the wife." For it is a natural iniquity that the wife's conjugal affection, and all her cares and fortune, should be devoted to one man and his offspring; while the affections of the husband <due to his first wife and children> are

---

6. See Pufendorf, *De officio* 2.2.4, point 1; Carmichael, *Notes on Puf.*, p. 129; Hutcheson, *System* 3.1.4, vol. II, pp. 156–57.

ejusque soboli debiti, a nova quavis uxore, aut pellice, earumque sobole interversi, {cum re etiam familiari} dispertiantur<, ejusque bona inter omnes dividenda permittantur,>.

Cohibendi igitur viri, ne plures simul habeant uxores; non ideo solùm quod iniquum <268> sit; verum quod omnem tollat e conjugio amicitiam; contentiones alat perpetuas; foeminas injuriosiùs tractatas, adulteriis objiciat; virorum animos vagis pervertat libidinibus, et ἀστόργους reddat; sobolem quibusdam submittat nimis numerosam, et ideo negligentius educandam, nullaque in parentem dissolutum pietate imbutam. Quinetiam, quum mares foeminis numero pares conservet Dei providentia; {siquidem viris plures simul habere uxores liceret,} plurimi a conjugio et sobole suscipienda excluderentur, humanis immunes vinculis, quibus praecipue colligantur societates; neque tamen {inde} populus fieret numerosior.[1]

3. Lex tertia est; "ut voluntatum et studiorum conjunctione, familiae communis prosperitati, liberis praecipuè <vero> communibus educandis et amplificandis, prospiciant."

Ut ad has leges observandas sint homines paratiores, a primis annis colenda est et fovenda ea verecundia, et pudicitia, quam ingenuo cuique altè infixit ipsa natura. Damnanda igitur omnis in sermone aut moribus obscoenitas, et impudica lascivia; quae pudorem minuit, et verecundiae laxat vincula, quibus continentur juniores, foeminae praecipuè, ne vitae se miserae et infami objiciant.

4. Est et quarta {conjugii} lex; "ut foedus <269> sit perpetuum, sola morte solvendum"; quod et verae amicitiae necessarium, postulatque fere sobolis, pro bona vitae parte nasciturae, educatio diuturna, utrique parenti [a natura commendata] [imposita]. Ab omni etiam humanitate abhorreret, conjugem repudiare amantem et fidelem, propter causas cum nulla turpi-

---

1. In 1742 edn. the whole paragraph (Cohibendi . . . numerosior) completed point 3 of this art.

allowed to be intercepted by, or dispersed among several women [by a new wife or mistress] and their children, and along with it his fortune.

Simultaneous polygamy is not to be allowed to men, not only on account of the inequality or iniquity now mentioned, but because it also destroys all friendship in marriage; must be the cause of perpetual contentions; must tempt women so injuriously treated into adulteries; must corrupt the minds of men with wandring lust, destroying their natural affection to their children; and must occasion to some an offspring too numerous, which therefor will be neglected, and be void of all sense of duty to such dissolute parents. And further since providence preserves the numbers of males at least equal to that of females, if 'tis allowed to men to have more wives at once, many must be excluded altogether from marriage or having offspring; and thus be free from these tender bonds which chiefly civilize and unite men in society: nor does polygamy contribute to make nations more populous{, but has rather the contrary effect}.[7]

3. The third article is that persons married should <261> by a perpetual union of interests and pursuits, consult the prosperity of their family, and chiefly the right education of their common children, and the improving their condition as they have opportunity.

That we may be the better fitted for observing these articles, from our infancy we should be enured to modesty and chastity; an high sense of which is deeply fixed by nature in the finest spirits. All obscenity and lasciviousness in discourse or behaviour is detestable; as it <abates modesty and> relaxes these bonds of modesty by which the young, and women especially, are restrained from exposing themselves to all infamy and misery.

4. The fourth article is, "that the bond be perpetual, to end only by death." This is necessary to make marriage a state of friendship; as also generally for the right [long lasting] education of children, who are successively born to us for a considerable part of life;[8] and this lasting duty or charge is imposed by nature equally on both parents. It would also be most inhuman to divorce or separate from a faithful and affectionate consort for

7. Cf. *Notes on Puf.*, p. 130.
8. The same argument is found in J. Locke, *Two Treatises* 2.7.80, and G. Carmichael, *Notes on Puf.*, p. 129.

tudine conjunctas; sterilitatem, nempè, aut valetudinem infirmam; aut casum tristem, a nemine mortalium praestandum, et repudiandae pariter deflendum; liberorum scil. communium interitum.

Quod ad imperium attinet, aut propriam aliquam potestatem conjugum alteri permittendam, amori ea omnis adversari videtur conjugiali, qui aequam potius commendat societatem. Neque quicquam aliud viris potiores tribuere videtur partes, quam quod gravioribus plerumque muneribus obeundis sint aptiores, quibus [postponenda] [cedere debunt] minus gravia, domi ab uxoribus obeunda.

Leges quatuor jam memoratae, adeo sunt necessariae, ut si quae his derogent pacta, quamvis iis temere consenserint vir et uxor, ea tamen sunt irrita.* Est igitur matrimonium, <270> "foedus inter marem et foeminam, de individuo vitae consortio, et sobole suscipienda et educanda, initum."

VI. Matrimonii impedimenta, vel offendunt contractum a primo {nullum aut} irritum fuisse, vel prius ratum rumpunt. Prioris generis quaedam sunt *naturalia,* quaedam *moralia.*

In naturalium numero, praeter manifestam infirmitatem corporis ad conjugium plane inhabilis, sunt pravitates quaedam insignes, et morbi saeviores et insanabiles, quae amicae vitae societati, aut sobolis vitalis procreationi repugnant; quales sunt fatuitas perpetua aut insania, lepra, aliique ejusmodi. Aetas deinde admodum provecta, {foeminae praesertim,} irritum reddit cum juniore initum conjugium. Si quidem {vir et foemina ambo}

---

* Si quis in causa polygamiae ad leges gentium haud prorsus barbararum provocet; perpendat is, leges etiam iniquissimas de servitute, et de hominum in sacris mactatione, apud plurimas gentes non minus invaluisse. Atque si polygamiam populo Judaico permissam fuisse doceant eorum leges; docet lex sanctior, hoc ipsos tantum [impune ferre voluisse] [impunitum reliquisse] Deum, pro gentis σκληροκαρδία, minime vero comprobasse. <Romanorum> *Concubinatus* [jure civili, coelebi solum, non marito, permissus, naturae jure legitimum erat matrimonium] [licita fuere coelibum conjugia, ast inaequalia, saepe post uxoris prioris obitum inita]. vid. *Heineccii* antiq, append. ad L. L. c. 38. &c.

---

9. Locke (*Two Treatises* 2.7.82) and Pufendorf (*De officio* 2.2.4, point 3) mitigate, but still ascribe to the husband, the right of governing the family. Hutcheson reduces this power further. See *System* 3.1.7, pp. 163–66, where he enlarges on this subject.

any causes which include no moral turpitude; such as barrenness, or infirmity of body; or any mournful accident which no mortal could prevent, and which must be equally afflicting to the person abandoned, the death of all the common children.

As to any proper power, or right of commanding, vested in either of the parties, it seems opposite to that tender affection the spring of marriage; which rather points out an equal friendly society. Nor seems there any other reason for giving any superiority to the husbands, except this, that men are generally more fit for <262> managing the more important business of the family, to which the less important <carried out by wifes> within doors should give place.[9]

The four articles [laws] above mentioned seem so necessary, that no covenants of the parties in opposition to them can be valid.* Marriage therefor may be defined "a covenant between a man and woman about perpetual faithful cohabitation and joint care <and education> of their common offspring."

VI. The *impediments* of marriage are either such as are deemed to make the contract from the first void; or, afterwards make void a valid contract. Of the former class some are natural and some moral.

Among the natural impediments, beside a manifest bodily weakness rendering one unfit for marriage, may be reckoned also some grievous disorders and miserable incurable diseases, inconsistent with a friendly society, or excluding all hopes of offspring that can live. Such as idiotism, and perpetual madness, leprosy, and some <263> other diseases. Very advanced years of either side<, especially of the women,> may justly be deemed to make void a marriage with one in the bloom of life. But if a couple both

---

* If any one in this matter insists that simultaneous polygamy was allowed in some civilized nations; let him remember that so were also human sacrifices, and a certain sort of slavery manifestly iniquitous and inhuman, in far more civilized [many] nations. And tho' a plurality of wives was allowed by the Jewish law; yet a far purer institution informs us, that it was permitted for *the hardness of their hearts;* or only allowed to pass with impunity, but not approved. The *concubinage* both in Heathen Rome and under the Christian emperors [according the Roman law] was allowed only to such as had no wives, and was a marriage naturally lawful. See *Heineccius' antiquities,* in the appendix to lib. i. c. 38. and the following ones. [Johann Gottlieb Heineccius, *Antiquitatum Romanarum jurisprudentiam illustrantium Syntagma,* Argentorati, 1724. The reference to the Christian emperors is not in the *Institutio,* but in *System* 3.1.6, p. 162 note, a further clue that the translator had a copy of Hutcheson's posthumous work.]

aetate provectiores, de convictu amico inter se paciscantur, nihil impedit. Tertium est impedimentum, si alterutrius aetas ita sit immatura, ut non adsit obligationi constituendae necessarius rationis usus. Absurdum enim est, ut quibus, nulla alia in re, pacto quovis se obligare, per aetatem permittitur, <271> in hac tamen longe gravissima iisdem liceat. Haec omnia legibus civilibus sunt sancienda.

Moralia, quae contractum a primo non obligasse ostendunt, impedimenta, censentur, contractus prior, et nimis arcta sanguinis conjunctio.

Quod ad prius attinet: si qui, mala utrinque fide, novum ineant contractum, prioris cum tertio initi non ignari; pactum irritum est, et paciscentes justis poenis se reddunt obnoxios. Ubi quidem unius tantum intervenerat dolus, ita alteri favendum, ut ob promissionem aut contractum clandestinum, non {eo invito} abrumpendum sit matrimonium perfectum, quod insecutus est convictus: prout in aliis negotiis, priora jura personalia cedunt juri reali: istiusmodi dolosis tamen poenae irrogandae. Ne vero etiam post matrimonia perfecta fraudibus sit locus, palam ante denuncianda omnia quae conficiuntur, et confectorum continuò publica fieri debet denunciatio.

An jure etiam naturali nuptias impediat arctior sanguinis nexus, altioris est indaginis. Inter parentes et liberos, {sive} in *linea recta,* quae dicitur, ascendentes et descendentes, in infinitum, nuptias {omninò} prohibere videtur lex naturalis; non solum ob aetatum discrimen insigne, verum multo magis, <272> quod amor et consuetudo conjugialis, ei adversetur {erga parentes} venerationi, quam liberis inseruit ipsa natura, et {educatio} confirmavit. De nuptiis consanguineorum in *linea transversa,* quas adferunt rationes viri docti, vix quicquam affirmant. Quia vero apud plurimas

---

10. In his letter to Hutcheson of Jan. 10th, 1743, Hume says that Hutcheson is too "much afraid to derive any thing of Virtue from Artifice or human Conventions" and neglects the "most satisfactory reason" for inspiring "an artificial Horror" toward marriage between collaterals "lest near Relations, having so many Opportunities in their

well advanced in years, covenant about a constant cohabitation, there's nothing blameable in it. A third impediment is, when either party is so young that they cannot have attained that use of reason which is necessary to their binding themselves by any contract. For it would be most absurd that persons who because of their immature years are deemed incapable of binding themselves in any other matter, yet should be deemed capable of it in this, which is far more important than any other{, and requires greater judgment}. <All these impediments are to be enacted by civil laws.>

The moral impediments which make void the contract from the first are *prior contracts* with others, and *too near consanguinity* or *affinity*.

As to the former: if two persons both <dishonestly> apprized of the prior contract with another join in marriage, the marriage should be deemed entirely void; and both parties should be severely punished. Where one of the parties was not apprized of the contract; the case of this person is so favourable [this person should be so favoured], that the marriage confirmed by cohabitation should not be made void <by the secret promise or covenant>, unless at the desire of this person: even as in other contracts, subsequent real rights take place against prior personal ones: but the guilty party deserves severe punishment. And that there may be no room for such frauds even after complete marriages, every state should take care that all marriages intended should be previously advertised and such as are celebrated also be divulged in the most publick manner. <264>

As to *consanguinity* invalidating marriages, there are higher debates. Among parents and children in the <so called> *direct line,* <between ascendants and descendants, without end,> the law of nature seems to prohibit all marriages; not only on account of a considerable difference of years, but because the conjugal affection and intimacy seems quite inconsistent with that reverence implanted by nature toward parents and confirmed by education. As to the inter-marriages of kindred in the *transverse line,* or collaterals, the {natural} reasons offered by ingenious men don't seem conclusive {to prove such marriages pernicious or impious}.[10] But as

Youth, might debauch each other." In *System* 3.1.10, pp. 170–73, Hutcheson argues in detail against the artificial account and sticks to the hypothesis of "some early divine prohibition," according to the talmudic tradition of the Noahide Laws.

gentes{*} legis Judaicae ignaras, ejusmodi nuptiae habebantur impurae et
nefariae, credibile est et eas in prima mundi aetate, lege aliqua positiva,
cujus diu manserunt vestigia, fuisse a Deo vetitas. Ea autem lex hoc praecipue spectasse videtur, ut familiae gentesque plurimae ea devinciantur caritate et benevolentia, quae ex affinitate et sanguinis conjunctione oriri solet.
Aliis forte [etiam sobolis nasciturae commoditatibus] [commoda hominibus nascituris] prospexit Deus, eo quod gentes varias, conjugiis inter se mis-
ceri jussit.

Jure Civili, ut Christianorum etiam moribus, prohibentur nuptiae omnibus qui sunt intra *quartum gradum:* et in hunc modum computantur
gradus: consanguineis communis fuerat stirps aliqua, a qua quot interve-
nerant utrinque generationes totidem sunt gradus. Simili etiam ratione,
quisque cum prioris conjugis cognatâ, intra quartum gradum, qui dicitur
affinitatis, matrimonium contrahere prohibetur. Jus vero *canonicum* <273>
eadem retinens verba, longius multo nuptiarum impedimenta aut prohi-
bitiones porrigit, gradus numerando [supputando] secundum generationes
in linearum tantum alterâ, ea quidem longiore, ubi non sunt aequales; adeo
ut reapse prohibeantur nuptiae inter eos qui sunt intra septimum juris civilis
gradum.

VII. Causae ob quas rumpuntur matrimonia, sunt legum praecipuarum
violationes: adulterium scil. aut obstinata desertio; capitalia item odia, et
injuriae atrociores, omnem amicitiae in posterum, aut tuti convictûs et jucundi, spem adimentes. Soluto has ob causas matrimonio, in conjugem
infidelem, et scelerum participes, graviore supplicio animadvertendum est;
quum injuriae in conjugio illatae, damna dent graviora, atque altiora men-
tibus infigant vulnera, quam quae extremis [capitalibus] coërcentur suppliciis, furta et rapinae. Alteri vero conjugi novum inire licet omnino matrimonium; nihil enim iniquius esset, quam ob acceptam injuriam, lege
etiam novam inferre, innocentibus a matrimonio cohibitis, atque a sobolis

---

* Levit. xviii. Tacit. Annal. 12.5. ff. 33. t.2. l. 17. ult. et L. 39. l. 53. Grot. II.5, 12.

---

* See Levit. xviii. and Tacitus's Annals, 12. 5. Digest. 33. t. 2. 1. 17. and last. and Lib.
39. 1. 53. and Grotius ii. 5. 12. [The reference to Justinian's Digest is wrong. The impediments for marriage from consanguinity are treated in Lib. 23, titulus 2, "De ritu
nuptiarum."]

we find that many nations who derived nothing from the* Jewish laws, held the same marriages of collaterals incestuous and impure; 'tis not improbable that they have been prohibited by some positive divine law in the earlier ages of the world; and that some vestiges of this law was preserved in many nations. The intention of this law has probably been to diffuse further among many families that good-will and endearment which frequently arises from consanguinity and affinity. The Deity may also have had in view some other advantages to human offspring to arise from such intermixtures of different families.

By the Roman law, and the customs of all Christians, marriage is prohibited to all within the *fourth degree.* And the degrees are thus computed. Persons a-kin have had some common parent: and as many generations as have interveened on both sides from this <265> stock, so many are the degrees. In like manner a man is prohibited to marry any such kinswoman of his former wife, as of his own; to wit, within the fourth degree. The canon law retaining the same words, has yet extended the prohibitions much further; as it computes the degrees according to the generations in one of the lines only; and by the longer of the two, if they are unequal: and thus prohibits all marriages within the seventh degree of the civil law.[11]

VII. The causes which break off a valid marriage are, any violation of the essential articles: such as adultery, obstinate desertion, capital enmity or hatred, and such gross outrages as take away all hopes of any friendly society for the future <or a safe and agreeable life together>. When a marriage is dissolved for such causes, the guilty party and the associate in the crime deserve the highest punishments; as these injuries in marriage do greater mischief, and cause deeper distress than stealing or robbery, for which capital punishments are inflicted. The innocent party should be allowed to marry again: for it would be strangely inhuman because one has suffered injury, that the law should inflict another hardship, by depriving them of

11. In *System* 3.1.10, vol. II, p. 174, Hutcheson's language is not so detached: "Among the other frauds of Popery, their canonists, to draw more money to their courts for dispensations, encreased the prohibition exceedingly." For other strictures against the church of Rome, "the fruitful source of all corruption and superstition," see also p. 168 and pp. 180–83.

novae suscipiendae solatio. Neque conjugi nocenti, si modo vitâ frui permittatur, adimenda est connubii ineundi potestas, nisi fortè cum sceleris
socio. Permittantur isti nuptiae, saltem cum iis qui similibus delictis sunt
infames. <274>

Quae in Evangelio habentur sententiae, repudia omnia, solâ adulterii
causa excepta,* prohibentes, sunt omnino *ellipticae;* quales et illae quae
omne vetant jusjurandum. Damnant scil. omnes quae apud Judaeos ad-
missae erant causas, eâ unicâ exceptâ. Aliam vero diserte ostendit {D.}
Paulus,† apertissima ratione, et latius patente, confirmatam; *desertionem*
nempe in qua obstinato animo perseveratum est.

In conjugio officia fido et constanti amore, omnique morum comitate,
una cum prudenti rei familiaris curâ, continentur. Quibus praecipue inserviet omnis virtutis cultura, mansuetudinis praecipue et patientiae; atque
ut uterque perturbatis animi motibus, quos negotia saepe excitabunt domestica, modum ponere assuescat. His sine virtutibus, vix gratus esse poterit convictus continuus, rerumque omnium societas. Quibus autem rationibus augeri possit res familiaris, ab iis petendum qui in artibus versantur
quaestuosis. <275>

* Matth. v. 32. Luc. xvi.18.
† 1 Cor. vii.15.

a new marriage and offspring. Nay if the guilty parties are allowed to live, they should not be hindered from marrying, except it be with the partners of their guilt. They should rather be obliged to marry persons equally infamous with themselves.

The prohibitions in the gospel of all divorces except in the case of adultery* seem *elliptical,* as those which prohibit all use of oaths.[12] They only condemn <266> all the causes assigned by the Jewish doctors, except that one. The apostle Paul† expresly allows another, and that for manifest reason, to wit, obstinate desertion.[13]

The duties of persons married consist chiefly in a faithful and constant affection, sweetness of manners, and prudent care of their families; and to this purpose 'tis necessary they improve their minds in all virtue; especially in meekness and calmness of temper; that they may restrain such passions as their family-affairs will be apt to excite. Without these virtues a continual society and community of all things can never be tolerable. As to the ways of improving their fortunes, this they must learn from other <profitable> arts, and not from philosophy.

* Matth. v. 32, Luke xvi. 18.
12. See above, p. 205 and note.
† 1. Corinth. vii. 15.
13. See *System* 3.1.11, vol. II, pp. 176–79 and note at p. 179. Hutcheson wants to show that the Scripture allows lawful cases of divorce beyond that of adultery ("unreasonable desertion" or "implacable hatred or enmity, sufficiently declared on one side").

CAPUT II

De Parentum et Liberorum Officiis.

I. Quum diu infirma maneat hominum soboles, se conservare nescia, aliorumque continua egens tutela, ut iis artibus et moribus quorum in vita est
usus imbuatur; hoc onus parentibus apertè imposuit Deus et natura, exi-
miam inserendo procreatorum curam. Tributa est igitur parentibus ea omnis potestas quam haec exigit tutela; eique liberos subjectos esse voluit natura. Ea parentum curâ et amore, satis plerumque cautum est liberorum
tempestivae manumissioni et libertati, quippe sine quâ beatè vivere nequeunt, cui rei parentes praecipue studere solent.

Consilii in liberis immaturis inopia, quique parentibus infixus est amor
gratuitus, duo parentum potestatis fundamenta, eam ostendunt haud esse
perpetuam; at tum demum desinere quum adoleverit eorum aetas et prudentia. Manet tamen idem parentum amor, ad omnia eos excitans officia,
quibus liberos adultos, vel ope vel consilio juvare possunt.

Ostendunt et eadem omnia, potestatem hanc ad supplicia quaevis graviora, quae aetatis <276> tenerae haud exigere potest tutela, neutiquam esse
porrigendam; multo minus ad vitam, aut omnem libertatem tollendam.
Nullo jure egerit parens qui liberos in perpetuam vendiderit servitutem, aut
onere quovis praegraverit, ultra impensarum modum quae in iis educandis,
viro prudenti erogandae viderentur.

II. Utrique etiam parenti pariter commissa est haec potestas; nisi quod in
re familiari administranda, potiores paulo sunt patris partes: eo tamen defuncto aut absente, omnem eam potestatem jure sibi vindicabit mater.

The Duties of Parents and Children.

I. As human offspring remains for a long time infirm, incapable of pre-serving itself, needing the constant care of others, both for preservation and instruction in these arts and manners which are necessary for life; <God and> nature has plainly imposed this charge upon the parents by that sin-gular affection implanted in them. Nature therefor must have designed that parents should assume all the power which is requisite for the discharge of this trust, and subjected children to it; while at the same time by this tender <care and> affection sufficient precaution is taken for the childrens ob-taining their liberty as soon as they can safely enjoy it; since without it they cannot be happy, which is the point that parents are most solicitous about.[1]

The want of judgment in our immature years, and the tender <and dis-interested> parental affection, the two only foundations of parental power, shew that it cannot be perpetual or during life; but must expire as soon as children grow up to mature strength of body and mind. And yet the pa-rental affection will always remain, exciting parents to all kind offices, when their children need their assistance or counsel.

The same considerations shew that this power cannot be extended to any of the more grievous punishments, <268> such as cannot be requisite for education in such tender years: much less can it extend to life or liberty. A parent has no right to sell his child to perpetual slavery, or to lay any burden upon it beyond the value of the necessary and prudent expences of its education.

II. This parental power belongs alike to both parents, only that in domestick affairs the power of the father is a little superior. But if he is dead or absent, it is wholly <rightly> vested in the mother.

1. See *System* 3.2.[1], vol. II, pp. 188–89.

Nugantur {isti} omnes qui potestatem hanc in sola fundari volunt{*} pro-creatione; ridiculè secuti, in re dissimillimâ, jurisconsultorum axiomata, de rerum inanimarum *specificationibus,* et *accessionibus,* vel de pecorum foe-turâ, quae nullum habent rationis usum, jurisve notitiam. Dei planè arte fabricata sunt liberorum et corpora et mentes, ut in aequalem vitae con-ditionem, et aequi juris usum tandem perveniant, licet aliquamdiu aliorum prudentia sint regendi. {Etenim} rerum dominia aliaque jura habent liberi, ab omni parentum potestate exempta; qui non aliud, in liberorum bona aliunde derivata, jus habent, quam tutores. {Hanc} a natura sibi <277> commissam tutelam qui abdicaverit, prolem exponendo aut negligendo, omnem {is} abdicat potestatem cum ea tutela conjunctam: quam omnem sibi acquisiverit, quisquis prolem abjectam alere voluerit et educare.

Liberis praebere tenentur parentes, idque sanctissimè, non solum ne-cessaria vitae praesidia, verum et ornamenta; eorumque uberiori foelicitati studere: praecipue vero, et doctrinâ et exemplo, mores eorum ad omnem virtutem conformare; citra quam liberis vita erit infoelix et ignominiosa [erubescenda], quantumvis rerum externarum copia abundet.

Quae erogant parentes in liberos queis nullae aliunde sunt facultates, ea donare intelliguntur; atque calculos ita subducere, ut ob victum et amictum pretium exigatur, nisi magna premuntur ipsi parentes inopia, ab omni abhorreret humanitate. Premente vero egestate, aut ubi liberis aliunde per-venerant opes, parentes omnia in liberos prudenter erogata jure reposcunt; eaque parenti egeno, liberi, etiam laboribus suis, praestare tenentur. Quan-tumvis igitur, pro communi parentum affectione [affectu], recte intelliga-

---

* Notantur hic *Hobbesius* et *Filmerus.*

---

* This is designed against *Hobbes* and *Filmer.*

2. This passage is rather implicit. Robert Filmer, quoting Grotius (*De iure belli* 2.5.1), derived the absolute power of father over children from begetting them. Locke (*Two Treatises* 1.6, 52–54) objected ironically that children are not the workmanship or artifact of parents, but—as Hutcheson says in the next sentence—are formed by the divine

'Tis trifling to found this power merely in generation,* or to follow < ri-
diculously> some law-maxims [the maxims of civilians] about <a quite different matter, as> the goods formed by our labour out of our own materials,
or other accessions of things animate or inanimate, [or the young of cattle]
which have no use of reason or no capacity of holding any rights.[2] Both
the bodies and souls of children are formed by the divine power, that they
may, as they grow up, arrive at the same condition of life, and an equality
of right with ourselves, tho' for some time they must be governed by the
wisdom of others. For children may have property, and other rights, quite
independent of their parents; who seem to have no other power over any
goods conveyed to their children by others than that of tutors or curators.
Whatever parents abandon this guardianship of their children committed
to them by nature, either by exposing or intirely neglecting them, forfeit
also the parental power connected with it: and any one acquires the whole
parental power who takes care of such children. <269>

Parents are most sacredly obliged to provide for their children all the
necessaries of life, and even to improve their condition as much as they can;
and above all to form their manners to all virtue by instruction and example:
for without this their lives must be miserable and infamous, tho' in the
greatest affluence.

What parents expend on children who have no stock of their own, is
justly presumed to be donation: and it would be inhuman in parents, who
are not in great distress, to charge food, clothing, {and necessary education},
as a debt upon their own children. But if the parents are in great distress,
or if any one of their children have a stock derived from some other friend,
parents may justly state such an account with their children, and exact payment from them {of all the prudent expences made upon their education};
and children in this case are bound to make such payment either by their
labours or otherways.[3] Altho' therefor from the common affections of par-

---

power. Hobbes in *De cive* 9, 2–3, and *Leviathan,* 1651, chapt. 20, 102–3, says that in the
state of nature the power over the child is in the mother "as she may either nourish, or
expose it." For Hutcheson this meant treating children as "specifications" of the father
(Filmer) or accessions of the mother (Hobbes). In *System* 3.2.2, vol. II, pp. 190–92,
Hutcheson enlarges on the subject. See also Pufendorf, *De officio* 2.2.4.

    3. See *System* 3.2.5, vol. II, p. 197.

tur, liberorum non minus quam sui causâ, parentes rem comparasse familiarem, unde et liberorum ad parentum haereditates succedendi jus innotescit; non tamen eo minus, <278> immo eo magis sancta est liberorum ad gratiam habendam et referendam obligatio: quo firmior enim, quo magis gratuita, atque ab ipsa natura profecta est amicitia et benevolentia, eo pluris est aestimanda, eoque major debetur gratia.

III. Parentum potestas legibus civilibus augeri potest, ut et ea quae magistratibus quibuslibet data est. {Etenim} imperium civile diversis causis innixum, et majora omnia spectans, pertinet ultra imperii *parentalis* fines. Quasi enim ex contractu, {imperatorum potestas} ad ea omnia recte extenditur, quae ab iis merito flagitari possunt, qui, ob communem plurium utilitatem consociati, omnium consilio et viribus proteguntur, cunctaque vitae civilis commoda et ornamenta sortiuntur, quique haec omnia posteris tradere sanctissimè tenentur. Jure [Minores] igitur <aut> pupilli obsides tradi possunt exteris; ad extrema etiam pericula adeunda, quum civitatis hoc exigit salus, rectè adiguntur.

IV. Liberi quamvis adulti, ad pietatem in parentes observantiamque, et ad gratiam referendam, sanctissime tenentur; non solum ob parentum merita, quibus {digna} rarò liberi [rependere] [vicem reddere] possunt; verum, ut Deum sequantur ducem et naturam, qui nos his parentibus ortos, cumque his sanguine, caritate, et veneratione ab incunabulis inchoatâ, <279> conjunctos esse voluerunt. Eorum igitur mores, parum licet commodos, amicissimè ferre decet; prout et illi, olim, nostros diu pertulerunt. In matrimonio praecipuè contrahendo, parentum auctoritatem sequi tenentur liberi; quum parentum multum intersit, quibus liberi, in vitae communitate omnium arctissima, se adjungant; unde nascituri sunt nepotes, in

ents we justly conclude, that their private fortunes are acquired for their children as well as themselves; whence appears the right of children to succeed to the inheritances of their parents; yet children are not to look upon themselves as less bound to gratitude on this account: nay they are rather the more bound. For the more firm and disinterested any affection [friendship and benevolence] is, and the more deeply it is rooted in the person's nature, the more it is to be valued, and the stronger is our obligation to gratitude.

III. Parents may acquire by civil law a further <270> power over their children, as the law commits power to any magistrates. For civil power having different foundations and greater ends, extends beyond the parental. And children, as they have from their birth enjoyed protection and the other advantages of a civilized life in a society constituted for the good of all, are plainly bound to perform to the community on their part* all that's due from good citizens; and particularly to preserve that constitution, and transmit the same to future ages.[4] Minors therefor may justly be delivered as hostages <to foreigners>, or be obliged to {military} services of the greatest danger in great exigences.

IV. Children even when adult owe all reverence and gratitude to their parents, not only in return for benefits received, which scarce any duty of theirs can sufficiently compensate; but also out of regard to God <and nature>, by whose providence it was ordered, that we descended from such parents, united with them in tyes of blood and natural affection, and an habitual reverence from our cradles. They ought therefor to bear with patience any weaknesses or froward humours of aged parents, as the parents long bore their childish follies. Particularly 'tis the duty of children to consult the satisfaction of their parents in entring into marriage; since the parent is also deeply concerned in this important step; by which their children enter into a strict society for life with others, from whence must proceed grand-

---

* See Book II. ch. xiv. 2. of obligations resembling those from contracts: and the following ch. v. 2.

4. See *System* 3.2.5, vol. II, p. 198.

eorum jura et nomina saepe, semper in στοργὴν, successuri.

Parentum imperium saepe excipit potestas patrisfamilias; quae tanta est, quantam, suo consensu, vel palam declarato vel tacitò, eam fecerunt liberi adulti, aut alii, qui sua sponte, potestatis quam arrogavit conscii, in ipsius degunt domo.

children to their parents, to succeed sometimes <271> to their names and fortunes, and always to their tenderest affections.

After the proper parental power expires, there often succeeds that of the *head of a family;* which is of such extent as the domesticks make it by their own consent express or tacit, by voluntarily continuing in, or entering into, a family, where they knew such a degree of power was assumed.

CAPUT III

De Herorum et Servorum Jure.

I. Aucto hominum genere, subinde extiterunt plures suis {solùm} laboribus alendi, quibus nempe nulla rerum necessariarum erat [suppetebat] aliunde copia; alii vero <fuere> opulenti, plurium ministerio et operis, ad vitam [faciliùs agendam] [faciliorem], indigentes. Hinc orta est conditio servilis, pactis innixa. Quae utrum a primo perpetua fuerat, an temporaria, parum attinet exquirere; quum utrobique, excepta diuturnitate [duratione], eadem fuere jura et obligationes, quae sequuntur sunt magis ad rem: <280>

1. Sani hominis et validi labores et operae longe pluris sunt aestimandae, quam ipsius victus simplicior et amictus: quippe videmus istiusmodi homines operis suis, aliquid etiam ad voluptatem et ornatum, aut ad familiam alendam, comparare. Si quis igitur incautus nihil ultra victum et amictum, pro operis suis fuerat stipulatus; ex eo contractu, utpote apertè oneroso, jure pleno{*} exigere potest ut quod deest ad aequalitatem ipsi suppleatur.

2. Ubi nihil de operarum genere diserte convenit, intelligitur servum sibi suscepisse eas solum operas, quas heri non inhumani a servis solent exigere; seque hero modicè castigandum permisisse, quoties cessaverit, aut familiae statum turbaverit. Caetera omnia hominum jura naturalia aut adventitia ipsi servo manent intacta.

3. Si quidem satis innotuerit, in moribus esse, patresfamilias sejunctos [segreges], in domesticos suos imperium aliquod civile sibi arrogare; huic etiam, quousque non ab humanitate abhorret, servum se subjecisse merito colligitur. Servi quidèm operas jure exigit herus; caetera retinet jura servus, quae cuivis ex populo manent sub imperio civili; omnia certe jura naturalia

---

* Vid. Lib. II.c.ix.5. et c.xiii.4.

1. Cf. Pufendorf, *De officio* 2.4.1.
2. Titius, cited by Carmichael, *Notes on Puf.,* p. 139.

The Rights of Masters and Servants.

I. When mankind were considerably multiplied, there would be many who had no other fund of support than their labours; and others of greater opulence, who for their ease would need much of the labours and services of others. And hence the relation of master and servant would arise, founded on some contract.[1] Nor is it of consequence whether such contracts at first were for life, or only for a certain term: since excepting the point of duration, the rights and obligations were the very same.[2] The points following are of more consequence.

1. The labours <and services> of any person sound in body and mind, are of much more value than the bare simple food and clothing of a servant; as we plainly see that such can purchase all this by their labours, and something further for the support of a family, and even for some pleasure and ornament. If any one therefor has incautiously insisted for no more in his contract; yet as the contract is plainly onerous, he has a right to have this inequality redressed.*

2. Where the labours were not specified, the servant is deemed to have engaged only for such as men of humanity in such stations commonly exact from their servants; and to have submitted only to such coercion <273> of his master as is necessary for the good order of a family, if he should neglect his work or misbehave. But he retains all other natural or acquired rights.

3. If indeed the custom is known to have obtained, that <separate> heads of families assume a sort of civil power over their domesticks; the servant is justly deemed to have consented to this also, as far as it is managed consistently with humanity. The servant is <justly> bound to perform his work; but retains all the rights of subjects under civil government; particularly all

---

* Book II. xii. 4. [See Book II, chapt. ix.5 and chapt. xiii.4. The section referred to by the translator is wrong.]

quae alienari nequeunt: et ad omnem vim iis defendendis necessariam, <281> contra herum ea violaturum, recte procurrit.

4. Ubi de certis tantum operis pactum fuit, ad has solas obligatur servus. Quin imo, licet quascunque praestare posset operas susceperit, easque perpetuas; non tamen idcirco dominus eum invitum alteri emancipare poterit: quum servi plurimum intersit cui serviat domino, et in quâ domo. Servorum autem hujusmodi omnium libera nascitur proles.

II. Hactenus de servitute sponte contracta. Deterior longe istiusmodi servorum conditio, qui ob grave damnum a se datum, quod alia nequeunt pensare [compensare] ratione, aut qui ob delictum atrox, poenae nomine, ad perpetuas operas <praestandas> addicuntur.

Neque tamen vel hi omnia hominum amittunt jura: ea enim sola, quae damno reparando inserviunt, quibusve ne similes in posterum injuriae inferantur caveri poterit, ipsis adimenda. In sceleratissimos, si modo ipsorum vitae parcatur, postquam, ad omnes a similibus delictis deterrendos, publicas poenas pertulerunt, non est ultra saeviendum, quum labores ipsis impositos non detrectant. Immo juris quicquid ipsis manet, recte per vim defendent. Quum vero in servitute his de causis constituenda, aliorum tantum spectetur utilitas, herus istiusmodi servum invitum, ad alterum transferre potest. <282> Nulla vero de causa, ex hominum numero, in belluarum, aut rerum inanimarum ordinem, servi jure detrudi possunt, ita ut nullius juris sint participes.

In hanc deterrimam conditionem, omnes in bello captos detruserunt olim gentes haud caetera barbarae, {temerè in semet legem sancientes iniquissimam, atque} mirum in modum conspirantes ad gravissimas contu-

such as are naturally unalienable: and may justly defend them, even by violence, against any invasions of them by his master.

4. Where the services have been specified in the contract, the servant is bound to no other. Nay tho' they were not, and the contract was perpetual or for life, yet the master cannot transfer him to another without his own consent; since 'tis of high importance to the servant what master he is subjected to, and in what family.[3] And for the children of such servants they are all born free.[4]

II. Hitherto we have treated of service founded on contract. But there is a far worse kind, to wit, of those who for some great damage done, which they can no other way repair; or on account of some great crime, are adjudged by way of punishment unto perpetual labours to others.

And yet even in these cases, they don't lose all the rights of mankind, but only such as are naturally fit to compensate the damage, or are necessary to give security to the publick against like injuries for the future. <274> If the lives even of the worst criminals are spared; after they have endured all such publick punishments as the safety of society may require, 'tis unjust to treat them with any further cruelty; provided they are willing to perform the labours they are condemned to. And they have a right to defend themselves even by violence, against {new injuries, or} violations of any rights still remaining to them.[5] But as slavery of this kind is constituted solely for the behoof of others; the master may transfer to another such a slave without his own consent. But no cause whatsoever can degrade a rational creature from the class of men into that of brutes or inanimate things, so as to become {wholly the property of another,} without any rights of his own.

<In times past> Nations in other respects not barbarous, condemned all captives in war into this most miserable condition; establishing an inhuman law even against themselves, and strangely conspiring to subject themselves and their posterity, upon many very possible contingencies, to the most

---

3. See Pufendorf, *De officio* 2.4.3.

4. Hutcheson, with Carmichael (*Notes on Puf.,* pp. 142–44 and note) and against Pufendorf and Barbeyrac rejects the idea of the slave as property and children born by a mother-slave as her fruit. See also *System* 3.3.1, vol. II, pp. 199–201.

5. See *System* 3.3.1, vol. II, p. 201.

melias et aerumnas, sibi fortè, aut posteris, olim arcessendas. Qua de re hi veri videntur aphorismi.{*}

1. Qui injustam in bello causam tuetur, nullum in res aut homines captos jus acquirit, quo salva fide et justitia uti possit, quamvis rebus captis impune frui liceat; quod jure quodam munitur externo; de quo alias.{†}

2. Qui justam habuit belli causam, intra justos tamen petendi fines se continere debet: neque quicquam a victis exigere <potest> nisi vel poenae nomine, vel damni reparandi; vel ut in posterum de non laedendo caveatur.{‡}

3. Poenae nomine nihil ab iis exigi potest qui nihil ad bellum attulerunt, vel faciendo vel non faciendo secus quam debebant; quae longe plurium civium adultorum est causa: ne de uxoribus dicamus et liberis, qui duas aut tres conficiunt civitatis cujusque <283> partes; quibusque bonorum omnium dominium cum patribus familias est commune. Nec, si tributa in belli sumptus pependerant patres familias, ullo ob id crimine sunt obstricti. Haec sub gravi solverant necessitate, per vim alias et supplicia extorquenda. Quamvis etiam, speciosis permoti rationibus a principibus suis denunciatis, bello consenserant; invicta erat ferè eorum ignorantia: neque quicquam eorum consensus ad bellum attulit, neque dissensus bellum prohibuisset: neque adeo arcta est conjunctio quaevis politica, ut unius delictum in alterum non consentientem transferri debeat.

4. [6.]¹ Quod ad ipsos attinet milites, qui consiliorum publicorum neque participes, neque fautores, speciosis illecti causis nomina dederunt; illis ob

---

* Hac de re vid. annot. *Carmichael.* in *Puffend.* lib. ii.c.4. et *Lockium* ibid. citatum.
† Vid. cap. ix. hujus libri, 4, 5.
‡ Vid. L. II.c.xv.5, 8.
1. The whole item was the sixth one in 1742 edn.

---

* See the following ch. ix. 4. <and 5>.
† See Book II. xv. 5, 8. On this subject of slavery many just reasonings are to be found in Mr. *Locke*'s 2d. book on government; and Mr. *Carmichael*'s notes on *Puffendorf,* Book II. ch. iv. [In the Latin text "On this subject . . . etc" is a distinct note placed before Hutcheson's list. So Hutcheson acknowledges that all his "maxims" (not just the second

miserable and ignominious treatment. Upon which subject the following maxims seem just.

1. Whoever makes war without a just cause acquired no right by such violence, over either persons or goods taken, which he can use with a good conscience, tho' he may detain them with external impunity, <granted by some external right> as we shall shew hereafter.*

2. One who has a just cause, yet should set just bounds to his demands: nor can he demand any thing from the conquered except either under the name of <275> *punishment, reparation of damage* done, or *precaution* against future injuries.†

3. None are punishable but such as either by some action or omission, contrary to their duty, have occasioned and contributed toward {these injuries done to us by} the war. {And 'tis plain,} this is seldom ever the case of the far greater part of the adult subjects of any state{, who are capable of a share in publick affairs}; not to speak of women and children, who make <two or> three fourths of every people, and ought to be deemed joint proprietors with the heads of families in their private properties. And tho' all heads of families payed tributes toward maintaining the war: this can't be deemed a crime in them, as they were under the immediate distress of their governors, who would otherways have levied these taxes by force{, and punished the refractory}. Grant they had consented to the war, following some specious reasons published by their governors; their ignorance generally was invincible: nor was their consent of such importance as to cause the war, nor would their dissent have prevented it. Nor can we ever suppose that any political union <is so close that it> can transfer the guilt of one person upon another who did not concur with him.[6]

4. Nay the very soldiers, all such at least as had no share of or influence in the publick councils, as they enlisted upon presumption of being em-

---

one) are based on Locke, *Two Treatises* 2. 16 and Carmichael's notes on Pufendorf. In fact from Locke, Hutcheson derives the idea that even in a just war, the conquerors have not the right to enslave a nation, but only the governors and, even in that case, they cannot deprive their females and children of their land and property. From Carmichael, who quotes Locke approvingly, stem the ideas that most of the conquered are innocent, that a slave is not to be considered a property or a merchandise, that children of slave are born free.

6. See *System* 3.3.3, vol. II, pp. 204–5.

ignorantiam, et parendi necessitatem, venia danda. Conscriptis enim imperata detrectare facinus est capitale. Ab illis igitur, poenae nomine, quicquam gravius exigere inhumanum esset; si modo ab iisdem in posterum satis caveri possit: quod, illaesa eorum libertate, eos apud se detinendo, aut in civitatem suam aut colonias adscribendo, victor semper sibi poterit praestare. Quae omnia suaderet humanitas, {bellique casus ancipites,} et fortunae bellicae maxima inconstantia.

5. [4.] Non alio juris fundamento quicquam <284> a civibus innoxiis postulat victor, damni reparandi nomine, quam quod substernitur *actionibus noxalibus et de pauperie;* quod scil. qui quaedam suae utilitatis praesidia sibi adscivit, ex quibus alii nullâ suâ culpâ damnum sunt passi, is vel damnum sarcire, vel, si malit, rem damnosam laeso dedere teneatur. Jure igitur aliquando a victis civibus id exigit victor, ut ipsorum deserant principes, belli injusti auctores; aut eos damna reparare cogant, aut ipsi ea reparent. Horum autem victis danda optio. Haec quidem de iis civibus qui imperia {civilia} primi constituerunt; aut de potentioribus, quorum auctoritate et consilio injustum bellum erat susceptum; quique poterant principes injusta molientes cohibuisse, apertius tenent: caeterorum, qui parum in Republica possunt, favorabilior est in ipso damno praestando causa.

6. [5.] Ubi primum vero hostes vel sponte victori damna data repararunt, vel ipse victor, rebus eorum per vim occupatis, damnorum compensationem est consecutus, una cum cautione in posterum, ad viri probi arbitrium; nihil amplius a civibus devictis exigere potest. Haec vero omnia, leniore multò ratione assequi possunt victores, quam adempta civibus innoxiis libertate. Ad damna [haec] autem praestanda primòtenentur qui imperio praesunt; his vero cessantibus, tenentur cives. <285>

ployed only in <276> just causes{, or persuaded by such reasons as their
governors publish}; they are excusable entirely, both on account of ignorance and necessity. To men once enlisted 'tis a capital crime to disobey
orders.[7] It must therefor be exceedingly inhuman to inflict any thing severe
upon them by way of punishment, provided we can be secured against
further dangers from them: and this we always may be from captives, by
keeping them in our own country, and mixing them with our citizens or
our colonies, without depriving them any way of their liberty. All this not
only humanity will recommend, but a consideration of the uncertain accidents of war, and the <greatest> inconstancy of fortune <in war>.

5. Under pretence of repairing damages, the conqueror can demand
nothing from the innocent citizens, except upon the same grounds that one
demands it for damage done by another's slaves or cattle, to wit this, "that,
whoever contrives or procures any thing for his own utility, by which others
without their fault receive hurt, is bound either to repair the damage, or
deliver up the goods, or contrivance whatever it was, to the person injured."
The conqueror may therefor justly demand from the conquered citizens, that
they abandon their unjust governors the causes of the war; or that they oblige
these governors to repair the damages; or that they repair them themselves:
and these three should be left to their choice. This holds most evidently as
to these first citizens who at first constituted the government; or those who
have great power in the state, by whose council the war was <wrongly>
undertaken; or who have it in their power to restrain <277> their princes
in their unjust designs. As to others who are of no weight in publick affairs,
their plea against even compensating of damages is more favourable.

6. But as soon as the defeated have repaired all damages, or the conqueror
has obtained reparation to himself by force and military execution; and has
also obtained security against future injuries, such as a wise arbiter judges
sufficient, he has no further demand upon the innocent citizens. Now he
may obtain all this in a {much easier, and} more merciful way, without
depriving the innocent citizens of their liberty. The governors are in the
first place bound to repair all damages, and the citizens only in the second
place when their governors cannot do it, or decline it.

7. See *System* 3.3.4, vol. II, p. 208.

7. Servorum omnium sobolem esse naturâ liberam, satis antea ostendimus.{*}

8. Qui hominem [servum] emit, aut <eum> emptum {in servitute} vi detinet, ipsius est ostendere eum jure libertatem amisisse. {Rei de qua disceptatur} antiquus semper adest dominus; quum adultos quosque sui juris constituat natura. Possessoris igitur violenti est probare se jure possidere; non [liberale judicium implorantis, ostendere] [servi, probare propositionem negantem] se non jure libertatem amisisse.

9. Neque dixeris, captivos nisi vendi possent, interemptum iri, ideoque vitam ipsam emptoribus debere. Esto. Hinc tamen non alia emptoribus nascuntur jura, quam quae negotium utile gerenti, aut vitam civis contra latrones defendenti, aut captum a piratis redimenti, aut morbos et vulnera graviora, sine ope medicâ lethalia, sananti. His omnibus impensae, et laborum curaeque pretia, quodque *aequius melius,* sunt persolvenda: nullum tamen imperii herilis jus inde nasci potest.

III. Ut servi cujusque, qui jure alteri subjicitur, officium est, strenuam et fidam, domino, aut hero potius, operam praestare; Deumque communem omnium dominum, omnia intuentem, in omni ministerio praecipuè respicere: ita domini est, nihil ultra <286> juris sui limites a servo exigere, atque ab omni abstinere saevitia, ut decet hominem, communis cognationis, humanaeque conditionis instabilis memorem; quique novit animos servorum et corpora, eâdem, qua nostra, materiâ constare, et paribus elementis; Deoque, communi omnium parenti, et domino, vitae actae rationem esse reddendam.

---

* L. II.c.xiv.3.

---

* Book II. xiv. 3. {See Mr. Locke on govern. Book II. as also *Hooker's. Ecles. Polity,* and *Sidney* on *Government.*} [Richard Hooker, *Of the Laws of Ecclesiastical Polity* (London, 1593); Algernon Sidney, *Discourses Concerning Government* (London, 1698).]

7. The children of slaves of any sort are all born free,* as we shewed above.

8. Whoever purchases a person for a slave, or detains him as such, is always bound to shew that this person was deprived of his liberty upon some just ground. The original proprietor of the matter in question is always at hand: since nature made every man master of himself, or of his own liberty. 'Tis plainly therefor incumbent upon the violent possessor to prove his title; and not upon the person {deforced, and} claiming his liberty, to prove {a negative[8]}, that he did not lose, or forfeit his liberty. {[Without a previous inquiry of this kind no man can in this case be a fair purchaser.]}[9]

9. Nor is it justly pleaded here, that captives would <278> be put to death if they could not be made slaves and sold as such: and that therefor they owe their lives and all to the purchasers. But sure no higher sort of title arises to the purchasers in this case, than to such as have done any other useful service of equal importance; such as, rescuing a fellow-citizen from robbers or murderers, ransoming them from pyrates, curing diseases or wounds which without the aid of art would have been deadly.[10] All such persons should have all expences refunded to them, and a generous compensation for their labours and art. But who ever alleged that they could claim the persons they thus served as their slaves?

III. As it is the duty of servants who are justly subjected to others, to perform their work with diligence and fidelity <to heir lord or rather master>; regarding God the common master of all, who is ever present with us: so 'tis the duty of masters to exact no more from servants than what they have a right to, and to abstain from all cruelty and insolence; as it becomes those who remember that all are of one blood, and naturally allied to each other, and that fortune is inconstant, that the souls and bodies of servants are of the same stuff with our own, and of a like constitution; and that all of us must give an account of our conduct to God the common Parent and Lord of all.

8. See Carmichael, *Notes on Puf.,* p. 141 for the same argument. See also *System* 3.3.6, vol. II, pp. 210–11.

9. Square parenthesis in the original text.

10. See *System* 3.3.5, vol. II, p. 210.

De Civitatum Origine et Causis.

I. De domesticis societatibus [hactenus.] [satis dictum:] ad civitatum causas et jura explicanda progredimur. Per societates et conjunctiones jam memoratas, si nemo suo deesset officio, copiosa satis esset hominum vita et jucunda. Ad civitates igitur et imperia civilia constituenda [impulit metus] [permoti fuerunt homines metu] malorum quae vel ex hominum imbecillitate vel improbitate oriri possent. Haud tamen idcirco naturae contraria dicenda est vita civilis: quicquid enim monstrabit ea ratio quam nobis natura inseruit, ad mala prohibenda, aut commoda consequenda, necessarium esse aut utile, illud omne est maxime secundum animantis providi et sagacis naturam. Jure igitur dicuntur homines φύσει ζῶα πολιτικὰ.

Fingamus autem omnes ita esse probos, ut ea sola consultò velint <aut cupiant>, quae ipsis justa videntur; erroribus tamen de suo et aliorum <287> jure, suae utilitatis appetitione et perturbationum impetu {deceptos}, saepe esse obnoxios: lites hinc saepe exsurgere necesse esset. Fingamus et plures esse ita suspiciosos, ut lites ortas arbitris permittere nollent, timentes quisque alterius gratiam, aut artes, quibus arbitros corrumpere posset. Huc si accedat nimia utrinque virium suarum fiducia, et in sua sententiâ

The Original of Civil Government.

I. Having finished the account of domestick society, we proceed to shew the origin and rights of civil society [states], {[in which 'tis universally understood, there is included a right vested in some person or council to decide all controversies arising amongst large numerous bodies, to direct the actions of all for the common interest, and to compell all by force to obey their orders.]}[1] By the associations <and conjunctions> already explained, if all men were faithful in discharging their duties, human life must have sufficient affluence and pleasure. It must therefore have been some fear of mischiefs to arise either from the weakness or vices of men, which has moved them to subject themselves to civil power [to constitute states and civil power]. But we must not therefor, call civil society *unnatural* or contrary to nature. For whatever that reason, nature has endued us with, shews to be necessary or very conducive to obtain those advantages we naturally desire, or avert the contrary evils, must plainly be deemed natural to a creature endued naturally with reason and forethought. Men therefor are justly called "creatures [animals] fitted by nature for civil polity."[2]

Let us suppose all men so just that none would do to others any thing he judged injurious, but that they are pretty liable to mistakes about their own and others rights, through their strong selfish desires, and the <280> byass of impetuous passions: this would frequently occasion controversies among them. Let us further suppose that many honest men are yet too suspicious, so that they won't submit their disputes to the arbitration of others, each fearing perhaps the interest of his adversary with the arbiters, or his art in seducing them:[3] if there be added to this, too much confidence

1. Square parenthesis in the original text. This definition is not in the *Institutio*.
2. Aristotle, *Politica*, 1253a.3, 1278b.19. See *System* 3.4.1, vol. II, p. 212.
3. Cf. *System* 3.4.2, vol. II, p. 214.

tuendâ pervicacia, non sine saevis belli malis lites in libertate dirimentur.

Quin et imperia civilia hominibus propius commendavit ipsa natura. Mortalium nonnulli caeteris multo sunt solertiores; quod et caeteri non raro fatebuntur: poterunt hi solertiores et sagaciores plurima in communem excogitare utilitatem, omnium viribus exsequenda; poterunt et optimas monstrare rationes, quibus sibi quisque et suis consulere posset, si modo eorum monitis paruerint. Quod si {his ingenii viribus et} solertiae conjunctae sint virtutes praeclarae, bonitas, justitia, fortitudo; earum significatio fidem apud omnes conciliabit, et omnium accendet studia, ad viros his ornatos virtutibus, honoribus et potestate ornandos et amplificandos; hisque auctoribus, foelicia omnia et laeta arbitrabuntur se consecuturos. Ad civitates igitur constituendas non solum injuriarum metus, verum et virtutes hominum egregiae, <288> et naturalis virtutum comprobatio, plurimum contulisse videtur.

II. Si vero etiam spectetur plurium improbitas, morumque depravationes, avaritia, ambitio, luxuries; tum vero patebit sine potestate civili, hominum non modo utilitati, et foelicitati, sed nedum saluti, satis consuli posse: eâque solâ, malis hisce ab hominum vitiis oriundis, optimum, et in improvidi et incauti cujusque oculos incurrens, remedium adhiberi. In magno enim concilio, quamvis ita vigeat injustitia, ut occasione oblata, quisque sui causa, injusta ageret; idem tamen alium {sui ordinis} moribus parem, eademque peragentem, si modo ipse nullum inde capiat fructum, odio habebit et damnabit. Ab istiusmodi igitur hominum concilio, alîus cujusque improbitatem damnantium, quamvis suae quisque secretò indulgeret, nunquam leges condentur iniquae. Quemque suam profiteri injustitiam pudebit; et sibi quisque ab aliorum metuet improbitate, nisi justis et aequis

on both sides in their own force, and obstinacy in opinion; their controversies in natural liberty can be decided no other way than by {violence
and} all the mischiefs of war.

But there's something in our nature which more immediately recommends civil power to us. Some of our species are manifestly superior in
wisdom to the vulgar, as the vulgar are often sensible. These of superior
<skills and> sagacity, {as all must own,} are capable of contriving and in-
venting many things of consequence to the common utility {of multi-
tudes}, and of pointing out more effectual methods for each one to promote
his own interest, if their directions are complied with. If to these abilities
be added also eminent moral virtues, goodness, justice, fortitude; the appearance of such excellencies obtains the trust and confidence of all, and
kindles their zeal to promote such persons to honour and power; as they
conclude that under their direction all may obtain every sort of prosperity.[4]
'Tis highly probable therefor that not only the dread of injuries, but eminent virtues, and our natural high approbation of them have engaged men
at first to form civil societies.

II. But if we consider how much injustice, depravation of manners, avarice,
ambition, and luxury prevail among men: it will be manifest, that without
civil <281> power, men cannot be preserved in safety, not to speak of any
high advantages or pleasures to be enjoyed in society: and that it is by civil
power alone an effectual remedy, and such a one as must strike the senses
of the most inconsiderate, can be found for the evils to be dreaded from
these vices of men. For tho' all the members of a large assembly were so
unjust, that upon a fit opportunity each one for his own interest would do
injuries to others; yet each one would abhor like injustice done by his fellow,
when he had no share in the gain of it. An assembly therefor of such men,
of whom each condemned that injustice in his neighbour which he would
indulge in himself, will never make unjust decrees for their whole body.[5]
Each one will be ashamed to own his dishonesty, and will live in dread of

4. See *System* 3.4.1, vol. II, p. 213.
5. See *System* 3.4.2, vol. II, p. 215.

legibus, et poenâ repraesentata, coërceantur.

Neque alia ratione hominibus satis caveri poterit. Licet enim non adeo depravati essent homines, plurimosque incitaret humanitas et recti honestique sensus, ad vicinos ab injuriis defendendos; <illi> ex metu tamen aut ignavia saepe hoc desererent officium, ubi <289> cum periculo esset conjunctum. Quinetiam ipsorum fortium et proborum multitudo, nisi uno regatur consilio, pro diversis, de opis ferendae ratione, sententiis, et quorundam pertinaciâ, in diversa omnia abiret; disjunctaque et discors, paucioribus et minus strenuis conjunctis praedae esset et ludibrio.

His {libertatis solutae} incommodis perspectis, credibile est, prudentiores et sagaciores hoc praecipuum excogitasse remedium, ut magnus hominum numerus inter se paciscantur, de societate ineunda, in singulorum, communemque omnium salutem et utilitatem, communi prudentiorum consilio regenda: cujus commoditatibus palam expositis, alios etiam sibi socios adscivisse{, iisque societatis arctioris ineundae auctores extitisse}.

III. Qui civitatum originem ambitiosorum adscribunt violentiae; id [quidem] [jam antea, alia ratione] factum statuunt, [ante eam vim, quam ejusdem causam esse volunt] [cujus de prima origine & causa anquirunt]. Nemo enim unus, sine plurium antea sibi subjectorum ope, hominum multitudinem, civitati constituendae idoneam, sibi poterat subjicere. Constituta igitur fuit civitas, ante eam vim cui primum civitatum ortum adscribunt.

---

6. Cf. *System* 3.4.2, vol. II, pp. 216–17.

7. See Carmichael, *Notes on Puf.,* pp. 146–47, for the same argument directed against Titius and Barbeyrac, who rejected Pufendorf's idea of general agreement as

receiving injuries from others, unless they are all restrained by equal laws enforced by proper punishments.

Nor is there any other way of preserving society in safety. For altho' men were not generally so depraved, and that even humanity and conscience [the sense of what is right and honourable] {restrained the generality from injuries, and} inclined them to give aid to any who happened to be wronged: yet multitudes would omit this duty through fear and cowardice, if it exposed themselves to danger. Nay further; a sufficient number of honest brave men, if they were not directed by some head, and that united in their efforts, would run into the most different measures, according to their different sentiments (and obstinacy); and when thus disjoined would become a prey <and laughing-stock> even to a smaller number of less bravery, who were united in their counsels.

'Tis therefor very probable that some of the wiser <282> and more sagacious, observing these inconveniences of a state of anarchy, fell upon this as the only remedy, that a large number of men should covenant with each other about entering into a firm society, to be regulated by the counsel of the wiser few, in all matters relating to the safety and advantage either of individuals or the whole body. And discerning the many conveniencies to ensue upon such a project, have explained it to others, and persuaded them to put it in execution.[6]

III. They who ascribe the first origin of all civil power [states] to the violence of ambitious men, plainly presuppose that already existing, whose original they are searching for [before the force that are claiming to be its cause]: as no one man could have force enough, without a large number of others already subjected {to his direction and government,} to compell a multitude sufficient to form a state, to submit themselves to his power. A civil power therefor was constituted previously to that conquest they suppose to have produced the first civil power.[7]

---

the origin of civil society, and ascribed it to the violence of ambitious and cunning men (cf. Titius, *Observationes,* nos. 547 and 555, and Pufendorf, *De iure nat.* 7.1.6, Barbeyrac's note 1).

Si quis dixerit, patremfamilias opulentum, suis et domesticorum viribus vicinos sibi subjicere potuisse: Esto. At non nomina, sed <290> res ipsae sunt spectandae. Regio enim imperio nonnunquam utebantur patresfamilias opulentiores: atque insuper, justas nos imperii justi causas quaerimus, non injusti violentas.

IV. Ad communem utilitatem plurimum hoc conferre, quod imperitiorum multitudo prudentiorum regatur consilio et ratione, negaverit nemo. Quod si ex inepta Reipub. forma eveniat, ut parum prudentibus, aut improbis nimia permittatur potestas, hoc etiam plurimum obesse posse, fatebuntur omnes; prout in aliis rebus, rei optimae cujusque pessima poterit esse depravatio. Nihil tamen hinc vitae civilis utilitati aut dignitati detrahetur. {Etenim} ingenii vires hominibus a Deo sunt datae, ut optimas, ex innumeris quae excogitari possunt, imperii formas sibi eligant.

Est igitur civitas "liberorum hominum coetus, sub uno imperio in communem omnium utilitatem consociatus." Communem omnium utilitatem potestatis civilis finem esse, inter omnes convenit. Hoc contendit populus; in hoc se jactant Reges omnes, qui non insano scelere, humanae conditionis obliti, Dei opt. max. jura sibi arrogant, aut iis etiam ampliora. Quicquid est civile, id toto coelo, ut aiunt, distat a dominatione *despotica.* Ea sola igitur potestas civilis <291> est justa, quae communi inservit utilitati. Quae huic obstat, utcunque populi hebetioris et incauti consensu constituta, nullo munitur jure. Vitium contractui inhaesit; quia in iis erratum est, quae hic praecipuè spectari omnibus est notissimum.

Should one allege that a potent head of a family, with his numerous domesticks, might have {conquered and thus} compelled his neighbours around to submit to him {as their prince}. This may have happened no doubt. But we are not to regard names, but things themselves. Heads of families no doubt sometimes had a proper regal power over their domesticks. And further, we are not inquiring into the possible injurious methods of usurpation, but into the probable just causes of just power.[8]

IV. That it must conduce much to the interest of a multitude to be governed by a council of the wise, <283> no man can deny. And altho' under some foolish plans of government, power [too much authority] may often be intrusted to bad hands, and thence great mischiefs arise, as the corruptions of the best things may be most pernicious; yet this is no dishonour to civil government, as if it were in general of little use or pernicious. For God has given men sufficient powers of reason to choose some of the more prudent convenient forms out of the innumerable multitudes conceivable.

A state or civil society is, "a society of free men united under one government for their common interest." That the common interest of the whole body is the end of all civil polity, is owned by all. This all subjects insist upon; and all governors [kings] glory in it as their dignity; except some vain monsters, who forgetting their mortal state, arrogate to themselves the rights of almighty God, or even powers more extensive. The very notion of civil life, or polity, is opposite to despotism{, or the power of masters over slaves}.[9] That civil power therefor alone is just which is naturally adapted to this end: other power tho' granted by the rash deed of an ignorant people, has no foundation of right. There was an essential defect in the deed granting it, as it was founded in an error about what is owned by all to be most essential in such contracts.

8. Cf. *System* 3.4.6, vol. II, pp. 224–25.
9. Cf. *System* 3.4.4, vol. II, p. 221.

{Hic} mirari subit, quorundam{*} non indoctorum orationes, in vitae civilis incommodis et oneribus molestis depingendis, ita nonnunquam exultare, ac si ab ea vita ineundâ homines vellent deterrere; quod tamen ne fiat, libertatis statum, pari modo, deformant, [in larvam] [larvarum] omnium maxime horribilem. Utrique quidem statui sua sunt commoda et incommoda. Non levia in libertate solutâ mala sunt subinde metuenda; atqui non continua. Malis {quidem} in vita civili metuendis, nisi in civitate constituenda aberat omnino prudentia, [paria, immo majora, eademque crebriora, in homines solutos cadere possunt: atque etiam, in vita civili,] [graviora quidem & craebriora, in libertate sunt metuenda,] contra ea mala, aliorum auxilia certius quisque sibi polliceri potest.

---

* Notatur hic *Puffendorfii* opus et majus et minus, una cum *Hobbesio,* quem plane secutus videtur *Puffendorfius.*

One can scarce avoid wondering how some* ingenious authors seem to pique themselves upon aggravating and exaggerating all the burdens of civil subjection, <284> as if they designed to deter men from entering into it; but then least they should do so, they paint a state of liberty {and anarchy} as the most frightful monster of all. Whereas 'tis plain both states have both their advantages and disadvantages. There are no doubt many dangers [not light evils to be repeatedly feared] in a state of liberty, but these not continual: generally they are <equal and even> greater and more frequent than in civil life; unless a people have been exceedingly incautious in the plan of power they constituted: as in civil life we have a much surer prospect of protection from injuries by the united force of all. {Nor are there any evils peculiar to a civil life under regular government; the like or worse, men were also† exposed to in liberty: [as it will appear by considering the several parts of civil power in the following chapter.]}

---

* The author has here in view *Hobbes;* and *Puffendorf,* both in his greater and lesser book, who has too blindly followed Hobbes {, nay even transcribed his very words}. [The translator, as well Hutcheson, may have in mind those passages of Pufendorf, such as *De iure nat.* 2.2.2 or *De officio* 2.1.9, where Pufendorf is echoing Hobbes, *De cive* 1.13.]

† {Thus subjects are bound to pay taxes, for the common interest, for fortifying or defending the state. But each one in liberty must on his part be at greater charges, either for his own conveniency, for fortifying his house and arming his domesticks, or for hiring assistance. Each subject may be obliged to hazard his life for the state. But so each one in anarchy may more frequently for his own defence. Subjects submit to a power of life and death over themselves in criminal jurisdictions. But so each one in anarchy is subjected to a worse power of any inraged person who alleges he is injured by him, and intituled to use force for redress. If by a power of life and death one means an arbitrary power in a governor, upon any caprice, without a crime alleged, to take mens lives away; no such power is in any wise polity; nor can any human deed constitute it.} [The translator derives the added text and this note from what Hutcheson says in *System* 3.4.5, vol. II, pp. 222–23.]

CAPUT V

De interna Civitatum Structura,
et summi Imperii Partibus.

I. Quum imperatorum nemo suum sibi populum progenuit, neque, si pro-
genuisset, <292> potestatem parentis in fratres adultos, ad haeredem trans-
mittere posset; {(}quippe quae parentum στοργή, et immaturo liberorum
judicio, tanquam unico fundamento, innitatur;{)} a *parentali* neutiquam
deducenda est potestas civilis{, quamvis ejusdem exemplum quoddam ad-
umbratum fuerit}. Neque, in populum universum justiùs arrogari potest
potestas herilis; quod ex jam dictis satis constat. Neque deinde oraculo Deus
reges, aut alios creat magistratus, modumve imperii certum, aut fines constituit. Nec denique vires nullo jure innixae justam potestatem tribuere possunt. {Restat} igitur {ut ipsius} Populi conventione et decreto verum omne
jus imperii constituatur.

In casibus forte rarioribus, res aliter se habere potest. Quum enim populi
salus et foelicitas sit unicus imperii finis; ubi satis huic consulitur, a viro
prudente et praepotente, {eâ scil.} formâ imperii praescripta, quam omnes
periculo <tandem> facto libenter sunt amplexuri; poterit idem, non inique,
populum rudem et rerum civilium imperitum, licet nondum consentientem, imperii [forma continere legitima] [formam praeferibere legitimam],
communi foelicitati inserviente, quam omnes {eidem assueti} suffragiis suis
mox sunt comprobaturi. Quum vero nemo de sua salute dubius et metuens,
cui praecipua hominum jura, minime contra potentiorum <293> vim tuta
esse et munita videntur, beatus esse possit; {idcirco} nisi vel antecedat populi

The Internal Structure of States:
and the Several Parts of Supreme Power.

I. As no governors are the natural parents or progenitors of their people, nor if they were, could they transmit to any one heir the parental power over his adult brethren: as this power is founded solely upon the parental affection, and the weakness of immature years: the parental power can never be the foundation of the civil, tho' it be a natural sketch or emblem of it. Nor can any person have such power over a whole people as masters have over slaves; as appears from what was already said.[1] Nor has God by any revelation nominated magistrates, shewed the nature or extent of their powers, or given a plan of civil polity for mankind. Nor lastly can mere force without some foundation of right constitute any just power. It must therefor remain that some *deed* or *contract* of a people must be the sole natural origin of all just power.[2]

In some extraordinary circumstances the case may be otherways. For since the good [safety and happiness] of the whole body, {as all allow,} is the sole end of all civil power; if any person of eminent wisdom and great power consults this end sufficiently, in prescribing a legal plan <for the common good>, which all upon trial shall soon heartily embrace, he may perhaps without any iniquity impose this plan upon a rude and unexperienced people, which upon experience they <286> shall soon approve, tho' he could not obtain their previous consent to it. But as no people can be happy while they live in perpetual doubts and fears, as to the security of their highest interests [rights] from the invasions of men in power; we may pronounce in general that there can be no right to power except what is

---

1. Cf. Locke, *Two Treatises* 2.15.
2. Cf. Locke, *Two Treatises* 2.16.175. See also *System* 3.5.1, vol. II, pp. 225–26.

consensus, vel subsequatur, justum esse nequit imperium.

II. In potestate civili, ratione et via constituendâ, haec tria ut concurrant est necesse; primo, Pactum omnium inter se, quo convenit, ut <in> unum populum, communi regendum consilio, conficiant [coalescant]: deinceps sequitur populi decretum, imperii formam modumque constituens, rectoresque designans. <Tertio> denique, pactum inter rectores designatos, et populum, hunc ad obsequium, illos ad imperii sibi in communem utilitatem {permissi} administrationem fidelem adstringens. In primis quidem civitatibus constituendis, vix est credibile popellum rudem et incautum, egregias quorundam virtutes suspicientem, haec omnia hoc ordine disertis transegisse verbis. In omni tamen justa imperii civilis constitutione,{*} actum est aliquid, quod horum omnium vim in se continet; quum omnibus satis notus sit unicus potestatis deferendae et suscipiendae finis.

Qua autem ratione in posteros eorum qui primi civitatem constituerunt, transmittatur haec obligatio civilis, ex his monitis constabit.

1. Civium quisque non sibi solum, verum <294> et liberis, a civitate defensionem stipulatur, et omnia vitae civilis commoda. Liberis gestum est negotium utilissimum; unde {et} citra suum consensum, ad ea omnia, pro ipsorum viribus, facienda praestanda adstringuntur, quae ob istiusmodi commoda ab adultis jure flagitari poterant. Nihil autem aequius quam ut singuli, pro virili parte, eam tueantur civitatem, neque ab ea intempestive discedant, cujus beneficio diu protecti, innumeris potiti fuerant vitae ex-

---

* Vid. *Carmichael.* annotat. ad *Puffend.* L. II.c.vi.9.

---

* See Mr. Carmichaell's notes on Puffendorf, Lib. II. vi. 9. [*Notes on Puf.,* pp. 148–49.]

3. See Pufendorf, *De officio* 2.6.7–9, *De iure nat.* 7.2.6–8. Cf. also *System* 3.5.2, vol. II, pp. 227–28.

4. Locke, on the contrary, says that no one can "by any *Compact* whatsoever, bind his *Children* or *Posterity*" (*Two Treatises* 2.8.116). The difference from Locke is slightly

either founded upon, or speedily obtains, the hearty consent of the body of the people.

II. To constitute a state or civil polity {in a regular manner} these three deeds are necessary; first a *contract* of each one with all, that they shall unite into one society to be governed by one counsel. And next a *decree* or *ordinance* of the people, concerning the plan of government, and the nomination of the governors; and lastly another *covenant* or *contract* between these governors and the people, binding the rulers to a faithful administration of their trust [of the granted power for the common good], and the people to obedience. 'Tis true that in the first constitutions of power [of states], 'tis scarce credible that a rude and incautious multitude, full of admiration of the shining virtues of some more eminent characters, took these three formal steps. But then in every just constitution of <civil> power,* something was originally done which plainly included the whole force of these three transactions; since the end known and professed by all sides in this constitution of power was the common good of the whole body [since is well known to all the only end of bestowing and receiving authority].[3]

As to the transmitting of these civil obligations to posterity, the following observations will explain it.

1. Each citizen in subjecting himself to civil power <287> stipulated protection from the whole body, with all the other advantages of a civilized life, not only for himself but for his posterity: and in this{, tho' uncommissioned,} did them a most important service.[4] They are bound therefor,{†} whether they consent or not, to perform to the body of the state, as far as their power goes, all that which could reasonably be demanded from persons adult for such important benefits received. Now 'tis highly reasonable that all such should on their parts contribute to the defence and support of that state, by which they have been so long protected <and profited>

---

more explicit in the corresponding paragraph of *System* 3.5.3, vol. II, pp. 228–31. In his letter to Hutcheson of Jan. 10th, 1743, p. 48, Hume writes: "You imply a Condemnation of Locke's Opinion, which being the receiv'd one, I cou'd wisht the Condemnation had been more express."

† {This is an obligation *quasi ex contractu.* See Book II. xiv. 2.} This added note is suggested by *System* 3.5.3, point 2, vol. II, pp. 229.

cultae commodis; utque haec a majoribus accepta ad posteros transmittant.

2. Quum non sine gravi periculo, manerent agri intra civitatis fines ab ipsius imperio immunes, hosti aut fugitivis recipiendis patentes; jure censentur omnes cives agros suos ita imperio subjecisse civili, ut eorum dominium {aut usus}, nemini qui non civitati subjectus degat, cedere possit.

3. Libero tamen quovis tempore, iniquum videtur cives prohibere, ne, solo mutato agrisque venditis, civitate etiam mutari possint. Reipub. enim, singuli plerumque, per tributa, aliaque ipsis onera {quotannis} imposita, [beneficia accepta pensant:] [beneficiorum acceptorum compensationem praestant.] neque aequum fuerit eos impedire, quo minus alibi melius sibi consulant. Nec metus ne civitas ulla penitùs deseratur, nisi quae vel pessime sit instituta vel administrata: qua quidèm in <295> causa, potiore jure cives postulant ut civitate mutari liceat, neque in civitate inviti manere cogantur.

III. Civitas in hunc modum constituta personae unius rationem subit, cui jura competunt ab omni privatorum jure [disjuncta] [diversa]; quin et obligationibus, quibus tenetur nemo privatus, adstringitur: rerumque omnium administrationem certis hominibus aut conciliis committit. Inter diversas istiusmodi civitates, in libertate quippe naturali degentes, idem fere jus, eaedemque leges naturales, quae inter singulos in primaeva libertate vigebant; eadem, aut iis simillima, sunt civitatum jura perfecta; eadem debentur mutuo officia humana; similis est pactorum obligatio; idem se suaque per vim defendendi jus: eadem {denique inter se} ratio est omnium

in a civilized life, and not desert it unseasonably; but transmit that association {with its beneficent influence} <received from the ancestors> to
posterity.

2. As it must be extremely dangerous to any political body settled in any
district, that any lands within the same should remain exempt from the
civil power of the united body, to be a receptacle to fugitives or foreign
enemies; 'tis justly presumed that {when any body of men possessing such
a district of land constitute a civil power}, each one thus subjects his lands
to it, that no person can hold the same without also subjecting himself to
it, and uniting with the body politick [that its property or use can not be
transferred to anybody that is not subjected to the state].[5]

3. And yet, in times of ease and peace, it would seem unjust and dishonourable to any state to hinder its citizens from selling their lands, re-
moving to any other state they please, and freeing themselves from their
former political relation. For the several subjects by the taxes or tributes
they pay annually, compensate <288> all the ordinary advantages they receive from the community: and it would be unjust to hinder them to consult better their own interest if they can elsewhere.[6] Nor is there danger
that any state will be deserted by many of its subjects, unless it be either
miserably constituted or administered; and in such cases the citizens have
a better right to quit it, and cannot be compelled to remain its subjects.

III. A state constituted in this manner becomes as *one person* in law,[7] holding
rights different from those of the several members; and under *obligations*,
which bind no individual; and committing to certain persons or councils
the management of its common interests. Among several states thus constituted, as they are all with respect to each other in natural liberty {and
independence}, the like rights and laws obtain as among individuals in liberty. States have their [the same or very similar] perfect rights, and obligations to each other, and are bound to offices of humanity, in a like manner
as individuals in natural liberty: and have like rights of self-defence <by

5. Cf. Locke, *Two Treatises* 2.8.117 and 120.
6. Cf. Locke, *Two Treatises* 2.8.121.
7. See Pufendorf, *De officio* 2.6.10, *De iure nat.* 7.2.13.

civitatum, quae non sub vicinae cujuspiam ditione tenentur, sive eae majores sint sive minores; quocunque demum nomine vocentur, sive humili,
sive glorioso. Facili igitur nominum et personarum mutatione, *jus naturale
privatum* sit jus fere omne *publicum,* cujus necessaria est obligatio. De *voluntario jure publico,* aliàs.

IV. Potestatis quae ad civitatem regendam exigitur, partes, aut summi jura
imperii, sunt vel *majora* vel *minora.* Majora, intra civitatis fines exsequenda,
immanentia, <296> a quibusdam appellantur: quae exteros respiciunt,
transeuntia dicuntur. Prioris generis sunt, primò, *jura legum jubendarum*
quibus civium actiones sunt regendae, et jura ipsis tuenda, legum naturalium habita semper ratione.

2. Jus deinde *exigendi tributa* {ea} omnia, aut reditus publicos, quos prudens exigerit reipublicae administratio: quod jus in priori contineri potest.
Tributa dixerunt Romani quae a civibus persolvebantur; *vectigalia,* quae a
provinciis subactis. Ex quibus omnibus, quae ad principum familias sus-
tinendas destinantur, *res Fisci* dicuntur; quae vero in Reipub. usus impen-
denda sunt, ad *aerarium* deferuntur. In priora, principibus electione nova
creatis, jus est quale *usufructuariis;* {in regnis} haereditariis vero, jus {regis
idem ferè quod} *feudatarii:* neutris licet privatis suis debitis imperii suc-
cessores onerare. Aerarii autem in Reipub. usus administratio sola rectoribus quibusvis commissa intelligitur.

3. Tertium est jus *legum exsequendarum,* quae *executiva* dicitur potestas;
jurisdictionem omnem continens ad lites dirimendas, et jus magistratus
creandi et ministros, ad rempublicam administrandam, et tributa exigenda.

Jura *transeuntia* ad haec reducuntur capita. <297> 1. *Jus belli,* quod in
se omne belli gerendi arbitrium continet, in [militibus conscribendis] [ex-
ercitu conscribendo], ducibusque sive summis sive inferioribus constituendis.

violence>. This is the case of all states which are independent, whether greater or smaller, whatever names and titles they bear, more humble or more ostentatious. By an easy substitution therefor of states for individuals, the natural law with respect to individuals in liberty, makes all that *publick law* of states with respect to each other, which is of necessary obligation. As to voluntary or positive *publick law,* we shall touch at it hereafter.{*}

IV. The several powers requisite for governing a people <or rights of sovereign power> are divided into the *greater* and *lesser.* Of these <289> greater powers some are executed within the bounds of the state <and called internal>, and others respecting other states are to be exerted abroad <and called external>. Of the former class, is that of *making laws* to regulate the behaviour of the subjects [citizens], and maintain their rights, still regarding the law of nature.[8]

2. Another is, that of *exacting all such tributes* or <public> revenues as the <wise> administration of the state requires: this some make a branch of the former. Revenues are sometimes raised from subjects [citizens] <and called *tributa* by the Romans>, sometimes from conquered provinces <and called *vectigalia*>; some destined for support of the families of the supreme governors, and some for the publick uses of the state. As to the former, elective princes are deemed only as life-renters, and hereditary princes have a right like that in fiefs, to be transmitted unburdened to their heirs. As to the other branch, princes can only be deemed administrators or trustees for the whole state.

3. A third branch of power is the *executive,* containing all jurisdiction civil and criminal; and the right of constituting magistrates, and judges to take care of all publick affairs, and decide controversies, as also officers to collect the tributes.

The powers to be exerted abroad are first those of *war,* in enlisting soldiers, and appointing officers, and directing all military operations.

---

* {Ch. ix. and x. of this book.}
8. Hutcheson's list of powers is in part different from Pufendorf's list (*De officio* 2.15 or *De iure nat.* 7.4.1–8) and Locke's (*Two Treatises* 2.12). See also *System* 3.5.5–7, vol. II, pp. 234–38.

2. Jura *foederum faciendorum;* cui connexum est jus legatos mittendi, ad foedera, quae aut pacem reducant, aut commercia conservent, transigenda.

Ab his diversum est *jus imperii eminens,* quo in casibus gravioribus et insolitis recte utuntur imperatores, [invadentes in] [contra] ea civium jura, quae libero quovis tempore, sunt {iisdem} sanctissime conservanda; quandam, {exempli causa,} rei familiaris partem, aut operas, etiam cum summo conjunctas periculo, exigentes, ultra quam aliàs praestare tenentur. Huic imperatorum juri, respondent in statu libero insolita ea quae premente necessitate oriuntur jura.

Minora imperii jura haec sunt; "Dignitates civiles tribuendi [conferendi], nummos cudendi, nundinas feriasque permittendi, liberos, [natalium infamiâ sublatâ, legitimos reddendi,] [legitimandi] {*universitates* constituendi,} aetatis veniam largiendi, poenas remittendi, debitoribus inducias dandi"; et id genus alia; quibus, utpote facilibus, neque civitati omni necessariis, non immoramur.

V. Summum in civitate imperium is homo, aut plurium concilium, habere censetur, <298> qui majora quae diximus imperii jura, vel omnia, vel pleraque, [suo arbitratu] [pro suo prudentia] exsequi potest; neque alterius, aut hominis aut concilii, potestati {ita} subjicitur, ut ejus voluntate ipsius actus fieri possint irriti. Summam saepe habet potestatem, qui non habet infinitam, nullisve limitibus circumscriptam; immo qui ne vel perpetuam; neque imperio successuros designare, aut leges quibus civitas erat fundata immutare potest. Summus ille erit imperator, cui praecipuae potestatis civilis partes permittuntur, suo arbitratu, intra certos fines, in reipublicae utilitatem exercendae: qui neque alterius jussu, aut mandato subinde interposito, civitatem regit; cujusque actus, intra potestatis sibi permissae fines, a nullius consensu vim sortiuntur.

In omni civitate, summa alicubi reperitur potestas, quae *majestas* dicitur, vel apud regem, vel senatum, vel populum. Neque eam imminuunt cum exteris inita foedera, quamvis incommoda, nisi majora civitati ipsi adimant

2. The power of making *treaties,* either for settling peace, or maintaining commerce, and of constituting ambassadors for this purpose.

There's beside all these a certain *extraordinary right* in the supreme governors of any people, in great exigencies, to incroach upon those rights of the subjects <290> which for ordinary are to be religiously maintained to them: as when it happens to be absolutely necessary, in some perilous emergencies, either to compell them to some extraordinary dangerous services, or to contributions of their goods beyond the ordinary proportions. This right in civil life answers to these extraordinary rights of necessity, we formerly{*} mentioned in natural liberty.

The smaller rights commonly vested in the supreme governor, are those of conferring civil honours, coining of money, granting to hold fairs or markets, legitimating of children, erecting corporations, admitting minors as if they were of due age, pardoning criminals, giving protections to debtors, and such like; which we briefly pass over as of less importance, and not always necessary in every state.[9]

V. Those persons or councils have the supreme power, who are intrusted with the greater branches of power above mentioned, or the greater part of them, so that they can exert them according to their own judgment, and no other person or council can rescind their deeds. Many have supreme power who don't hold it unlimited, nor even for life: such too as cannot alter the order of succession, or abolish any of the fundamental laws of the state. He is supreme to whom the chief parts of civil power are committed, tho' within certain limits, to be executed by his own order for the good of the body, so that he does not act by new commands, or commissions from any other; and whose <291> deeds<, within the allowed limits of power,> derive not their force from the consent of any superior.

In every state the same quantity of power is deemed to be lodged some where or other; either with a monarch, a senate, or popular assembly{, or at least with the whole body of the people}. Nor is it any diminution of the supremacy or independence of a state that it is bound by its treaties

* {Book II. ch. 16. art. 3. near the end.}
9. See Carmichael, *Notes on Puf.,* p. 158.

imperii jura, aut prohibeant ne sui juris *persona* quae dicitur *politica* maneat.

Si quidem pluribus civitatibus hoc, quacunque de causa, eveniat, ut uni homini aut uni concilio perpetuo, quarundam imperii partium concedatur administratio; illae civitatum *systema* constituunt: quales, ex noto <299> apud antiquos exemplo, civitates dicuntur *Achaicae.* In unam autem civitatem plures tum demum coalescere dicuntur, et unam gerere personam, quum uni homini, aut uni concilio, aut iisdem vel hominibus, vel conciliis, permittuntur omnes potestatis partes majores, quà omnium fines patent, administrandae.

with others, even tho' they be very inconvenient ones; provided the state can still exercise all the greater parts of civil power, and can govern itself independently of others.

If a number of states enter into such a strict alliance <for whatever cause>, as to constitute some one person or permanent common council for them all, and commit to this person or council some parts of the supreme power, to be executed for them all; they are called a *system of states,* or *Achaian states,* from a famous instance of that kind. But independent states then incorporate entirely into one, when the very same persons or councils have committed to them all the parts of the supreme power to be executed for them all.[10]

10. See *System* 3.5.8, vol. II, pp. 239–40.

CAPUT VI

De variis Rerumpublicarum Formis.

I,[1] Simplicium civitatum tria sunt genera. Ubi omnes imperii partes uni homini committuntur, dicitur *monarchia;* cujus varia sunt nomina: ubi concilio unico, idque ex optimatibus constat, *aristocratia;* si vero ex omnibus civibus, [aut honestioribus quibusdam ad rempublicam procurandam] [eorumve] delegatis constet concilium, dicitur *democratia.*

Concilium, cui permissa est potestas, id voluisse censetur quod pluribus placuit; nisi lege aut decreto quodam primario, quo civitas fundatur, cautum sit, quota concilii pars rerum publicarum administrationi sit necessaria. Praecavenda etiam sallacia satis nota, semperque metuenda ubi quaestio [tripartita aut quadripartita] [trimembris] decidenda est{: quod scil. incidere possit, ut eam sententiam quae longè <300> pluribus displicet, comprobent tamen plures, quam qui reliquarum unam ullam. Quod fiet quaestione}<, ea> vel ad bimembres duas reducta, vel membro uno {aut altero}, suffragiis de eo prius latis, excluso: quod etiam in magistratibus, ubi plures sunt petitores, creandis observandum.

(II.) Generis cujusque simplicis {civitatum} plures sunt partes. Monarchia enim vel est *absoluta* et interminata, ubi {scilicet} unius prudentiae tota permittitur reipublicae administratio, nullis positis limitibus, praeter eos qui ex politiae omnis natura et fine intelliguntur; vel est *terminata,* ubi legibus quibus civitas fundatur, aut in ipsa potestate deferenda, certis terminis

---

1. By mistake Hutcheson did not number this and the following section.

Of the Various Plans of Government.

I. The simple forms of government are divided into three classes, according as the power is committed to one person or to one council. When it is committed to one person, it is called monarchy <and has different names>; when to a council of some few eminent citizens, it is an aristocracy; and when it is committed to a popular assembly either of all the free citizens, or of some more reputable persons deputed by them, 'tis democracy.

When power is committed to a council, that is deemed the will of the council which is determined by the major part; unless by some fundamental law, a certain number of members is made necessary for determining any matters of publick administration, as a *quorum*{; and what proportion of this number, can make any alterations}. Precaution should also be taken against an inconvenience which may always happen when a question of three or more parts is put to a vote, that that part to which a great majority may be most averse, may yet have more votes than any one of the other parts{, and thus be enacted}. This may always be prevented by reducing a complex question into two {or more simple ones}, of two parts each; or by excluding by previous votes one or two of the parts of the complex question{, so as only two parts shall remain for <293> the last decisive vote}. A like method may be taken where many candidates set up for the same office.[1]

II. Of each of these simple kinds there are many species. Monarchy is either *absolute,* <and unlimited,> where the whole administration is committed to the prudence of the monarch, without any other limits than those which are always understood from the general <nature and> end of all civil government; <when the power is bound by the fundamental laws of the state>

---

1. See *System* 3.6.1, vol. II, pp. 240–41.

circumscribitur imperium, populique jura quaedam sanctiora {inde} eximuntur. Utriusque generis monarchae vel jure haereditario succedunt, vel a populo creantur aut eliguntur: idque vel in perpetui imperii jus, vel temporarii.

Aristocratiae pariter plura sunt genera, hisque consimilia: *absoluta* nempe, sive infinita; aut *terminata,* et lege circumscripta: *haereditaria,* aut creationibus novis reficienda; *perpetua,* aut *temporaria.* In hac temporaria, pro certo tempore suffragii jure gaudent senatores; quo peracto, sufficiuntur in eorum locum alii: quod si populi suffragiis fiat, et civis cujuscunque, qui se petitorem <301> profiteatur, habenda sit ratio, *democraticum* potius videtur concilium: sin per cooptationem reficiatur senatus; aut optimatibus solis petere liceat; erit aristocraticum. Si ex censu majore petendi jus oriatur, proprie *oligarchicum* dicitur; aut ubi agrorum quorundam domini, eo ipso fiunt senatores <quod eos jure possideant>. Ubi vero hi soli qui, honoribus functi, gratiam fidemque consecuti sunt, creari possunt; a quibusdam, κατ' ἐξοχὴν *aristocratia,* aut *politia* dicitur.

Conciliorum popularium dissimilia [diversa] etiam genera; comitia *curiata* et *centuriata* duorum exhibent exempla. In illis suffragii pari jure utebantur [gaudebant] cives omnes; in his pro ratione census; quae {idcirco} dicebantur *timocratica.* Sorte etiam alicubi definiebatur, quibus dandum esset in comitiis suffragii jus. Alicubi ex tribubus aut curiis diversis, quibus distinctus fuerat populus, {ad rem communem gerendam} eligebantur delegati, qui concilium constituerent populare.

Junctarum et multiplicium formarum ingens est numerus, prout cum diversis monarchiae generibus conjunguntur concilia varia [diversa], vel senatoria vel popularia; atque prout variae imperii partes vel regi, vel senatui, vel concilio populari, vel omnibus simul permittuntur.

---

* {The characters of aristocracy, are *cooptation* by the senate, to a perpetual seat, and a limitation to certain eminent families, distinguished by fortune, or bearing great offices. The characters of democracy are *popular elections, temporary seats,* and *access to all* citizens

or it is *limited* in the original conveyance of the power; and certain rights reserved to the people and exempted from it. And then each of these kinds are subdivided into *hereditary* and *elective:* the elective princes again may either be chosen for *life,* or for a *certain term.*

There are likeways several kinds of *aristocracys, absolute,* <or unlimited,> or *limited* <and circumscribed by law>: *hereditary* or *elective; perpetual* or *temporary.*{*} In this last sort the senators hold their seats for a certain term; upon the expiration of which, others are substituted in their places. If such new senators are elected by the people, and any free citizen may stand candidate, the council is rather *democratical:* but if the places are filled by the votes of the remaining members of the council; or only some eminent families can be candidates, it is *aristocratical.* When the seat in the senate depends upon a certain quantity of wealth; or is held in virtue of certain <294> lands justly possessed; 'tis called properly *oligarchical.* When these alone can be elected who have discharged certain great offices with approbation, this is deemed *aristocracy* in the properest sense, <or politia> {and the plan of it most commended by some great authors of antiquity}.

There are also different kinds of *democracies*{, as the popular assembly is differently constituted}. We have examples of two ways in the *comitia curiata,* and *centuriata* of the Romans. In the former all citizens voted equally: In the later according to their fortunes <and for that reason called timocratic>. In some states the lot determined the members of the assembly: in others the people being divided into a number of tribes, counties, or districts, and these again subdivided; each division sends so many delegates or deputies, chosen by themselves, to be members of the popular assembly.

The complex forms are innumerable, according as any of the different sorts of senates jointly share the supreme power, with any of the sorts of monarchy; and again as any of those complex kinds are again conjoined with one or other of the popular assemblies: and then as such or such parts of the supreme power are vested in one or other of these councils, or in the monarch; or in all three jointly.[2]

---

to stand candidates. There's in many constitutions a mixture of these different characters.} [This note added by the translator is not suggested by Hutcheson's *System.*]

2. See *System* 3.6.2, vol. II, pp. 241–43.

III. Ut formas praestantiores a deterioribus <302> secernere valeamus, haec pauca sedulo sunt spectanda.

1. Ut foelix sit reipublicae status, quatuor hisce in {omni} politia prospiciendum [retinenda]; ut scil. imperatoribus adsit prudentia, optima quaeque prospiciens; {deinde ut adsit} fides communi consulens prosperitati; {tum} ut conservetur concordia; denique ut reipublicae negotia et celeriter et secreto possint expediri. De his ubi satis est cautum, non melius communi civium prosperitati, per politiam consuli poterit.

2. Ubicunque non uni homini aut concilio, sed pluribus datae sunt summae potestatis partes; inter eos intervenire debet aliquis *imperii nexus,* ne in omnia contraria abire possint: ne scil. Rex, inconsulto aut invito concilio, vel senatorio, vel populari, quicquam gravius moliri queat; nec concilia, rege inconsulto aut invito; neve unum concilium, altero invito. Si hac de re satis cautum fuerit, melius inter diversos, sive diversa quae dicuntur *subjecta,* dividuntur imperii partes, quam si omnes uni, sive regi sive concilio, mandarentur.

3. Stabile neutiquam erit imperii jus, nisi rerum dominio aut opibus fultum: aliter fluctuationibus et seditionibus perpetuis civitas vexabitur. Rerum enim dominia potentiam secum ferunt, quae jura nullis opibus subnixa <303> evertet, aut ipsa labantibus [cum] divitiis collabetur. Stabile tum demum erit regnum haereditarium, ubi agris suffultum est aut provinciis haereditariis: stabile senatus imperium, ubi agrorum bona pars est senatorum: stabilis civitas popularis, ubi vigent leges agrariae; aut ubi alia quavis ratione agri inter plurimos dividuntur dominos. Quamvis autem seduli et solertiores, non nisi gravi de causa sunt cohibendi, quo minus rem suam familiarem bonis artibus augeant; (quod democratia vel optima permittet, quantum exigere potest vitae vel jucunditas vel voluptas quaevis, viro bono expetenda,) non tamen cum plurium salute, aut libertate, pensanda est inanis paucorum vel ambitio, vel luxuries, vel avaritia. In omni igitur populo

III. That we may discern which of these forms is preferable, the following <few> observations seem proper.

1. In constituting of a state these four points are to be aimed at; that first, there be sufficient *wisdom* in the government to see what is best for the state; and then *fidelity* to choose what is best; and next that *concord* be maintained; and lastly a *secret and speedy execution.* <295> If in any plan sufficient precaution is taken for all these, a people cannot desire more from its civil polity.

2. Where the parts of the supreme power are placed in different subjects or bodies; there must be some such political bonds between them, as shall prevent their acting in opposition to each other; that the prince, for instance, may do nothing of high importance without consent of the senate or popular assembly; nor these bodies do any thing without consent of the prince; nor one of these bodies without the concurrence of the other. If any sufficient precautions of this kind be taken, the civil power is better lodged by parts in different bodies, than all committed to either a monarch, or to any one council.

3. The power wheresoever lodged will never remain stable unless it has large *property* for its foundation; without this it must be fluctuating, and exposed to frequent seditions. Wealth carries force along with it, which will overturn rights not supported by wealth; or be wrested from the owners by the civil power [or the power of the state will collapse with fluctuating wealth]. An hereditary monarchy needs for its stability large crownlands, or hereditary provinces{, belonging to the monarch's family}. A senate will not remain stable unless a large share of the lands are the property of the senators: and lands must be dispersed among great multitudes, and preserved thus dispersed by agrarian laws, to make a stable democracy; or some other causes must keep property much diffused. And altho' the diligent and active should not, without weighty causes, be any way restrained in their just acquisitions: (and indeed <296> the best sorts of democracy may allow them to acquire as much as can be requisite for any elegance or pleasure of life that a wise man could desire) yet we are never to put in the ballance with the liberty or safety of a people, the gratifying the vain ambition, luxury, or avarice of a few. It may therefor often be just to prevent by agrarian

libero, jure per leges agrarias praecavetur, ne nimiae evadant [sint] paucorum opes, et toti civitati metuendae.

4. Cavendum etiam, ne iniqua, aut parum civilia, cuivis ordini tribuantur jura, quibus caeteri omnes a republica {capessenda} summisque honoribus excludantur; perpetuis enim seditionibus materiam praebebunt.

5. Quum parum referat qualis sit civitatis institutio, si modo solis prudentibus et bonis commissa sit potestas; cui tamen rei nulla ratione satis caveri poterit; hoc in civitate constituenda praecipuè erit spectandum, <304> ut insidis et malis, quamvis potestatem adepti fuerint, nulla aut exigua ad peccandum sint invitamenta; aut saltem nullae impunitatis, aut commodi sui augendi spes, ubi perfidè rempublicam administraverint.

6. Quis vero ad [coetum civilem] [civitatem] optimè constituendum hominum numerus potissimum requiratur, definiri nequit. Paucis neque vires neque opes suppetent, quibus se contra praedonum manus defendant, aut ea comparent, quae ad uberiorem faciunt vitae ornatum aut jucunditatem. Ubi contra, magnus est numerus civium magnam regionem occupantium, non adeo accurate omnia procurari, aut a civibus fraudes, injuriae, et vexationes prohiberi poterunt: paucioribus praeterea patebit aditus ad rempublicam, ut virtutes latius patentes addiscant atque exerceant, quam si ab iisdem hominibus plures constitutae fuissent civitates. Ubi quidem ingentes civitates sunt constitutae, neque jam hominibus <non> est integrum, ut se in civitates dividant commodissimas; vicinis omnibus forte profuerit, sui contra nimias vicinorum opes defendendi gratia, in majores congregare civitates. Quemadmodum etiam, inter cives, ad paucorum nimias opes praecavendas, et potentiam caeteris metuendam, justae sunt leges agrariae, eodem jure civitates vicinae nimias alterius cujusque opes <305>

---

3. *System* 3.6.3, vol. II, pp. 243–47, contains the same three points. Hutcheson emphasizes the relevance of large landed property for the stability of the civil power in whatever form of government. James Harrington in his *Oceana* (1656) considers the agrarian law limiting and evenly distributing land to the people fundamental law to a long lasting commonwealth. For his defence of the agrarian laws against detractors, see *Oceana,* part 3.1.]

laws such vast wealth coming into a few hands, that {a cabal of them} might endanger the state.[3]

4. No such insolent or oppressive privileges should be granted to any one order in the state, as would exclude all others from publick offices of dignity or profit. For they will become occasions of perpetual seditions.{*}

5. As it would be of little consequence what were the form of polity, were it provided that none but good and wise men got into power; (which perhaps no precaution can ensure) the main drift of good policy is, to provide that even tho' bad men come into power, they shall either have small temptations to abuse it, or at least no hopes of gain and impunity in doing so.[4]

6. As to the fittest number for making an happy state, nothing can be precisely determined. If the number is small, there won't be strength enough against bands of the avowedly unjust{, who may attack it by surprize}; nor will there be sufficient wealth to execute any wise designs for the improvement of life. On the other hand when the numbers and the extent of a country <297> is very large, no governors can take sufficient care of all their interests, and prevent frauds, extortions and oppressions{, even by the avarice of the deputy-magistrates, as access to complain must be more difficult}. And besides, far fewer men can be employed in the greater and more important state-affairs, and thus improve in that most important part of wisdom [and thus learn to cultivate more extensive virtues], than if out of the same numbers and the same tract of ground, several distinct independent societies had been framed. Indeed this is seldom matter of choice, what numbers should unite. For if once vast empires are formed, it becomes necessary to any little states around them to incorporate together, as many of them as may be, for their defence against a potent neighbour.[5] But as agrarian laws are often justifiable in a state, to prevent the immoderate increase of wealth in the hands of a few <and to prevent the fear of their power>; 'tis equally just, for the same reasons, that smaller neighbouring

---

* {Of this we have a clear instance in the Roman state, till the plebeians got access even to the consulate.} [Also this footnote is a free addition by the translator.]

4. See *System* 3.6.3, vol. II, p. 252.

5. See *System* 3.6.3, vol. II, pp. 249–51.

merito habent suspectas, siquidem ejusdem etiam mores cupiditate vincendi inflammentur; iisque, opibus augendis, per vim, si aliter fieri nequeat, modum ponere licet, antequam tantae evaserint ut libertati et saluti suae cautum esse nequeat.

IV. Monarchia simplex has habet opportunitates; {quod} civitatis concordiae consulat; et per eam secretò et expeditè res geri possint. In monarchia autem haereditaria, neque de prudentia regis, neque de fide caveri poterit. De electorum prudentia melius cavetur; non item de fide: et {hujusmodi} rege defuncto, seditionibus bellisque civilibus janua patebit. In haereditaria absoluta sive infinita, sunt omnia incerta. In haereditaria terminata, non de prudentia, at melius multo cautum est de fide; quum rex leges eas quibus fundata erat civitas violando, aut potestatis sibi commissae fines transiliendo, se planè tyrannum profiteatur; ipsiusque perfidiâ regni jus omne abdicatum esse facile inter omnes constet. Unde etiam populo jus oritur, ut, eo deturbato, novum creare regem, aut novam Reipub. formam instituere liceat. <Ast> In regnis verò {legibus} terminatis et circumscriptis, perpetuae ferè vigent factiones, et bella subinde nascuntur civilia.

In simplicioribus aristocratiis haereditariis, <306> de senatorum prudentia rarô, de fide nunquam satis cautum est, neque quidem de concordia, aut expedita et arcana Reipub. administratione. Inter senatores ad munus electos, melius de prudentia et fide, parum vero de concordia, aut negotiis celeriter et secretò gerendis, caveri poterit.

In concilio populari fides semper vigebit, et tum demum prudentia, ubi vel censui respondet suffragii jus, vel consilium ex honestioribus paucis a

states should take timely precautions, and that by violence too, if gentler methods are not like to succeed, that no neighbour-state should acquire such force as may enslave all around; especially if they see a prevalent disposition in all {the institutions and} manners of any neighbour-state toward {military affairs and} conquest.[6]

IV. <Simple> Monarchy has these peculiar advantages, that it is adapted to preserve concord, and make a secret and speedy execution of any design. But then in hereditary monarchies there's small security for either the wisdom or fidelity of the monarch. In elective monarchies there's greater probability for wisdom; but rather less for fidelity: and upon the death of each monarch <298> there's an open gate to civil wars. Under an absolute hereditary monarchy nothing is secure. Under the limited hereditary, no better precaution is taken for wisdom, but there is better precaution as to a faithful administration: since if the monarch violates the fundamental laws, or breaks over the bounds set by them to his power, he plainly declares himself a tyrant{, and forfeits his right}; which all the subjects must plainly see: and hence will more readily agree in dethroning him to set up another, or to constitute some better plan. But then in the limited monarchies there generally prevail factions, which sometimes [repeatedly] turn into civil wars.[7]

In the simpler hereditary aristocracies scarce sufficient precaution is taken for wisdom, and scarce any for fidelity, concord, or secret and speedy execution. In the elective are better precautions for wisdom and fidelity, but no better for concord or execution.

In democracies we are always secured as to fidelity; and may have a tolerable prospect as to wisdom too, when mens votes are according to their fortunes; or when the assembly is made up of deputies elected by the peo-

---

6. More literally: "'tis equally right that smaller neighbouring states, when justly suspicious of the wealth of anyone of the others, especially if the latter is excited by an ambition of conquest, put limits to its increase of wealth, even by violence if it is not possible otherwise, before it turns out to be so great that their safety and liberty is no more secured."

7. See *System* 3.6.4, vol. II, pp. 252–54.

populo delegatis constat. Neque tamen inter hosce speranda concordia, aut expedita et arcana reip. administratio.

In magno quovis concilio per tabellas optime feruntur suffragia: sic enim non metuendae erunt potentiorum offensiones, neque suffragia largitionibus corrumpere in promptu erit. Atque licet, pudore sublato, locus sit gratiae, odio, et invidiae; his {tamen} rariùs, nisi objustam causam, populi pars major incitabitur. Sin autem sors, aliqua ex parte immisceatur, omnis excludi poterit largitio; gratiaeque, odio, aut invidiae grassanti saepe obstruetur iter.{*} Sola tamen sorte res decidere graviores, aut magistratus delegatosve designare [constituere], parum erit tutum; quum sorti, quantumvis omni gratia et contumelia vacet, nulla sit prudentia rerumve judicium.

V. Rerumpub. formas simpliciores parum < 307 > esse commodas, haec satis ostendunt. Neque antiquissima quaeque sunt optima; sic enim ad pelles, antra, glandesque redire oporteret. Quod a {regum} adulatoribus jactari solet, monarchiam primum in terris nomen imperii fuisse, monarchiae neutiquam est honorificum. Hoc enim est dicere, rudi eam et incauto popello placuisse, prudentioribus et cultioribus haud diu placituram. Etenim in nullo rerum genere minus sperare licet prima quaeque opera perfecta fore et absoluta, quam in civitatibus constituendis, ubi maxima opus est rerum notitia et prudentia, [non sine meditatione alta] [multa meditatione], vitaeque usu diuturno et vario, comparandâ. Quae formas quasque simplices comitantur incommoda graviora, ad mixtas et multiplices confugiendum esse docent: mixtarum autem eam esse optimam ubi tres illae artificiosè

---

* De hisce omnibus legatur *Harringtonius.*

ple: but there's no security of concord, or of speedy and secret execution {in any pure democracy}.[8]

The most convenient way of voting in all large councils or assemblies is by the ballot: as by this means, men need not dread the resentments of men in power; and 'tis less easy to use any indirect influence [to corrupt the ballot by bribery]. And altho' in the ballot there's no restraint of shame, but a door opened for private favour, hatred, and envy; yet it seldom happens that these passions work in the majority of a people without some just or probable <299> cause. But if something of the lot be also intermixed,* it may often quite defeat great cabals, and their arts of corruption, and stop the power of malice and envy. But the lot alone must be quite unfit to determine any point of consequence, or to advance any persons to offices; for tho' no man is affronted by a disappointment this way, nor is there any room for partial favour; yet it is plainly void of all prudence or wisdom.

V. We have said enough to shew that none of the simple forms of government are well adapted to preserve any state happy. Nor is it of any avail to plead antiquity here. If all the most antient ways were best, we should return to caves and beast-skins for our shelter and dress. What flatterers of princes often tell us, that monarchy was the earliest form, is rather dishonourable to it; importing indeed that it at first pleased a rude and unexperienced populace, but could not continue to please upon experience and the increase of wisdom. And indeed in nothing could one less expect that the first essays would be perfect, than in the constitution of civil polity; a work requiring the greatest knowledge and prudence, to be acquired only by much thought and experience of human life. The several great inconveniences attending each of the simple forms shew the necessity of having recourse to the mixt and complex; and the several great advantages peculiar to each of the simple, shew that those mixed forms are best where all the

---

8. The observations on aristocracies and democracies in *System* 3.6.5–6, vol. II, pp. 254–58, are much more detailed than in the *Institutio*.

* All these points are fully explained by *Harrington*. [Cf. *System* 3.6.6 and 7, point 8, vol. II, pp. 257 and 264. James Harrington, in his *Oceana*, part 3 (1656), plans a complex system of secret ballots, drawing representatives by lot and rotation of magistrates in order to avoid corruption and sedition.]

inter se compinguntur formae, monstrant singularum seorsim haud leves opportunitates: quod et antiquorum gravissimis placuit.

Concilio igitur populari, quod ex {honestioribus ad rem communem gerendam} delegatis constet, quibus idcirco nunquam fides, raro prudentia deesse poterit, maximae imperii partes committendae. Leges igitur sanciat istud concilium, et de rebus statuat gravissimis. Per leges etiam agrarias, haud ita arctas tamen ut industriae modicaeve vitae <308> elegantiae adversentur, concilio isti {sua} conservanda est potestas.

Senatui item ex paucis, a populo electis, quorum in Reipub. negotiis diu spectata fuit prudentia et fides, permittatur, ut de legibus et Repub. disceptent, et ad concilium populare referant; ita ut sine senatus auctoritate nihil gravius fieri possit. In utroque concilio etiam, ita decedentibus succedant homines novi, sive ea legibus annalibus instituatur *rotatio,* ut neque concilia ex novis omnibus constent, neque cuiquam suffragii perpetuum jus sit, aut potestas perpetua. In omnibus pariter magistratibus prosunt leges annales, ut caveatur ne quis nimiam sibi comparet potentiam aut gratiam; utque [quam plurimi] [plures] eam usu addiscant prudentiam, easque artes quae Reipub. sunt necessariae aut utiles; ne necesse sit ut tota civitas unum tantum aut paucos spectet, spemque omnem in iis solis collocet. Ubi vigent istiusmodi leges, Reipub. non deerunt imperatorum, aut magistratuum officio functorum, prudentia et virtus: neutiquam enim aegre ferent, quod pro legum sanctarum praescripto, tempore definito munera deponant.

Ad subita autem et inopina pericula avertenda, atque ad negotia secretò et celeriter obeunda, necessaria est potestas quaedam regia aut dictatoria,

three kinds are artfully compounded: <300> and this was the opinion of the wisest men of antiquity.{*}

As a council of delegates or deputies duly elected by a general popular interest can never want fidelity or good intention, and seldom can be deficient in wisdom, it may seem advisable that a large share of the civil power should be lodged in such a body; such as that of enacting laws and even determining definitively the most weighty affairs in deliberation. And this part of a constitution should be secured by agrarian laws: not so strait however as to discourage industry, or exclude any innocent elegance or ornament of life.

If there be also a *senate* of a few <elected by the people> who have approved their abilities and fidelity in discharging the great offices of the common-wealth; it may safely be intrusted with the sole right of deliberating, debating, and proposing business to the popular assembly <so that no weighty affair is decided without the authority of the senate>. In both councils it may be proper to contrive <by annual laws> a rotation, by new members gradually succeeding to the old, so that neither council may have above one third of [may be formed by all][9] unexperienced new men, nor yet any one man continue a member perpetually [has a perpetual right of voting or authority]. Laws limiting the times that any {general, minister of state, or} magistrate can continue in office have also great advantages, to prevent any person's so rooting himself in power or popularity, as to be dangerous to the constitution; and to train up greater numbers in political wisdom, by experience in all the important offices; so that the state may never be obliged to have all its hopes depending upon one mortal life. Where such laws are sacredly established, the <301> state will never want the benefit of the wisdom or experience of such as have served out their legal time. For it will be no matter of offence that at the expiration of it they must lay down their offices according to law.

And lastly, for sudden unexpected exigences or dangers, and for the secret and speedy execution of what the publick interest may require, some sort

---

* {*Plato, Aristotle, Zeno, Cicero.*} [See *System* 3.6.7, vol. II, pp. 258–59. Here Hutcheson refers to Aristotle, *Politica*, books IV–VI, and to Harrington.]

9. Hutcheson mentions the Harringtonian rotation of one third of the representatives only in *System* 3.6.8, vol. II, p. 261.

nullo tamen alio fundamento <309> praeter ipsas leges innixa; cui permittendum belli arbitrium, legumque tutela et administratio. Arbitri etiam
officio fungetur rex, si qua inter senatum et populum suboriatur contentio.

Magistratuum creandorum jus, tribus hisce potestatibus simul permittendum, aut inter eas dividendum: ut scil. quibus majore opus est prudentia, a senatu eligantur; quorum opera celeriore [celeri] et expeditiore opus
fuerit, a rege; quique populi jura tueantur et conservent, a populo aut concilio populari creentur.

Profuerit etiam plurimum *censoriam* semper adesse potestatem, ut civium mores emendentur, omnesque flagitiosi et improbi, cujuscunque fuerint ordinis aut dignitatis civilis, de loco dimoveantur.

of regal or dictatorial power is requisite; but such an one as has no other foundation of its force but the laws themselves. And to this power may be committed the command in war, and the execution of the laws. This third branch may be as an arbitrator, {holding the ballance between the two other parts of the constitution,} if there should arise any high contention between the senatorial order and the plebeian.[10]

The power of promoting to all sorts of offices may be some way vested in these three jointly, or divided among them; so that offices requiring great abilities and wisdom should be filled by the nomination of the senate; such officers as are to be employed in speedy execution, to be nominated by the prince: and such as are to protect the rights of the people, and administer justice among them, to be elected by the people.

A censorial power too would be of the highest use, to reform, or prevent the corruption of manners; by degrading persons of any dignity whatsoever, as soon as they run into a dissolute course of debauchery.[11]

10. See *System* 3.6.5–8. point 7, vol. II, p. 263.
11. *Ibidem*, point 10, p. 265.

CAPUT VII

De summi Imperii Jure, ejusque acquirendi rationibus.

I. [Rerumpub. Rectoribus] [Qui summo cum imperio sunt] ea est potestas, ea jura, quae primaria populi tribuerunt decreta. In omnibus quidem civitatibus, eadem alicubi, saltem apud populum universum, sita est potestas. Quae tamen vel regi, vel concilio, vel utrique committitur <potestas>, <310> in diversis civitatibus [longissimè diversa] [diversissima] est. In quibusdam enim, quaedam populi jura, ab omni imperantium potestate eximuntur: in aliis, omnia eorum prudentiae et fidei permittuntur. Quum tamen solus imperii constituendi finis, quod omnes agnoscunt, sit populi salus et foelicitas; quaecunque [eidem accommodata non est] [hinc aberrat] potestas, ea est injusta; quam populus, qui temere eam donaverat, repetere aut abrogare poterit, quum idipsius exegerit salus. Neque quicquam fingi potest perfidum magis aut fastuosum, quam ut [si] hi, quibus in populi salutem et utilitatem commissa erat potestas, eam, licet populo pestiferam, sui causa per vim retinere conentur.

Optandum quidem foret, ut potestas olim permissa, amicis potius disceptationibus, quam vi repetatur: neque ubi vel mediocriter communi consultum est saluti et prosperitati, ad vim et bella civilia, leviori aliqua de causa, decurrendum. Verum ubi haud satis de populi libertate et salute cau-

The Rights of the Supreme Power: and the Methods of Acquiring it.

I. The persons vested with the supreme power, have it <and the consequent rights> with that extent which the constitution or fundamental laws <of the people> have given them.[1] The sum of *civil power* in all states is the same; the same quantity of it in every state resides some-where or other, at least with the body of the people. But the powers vested in the king, or in any councils, in one state, may be very different from what is vested in like persons or councils in others. For in some, certain rights of the people are expresly exempted from the power of any prince or political council; but in others, there's no such exemptions [all the rights of the people are trust to their wisdom and fidelity]. But as the end of all civil power is acknowledged by all to be the safety and happiness of the whole body; any power not naturally conducive to this end is unjust; which the people, who rashly granted it under an error, may justly abolish again, when they find it necessary to their safety to do so.[2] Nor can any thing be conceived more insolent or perfidious, than that persons intrusted with power solely for the good of a people, should strive to retain it by force, for their own grandeur, when it is found destructive to the people.

It were to be wished that in these cases, such powers should be abolished in a peaceable manner, by mutual <303> consent, rather than by force. Nor is it justifiable in a people to have recourse for any lighter causes to violence and civil wars against their rulers, while the publick interests are tolerably secured and consulted. But when it is evident, that the publick liberty and

---

1. See *System* 3.7.1, vol. II, p. 266. These opening paragraphs are to be contrasted with what Pufendorf says in *De officio* 2.9 on the supremacy, superiority and particular sanctity of the sovereign authority. See also Carmichael, *Notes on Puf.*, pp. 162–65.

2. See *System* 3.7.3, vol. II, p. 271, and vol. 4, p. 276.

tum esse constat, pluraque mala, ex ipsa imperii formâ fore nascitura, eaque diuturniora, quam ex rerum commutatione violenta; tum demum et per extrema omnia {res novare}, imperiique formam modumque immutare licitum erit et honestum.

Quae de proprio rectorum civilium, praecipuè regum, jure divino, et sanctitate quadam <311> inviolabili jactantur, mera sunt adulantium somnia. Divinum est jus omne quod Dei et naturae lege sancitur. Divina sunt populi pariter ac imperantium jura. Immo, quandoquidem haec in illorum tutelam sunt constituta, illa his sunt et graviora et sanctiora. Imperantis quidem jus, singulorum seorsim jure quovis gravius est; universorum verò neutiquam. Plurima civis privatus perferre patique debet iniqua, potius quam contra regem caetera aequum et reipub. utilem, quicquam hostile moliretur; si modo sibi soli periculum immineat. Verum ubi communia omnium jura a rege pessundantur; quaeque uni intentantur, aliis omnibus mox metuenda erunt; tum vero manifesta regis perfidia, omneque imperii jus amissum.

II. Populo jura sua contra rectores quoscunque per vim defendere licet. Si quidem ii quorum imperium est legibus circumscriptum, ea invadant jura, quae populus in imperio deferendo sibi retinuit et reservavit; non dubium est quin populo, [juris sui tuendi causa, ad vim procurrere] [iura sua per vim defendere] liceat. Quin et ad rectores, quorum imperium absolutum est nullisque legibus circumscriptum, coërcendos, vis recte adhibetur; ubi civili animo exuto dominatum occupare conantur, in suam libidinem aut utilitatem, communi <312> spretâ, omnia convertentes; vel ubi animum in cives hostilem produnt; aut ita nequiter rempub. administrant, ut ne vel sanctissima populi jura, quaeque ad vitam tolerabilem sunt necessaria, tuta

safety is not tolerably secured, and that more mischiefs, and these of a more lasting kind, are like to arise from the continuance of any plan of civil power than are to be feared from the violent efforts for an alteration of it, then it becomes lawful, nay honourable, to make such efforts, and change the plan of government.

What is alleged about some peculiarly divine right, and inviolable sanctity of governors, especially monarchs, is a mere dream of court-flatterers. In one sense every right is divine which is constituted by the law of God and nature. The rights of the people are thus divine, as well as those of princes: nay since the later were constituted for the defence and protection of the former; the former should be deemed the more divine and sacred. The rights of the governor, as they are more important than those of any one private man, may be deemed more sacred than his private rights; but can never be deemed more sacred than the rights of the whole body. A good subject [citizen] ought to bear patiently many injuries done only to himself, rather than take arms against a prince in the main good and useful to the state; provided the danger only extends to himself. But when the common rights of the community are trampled upon; and what at first is attempted against one, is to be made a precedent against all the rest, then as the governor is plainly perfidious to his <304> trust, he has forfeited all the power committed to him.[3]

II. In every sort of government the people has this right of defending themselves <by violence> against the abuse of power. If the prince's power be limited, and yet he breaks over its bounds, invading such rights as the people had reserved in the very constitution of the power; the people's right of resistance is unquestionable. But even in absolute governments they have the same right; if their governor, ceasing to use his power {as if he owned it destined} for the good of the body, should govern the whole state as his own property; and neglecting the common safety of all, turn every thing to the gratification of his own lust or avarice; or if he plainly declares a hatred of his people; or conducts all affairs in such a wretched manner, that not even the most sacred rights of the people, such as are necessary to any

3. See *System* 3.7.2, vol. II, p. 268–70.

maneant. Neque qui hoc populo tribuit, dabit quoque eum regibus esse superiorem: servis enim vel in deterrima conditione degentibus jus est, ut contra dominorum injurias atrociores se per vim defendant.

Si hìc moveatur quaestio, cujus hac in causa sit judicium, numnam qui summo imperio praesunt <et> rempub. male administrârint, suâque perfidia jus omne amiserint? Si non populi, quod ipsius causa agatur; ob eandem causam, neque imperantis erit judicium. Ad aequos igitur decurrendum esset arbitros, vel nostrates, vel externos, si res sineret: sin minus, populi certe potius erit judicium, a quo magistratibus olim mandatum erat imperium, cujusque negotia geruntur, cujus etiam gratiâ potestas omnis fuit constituta. De re fere quavis humanum est errare{: neque errorum immunes sunt ipsi rectores}. Saepe de jure publico, saepe de privato sui defendendi jure erratum est; nontamen ideo tollenda sunt haec hominum jura, sive privata sive publica.

His quidem in rebus gravissimis, cuncta cautissimé pensitanda; neque ob leviores <313> imperantium injurias aut errores, quales in homines haud improbos aliquando cadere possunt, in bella civilia, omnium saepe saevissima, cives sunt conjiciendi. Ubi vero alia ratione populus salvus esse nequit; et perfidis dolosisque facinoribus, imperii jus omne amiserunt imperantes; jure per vim regno exui possunt, aliis in eorum locum suffectis, aut nova imperii formâ constitutâ.

Neque motibus civilibus bellisve fovendis apta est haec, de sancto populi jure se contra tyrannos defendendi, doctrina. Immo contrariis feré dog-

tolerable life, remain secure to them.[4] Nor does this doctrine of resistance give to the people a civil superiority over their governors: for even slaves adjudged to the most miserable subjection {for their crimes}, may have a right to defend themselves <by violence> against certain [the fiercest] injuries their masters may attempt against them.

As to that question, who shall be judge in this disputed point, whether the governors by their perfidy and mal-administration have forfeited their right? If 'tis alleged, the people cannot judge as they are parties: for the same reason the governors cannot judge. The only recourse then should be to impartial arbiters, either within the state, or in some other nation, if this could be safe: but if not; surely the people have a better <305> claim to judge in this point; since *they* at first entrusted their governors with such powers, and the powers were designed for the management of the people's interests, and were constituted for their behoof. 'Tis true there are great dangers of mistakes on this head: but the governors are not exempted from errors more than the people. Men have often erred both about publick rights, and the private ones too of self-defence: but we must not for that reason deny that they have such rights.[5]

In this most important matter, no doubt, persons concerned are bound to use the utmost caution, and weigh all things on both sides. Nor ought we to involve our fellow-citizens in civil-wars, the most miserable [savage] of all wars, for any such lighter injuries, or wrong conduct of our governors, as may be incident sometimes to persons in the main good and of upright intentions. But when there's no other way of preserving a people; and when their governors by their perfidious frauds have plainly forfeited their right; they may justly be divested of their power <by violence>, and others put into their places, or a new plan of power established.

Nor does this doctrine of the right of resistance in defence of the rights of a people, naturally tend to excite seditions and civil wars. Nay they have

4. Hutcheson, as well as Carmichael (*Notes on Puf.,* pp. 169–71), plays down the differences between absolute and limited governments made by Pufendorf in relation to the people's right of resistance.

5. See *System* 3.7.4, vol. II, p. 273–74.

matis haec mala praecipue imputanda. Nimia fere semper fuit populi patientia, et inepta imperantium veneratio; quae tot civitatum monstra, aut potius miseros et abjectos servorum greges, sub dominis saevissimis et nequissimis, jura omnia divina et humana impudenter miscentibus, per terrarum orbem pepererunt.[1]

III. Tyranno exturbato, aut rege qui ad munus electus fuit extincto, ubi nihil de successione est praestitutum, aut denique stirpe regia extincta in regnis haereditariis, nascitur *interregnum.* His in casibus, quamvis nihil legibus publicis sit cautum, haud quidem tollitur populi conjunctio civilis: primo enim, quod diximus, pacto obligantur omnes, ut communi consilio communi prospiciant saluti. Existet aliquamdiu democratia <314> quaedam, ubi plurium aut praestantiorum, qui reipub. negotia gerere solebant, suffragiis erit statuendum, qualis in posterum futura sit reipub. forma, quibusque deinceps permittendum imperium. Neque paucioribus, caeteris invitis, civilis vinculi licet esse immunibus; nisi pars major planè iniquas et pestiferas reipub. administrandae rationes ineant.

IV. Principibus quorum probitas fidesque satis est spectata, debetur pietas omnis et observantia; iique cum summo civium periculo, sive contra caecos tumultus, sive aperta bella, sunt defendendi; neque culpis eorum aut vitiis levioribus, qualia aliquando in viros minime malos cadere possunt, cives ab ea obligatione exsolvuntur. Si vero hoc incidat ut devincantur et a dignitate deturbentur, vel ab imperii competitoribus, vel hostibus externis, ita ut

---

1. In 1742 edn. this paragraph was at the end of art. iv.

6. Cf. *System* 3.7.6, vol. II, pp. 279–80, and Locke, *Two Treatises* 2.18, sections 207–8, and 2.19, sections 223–26.
7. See Pufendorf, *De officio* 2.10.4 and *De Iure nat.* 7.7.7–10.

been more frequently occasioned by the contrary tenets.[6] In all ages there has been too much patience in the body of the people, and too stupid a veneration for their princes or rulers; which {for each one free kingdom or state} <in the whole world> has produced many monstrous <states or rather> herds of miserable abject slaves or beasts of burden, {rather than civil <306> polities of rational creatures}, under the most inhuman and worthless masters, trampling upon all things human and divine with the utmost effrontery.

III. Upon dethroning a tyrant, or upon the natural extinction of a royal family, or the death of an elective prince<, where there is no rule of succession>, there arises an *interregnum*. In which case, even altho' there be nothing expresly provided in the constitution, yet the political union of the people is not quite dissolved. They all continue bound by that first covenant we mentioned, to consult their common interest by joint counsels.[7] They seem to be in a sort of {simple} democracy for some time; in which it should be determined by plurality of votes of the whole, or of those at least who used to be concerned in the publick affairs, what shall be their future form of polity and who are to be promoted to the government.[8] Nor is it just that any smaller part, without consent of the rest, should break off from the political union; unless the majority are setting up some unjust or destructive plan of polity.

IV. To princes, or rulers of any kind, who have evidenced integrity and fidelity in their trust, the highest deference and honour is due {from their subjects}; they should be supported and defended with the lives and fortunes of all, whether against rebels or foreign enemies. Nor are subjects [citizen] freed from this obligation, by any such lighter faults or mistakes of their governors, as may be incident to men in the main upright {and faithful to their trust}. But if {after all the efforts of their subjects,} such princes are conquered and dethroned, either by some competitor or some

8. That "interregna have the character of a temporary democracy" is what Pufendorf says in *De interregnis* (*Dissertationes academicae selectae,* Upsaliae 1677, pp. 261–301), and Carmichael quotes approvingly (*Notes on Puf.,* p. 184).

nulla spes sit reliqua, eos jus suum antiquum recuperare posse; principum est regumve de jure suo ultro cedere: immo id omne pro extincto est habendum; quum omnis inter imperantes et populum obligatio sit mutua, mutuisque officiis conservanda: quae quum ab altera parte praestari nequeunt, nulla alteri sunt praestanda. Omnibus igitur prius tentatis, populus jure se victori submittet, quum suae saluti aliter consulere nequeat. <315> Mirae quidem foret arrogantiae, si quis suae dignitatis aut utilitatis causa, totam civitatem et populum pessundatum velit et laniatum.

V. Quemadmodum naturalis *libertas* est jus pro sua cujusque voluntate agendi, intra legum naturalium limites, (quae nulla foret si nullae essent leges, hanc libertatem caeteraque jura cuique munientes;) sic dicimus populum esse *liberum,* quum non ad alterius praescriptum, sed [suo arbitratu] [ad suum arbitrium] intra legum civilium sines, cuique [manet] [permissa est] agendi facultas. Non igitur leges libertati repugnant, sed acerba aut morosa hominum imperia. Liber Romanis dicebatur populus, ubi concilio populari imperii summa erat permissa, et parendi imperandique vices obtinebantur.

VI. Vix alia ratione quam populi decreto voluntario, potestatem civilem jure constitui posse, satis jam disputatum [dictum]; neque imperatores aliam habere sanctitatem aut majestatem, quam quae hinc oritur, quod hominum multitudo jura, quisque sua, uni homini aut concilio permiserat administranda. Ex quadam libertatis naturalis parte, a singulis ad imperantem translata, aut ex singulorum dominiis eidem aliquatenus subjectis, nascitur legum condendarum potestas. In libertate, quisque vitae necisque jus hactenus <316> in se habebat, ut officia honesta quantocunque cum periculo suscipere liceret; quumque communis hoc postulat utilitas, aliis se dirigen-

foreign <307> power, so that there remain no probable hopes of their re-
covering their just rights; 'tis their duty in such cases to quit their claim:
nay 'tis justly deemed extinct: since all obligations between governors and
subjects are mutual; depending upon mutual offices. And when it becomes
impossible for one side to perform his part, the other is freed from his obligation. The people therefor, after their utmost efforts for their old rulers
have proved unsuccessful, may justly submit to the conqueror, when they
cannot otherways consult their own safety. It would indeed be strange arrogance in any prince to expect that a whole people should be bound, by
a vain zeal for his dignity and interest, to expose themselves to all the rage
and fury of a conqueror{, to no valuable purpose}.[9]

V. As natural liberty is "the right of acting as one inclines within the bounds
of the law of nature"; (nor could we hold any such liberty were there no
laws to defend it from the force of the stronger:) so we say a people enjoys
liberty when "each one is allowed to act as he inclines, within the bounds
of civil law, and not subjected to the caprice of any other." We should never
look upon laws as eversive of liberty; but that 'tis sole enemy is the capricious humourous will or command of men in power. The Romans indeed
in speaking of a *free people,* generally meant a democratical state; where
men had their turns of commanding, as well as of obeying.[10]

VI. It was already shewn that civil power can scarce be constituted justly
any other way than by the consent of the people; and that rulers have no
other <308> sacred rights or majesty, than what may arise from this: that
of a large multitude of men, each one for himself subjected part of his
rights to the administration of a certain person or council. And thus from
a part of our natural liberty transferred to the ruler, and our property in a
certain degree subjected to his disposal, arises the legislative power. In natural liberty also each one had a right to expose his life to the greatest dangers,
in any honourable services in defence of his family or his neighbours, and
when the common interest required it he could commit himself to the di-

9. See *System* 3.7.5, vol. II, pp. 278–79.
10. See *System* 3.7.7, vol. II, p. 281–82.

dum in his officiis obeundis permittere{: unde imperii militaris jus}. In libertate etiam, inter hominum jura erat, ut eum qui ipsis injuriam intentaverat aut fecerat, summis coércerent suppliciis; communique innocuorum saluti, si ita facto opus esset, ejusdem caede prospicerent. Hinc oritur jus omne poenas delictis aequas irrogandi, sive jurisdictio quae *criminalis* dicitur. Neque ad potestatem aliquam a Deo proximè derivatam, ad haec aut alia majestatis jura explicanda, decurrendum.

VII. Neque una reipub. forma prae caeteris, alia de causa, divina est habenda, quam quod per eam optimè communi consulatur prosperitati; quod in monarchiis infinitis et haereditariis minime contingit. Quid? quod nulla lege divina, naturali aut positiva, monstratur succedendi, ratio; num scil. satis sit successio quaevis haereditaria, eaque vel agnationis, vel cognationis jure; an contra exigatur *linealis.* De re familiari ad cognatos transmittenda, non leves sunt juris naturalis obscuritates; licet, re generaliter spectata, manifestum sit, bona in familiae aut gentis utilitatem acquisita, sanguinis sequi debere conjunctionem. Quod vero ad imperia attinet, <317> (non in unius familiae dignitatem, sed in populi universi utilitatem destinata,) nulla subest causa, cur in iis deferendis spectetur sanguinis conjunctio; multo minus cur linealis admittatur successio qualiscunque.{*} Ex legibus humanis aut populi scitis, saepe temerariis et incautis, haec omnia nascuntur.

---

* Vid. Lib. II.viii.4.

---

11. See *System* 3.8.3, vol. II, pp. 286–89, where Hutcheson refers to Locke, *Two Treatises* 1.11. Hutcheson, following Locke's arguments against Robert Filmer, sees a contradiction between the pretended divine institution of hereditary government and the positive character of the laws of succession.

* See Book II. Ch. 8. 4. {The decisions of some questions about the succession in hereditary lineal kingdoms, turn upon very fantastick reasons. Some allege proximity as a natural reason; and yet an elder cousin-germain's grandchild, shall often be preferred

rection of others in such services; and hence the right of military command. <In natural liberty> Men had also this right of repelling injuries, and punishing by violence any one who attempted or executed any injury, and even of putting him to death if this was necessary for the common safety: and hence arises all *criminal jurisdiction,* even to the inflicting of capital punishments [or the right of imposing just punishments on crimes]. Nor need we have recourse to any extraordinary grants or commissions from God to explain any of these rights of civil sovereigns.

VII. Nor can any one form of government be esteemed more divine than others, on any other account than that it is better adapted to promote the prosperity of the community; which can least of all be alleged of absolute hereditary monarchies. Need we suggest here that no divine law natural or positive determines the order of succession to monarchies, whether the *general hereditary,* and that either by males only, or also by females; or the *lineal hereditary.*[11] In the succession to private fortunes, tho' this be manifest in general, that the goods plainly acquired for the behoof <309> of a man's family and kinsmen, should descend to his family or kinsmen upon his decease; yet there are not a few difficulties in determining the proportions. But as to civil governments, which, 'tis obvious, were never constituted for the behoof of a family, but for the interest of a whole nation; there seems no natural reasons that the succession to them should depend upon the proximity of blood to the former possessor; and much less that the lineal succession should be regarded.* All such right of succession must arise from human laws, or decrees of a people, and these sometimes very incautious and imprudent.

---

to a younger cousin-germain. They say too that seniority is a natural reason of preference; and yet the infant-grandchild of a deceased elder-brother takes before a second-brother of mature years. The preeminence of sex too is made a great matter; and yet the infant-grand-daughter by an elder-uncle deceased, shall take before a younger-uncle. In general, these potent causes of preference, proximity, seniority, and the sex, are not regarded as they are found in the competitors themselves; but as they were perhaps in their great-grandfathers or great-grandmothers, deceased an age or two before.} [This added footnote derives from what Hutcheson says in *System* 3.8.3, vol. II, p. 287–88.]

VIII. Illud autem jus, vulgo jactatum, quo in populum devictum imperium civile sibi arrogat victor, non meliore plerumque innititur fundamento, quam quod {sibi} [arrogant latrones ac praedones maritimi] [latronibus ac praedonibus maritimis arrogatur]. Nam primo, qui justam bellandi causam non habuit, nihil quicquam ullo jure capit aut detinet. <(2)> Deinde, fingatur causa vel justissima, certi tamen, ut ante dictum,{*} sunt petendi fines: neque contra hostes quicquam jure aget victor, quod neque ad injuriam avertendam, neque ad damnum reparandum, neque ad injurias in posterum praecavendas, necessarium est aut utile: si quid amplius exegerit, justitiae fines transit. Ad injuriam vero avertendam, aut damnum pensandum, nunquam necessarium est aut utile, ut civitati et populo victo, in provinciam redacto, adimatur libertas publica et majestas. Immo communi plerumque repugnat utilitati, ut civitates opes suas sic augeant, potentiamque adipiscantur vicinis metuendam. Diu <318> plerumque antequam debellatur civitas, victorique subjicitur, depulsa est omnis injuria, damnumque cumulatissime pensatum. Pensationem [pensatur. Compensationem] fere semper sibi prius arripiunt victores, ex rebus hostium mobilibus, quam eorundam penitus devincatur civitas. Hac ratione damnum lubentes praestarent hostes devicti, vel si opus sit, stipendium quotannis penderent (quibus certè omnia damna cumulatissime reparari possunt) potius quam, a missâ patriae civitatis libertate, exteris se subjicerent.

Quod ad cautionem attinet: quibus {rationibus}, ab injuriis a civitate devicta, haud tamen exhausta, in posterum inferendis, satis cautum est, iis multo magis, a civitate {jam} exhausta et tantum non deleta, cautum erit. A civitate autem opibus valente satis cautum est traditis obsidibus, navi-

---

* Lib. II.xv.5, 8. Lib. III.iii.2.

---

* {Upon this subject see *Locke on Government;* whose reasonings are well abridged in Mr. *Carmichaell's* notes on Puffendorf's smaller book. Book II. ch. x.} [See Locke, *Two Treatises* 2. 16 and Carmichael, *Notes on Puf.,* pp. 175–80.]

VIII. As to that much celebrated *right of conquest,* by which the conqueror claims the civil power to himself {and his heirs} over the conquered people; it has little better foundation generally than the claim of robbers and pirates {upon persons and their goods which <310> have fallen into their hands}.{*} For first, unless the conqueror had a just cause, he acquires <and detains> no right. And then tho' his cause was just [suppose his cause the most just], yet, as we said above,† his claim has certain bounds; nor has he a right to exact more from the vanquished than what is requisite <or useful> to repell the injury attempted, to repair all damages done, or to obtain sufficient security against injuries for the future. If he insists on more, he has no justice on his side in such demands. Now it is never necessary <or advantageous>, either for averting of injuries, or repairing of damages, that the conquered should be deprived of their liberty, or independency, and be reduced into the form of a province to the conqueror. Nay 'tis generally very pernicious to the common interests of mankind, that states should thus enlarge their power, and make it formidable to all around them. All present danger to the victorious is averted, and full reparation of damages generally obtained, long before their enemies are entirely subdued {and over-run by their arms}. The conquerors generally soon take to themselves abundant compensation out of the moveable goods of the conquered: and every state when thoroughly defeated, would always consent to make compensation this way, nay would pay an annual contribution for a certain term, to make up what was awanting; rather than lose their liberty and sovereignty, and be subjected to foreigners. <311> And surely by these ways all damages could be abundantly repaired.{‡}

As to securities against future injuries: surely such securities as are universally allowed to be sufficient against a state yet retaining much of its strength, shall be more than sufficient against one wholly exhausted and almost ruined by war: now {in all treaties,} these are deemed sufficient securities against states yet retaining much of their force, if they deliver hos-

† Book II. ch. xv. 5. 8. and Book III. ch. iii. 2.

‡ {The reasonings in this and the following articles are designed against the pleas of *Grotius* and *Puffendorf* for the rights of conquest, and *patrimonial kingdoms,* or *principalities,* founded on it.}

busve armatis, vel oppidis in confinio munitis; vel victoris praesidiis in urbes munitas acceptis. Immo saepe sufficit quod earum urbium munimenta diruantur. Neque ulla est civitas devicta, quin omnia haec lubens praestaret, potius quam vicinae civitati provincia fieret.

IX. Si quid poenae nomine, ad omnes ab injuriis deterrendos, sit exigendum, id a solis delinquentibus exigi debet. Populi vero devicti pars longe maxima, nullo crimine <319> obligatur, ideo quod a rectoribus suis ciebantur bella {vel} maxime nefaria. A victis igitur hoc solum jure exigere potest victor, ut rectores suos injustos aut dedant aut defendere desinant, ut de illis poenas factis dignas sumat. At propter ea quae injustè aut inhumaniter in bello fiunt publico, poenas exigere vetat communis utilitas. In civitate semper spes est, magistratus, viribus suis legumque auctoritate sublevatos, poenas de civibus crimine obstrictis sumere posse: At civitatum bella gerentium vires, per socios et foederatos, ita plerumque sunt aequales, ut anceps sit belli fortuna; quibusque causae sunt justissimae, exitus tamen sit incertus. Ab omni igitur in devictos saevitia abstinendum, ne ad hostes exemplum transferatur, qui causam injustam tuentur, quae {tamen} ipsis justa videatur. Neque ideo quod causam suam justam putant victores, legem saevam, contra se forte aut suos postea valituram, sanciant.

Neque credibile est ullam conventionem tacitam inter civitates dissidentes intercessisse, ut ibi imperium foret unde victoria fuerit. Contraria omnia palam testatur qui bellum movet, nisi ubi disertis verbis istiusmodi pactum fuit initum. Ipso bello, se omni ratione, jura sua defensurum aut persecuturum, significat et denunciat: neque populus, <320> quamvis debellatus, qui novis sociis aut opibus adscitis bellum renovaverit, fidem vio-

tages, give up their fleets, {or a great part of them,} surrender frontier towns with their fortifications, or receive garrisons of their neighbours into them [into their walled cities], or even if they dismantle them{, or demolish all the fortifications}. Nor is there any state that would not rather consent to all these, rather than become a province subjected to another [to a neigbour-state].

IX. If it be alleged that punishments should also be inflicted as a further security by deterring others: yet surely none should be punished but the guilty. Now the far greater part of any conquered people were involved in no guilt by their governors having entered into even the most unjust wars.{*} The conqueror therefor can demand no more of the body of a people than that they either give up their injurious governors, or desist to defend them any further, that the victor may punish them as they deserve. But as to any thing done unjustly or inhumanly in publick wars, the common <312> interest of mankind would dissuade from making it matter of proper punishment. Within the bounds of any regular polity, 'tis generally highly probable or certain that the power of the laws and magistrates will be superiour to that of any criminal citizens; and that therefor they may be brought to justice. But in publick wars, the forces of the parties by their confederates and allies are so generally brought to a parity, that the event is very uncertain: and the just cause is often unsuccessful. This should restrain conquerors even in the justest causes from any severities{, under the notion of punishment}; as they will become precedents to others in very bad causes, which yet they may judge to be just. The victorious therefor should beware of establishing a precedent, which may be followed thereafter against themselves or their friends.

'Tis vain to allege any tacit convention between the parties in war, that that side shall have the civil power over both which happens to be victorious. Taking arms is rather an open declaration of the contrary, that neither side intends to submit its rights of any sort to the other; unless in those cases where there has been such covenants expresly made; nor was it ever, in any other case, deemed perfidious, that the party defeated rallys its forces,

* {See Book III. ch. iii. 2.}

lasse censetur. Quid, quod nemo dixerit, eum cui causa sua videtur justa, tali legi consensisse: atqui sine hujus consensu, alterius partis, {quicquid de ipsius causa senserit,} intervenisse consensum, colligi nequit. Hi denique victorum fautores, solos imperantes consensisse volunt: quo vero jure hi, quorum in tutelam permittitur populus, populi jura omnia, vel absolutè, vel sub conditione, alienare possunt? Finge istud disertis verbis {ab iis} pactum fuisse; ob id ipsum, homines illi perfidi et audaces, omne imperandi jus amiserunt; neque quae ab iis transiguntur civitatem obligare possunt.

X. Quum igitur {illi} scriptores <fere> omnes, qui regna quaedam *patrimonialia* esse contendunt, quae regis arbitrio alienari, aut dividi possunt, ea ex sola ferè victoria profecta statuant; nullo idcirco jure ea arrogari, satis [docuimus] [ex dictis constat]. Quinetiam, si forte accidat ut populus aliquis, ab saevis hostibus ingruentibus perterritus, populo potentiori se suaque omnia dedat, solum hoc stipulatus, ut contra calamitatem imminentem protegatur; nihilo {tamen} magis ea pactione regnum patrimoniale constituitur.{*} Ne quid enim de metus exceptione dicatur; aut quod pactum istud <321> plane onerosum, sit tamen inaequale; ex ipso pacto {reique natura} patet, quod colligi nequeat, tale quicquam fuisse factum. Quippe, qui se civitati excultae, humanae, imperiumque lene exercenti dedunt, minimé censeri poterunt consensisse, ut {istius arbitratu, quovis modo vexentur aut lacerentur; utque} <et> alteri cuivis vel regi vel populo barbaro subjiciantur; aut saeviore regantur imperio, quam exercebant illi cui se dedi-

---

* Notatur hic Grot. vid. Lib. I.c.iii.12.

---

12. For the patrimonial kingdoms, see Pufendorf, *De officio* 2.9.7 and *De iure nat.* 7.6.16; Carmichael says that "patrimonial kingdoms scarcely ever have a just beginning," that they "are imperfect states," that their ownership "does not include civil government over the people" (*Notes on Puf.,* pp. 180–82).

{makes new levies,} or gets new allies to continue the war. Can any one pretend, that that side which has a just cause [which judges his cause to be just], {defending or prosecuting its own rights,} makes any such convention? and if one side is known not to do it, we can never presume it on the other side <however it judges its own cause>. The patrons of this right of conquest too, can allege only that the supreme governors <313> consented, and not the body of the people: but with what shadow of right can any governors, whose power was granted to them only in trust for protection of the people, pretend to alienate or transfer the whole people with all their rights to another, either absolutely or upon any contingency? suppose the governors made such an express convention: by this audacious perfidy they plainly forfeit their power; nor is the state bound by such a deed.

X. Since therefor all the authors who plead that certain civil sovereignties are *patrimonial,* so that they may be sold, divided{, or any way transferred}at the pleasure of the sovereign, suppose also that they are generally founded in conquest; what is said above shews that such power has no just foundation.[12] Nay if it should happen that a state in the greatest consternation, upon an invasion from barbarians [enemies], should by their own deed submit themselves and all their rights to some potent neighbour, demanding nothing from them but protection; yet even such a deed cannot constitute a patrimonial power.* For not to mention the exception of unjust force and terror; or that this covenant being plainly of the onerous kind, yet does not maintain the essential equality: the very nature of the covenant, and the matter of it, shews that no patrimonial power could be intended in it. A state by submitting itself to a humane, civilized neighbour which exercised a gentle rule over its subjects, cannot be deemed to have consented also to any manner of oppression or vexations that thereafter this neighbour may inflict on them; nor that <314> they should be made over to any barbarous prince or people at the pleasure of those entrusted themselves to.

---

* The reasons here confuted are found in Grotius, L. I. iv. [The corresponding footnote of the *Institutio* refers to *De jure belli* 1.3.12. See also *System* 3.8.7, vol. II, pp. 297–99.]

derunt. Quinetiam si quid istiusmodi moliatur haec civitas dominans, jure sibi jugum excutient qui longè alia lege se isti subjecerunt. Ad arbitros {enim} provocare licet et deditiis, si quid crudelius ipsis sit impositum, ultra {id,} quod salutis et defensionis pretium, jure exigi poterat.

Neque ex populi devicti pacto aut promisso, quod vis minax extorserat, victorijus imperii nascitur. Eam enim vim esse injustam satis ostendimus.{*} Sin verò a victore, aequa reipub. forma populo devicto constituatur, quae satis ipsius conservat jura, communemque tuetur prosperitatem; ita ut populus, post periculum factum, ei formae se submittere non recuset; ex hoc consensu imperii jus oriri quodque praecesserat vitium purgari poterit.

XI. Quum insuper nullis causis naturalibus <322> libus {et necessario obligantibus}, sed solo populi decreto, innitatur cujusvis ex regia sobole aut gente jus, ut regi defuncto succedat; decreti hujus verba eodem modo sunt interpretanda, quo {istiusmodi verba} in caeteris legibus de *successionibus haereditariis:* eaque censenda est hac de re fuisse populi voluntas, quae verbis iisdem aliis de rebus declaratur. Ubi igitur, in aliis bonis haereditariis, quisque delicto suo, jus suum, non solum pro se, verum etiam pro liberis et cognatis amittit, idem etiam de imperii jure haereditario est censendum. Immo, rei familiaris dispar [dissimilis] est ratio. Ea familiae alendae et amplificandae gratia acquisita fuit: unde liberi, et saepe cognati, jure postulant ut ex re familiari alantur et amplificentur: durumque est et iniquum, ut unius delictum immerentibus noceat, bonaque, quae naturae lege iis rediissent, intervertat. De imperii jure omnia alia dicenda; quod neutiquam ob regiam stirpem, aut ob aliquid quod ipsi regi, ejusve soboli debebatur;

* Lib. II.xv.5, 8. Lib. III.iii.2.

Nay if this superior state should attempt any thing very oppressive of this nature, the subject-people may justly shake off the yoke: since it was plainly upon other terms that they subjected themselves. They have a right to demand arbitration, as to the equity of any thing imposed beyond what should be deemed a just compensation for the protection received.

Nor can any right of sovereignty arise from any seeming consent of the conquered, which was only extorted by present force. For we shewed* above that such force is plainly unjust. But if the victor establishes among the vanquished such an equitable plan of civil power, as sufficiently consults their future safety and prosperity, so that upon experience of it they are truly satisfied to submit to it; this subsequent consent becomes a just foundation of his power, and is a sort of civil expiation of the injury done in the conquest.

XI. But further, as the right of any person of the royal-blood to succeed upon the demise of his predecessor, is not founded on any natural causes, but solely upon some {old law or} decree of the state [people]: the words of such laws or deeds are to be understood in the same way as like words about other matters deemed hereditary; and thus we are to collect from them what was the intention of the people in such deeds. When therefor this universally obtained in any country, that when the present possessor of any thing hereditary forfeits it, he forfeits not only for himself but all his kindred; <315> we justly conclude that the peoples intention was that the forfeitures of the hereditary sovereignty should be in the same manner. The plea against extending forfeitures to the whole kindred of the person forfeiting, is very strong and plausible as to private fortunes, which all know were acquired chiefly for the behoof of the proprietor and his family; and this according to a natural obligation: so that children and kinsmen too have a natural claim to be supported and have their condition advanced out of such fortunes: and 'tis unjust that the fault of one of the joint proprietors should prejudice the rest, and prevent their obtaining what they are naturally entitled to. But as to hereditary sovereignties the case is quite different. They were not constituted for the behoof of the royal family, nor

* § 8th of this chap. [The *Institutio* rightly refers to 2.15.5 and 8 and 3.3.2.]

sed ipsius civitatis gratiâ, utque praecaveantur mala ex novorum regum creationibus subinde metuenda, constitutum fuit. Potiore igitur jure in *causam commissi* cadunt regna haereditaria, quam privatorum haereditates.

Ut igitur populus suo jure perfidum regem de solio deturbat; potiore certè jure <323> praecavere potest, ne quis succedat qui reipub. administrandae est ineptus; qui ea fovet dogmata, quae sanctissima populi jura pessundare eum promovebunt, quum primùm potestatem fuerit adeptus; qui insana quadam superstitione percitus, summae potestatis partes haud leves, ad regem quendam exterum, sub falso pontificis nomine, transferet; aut qui se jure divino munitum credit, quo fretus <omnia> civitatis jura audacissime perrumpet, omnesque imperii sibi permissi limites transiliet; seque officio defuturum existimabit, nisi cives summorum cruciatuum metu cogat, ut dogmata absurdissima credant, vel saltem credere simulent; cultumque Deo praestent quem nefarium putant. Qui regni haeres talia profitetur dogmata, {eave palam ejurare rogatus detrectat,} potiore jure excluditur, quam qui plane fatuus est aut insanus: quum istiusmodi dogmata populo libero magis sint perniciosa, quam ulla regis fatuitas aut insania.

XII. Quae de regibus diximus, de cunctis tenent civitatum rectoribus, atque de populi ipsius in provincias aut colonias imperio. Si qui cives, populi aut magistratuum permissu, e civitate suis sumptibus migrent, novas sibi sedes quaesituri; illi [civitatem liberam, ditionisque omnis externae immunem] [sociam civitatem] sibi jure constituunt. Qui publicis <324> impensis ea mittuntur lege, ut coloniae modo sub civitatis ditione maneant, ad ejusdem potentiam aut opes augendas; haud aequum est ut eorum quam civium

founded in consequence of any just claim they had for their own behoof;
but for the interest of the whole nation, and chiefly to prevent the mischiefs
to be apprehended in new elections of sovereigns: and therefore they are
much more justly made liable to entire forfeitures from the whole family,
than any private fortunes.

As therefor a people may justly dethrone a perfidious prince; they have
a better right to exclude from the succession any one who shews himself
plainly unfit for the trust: and such are those who hold tenets {about divine
rights} which must excite them to trample upon the most sacred rights of
the people, as soon as they get into power; or those who possessed with
some furious superstition will subject their crown, or alienate no small parts
of the supreme power, to some foreign prince, <316> under the shew of a
religious character [under the false name of pontifex];[13] and at the same
time think themselves commissioned by God to break through in the most
audacious manner the fundamental laws or constitution, and all limits set
by it to their power; and to force the subjects by the severest tortures either
to believe, or falsely profess to believe, the most monstrous absurdities in
religion, and to worship God in a way they judge impious. Any heir apparent who professes such tenets, or refuses upon a just demand to renounce
and abjure them in the most solemn manner, may be excluded from succession with much better ground than if he were an ideot or a madman;
as the holding of such tenets must make him more dangerous to a free
people than any folly or madness.

<XII>: What we have said relates not only to monarchs but all sorts of
governours, and to the power of a state itself over its colonies, or provinces.
If any citizens, with permission of the <people or> government, leave their
country, and at their own expence find new habitations; they may justly
constitute themselves into an independent state{, in amity with their
mother-country}. If any are sent off at the publick charge as a colony, to
make settlements subject to the state, for augmenting its commerce and
power; such persons should hold all the rights of the other subjects, and

13. The reference to King James II is as explicit here as in *System* 3.8.11, vol. II, p. 305–
6. A more serene condemnation of the king is in Carmichael, *Notes on Puf.*, pp. 185–87.

caeterorum deterior sit conditio. Jura omnia, illis concessa, sunt religiose conservanda. Si quid durius in colonos patria civitas statuerit, ipsique satis per se sibi prospicere possint; aut si tyrannide oppressa sit civitas, ipsiusve forma in deteriora omnia immutata; hoc sibi jure arrogabunt coloni, ut sui sint in posterum juris, sociae civitatis officia praestare parati. Neque pacta, in quibus contrahendis, de iis quae in istiusmodi negotiis praecipuè spectari solent, erratum est, magnum hominum numerum, civitati beatae constituendae idoneum, ad ea subeunda adstringunt, quae ipsorum prosperitati et saluti adversantur. Neque quicquam graviora in hominum vitam mala invexit, quam vana et insolens, sive regum sive populorum, cupiditas, imperii sui fines porrigendi, aliosque populos in suam ditionem redigendi, dum neque suae neque eorum foelicitati prudenter consulunt. Hinc ingentia et immania exsurrexerunt imperia, vicinis omnibus gravia et pestifera, et brevi, cum misera hominum strage ruitura. <325>

whatever grants are made to them are to be faithfully observed. If the mother-country attempts any thing oppressive toward a colony, and the colony be able to subsist as a sovereign state by itself; or if the mother-country lose its liberty, or have its plan of polity miserably changed to the worse: <317> the colony is not bound to remain subject any longer: 'tis enough that it remain a friendly state. Nor are we to imagine that any early covenants founded upon errors about the most essential points in view, can still bind large societies of men fit to subsist as happy independent states, to continue in a submission eversive of all prosperity and safety. Nor has any thing occasioned more misery in human life than a vain and insolent ambition, both in princes and popular states of extending their empires, and bringing every neighbouring state under subjection to them; without consulting the real felicity either of their own people or of their new acquisitions. And hence have arose these vast unwieldy empires; the plagues of all around them; which after some time are ruined by their own bulk, with vast destruction of mankind.[14]

14. For the same defense of the rights of the American colonies see *System* 3.8.12, vol. II, pp. 306–9.

CAPUT VIII

De Legibus condendis, et de Jurisdictione.

I. Inter imperii jura *immanentia,* est legum jubendarum et administrandarum potestas. Omnis lex aliquam civitatis utilitatem spectare debet, legibusque ea omnia sancienda quae communi inserviunt prosperitati, quantum penes homines est eam procurare aut augere. Si quidem in ipsa imperii constitutione, ea tantummodo potestas rectoribus permissa fuerit, quae in rebus externis tuendis versatur; illi de civium animis virtute colendis, aut de cultu religioso, nihil pro imperio statuere poterunt. Verum ubi eorum arbitratui conceduntur certi reditus, in communem utilitatem impendendi, aut ubi totius [plena] reipublicae administratio ipsis est permissa; quum ex hominum virtute pendeat praecipuè eorum foelicitas, hoc illis qui reipub. praesunt imprimis curae esse debet, ut per disciplinam et institutionem, primis ab annis, imbuantur civium animi iis sententiis et moribus, quibus ad omnia virtutis officia reddantur paratiores.

Cuique tamen conservandum jus illud sanctissimum suo utendi judicio; cui aperte <326> repugnant leges omnes poenaeque latae de hominum sententiis, sive celatis, sive palam factis, si modo civium moribus non sint pestiferae. Immo, etsi istiusmodi dogmata ab iis divulgentur qui ad ea divulganda religione se putant adstrictos, satius est plerumque, cautione, de non laedendo, officiisque civilibus praestandis, a caeteris exactâ, in ea tantum facinora gravius animadvertere, quae religione malesuadâ perciti admise-

CHAPTER VIII

<318>

Of Civil Laws and their Execution.

I. The power of making and executing laws is the most important internal power. Every law should be intended for some real utility to the state; and as far as human power can go, laws should enjoin whatever is of consequence to the general prosperity. But if in the very constitution of the civil polity, the sovereign or chief magistrate is only entrusted with such power as is requisite for the preservation of the secular rights [external goods] of men; then they cannot exert any sort of coercive power about the means of forming mens minds to religion or inward virtue. But when they are entrusted with certain revenues, to be employed for the publick utility at their discretion; and where they are not expresly restricted to the care of the secular rights of men; since human happiness chiefly depends upon virtue, the civil governors must think it belonging to their office, to instill into the minds of their subjects the true sentiments of religion and virtue, {and to influence their hearts to relish them,} by the best instruction and discipline from their infancy, that they may be furnished for all the honourable [virtuous] offices of life.[1]

But at the same time they must maintain to all, their sacred right of judging for themselves; which would be plainly encroached upon by any penal laws about such opinions, whether secret or divulged, which don't <319> lead to any practices destructive to society.[2] Nay tho' such <religious> tenets should be divulged by men who imagine themselves bound in conscience to divulge them; it would generally be more advisable only to insist that such persons give proper security that they will give no disturbance to the state, and bear their share in all services required of them for the publick; and to punish rigorously only the injuries done in conse-

1. See *System* 3.9.1, vol. II, pp. 310–11.
2. See *System* 3.9.1, vol. II, pp. 312–13.

runt, quam poenas ob ipsas sententias divulgatas irrogare. Istiusmodi dogmata pleraque melius saniorum hominum prudentiae et ingenio explo-
denda permittuntur.

Quum tamen in civitate omni, civium pars longe maxima suo judicio
strenue uti nolit; [plurimique] [ast plurimi], speciosa decepti pietatis aut
acrioris judicii ostentatione, quae prae se ferre solent homines quidam astuti
et vafri, his se temerè tradant ducendos; eorum est qui reipub. praesunt
cavere, ut constituantur viri graves et docti, qui sententias omnes saniores,
et de religione et officiis civilibus, populum doceant, easque uberius et fusius illustrent, rationibusque et argumentis confirment, ne malis aliorum
artibus ab officiis honestis detorqueatur. Et, si modo vel mediocris adsit
principibus viris prudentia, neque absurda plane aut inhumana foveant
dogmata, populum, ejusve saltem partem <327> longe maximam, habe-
bunt flexibilem, ut quocunque duxerint sequutura sit: ita ut nihil a diversis
paucorum sententiis sit metuendum.

Ubi exigitur ut populus sacrorum ritibus, aut dogmatis, vanis, falsis et
stolidis, aut inutilibus quantumvis veris, assentiantur, et dissentientibus ir-
rogantur poenae; gravis plerumque pernicies civitati oritur: quum, ut diversa sunt hominum ingenia, in his praecipuè rebus, ad sententias longissimè
diversas semper sunt proclives. Cives vel optimi his de causis vexati civitatem deserent; seditionibus discordiisque permiscebuntur omnia; atque ab
officiis civilibus, artibusque reipub. profuturis, ad nugas saepe ineptiasque
civium animi avocabuntur. Ob sententias igitur de religione, quantumvis
falsas, aut sacrorum ritus quoslibet, dummodo nemini noceant, cives boni
haud vexandi, ullove civium jure excludendi.

II. Ad virtutem omnem in civitate fovendam praecipuè conducunt imperatorum exempla; a quibus si probi soli, morumque integritate spectati, ad

quence of such dangerous opinions; rather than to inflict any penalties on men for these opinions themselves. 'Tis often better to leave such tenets to be exploded by the juster reasonings of wise men{, than to proceed to any severities on account of the tenets themselves}.

But as the far greater part of every people will not use this right; but induced by specious appearances of sanctity, and ostentation of superior wisdom in some designing men, will incautiously give up themselves to be led by them; it must plainly be the business of the magistrate {to get this *leading* into his own hands}; by appointing [to appoint] men of character and learning to teach the people the just sentiments of religion and virtue [and civil offices], and to confirm them by the most effectual reasonings <and arguments>; that they may not be perverted by the wicked arts of others.[3] And if men in power have any tolerable wisdom, and hold any tolerable scheme of religion, they will always find the far greater part of the people very tractable to follow as they lead them, so that little need be apprehended from a few who may dissent from the publick schemes.

The exacting by law, under any penalties, that people should conform in opinion and practice to any tenets <320> or rites of worship, that are either false and absurd, or tho' true yet of little consequence, generally occasions great mischief to any state; since according to the different genius's and tempers of men, they have and always will run into different opinions and practices in matters of religion: and thence some of the most useful hands will desert the country when they are harrassed about such matters: the state will be plagued with sedition and discord: and the activity of men turned off from the services and occupations which are most useful to the community, and occupied upon trifles. No good subject should meet with any vexation, or be excluded from any civil right, on account of any opinions<, however false,> or modes of worship which don't hurt any of their neighbours.[4]

II. The example of those in supreme power will have the highest influence in promoting the virtue of the people: {especially} if they advance to hon-

3. Cf. Pufendorf, *De officio* 2.11.4.
4. See *System* 3.9.2, vol. II, pp. 313–14.

honores evehantur, ardentiora accendentur omnis honestatis studia. Virtutis speciem populus favore nunquam non prosequitur. A populo verè libero soli ferè morum probitate insignes, ad honores provehentur; [neque honores et imperia <328> eorum mores immutabunt, si, legum annalium praescripto, ea brevi] [praecipue si, secundum leges annales, brevi ipsis numera] sint deponenda. Qualis est ipse rex, qui a rege creantur sunt futuri.

Post pietatem erga Deum, in qua sita est summa cujusque foelicitas, quaeque ad alias omnes virtutes fovendas plurimum confert, virtutes in civitate praecipuè colendae sunt *temperantia, justitia, fortitudo,* et *diligentia.*

Temperantiam, qua non solum libidines corporis voluptatem respicientes cohibentur, verum omnis luxuria, sumptusque nimii in vitae ornatum et splendorem erogandi, civitati necessariam esse fatebuntur omnes, quibus ipsius natura est perspecta. Certus est voluptatis modus, et gratus et innocuus, a Deo et natura concessus, cui fruendae plurima benignissime ipsa machinata est. Neque damnandus est voluptatum usus, si modo nulli officio adversentur, neque ad hominum mentes ita effoeminandas aut depravandas pertineant, ut absentium voluptatum desiderio crucientur, aut vitae officia deserant, iisve voluptates anteponant. Luxuria igitur est "voluptatum appetitio nimia, quae officio adversatur." Neque voluptatum modus definiri potest, nisi et facultatum, et necessitudinum, et officiorum, et valetudinis ratio habeatur. Luxuria autem, quum <329> facultatum sit prodiga, hominesque faciat rerum plurimarum indigentes et avidos, atque ad officia quae patriae aut amicis debentur <relinquendae>, quum voluptati repugnant, relinquenda [reddat] proclives; cives etiam ad patriam vel tyranno vel hosti prodendam incitabit; si quando ea ratione opes in luxum

---

5. See *System* 3.9.3, vol. II, p. 317.

6. Whereas Pufendorf explains the duties of sovereigns (*De officio* 2.11, *De iure nat.* 7.9) and Barbeyrac, in his long note 8 to *De iure nat.* 7.9.2, lists the virtues requisite to

ours only such as are of approved integrity and purity of manners<, the zeal for all that is virtuous will be much stronger>. The populace in their elections, if they are truly free, always follow some appearance of virtue; and will seldom promote any but such as are of distinguished integrity. Nor will honour or power alter the tempers of the persons advanced, if there are proper terms fixed by law for the holding of offices{; so that upon expiration of the term, they must return into the common condition of the people}. Where the power of promoting to offices is in the monarch, the men promoted will probably resemble their political creator.[5]

Next to *piety toward God,* the great source of happiness, and the strongest incentive to all other virtues, <321> the virtues to be most cultivated in a state are, *temperance, justice, fortitude,* and *industry.*[6]

[7]Such temperance as restrains not only excessive impulses toward <sensual> pleasure, but all luxury and immoderate expences on the shew and grandeur of life, must be allowed, by all who consider it, to be necessary to {the prosperity of} any state. There is a certain measure of sensual pleasures and elegance both grateful and innocent; to provide us to this degree God and nature have produced many fruits and other materials with exquisite art. Nor is there any moral turpitude in the enjoyment of any pleasure, if it be inconsistent with no duty of life, nor tends so to soften or weaken the mind that it shall be distressed in the want of it, or be apt to neglect and counteract its duty to obtain it. Luxury therefor should be defined, "such an excessive desire or use of the lower pleasures, as is inconsistent with discharging the offices of life." Nor is it possible precisely to fix general measures of lawful enjoyment for all; they must be various as their fortunes, attachments, dependent friends, and even bodily constitutions are various. Now luxury, in this notion of it, as it lavishes out mens fortunes, and yet increases their keen desires, making them needy, and craving; it must occasion the strongest temptations to desert their duty to their country <and friends>, whenever it is inconsistent with pleasure: it must lead the citizens to betray their country, either to a tyrant at home, or a

---

the sovereign, Hutcheson turns to the virtues to be encouraged among citizens and is back to the four cardinal virtues, with industry instead of wisdom.

7. Not a new paragraph in the *Institutio.*

profundendas [impendendas] sibi comparare possint. Luxuriosis enim omnia venalia.

Neque dixeris luxuriam ad artes et opificia fovenda vel necessariam vel utilem. Etenim sine ulla luxurie foveri possunt artes omnes aut necessariae aut elegantiores. Opulentioribus sine crimine coëmere licet opera quaevis artificiosa et elegantiora, quatenus sinit officiorum et necessitudinum ratio. Quique, pro sua benignitate, plurimas sibi negant voluptates, iidem eas ipsas, aut alias saltem civitati pariter profuturas, soboli, cognatis, amicis, fruendas plerumque largiuntur. Hi igitur una cum amicis, magis opificibus prosunt quam luxuriosi.

Quid, quod et sobrius quisque et providus, diuturna in vita et copiosâ, plura fere consumat quam prodigus, qui plurium annorum morbis et inedia, brevis luxuriae poenas pendit. Quumque mores superiorum imitari soleant inferiores, cito ad infimos, ipsosque opifices, descendet haec pestis; quorum operae idcirco cariùs erunt emundae: <330> merces igitur {nostratium}, pretio aucto, exteri non sunt coëmpturi, quum vilius veneant quae in civitatibus aliis, ubi viget sobrietas et temperantia, conficiuntur.

III. De diligentia et industria fovenda vix dicere attinet, quum ab ea ferè sola civitatis cujusque opes pendeant et potentia. Fovenda est agricultura, ne quid, ad populum alendum, de civitatis opibus decedat; utque fruges suppetant et frumentum exteris vendendum, nostratibusque materies omnis, in qua elaborent opifices; quae, alioqùi ab exteris esset emenda. Fovendae pariter omnes artes et simpliciores et elegantiores, ne exterorum operis et opificiis emendis civitatis opes dilabantur. Exercenda etiam

foreign enemy, when they cannot otherways get funds for their luxury. With the luxurious generally every thing is venal.

Nor is it justly alleged, that luxury is necessary or <322> useful to encourage arts and manufactures. For arts and industry may be encouraged to the highest without any luxury, at least all innocent, necessary, or elegant arts. Men of higher fortunes may without any luxury purchase the most ingenious and nice manufactures, as far as their several obligations in life allow it. And if any such deny themselves such expences, from views of a finer liberality, in raising the condition of indigent friends; they along with their families, kinsmen, and friends thus supported, may make a much greater consumption of the very same products and manufactures, or of others equally deserving encouragement in the state; and thus they with their dependents are more beneficial to artificers.[8]

Need we mention too, that a sober, frugal oeconomist [provident man], in a long and healthy copious life, generally makes greater consumption than a prodigal of equal fortune; who is often punished with a long tract of diseases and penury, for the extravagance of a few years. And then, as lower orders are always imitating the manners of their superiors; the plague of luxury will soon infect the very lowest, and even the mechanicks. Then they cannot subsist without higher prices for their labours; the manufactures must consequently rise in their prices, and cannot be vended abroad, if any more industrious and sober country can afford the like in foreign markets at lower prices.

III. 'Tis scarce necessary to shew the necessity of *diligence* and industry, since the wealth and power of a nation depends almost wholly upon them. Agriculture is necessary, to prevent a constant drain for the food of <323> our people, to obtain grain for exportation, and furnish the very materials for many of our artizans, which otherways we must buy abroad. And in like manner all mechanick arts, either simpler, or more elegant, should be encouraged, lest our wealth be drained by our buying foreign manufactures.

---

8. Cf. *System* 3.9.4, vol. II, pp. 320–21. Hutcheson clearly reacts to Mandeville's thesis and uses some of the arguments put forward in his "Observations on the Fable of the Bees," *The Dublin Weekly Journal*, Nos. 45–47, 1726.

mereatura, et piscatus, ubi ejusdem est copia. Quin et mercibus, sive nostris sive alienis, vehendis, construendae sunt naves; artesque nauticae addiscendae, quae et divitiis augendis inserviunt, et civitati in bello protegendae. Neque artibus hisce suus deesse debet honos, ne honestiore loco natis <non> prorsus indignae censeantur.

IV. Justitiam civitati necessariam esse nemo negat. Ubi enim non vigent leges et judicia, (sine quibus, quae vel natura tribuit vel industria, nemini sunt tuta,) omnes ab industria deterrentur. Quin etiam quum mercium omnium, pro mercatorum <331> periculis, augeantur pretia; ubi non viget justitia, quae damna {mercatoribus} dant emptores fraudulenti, ea mercium pretio sunt reparanda; eisque onerabuntur emptores probi et candidi. Quaevis igitur gens vicina, ubi conservatur rerum contractarum fides, similes merces viliùs vendere poterit. Civitas igitur ubi impunitae sunt fraudes fallaciaeque, praecipua ex commerciis et opificiis emolumenta est amissura.

De judiciis legibusque interpretandis longum esset dicere. Hoc tantum monemus, legibus paucis et simplicioribus cives satis protegi posse, si modo ita constituantur judicia, ut solis probis et aequis, fideique spectatae judicibus, lites dijudicandae permittantur. Multum etiam profuerit si calumniatoribus et temerè litigantibus poenae graviores irrogentur[: quarum exempla] [Antiquiores] Romanorum leges exhibent aliis civitatibus imitanda.{*}

V. Virtutes artesque bellicae civibus quibuslibet honestioribus sunt dignissimae. Nulli igitur militiae munus perpetuum esse debet; omnibus vero per vices obeundum. [Atque licet ubi mos invaluit, ut] [Quamvis autem ubi]

---

* Inst. Lib. IV. tit. 16. cum Comment. *Vinnii.*

---

9. See *System* 3.9.4, vol. II, pp. 318–20.
* <Inst. Lib. IV. tit. 16. cum Comment. *Vinnii.*> [Arnoldus Vinnius, *In quattuor*

Merchandize and fishery<, where abundant> are of great consequence: nay the very building of ships too, that we may not lose the profit of the carriage either of our own or foreign goods, and with this, the training of sailors; which contributes both to the increase of wealth and to the defence of the state in war. The mechanick trades should be held in reputation, so that people of better fortunes and families may not deem it below them to be concerned in them.[9]

IV. That justice is necessary cannot be a question. For if laws and justice don't prevail{, as without them no right natural or acquired can be safe, all industry must languish}. Nay as merchants must augment their prices in proportion to all their casual losses: where there's much injustice, the merchants must charge in the price of their goods the losses they sustain by the frauds of the unjust; and thus the best citizens must be loaded with this burden: nay further, any neighbouring state where justice more prevails, if other circumstances be equal, can undersell us, on this account. Where therefor justice is not maintained, the commerce <and manufacture> of a nation must sink, with all its attendant profits.

To examine into the best methods of *administring justice,* would require long dissertations. We only briefly suggest, that a small number of simple easy laws <324> might sufficiently protect and regulate the citizens, if there were such a contrivance for the courts of judicature, as would entrust the decision of suits to men of great goodness and equity and approved integrity. <Also>, severe restraints upon vexatious or oppressive suits would be of the highest advantage. The earlier laws {and constitutions} of the Romans about these matters are <examples> worthy of imitation.*

V. Military arts and virtues are accomplishments highly becoming all the more honourable citizens. Warfare therefor should be no man's perpetual profession; but all ought to take their turns in such services. And however it may be observed, that, when according to modern custom, armies are

---

libros Institutionum imperialium commentarius academicus & forensis, Amstelodami, 1692. The title 16 of the fourth book of Justinian's *Intitutions* prescribes fines and penalties for litigious goers to law. Hutcheson enlarges on this subject in *System* 3.9.5, pp. 322–23.

in perpetuam militiam conscribantur hi fere soli, qui aliis muneribus sunt inutiles, nebulones, civitatis purgamenta, {usu veniat, ut} quicunque aliquot stipendia meruit, pacis artibus <332> exercendis parum idoneus reddatur; aliter se res haberet, si per vices haec munera civibus optimis essent obeunda. Quae res maximas praeterea haberet opportunitates: rerum militarium scientiam haberent omnes: deleto uno exercitu, non deficeret alter: deletis imperatoribus, plures praestò essent ei muneri aptissimi: populi denique armati armisque assueti jura, non facile pessundaret vel civis ambitiosus et audax, vel hostis.

VI. Legibus atque ipsa reipub. formâ cavendum est, ne qui cives vel inter se, vel cum exteris, sive regibus sive sacerdotibus, arctius quam cum patria conjungantur; neve aliunde spes habeant majores. Civesque ab eorum errore abducendi, qui pacta, a majoribus scelerata fraude deceptis inita, contra patriae salutem et prosperitatem valere credunt. Ad veram enim religionem conservandam, neque necessarium est neque utile, {ut} sacerdotibus imperia civilia qualiacunque permittantur; multo minus ut omnes ubique gentium sacerdotes, una regantur potestate, quae in pluribus civitatibus honores et dignitates, immo opes ingentes, et proventus fere regios, largiri possit; et cui in plurimis rebus gravioribus, ad opes potentiamque pertinentibus, ultimum permittatur judicium.

VII. Legibus civilibus sancienda et <333> confirmanda praecipuè juris naturalis praecepta; et de negotiis et *actionibus* formulae constituendae, ad fraudes praecavendas aptissimae. In rebus suis gerendis, ipsisque opificiis,

made up of the very dregs of a people, fellows too dissolute and worthless for any other occupation, whosoever takes to this way of life for a few years is made unfit for any other [peaceful] occupation for the future; yet the case would be quite otherways if all the best citizens served in our armies by turns. This method too would bring along with it these grand advantages: all the people would be trained and skilled in military service. Should one of our armies be entirely cut off, we could have another {of veterans} immediately: were the chief officers cut off; we would have others of equal experience in readiness to take the command: and it would be no easy matter for either any ambitious citizen at home, or any foreign invader, to trample upon the rights of an armed people well trained in military service.[10]

VI. The laws and whole constitution of the state should be such as may prevent any smaller bodies of citizens <325> to be more strongly attached to each other, or to any foreign interest, whether of prince or bishop, than they are to their own country, or have greater dependance and expectations of promotion by them. And the citizens should be taught that no antient engagements, obtained from their ancestors by the most impious frauds, can be of any validity against the prosperity of their country. For it cannot be of use to <true> religion that ecclesiasticks should have {great} secular power of any kind; and much less that all ecclesiasticks through the world should be deemed as a great corporation to be governed by a common prince or council; who too should have power to promote, in many nations, what favourites they pleased, to high dignities and <almost> princely revenues; and to whom there should lye appeals from the highest courts of the several nations, in matters upon which wealth and power depend.

VII. It is one great design of civil laws to strengthen by political sanctions the several laws of nature; and to appoint such forms of business, and of process in courts, as may prevent frauds {and promote justice}. The populace [People] often needs also to be taught, and engaged by laws, into the best methods of managing their own affairs, and exercising their mechanick

10. A more detailed support for a popular militia is in *System* 3.9.6, pp. 323–25.

docendus est populus; eaque omnia definienda quae lege naturali non satis definiuntur.

Ex legum civilium systemate vel optimo, quibusdam nasci solent jura quaedam externa, quae impunè, licet parum honestè, persequi possunt: neque iis vim, aut actionem in foro, opponere licebit: sanctissima etiam officia plurima cujusque pudori permittenda. Sunt et legum beneficia quaedam ejusmodi, ut quamvis iis uti nollet vir bonus, petenti tamen haud recte negari poterunt. Quae quidem pactiones aut testamenta legibus civilibus non confirmantur, quoniam absunt praescriptae formulae, ea vir bonus saepe rata habebit, si modo neque testatoris aut paciscentis potestatem excesserint, neque quicquam iniqui aut inhumani contineant.{*} Si vero in horum alterutro erratum fuerit, legum beneficio jure uti poterit.

VIII. Leges praemiis et poenis sanciuntur. Omni civium jure et beneficiis frui, legum civilium commune est praemium; quibusdam propria sunt praemia, honores, dignitates, divitiae. *Honor naturalis* est "aliorum <334> bona de nobis ob praestantiam nostram opinio." *Honores civiles* sunt "ea cultus et observantiae indicia, quae viris claris ex legum praescripto exhibentur."

Existimatio simplex, sive "viri innocui et hominum societate non indigni, fama," nemini a reipub. rectoribus causa indictâ est eripienda. Existimatio eximia, quae a quibusdam *intensiva* dicitur, a nemine jure pleno exigi potest. Nemo enim ad alterius voluntatem judicare, aut magni eos aestimare potest, in quibus non cernit virtutes eximias. De externis vero honoris in-

---

* Vid. *Barbeyracii* orationes *De legum Permissione* et *Beneficiis.*

---

* On these two heads there are two good orations of Barbeyraque, annexed to his translation of the smaller book of Puffendorf, *De legum permissione et beneficiis.* [Jean Barbeyrac, *Discours sur la permission des loix, où l'on fait voir, que ce qui est permis par le loix, n'est pas toujours juste et honnête,* (Amsterdam, 1716) and *Discours sur le bénéfice des loix, où l'on fait voir, qu'un honnête homme ne peut pas toujours se prévaloir des droits et des*

arts: and in general, civil laws should more precisely determine many points in which the law of nature leaves much latitude.

From the very best body of civil laws certain external rights must arise, which tho' no man can insist upon with a good conscience, yet if the persons to whom they are granted claim them, they must hold them with <326> impunity: nor can any one rightly have recourse to violence against such rights, or obtain redress at law. Many also of the most sacred duties {can be no matters of compulsion, but} must be left to {the honour and} conscience of those concerned. There are certain benefits granted by law, which no good man would claim, but when claimed they cannot be refused.* Any such covenants or testaments too as for want of the legal formalities are not confirmed by human laws, a good man would often think himself bound to hold as valid, if there's nothing appointed in them beyond the moral power of the parties or testator, nor contrary to equity <or humanity>. But if they are wrong in either of these respects, a {good} man may take the benefit of the law.

VIII. The *sanctions* of laws are *rewards* and *punishments.* There's this common reward annexed to obedience to civil laws, that these who obey them continue to enjoy all the <rights and> advantages of civil life. Some few civil laws have peculiar rewards, such as honours, <dignities,> and premiums in money. The natural honour is "the good opinion others entertain of our moral excellencies." Civil honours are "these external indications of deference which are appointed by law."

The *simple estimation,* or character of common honesty, is so much every man's right, that no governors can deprive one of it at pleasure, without a cause determined in judgment. The higher estimation, or *intensive,* as some call it, is not a matter of perfect right; <327> as no man can at the command of others form high opinions of any person, without he is persuaded of his merit. But as to external marks of deference, and precedencys, the civil

---

privilèges que le loix donnent. Amsterdam, 1717. Both orations are translated in Pufendorf, *The Whole Duty of Man According to the Law of Nature.* Together with Two Discourses and a Commentary by Jean Barbeyrac, ed. Ian Hunter and David Saunders (Indianapolis: Liberty Fund, 2002). See *System* 3.9.9, vol. II, pp. 328–29. This footnote in the *Institutio* is placed after the next sentence.]

diciis, ut de omni jure quod res externas spectat, eorum est definire qui reipub. praesunt: qui si justis tantum de causis honores {civiles} largiantur, magni apud omnes sapientes erunt <honores civiles>: sin saepius aliter fiat, viles erunt et despiciendi, solâque simulatione aut sannis excipiendi. Quales saepe conspiciuntur honores haereditarii, ubi nulla est potestas censoria.

IX. Proprie vereque huc spectant omnes *poenae,* ut improbis earum metu ab injuriis absterritis, caeteri tuto vitam degant: *castigatio,* ipsius qui delictum admiserat utilitatem spectat; et *damni reparatio,* laesi; quae etiam nullo antecedente delicto, jure nonnunquam exigitur.

Non ex odio aut ira, neque ex ea indignatione quam in proborum animis excitat <335> delicti turpitudo, poenae praecipue irrogandae; sed ex communis potius utilitatis conservandae studio, et innocuorum curâ. Unica igitur poenarum mensura non est ipsa delicti turpitudo, sed communis potius omnium utilitas ex poenis oritura. Impunita igitur et inulta recte manent delicta quaedam turpissima. Contra ea, si aliter salva nequit esse civitas, gravioribus rectè coërcentur suppliciis, quae non adeo magnam ingenii pravitatem produnt. Ingratis, aut inhumanis, nulla irrogatur poena: severius puniuntur qui *majestatis crimen,* licet sub fallaci juris specie, admiserunt. Ob utrumque severius animadvertendum in eos qui potestate civili sibi permissa perfidiose abutentes, cives suos vexant et spoliant.

Quamvis necesse non sit {(nec quidem saepè fieri potest,) ut ipsa agendi consilia turpia, aut} primi voluntatis motus improbi poenis coërceantur; quales nonnunquam in bonorum animis subitò existunt, quosque ipsi ultro

powers have a right to determine about them, as they do about other civil rights. If these are conferred only upon real merit, they will be of high account with wise men. But if they are often conferred injudiciously, they will grow mean and despicable to wise men, and matter of scorn and jest: as they are often seen where they are hereditary, and there's no censorial power to degrade the unworthy.[11]

IX. The true end of all punishment is this, that all bad men by the terror of them may be restrained from doing any thing injurious, and thus the community be preserved in safety. *Chastisement* {as distinguished from punishment,} has in view only the reformation of the sufferer [the person who confesses his crime]: and *reparation of damage,* aims at the utility of the one who sustained the loss: to this men are often bound even without any preceeding crime or fault.[12]

Neither anger, nor hatred of the criminal, nor even that honest indignation at moral evil, which is natural to every good man, should be the sole [chief] springs of punishing: but rather a {calm} regard to the common interest, and the safety of the innocent. The true measure of punishment is not to be taken from the degrees of moral turpitude, but the exigence of society. A great deal of high moral turpitude must pass unpunished: and yet on the other hand if the safety of the community require it, some actions which shew smaller depravity of temper, must be punished severely. Thus <328> no penalties are inflicted on ingratitude, and want of humanity; while any insurrection against the supreme power, tho' upon plausible pretences of the right of some competitor, must be punished severely. But the crimes which deserve the highest punishments on both accounts, are the publick ones of men in power, perverting what was intrusted to them for the safety of others, to the oppression <and spoliation> of the citizens.[13]

Though it may not be necessary to punish the first motions or hasty intentions of wickedness, nor is it often practicable; as such rash motions may upon sudden provocation arise in the breasts of good men, who will

---

11. See Pufendorf, *De officio* 2.14 and *System* 3.9.10, pp. 329–31.
12. For these and the following sentence, see Pufendorf, *De officio* 2.13.6–8.
13. See *System* 3.9.10, vol. II, pp. 333–35.

mox sunt repressuri: qui tamen in externos proruperunt actus istiusmodi, qui casu tantummodo, aut per aliorum vim et solertiam, irriti fuerunt, quibusque capitale ostenditur odium, et laedendi consilium, summis illi sunt coërcendi suppliciis. Exigit quidem nonnunquam communis utilitas, ut <336> facinoribus parum honestis praemia decernantur [sit praemium], utque nefariis ignoscatur.

Damnanda in judiciis est ea προσωποληψία quae <eas> respicit sontium necessitudines, aut facinorum adjuncta et qualitates eas, quae neque delicti turpitudinem, neque poenae sensum, communemve utilitatem afficiunt [respiciunt]. Quae enim vel hominum vel facinorum adjuncta aut qualitates, horum quodvis afficiunt, ea omnino spectanda. Unde, caeteris paribus, pro reorum censu, augendae sunt poenae pecuniariae; et pro corporis robore, poenae quae corpore luuntur: poenae, contra, cum infamia conjunctae, pro majore reorum dignitate sunt minuendae.

Non tamen, pro majore delictorum atrocitate, sine fine augenda <sunt> supplicia et cruciatus. Ex crebris enim cruciatuum saeviorum spectaculis, imminui solet apud cives morum mansuetudo, saeviusque nascitur ingenium.

X. Ob delictum alienum nemo poenis est obnoxius: neque ob patris familias delictum recte publicatur tota res familiaris: ex ea prius praestanda omnia, quae jure suo, naturâ pactove constituto, postulare possunt conjux, et liberi, aut alii innoxii. Neque ob ullum delictum poena universitati recte irrogatur. Puniendi soli qui deliquerunt, sive privati, sive universitatis rectores. Ipsi <337> quidem universitati aliquando recte adimuntur ea, sive jura, sive propugnacula aut arma, quibus ad nocendum fuerat instructa, si aliter de non laedendo cautum esse nequeat. Ad damnum ex bonis {suis} publicis prae-

soon restrain them of themselves: yet such as have proceeded to any external actions which might have effectually accomplished the evil, but were prevented by accident, or force, or the timely aid of others, and which shew furious malice and obstinate purposes of injury, these deserve as high punishments as if they had obtained their effect. Sometimes indeed the publick interest may require the granting even rewards to some bad actions, and pardoning the greatest criminals.

The *respect of persons* which is highly culpable in judgment, is when any regard is had to such qualities of actions or circumstances of the guilty as neither affect the turpitude of the crime, nor the sense of the punishment, nor the common interest of society. But circumstances which affect any of these three must always be regarded. And therefor when other circumstances are equal, pecuniary fines are to be enlarged for equal crimes according to the fortunes of the criminals, and corporal punishments according to their strength of body; <329> and ignominious ones are to be abated according to the dignity of the persons.[14]

But we must not go on in increasing without bounds the severities of punishment upon the higher crimes. For frequent spectacles of tortures have a tendency to diminish our natural compassion and tenderness of heart, and to make the tempers of men more savage and cruel.

X. 'Tis unjust to punish any man for the crimes of others; nor is it equitable to confiscate the whole fortune of a family for any crime of the head of it. All the natural claims of the wife and children to a support out of it, as well as debts due to any innocent persons, should first be discharged.[15] Nor is it naturally just to punish any bodies-corporate for any crimes; the guilty only in such cases should be punished, whether private persons or magistrates of the corporation.[16] It may sometimes be just to take from the corporation either these privileges, or fortifications, or arms, by which the criminal members of it were encouraged or enabled to do injuries to their neighbours, if security against like injuries can be obtained no other way.

14. Cf. Pufendorf, *De officio* 2.13.18. See also *System* 3.9.13, vol. II, pp. 336–38.
15. Compare Pufendorf, *De officio* 2.13.20.
16. Compare Pufendorf, *De officio* 2.13.19. See also *System* 3.9.15, vol. II, pp. 339–40.

standum nonnunquam tenebitur universitas, aut, ubi illa desunt, ex privatorum bonis; quum quae singuli suae utilitatis causa adsciverant sibi praesidia, aliis evadunt damnosa.

XI. Leges per quas imponuntur tributa, nisi majora sint quam sumptus
quos civitatis tutela exigit, justissimo innituntur fundamento; quum populi
totius negotiis expediundis erogentur. Eae igitur leges non sine furti crimine
a civibus violantur. Neque haec injuria tam rectoribus ipsis obest, quam
civibus aliis magis probis, qui quod defuerit supplere adiguntur, aliisque,
ea de causa, damnis premuntur et oneribus. Tributa autem, nisi instituto
civium censu, aequa ratione imperari nequeunt.

XII. Civium adversum rectores suos haec sunt officia: imprimis, rectorum
justis et legibus et imperiis parere tenentur, idque sanctissimè.

2. Deinde, quum quod imperatum est in imperantis continebatur potestate, civibus plerumque parendum, quamvis non satis honestè et prudenter imperatum judicent: quod <338> in bellicis praecipuè patet imperiis.
Si enim civibus permittatur de imperiis judicium, neque ipsis parendum
foret, quoties mandata civitati parum commoda videntur; tolleretur omnis
disciplina militaris, et in multitudinem solutam et inconditam exercitus
converteretur.

3. Hinc etiam efficitur, quod in iis rebus quae imperantium arbitrio permittuntur, cives rectè, immo honestè, ea imperia exsequi possunt quae imperatoribus foedo vertenda sunt vitio; quum, ruptis disciplinae vinculis,

The corporation may sometimes be bound to compensate damages out of its publick stock, or <when they are wanting> even the private fortunes of its members{, when the criminals can't be found, or cannot repair the dam- age}; if it has been occasioned or encouraged by any of these advantages, privileges or fortifications, which the body had obtained for their own be- hoof [if the defences received for their own utility, come out detrimental to others].

XI. Every government has the justest right to exact tributes from the sub- jects by law, provided they are no more than what are requisite for the pru- dent administration <330> of publick affairs; as this publick expence is made for the behoof of all. The violating such laws by any subject [citizen] is equally criminal with theft. Nor is the injury so properly done to the governors, as to our fellow-subjects; who must be obliged to make up de- ficiencies occasioned by these frauds, some other way, and must be sub- jected to other burdens on this account; beside many other inconveniences. There is no other possible method, of making men contribute in just pro- portions to the publick charge, than by instituting a *census*, or valuation of all their fortunes.[17]

XII. These are the obligations of subjects toward their governors: first, they are sacredly bound to obey all their just laws and commands: and secondly, if the thing commanded be a matter committed to the power of the gov- ernor; 'tis generally the duty of subjects [citizen] to obey, even when they judge that the orders are <not quite honourable and> imprudent. This holds most obviously in military operations. For to allow the inferior to judge of his orders, and only to obey when he thinks them prudent for the good of the state, would destroy all military discipline, and reduce an army into a tumultuous mob.

3. Hence it follows that in matters committed to the wisdom of gov- ernors, the subjects [citizens] may act a just nay an honourable part in obey- ing such orders as were very criminal to their governor: the subject by obey- ing is preventing the greatest mischief; since from the relaxing of all order

17. Cf. Pufendorf, *De officio* 2.11.10 and *System* 3.9.16, vol. II, pp. 340–42.

mala multo graviora plerumque sint metuenda, quam quae ex imperatis peractis essent oritura.

4. Sin autem adeo nefaria et pestifera videantur imperia, ut gravior inde civitati oritura sit pernicies, quam si penitus evertatur istorum imperatorum potestas; rectè imperia detrectabunt cives: {sedulo} cavendum tamen ne temere iis de rebus judicent.

5. Ubi aliquid imperatur quo divini Numinis majestas impiè laeditur, quove violantur hominum immerentium jura perfecta, aut quod imperantis potestati non erat permissum; imperium istud neminem obligat: immo saepe honestissimum est, quaevis potius perferre supplicia, quam, exemplo perniciem in totam civitatem trahente, istiusmodi parere imperiis. Quo jure imperantibus vim <339> aliquando opponere possunt cives, satis antea dictum.{*}

Communia civium officia, ex conjunctionis civilis indole et causis; singulorum propria, ex ipsorum statu, conditione, et muneribus susceptis, satis innotescunt.

---

* Lib. III.c.vii.2.

and government, far greater evils must generally ensue, than from the execution of very imprudent orders.

4. But if the thing commanded seems to the subject [citizen] <331> so entirely pernicious and ruining to the state, that it were better to break through and destroy the authority of such commanders, than to execute such destructive orders: the subject [citizen] may refuse obedience. But in such matters they should use the utmost caution that they don't judge amiss.

5. Where we are commanded to do any act directly irreverent and impious toward God, or contrary to the perfect rights of others; or where the matter commanded was not committed to the power of the commander; we are under no obligation to obedience. Nay 'tis often highly honourable to endure rather any punishment, than submit to a precedent that may be ruinous to our country. We shewed above* in what cases it is lawful for subjects [citizens] to resist their governors.[18]

The common duties of all subjects [citizens] must easily appear from the nature and origin of civil power and the political union. Their peculiar duties arise from their several stations, relations, and offices in the state.

---

* Book III. vii. 2.

18. Compare Pufendorf, *De officio* 2.12.8–9. See also *System* 3.9.17, vol. II, pp. 342–43. In the following section of *System*, 343–47, the citizen's obligations to obedience are discussed in relation to the right of resistance.

CAPUT IX

De Jure Belli.

I. Belli, pacis, et foederum jura dicuntur *transeuntia,* quia exteros ferè spectant. Belli jura praecipua, in superiore libro satis explicavimus, ubi de privatorum bellis agebamus, monstratis eorum causis et terminis. Quae fere omnia conveniunt bellis civitatum, quae libertatis statum inter se conservant, qualem inter homines singulos ipsa natura constituit.

Bellorum publicorum minus solennium perfacilis est cognitio, ex magistratuum jure antea explicato, quo cives reprimunt tumultuantes, eoque civium jure, quod contra eos vicissim qui summo imperio praesunt tueri possunt.{*} "Bellum eorum jussu quibus <340> summa est potestas utrinque susceptum," dicitur *solenne,* sive *justum.* Neque semper necessarium est ut publicè indicatur aut denuncietur; quod tamen populo cultiore plerumque dignum est, neque sine causa graviori omittendum. Ab eo qui se contra vim defendit illatam, haud necessariò prius bellum indicitur; neque quidem semper ab eo qui vim infert: quoties scil. res subito est gerenda, neque bellum prius indici poterat, nisi omissâ rei bene gerendae occasione commodissima.

Qui viri graves et docti bellum necessario prius indicendum statuerunt, jus Romanorum foeciale temerè secuti sunt. Quum autem per vim decer-

* Ibid.

CHAPTER IX <332>

The Laws of War.

I. The rights of war and treaties <called external> are of that class which respect foreigners. The principal matters of right in war, as to their causes and bounds, were explained in the former book,{*} when treating of war among persons in natural liberty. The same maxims hold in the publick wars of states, which with respect to each other are in the same state of natural liberty.

As to publick wars of a less solemn kind, {without the order of sovereign states on both sides;} they may be sufficiently understood from what was already said about the right of governors to repress tumults and insurrections, and from the right of resistance that subjects may have in defence of themselves against {perfidious} governors.† "A war undertaken by order of independent states on both sides" is called a *solemn* <or *just*> war. Nor need we add to the definition [Nor it is always necessary], that it be *previously proclaimed;* tho' it be highly becoming every civilized nation, {when they have recourse to force, to let all around know the grounds of it,} as soon as they can conveniently [when more weighty reasons are not opposing to it]. But 'tis plainly not incumbent on the nation invaded by another, to make a previous declaration before it defends itself. Nor is it always necessary that the aggressor should make such previous <333> declaration; as perhaps his surest method of obtaining his right may be by surprizing the enemy; and a previous declaration might prevent his best opportunity of success.[1] What has led ingenious and learned men to make a previous proclamation necessary, was too great a deference to the *foecial laws* among the

---

* {Ch. xv.} [2.15.6–8.]
† Book III, vii.2.
1. A new paragraph in the *Institutio.*

tare praeter naturam sit; viro bono indignum est ut ad id confugiat, nisi causis, ubi primum tuto fieri potest, palam indicatis; ut sciant omnes eum alia ratione jura sua tueri aut persequi non potuisse.

In bellis civilibus, <quae saepe speciosis de causis utrinque suscipiuntur> eodem favore utramque partem prosequi debent vicini omnes, quo illos quos inter bellum solenne geritur: quum in bellis civilibus, ab altera parte non minus justae, ab altera speciosae, {saepe} sint belli causae, quam quae in bellis solennibus: neque qui probabili de causa bella civilia movet, ullo hominum jure se abdicasse censendus <est>. <341>

II. Belli jura vel eos inter quos bellum geritur, vel vicinos neutri parti se adjungentes spectant, "Quae recta ratio monstrat in communem utilitatem necessariò esse observanda," ea dicuntur *juris* esse *publici et necessarii:* "quae vero in morem vetustas gentium approbatione perduxit," ita tamen ut aliis atque aliis moribus mutari, aut significatione prius factâ confestim tolli possint, ea sunt *juris gentium voluntarii.*

[Quae belli causae sint justae, antea docuimus*] [Belli causas antea diximus.] Hoc solum de civitatibus monendum, quod quemadmodum inter cives, *damni infecti* datur actio, nimiaeque paucorum opes, quamvis eas sine injuria congerere velint, legibus tamen agrariis prohibentur: sic{, si de periculo imminente, ratione leniori caveri nequeat,} justa aliquando erit belli causa, nimia vicinae civitatis potentia, indies magis magisque gliscens; praecipue ubi animum ostendunt cives laudis bellicae nimis avidum, atque a pacis artibus alienum: ita ut vicinis vitam tutò degere non liceat, nisi ipsi

---

* Lib. II.c.xv.6.

2. The great deference was rather to the authority of Cicero, often quoted by all the natural law jurists. In *De officiis,* 1.36 Cicero refers to the Roman "ius fetialis" and states that no war can be just unless there is a previous claim for damage and formal declaration, which was made by an appointed college of priests, the *fetiales.*

3. In *System* 3.10.1, vol. II, p. 348, Hutcheson refers to the work of the Dutch jurist Cornelius van Bynkershoek (1673–1743), *Quaestionum juris privati libri quatuor* (Lug-

Romans.[2] But as contending by violence is not agreeable to {the rational and social} nature, 'tis unworthy of a good man, when he is forced to betake himself to it, not to declare openly, as soon as he can with safety, his motives and intentions, that all may see that he could not otherways obtain his right.[3]

As in civil wars there are often specious reasons on both sides; all neighbouring states should shew the same favour to both the contending parties as to these engaged in solemn wars. Nay in civil wars there are as frequently as in the solemn, just causes on one side, and specious ones on the other. Nor is either of the parties engaged in them to be deemed {like robbers or pirates,} abdicating or forfeiting all the rights of mankind.

II. The laws of war either respect the contending parties or neutral states. "What right reason shews necessary to be observed in war for the general interest of mankind" may be called *the law of nations of necessary obligation.* But "what a long tract of time has made customary, with a tacit approbation or consent of nations"; which however might be altered by contrary custom, or taken away at once by a timeous premonition of all concerned, we may call the *voluntary law of nations.*[4] <334>

The just causes of war were explained in the former book.* But with respect to neighbouring states we may suggest, that as among citizens there are allowed actions at law for prevention of damages not yet done, and agrarian laws restrain such excessive acquisitions of wealth as may prove dangerous to the society, tho' the acquisitions are not to be made by injurious means; so sometimes among neighbouring states, a dangerous increase of power in any one of them may give a just cause of war, if no gentler securities can be obtained: especially when the people of that state shew a general ambition of military glory and conquest, and quit all peaceful arts: so that their neighbours must be in perpetual dangers, unless they

---

duni Batavorum, 1744), book 1, chapt. 2, where it is argued against Grotius that wars may be lawful without a formal declaration. The whole first book of Bynkershoek's work considers the matter treated by Hutcheson in this chapter.

4. This distinction between natural and customary or voluntary law of nations is discussed by Carmichael, *Notes on Puf.,* pp. 202–3.

* Ch. xv. [2.15.6.]

pariter, mitioribus omissis artibus, ad studia bellica se totos convertant: <praesertim ubi ab ista civitate, haud aliter vicinis ut non laedantur satis caveri potest.> hoc tamen inter jura rariora censendum.

In bellis publicis iidem sunt petendi sines et justa initia, sive *termini a quo,* et *ad quem,* quae in bellis privatis. <342> Belli gerendi rationes sunt aut vis aperta, aut istiusmodi fallendi artes,{*} quae nullam de sententiis nostris communicandis pacti vim continent. Vis autem in sola acie, aut contra repugnantes, licita est et probanda; quamvis pro more illo, qui ubique gentium invaluit, inhumanissimo, omnia in quoslibet ex hostili populo, externâ juris specie, impune fieri possint. Est hoc quoque receptum, hostem fictis fallere narrationibus, aut sermone quovis, si pacti forma penitus absit. Quum vero pactis solis pax reduci possit, aut, manente bello, averti saevitia ab omni abhorrens humanitate; neque hostem foederis aut pacti specie decipere receptum est, neque umbrâ quidem justitiae fieri potest.

III. Sunt et quaedam alia, pacto tacito aut consuetudine, introducta, quorum obligatio tolli potest, si modo illi quorum interest tempestive praemoneantur: ne scil. quisquam venenis in bello utatur; aut sicarios, ad reges ducesve hostiles clam necandos, ex ipsorum civibus aut militibus conducat. Ut sacri sanctique inter hostes sint nuncii quivis aut legati, juris est naturalis et necessarii; quum illorum tantum interventu, sine partis alterutrius internecione, pax bello mutari, aut belli gerendi rationes humaniores iniri possint. Jure tantum voluntario receptum <343> est, ut etiam privatis rogantibus, modo sint inermes, iter per hostium fines facere, aut in hostium agris aut urbibus aliquamdiu commorari liceat.

* Lib. II.c.x.2, 3.

also quit the innocent arts of peace, and are always a training to war. But this is an instance of these *extraordinary rights* which seldom occur.

In publick wars the term of commencement, and the term of ending, <that is *termini a quo,* and *ad quem*> {or the bounds of our demands}, may be fixed the same way as those of private persons in natural liberty{; of which formerly}[5].

The just methods of carrying on war are open violence, or such arts of deceiving as carry along with them no profession or tacit engagement [agreement] of communicating our sentiments to the enemy.* Violence is justifiable only against men in battle, or such as violently obstruct our obtaining our rights; altho' by the inhuman customs which have prevailed, men may exercise with impunity any sort of cruelties toward their enemies <as an external right>. 'Tis also very ordinary to deceive enemies <335> by any false narrations, or any sort of discourse, except such as imports making some covenant or treaty with them. But as it is by treaties alone that either peace can be restored, or more humane methods of war maintained, and horrid mutual cruelties prevented; it never was, nor ought it to be allowed to deceive enemies by any form of treaties.[6]

III. There are many other obligations introduced by long custom importing tacit covenants; which however could be taken away by a timeous premonition of all concerned. Such as, that none should use poisons in war, or employ any of the enemies subjects or soldiers to assassinate their prince or their generals.[7] That all messengers or envoys, or ambassadors sent on either side should have protection to their persons, is indeed matter of <natural and> necessary obligation; since it is by their means alone that peace can be obtained, without the entire destruction of one side, or any humane methods of war preserved. But 'tis matter only of voluntary right that passports should be mutually allowed, to any subjects of the hostile nation who come unarmed, to travel through their countries, or to reside in their cities.[8]

5. See Book II. xv. 7–8.
* Book II. x. 2 and 3.
6. Cf. Pufendorf, *De officio* 2.16.5.
7. See *ibidem,* 2.16.12.
8. See *System* 3.10.5, vol. II, pp. 352–56.

IV. Quo jure res civium ab hoste capiuntur paucis expediendum.

1. Tenentur gentes pace utentes, cives suos omnes, a latrociniis, aut injuriis quibuslibet, vicinis inferendis, coërcere: aut si quem vicinae gentis civem laeserint, eos cogere, ut damnum abs se datum reparent. De civibus loquimur, qui non praedonum more vitam exuere civilem.

2. Rebus repetitis neque redditis, civitas laesa jure bellum movet; res suas, aut civium suorum, apud hostem detentas, jure occupat: cujus si non sit copia, damni pensationem [compensationem] ab iis qui damnum dederant, vel ab ipsa exigit civitate, quae eos defendendo, iisve receptum praebendo, in se crimen derivavit. Eadem omnia apertiora, si publico consilio injuria fuit illata.

3. Ubi civitatis iniquae bona publica occupandi deest copia; civium hostilium bona privata, civitas laesa jure occupabit, donec omne damnum ab injuria ortum sit pensatum [compensatum]. Quum enim in civium omnium utilitatem civitas fuerat constituta, civilisque imperantibus tributa potestas; tenentur cives ea praestare damna, quae ex eo orta sunt <344> praesidio, quod utilitatis suae causâ sibi adsciverant: atqui civitatum rectores, ex eo quod praedones protexerint, eos ad injurias hasce inferendas incitarunt, easque defenderunt.

4. Qui verò <innocui> cives hostiles damna haec, insontes, ex causa publica perferunt, jure a suis imperatoribus hoc exigunt, ut publicè haec ipsis praestentur, aut ex eorum bonis qui sua culpâ damnis causas praebuerunt. Aequius quidem foret et facilius, si civium hostilium bona capta, pignoris in modum detinerentur, donec laesae civitati aliunde fieret compensatio; eâque publicè factâ, tum demum sua privatis restituerentur. Mos tamen invaluit diversus. Captae res mobiles dominos omnino mutasse censentur, ubi primum in hostium delatae praesidia, vel ei qui eas ceperat, vel civitati

IV. Upon what grounds of justice the goods of the subjects of hostile states are seized mutually, comes next to be explained.

1. All states in amity are bound to restrain their subjects from depredations, or any way injuring the subjects of states around them: and when such injuries are done, they are obliged to compel the authors of them to make reparation. We speak now of subjects <336> who are amenable by law, and not of pirates or robbers.

2. When such reparation is demanded and refused, the injured state may justly have recourse to force, seizing the <public or private> goods wrongfully taken, or if they can't find them, taking to their value from the authors of the injury, or from the state, which by defending the depredators <and offering refuge to them> bring the guilt upon themselves. And this right is still more obvious if the injuries have been done by publick order.

3. If there's no opportunity of seizing the publick goods of the injurious state, the injured may seize the private goods of any citizens of that state <to compensate the damage that has arisen from the injury>. For as the political constitution and the civil power was erected for the behoof of all the subjects [citizens], they are bound to repair any damages arising from this contrivance which they fell upon for their own utility.{*} And the civil powers by giving their protection, have plainly supported and excited their subjects to such injuries.

4. But then these innocent subjects who suffer thus by these reprisals, on account of their community, may justly claim from their community to have their losses repaired, out of the common stock, or out of the goods of the depredators. It certainly would be the more equitable and clear way, that goods thus seized as reprisals from the innocent subjects were only detained as pledges, till the injured state received reparation another way, and then were restored to the owners. But a contrary custom has prevailed;{†} and the old property <337> is on all sides deemed to be extinguished, as soon as such <moveable> goods taken are brought into any fortresses of the captors, and adjudged, either to them or their community:

* {Book II. xiv. [xv] 2. and Book III. iii. 2, art. 5.}

† {Probably with a view to make the soldiers more active in distressing the enemy: as large shares of the goods taken are usually given to the captors.} [This added footnote is not derived from the parallel section of *System* 3.10.7, vol. II, pp. 355–56.]

fuerint adjudicatae; ita ut postea receptae, a priore domino postliminii jure vindicari nequeant: neque ulli in posterum vindiciarum liti pateant, postquam, specioso quovis titulo acquisitae, intra civitatis non hostilis fines pervenerunt.

V. Quae civitates medias, neutri bellantium palam faventes, spectant jura, breviter attingemus. 1. Vicina quaevis civitas, nullo de auxiliis alterutri praebendis foedere devincta, vicinorum bellis neque invita <345> implicari, neque ex iis damna pati debet.

2. Si foedere de auxiliis mittendis utrique adstringatur media civitas; vel neutri mittenda auxilia; vel si malit, illi cujus causa sibi justa videtur; et tum demum bello se immiscebit. Istiusmodi enim foedera tunc modò obligant, quum bello subest causa justa; neque paciscentium quemquam ad bellum iis, quibus priore foedere publico devincti erant, inferendum adstringunt.

3. Res mobiles ab utravis parte captas et abjudicatas, jure emit, aut, {alio} quovis titulo legitimo, sibi comparat civitas media; neque eas domini priores jure vindicabunt. Ad mediam civitatem ejusve cives non attinet judicare, quo jure res captae fuerant. Saepenumero ne vel norunt quod istae res venales praedae pars fuerant.

4. Rerum immobilium alia longè ratio. Eas civitati sibi non inimicae fuisse ereptas, mediam civitatem latere nequit: sua autem emptione domini prioris jus, ad eas per vim recipiendas, praecluderetur. Quae quidem urbi cuivis, castello, aut praedio, debebantur a vicinis servitutes reales, aut pensiones annuae, illae novo possessori postulanti jure praestantur: idque denegare tacitum in se haberet contra causam ejus judicium: quaeque hujusmodi novo possessori praestita fuerant, <346> ea antiquus dominus, rebus

---

9. See Grotius, *De jure belli* 3.9.14–15. *Postliminium* is originally the recovery of rights by a returning Roman citizen who had been a prisoner of war.

10. This section is parallel to *System* 3.10.8, vol. II, pp. 356–62, but perhaps more

so that should they even be retaken afterwards, the old proprietors cannot claim them <by right of *postliminium.*>[9] Nor can {they be taken by violence, or} any claim be made upon them by the old proprietors, after they are any way legally acquired by any subjects of a neutral state, and brought within their territories.

V. The principal laws with respect to neutral states are briefly these. 1. A neighbour-state under no engagement to send auxiliaries to either side, ought neither to be involved in the war, nor sustain any damage by it.[10]

2. If the neutral state by some former treaties be obliged to send auxiliaries to both upon the event of wars; when its two confederates are at war with each other, it ought to send aids to neither; or if it is inclined to engage in war, it should send aids to that state whose cause it judges to be just. For all such offensive and defensive alliances bind only upon supposal that the cause be just: nor can they bind the neutral state to make war upon such as are allied to them by solemn treaties.

3. A neutral state may justly purchase, or take by any other title, any moveable spoils taken on either side after they are adjudged as lawful prize: nor can the former proprietors have any further claim upon them. The neutral states or their citizens are no competent <338> judges of the justice of the war and the captures; and they may frequently be ignorant whether the goods they purchase are prizes taken in war or not.

4. But as to lands, forts, or cities [as to immoveable things] the case is different. The neutral state must know by what title they are held, and that they were taken from a state in amity with them: and by purchasing them they must preclude that state from retaking them again. What annual rents or services may be due {by any district or smaller town}, to any {great} city or fort <or land> {lately taken by the enemy}, may justly be paid by such as are neutral, to the present possessor; and the refusal of such payment might be deemed a declaration against the justice of the capture. If such great cities or forts [things] be again recovered by the old governors, the

---

orderly. Grotius, devoted only a brief chapter to neutral states (*De jure belli* 3, 17). The first book of Bynkershoek's *Quaestionum juris privati libri quatuor* has many chapters devoted to the matter (1.9–16 and 22).

suis immobilibus receptis, repetere nequit. Nullo tamen jure novus possessor, nisi bello finito, ipsas servitutes in perpetuum abolere, aut sortem debitam remittere potest, ita ut domini prioris, rebus suis receptis, jus tollatur.

5. Quicquid eorum, qui bellum gerunt, uni, a civitate media concessum fuerit, idem alteri concedendum; sive uni concesserit, ut milites ex suis civibus conscribat; sive copias suas militares eidem conducendas praebuerit; sive armis militaribus aut commeatibus supportatis adjuverit; ea omnia alteri etiam facienda. Arma quidem hostium alterutri vendere, aut commeatum etiam, in urbem aliquam aut regionem armis obsessam, invehere, civitatibus mediis negatur, nisi bello se immiscere velint.

6. Civitas media neutiquam prohibenda, ne, cum earum utrâque quae bellum inter se gerunt, commercia exerceat, nisi forte in armis aut apparatu bellico invehendo. Utrique naves onerarias locare, et, ex earum mercibus vehendis, justum sibi lucrum captare potest. Quod cum sit, hostium merces, non vero ipsae civitatis mediae naves, jure capi possunt et publicari. Civitas etiam media eorum naves, inter quos bellum geritur, ad merces suas vehendas conducere potest: <347> quae naves si ab hoste capiantur, jure publicantur; non vero mediae civitatis merces. Neque pignorisjus quodvis aut hypothecae, in res captas olim constitutum, amittit civitas media.

7. Merito item receptum, ut neutri, intra mediae civitatis sines, hostibus suis vim inferre liceat, homines ipsos eorumve naves aut merces capiendo aut perdendo. Porrigi autem censentur civitatis cujusque fines, non solum ad portus, sed etiam ad maris sinus intra agros ejus recedentes, et littora, partesque maris propinquiores, unde aut ipsi ab hostibus, aut hostes ab ipsis, tormentis bellicis laedi possint. Si enim bellantibus intra mediae civitatis fines sibi invicem vim inferre liceret; bellum alienum in civitatem mediam, non sine plurimis incommodis et periculis, transportaretur: omniaque interea cum bellantium utroque commercia penitus tollerentur.

---

11. More literally: "But the new possessor (unless the war is ended) has no right to abolish for ever these services or the payments of debts, so that the old proprietor, when he recovers his possession, can not claim what is due to him [by the neutral state]."

payments made to the enemy during his possession must be sustained as good; nor can the repayment of the same sums or services be demanded. But if the violent possessor <before the end of war> pretends to sell or alienate or relinquish for ever any such rents or services due by a neutral territory, or to exact payments of old debts, or to abolish them, the deed will not be valid against the old proprietor when he recovers his old possessions again.[11]

5. Whatever new favour is granted, by a neutral state to one of the parties in war, it must grant the like to the other{, if it would preserve neutrality}; such as the allowing any of its subjects to enlist, or hiring out its troops, or supplying with military stores. Indeed the sending arms or military stores, by way of merchandize, to either of the states in war, is deemed commonly by the other a breach of the neutrality; <339> and they are accordingly seizable: and so are even common provisions into any place besieged.[12]

6. Neutral states must not be hindered in their commerce with either of the parties, except in arms or military stores{; the nature of which too 'tis not easy to define}. A neutral state may set to freight its merchant-ships to either side for trade. If they are taken, the enemy's cargo is justly seizable, but not the ship. Neutral states may freight the ships of either side; and if they are taken, the cargo cannot be made a prize, but the ship may. Nor should any neutral state lose any right of pledge or mortgage formerly constituted, in any goods {moveable or immoveable} which happen to be taken in war.

7. Neither of the parties at war ought to use any violence against each other within the territories of a neutral state, by taking men, ships, or other goods of their enemies, {found in neutral ports}. And the territory of each includes not only their harbours, but any narrow bays running far into the land, the shoars, and such contiguous parts of the sea as are within reach of any military engines. For if such violence were allowed, a neutral state might suffer greatly by being made a seat of war; and their commerce with both sides must be entirely obstructed.

12. More literally: "Indeed neutral states can not sell arms or carry provisions into a city or a place besieged, if they do not want to mix in the war."

8. Quod ad perfugas attinet: bellantium neutri permittitur, ut, intra mediae civitatis fines, imperium aut jurisdictionem cum vi conjunctam in cives
proprios exerceat, nisi potestate prius a media civitate impetrata. Homines
{quidèm} atrociorum scelerum rei, minimè in media civitate protegendi;
sed capti, suis ad supplicium sunt tradendi. Qui vero milites ab utrovis ad
mediam confugerunt <348> civitatem, aut qui religionis ergô, aut ob si-
multates civiles, aut quaecunque speciosis de causis ab aliqua reipub. fac-
tione incoepta fuerant, patriâ sunt profugi; de iis invaluit mos, idemque
humanissimus, ut tutum in omni civitate vicina receptum habeant et
protegantur; dummodo nihil hostile contra suae civitatis rectores illic
moliantur.

8. As to deserters and fugitives; neither of the contending parties can exercise any jurisdiction conjoined with force, over their own citizens within the bounds of a neutral state, except by commission first obtained from the civil powers of the neutral state. No state indeed should protect such as have been guilty of the <340> more atrocious, detestable crimes; such criminals should be seized and delivered up to justice. But as to deserters in war from either side, or persons who have fled on account of religion, or any state-crimes they committed, in conjunction with any state-faction, upon some plausible shews of right; a humane custom has obtained that they should find protection in all other states, while they don't make any new attempts against the civil powers of their country.

CAPUT X

De Foederibus, Legatis, et Civitatum Interitu [Deletione].

I. Bella foederum ope plerumque componuntur; quorum jura praecipua de singulorum pactis agentes docuimus. In foederibus vero pacem reducentibus, vis et metûs exceptioni vix est locus: alioquin controversiae veteres, quae bellis causam dederant, semper renasci possent. Valebit tamen ea exceptio, quoties illata fuerit vis apertè iniquissima, nulla juris specie innixa; aut ubi pacis leges impositae ab omni aequitate et humanitate abhorrent.

[1]Quod ubi evenerit, ad arbitros provocare licebit; parte vero altera id detrectante, <349> non aliud perfugium restabit, quam ut utraque pro se judicet, quantumque fieri potest sibi consulat.

Foedera sunt vel *realia,* vel *personalia:* Haec rariùs inita, ipsos civitatum rectores praecipue spectant, cumque ipsis intereunt: realia populum spectant, qui sensu quodam immortalis dici potest. Sunt etiam foedera vel aequalia, vel inaequalia: nec omnia foedera inaequalia populi majestatem imminuunt.{[*]}

Ad foedera firmanda dabantur olim *obsides.* Qui mos ideo exolevisse videtur, quod haud sine summâ morum saevitia et immanitate, obsides immeriti durius tractari poterant, ubi suae civitatis perfidiâ violatum esset foedus.

---

1. In 1742 edn. not a new paragraph.
* Vid. Lib. III.v.5.

---

* {Book II. ix.}
1. Cf. *System* 3.10.10, vol. II, pp. 363–65; Pufendorf, *De iure nat.* 8.8.1; Grotius, *De jure belli* 2.17.19 and 3.19.11.

Of Treaties and Ambassadors, and the Entire Dissolution of States.

I. <Wars in general are setled by treaties>. The chief laws of nature about treaties were explained in the doctrine of contracts in natural liberty.{*} But we must remember that the exception of unjust force and fear cannot be admitted against the obligation of any treaties of peace; otherwise the old controversies <that occasioned the war> might always be kept a-foot. And yet such exceptions may justly take place when the war is manifestly and avowedly unjust on one side; or if the terms imposed {by the more potent side} are manifestly injurious and contrary to all humanity. In these cases the party injured may insist upon an arbitration; and if the other side refuse to submit to it, each side must by force consult its own safety and the maintenance of its rights{, by what aids it can find}.[1]

Treaties are divided into *real,* and *personal:* the personal, which are less in use, are entered into in favour of the prince's person, and cease to bind upon his demise. The *real,* respect the body of the people, or the nation, which is deemed immortal.[2] Treaties are also divided into the *equal,* {such as bring equal or proportionable burdens on each side,} and *unequal* {which bring unequal burdens}.[3] But 'tis not every unequal treaty that any way impairs or diminishes the† majesty and independency of the side submitting to the greater burden. <342>

Hostages in former ages were securities commonly given for performance of treaties, but they are now gone into disuse; because it would be exceedingly <barbarous and> inhumane to treat the innocent hostages any way harshly because of the perfidy of their country.

2. Cf. Pufendorf, *De officio* 2.17.7.
3. Cf. *ibidem* 2.17.3–4.
† Book III. v. 5.

II. In foederibus faciendis adhibentur *legati*, aut internuntii. Qui omnes, quibuscunque nominibus sint insignes, eodem utuntur jure naturali, quum ad liberae civitatis negotia obeunda veniunt. Legatos sanctos habendos antea dictum. Jure etiam postulant, ut apud eos ad quos mittuntur mandata exponant. Ut etiam iis petentibus {ibidem} <in ea civitate ad quam missi fuerant> commorari concedatur, humanitas quidem suaderet; pleno tamen jure non est postulandum: quum legati, praesertim solertiores, speculatorum munere saepius fungi <350> soleant: dumque commorantur, eo solo proteguntur [gaudent] jure naturali et necessario, quo et inquilini.

Jure autem publico et voluntario, [plurimas habent immunitates et beneficia] [plurimis gaudent immunitatibus, privilegiis, & beneficiis], et ipsi legati, et omnis eorum comitatus necessarius. Quae omnia tamen, vicinis maturè praemonitis, civitas quaevis sine injuria immutare poterit.

1. Hoc imprimis receptum, quod legatus in forum alienum non sit vocandus, eidemque cui antea jurisdictioni obnoxius sit. Quod hoc consilio institutum videtur, quod quo vigilantius munere suo fungitur {legatus}, eo magis civitatis ubi commoratur populo suspectus erit et invisus; ideoque si illic causam dicere cogeretur, metus esset, ne coram judicibus minus aequis agendum foret. Sibi caveant igitur isti cives, neque cum legato inter ipsos commorante, quem in jus vocare nequeunt, contractus ineant. At si quid gravius admiserit legatus, domum est remittendus: bellumque, si opus fuerit, regi populove a quo missus fuerat, indicendum, nisi illi irrogentur poenae, aut omne [a se illatum] [quod dederat] damnum praestare cogatur. Ubi quidem mercaturae se immiscuit legatus, merces civitati ubi commoratur subjiciuntur, nisi legationi obeundae sint necessariae.

---

4. This section is parallel to *System* 3.10.12–14, vol. II, pp. 366–71, and perhaps a more orderly account. Grotius devoted a chapter to the right of legacies (*De jure belli* 2, 18). See also footnote 1 by Jean Barbeyrac to Pufendorf, *De iure nat.* 8.9.12. In *System*

II. In making treaties *ambassadors* <or intermediaries> are employed. Their rights are all the same, whatever names are given them, if they are entrusted to transact the affairs of a sovereign state. Their persons should be sacred and inviolable, as we said above. They have a just natural right to demand that their proposals should be delivered. But as to an allowance to reside any time in the state to which they are sent, they may claim it as due out of humanity, but cannot insist on it as a perfect right. Since the business of the more active ambassadors is much the same with that of spies upon the nations where they reside. If they are allowed to reside; the law of nature would give them no higher rights or immunities, than any other foreigner might claim without any publick character.[4]

But by the voluntary laws of nations, they have many singular privileges and immunities, both for themselves and all their necessary retinue: all which however any state might without any iniquity refuse to grant them, if they give timeous intimation of their design to do so to all concerned.

1. This is customary in the first place, that no action can be brought against an ambassador or his necessary retinue{, such as his secretaries, or domesticks,} in any courts to which he was not subject previously to his taking this character. What has been in view <343> in this custom, was this; that an ambassador, the more vigilant he is in his office, will be generally so much the more disliked and hated in the state where he resides: and therefor were he subject to its courts, he would not have a fair hazard for justice in a nation prejudiced against him. The subjects of the state where he resides may easily abstain from any contracts with him in which they may be wronged, since they can have no action against him. Should an ambassador {or his retinue} commit any outragious crimes; he may be sent home, and justice demanded of his constituents; the refusal of which may be a just cause of war. If any ambassador intermeddles in trade, his merchant-goods, except such as are necessary for his support in his embassy, are liable to attachments or arrests for the debts he contracts in trade [are subject to the state where he resides].

Hutcheson refers to Cornelius van Bynkershoek's *De Foro Legatorum Liber Singularis* and to the Dutch diplomat (1606–1682) Abraham de Wicquefort's *L'Ambassadeur et ses fonctions*, 1682.

2. Legato ipsiusque comitibus necessariis <351> (quorum numerum et nomina rogatus exhibere tenetur,) asylum praestat ipsius domus. Magistratuum tamen ibidem in cives suos, aut inquilinos alios, potestatem imminuere nequit, iisdem etiam praestando asylum. Quantus autem cum legato admittendus sit comitatus, civitatis ubi commoraturus est judicio permittendum.

3. Legato in suos jus idem est quod patrifamilias, aut quantum, in eorum litibus privatis, ipsi sua dederat civitas. Supplicii vero gravioris de suis sumendi jus, nisi civitatis ubi commoratur permissu, sibi arrogare nequit legatus, aut ipse quidem rex in aliena civitate degens.

4. Adversum legatos *interdictis* est locus, ut a vi cives nostri defendantur; qui, et per se, vim vi jure repellere possunt.

5. Exulem quempiam aut perfugam facinorosum legatum accipere, nulla tenetur civitas: eum tamen jure in vincula non conjiciet, neque ad supplicium detinebit.

6. Quales legatis honores sint deferendi, et quinam praestantiores habendi, solis civitatum pactis est definiendum. Eo praestantior habendus videretur quisque, quo prudentius instituatur civitas cujus negotia obit, aut quo ipse reliquis virtute et honore sit insignior. Regia potestas haereditaria nullisque limitibus circumscripta, ad legatos honestandos <352> nihil affert, si veras rerum causas, non mores a regnis barbaris deductos, spectare velimus.

III. De civili vinculo solvendo haec breviter monenda. Primo, Civilem nexum [obligationem] perpetuo solvi exilio, non vero temporario, neque relegatione quamvis perpetuâ.

2. An ambassador's house is deemed a sanctuary to himself and all his retinue and attendants: of which however a list may justly be demanded upon his admission; and the state where he is to reside have a right to fix what retinue of his they will receive {or grant immunities to}. But an ambassador by this privilege must not impair the jurisdiction of the state where he resides over its own subjects, by making his house a sanctuary for any criminals among them.

3. An ambassador has the ordinary power of the head of a family over his own domesticks; or such jurisdiction in their civil actions as his constituents have granted him. But neither an ambassador, nor even a prince residing in a foreign state, has a criminal jurisdiction or power of inflicting capital punishments upon <344> his own subjects, except by permission of the state where he resides.

4. *Inhibitions* may justly be used against an ambassador, to restrain him from any outrages against our subjects: and they themselves have the natural right of repelling force by force.

5. No state is bound to admit any exiled criminal or fugitive subject of theirs, as an ambassador from any neighbouring state. But if such a one is sent with such commission, he cannot justly be seized or punished{, but he may be immediately ordered to quit our country}.

6. The honours and precedencies of ambassadors must be determined by express conventions or the tacit ones of long custom. The sole natural causes of precedency would be the superior excellency of the constitution of the state he represents; or his own superior personal worth <or virtue>. The absolute or hereditary power of his constituent is the worst reason of all; if we regard true merit, and not customs introduced by barbarians.

III. As to the dissolution of our political relations, we may <briefly> observe: that by perpetual banishment, one ceases to be a subject any further. But it is not so in temporary banishments; much less [nor] in perpetual confinements {to any remote parts of the state}.[5]

5. These last three sections of the *Institutio* are more orderly and complete than the parallel sections of *System* 3.11.1–3, vol. II, pp. 372–76.

2. Nemini jus esse plenum, civitatem suam ipsâ inconsultâ deserere, nisi legibus permittatur.

3. Ubi vel per vim externam, vel factionem praepotentem, multum immutata fuerit reipub. forma; civibus diffentientibus saluti suae alibi gentium melius consulere, immo et provinciis se in libertatem vindicare, licebit: quippe quae, ut antea dictum,{*} sua solum voluntate, Reip. longe aliter ac nunc est constitutae, subjiciebantur.

4. In melius mutatâ repub. eam nulla juris specie cives deserere possunt.

5. Utcunque ab ipsius civibus immutetur reipub. forma, manent omnia cum externis inita foedera *realia*.

IV. Quo jure civitas regionis suae partem aliquam aut provinciam, cum populo illic degente, hosti, aut extero cuivis dedere possit, ex [iis quae antè diximus†] [dictis] facilè intelligitur. Primo, quum communis utilitatis causa, in quâ sua cujusque continetur, <353> civitatis aut populi partes quaeque, ut etiam provinciae, se toti civitati subjecerunt; nullo jure civitas partes sui quasvis, aut provincias, invitas extero cuivis dedere poterit, easve obligare, ut se isti subjiciant quamvis aliter melius sibi consulere possint. At contra, quum ad ea quae fieri nequeunt praestanda nulla civitas obligetur, si sui partem aliquam aut provinciam civitas defendere nequeat, eam jure indefensam relinquet; et, si aliter suae saluti consulere nequeat, ne eam amplius defendat pacto se adstringet: quo tamen pacto, nulla huic parti aut provinciae imponitur obligatio, quo minus sibi alia ratione prospiciat, vel novos adsciscendo socios, vel tertiae cuivis civitati se adjungendo, aut subjiciendo, quo ab hoste ingruente protegatur. Pactum enim illud {de communi omnium defensione}, quo in civitatem coaluit populus, illudve quo

---

* Vid. Lib. III.c.vii.8, 9, 10.
† Lib. III.c.iv et v.

2. No man can claim it as his perfect right to quit his country without the permission of the civil powers or the laws, while it remains unaltered.

3. Where the old constitution is much altered, either by foreign force or any potent faction; subjects <345> who dissent from these changes have a right to consult their own safety elsewhere. And provinces may resume their independency if they can: as they were subjected, as we said above,* only by their own consent, and that to a state constituted in a very different manner.

4. But upon any improvements made in a constitution, subjects [citizens] can have no just right to desert it.

5. Whatever changes be made by the citizens themselves in their own constitution, their treaties with foreigners still remain obligatory on both sides.

IV. We may from what was said above† see, what right any state can have to give up any part of its district, or any province with the people dwelling in it, to an enemy, or any foreign potentate. For first, as the several parts of any community, and even provinces, submitted themselves to the whole body for the common utility of the whole, in which each one was to share; the community has no right to give up or alienate any parts or any provinces without their own consent; or to oblige them to be subject to any other power, when they think they can otherways better consult their own interest. But on the other hand, as there can be no obligation to impossibilities; if a state cannot defend its more exposed parts, or its provinces; it must leave them unprotected: nay, if the safety of the whole cannot otherways be maintained, it may bind itself by a treaty to give no further defence to these parts or provinces. But such a treaty imposes no obligation upon the part or province so deserted, to <346> submit to this new claimant. It may justly consult its own interest any other way; either by obtaining new confederates, or giving itself up to some other state upon as good terms as it can; that it may be protected against the present invader. For that covenant about the common defence of all, by which the several parts were

* Book III. vii. 8, 9, 10.
† <Book III.iv and v.>

provincia se subjecerat, in eo casu, ejusdemmodi est cum pactis de iis quae fieri nequeunt praestandis.

Quod de populi parte aut provincia, idem dicendum de cive strenuo et forti, quem ob virtutem invisum, hostis sibi tradi postulat: qui quidem, gravi premente necessitate, nonnunquam esset deserendus, neque amplius defendendus; ut dedatur vero, aut prohibeatur quo minus alibi suae saluti consulat, minime convenit. <354>

V. De civitatum *interitu* [deletione] haec tenenda. Civitate penitus devictâ, civibus quibusvis, provinciis item, sibi quantum possunt prospicere licet; sive alii se adjungere velint civitati, sive novam sibi in provincia constituere. Civium quidem est, pro patria omnia subire pericula, neque temere de ejus salute spem deponere. Si tamen sat patriae sit datum, neque tamen defendi possit, jure, qua ratione possunt, sibi suisque prospiciunt.

2. Si quo casu insperato reviviscat civitas, quae aliquamdiu extincta jacebat [fuerat]; ei se adjungere tenentur cives omnes et provinciae, nisi interea novo atque aequo foedere teneantur. Quae autem foedera, a civibus dissipatis, aut a provinciis, bona fide, dum antiqua civitas extincta fuit, cum exteris jungebantur, eorum firma manebit obligatio.

3. Quae diu deleta [extincta] fuit civitas, civitati victrici in provinciae modum subjecta, omnia amisit in cives profugos aut provincias suas jura. Neque si in iisdem finibus qui a civitate antiqua occupabantur, nova olim constituatur, ea prioris jura sibi arrogare poterit. Diversae saepe civitates populique, temporibus diversis, eosdem occupant agros: agrisque mutatis, eadem manet civitas; immo quum vel nullos prorsus habeat.

united into one state, is now come into the case of contracts{*} about what proves impossible to be performed.

What is said about any part of a people or a province, holds also as to any brave citizen, whom an enraged enemy demands to be given up to him. Such a brave man in cases of the utmost extremity may be as it were abandoned; or no further protected. But his country has not a right to seize and deliver him to the enemy, or to hinder him to consult his safety elsewhere.

V. As to the entire dissolution of states; these maxims hold: when a state is entirely conquered, the several subjects of it, and the provinces too, have a right to secure themselves as well as they can; whether by adjoining themselves to any other state, or by attempting to set up a new sovereign state to themselves in the province. Citizens no doubt are bound to hazard all for their country, and not to despair too hastily about its safety. But if they have made all possible efforts for their country, and yet all in vain, they may justly consult their own safety as they can.

2. If by any unexpected accidents, a state which seemed extinct and conquered for some considerable time, finds opportunity of setting up again independently, <347> its former subjects and provinces seem bound to reunite themselves to it; provided that during the conquest they came under no new and just engagements {inconsistent with this re-union}. For such engagements as the citizens or provinces of the ruined state have entered into with foreigners, without any fraud, while their former country seemed destroyed, must be as obligatory as any.

3. A state which has long continued conquered, and was made a province to the conqueror, has lost all its rights over any of its former citizens who have fled to other countries, and over its former provinces. And tho' after a course of ages a new state should be formed in the same tracts of land formerly occupied by the old state; this new state can claim none of the peculiar rights of the old one. The states occupying the same lands in different ages may be quite different political bodies: and the political body may remain the same when they change entirely their lands, nay while they have none at all in possession.

* {Book III. vii. 8, 9, 10.}

Manente civitate unus omnium debet esse <355> animus, omnia pro patria et facere et pati, quae antiquissimae sanctissimaeque civitatis, in qua continetur universum genus humanum, cujusque rector et parens est Deus, legibus non adversantur. "Cari sunt liberi, cari conjuges, parentes, propinqui, amici, familiares; omnes tamen omnium caritates patria una complexa est: pro qua vir bonus non dubitabit mortem oppetere, si ei sit profuturus."[2]

FINIS.

---

2. Cicero, *De officiis* 1.57.5: "Cari sunt parentes, cari liberi, propinqui, familiares, sed omnes omnium caritates patria una complexa est, pro qua quis bonus dubitet mortem oppetere, si ei sit profuturus?"

While our country remains, all good men should be united in this purpose, to deem nothing too hard to be endured or done for its interest; provided it be consistent with the laws of that more antient and sacred association of all mankind, of which God is the parent and governor. "Our children are dear to us, our wives are dear, so are our parents, our kinsmen, our friends and acquaintance. But our country contains within it all these objects of endearment, and preserves them to us: and therefor every good man should be ready to lay down his life for it, if he can thus do it service."[6]

FINIS

6. Cicero, *De officiis* 1.57.5.

BIBLIOGRAPHY OF ANCIENT LITERATURE
REFERRED TO BY HUTCHESON

Andronicus. *De passionibus*

Aristotle. *Ethica Nicomachea*

———. *Politica*

Cicero. *De finibus bonorum et malorum*

———. *De officiis*

———. *Tusculanae disputationes*

———. *De natura deorum*

———. *De inventione*

———. *Lelius de amicitia*

———. *Cato maior de senectute*

———. *Pro Milone*

Epictetus. *Enchiridion*

———. *Dissertationes ab Arriano digestae*

Livius. *Ab urbe condita libri*

Horace. *Carmina*

———. *Epistulae*

Justinian. *Corpus iuris civilis*

Nemesius. *De natura hominis*

Ovid. *Metamorphoses*

Persius. *Saturae*

Plato. *Phaedrus*

———. *Respublica*

———. *Timaeus*

Tacitus. *Annales*

Xenophon. *Memorabilia*

The list comprises works referred to by Hutcheson and by the Editor in the notes and Introduction.

Barbeyrac, Jean. *Discours sur le benéfice des loix, où l'on fait voir, qu'un honnête homme ne peut pas toujours se prévaloir des droits et des privilèges que le loix donnent.* Amsterdam, 2d ed. 1717. (See below, Pufendorf.)

———. *Discours sur la permission des loix, où l'on fait voir, que ce qui est permis par le loix, n'est pas toujours juste et honnête,* Amsterdam, 1716. (See below, Pufendorf.)

Bynkershoek, Cornelis van. *De dominio maris dissertatio.* 1702. A photographic reproduction of the second edition, in *Opera minora,* 1744, pp. 352–424. New York: Oxford University Press, 1923.

———. *De foro legatorum liber singularis. A monograph on the jurisdiction over ambassadors in both civil and criminal cases.* A photographic reproduction of the text of 1744 with an English translation by Gordon J. Laing and an introduction by the late Jan de Louter. Oxford: Clarendon Press, 1946.

———. *Quaestionum juris privati libri quatuor.* Leiden, 1744.

———. *Traité du juge competent des ambassadeurs: Tant pour le civil, que pour le criminel.* Traduit du Latin de Mr. de Bynkerhoek par Jean Barbeyrac. The Hague, 1723.

Campbell, Archibald. *An Enquiry into the Original of Moral Virtue.* Edinburgh, 1733.

Carmichael, Gershom. *Natural Rights on the Threshold of the Scottish Enlightenment: The Writings of Gershom Carmichael,* ed. J. Moore and M. Silverthorne. Indianapolis: Liberty Fund, 2002.

Cumberland, Richard. *De legibus naturae,* 1672. Translated by John Maxwell, London, 1727.

Filmer, Robert. *Patriarcha, or the Natural Power of Kings.* London, 1680.

Greig, J. Y. T. *The letters of David Hume.* Oxford: Clarendon Press, 1932.

Grotius, Hugo. *De iure belli ac pacis libri tres, in quibus ius naturae et gentium, item iuris publici praecipua explicantur.* Paris, 1625.

———. *Les Droit de la guerre et de la paix.* Trans. Jean Barbeyrac, 2 vols., Amsterdam, 1724.

Haakonssen, Knud. *Natural Law and Moral Philosophy: From Grotius to the Scottish Enlightenment.* Cambridge: Cambridge University Press, 1996.

Harrington, James. *The Commonwealth of Oceana.* London, 1656.

Heineccius, Johann Gottlieb. *Antiquitatum Romanarum jurisprudentium illustrantium Syntagma, secundum ordinem Institutionum Justiniani digestum, in quo multa iuris romani atque auctorum veterum loca explicantur atque illustrantur.* Strassbourg, 1724.

Hooker, Richard. *Of the Laws of Ecclesiastical Polity.* London, 1593.

Hume, David. *A Treatise of Human Nature.* London, 1739–40.

Hutcheson, Francis. *An Essay on the Nature and Conduct of the Passions and Affections. With Illustrations on the Moral Sense.* London, 1742.

———. *An Inquiry into the Original of our Ideas of Beauty and Virtue; In Two Treatises. I. Concerning Beauty, Order, Harmony, Design. II. Concerning Moral Good and Evil.* London,1738.

———. *Synopsis metaphysicae, ontologiam & pneumatologiam complectens.* Glasgow, 1744.

———. *Philosophiae moralis institutio compendiaria, Ethices & Jurisprudentiae Naturalis elementa continens.* Glasgow, 1742, 2d ed. 1745.

———. *A Short Introduction to Moral Philosophy.* Glasgow, 1747.

———. *A System of Moral Philosophy.* London, 1755.

———. "Observations on the Fable of the Bees," *The Dublin Weekly Journal* 4, 12, and 19 February 1726. Reprinted in *Collected Works,* vol. VII. New York: Garland, 1971.

———. "Reflections upon Laughter," *The Dublin Weekly Journal,* 5, 12, and 19 June 1725. Reprinted in *Collected Works,* vol. VII. New York: Garland, 1971.

Iustinianus. *Corpus iuris civilis.*

King, William. *De Origine Mali.* London, 1702.

La Bruyère, Jean de. *Les caractères de Théophraste traduit du Grec avec Les caracterères ou le moeurs de ce siècle.* Bruxelles, 1688.

Leechman,William. Preface to *A system of Moral Philosophy.* Glasgow, 1755.

Leibniz, Gottfried Wilhelm von. *Jugement d'un anonyme sur l'orginal de cet abrégé* [De officio]*: avec des réflexions du Traducteur.* (Published in Pufendorf, *Les Devoirs de l'homme, et du citoien.* pp. 429–95; see below.)

Locke, John. *An Essay concerning Human Understanding.* London, 1690.

———. *Two Treatises of Government.* London, 1690.

Malebranche, Nicolas. *De la recherche de la verité: Ou l'on traite de la nature de l'esprit de l'homme et de l'usage qu'il en doit faire pour éviterl'erreur dans les Sciences.* Paris, 1674–78. (First English translation by Thomas Taylor with the title *Father Malebranche's Treatise concerning the Search after Truth.* Oxford, 1694.)

Mautner, Thomas. *Francis Hutcheson: On Human nature.* Cambridge: Cambridge University Press, 1993.

Moore, James. "The Two Systems of Francis Hutcheson: On the Origins of the Scottish Enlightenment." In *Studies in the Philosophy of Scottish Enlightenment,* edited by M. A. Stewart, 1990, pp. 37–59.

More, Henry. *Enchiridion Ethicum,* 1679, 2d ed., in *Opera Omnia,* London, 1629.

More, Thomas. *The Utopia of Sir Thomas More.* In Latin from the edition of March 1518, and in English from the first edition of Ralph Robynson's translation in 1551, with additional translations, introduction and notes, by J. H. Lupton. Oxford: Clarendon Press, 1895.

Pufendorf, Samuel von. *De jure naturae et gentium libri octo.* Lund, 1672.

———. *Le droit de la nature et des gens ou systeme general des principes les plus importans de la morale, de la jurisprudence, et de la politique.* Trans. Jean Barbeyrac, 2 vols., Basle, 1732.

———. *De officio hominis et civis iuxta legem naturalem libri duo.* Lund, 1673.

———. *Les Devoirs de l'homme, et du citoien.* Ed. J. Barbeyrac. Amsterdam, 1718.

———. *The Whole Duty of Man According to the Law of Nature. Together with Two Discourses and a Commentary by Jean Barbeyrac.* Edited by Ian Hunter and David Saunders. Indianapolis: Liberty Fund, 2002.

Scott, William Robert. *Francis Hutcheson: His Life, Teaching and Position in the History of Philosophy.* Cambridge: Cambridge University Press, 1900.

Shaftesbury, Anthony Ashley Cooper, Third Earl of. *Characteristicks of Men, Manners, Opinions, Times.* London, 1714. 2d ed. Edited by L. E. Klein, Cambridge: Cambridge University Press, 1999.

Sidney, Algernon. *Discourses Concerning Government.* London, 1698.

Titius, Gottlieb Gerhard. *Observationes in Samuelis L. B. de Pufendorf De officio hominis et civis juxta legem naturalem libri duos.* Leipzig, 1703.

Vinnius, Arnoldus. *In quattuor libros Institutionum imperialium Commentarius academicus et forensic.* Amsterdam, 1692.

Wicquefort, Abraham van. *L'Ambassadeur et ses fonctions.* La Haye, 1681.

INDEX

abortion, 210

absolute or unlimited monarchies, 246

acceptilation, 213

accessions and improvements, 143

Achaian states, 245

acquisition of property, 137–44

actions: consequences of, 124–25; estimating morality of, 116–26; human nature and, 34–38; importance of, 117, 123–24; imputation of, 126; voluntary and involuntary, 117–18; will, morality of actions relating to, 120–22

adventitious rights, 127, 129, 133. *See also* economics and politics

agents: contracts by, 168; estimation of virtue and abilities of, 123–25

Albans, 208*n*

alienable and inalienable rights, 114–15

ambassadors, 285–86

ambition, 44

American colonies, 265*n*

Andronicus, 45

anger, 30, 44, 45, 93, 120–21

animals, rights over, 133–35

arbitration, 213–14

aristocracies, 246, 247, 250

Aristotle: Cicero and Stoic ideas, xxi; on civil government and civil society, 235*n*, 252*n*; on good, 67*n*; on human nature and moral sense, xxi, 29*n*, 37*n*, 42*n*, 45; *Institutio*

influenced by, x, xiv, xvii, xx, 3; on moderation in passions, 90*n*, 92*n*, 94*n*, 95; moral philosophy, purpose of, 23*n*, 24*n*; *noetic* and *dianoetic* propositions, 109*n*; on types of virtue, 70*n*, 71*n*, 74*n*, 75, 90*n*

Arnauld, Antoine, 190*n*

Arrian, 25*n*, 101*n*

arts: as admirable profession, 96; good derived from pleasures of, 58–60; no proper evil or pain associated with, 65–66; sense of beauty and, 32–33

assertions: contracts distinguished from, 157; oaths and vows distinguished, 177

association of ideas, 46–47

avarice, 44, 92

aversion, 28–29, 30, 44

bail in confirmation of contract, 191

ballot, voting by, 251

banishment, 286

bankruptcy and presumptive property, 148

Barbeyrac, Jean: on ambassadors, 285*n*; on civil government and civil society, 237*n*; on civil law, 272*n*; Hutcheson influenced by, xvi, 5; on property, 134*n*, 152*n*; on rights, 113*n*; on slavery, 231*n*

barter or exchange, contracts of, 187–88

This book is set in Adobe Garamond, a modern adaptation by Robert Slimbach of the typeface originally cut around 1540 by the French typographer and printer Claude Garamond. The Garamond face, with its small lowercase height and restrained contrast between thick and thin strokes, is a classic "old-style" face and has long been one of the most influential and widely used typefaces.

Printed on paper that is acid-free and meets the requirements of the American National Standard for Permanence of Paper for Printed Library Materials, z39.48-1992. ♾

Book design by Louise OFarrell
Gainesville, Florida
Typography by Apex Publishing, LLC
Madison, Wisconsin
Printed and bound by Worzalla Publishing Company
Stevens Point, Wisconsin